THIRD EDITION

Hadoop: The Definitive Guide

Tom White

O'REILLY®

Beijing · Cambridge · Farnham · Köln · Sebastopol · Tokyo

SHROFF PUBLISHERS & DISTRIBUTORS PVT. LTD.

Mumbai   *Bangalore*   *Kolkata*   *New Delhi*

Hadoop: The Definitive Guide, Third Edition

by Tom White

Published by O'Reilly Media, Inc., 1005 Gravenstein Highway North, Sebastopol, CA 95472.

O'Reilly books may be purchased for educational, business, or sales promotional use. Online editions are also available for most titles (*http://my.safaribooksonline.com*). For more information, contact our corporate/institutional sales department: (800) 998-9938 or *corporate@oreilly.com*.

Editors: Mike Loukides and Meghan Blanchette
Production Editor: Rachel Steely
Copyeditor: Genevieve d'Entremont
Proofreader: Kevin Broccoli

Indexer: Kevin Broccoli
Cover Designer: Karen Montgomery
Interior Designer: David Futato
Illustrator: Robert Romano

May 2012: Third Edition.

Revision History for the First Edition:

2012-01-27 Early release revision 1

2012-05-07 First release

See http://oreilly.com/catalog/errata.csp?isbn=9781449311520 for release details.

Fourth Indian Reprint: June 2013

ISBN 13: 978-93-5023-756-4

Published by **Shroff Publishers and Distributors Pvt. Ltd.** C-103, MIDC, TTC Industrial Area, Pawane, Navi Mumbai 400 705, Tel: (91 22) 4158 4158, Fax: (91 22) 4158 4141, e-mail: spdorders@shroffpublishers.com. Printed at Rose Fine Art, Mumbai.

For Eliane, Emilia, and Lottie

Table of Contents

Foreword xv

Preface xvii

1. Meet Hadoop 1
Data!   1
Data Storage and Analysis   3
Comparison with Other Systems   4
    Rational Database Management System   4
    Grid Computing   6
    Volunteer Computing   8
A Brief History of Hadoop   9
Apache Hadoop and the Hadoop Ecosystem   12
Hadoop Releases   13
    What's Covered in This Book   15
    Compatibility   15

2. MapReduce 17
A Weather Dataset   17
    Data Format   17
Analyzing the Data with Unix Tools   19
Analyzing the Data with Hadoop   20
    Map and Reduce   20
    Java MapReduce   22
Scaling Out   30
    Data Flow   30
    Combiner Functions   33
    Running a Distributed MapReduce Job   36
Hadoop Streaming   36
    Ruby   36
    Python   39

Hadoop Pipes   40
    Compiling and Running   41

3. The Hadoop Distributed Filesystem **43**
The Design of HDFS   43
HDFS Concepts   45
    Blocks   45
    Namenodes and Datanodes   46
    HDFS Federation   47
    HDFS High-Availability   48
The Command-Line Interface   49
    Basic Filesystem Operations   50
Hadoop Filesystems   52
    Interfaces   53
The Java Interface   55
    Reading Data from a Hadoop URL   55
    Reading Data Using the FileSystem API   57
    Writing Data   60
    Directories   62
    Querying the Filesystem   62
    Deleting Data   67
Data Flow   67
    Anatomy of a File Read   67
    Anatomy of a File Write   70
    Coherency Model   72
Data Ingest with Flume and Sqoop   74
Parallel Copying with distcp   75
    Keeping an HDFS Cluster Balanced   76
Hadoop Archives   77
    Using Hadoop Archives   77
    Limitations   79

4. Hadoop I/O **81**
Data Integrity   81
    Data Integrity in HDFS   81
    LocalFileSystem   82
    ChecksumFileSystem   83
Compression   83
    Codecs   85
    Compression and Input Splits   89
    Using Compression in MapReduce   90
Serialization   93
    The Writable Interface   94

Writable Classes   96
Implementing a Custom Writable   103
Serialization Frameworks   108
Avro   110
Avro Data Types and Schemas   111
In-Memory Serialization and Deserialization   114
Avro Datafiles   117
Interoperability   118
Schema Resolution   121
Sort Order   123
Avro MapReduce   124
Sorting Using Avro MapReduce   128
Avro MapReduce in Other Languages   130
File-Based Data Structures   130
SequenceFile   130
MapFile   137

5. Developing a MapReduce Application **143**
The Configuration API   144
Combining Resources   145
Variable Expansion   146
Setting Up the Development Environment   146
Managing Configuration   148
GenericOptionsParser, Tool, and ToolRunner   150
Writing a Unit Test with MRUnit   154
Mapper   154
Reducer   156
Running Locally on Test Data   157
Running a Job in a Local Job Runner   157
Testing the Driver   160
Running on a Cluster   161
Packaging a Job   162
Launching a Job   163
The MapReduce Web UI   165
Retrieving the Results   168
Debugging a Job   170
Hadoop Logs   175
Remote Debugging   177
Tuning a Job   178
Profiling Tasks   179
MapReduce Workflows   181
Decomposing a Problem into MapReduce Jobs   181
JobControl   183

Apache Oozie 183

6. How MapReduce Works **189**
Anatomy of a MapReduce Job Run   189
Classic MapReduce (MapReduce 1)   190
YARN (MapReduce 2)   196
Failures   202
Failures in Classic MapReduce   202
Failures in YARN   204
Job Scheduling   206
The Fair Scheduler   207
The Capacity Scheduler   207
Shuffle and Sort   208
The Map Side   208
The Reduce Side   210
Configuration Tuning   211
Task Execution   214
The Task Execution Environment   215
Speculative Execution   215
Output Committers   217
Task JVM Reuse   219
Skipping Bad Records   220

7. MapReduce Types and Formats **223**
MapReduce Types   223
The Default MapReduce Job   227
Input Formats   234
Input Splits and Records   234
Text Input   245
Binary Input   249
Multiple Inputs   250
Database Input (and Output)   251
Output Formats   251
Text Output   252
Binary Output   253
Multiple Outputs   253
Lazy Output   257
Database Output   258

8. MapReduce Features **259**
Counters   259
Built-in Counters   259
User-Defined Java Counters   264

	User-Defined Streaming Counters	268
	Sorting	268
	Preparation	269
	Partial Sort	270
	Total Sort	274
	Secondary Sort	277
	Joins	283
	Map-Side Joins	284
	Reduce-Side Joins	285
	Side Data Distribution	288
	Using the Job Configuration	288
	Distributed Cache	289
	MapReduce Library Classes	295

9. Setting Up a Hadoop Cluster **297**

Cluster Specification	297
Network Topology	299
Cluster Setup and Installation	301
Installing Java	302
Creating a Hadoop User	302
Installing Hadoop	302
Testing the Installation	303
SSH Configuration	303
Hadoop Configuration	304
Configuration Management	305
Environment Settings	307
Important Hadoop Daemon Properties	311
Hadoop Daemon Addresses and Ports	316
Other Hadoop Properties	317
User Account Creation	320
YARN Configuration	320
Important YARN Daemon Properties	321
YARN Daemon Addresses and Ports	324
Security	325
Kerberos and Hadoop	326
Delegation Tokens	328
Other Security Enhancements	329
Benchmarking a Hadoop Cluster	331
Hadoop Benchmarks	331
User Jobs	333
Hadoop in the Cloud	334
Apache Whirr	334

10. Administering Hadoop **339**
  HDFS   339
    Persistent Data Structures   339
    Safe Mode   344
    Audit Logging   346
    Tools   347
  Monitoring   351
    Logging   352
    Metrics   352
    Java Management Extensions   355
  Maintenance   358
    Routine Administration Procedures   358
    Commissioning and Decommissioning Nodes   359
    Upgrades   362

11. Pig **367**
  Installing and Running Pig   368
    Execution Types   368
    Running Pig Programs   370
    Grunt   370
    Pig Latin Editors   371
  An Example   371
    Generating Examples   373
  Comparison with Databases   374
  Pig Latin   375
    Structure   376
    Statements   377
    Expressions   381
    Types   382
    Schemas   384
    Functions   388
    Macros   390
  User-Defined Functions   391
    A Filter UDF   391
    An Eval UDF   394
    A Load UDF   396
  Data Processing Operators   399
    Loading and Storing Data   399
    Filtering Data   400
    Grouping and Joining Data   402
    Sorting Data   407
    Combining and Splitting Data   408
  Pig in Practice   409

	Parallelism	409
	Parameter Substitution	410

12. Hive **413**

Installing Hive	414
The Hive Shell	415
An Example	416
Running Hive	417
Configuring Hive	417
Hive Services	419
The Metastore	421
Comparison with Traditional Databases	423
Schema on Read Versus Schema on Write	423
Updates, Transactions, and Indexes	424
HiveQL	425
Data Types	426
Operators and Functions	428
Tables	429
Managed Tables and External Tables	429
Partitions and Buckets	431
Storage Formats	435
Importing Data	441
Altering Tables	443
Dropping Tables	443
Querying Data	444
Sorting and Aggregating	444
MapReduce Scripts	445
Joins	446
Subqueries	449
Views	450
User-Defined Functions	451
Writing a UDF	452
Writing a UDAF	454

13. HBase **459**

HBasics	459
Backdrop	460
Concepts	460
Whirlwind Tour of the Data Model	460
Implementation	461
Installation	464
Test Drive	465
Clients	467

Java	467
Avro, REST, and Thrift	470
Example	472
Schemas	472
Loading Data	473
Web Queries	476
HBase Versus RDBMS	479
Successful Service	480
HBase	481
Use Case: HBase at Streamy.com	481
Praxis	483
Versions	483
HDFS	484
UI	485
Metrics	485
Schema Design	486
Counters	486
Bulk Load	487
14. ZooKeeper	**489**
Installing and Running ZooKeeper	490
An Example	492
Group Membership in ZooKeeper	492
Creating the Group	493
Joining a Group	495
Listing Members in a Group	496
Deleting a Group	498
The ZooKeeper Service	499
Data Model	499
Operations	501
Implementation	506
Consistency	507
Sessions	509
States	511
Building Applications with ZooKeeper	512
A Configuration Service	512
The Resilient ZooKeeper Application	515
A Lock Service	519
More Distributed Data Structures and Protocols	521
ZooKeeper in Production	522
Resilience and Performance	523
Configuration	524

15. Sqoop **527**

Getting Sqoop   527
Sqoop Connectors   529
A Sample Import   529
   Text and Binary File Formats   532
Generated Code   532
   Additional Serialization Systems   533
Imports: A Deeper Look   533
   Controlling the Import   535
   Imports and Consistency   536
   Direct-mode Imports   536
Working with Imported Data   536
   Imported Data and Hive   537
Importing Large Objects   540
Performing an Export   542
Exports: A Deeper Look   543
   Exports and Transactionality   545
   Exports and SequenceFiles   545

16. Case Studies **547**

Hadoop Usage at Last.fm   547
   Last.fm: The Social Music Revolution   547
   Hadoop at Last.fm   547
   Generating Charts with Hadoop   548
   The Track Statistics Program   549
   Summary   556
Hadoop and Hive at Facebook   556
   Hadoop at Facebook   556
   Hypothetical Use Case Studies   559
   Hive   562
   Problems and Future Work   566
Nutch Search Engine   567
   Data Structures   568
   Selected Examples of Hadoop Data Processing in Nutch 571
   Summary   580
Log Processing at Rackspace   581
   Requirements/The Problem   581
   Brief History   582
   Choosing Hadoop   582
   Collection and Storage   582
   MapReduce for Logs   583
Cascading   589
   Fields, Tuples, and Pipes   590

Operations   593
Taps, Schemes, and Flows   594
Cascading in Practice   595
Flexibility   598
Hadoop and Cascading at ShareThis   599
Summary   603
TeraByte Sort on Apache Hadoop   603
Using Pig and Wukong to Explore Billion-edge Network Graphs   607
Measuring Community   609
Everybody's Talkin' at Me: The Twitter Reply Graph   609
Symmetric Links   612
Community Extraction   613

A. Installing Apache Hadoop   617

B. Cloudera's Distribution Including Apache Hadoop   623

C. Preparing the NCDC Weather Data   625

Index 629

Foreword

Hadoop got its start in Nutch. A few of us were attempting to build an open source web search engine and having trouble managing computations running on even a handful of computers. Once Google published its GFS and MapReduce papers, the route became clear. They'd devised systems to solve precisely the problems we were having with Nutch. So we started, two of us, half-time, to try to re-create these systems as a part of Nutch.

We managed to get Nutch limping along on 20 machines, but it soon became clear that to handle the Web's massive scale, we'd need to run it on thousands of machines and, moreover, that the job was bigger than two half-time developers could handle.

Around that time, Yahoo! got interested, and quickly put together a team that I joined. We split off the distributed computing part of Nutch, naming it Hadoop. With the help of Yahoo!, Hadoop soon grew into a technology that could truly scale to the Web.

In 2006, Tom White started contributing to Hadoop. I already knew Tom through an excellent article he'd written about Nutch, so I knew he could present complex ideas in clear prose. I soon learned that he could also develop software that was as pleasant to read as his prose.

From the beginning, Tom's contributions to Hadoop showed his concern for users and for the project. Unlike most open source contributors, Tom is not primarily interested in tweaking the system to better meet his own needs, but rather in making it easier for anyone to use.

Initially, Tom specialized in making Hadoop run well on Amazon's EC2 and S3 services. Then he moved on to tackle a wide variety of problems, including improving the MapReduce APIs, enhancing the website, and devising an object serialization framework. In all cases, Tom presented his ideas precisely. In short order, Tom earned the role of Hadoop committer and soon thereafter became a member of the Hadoop Project Management Committee.

Tom is now a respected senior member of the Hadoop developer community. Though he's an expert in many technical corners of the project, his specialty is making Hadoop easier to use and understand.

Given this, I was very pleased when I learned that Tom intended to write a book about Hadoop. Who could be better qualified? Now you have the opportunity to learn about Hadoop from a master—not only of the technology, but also of common sense and plain talk.

—Doug Cutting
Shed in the Yard, California

Preface

Martin Gardner, the mathematics and science writer, once said in an interview:

> Beyond calculus, I am lost. That was the secret of my column's success. It took me so long to understand what I was writing about that I knew how to write in a way most readers would understand.[1]

In many ways, this is how I feel about Hadoop. Its inner workings are complex, resting as they do on a mixture of distributed systems theory, practical engineering, and common sense. And to the uninitiated, Hadoop can appear alien.

But it doesn't need to be like this. Stripped to its core, the tools that Hadoop provides for building distributed systems—for data storage, data analysis, and coordination—are simple. If there's a common theme, it is about raising the level of abstraction—to create building blocks for programmers who just happen to have lots of data to store, or lots of data to analyze, or lots of machines to coordinate, and who don't have the time, the skill, or the inclination to become distributed systems experts to build the infrastructure to handle it.

With such a simple and generally applicable feature set, it seemed obvious to me when I started using it that Hadoop deserved to be widely used. However, at the time (in early 2006), setting up, configuring, and writing programs to use Hadoop was an art. Things have certainly improved since then: there is more documentation, there are more examples, and there are thriving mailing lists to go to when you have questions. And yet the biggest hurdle for newcomers is understanding what this technology is capable of, where it excels, and how to use it. That is why I wrote this book.

The Apache Hadoop community has come a long way. Over the course of three years, the Hadoop project has blossomed and spun off half a dozen subprojects. In this time, the software has made great leaps in performance, reliability, scalability, and manageability. To gain even wider adoption, however, I believe we need to make Hadoop even easier to use. This will involve writing more tools; integrating with more systems; and

---

1. "The science of fun," Alex Bellos, *The Guardian*, May 31, 2008, *http://www.guardian.co.uk/science/2008/may/31/maths.science*.

writing new, improved APIs. I'm looking forward to being a part of this, and I hope this book will encourage and enable others to do so, too.

Administrative Notes

During discussion of a particular Java class in the text, I often omit its package name to reduce clutter. If you need to know which package a class is in, you can easily look it up in Hadoop's Java API documentation for the relevant subproject, linked to from the Apache Hadoop home page at *http://hadoop.apache.org/*. Or if you're using an IDE, it can help using its auto-complete mechanism.

Similarly, although it deviates from usual style guidelines, program listings that import multiple classes from the same package may use the asterisk wildcard character to save space (for example, `import org.apache.hadoop.io.*`).

The sample programs in this book are available for download from the website that accompanies this book: *http://www.hadoopbook.com/*. You will also find instructions there for obtaining the datasets that are used in examples throughout the book, as well as further notes for running the programs in the book, and links to updates, additional resources, and my blog.

What's in This Book?

The rest of this book is organized as follows. Chapter 1 emphasizes the need for Hadoop and sketches the history of the project. Chapter 2 provides an introduction to MapReduce. Chapter 3 looks at Hadoop filesystems, and in particular HDFS, in depth. Chapter 4 covers the fundamentals of I/O in Hadoop: data integrity, compression, serialization, and file-based data structures.

The next four chapters cover MapReduce in depth. Chapter 5 goes through the practical steps needed to develop a MapReduce application. Chapter 6 looks at how MapReduce is implemented in Hadoop, from the point of view of a user. Chapter 7 is about the MapReduce programming model and the various data formats that MapReduce can work with. Chapter 8 is on advanced MapReduce topics, including sorting and joining data.

Chapters 9 and 10 are for Hadoop administrators and describe how to set up and maintain a Hadoop cluster running HDFS and MapReduce.

Later chapters are dedicated to projects that build on Hadoop or are related to it. Chapters 11 and 12 present Pig and Hive, which are analytics platforms built on HDFS and MapReduce, whereas Chapters 13, 14, and 15 cover HBase, ZooKeeper, and Sqoop, respectively.

Finally, Chapter 16 is a collection of case studies contributed by members of the Apache Hadoop community.

What's New in the Second Edition?

The second edition has two new chapters on Hive and Sqoop (Chapters 12 and 15), a new section covering Avro (in Chapter 4), an introduction to the new security features in Hadoop (in Chapter 9), and a new case study on analyzing massive network graphs using Hadoop (in Chapter 16).

This edition continues to describe the 0.20 release series of Apache Hadoop because this was the latest stable release at the time of writing. New features from later releases are occasionally mentioned in the text, however, with reference to the version that they were introduced in.

What's New in the Third Edition?

The third edition covers the 1.x (formerly 0.20) release series of Apache Hadoop, as well as the newer 0.22 and 2.x (formerly 0.23) series. With a few exceptions, which are noted in the text, all the examples in this book run against these versions. The features in each release series are described at a high level in "Hadoop Releases" on page 13.

This edition uses the new MapReduce API for most of the examples. Because the old API is still in widespread use, it continues to be discussed in the text alongside the new API, and the equivalent code using the old API can be found on the book's website.

The major change in Hadoop 2.0 is the new MapReduce runtime, MapReduce 2, which is built on a new distributed resource management system called YARN. This edition includes new sections covering MapReduce on YARN: how it works (Chapter 6) and how to run it (Chapter 9).

There is more MapReduce material, too, including development practices such as packaging MapReduce jobs with Maven, setting the user's Java classpath, and writing tests with MRUnit (all in Chapter 5); and more depth on features such as output committers, the distributed cache (both in Chapter 8), and task memory monitoring (Chapter 9). There is a new section on writing MapReduce jobs to process Avro data (Chapter 4), and one on running a simple MapReduce workflow in Oozie (Chapter 5).

The chapter on HDFS (Chapter 3) now has introductions to high availability, federation, and the new WebHDFS and HttpFS filesystems.

The chapters on Pig, Hive, Sqoop, and ZooKeeper have all been expanded to cover the new features and changes in their latest releases.

In addition, numerous corrections and improvements have been made throughout the book.

Conventions Used in This Book

The following typographical conventions are used in this book:

Italic
> Indicates new terms, URLs, email addresses, filenames, and file extensions.

`Constant width`
> Used for program listings, as well as within paragraphs to refer to program elements such as variable or function names, databases, data types, environment variables, statements, and keywords.

`Constant width bold`
> Shows commands or other text that should be typed literally by the user.

`Constant width italic`
> Shows text that should be replaced with user-supplied values or by values determined by context.

 This icon signifies a tip, suggestion, or general note.

 This icon indicates a warning or caution.

Using Code Examples

This book is here to help you get your job done. In general, you may use the code in this book in your programs and documentation. You do not need to contact us for permission unless you're reproducing a significant portion of the code. For example, writing a program that uses several chunks of code from this book does not require permission. Selling or distributing a CD-ROM of examples from O'Reilly books does require permission. Answering a question by citing this book and quoting example code does not require permission. Incorporating a significant amount of example code from this book into your product's documentation does require permission.

We appreciate, but do not require, attribution. An attribution usually includes the title, author, publisher, and ISBN. For example: "*Hadoop: The Definitive Guide*, Third Edition, by Tom White. Copyright 2011 Tom White, 978-1-449-31152-0."

If you feel your use of code examples falls outside fair use or the permission given here, feel free to contact us at *permissions@oreilly.com*.

Safari® Books Online

Safari Books Online (*www.safaribooksonline.com*) is an on-demand digital library that delivers expert content in both book and video form from the world's leading authors in technology and business. Technology professionals, software developers, web designers, and business and creative professionals use Safari Books Online as their primary resource for research, problem solving, learning, and certification training.

Safari Books Online offers a range of product mixes and pricing programs for organizations, government agencies, and individuals. Subscribers have access to thousands of books, training videos, and prepublication manuscripts in one fully searchable database from publishers like O'Reilly Media, Prentice Hall Professional, Addison-Wesley Professional, Microsoft Press, Sams, Que, Peachpit Press, Focal Press, Cisco Press, John Wiley & Sons, Syngress, Morgan Kaufmann, IBM Redbooks, Packt, Adobe Press, FT Press, Apress, Manning, New Riders, McGraw-Hill, Jones & Bartlett, Course Technology, and dozens more. For more information about Safari Books Online, please visit us online.

How to Contact Us

Please address comments and questions concerning this book to the publisher:

O'Reilly Media, Inc.
1005 Gravenstein Highway North
Sebastopol, CA 95472
800-998-9938 (in the United States or Canada)
707-829-0515 (international or local)
707-829-0104 (fax)

We have a web page for this book, where we list errata, examples, and any additional information. You can access this page at:

http://www.oreilly.com/catalog/9781449311520

To comment or ask technical questions about this book, send email to:

bookquestions@oreilly.com

For more information about our books, courses, conferences, and news, see our website at *http://www.oreilly.com*.

Find us on Facebook: *http://facebook.com/oreilly*

Follow us on Twitter: *http://twitter.com/oreillymedia*

Watch us on YouTube: *http://www.youtube.com/oreillymedia*

Acknowledgments

I have relied on many people, both directly and indirectly, in writing this book. I would like to thank the Hadoop community, from whom I have learned, and continue to learn, a great deal.

In particular, I would like to thank Michael Stack and Jonathan Gray for writing the chapter on HBase. Thanks also go to Adrian Woodhead, Marc de Palol, Joydeep Sen Sarma, Ashish Thusoo, Andrzej Białecki, Stu Hood, Chris K. Wensel, and Owen O'Malley for contributing case studies for Chapter 16.

I would like to thank the following reviewers who contributed many helpful suggestions and improvements to my drafts: Raghu Angadi, Matt Biddulph, Christophe Bisciglia, Ryan Cox, Devaraj Das, Alex Dorman, Chris Douglas, Alan Gates, Lars George, Patrick Hunt, Aaron Kimball, Peter Krey, Hairong Kuang, Simon Maxen, Olga Natkovich, Benjamin Reed, Konstantin Shvachko, Allen Wittenauer, Matei Zaharia, and Philip Zeyliger. Ajay Anand kept the review process flowing smoothly. Philip ("flip") Kromer kindly helped me with the NCDC weather dataset featured in the examples in this book. Special thanks to Owen O'Malley and Arun C. Murthy for explaining the intricacies of the MapReduce shuffle to me. Any errors that remain are, of course, to be laid at my door.

For the second edition, I owe a debt of gratitude for the detailed review and feedback from Jeff Bean, Doug Cutting, Glynn Durham, Alan Gates, Jeff Hammerbacher, Alex Kozlov, Ken Krugler, Jimmy Lin, Todd Lipcon, Sarah Sproehnle, Vinithra Varadharajan, and Ian Wrigley, as well as all the readers who submitted errata for the first edition. I would also like to thank Aaron Kimball for contributing the chapter on Sqoop, and Philip ("flip") Kromer for the case study on graph processing.

For the third edition, thanks go to Alejandro Abdelnur, Eva Andreasson, Eli Collins, Doug Cutting, Patrick Hunt, Aaron Kimball, Aaron T. Myers, Brock Noland, Arvind Prabhakar, Ahmed Radwan, and Tom Wheeler for their feedback and suggestions. Rob Weltman kindly gave very detailed feedback for the whole book, which greatly improved the final manuscript. Thanks also go to all the readers who submitted errata for the second edition.

I am particularly grateful to Doug Cutting for his encouragement, support, and friendship, and for contributing the Foreword.

Thanks also go to the many others with whom I have had conversations or email discussions over the course of writing the book.

Halfway through writing this book, I joined Cloudera, and I want to thank my colleagues for being incredibly supportive in allowing me the time to write and to get it finished promptly.

I am grateful to my editor, Mike Loukides, and his colleagues at O'Reilly for their help in the preparation of this book. Mike has been there throughout to answer my questions, to read my first drafts, and to keep me on schedule.

Finally, the writing of this book has been a great deal of work, and I couldn't have done it without the constant support of my family. My wife, Eliane, not only kept the home going, but also stepped in to help review, edit, and chase case studies. My daughters, Emilia and Lottie, have been very understanding, and I'm looking forward to spending lots more time with all of them.

Meet Hadoop

In pioneer days they used oxen for heavy pulling, and when one ox couldn't budge a log, they didn't try to grow a larger ox. We shouldn't be trying for bigger computers, but for more systems of computers.

—Grace Hopper

Data!

We live in the data age. It's not easy to measure the total volume of data stored electronically, but an IDC estimate put the size of the "digital universe" at 0.18 zettabytes in 2006 and is forecasting a tenfold growth by 2011 to 1.8 zettabytes.[1] A zettabyte is 10^{21} bytes, or equivalently one thousand exabytes, one million petabytes, or one billion terabytes. That's roughly the same order of magnitude as one disk drive for every person in the world.

This flood of data is coming from many sources. Consider the following:[2]

- The New York Stock Exchange generates about one terabyte of new trade data per day.
- Facebook hosts approximately 10 billion photos, taking up one petabyte of storage.
- Ancestry.com, the genealogy site, stores around 2.5 petabytes of data.
- The Internet Archive stores around 2 petabytes of data and is growing at a rate of 20 terabytes per month.
- The Large Hadron Collider near Geneva, Switzerland, will produce about 15 petabytes of data per year.

1. From Gantz et al., "The Diverse and Exploding Digital Universe," March 2008 (*http://www.emc.com/ collateral/analyst-reports/diverse-exploding-digital-universe.pdf*).

2. *http://www.intelligententerprise.com/showArticle.jhtml?articleID=207800705*, *http://mashable.com/ 2008/10/15/facebook-10-billion-photos/*, *http://blog.familytreemagazine.com/insider/Inside +Ancestrycoms+TopSecret+Data+Center.aspx*, *http://www.archive.org/about/faqs.php*, and *http://www .interactions.org/cms/?pid=1027032*

So there's a lot of data out there. But you are probably wondering how it affects you. Most of the data is locked up in the largest web properties (like search engines) or in scientific or financial institutions, isn't it? Does the advent of "Big Data," as it is being called, affect smaller organizations or individuals?

I argue that it does. Take photos, for example. My wife's grandfather was an avid photographer and took photographs throughout his adult life. His entire corpus of medium-format, slide, and 35mm film, when scanned in at high resolution, occupies around 10 gigabytes. Compare this to the digital photos that my family took in 2008, which take up about 5 gigabytes of space. My family is producing photographic data at 35 times the rate my wife's grandfather's did, and the rate is increasing every year as it becomes easier to take more and more photos.

More generally, the digital streams that individuals are producing are growing apace. Microsoft Research's MyLifeBits project (*http://research.microsoft.com/en-us/projects/mylifebits/default.aspx*) gives a glimpse of the archiving of personal information that may become commonplace in the near future. MyLifeBits was an experiment where an individual's interactions—phone calls, emails, documents—were captured electronically and stored for later access. The data gathered included a photo taken every minute, which resulted in an overall data volume of one gigabyte per month. When storage costs come down enough to make it feasible to store continuous audio and video, the data volume for a future MyLifeBits service will be many times that.

The trend is for every individual's data footprint to grow, but perhaps more important, the amount of data generated by machines will be even greater than that generated by people. Machine logs, RFID readers, sensor networks, vehicle GPS traces, retail transactions—all of these contribute to the growing mountain of data.

The volume of data being made publicly available increases every year, too. Organizations no longer have to merely manage their own data; success in the future will be dictated to a large extent by their ability to extract value from other organizations' data.

Initiatives such as Public Data Sets on Amazon Web Services (*http://aws.amazon.com/publicdatasets/*), Infochimps.org (*http://infochimps.org/*), and theinfo.org (*http://theinfo.org/*) exist to foster the "information commons," where data can be freely (or in the case of AWS, for a modest price) shared for anyone to download and analyze. Mashups between different information sources make for unexpected and hitherto unimaginable applications.

Take, for example, the Astrometry.net (*http://astrometry.net/*) project, which watches the Astrometry group on Flickr for new photos of the night sky. It analyzes each image and identifies which part of the sky it is from, as well as any interesting celestial bodies, such as stars or galaxies. This project shows the kind of things that are possible when data (in this case, tagged photographic images) is made available and used for something (image analysis) that was not anticipated by the creator.

It has been said that "more data usually beats better algorithms," which is to say that for some problems (such as recommending movies or music based on past preferences), however fiendish your algorithms are, often they can be beaten simply by having more data (and a less sophisticated algorithm).[3]

The good news is that Big Data is here. The bad news is that we are struggling to store and analyze it.

Data Storage and Analysis

The problem is simple: although the storage capacities of hard drives have increased massively over the years, access speeds—the rate at which data can be read from drives —have not kept up. One typical drive from 1990 could store 1,370 MB of data and had a transfer speed of 4.4 MB/s,[4] so you could read all the data from a full drive in around five minutes. Over 20 years later, one terabyte drives are the norm, but the transfer speed is around 100 MB/s, so it takes more than two and a half hours to read all the data off the disk.

This is a long time to read all data on a single drive—and writing is even slower. The obvious way to reduce the time is to read from multiple disks at once. Imagine if we had 100 drives, each holding one hundredth of the data. Working in parallel, we could read the data in under two minutes.

Using only one hundredth of a disk may seem wasteful. But we can store one hundred datasets, each of which is one terabyte, and provide shared access to them. We can imagine that the users of such a system would be happy to share access in return for shorter analysis times, and, statistically, that their analysis jobs would be likely to be spread over time, so they wouldn't interfere with each other too much.

There's more to being able to read and write data in parallel to or from multiple disks, though.

The first problem to solve is hardware failure: as soon as you start using many pieces of hardware, the chance that one will fail is fairly high. A common way of avoiding data loss is through replication: redundant copies of the data are kept by the system so that in the event of failure, there is another copy available. This is how RAID works, for instance, although Hadoop's filesystem; the Hadoop Distributed Filesystem (HDFS), takes a slightly different approach, as you shall see later.

The second problem is that most analysis tasks need to be able to combine the data in some way, and data read from one disk may need to be combined with the data from any of the other 99 disks. Various distributed systems allow data to be combined from

---

3. The quote is from Anand Rajaraman writing about the Netflix Challenge (*http://anand.typepad.com/ datawocky/2008/03/more-data-usual.html*). Alon Halevy, Peter Norvig, and Fernando Pereira make the same point in "The Unreasonable Effectiveness of Data," IEEE Intelligent Systems, March/April 2009.

4. These specifications are for the Seagate ST-41600n.

multiple sources, but doing this correctly is notoriously challenging. MapReduce provides a programming model that abstracts the problem from disk reads and writes, transforming it into a computation over sets of keys and values. We look at the details of this model in later chapters, but the important point for the present discussion is that there are two parts to the computation, the map and the reduce, and it's the interface between the two where the "mixing" occurs. Like HDFS, MapReduce has built-in reliability.

This, in a nutshell, is what Hadoop provides: a reliable shared storage and analysis system. The storage is provided by HDFS and analysis by MapReduce. There are other parts to Hadoop, but these capabilities are its kernel.

Comparison with Other Systems

The approach taken by MapReduce may seem like a brute-force approach. The premise is that the entire dataset—or at least a good portion of it—is processed for each query. But this is its power. MapReduce is a *batch* query processor, and the ability to run an ad hoc query against your whole dataset and get the results in a reasonable time is transformative. It changes the way you think about data and unlocks data that was previously archived on tape or disk. It gives people the opportunity to innovate with data. Questions that took too long to get answered before can now be answered, which in turn leads to new questions and new insights.

For example, Mailtrust, Rackspace's mail division, used Hadoop for processing email logs. One ad hoc query they wrote was to find the geographic distribution of their users. In their words:

> This data was so useful that we've scheduled the MapReduce job to run monthly and we will be using this data to help us decide which Rackspace data centers to place new mail servers in as we grow.

By bringing several hundred gigabytes of data together and having the tools to analyze it, the Rackspace engineers were able to gain an understanding of the data that they otherwise would never have had, and, furthermore, they were able to use what they had learned to improve the service for their customers. You can read more about how Rackspace uses Hadoop in Chapter 16.

Rational Database Management System

Why can't we use databases with lots of disks to do large-scale batch analysis? Why is MapReduce needed?

The answer to these questions comes from another trend in disk drives: seek time is improving more slowly than transfer rate. Seeking is the process of moving the disk's head to a particular place on the disk to read or write data. It characterizes the latency of a disk operation, whereas the transfer rate corresponds to a disk's bandwidth.

If the data access pattern is dominated by seeks, it will take longer to read or write large portions of the dataset than streaming through it, which operates at the transfer rate. On the other hand, for updating a small proportion of records in a database, a traditional B-Tree (the data structure used in relational databases, which is limited by the rate it can perform seeks) works well. For updating the majority of a database, a B-Tree is less efficient than MapReduce, which uses Sort/Merge to rebuild the database.

In many ways, MapReduce can be seen as a complement to a Rational Database Management System (RDBMS). (The differences between the two systems are shown in Table 1-1.) MapReduce is a good fit for problems that need to analyze the whole dataset in a batch fashion, particularly for ad hoc analysis. An RDBMS is good for point queries or updates, where the dataset has been indexed to deliver low-latency retrieval and update times of a relatively small amount of data. MapReduce suits applications where the data is written once and read many times, whereas a relational database is good for datasets that are continually updated.

Table 1-1. RDBMS compared to MapReduce

	Traditional RDBMS	MapReduce
Data size	Gigabytes	Petabytes
Access	Interactive and batch	Batch
Updates	Read and write many times	Write once, read many times
Structure	Static schema	Dynamic schema
Integrity	High	Low
Scaling	Nonlinear	Linear

Another difference between MapReduce and an RDBMS is the amount of structure in the datasets on which they operate. *Structured data* is data that is organized into entities that have a defined format, such as XML documents or database tables that conform to a particular predefined schema. This is the realm of the RDBMS. *Semi-structured data*, on the other hand, is looser, and though there may be a schema, it is often ignored, so it may be used only as a guide to the structure of the data: for example, a spreadsheet, in which the structure is the grid of cells, although the cells themselves may hold any form of data. *Unstructured data* does not have any particular internal structure: for example, plain text or image data. MapReduce works well on unstructured or semi-structured data because it is designed to interpret the data at processing time. In other words, the input keys and values for MapReduce are not intrinsic properties of the data, but they are chosen by the person analyzing the data.

Relational data is often *normalized* to retain its integrity and remove redundancy. Normalization poses problems for MapReduce because it makes reading a record a nonlocal operation, and one of the central assumptions that MapReduce makes is that it is possible to perform (high-speed) streaming reads and writes.

A web server log is a good example of a set of records that is *not* normalized (for example, the client hostnames are specified in full each time, even though the same client may appear many times), and this is one reason that logfiles of all kinds are particularly well-suited to analysis with MapReduce.

MapReduce is a linearly scalable programming model. The programmer writes two functions—a map function and a reduce function—each of which defines a mapping from one set of key-value pairs to another. These functions are oblivious to the size of the data or the cluster that they are operating on, so they can be used unchanged for a small dataset and for a massive one. More important, if you double the size of the input data, a job will run twice as slow. But if you also double the size of the cluster, a job will run as fast as the original one. This is not generally true of SQL queries.

Over time, however, the differences between relational databases and MapReduce systems are likely to blur—both as relational databases start incorporating some of the ideas from MapReduce (such as Aster Data's and Greenplum's databases) and, from the other direction, as higher-level query languages built on MapReduce (such as Pig and Hive) make MapReduce systems more approachable for traditional database programmers.[5]

Grid Computing

The High Performance Computing (HPC) and Grid Computing communities have been doing large-scale data processing for years, using such Application Program Interfaces (APIs) as Message Passing Interface (MPI). Broadly, the approach in HPC is to distribute the work across a cluster of machines, which access a shared filesystem, hosted by a Storage Area Network (SAN). This works well for predominantly compute-intensive jobs, but it becomes a problem when nodes need to access larger data volumes (hundreds of gigabytes, the point at which MapReduce really starts to shine), since the network bandwidth is the bottleneck and compute nodes become idle.

5. In January 2007, David J. DeWitt and Michael Stonebraker caused a stir by publishing "MapReduce: A major step backwards," in which they criticized MapReduce for being a poor substitute for relational databases. Many commentators argued that it was a false comparison (see, for example, Mark C. Chu-Carroll's "Databases are hammers; MapReduce is a screwdriver," and DeWitt and Stonebraker followed up with "MapReduce II," where they addressed the main topics brought up by others.

MapReduce tries to collocate the data with the compute node, so data access is fast because it is local.[6] This feature, known as *data locality*, is at the heart of MapReduce and is the reason for its good performance. Recognizing that network bandwidth is the most precious resource in a data center environment (it is easy to saturate network links by copying data around), MapReduce implementations go to great lengths to conserve it by explicitly modelling network topology. Notice that this arrangement does not preclude high-CPU analyses in MapReduce.

MPI gives great control to the programmer, but requires that he explicitly handle the mechanics of the data flow, exposed via low-level C routines and constructs such as sockets, as well as the higher-level algorithm for the analysis. MapReduce operates only at the higher level: the programmer thinks in terms of functions of key and value pairs, and the data flow is implicit.

Coordinating the processes in a large-scale distributed computation is a challenge. The hardest aspect is gracefully handling partial failure—when you don't know whether or not a remote process has failed—and still making progress with the overall computation. MapReduce spares the programmer from having to think about failure, since the implementation detects failed map or reduce tasks and reschedules replacements on machines that are healthy. MapReduce is able to do this because it is a *shared-nothing* architecture, meaning that tasks have no dependence on one other. (This is a slight oversimplification, since the output from mappers is fed to the reducers, but this is under the control of the MapReduce system; in this case, it needs to take more care rerunning a failed reducer than rerunning a failed map because it has to make sure it can retrieve the necessary map outputs, and if not, regenerate them by running the relevant maps again.) So from the programmer's point of view, the order in which the tasks run doesn't matter. By contrast, MPI programs have to explicitly manage their own checkpointing and recovery, which gives more control to the programmer but makes them more difficult to write.

MapReduce might sound like quite a restrictive programming model, and in a sense it is: you are limited to key and value types that are related in specified ways, and mappers and reducers run with very limited coordination between one another (the mappers pass keys and values to reducers). A natural question to ask is: can you do anything useful or nontrivial with it?

The answer is yes. MapReduce was invented by engineers at Google as a system for building production search indexes because they found themselves solving the same problem over and over again (and MapReduce was inspired by older ideas from the functional programming, distributed computing, and database communities), but it has since been used for many other applications in many other industries. It is pleasantly surprising to see the range of algorithms that can be expressed in MapReduce, from

---

6. Jim Gray was an early advocate of putting the computation near the data. See "Distributed Computing Economics," March 2003, *http://research.microsoft.com/apps/pubs/default.aspx?id=70001*.

image analysis, to graph-based problems, to machine learning algorithms.[7] It can't solve every problem, of course, but it is a general data-processing tool.

You can see a sample of some of the applications that Hadoop has been used for in Chapter 16.

Volunteer Computing

When people first hear about Hadoop and MapReduce, they often ask, "How is it different from SETI@home?" SETI, the Search for Extra-Terrestrial Intelligence, runs a project called SETI@home (*http://setiathome.berkeley.edu/*) in which volunteers donate CPU time from their otherwise idle computers to analyze radio telescope data for signs of intelligent life outside earth. SETI@home is the most well-known of many *volunteer computing* projects; others include the Great Internet Mersenne Prime Search (to search for large prime numbers) and Folding@home (to understand protein folding and how it relates to disease).

Volunteer computing projects work by breaking the problem they are trying to solve into chunks called *work units*, which are sent to computers around the world to be analyzed. For example, a SETI@home work unit is about 0.35 MB of radio telescope data, and takes hours or days to analyze on a typical home computer. When the analysis is completed, the results are sent back to the server, and the client gets another work unit. As a precaution to combat cheating, each work unit is sent to three different machines and needs at least two results to agree to be accepted.

Although SETI@home may be superficially similar to MapReduce (breaking a problem into independent pieces to be worked on in parallel), there are some significant differences. The SETI@home problem is very CPU-intensive, which makes it suitable for running on hundreds of thousands of computers across the world[8] because the time to transfer the work unit is dwarfed by the time to run the computation on it. Volunteers are donating CPU cycles, not bandwidth.

MapReduce is designed to run jobs that last minutes or hours on trusted, dedicated hardware running in a single data center with very high aggregate bandwidth interconnects. By contrast, SETI@home runs a perpetual computation on untrusted machines on the Internet with highly variable connection speeds and no data locality.

---

7. Apache Mahout (*http://mahout.apache.org/*) is a project to build machine-learning libraries (such as classification and clustering algorithms) that run on Hadoop.

8. In January 2008, SETI@home was reported at *http://www.planetary.org/programs/projects/setiathome/setiathome_20080115.html* to be processing 300 gigabytes a day, using 320,000 computers (most of which are not dedicated to SETI@home; they are used for other things, too).

A Brief History of Hadoop

Hadoop was created by Doug Cutting, the creator of Apache Lucene, the widely used text search library. Hadoop has its origins in Apache Nutch, an open source web search engine, itself a part of the Lucene project.

The Origin of the Name "Hadoop"

The name Hadoop is not an acronym; it's a made-up name. The project's creator, Doug Cutting, explains how the name came about:

> The name my kid gave a stuffed yellow elephant. Short, relatively easy to spell and pronounce, meaningless, and not used elsewhere: those are my naming criteria. Kids are good at generating such. Googol is a kid's term.

Subprojects and "contrib" modules in Hadoop also tend to have names that are unrelated to their function, often with an elephant or other animal theme ("Pig," for example). Smaller components are given more descriptive (and therefore more mundane) names. This is a good principle, as it means you can generally work out what something does from its name. For example, the jobtracker[9] keeps track of MapReduce jobs.

Building a web search engine from scratch was an ambitious goal, for not only is the software required to crawl and index websites complex to write, but it is also a challenge to run without a dedicated operations team, since there are so many moving parts. It's expensive, too: Mike Cafarella and Doug Cutting estimated a system supporting a one-billion-page index would cost around half a million dollars in hardware, with a monthly running cost of $30,000.[10] Nevertheless, they believed it was a worthy goal, as it would open up and ultimately democratize search engine algorithms.

Nutch was started in 2002, and a working crawler and search system quickly emerged. However, they realized that their architecture wouldn't scale to the billions of pages on the Web. Help was at hand with the publication of a paper in 2003 that described the architecture of Google's distributed filesystem, called GFS, which was being used in production at Google.[11] GFS, or something like it, would solve their storage needs for the very large files generated as a part of the web crawl and indexing process. In particular, GFS would free up time being spent on administrative tasks such as managing storage nodes. In 2004, they set about writing an open source implementation, the Nutch Distributed Filesystem (NDFS).

---

9. In this book, we use the lowercase form, "jobtracker," to denote the entity when it's being referred to generally, and the CamelCase form JobTracker to denote the Java class that implements it.

10. See Mike Cafarella and Doug Cutting, "Building Nutch: Open Source Search," *ACM Queue*, April 2004, *http://queue.acm.org/detail.cfm?id=988408*.

11. Sanjay Ghemawat, Howard Gobioff, and Shun-Tak Leung, "The Google File System," October 2003, *http://labs.google.com/papers/gfs.html*.

In 2004, Google published the paper that introduced MapReduce to the world.[12] Early in 2005, the Nutch developers had a working MapReduce implementation in Nutch, and by the middle of that year. All the major Nutch algorithms had been ported to run using MapReduce and NDFS.

NDFS and the MapReduce implementation in Nutch were applicable beyond the realm of search, and in February 2006 they moved out of Nutch to form an independent subproject of Lucene called Hadoop. At around the same time, Doug Cutting joined Yahoo!, which provided a dedicated team and the resources to turn Hadoop into a system that ran at web scale (see the sidebar "Hadoop at Yahoo!" on page 11). This was demonstrated in February 2008 when Yahoo! announced that its production search index was being generated by a 10,000-core Hadoop cluster.[13]

In January 2008, Hadoop was made its own top-level project at Apache, confirming its success and its diverse, active community. By this time, Hadoop was being used by many other companies besides Yahoo!, such as Last.fm, Facebook, and the *New York Times*. Some applications are covered in the case studies in Chapter 16 and on the Hadoop wiki (*http://wiki.apache.org/hadoop/PoweredBy*).

In one well-publicized feat, the *New York Times* used Amazon's EC2 compute cloud to crunch through four terabytes of scanned archives from the paper, converting them to PDFs for the Web.[14] The processing took less than 24 hours to run using 100 machines, and the project probably wouldn't have been embarked upon without the combination of Amazon's pay-by-the-hour model (which allowed the NYT to access a large number of machines for a short period) and Hadoop's easy-to-use parallel programming model.

In April 2008, Hadoop broke a world record to become the fastest system to sort a terabyte of data. Running on a 910-node cluster, Hadoop sorted one terabyte in 209 seconds (just under 3½ minutes), beating the previous year's winner of 297 seconds (described in detail in "TeraByte Sort on Apache Hadoop" on page 603). In November of the same year, Google reported that its MapReduce implementation sorted one terabyte in 68 seconds.[15] As the first edition of this book was going to press (May 2009), it was announced that a team at Yahoo! used Hadoop to sort one terabyte in 62 seconds.

Since then, Hadoop has seen rapid mainstream enterprise adoption. Hadoop's role as a general-purpose storage and analysis platform for big data has been recognized by

---

12. Jeffrey Dean and Sanjay Ghemawat, "MapReduce: Simplified Data Processing on Large Clusters ," December 2004, *http://labs.google.com/papers/mapreduce.html*.

13. "Yahoo! Launches World's Largest Hadoop Production Application," 19 February 2008, *http://developer .yahoo.net/blogs/hadoop/2008/02/yahoo-worlds-largest-production-hadoop.html*.

14. Derek Gottfrid, "Self-service, Prorated Super Computing Fun!" 1 November 2007, *http://open.blogs .nytimes.com/2007/11/01/self-service-prorated-super-computing-fun/*.

15. "Sorting 1PB with MapReduce," 21 November 2008, *http://googleblog.blogspot.com/2008/11/sorting-1pb -with-mapreduce.html*.

the industry, and this fact is reflected in the number of products that use or incorporate Hadoop in some way. There are Hadoop distributions from the large, established enterprise vendors, including EMC, IBM, Microsoft, and Oracle, as well as from specialist Hadoop companies such as Cloudera, Hortonworks, and MapR.

Hadoop at Yahoo!

Building Internet-scale search engines requires huge amounts of data and therefore large numbers of machines to process it. Yahoo! Search consists of four primary components: the *Crawler*, which downloads pages from web servers; the *WebMap*, which builds a graph of the known Web; the *Indexer*, which builds a reverse index to the best pages; and the *Runtime*, which answers users' queries. The WebMap is a graph that consists of roughly 1 trillion (10^{12}) edges, each representing a web link, and 100 billion (10^{11}) nodes, each representing distinct URLs. Creating and analyzing such a large graph requires a large number of computers running for many days. In early 2005, the infrastructure for the WebMap, named *Dreadnaught*, needed to be redesigned to scale up to more nodes. Dreadnaught had successfully scaled from 20 to 600 nodes, but required a complete redesign to scale out further. Dreadnaught is similar to MapReduce in many ways, but provides more flexibility and less structure. In particular, each fragment in a Dreadnaught job can send output to each of the fragments in the next stage of the job, but the sort was all done in library code. In practice, most of the WebMap phases were pairs that corresponded to MapReduce. Therefore, the WebMap applications would not require extensive refactoring to fit into MapReduce.

Eric Baldeschwieler (Eric14) created a small team and we started designing and prototyping a new framework written in C++ modeled after GFS and MapReduce to replace Dreadnaught. Although the immediate need was for a new framework for WebMap, it was clear that standardization of the batch platform across Yahoo! Search was critical and by making the framework general enough to support other users, we could better leverage investment in the new platform.

At the same time, we were watching Hadoop, which was part of Nutch, and its progress. In January 2006, Yahoo! hired Doug Cutting, and a month later we decided to abandon our prototype and adopt Hadoop. The advantage of Hadoop over our prototype and design was that it was already working with a real application (Nutch) on 20 nodes. That allowed us to bring up a research cluster two months later and start helping real customers use the new framework much sooner than we could have otherwise. Another advantage, of course, was that since Hadoop was already open source, it was easier (although far from easy!) to get permission from Yahoo!'s legal department to work in open source. So we set up a 200-node cluster for the researchers in early 2006 and put the WebMap conversion plans on hold while we supported and improved Hadoop for the research users.

Here's a quick timeline of how things have progressed:

- 2004: Initial versions of what is now Hadoop Distributed Filesystem and MapReduce implemented by Doug Cutting and Mike Cafarella.

- December 2005: Nutch ported to the new framework. Hadoop runs reliably on 20 nodes.
- January 2006: Doug Cutting joins Yahoo!.
- February 2006: Apache Hadoop project officially started to support the standalone development of MapReduce and HDFS.
- February 2006: Adoption of Hadoop by Yahoo! Grid team.
- April 2006: Sort benchmark (10 GB/node) run on 188 nodes in 47.9 hours.
- May 2006: Yahoo! set up a Hadoop research cluster—300 nodes.
- May 2006: Sort benchmark run on 500 nodes in 42 hours (better hardware than April benchmark).
- October 2006: Research cluster reaches 600 nodes.
- December 2006: Sort benchmark run on 20 nodes in 1.8 hours, 100 nodes in 3.3 hours, 500 nodes in 5.2 hours, 900 nodes in 7.8 hours.
- January 2007: Research cluster reaches 900 nodes.
- April 2007: Research clusters—two clusters of 1000 nodes.
- April 2008: Won the 1-terabyte sort benchmark in 209 seconds on 900 nodes.
- October 2008: Loading 10 terabytes of data per day onto research clusters.
- March 2009: 17 clusters with a total of 24,000 nodes.
- April 2009: Won the minute sort by sorting 500 GB in 59 seconds (on 1,400 nodes) and the 100-terabyte sort in 173 minutes (on 3,400 nodes).

—Owen O'Malley

Apache Hadoop and the Hadoop Ecosystem

Although Hadoop is best known for MapReduce and its distributed filesystem (HDFS, renamed from NDFS), the term is also used for a family of related projects that fall under the umbrella of infrastructure for distributed computing and large-scale data processing.

All of the core projects covered in this book are hosted by the Apache Software Foundation (*http://hadoop.apache.org/*), which provides support for a community of open source software projects, including the original HTTP Server from which it gets its name. As the Hadoop ecosystem grows, more projects are appearing, not necessarily hosted at Apache, that provide complementary services to Hadoop or build on the core to add higher-level abstractions.

The Hadoop projects that are covered in this book are described briefly here:

Common
    A set of components and interfaces for distributed filesystems and general I/O (serialization, Java RPC, persistent data structures).

Avro

A serialization system for efficient, cross-language RPC and persistent data storage.

MapReduce

A distributed data processing model and execution environment that runs on large clusters of commodity machines.

HDFS

A distributed filesystem that runs on large clusters of commodity machines.

Pig

A data flow language and execution environment for exploring very large datasets. Pig runs on HDFS and MapReduce clusters.

Hive

A distributed data warehouse. Hive manages data stored in HDFS and provides a query language based on SQL (and which is translated by the runtime engine to MapReduce jobs) for querying the data.

HBase

A distributed, column-oriented database. HBase uses HDFS for its underlying storage, and supports both batch-style computations using MapReduce and point queries (random reads).

ZooKeeper

A distributed, highly available coordination service. ZooKeeper provides primitives such as distributed locks that can be used for building distributed applications.

Sqoop

A tool for efficient bulk transfer of data between structured data stores (such as relational databases) and HDFS.

Oozie

A service for running and scheduling workflows of Hadoop jobs (including MapReduce, Pig, Hive, and Sqoop jobs).

Hadoop Releases

Which version of Hadoop should you use? The answer to this question changes over time, of course, and also depends on the features that you need. "Hadoop Releases" on page 13 summarizes the high-level features in recent Hadoop release series.

There are a few active release series. The 1.x release series is a continuation of the 0.20 release series and contains the most stable versions of Hadoop currently available. This series includes secure Kerberos authentication, which prevents unauthorized access to Hadoop data (see "Security" on page 325). Almost all production clusters use these releases or derived versions (such as commercial distributions).

The 0.22 and 2.x release series[16] are not currently stable (as of early 2012), but this is likely to change by the time you read this as they undergo more real-world testing (consult the Apache Hadoop releases page for the latest status). 2.x includes several major new features:

- A new MapReduce runtime, called MapReduce 2, implemented on a new system called YARN (Yet Another Resource Negotiator), which is a general resource management system for running distributed applications. MapReduce 2 replaces the "classic" runtime in previous releases. It is described in more depth in "YARN (MapReduce 2)" on page 196.

- HDFS federation, which partitions the HDFS namespace across multiple namenodes to support clusters with very large numbers of files. See "HDFS Federation" on page 47.

- HDFS high-availability, which removes the namenode as a single point of failure by supporting standby namenodes for failover. See "HDFS High-Availability" on page 48.

Table 1-2. Features supported by Hadoop release series

Feature	1.x	0.22	2.x
Secure authentication	Yes	No	Yes
Old configuration names	Yes	Deprecated	Deprecated
New configuration names	No	Yes	Yes
Old MapReduce API	Yes	Yes	Yes
New MapReduce API	Yes (with some missing libraries)	Yes	Yes
MapReduce 1 runtime (Classic)	Yes	Yes	No
MapReduce 2 runtime (YARN)	No	No	Yes
HDFS federation	No	No	Yes
HDFS high-availability	No	No	Yes

Table 1-2 only covers features in HDFS and MapReduce. Other projects in the Hadoop ecosystem are continually evolving too, and picking a combination of components that work well together can be a challenge. Thankfully, you don't have to do this work yourself. The Apache Bigtop project (*http://incubator.apache.org/bigtop/*) runs interoperability tests on stacks of Hadoop components and provides Linux packages (RPMs and Debian packages) for easy installation. There are also commercial vendors offering Hadoop distributions containing suites of compatible components.

16. As this book went to press, the Hadoop community voted for the 0.23 release series to be renamed as the 2.x release series. This book uses the shorthand "releases after 1.x" to refer to releases in the 0.22 and 2.x (formerly 0.23) series.

What's Covered in This Book

This book covers all the releases in Table 1-2. In the cases where a feature is available only in a particular release, it is noted in the text.

The code in this book is written to work against all these release series, except in a small number of cases, which are called out explicitly. The example code available on the website has a list of the versions that it was tested against.

Configuration names

Configuration property names have been changed in the releases after 1.x, in order to give them a more regular naming structure. For example, the HDFS properties pertaining to the namenode have been changed to have a `dfs.namenode` prefix, so `dfs.name.dir` has changed to `dfs.namenode.name.dir`. Similarly, MapReduce properties have the `mapreduce` prefix, rather than the older `mapred` prefix, so `mapred.job.name` has changed to `mapreduce.job.name`.

For properties that exist in version 1.x, the old (deprecated) names are used in this book because they will work in all the versions of Hadoop listed here. If you are using a release after 1.x, you may wish to use the new property names in your configuration files and code to remove deprecation warnings. A table listing the deprecated properties names and their replacements can be found on the Hadoop website at *http://hadoop.apache .org/common/docs/r0.23.0/hadoop-project-dist/hadoop-common/DeprecatedProperties .html*.

MapReduce APIs

Hadoop provides two Java MapReduce APIs, described in more detail in "The old and the new Java MapReduce APIs" on page 27. This edition of the book uses the new API for the examples, which will work with all versions listed here, except in a few cases where a MapReduce library using new API is not available in the 1.x releases. All the examples in this book are available in the old API version (in the `oldapi` package) from the book's website.

Where there are material differences between the two APIs, they are discussed in the text.

Compatibility

When moving from one release to another, you need to consider the upgrade steps that are needed. There are several aspects to consider: API compatibility, data compatibility, and wire compatibility.

API compatibility concerns the contract between user code and the published Hadoop APIs, such as the Java MapReduce APIs. Major releases (e.g., from 1.x.y to 2.0.0) are allowed to break API compatibility, so user programs may need to be modified and recompiled. Minor releases (e.g., from 1.0.x to 1.1.0) and point releases (e.g., from 1.0.1 to 1.0.2) should not break compatibility.[17]

 Hadoop uses a classification scheme for API elements to denote their stability. The preceding rules for API compatibility cover those elements that are marked InterfaceStability.Stable. Some elements of the public Hadoop APIs, however, are marked with the InterfaceStability.Evolving or InterfaceStability.Unstable annotations (all these annotations are in the org.apache.hadoop.classification package), which mean they are allowed to break compatibility on minor and point releases, respectively.

Data compatibility concerns persistent data and metadata formats, such as the format in which the HDFS namenode stores its persistent data. The formats can change across minor or major releases, but the change is transparent to users because the upgrade will automatically migrate the data. There may be some restrictions about upgrade paths, and these are covered in the release notes. For example, it may be necessary to upgrade via an intermediate release rather than upgrading directly to the later final release in one step. Hadoop upgrades are discussed in more detail in "Upgrades" on page 362.

Wire compatibility concerns the interoperability between clients and servers via wire protocols such as RPC and HTTP. There are two types of client: external clients (run by users) and internal clients (run on the cluster as a part of the system, e.g., datanode and tasktracker daemons). In general, internal clients have to be upgraded in lockstep; an older version of a tasktracker will not work with a newer jobtracker, for example. In the future, rolling upgrades may be supported, which would allow cluster daemons to be upgraded in phases, so that the cluster would still be available to external clients during the upgrade.

For external clients that are run by the user—such as a program that reads or writes from HDFS, or the MapReduce job submission client—the client must have the same major release number as the server, but is allowed to have a lower minor or point release number (e.g., client version 1.0.1 will work with server 1.0.2 or 1.1.0, but not with server 2.0.0). Any exception to this rule should be called out in the release notes.

---

17. Pre-1.0 releases follow the rules for major releases, so a change in version from, say, 0.1.0 to 0.2.0 constitutes a major release, and therefore may break API compatibility.

MapReduce

MapReduce is a programming model for data processing. The model is simple, yet not too simple to express useful programs in. Hadoop can run MapReduce programs written in various languages; in this chapter, we look at the same program expressed in Java, Ruby, Python, and C++. Most important, MapReduce programs are inherently parallel, thus putting very large-scale data analysis into the hands of anyone with enough machines at her disposal. MapReduce comes into its own for large datasets, so let's start by looking at one.

A Weather Dataset

For our example, we will write a program that mines weather data. Weather sensors collect data every hour at many locations across the globe and gather a large volume of log data, which is a good candidate for analysis with MapReduce because it is semistructured and record-oriented.

Data Format

The data we will use is from the National Climatic Data Center (NCDC, *http://www .ncdc.noaa.gov/*). The data is stored using a line-oriented ASCII format, in which each line is a record. The format supports a rich set of meteorological elements, many of which are optional or with variable data lengths. For simplicity, we focus on the basic elements, such as temperature, which are always present and are of fixed width.

Example 2-1 shows a sample line with some of the salient fields highlighted. The line has been split into multiple lines to show each field; in the real file, fields are packed into one line with no delimiters.

Example 2-1. Format of a National Climate Data Center record

```
0057
332130   # USAF weather station identifier
99999    # WBAN weather station identifier
19500101 # observation date
0300     # observation time
4
+51317   # latitude (degrees x 1000)
+028783  # longitude (degrees x 1000)
FM-12
+0171    # elevation (meters)
99999
V020
320      # wind direction (degrees)
1        # quality code
N
0072
1
00450    # sky ceiling height (meters)
1        # quality code
C
N
010000   # visibility distance (meters)
1        # quality code
N
9
-0128    # air temperature (degrees Celsius x 10)
1        # quality code
-0139    # dew point temperature (degrees Celsius x 10)
1        # quality code
10268    # atmospheric pressure (hectopascals x 10)
1        # quality code
```

Datafiles are organized by date and weather station. There is a directory for each year from 1901 to 2001, each containing a gzipped file for each weather station with its readings for that year. For example, here are the first entries for 1990:

```
% ls raw/1990 | head
010010-99999-1990.gz
010014-99999-1990.gz
010015-99999-1990.gz
010016-99999-1990.gz
010017-99999-1990.gz
010030-99999-1990.gz
010040-99999-1990.gz
010080-99999-1990.gz
010100-99999-1990.gz
010150-99999-1990.gz
```

Since there are tens of thousands of weather stations, the whole dataset is made up of a large number of relatively small files. It's generally easier and more efficient to process a smaller number of relatively large files, so the data was preprocessed so that each year's readings were concatenated into a single file. (The means by which this was carried out is described in Appendix C.)

Analyzing the Data with Unix Tools

What's the highest recorded global temperature for each year in the dataset? We will answer this first without using Hadoop, as this information will provide a performance baseline and a useful means to check our results.

The classic tool for processing line-oriented data is *awk*. Example 2-2 is a small script to calculate the maximum temperature for each year.

Example 2-2. A program for finding the maximum recorded temperature by year from NCDC weather records

```
#!/usr/bin/env bash
for year in all/*
do
  echo -ne `basename $year .gz`"\t"
  gunzip -c $year | \
    awk '{ temp = substr($0, 88, 5) + 0;
           q = substr($0, 93, 1);
           if (temp !=9999 && q ~ /[01459]/ && temp > max) max = temp }
         END { print max }'
done
```

The script loops through the compressed year files, first printing the year, and then processing each file using *awk*. The *awk* script extracts two fields from the data: the air temperature and the quality code. The air temperature value is turned into an integer by adding 0. Next, a test is applied to see whether the temperature is valid (the value 9999 signifies a missing value in the NCDC dataset) and whether the quality code indicates that the reading is not suspect or erroneous. If the reading is OK, the value is compared with the maximum value seen so far, which is updated if a new maximum is found. The END block is executed after all the lines in the file have been processed, and it prints the maximum value.

Here is the beginning of a run:

```
% ./max_temperature.sh
1901    317
1902    244
1903    289
1904    256
1905    283
...
```

The temperature values in the source file are scaled by a factor of 10, so this works out as a maximum temperature of 31.7°C for 1901 (there were very few readings at the beginning of the century, so this is plausible). The complete run for the century took 42 minutes in one run on a single EC2 High-CPU Extra Large Instance.

To speed up the processing, we need to run parts of the program in parallel. In theory, this is straightforward: we could process different years in different processes, using all the available hardware threads on a machine. There are a few problems with this, however.

First, dividing the work into equal-size pieces isn't always easy or obvious. In this case, the file size for different years varies widely, so some processes will finish much earlier than others. Even if they pick up further work, the whole run is dominated by the longest file. A better approach, although one that requires more work, is to split the input into fixed-size chunks and assign each chunk to a process.

Second, combining the results from independent processes may need further processing. In this case, the result for each year is independent of other years and may be combined by concatenating all the results and sorting by year. If using the fixed-size chunk approach, the combination is more delicate. For this example, data for a particular year will typically be split into several chunks, each processed independently. We'll end up with the maximum temperature for each chunk, so the final step is to look for the highest of these maximums for each year.

Third, you are still limited by the processing capacity of a single machine. If the best time you can achieve is 20 minutes with the number of processors you have, then that's it. You can't make it go faster. Also, some datasets grow beyond the capacity of a single machine. When we start using multiple machines, a whole host of other factors come into play, mainly falling into the category of coordination and reliability. Who runs the overall job? How do we deal with failed processes?

So, although it's feasible to parallelize the processing, in practice it's messy. Using a framework like Hadoop to take care of these issues is a great help.

Analyzing the Data with Hadoop

To take advantage of the parallel processing that Hadoop provides, we need to express our query as a MapReduce job. After some local, small-scale testing, we will be able to run it on a cluster of machines.

Map and Reduce

MapReduce works by breaking the processing into two phases: the map phase and the reduce phase. Each phase has key-value pairs as input and output, the types of which may be chosen by the programmer. The programmer also specifies two functions: the map function and the reduce function.

The input to our map phase is the raw NCDC data. We choose a text input format that gives us each line in the dataset as a text value. The key is the offset of the beginning of the line from the beginning of the file, but as we have no need for this, we ignore it.

Our map function is simple. We pull out the year and the air temperature because these are the only fields we are interested in. In this case, the map function is just a data preparation phase, setting up the data in such a way that the reducer function can do its work on it: finding the maximum temperature for each year. The map function is also a good place to drop bad records: here we filter out temperatures that are missing, suspect, or erroneous.

To visualize the way the map works, consider the following sample lines of input data (some unused columns have been dropped to fit the page, indicated by ellipses):

```
0067011990999991950051507004...9999999N9+00001+99999999999...
0043011990999991950051512004...9999999N9+00221+99999999999...
0043011990999991950051518004...9999999N9-00111+99999999999...
0043012650999991949032412004...0500001N9+01111+99999999999...
0043012650999991949032418004...0500001N9+00781+99999999999...
```

These lines are presented to the map function as the key-value pairs:

```
(0, 0067011990999991950051507004...9999999N9+00001+99999999999...)
(106, 0043011990999991950051512004...9999999N9+00221+99999999999...)
(212, 0043011990999991950051518004...9999999N9-00111+99999999999...)
(318, 0043012650999991949032412004...0500001N9+01111+99999999999...)
(424, 0043012650999991949032418004...0500001N9+00781+99999999999...)
```

The keys are the line offsets within the file, which we ignore in our map function. The map function merely extracts the year and the air temperature (indicated in bold text), and emits them as its output (the temperature values have been interpreted as integers):

```
(1950, 0)
(1950, 22)
(1950, -11)
(1949, 111)
(1949, 78)
```

The output from the map function is processed by the MapReduce framework before being sent to the reduce function. This processing sorts and groups the key-value pairs by key. So, continuing the example, our reduce function sees the following input:

```
(1949, [111, 78])
(1950, [0, 22, -11])
```

Each year appears with a list of all its air temperature readings. All the reduce function has to do now is iterate through the list and pick up the maximum reading:

```
(1949, 111)
(1950, 22)
```

This is the final output: the maximum global temperature recorded in each year.

The whole data flow is illustrated in Figure 2-1. At the bottom of the diagram is a Unix pipeline, which mimics the whole MapReduce flow and which we will see again later in this chapter when we look at Hadoop Streaming.

Figure 2-1. MapReduce logical data flow

Java MapReduce

Having run through how the MapReduce program works, the next step is to express it in code. We need three things: a map function, a reduce function, and some code to run the job. The map function is represented by the Mapper class, which declares an abstract map() method. Example 2-3 shows the implementation of our map method.

Example 2-3. Mapper for the maximum temperature example

```java
import java.io.IOException;

import org.apache.hadoop.io.IntWritable;
import org.apache.hadoop.io.LongWritable;
import org.apache.hadoop.io.Text;
import org.apache.hadoop.mapreduce.Mapper;

public class MaxTemperatureMapper
  extends Mapper<LongWritable, Text, Text, IntWritable> {

  private static final int MISSING = 9999;

  @Override
  public void map(LongWritable key, Text value, Context context)
      throws IOException, InterruptedException {

    String line = value.toString();
    String year = line.substring(15, 19);
    int airTemperature;
    if (line.charAt(87) == '+') { // parseInt doesn't like leading plus signs
      airTemperature = Integer.parseInt(line.substring(88, 92));
    } else {
      airTemperature = Integer.parseInt(line.substring(87, 92));
    }
    String quality = line.substring(92, 93);
    if (airTemperature != MISSING && quality.matches("[01459]")) {
      context.write(new Text(year), new IntWritable(airTemperature));
    }
  }
}
```

The Mapper class is a generic type, with four formal type parameters that specify the input key, input value, output key, and output value types of the map function. For the present example, the input key is a long integer offset, the input value is a line of text, the output key is a year, and the output value is an air temperature (an integer). Rather than use built-in Java types, Hadoop provides its own set of basic types that are optimized for network serialization. These are found in the `org.apache.hadoop.io` package. Here we use `LongWritable`, which corresponds to a Java `Long`, `Text` (like Java `String`), and `IntWritable` (like Java `Integer`).

The `map()` method is passed a key and a value. We convert the `Text` value containing the line of input into a Java `String`, then use its `substring()` method to extract the columns we are interested in.

The `map()` method also provides an instance of `Context` to write the output to. In this case, we write the year as a `Text` object (since we are just using it as a key), and the temperature is wrapped in an `IntWritable`. We write an output record only if the temperature is present and the quality code indicates the temperature reading is OK.

The reduce function is similarly defined using a `Reducer`, as illustrated in Example 2-4.

Example 2-4. Reducer for the maximum temperature example

```
import java.io.IOException;

import org.apache.hadoop.io.IntWritable;
import org.apache.hadoop.io.Text;
import org.apache.hadoop.mapreduce.Reducer;

public class MaxTemperatureReducer
  extends Reducer<Text, IntWritable, Text, IntWritable> {

  @Override
  public void reduce(Text key, Iterable<IntWritable> values,
      Context context)
      throws IOException, InterruptedException {

    int maxValue = Integer.MIN_VALUE;
    for (IntWritable value : values) {
      maxValue = Math.max(maxValue, value.get());
    }
    context.write(key, new IntWritable(maxValue));
  }
}
```

Again, four formal type parameters are used to specify the input and output types, this time for the reduce function. The input types of the reduce function must match the output types of the map function: `Text` and `IntWritable`. And in this case, the output types of the reduce function are `Text` and `IntWritable`, for a year and its maximum temperature, which we find by iterating through the temperatures and comparing each with a record of the highest found so far.

The third piece of code runs the MapReduce job (see Example 2-5).

Example 2-5. Application to find the maximum temperature in the weather dataset

```
import org.apache.hadoop.fs.Path;
import org.apache.hadoop.io.IntWritable;
import org.apache.hadoop.io.Text;
import org.apache.hadoop.mapreduce.Job;
import org.apache.hadoop.mapreduce.lib.input.FileInputFormat;
import org.apache.hadoop.mapreduce.lib.output.FileOutputFormat;

public class MaxTemperature {

  public static void main(String[] args) throws Exception {
    if (args.length != 2) {
      System.err.println("Usage: MaxTemperature <input path> <output path>");
      System.exit(-1);
    }

    Job job = new Job();
    job.setJarByClass(MaxTemperature.class);
    job.setJobName("Max temperature");

    FileInputFormat.addInputPath(job, new Path(args[0]));
    FileOutputFormat.setOutputPath(job, new Path(args[1]));

    job.setMapperClass(MaxTemperatureMapper.class);
    job.setReducerClass(MaxTemperatureReducer.class);

    job.setOutputKeyClass(Text.class);
    job.setOutputValueClass(IntWritable.class);

    System.exit(job.waitForCompletion(true) ? 0 : 1);
  }
}
```

A Job object forms the specification of the job and gives you control over how the job is run. When we run this job on a Hadoop cluster, we will package the code into a JAR file (which Hadoop will distribute around the cluster). Rather than explicitly specify the name of the JAR file, we can pass a class in the Job's setJarByClass() method, which Hadoop will use to locate the relevant JAR file by looking for the JAR file containing this class.

Having constructed a Job object, we specify the input and output paths. An input path is specified by calling the static addInputPath() method on FileInputFormat, and it can be a single file, a directory (in which case the input forms all the files in that directory), or a file pattern. As the name suggests, addInputPath() can be called more than once to use input from multiple paths.

The output path (of which there is only one) is specified by the static setOutput Path() method on FileOutputFormat. It specifies a directory where the output files from the reducer functions are written. The directory shouldn't exist before running the job because Hadoop will complain and not run the job. This precaution is to prevent data loss (it can be very annoying to accidentally overwrite the output of a long job with another).

Next, we specify the map and reduce types to use via the setMapperClass() and setReducerClass() methods.

The setOutputKeyClass() and setOutputValueClass() methods control the output types for the map and the reduce functions, which are often the same, as they are in our case. If they are different, the map output types can be set using the methods setMapOutputKeyClass() and setMapOutputValueClass().

The input types are controlled via the input format, which we have not explicitly set because we are using the default TextInputFormat.

After setting the classes that define the map and reduce functions, we are ready to run the job. The waitForCompletion() method on Job submits the job and waits for it to finish. The method's Boolean argument is a verbose flag, so in this case the job writes information about its progress to the console.

The return value of the waitForCompletion() method is a Boolean indicating success (true) or failure (false), which we translate into the program's exit code of 0 or 1.

A test run

After writing a MapReduce job, it's normal to try it out on a small dataset to flush out any immediate problems with the code. First, install Hadoop in standalone mode—there are instructions for how to do this in Appendix A. This is the mode in which Hadoop runs using the local filesystem with a local job runner. Then, install and compile the examples using the instructions on the book's website.

Let's test it on the five-line sample discussed earlier (the output has been slightly reformatted to fit the page):

```
% export HADOOP_CLASSPATH=hadoop-examples.jar
% hadoop MaxTemperature input/ncdc/sample.txt output
12/02/04 11:50:41 WARN util.NativeCodeLoader: Unable to load native-hadoop library
for your platform... using builtin-java classes where applicable
12/02/04 11:50:41 WARN mapred.JobClient: Use GenericOptionsParser for parsing the
arguments. Applications should implement Tool for the same.
12/02/04 11:50:41 INFO input.FileInputFormat: Total input paths to process : 1
12/02/04 11:50:41 INFO mapred.JobClient: Running job: job_local_0001
12/02/04 11:50:41 INFO mapred.Task:  Using ResourceCalculatorPlugin : null
12/02/04 11:50:41 INFO mapred.MapTask: io.sort.mb = 100
12/02/04 11:50:42 INFO mapred.MapTask: data buffer = 79691776/99614720
12/02/04 11:50:42 INFO mapred.MapTask: record buffer = 262144/327680
12/02/04 11:50:42 INFO mapred.MapTask: Starting flush of map output
12/02/04 11:50:42 INFO mapred.MapTask: Finished spill 0
12/02/04 11:50:42 INFO mapred.Task: Task:attempt_local_0001_m_000000_0 is done. And i
s in the process of commiting
12/02/04 11:50:42 INFO mapred.JobClient:  map 0% reduce 0%
12/02/04 11:50:44 INFO mapred.LocalJobRunner:
12/02/04 11:50:44 INFO mapred.Task: Task 'attempt_local_0001_m_000000_0' done.
```

```
12/02/04 11:50:44 INFO mapred.Task:  Using ResourceCalculatorPlugin : null
12/02/04 11:50:44 INFO mapred.LocalJobRunner:
12/02/04 11:50:44 INFO mapred.Merger: Merging 1 sorted segments
12/02/04 11:50:44 INFO mapred.Merger: Down to the last merge-pass, with 1 segments
left of total size: 57 bytes
12/02/04 11:50:44 INFO mapred.LocalJobRunner:
12/02/04 11:50:45 INFO mapred.Task: Task:attempt_local_0001_r_000000_0 is done. And
is in the process of commiting
12/02/04 11:50:45 INFO mapred.LocalJobRunner:
12/02/04 11:50:45 INFO mapred.Task: Task attempt_local_0001_r_000000_0 is allowed to
commit now
12/02/04 11:50:45 INFO output.FileOutputCommitter: Saved output of task 'attempt_local
_0001_r_000000_0' to output
12/02/04 11:50:45 INFO mapred.JobClient:  map 100% reduce 0%
12/02/04 11:50:47 INFO mapred.LocalJobRunner: reduce > reduce
12/02/04 11:50:47 INFO mapred.Task: Task 'attempt_local_0001_r_000000_0' done.
12/02/04 11:50:48 INFO mapred.JobClient:  map 100% reduce 100%
12/02/04 11:50:48 INFO mapred.JobClient: Job complete: job_local_0001
12/02/04 11:50:48 INFO mapred.JobClient: Counters: 17
12/02/04 11:50:48 INFO mapred.JobClient:    File Output Format Counters
12/02/04 11:50:48 INFO mapred.JobClient:      Bytes Written=29
12/02/04 11:50:48 INFO mapred.JobClient:    FileSystemCounters
12/02/04 11:50:48 INFO mapred.JobClient:      FILE_BYTES_READ=357503
12/02/04 11:50:48 INFO mapred.JobClient:      FILE_BYTES_WRITTEN=425817
12/02/04 11:50:48 INFO mapred.JobClient:    File Input Format Counters
12/02/04 11:50:48 INFO mapred.JobClient:      Bytes Read=529
12/02/04 11:50:48 INFO mapred.JobClient:    Map-Reduce Framework
12/02/04 11:50:48 INFO mapred.JobClient:      Map output materialized bytes=61
12/02/04 11:50:48 INFO mapred.JobClient:      Map input records=5
12/02/04 11:50:48 INFO mapred.JobClient:      Reduce shuffle bytes=0
12/02/04 11:50:48 INFO mapred.JobClient:      Spilled Records=10
12/02/04 11:50:48 INFO mapred.JobClient:      Map output bytes=45
12/02/04 11:50:48 INFO mapred.JobClient:      Total committed heap usage (bytes)=36923
8016
12/02/04 11:50:48 INFO mapred.JobClient:      SPLIT_RAW_BYTES=129
12/02/04 11:50:48 INFO mapred.JobClient:      Combine input records=0
12/02/04 11:50:48 INFO mapred.JobClient:      Reduce input records=5
12/02/04 11:50:48 INFO mapred.JobClient:      Reduce input groups=2
12/02/04 11:50:48 INFO mapred.JobClient:      Combine output records=0
12/02/04 11:50:48 INFO mapred.JobClient:      Reduce output records=2
12/02/04 11:50:48 INFO mapred.JobClient:      Map output records=5
```

When the hadoop command is invoked with a classname as the first argument, it
launches a Java Virtual Machine (JVM) to run the class. It is more convenient to use
hadoop than straight java because the former adds the Hadoop libraries (and their dependencies) to the classpath and picks up the Hadoop configuration, too. To add the
application classes to the classpath, we've defined an environment variable called
HADOOP_CLASSPATH, which the hadoop script picks up.

> When running in local (standalone) mode, the programs in this book
> all assume that you have set the HADOOP_CLASSPATH in this way. The com-
> mands should be run from the directory that the example code is
> installed in.

The output from running the job provides some useful information. For example, we can see that the job was given an ID of `job_local_0001`, and it ran one map task and one reduce task (with the IDs `attempt_local_0001_m_000000_0` and `attempt_local_0001_r_000000_0`). Knowing the job and task IDs can be very useful when debugging MapReduce jobs.

The last section of the output, titled "Counters," shows the statistics that Hadoop generates for each job it runs. These are very useful for checking whether the amount of data processed is what you expected. For example, we can follow the number of records that went through the system: five map inputs produced five map outputs, then five reduce inputs in two groups produced two reduce outputs.

The output was written to the *output* directory, which contains one output file per reducer. The job had a single reducer, so we find a single file, named *part-r-00000*:

```
% cat output/part-r-00000
1949    111
1950    22
```

This result is the same as when we went through it by hand earlier. We interpret this as saying that the maximum temperature recorded in 1949 was 11.1°C, and in 1950 it was 2.2°C.

The old and the new Java MapReduce APIs

The Java MapReduce API used in the previous section was first released in Hadoop 0.20.0. This new API, sometimes referred to as "Context Objects," was designed to make the API easier to evolve in the future. It is type-incompatible with the old, however, so applications need to be rewritten to take advantage of it.

The new API is largely complete in the latest 1.x release series (which is a continuation of the 0.20 series), except for a few MapReduce libraries that are missing (check in the latest release to see whether the library you want to use is available in a subpackage of `org.apache.hadoop.mapreduce.lib`).

Previous editions of this book were based on 0.20 releases and used the old API throughout. In this edition, the new API is used as the primary API, except in a few places. However, should you wish to use the old API, you can, since the code for all the examples in this book is available for the old API on the book's website. (A few of the early 0.20 releases deprecated the old API, but the deprecation was removed in later releases, so that all 1.x and 2.x releases now support both the old and new APIs without causing deprecation warnings.)

There are several notable differences between the two APIs:

- The new API favors abstract classes over interfaces, since these are easier to evolve. This means that you can add a method (with a default implementation) to an abstract class without breaking old implementations of the class.[1] For example, the `Mapper` and `Reducer` interfaces in the old API are abstract classes in the new API.

- The new API is in the `org.apache.hadoop.mapreduce` package (and subpackages). The old API can still be found in `org.apache.hadoop.mapred`.

- The new API makes extensive use of context objects that allow the user code to communicate with the MapReduce system. The new `Context`, for example, essentially unifies the role of the `JobConf`, the `OutputCollector`, and the `Reporter` from the old API.

- In both APIs, key-value record pairs are pushed to the mapper and reducer, but in addition, the new API allows both mappers and reducers to control the execution flow by overriding the `run()` method. For example, records can be processed in batches, or the execution can be terminated before all the records have been processed. In the old API this is possible for mappers by writing a `MapRunnable`, but no equivalent exists for reducers.

- Job control is performed through the `Job` class in the new API, rather than the old `JobClient`, which no longer exists in the new API.

- Configuration has been unified. The old API has a special `JobConf` object for job configuration, which is an extension of Hadoop's vanilla `Configuration` object (used for configuring daemons; see "The Configuration API" on page 144). In the new API, job configuration is done through a `Configuration`, possibly via some of the helper methods on `Job`.

- Output files are named slightly differently: in the old API both map and reduce outputs are named *part-nnnnn*, whereas in the new API map outputs are named *part-m-nnnnn*, and reduce outputs are named *part-r-nnnnn* (where *nnnnn* is an integer designating the part number, starting from zero).

- User-overridable methods in the new API are declared to throw `java.lang.Inter ruptedException`. This means that you can write your code to be responsive to interrupts so that the framework can gracefully cancel long-running operations if it needs to.[2]

- In the new API, the `reduce()` method passes values as a `java.lang.Iterable`, rather than a `java.lang.Iterator` (as the old API does). This change makes it easier to iterate over the values using Java's for-each loop construct:

  ```
  for (VALUEIN value : values) { ... }
  ```

Example 2-6 shows the `MaxTemperature` application rewritten to use the old API. The differences are highlighted in bold.

---

1. Technically, such a change would almost certainly break implementations that already define a method with the same signature as the new one, but as the article at *http://wiki.eclipse.org/Evolving_Java-based _APIs#Example_4_-_Adding_an_API_method* explains, for all practical purposes this is treated as a compatible change.

2. "Dealing with InterruptedException" (*http://www.ibm.com/developerworks/java/library/j-jtp05236 .html*) by Brian Goetz explains this technique in detail.

When converting your Mapper and Reducer classes to the new API, don't
forget to change the signature of the map() and reduce() methods to the
new form. Just changing your class to extend the new Mapper or
Reducer classes will *not* produce a compilation error or warning, because
these classes provide an identity form of the map() or reduce() method
(respectively). Your mapper or reducer code, however, will not be invoked, which can lead to some hard-to-diagnose errors.

Annotating your map() and reduce() methods with the @Override an-
notation will allow the Java compiler to catch these errors.

Example 2-6. Application to find the maximum temperature, using the old MapReduce API

```java
public class OldMaxTemperature {

  static class OldMaxTemperatureMapper extends MapReduceBase
    implements Mapper<LongWritable, Text, Text, IntWritable> {

    private static final int MISSING = 9999;

    @Override
    public void map(LongWritable key, Text value,
        OutputCollector<Text, IntWritable> output, Reporter reporter)
        throws IOException {

      String line = value.toString();
      String year = line.substring(15, 19);
      int airTemperature;
      if (line.charAt(87) == '+') { // parseInt doesn't like leading plus signs
        airTemperature = Integer.parseInt(line.substring(88, 92));
      } else {
        airTemperature = Integer.parseInt(line.substring(87, 92));
      }
      String quality = line.substring(92, 93);
      if (airTemperature != MISSING && quality.matches("[01459]")) {
        output.collect(new Text(year), new IntWritable(airTemperature));
      }
    }
  }

  static class OldMaxTemperatureReducer extends MapReduceBase
    implements Reducer<Text, IntWritable, Text, IntWritable> {

    @Override
    public void reduce(Text key, Iterator<IntWritable> values,
        OutputCollector<Text, IntWritable> output, Reporter reporter)
        throws IOException {

      int maxValue = Integer.MIN_VALUE;
      while (values.hasNext()) {
        maxValue = Math.max(maxValue, values.next().get());
      }
      output.collect(key, new IntWritable(maxValue));
    }
```

```
    }

    public static void main(String[] args) throws IOException {
      if (args.length != 2) {
        System.err.println("Usage: OldMaxTemperature <input path> <output path>");
        System.exit(-1);
      }

      JobConf conf = new JobConf(OldMaxTemperature.class);
      conf.setJobName("Max temperature");

      FileInputFormat.addInputPath(conf, new Path(args[0]));
      FileOutputFormat.setOutputPath(conf, new Path(args[1]));

      conf.setMapperClass(OldMaxTemperatureMapper.class);
      conf.setReducerClass(OldMaxTemperatureReducer.class);

      conf.setOutputKeyClass(Text.class);
      conf.setOutputValueClass(IntWritable.class);

      JobClient.runJob(conf);
    }
}
```

Scaling Out

You've seen how MapReduce works for small inputs; now it's time to take a bird's-eye view of the system and look at the data flow for large inputs. For simplicity, the examples so far have used files on the local filesystem. However, to scale out, we need to store the data in a distributed filesystem, typically HDFS (which you'll learn about in the next chapter), to allow Hadoop to move the MapReduce computation to each machine hosting a part of the data. Let's see how this works.

Data Flow

First, some terminology. A MapReduce *job* is a unit of work that the client wants to be performed: it consists of the input data, the MapReduce program, and configuration information. Hadoop runs the job by dividing it into *tasks*, of which there are two types: *map tasks* and *reduce tasks*.

There are two types of nodes that control the job execution process: a *jobtracker* and a number of *tasktrackers*. The jobtracker coordinates all the jobs run on the system by scheduling tasks to run on tasktrackers. Tasktrackers run tasks and send progress reports to the jobtracker, which keeps a record of the overall progress of each job. If a task fails, the jobtracker can reschedule it on a different tasktracker.

Hadoop divides the input to a MapReduce job into fixed-size pieces called *input splits*, or just *splits*. Hadoop creates one map task for each split, which runs the user-defined map function for each *record* in the split.

Having many splits means the time taken to process each split is small compared to the time to process the whole input. So if we are processing the splits in parallel, the processing is better load-balanced when the splits are small, since a faster machine will be able to process proportionally more splits over the course of the job than a slower machine. Even if the machines are identical, failed processes or other jobs running concurrently make load balancing desirable, and the quality of the load balancing increases as the splits become more fine-grained.

On the other hand, if splits are too small, the overhead of managing the splits and of map task creation begins to dominate the total job execution time. For most jobs, a good split size tends to be the size of an HDFS block, 64 MB by default, although this can be changed for the cluster (for all newly created files) or specified when each file is created.

Hadoop does its best to run the map task on a node where the input data resides in HDFS. This is called the *data locality optimization* because it doesn't use valuable cluster bandwidth. Sometimes, however, all three nodes hosting the HDFS block replicas for a map task's input split are running other map tasks, so the job scheduler will look for a free map slot on a node in the same rack as one of the blocks. Very occasionally even this is not possible, so an off-rack node is used, which results in an inter-rack network transfer. The three possibilities are illustrated in Figure 2-2.

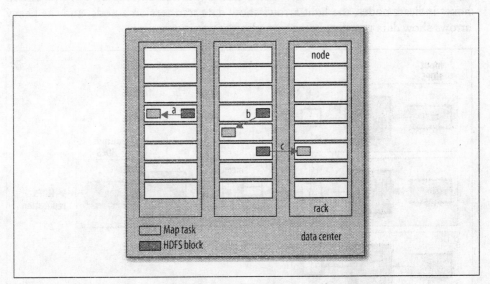

Figure 2-2. Data-local (a), rack-local (b), and off-rack (c) map tasks

It should now be clear why the optimal split size is the same as the block size: it is the largest size of input that can be guaranteed to be stored on a single node. If the split spanned two blocks, it would be unlikely that any HDFS node stored both blocks, so some of the split would have to be transferred across the network to the node running the map task, which is clearly less efficient than running the whole map task using local data.

Map tasks write their output to the local disk, not to HDFS. Why is this? Map output is intermediate output: it's processed by reduce tasks to produce the final output, and once the job is complete, the map output can be thrown away. So storing it in HDFS with replication would be overkill. If the node running the map task fails before the map output has been consumed by the reduce task, then Hadoop will automatically rerun the map task on another node to re-create the map output.

Reduce tasks don't have the advantage of data locality; the input to a single reduce task is normally the output from all mappers. In the present example, we have a single reduce task that is fed by all of the map tasks. Therefore, the sorted map outputs have to be transferred across the network to the node where the reduce task is running, where they are merged and then passed to the user-defined reduce function. The output of the reduce is normally stored in HDFS for reliability. As explained in Chapter 3, for each HDFS block of the reduce output, the first replica is stored on the local node, with other replicas being stored on off-rack nodes. Thus, writing the reduce output does consume network bandwidth, but only as much as a normal HDFS write pipeline consumes.

The whole data flow with a single reduce task is illustrated in Figure 2-3. The dotted boxes indicate nodes, the light arrows show data transfers on a node, and the heavy arrows show data transfers between nodes.

Figure 2-3. MapReduce data flow with a single reduce task

The number of reduce tasks is not governed by the size of the input, but instead is specified independently. In "The Default MapReduce Job" on page 227, you will see how to choose the number of reduce tasks for a given job.

When there are multiple reducers, the map tasks *partition* their output, each creating one partition for each reduce task. There can be many keys (and their associated values) in each partition, but the records for any given key are all in a single partition. The partitioning can be controlled by a user-defined partitioning function, but normally the default partitioner—which buckets keys using a hash function—works very well.

The data flow for the general case of multiple reduce tasks is illustrated in Figure 2-4. This diagram makes it clear why the data flow between map and reduce tasks is colloquially known as "the shuffle," as each reduce task is fed by many map tasks. The shuffle is more complicated than this diagram suggests, and tuning it can have a big impact on job execution time, as you will see in "Shuffle and Sort" on page 208.

Figure 2-4. MapReduce data flow with multiple reduce tasks

Finally, it's also possible to have zero reduce tasks. This can be appropriate when you don't need the shuffle because the processing can be carried out entirely in parallel (a few examples are discussed in "NLineInputFormat" on page 247). In this case, the only off-node data transfer is when the map tasks write to HDFS (see Figure 2-5).

Combiner Functions

Many MapReduce jobs are limited by the bandwidth available on the cluster, so it pays to minimize the data transferred between map and reduce tasks. Hadoop allows the user to specify a *combiner function* to be run on the map output, and the combiner function's output forms the input to the reduce function. Because the combiner function is an optimization, Hadoop does not provide a guarantee of how many times it will call it for a particular map output record, if at all. In other words, calling the combiner function zero, one, or many times should produce the same output from the reducer.

Figure 2-5. MapReduce data flow with no reduce tasks

The contract for the combiner function constrains the type of function that may be used. This is best illustrated with an example. Suppose that for the maximum temperature example, readings for the year 1950 were processed by two maps (because they were in different splits). Imagine the first map produced the output:

```
(1950, 0)
(1950, 20)
(1950, 10)
```

and the second produced:

```
(1950, 25)
(1950, 15)
```

The reduce function would be called with a list of all the values:

```
(1950, [0, 20, 10, 25, 15])
```

with output:

```
(1950, 25)
```

since 25 is the maximum value in the list. We could use a combiner function that, just like the reduce function, finds the maximum temperature for each map output. The reduce would then be called with:

```
(1950, [20, 25])
```

and the reduce would produce the same output as before. More succinctly, we may express the function calls on the temperature values in this case as follows:

```
max(0, 20, 10, 25, 15) = max(max(0, 20, 10), max(25, 15)) = max(20, 25) = 25
```

Not all functions possess this property.[3] For example, if we were calculating mean temperatures, we couldn't use the mean as our combiner function, because:

```
mean(0, 20, 10, 25, 15) = 14
```

but:

```
mean(mean(0, 20, 10), mean(25, 15)) = mean(10, 20) = 15
```

The combiner function doesn't replace the reduce function. (How could it? The reduce function is still needed to process records with the same key from different maps.) But it can help cut down the amount of data shuffled between the mappers and the reducers, and for this reason alone it is always worth considering whether you can use a combiner function in your MapReduce job.

Specifying a combiner function

Going back to the Java MapReduce program, the combiner function is defined using the Reducer class, and for this application, it is the same implementation as the reducer function in MaxTemperatureReducer. The only change we need to make is to set the combiner class on the Job (see Example 2-7).

Example 2-7. Application to find the maximum temperature, using a combiner function for efficiency

```
public class MaxTemperatureWithCombiner {

  public static void main(String[] args) throws Exception {
    if (args.length != 2) {
      System.err.println("Usage: MaxTemperatureWithCombiner <input path> " +
          "<output path>");
      System.exit(-1);
    }

    Job job = new Job();
    job.setJarByClass(MaxTemperatureWithCombiner.class);
    job.setJobName("Max temperature");

    FileInputFormat.addInputPath(job, new Path(args[0]));
    FileOutputFormat.setOutputPath(job, new Path(args[1]));

    job.setMapperClass(MaxTemperatureMapper.class);
    job.setCombinerClass(MaxTemperatureReducer.class);
    job.setReducerClass(MaxTemperatureReducer.class);
```

---

3. Functions with this property are called *commutative* and *associative*. They are also sometimes referred to as *distributive*, such as in the paper "Data Cube: A Relational Aggregation Operator Generalizing Group-By, Cross-Tab, and Sub-Totals," Gray et al. (1995).

```
    job.setOutputKeyClass(Text.class);
    job.setOutputValueClass(IntWritable.class);

    System.exit(job.waitForCompletion(true) ? 0 : 1);
  }
}
```

Running a Distributed MapReduce Job

The same program will run, without alteration, on a full dataset. This is the point of
MapReduce: it scales to the size of your data and the size of your hardware. Here's one
data point: on a 10-node EC2 cluster running High-CPU Extra Large Instances, the
program took six minutes to run.[4]

We'll go through the mechanics of running programs on a cluster in Chapter 5.

Hadoop Streaming

Hadoop provides an API to MapReduce that allows you to write your map and reduce
functions in languages other than Java. *Hadoop Streaming* uses Unix standard streams
as the interface between Hadoop and your program, so you can use any language that
can read standard input and write to standard output to write your MapReduce
program.

Streaming is naturally suited for text processing. Map input data is passed over standard
input to your map function, which processes it line by line and writes lines to standard
output. A map output key-value pair is written as a single tab-delimited line. Input to
the reduce function is in the same format—a tab-separated key-value pair—passed over
standard input. The reduce function reads lines from standard input, which the framework guarantees are sorted by key, and writes its results to standard output.

Let's illustrate this by rewriting our MapReduce program for finding maximum temperatures by year in Streaming.

Ruby

The map function can be expressed in Ruby as shown in Example 2-8.

Example 2-8. Map function for maximum temperature in Ruby

```
#!/usr/bin/env ruby
```

---

4. This is a factor of seven faster than the serial run on one machine using *awk*. The main reason it wasn't
   proportionally faster is because the input data wasn't evenly partitioned. For convenience, the input
   files were gzipped by year, resulting in large files for later years in the dataset, when the number of weather
   records was much higher.

```
STDIN.each_line do |line|
  val = line
  year, temp, q = val[15,4], val[87,5], val[92,1]
  puts "#{year}\t#{temp}" if (temp != "+9999" && q =~ /[01459]/)
end
```

The program iterates over lines from standard input by executing a block for each line from STDIN (a global constant of type IO). The block pulls out the relevant fields from each input line, and, if the temperature is valid, writes the year and the temperature separated by a tab character \t to standard output (using puts).

It's worth drawing out a design difference between Streaming and the Java MapReduce API. The Java API is geared toward processing your map function one record at a time. The framework calls the map() method on your Mapper for each record in the input, whereas with Streaming the map program can decide how to process the input—for example, it could easily read and process multiple lines at a time since it's in control of the reading. The user's Java map implementation is "pushed" records, but it's still possible to consider multiple lines at a time by accumulating previous lines in an instance variable in the Mapper.[5] In this case, you need to implement the close() method so that you know when the last record has been read, so you can finish processing the last group of lines.

Because the script just operates on standard input and output, it's trivial to test the script without using Hadoop, simply using Unix pipes:

```
% cat input/ncdc/sample.txt | ch02/src/main/ruby/max_temperature_map.rb
1950    +0000
1950    +0022
1950    -0011
1949    +0111
1949    +0078
```

The reduce function shown in Example 2-9 is a little more complex.

Example 2-9. Reduce function for maximum temperature in Ruby

```
#!/usr/bin/env ruby

last_key, max_val = nil, -1000000
STDIN.each_line do |line|
  key, val = line.split("\t")
  if last_key && last_key != key
    puts "#{last_key}\t#{max_val}"
    last_key, max_val = key, val.to_i
  else
    last_key, max_val = key, [max_val, val.to_i].max
```

5. Alternatively, you could use "pull" style processing in the new MapReduce API; see "The old and the new Java MapReduce APIs" on page 27.

```
    end
  end
  puts "#{last_key}\t#{max_val}" if last_key
```

Again, the program iterates over lines from standard input, but this time we have to store some state as we process each key group. In this case, the keys are the years, and we store the last key seen and the maximum temperature seen so far for that key. The MapReduce framework ensures that the keys are ordered, so we know that if a key is different from the previous one, we have moved into a new key group. In contrast to the Java API, where you are provided an iterator over each key group, in Streaming you have to find key group boundaries in your program.

For each line, we pull out the key and value. Then, if we've just finished a group (last_key && last_key != key), we write the key and the maximum temperature for that group, separated by a tab character, before resetting the maximum temperature for the new key. If we haven't just finished a group, we just update the maximum temperature for the current key.

The last line of the program ensures that a line is written for the last key group in the input.

We can now simulate the whole MapReduce pipeline with a Unix pipeline (which is equivalent to the Unix pipeline shown in Figure 2-1):

```
% cat input/ncdc/sample.txt | ch02/src/main/ruby/max_temperature_map.rb | \
    sort | ch02/src/main/ruby/max_temperature_reduce.rb
1949    111
1950    22
```

The output is the same as the Java program, so the next step is to run it using Hadoop itself.

The hadoop command doesn't support a Streaming option; instead, you specify the Streaming JAR file along with the jar option. Options to the Streaming program specify the input and output paths and the map and reduce scripts. This is what it looks like:

```
% hadoop jar $HADOOP_INSTALL/contrib/streaming/hadoop-*-streaming.jar \
    -input input/ncdc/sample.txt \
    -output output \
    -mapper ch02/src/main/ruby/max_temperature_map.rb \
    -reducer ch02/src/main/ruby/max_temperature_reduce.rb
```

When running on a large dataset on a cluster, we should use the -combiner option to set the combiner.

In releases after 1.x, the combiner can be any Streaming command. For earlier releases, the combiner had to be written in Java, so as a workaround it was common to do manual combining in the mapper without having to resort to Java. In this case, we could change the mapper to be a pipeline:

```
% hadoop jar $HADOOP_INSTALL/contrib/streaming/hadoop-*-streaming.jar \
    -input input/ncdc/all \
    -output output \
```

```
-mapper "ch02/src/main/ruby/max_temperature_map.rb | sort |
  ch02/src/main/ruby/max_temperature_reduce.rb" \
-reducer ch02/src/main/ruby/max_temperature_reduce.rb \
-file ch02/src/main/ruby/max_temperature_map.rb \
-file ch02/src/main/ruby/max_temperature_reduce.rb
```

Note also the use of -file, which we use when running Streaming programs on the cluster to ship the scripts to the cluster.

Python

Streaming supports any programming language that can read from standard input and write to standard output, so for readers more familiar with Python, here's the same example again.[6] The map script is in Example 2-10, and the reduce script is in Example 2-11.

Example 2-10. Map function for maximum temperature in Python

```python
#!/usr/bin/env python

import re
import sys

for line in sys.stdin:
  val = line.strip()
  (year, temp, q) = (val[15:19], val[87:92], val[92:93])
  if (temp != "+9999" and re.match("[01459]", q)):
    print "%s\t%s" % (year, temp)
```

Example 2-11. Reduce function for maximum temperature in Python

```python
#!/usr/bin/env python

import sys

(last_key, max_val) = (None, -sys.maxint)
for line in sys.stdin:
  (key, val) = line.strip().split("\t")
  if last_key and last_key != key:
    print "%s\t%s" % (last_key, max_val)
    (last_key, max_val) = (key, int(val))
  else:
    (last_key, max_val) = (key, max(max_val, int(val)))

if last_key:
  print "%s\t%s" % (last_key, max_val)
```

---

6. As an alternative to Streaming, Python programmers should consider Dumbo (*http://www.last.fm/dumbo*), which makes the Streaming MapReduce interface more Pythonic and easier to use.

We can test the programs and run the job in the same way we did in Ruby. For example, to run a test:

```
% cat input/ncdc/sample.txt | ch02/src/main/python/max_temperature_map.py | \
  sort | ch02/src/main/python/max_temperature_reduce.py
1949    111
1950    22
```

Hadoop Pipes

Hadoop Pipes is the name of the C++ interface to Hadoop MapReduce. Unlike Streaming, which uses standard input and output to communicate with the map and reduce code, Pipes uses sockets as the channel over which the tasktracker communicates with the process running the C++ map or reduce function. JNI is not used.

We'll rewrite this chapter's temperature example in C++, and then we'll see how to run it using Pipes. Example 2-12 shows the source code for the map and reduce functions in C++.

Example 2-12. Maximum temperature in C++

```cpp
#include <algorithm>
#include <limits>
#include <stdint.h>
#include <string>

#include "hadoop/Pipes.hh"
#include "hadoop/TemplateFactory.hh"
#include "hadoop/StringUtils.hh"

class MaxTemperatureMapper : public HadoopPipes::Mapper {
public:
  MaxTemperatureMapper(HadoopPipes::TaskContext& context) {
  }
  void map(HadoopPipes::MapContext& context) {
    std::string line = context.getInputValue();
    std::string year = line.substr(15, 4);
    std::string airTemperature = line.substr(87, 5);
    std::string q = line.substr(92, 1);
    if (airTemperature != "+9999" &&
        (q == "0" || q == "1" || q == "4" || q == "5" || q == "9")) {
      context.emit(year, airTemperature);
    }
  }
};

class MapTemperatureReducer : public HadoopPipes::Reducer {
public:
  MapTemperatureReducer(HadoopPipes::TaskContext& context) {
  }
  void reduce(HadoopPipes::ReduceContext& context) {
    int maxValue = INT_MIN;
    while (context.nextValue()) {
```

```
      maxValue = std::max(maxValue, HadoopUtils::toInt(context.getInputValue()));
    }
    context.emit(context.getInputKey(), HadoopUtils::toString(maxValue));
  }
};

int main(int argc, char *argv[]) {
  return HadoopPipes::runTask(HadoopPipes::TemplateFactory<MaxTemperatureMapper,
                              MapTemperatureReducer>());
}
```

The application links against the Hadoop C++ library, which is a thin wrapper for communicating with the tasktracker child process. The map and reduce functions are defined by extending the `Mapper` and `Reducer` classes defined in the `HadoopPipes` namespace and providing implementations of the `map()` and `reduce()` methods in each case. These methods take a context object (of type `MapContext` or `ReduceContext`), which provides the means for reading input and writing output, as well as accessing job configuration information via the `JobConf` class. The processing in this example is very similar to the Java equivalent.

Unlike the Java interface, keys and values in the C++ interface are byte buffers represented as Standard Template Library (STL) strings. This makes the interface simpler, although it does put a slightly greater burden on the application developer, who has to convert to and from richer domain-level types. This is evident in `MapTemperatureReducer`, where we have to convert the input value into an integer (using a convenience method in `HadoopUtils`) and then the maximum value back into a string before it's written out. In some cases, we can skip the conversion, such as in `MaxTemperatureMapper`, where the `airTemperature` value is never converted to an integer because it is never processed as a number in the `map()` method.

The `main()` method is the application entry point. It calls `HadoopPipes::runTask`, which connects to the Java parent process and marshals data to and from the `Mapper` or `Reducer`. The `runTask()` method is passed a `Factory` so that it can create instances of the `Mapper` or `Reducer`. Which one it creates is controlled by the Java parent over the socket connection. There are overloaded template factory methods for setting a combiner, partitioner, record reader, or record writer.

Compiling and Running

Now we can compile and link our program using the makefile in Example 2-13.

Example 2-13. Makefile for C++ MapReduce program

```
CC = g++
CPPFLAGS = -m32 -I$(HADOOP_INSTALL)/c++/$(PLATFORM)/include

max_temperature: max_temperature.cpp
    $(CC) $(CPPFLAGS) $< -Wall -L$(HADOOP_INSTALL)/c++/$(PLATFORM)/lib -lhadooppipes \
    -lhadooputils -lpthread -g -O2 -o $@
```

The makefile expects a couple of environment variables to be set. Apart from HADOOP_INSTALL (which you should already have set if you followed the installation instructions in Appendix A), you need to define PLATFORM, which specifies the operating system, architecture, and data model (e.g., 32- or 64-bit). I ran it on a 32-bit Linux system with the following:

```
% export PLATFORM=Linux-i386-32
% make
```

On successful completion, you'll find the max_temperature executable in the current directory.

To run a Pipes job, we need to run Hadoop in *pseudodistributed* mode (where all the daemons run on the local machine), for which there are setup instructions in Appendix A. Pipes doesn't run in standalone (local) mode, because it relies on Hadoop's distributed cache mechanism, which works only when HDFS is running.

With the Hadoop daemons now running, the first step is to copy the executable to HDFS so that it can be picked up by tasktrackers when they launch map and reduce tasks:

```
% hadoop fs -put max_temperature bin/max_temperature
```

The sample data also needs to be copied from the local filesystem into HDFS:

```
% hadoop fs -put input/ncdc/sample.txt sample.txt
```

Now we can run the job. For this, we use the Hadoop pipes command, passing the Uniform Resource Identifier (URI) of the executable in HDFS using the -program argument:

```
% hadoop pipes \
    -D hadoop.pipes.java.recordreader=true \
    -D hadoop.pipes.java.recordwriter=true \
    -input sample.txt \
    -output output \
    -program bin/max_temperature
```

We specify two properties using the -D option: hadoop.pipes.java.recordreader and hadoop.pipes.java.recordwriter, setting both to true to say that we have not specified a C++ record reader or writer, but that we want to use the default Java ones (which are for text input and output). Pipes also allows you to set a Java mapper, reducer, combiner, or partitioner. In fact, you can have a mixture of Java or C++ classes within any one job.

The result is the same as the other versions of the same program that we ran previously.

The Hadoop Distributed Filesystem

When a dataset outgrows the storage capacity of a single physical machine, it becomes necessary to partition it across a number of separate machines. Filesystems that manage the storage across a network of machines are called *distributed filesystems*. Since they are network-based, all the complications of network programming kick in, thus making distributed filesystems more complex than regular disk filesystems. For example, one of the biggest challenges is making the filesystem tolerate node failure without suffering data loss.

Hadoop comes with a distributed filesystem called HDFS, which stands for *Hadoop Distributed Filesystem*. (You may sometimes see references to "DFS"—informally or in older documentation or configurations—which is the same thing.) HDFS is Hadoop's flagship filesystem and is the focus of this chapter, but Hadoop actually has a general-purpose filesystem abstraction, so we'll see along the way how Hadoop integrates with other storage systems (such as the local filesystem and Amazon S3).

The Design of HDFS

HDFS is a filesystem designed for storing very large files with streaming data access patterns, running on clusters of commodity hardware.[1] Let's examine this statement in more detail:

Very large files
> "Very large" in this context means files that are hundreds of megabytes, gigabytes, or terabytes in size. There are Hadoop clusters running today that store petabytes of data.[2]

---

1. The architecture of HDFS is described in "The Hadoop Distributed File System" by Konstantin Shvachko, Hairong Kuang, Sanjay Radia, and Robert Chansler (Proceedings of MSST2010, May 2010, *http://storageconference.org/2010/Papers/MSST/Shvachko.pdf*).

2. "Scaling Hadoop to 4000 nodes at Yahoo!," *http://developer.yahoo.net/blogs/hadoop/2008/09/scaling_hadoop_to_4000_nodes_a.html*.

Streaming data access
> HDFS is built around the idea that the most efficient data processing pattern is a write-once, read-many-times pattern. A dataset is typically generated or copied from source, and then various analyses are performed on that dataset over time. Each analysis will involve a large proportion, if not all, of the dataset, so the time to read the whole dataset is more important than the latency in reading the first record.

Commodity hardware
> Hadoop doesn't require expensive, highly reliable hardware. It's designed to run on clusters of commodity hardware (commonly available hardware that can be obtained from multiple vendors)[3] for which the chance of node failure across the cluster is high, at least for large clusters. HDFS is designed to carry on working without a noticeable interruption to the user in the face of such failure.

It is also worth examining the applications for which using HDFS does not work so well. Although this may change in the future, these are areas where HDFS is not a good fit today:

Low-latency data access
> Applications that require low-latency access to data, in the tens of milliseconds range, will not work well with HDFS. Remember, HDFS is optimized for delivering a high throughput of data, and this may be at the expense of latency. HBase (Chapter 13) is currently a better choice for low-latency access.

Lots of small files
> Because the namenode holds filesystem metadata in memory, the limit to the number of files in a filesystem is governed by the amount of memory on the namenode. As a rule of thumb, each file, directory, and block takes about 150 bytes. So, for example, if you had one million files, each taking one block, you would need at least 300 MB of memory. Although storing millions of files is feasible, billions is beyond the capability of current hardware.[4]

Multiple writers, arbitrary file modifications
> Files in HDFS may be written to by a single writer. Writes are always made at the end of the file. There is no support for multiple writers or for modifications at arbitrary offsets in the file. (These might be supported in the future, but they are likely to be relatively inefficient.)

---

3. See Chapter 9 for a typical machine specification.

4. For an in-depth exposition of the scalability limits of HDFS, see Konstantin V. Shvachko's "Scalability of the Hadoop Distributed File System" (*http://developer.yahoo.net/blogs/hadoop/2010/05/scalability_of _the_hadoop_dist.html*) and the companion paper, "HDFS Scalability: The limits to growth" (April 2010, pp. 6–16), *http://www.usenix.org/publications/login/2010-04/openpdfs/shvachko.pdf*), by the same author.

HDFS Concepts

Blocks

A disk has a block size, which is the minimum amount of data that it can read or write. Filesystems for a single disk build on this by dealing with data in blocks, which are an integral multiple of the disk block size. Filesystem blocks are typically a few kilobytes in size, whereas disk blocks are normally 512 bytes. This is generally transparent to the filesystem user who is simply reading or writing a file of whatever length. However, there are tools to perform filesystem maintenance, such as *df* and *fsck*, that operate on the filesystem block level.

HDFS, too, has the concept of a block, but it is a much larger unit—64 MB by default. Like in a filesystem for a single disk, files in HDFS are broken into block-sized chunks, which are stored as independent units. Unlike a filesystem for a single disk, a file in HDFS that is smaller than a single block does not occupy a full block's worth of underlying storage. When unqualified, the term "block" in this book refers to a block in HDFS.

Why Is a Block in HDFS So Large?

HDFS blocks are large compared to disk blocks, and the reason is to minimize the cost of seeks. By making a block large enough, the time to transfer the data from the disk can be significantly longer than the time to seek to the start of the block. Thus the time to transfer a large file made of multiple blocks operates at the disk transfer rate.

A quick calculation shows that if the seek time is around 10 ms and the transfer rate is 100 MB/s, to make the seek time 1% of the transfer time, we need to make the block size around 100 MB. The default is actually 64 MB, although many HDFS installations use 128 MB blocks. This figure will continue to be revised upward as transfer speeds grow with new generations of disk drives.

This argument shouldn't be taken too far, however. Map tasks in MapReduce normally operate on one block at a time, so if you have too few tasks (fewer than nodes in the cluster), your jobs will run slower than they could otherwise.

Having a block abstraction for a distributed filesystem brings several benefits. The first benefit is the most obvious: a file can be larger than any single disk in the network. There's nothing that requires the blocks from a file to be stored on the same disk, so they can take advantage of any of the disks in the cluster. In fact, it would be possible, if unusual, to store a single file on an HDFS cluster whose blocks filled all the disks in the cluster.

Second, making the unit of abstraction a block rather than a file simplifies the storage subsystem. Simplicity is something to strive for in all systems, but is especially important for a distributed system in which the failure modes are so varied. The storage subsystem deals with blocks, simplifying storage management (because blocks are a fixed size, it is easy to calculate how many can be stored on a given disk) and eliminating metadata concerns (because blocks are just a chunk of data to be stored, file metadata such as permissions information does not need to be stored with the blocks, so another system can handle metadata separately).

Furthermore, blocks fit well with replication for providing fault tolerance and availability. To insure against corrupted blocks and disk and machine failure, each block is replicated to a small number of physically separate machines (typically three). If a block becomes unavailable, a copy can be read from another location in a way that is transparent to the client. A block that is no longer available due to corruption or machine failure can be replicated from its alternative locations to other live machines to bring the replication factor back to the normal level. (See "Data Integrity" on page 81 for more on guarding against corrupt data.) Similarly, some applications may choose to set a high replication factor for the blocks in a popular file to spread the read load on the cluster.

Like its disk filesystem cousin, HDFS's fsck command understands blocks. For example, running:

```
% hadoop fsck / -files -blocks
```

will list the blocks that make up each file in the filesystem. (See also "Filesystem check (fsck)" on page 347.)

Namenodes and Datanodes

An HDFS cluster has two types of nodes operating in a master-worker pattern: a *namenode* (the master) and a number of *datanodes* (workers). The namenode manages the filesystem namespace. It maintains the filesystem tree and the metadata for all the files and directories in the tree. This information is stored persistently on the local disk in the form of two files: the namespace image and the edit log. The namenode also knows the datanodes on which all the blocks for a given file are located; however, it does not store block locations persistently, because this information is reconstructed from datanodes when the system starts.

A *client* accesses the filesystem on behalf of the user by communicating with the namenode and datanodes. The client presents a filesystem interface similar to a Portable Operating System Interface (POSIX), so the user code does not need to know about the namenode and datanode to function.

Datanodes are the workhorses of the filesystem. They store and retrieve blocks when they are told to (by clients or the namenode), and they report back to the namenode periodically with lists of blocks that they are storing.

Without the namenode, the filesystem cannot be used. In fact, if the machine running the namenode were obliterated, all the files on the filesystem would be lost since there would be no way of knowing how to reconstruct the files from the blocks on the datanodes. For this reason, it is important to make the namenode resilient to failure, and Hadoop provides two mechanisms for this.

The first way is to back up the files that make up the persistent state of the filesystem metadata. Hadoop can be configured so that the namenode writes its persistent state to multiple filesystems. These writes are synchronous and atomic. The usual configuration choice is to write to local disk as well as a remote NFS mount.

It is also possible to run a *secondary namenode*, which despite its name does not act as a namenode. Its main role is to periodically merge the namespace image with the edit log to prevent the edit log from becoming too large. The secondary namenode usually runs on a separate physical machine because it requires plenty of CPU and as much memory as the namenode to perform the merge. It keeps a copy of the merged namespace image, which can be used in the event of the namenode failing. However, the state of the secondary namenode lags that of the primary, so in the event of total failure of the primary, data loss is almost certain. The usual course of action in this case is to copy the namenode's metadata files that are on NFS to the secondary and run it as the new primary.

See "The filesystem image and edit log" on page 340 for more details.

HDFS Federation

The namenode keeps a reference to every file and block in the filesystem in memory, which means that on very large clusters with many files, memory becomes the limiting factor for scaling (see "How Much Memory Does a Namenode Need?" on page 308). HDFS Federation, introduced in the 2.x release series, allows a cluster to scale by adding namenodes, each of which manages a portion of the filesystem namespace. For example, one namenode might manage all the files rooted under */user*, say, and a second namenode might handle files under */share*.

Under federation, each namenode manages a *namespace volume*, which is made up of the metadata for the namespace, and a *block pool* containing all the blocks for the files in the namespace. Namespace volumes are independent of each other, which means namenodes do not communicate with one another, and furthermore the failure of one namenode does not affect the availability of the namespaces managed by other namenodes. Block pool storage is *not* partitioned, however, so datanodes register with each namenode in the cluster and store blocks from multiple block pools.

To access a federated HDFS cluster, clients use client-side mount tables to map file paths to namenodes. This is managed in configuration using `ViewFileSystem` and the *viewfs://* URIs.

HDFS High-Availability

The combination of replicating namenode metadata on multiple filesystems and using the secondary namenode to create checkpoints protects against data loss, but it does not provide high-availability of the filesystem. The namenode is still a *single point of failure* (SPOF). If it did fail, all clients—including MapReduce jobs—would be unable to read, write, or list files, because the namenode is the sole repository of the metadata and the file-to-block mapping. In such an event the whole Hadoop system would effectively be out of service until a new namenode could be brought online.

To recover from a failed namenode in this situation, an administrator starts a new primary namenode with one of the filesystem metadata replicas and configures datanodes and clients to use this new namenode. The new namenode is not able to serve requests until it has i) loaded its namespace image into memory, ii) replayed its edit log, and iii) received enough block reports from the datanodes to leave safe mode. On large clusters with many files and blocks, the time it takes for a namenode to start from cold can be 30 minutes or more.

The long recovery time is a problem for routine maintenance too. In fact, because unexpected failure of the namenode is so rare, the case for planned downtime is actually more important in practice.

The 2.x release series of Hadoop remedies this situation by adding support for HDFS high-availability (HA). In this implementation there is a pair of namenodes in an active-standby configuration. In the event of the failure of the active namenode, the standby takes over its duties to continue servicing client requests without a significant interruption. A few architectural changes are needed to allow this to happen:

- The namenodes must use highly available shared storage to share the edit log. (In the initial implementation of HA this will require an NFS filer, but in future releases more options will be provided, such as a BookKeeper-based system built on Zoo-Keeper.) When a standby namenode comes up, it reads up to the end of the shared edit log to synchronize its state with the active namenode, and then continues to read new entries as they are written by the active namenode.

- Datanodes must send block reports to both namenodes because the block mappings are stored in a namenode's memory, and not on disk.

- Clients must be configured to handle namenode failover, using a mechanism that is transparent to users.

If the active namenode fails, the standby can take over very quickly (in a few tens of seconds) because it has the latest state available in memory: both the latest edit log entries and an up-to-date block mapping. The actual observed failover time will be longer in practice (around a minute or so), because the system needs to be conservative in deciding that the active namenode has failed.

In the unlikely event of the standby being down when the active fails, the administrator can still start the standby from cold. This is no worse than the non-HA case, and from an operational point of view it's an improvement, because the process is a standard operational procedure built into Hadoop.

Failover and fencing

The transition from the active namenode to the standby is managed by a new entity in the system called the *failover controller*. Failover controllers are pluggable, but the first implementation uses ZooKeeper to ensure that only one namenode is active. Each namenode runs a lightweight failover controller process whose job it is to monitor its namenode for failures (using a simple heartbeating mechanism) and trigger a failover should a namenode fail.

Failover may also be initiated manually by an administrator, for example, in the case of routine maintenance. This is known as a *graceful failover*, since the failover controller arranges an orderly transition for both namenodes to switch roles.

In the case of an ungraceful failover, however, it is impossible to be sure that the failed namenode has stopped running. For example, a slow network or a network partition can trigger a failover transition, even though the previously active namenode is still running and thinks it is still the active namenode. The HA implementation goes to great lengths to ensure that the previously active namenode is prevented from doing any damage and causing corruption—a method known as *fencing*. The system employs a range of fencing mechanisms, including killing the namenode's process, revoking its access to the shared storage directory (typically by using a vendor-specific NFS command), and disabling its network port via a remote management command. As a last resort, the previously active namenode can be fenced with a technique rather graphically known as *STONITH*, or "shoot the other node in the head," which uses a specialized power distribution unit to forcibly power down the host machine.

Client failover is handled transparently by the client library. The simplest implementation uses client-side configuration to control failover. The HDFS URI uses a logical hostname that is mapped to a pair of namenode addresses (in the configuration file), and the client library tries each namenode address until the operation succeeds.

The Command-Line Interface

We're going to have a look at HDFS by interacting with it from the command line. There are many other interfaces to HDFS, but the command line is one of the simplest and, to many developers, the most familiar.

We are going to run HDFS on one machine, so first follow the instructions for setting up Hadoop in pseudodistributed mode in Appendix A. Later we'll see how to run HDFS on a cluster of machines to give us scalability and fault tolerance.

There are two properties that we set in the pseudodistributed configuration that deserve further explanation. The first is fs.default.name, set to *hdfs://localhost/*, which is used to set a default filesystem for Hadoop. Filesystems are specified by a URI, and here we have used an hdfs URI to configure Hadoop to use HDFS by default. The HDFS daemons will use this property to determine the host and port for the HDFS namenode. We'll be running it on localhost, on the default HDFS port, 8020. And HDFS clients will use this property to work out where the namenode is running so they can connect to it.

We set the second property, dfs.replication, to 1 so that HDFS doesn't replicate filesystem blocks by the default factor of three. When running with a single datanode, HDFS can't replicate blocks to three datanodes, so it would perpetually warn about blocks being under-replicated. This setting solves that problem.

Basic Filesystem Operations

The filesystem is ready to be used, and we can do all of the usual filesystem operations, such as reading files, creating directories, moving files, deleting data, and listing directories. You can type hadoop fs -help to get detailed help on every command.

Start by copying a file from the local filesystem to HDFS:

```
% hadoop fs -copyFromLocal input/docs/quangle.txt hdfs://localhost/user/tom/
    quangle.txt
```

This command invokes Hadoop's filesystem shell command fs, which supports a number of subcommands—in this case, we are running -copyFromLocal. The local file *quangle.txt* is copied to the file */user/tom/quangle.txt* on the HDFS instance running on localhost. In fact, we could have omitted the scheme and host of the URI and picked up the default, hdfs://localhost, as specified in *core-site.xml*:

```
% hadoop fs -copyFromLocal input/docs/quangle.txt /user/tom/quangle.txt
```

We also could have used a relative path and copied the file to our home directory in HDFS, which in this case is */user/tom*:

```
% hadoop fs -copyFromLocal input/docs/quangle.txt quangle.txt
```

Let's copy the file back to the local filesystem and check whether it's the same:

```
% hadoop fs -copyToLocal quangle.txt quangle.copy.txt
% md5 input/docs/quangle.txt quangle.copy.txt
MD5 (input/docs/quangle.txt) = a16f231da6b05e2ba7a339320e7dacd9
MD5 (quangle.copy.txt) = a16f231da6b05e2ba7a339320e7dacd9
```

The MD5 digests are the same, showing that the file survived its trip to HDFS and is back intact.

Finally, let's look at an HDFS file listing. We create a directory first just to see how it is displayed in the listing:

```
% hadoop fs -mkdir books
% hadoop fs -ls .
Found 2 items
drwxr-xr-x   - tom supergroup          0 2009-04-02 22:41 /user/tom/books
-rw-r--r--   1 tom supergroup        118 2009-04-02 22:29 /user/tom/quangle.txt
```

The information returned is very similar to the Unix command ls -1, with a few minor differences. The first column shows the file mode. The second column is the replication factor of the file (something a traditional Unix filesystem does not have). Remember we set the default replication factor in the site-wide configuration to be 1, which is why we see the same value here. The entry in this column is empty for directories because the concept of replication does not apply to them—directories are treated as metadata and stored by the namenode, not the datanodes. The third and fourth columns show the file owner and group. The fifth column is the size of the file in bytes, or zero for directories. The sixth and seventh columns are the last modified date and time. Finally, the eighth column is the absolute name of the file or directory.

File Permissions in HDFS

HDFS has a permissions model for files and directories that is much like POSIX.

There are three types of permission: the read permission (r), the write permission (w), and the execute permission (x). The read permission is required to read files or list the contents of a directory. The write permission is required to write a file, or for a directory, to create or delete files or directories in it. The execute permission is ignored for a file because you can't execute a file on HDFS (unlike POSIX), and for a directory this permission is required to access its children.

Each file and directory has an *owner*, a *group*, and a *mode*. The mode is made up of the permissions for the user who is the owner, the permissions for the users who are members of the group, and the permissions for users who are neither the owners nor members of the group.

By default, a client's identity is determined by the username and groups of the process it is running in. Because clients are remote, this makes it possible to become an arbitrary user simply by creating an account of that name on the remote system. Thus, permissions should be used only in a cooperative community of users, as a mechanism for sharing filesystem resources and for avoiding accidental data loss, and not for securing resources in a hostile environment. (Note, however, that the latest versions of Hadoop support Kerberos authentication, which removes these restrictions; see "Security" on page 325.) Despite these limitations, it is worthwhile having permissions enabled (as it is by default; see the dfs.permissions property), to avoid accidental modification or deletion of substantial parts of the filesystem, either by users or by automated tools or programs.

When permissions checking is enabled, the owner permissions are checked if the client's username matches the owner, and the group permissions are checked if the client is a member of the group; otherwise, the other permissions are checked.

There is a concept of a super user, which is the identity of the namenode process. Permissions checks are not performed for the super user.

Hadoop Filesystems

Hadoop has an abstract notion of filesystem, of which HDFS is just one implementation. The Java abstract class `org.apache.hadoop.fs.FileSystem` represents a filesystem in Hadoop, and there are several concrete implementations, which are described in Table 3-1.

Table 3-1. Hadoop filesystems

Filesystem	URI scheme	Java implementation (all under org.apache.hadoop)	Description
Local	*file*	fs.LocalFileSystem	A filesystem for a locally connected disk with client-side checksums. Use RawLocalFileSystem for a local filesystem with no checksums. See "LocalFileSystem" on page 82.
HDFS	*hdfs*	hdfs.DistributedFileSystem	Hadoop's distributed filesystem. HDFS is designed to work efficiently in conjunction with MapReduce.
HFTP	*hftp*	hdfs.HftpFileSystem	A filesystem providing read-only access to HDFS over HTTP. (Despite its name, HFTP has no connection with FTP.) Often used with *distcp* (see "Parallel Copying with distcp" on page 75) to copy data between HDFS clusters running different versions.
HSFTP	*hsftp*	hdfs.HsftpFileSystem	A filesystem providing read-only access to HDFS over HTTPS. (Again, this has no connection with FTP.)
WebHDFS	*webhdfs*	hdfs.web.WebHdfsFileSystem	A filesystem providing secure read-write access to HDFS over HTTP. WebHDFS is intended as a replacement for HFTP and HSFTP.
HAR	*har*	fs.HarFileSystem	A filesystem layered on another filesystem for archiving files. Hadoop Archives are typically used for archiving files in HDFS to reduce the namenode's memory usage. See "Hadoop Archives" on page 77.
KFS (CloudStore)	*kfs*	fs.kfs.KosmosFileSystem	CloudStore (formerly Kosmos filesystem) is a distributed filesystem like HDFS or Google's GFS, written in C++. Find more information about it at *http://code.google.com/p/kosmosfs/*.
FTP	*ftp*	fs.ftp.FTPFileSystem	A filesystem backed by an FTP server.
S3 (native)	*s3n*	fs.s3native.NativeS3FileSystem	A filesystem backed by Amazon S3. See *http://wiki.apache.org/hadoop/AmazonS3*.

Filesystem	URI scheme	Java implementation (all under org.apache.hadoop)	Description
S3 (block-based)	s3	fs.s3.S3FileSystem	A filesystem backed by Amazon S3, which stores files in blocks (much like HDFS) to overcome S3's 5 GB file size limit.
Distributed RAID	hdfs	hdfs.DistributedRaidFileSystem	A "RAID" version of HDFS designed for archival storage. For each file in HDFS, a (smaller) parity file is created, which allows the HDFS replication to be reduced from three to two, which reduces disk usage by 25% to 30% while keeping the probability of data loss the same. Distributed RAID requires that you run a RaidNode daemon on the cluster.
View	viewfs	viewfs.ViewFileSystem	A client-side mount table for other Hadoop filesystems. Commonly used to create mount points for federated namenodes (see "HDFS Federation" on page 47).

Hadoop provides many interfaces to its filesystems, and it generally uses the URI scheme to pick the correct filesystem instance to communicate with. For example, the filesystem shell that we met in the previous section operates with all Hadoop filesystems. To list the files in the root directory of the local filesystem, type:

```
% hadoop fs -ls file:///
```

Although it is possible (and sometimes very convenient) to run MapReduce programs that access any of these filesystems, when you are processing large volumes of data, you should choose a distributed filesystem that has the data locality optimization, notably HDFS (see "Scaling Out" on page 30).

Interfaces

Hadoop is written in Java, and all Hadoop filesystem interactions are mediated through the Java API. The filesystem shell, for example, is a Java application that uses the Java FileSystem class to provide filesystem operations. The other filesystem interfaces are discussed briefly in this section. These interfaces are most commonly used with HDFS, since the other filesystems in Hadoop typically have existing tools to access the underlying filesystem (FTP clients for FTP, S3 tools for S3, etc.), but many of them will work with any Hadoop filesystem.

HTTP

There are two ways of accessing HDFS over HTTP: directly, where the HDFS daemons serve HTTP requests to clients; and via a proxy (or proxies), which accesses HDFS on the client's behalf using the usual DistributedFileSystem API. The two ways are illustrated in Figure 3-1.

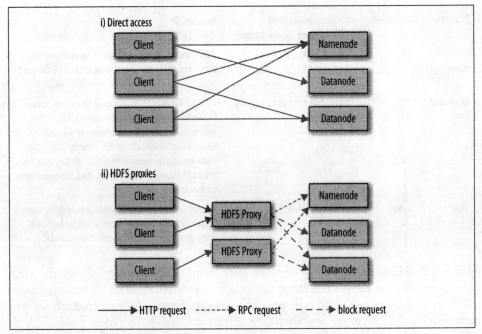

Figure 3-1. Accessing HDFS over HTTP directly and via a bank of HDFS proxies

In the first case, directory listings are served by the namenode's embedded web server (which runs on port 50070) formatted in XML or JSON, whereas file data is streamed from datanodes by their web servers (running on port 50075).

The original direct HTTP interface (HFTP and HSFTP) was read-only, but the new WebHDFS implementation supports all filesystem operations, including Kerberos authentication. WebHDFS must be enabled by setting dfs.webhdfs.enabled to true, which allows you to use *webhdfs* URIs.

The second way of accessing HDFS over HTTP relies on one or more standalone proxy servers. (The proxies are stateless so they can run behind a standard load balancer.) All traffic to the cluster passes through the proxy. This allows for stricter firewall and bandwidth-limiting policies to be put in place. It's common to use a proxy for transfers between Hadoop clusters located in different data centers.

The original HDFS proxy (in *src/contrib/hdfsproxy*) was read-only and could be accessed by clients using the HSFTP FileSystem implementation (*hsftp* URIs). From release 1.0.0, there is a new proxy called HttpFS that has read and write capabilities and exposes the same HTTP interface as WebHDFS, so clients can access both using *webhdfs* URIs.

The HTTP REST API that WebHDFS exposes is formally defined in a specification, so it is expected that over time clients in languages other than Java will be written that use it directly.

C

Hadoop provides a C library called *libhdfs* that mirrors the Java `FileSystem` interface (it was written as a C library for accessing HDFS, but despite its name it can be used to access any Hadoop filesystem). It works using the *Java Native Interface* (JNI) to call a Java filesystem client.

The C API is very similar to the Java one, but it typically lags the Java one, so newer features may not be supported. You can find the generated documentation for the C API in the *libhdfs/docs/api* directory of the Hadoop distribution.

Hadoop comes with prebuilt *libhdfs* binaries for 32-bit Linux, but for other platforms, you will need to build them yourself using the instructions at *http://wiki.apache.org/ hadoop/LibHDFS*.

FUSE

Filesystem in Userspace (FUSE) allows filesystems that are implemented in user space to be integrated as a Unix filesystem. Hadoop's Fuse-DFS contrib module allows any Hadoop filesystem (but typically HDFS) to be mounted as a standard filesystem. You can then use Unix utilities (such as `ls` and `cat`) to interact with the filesystem, as well as POSIX libraries to access the filesystem from any programming language.

Fuse-DFS is implemented in C using *libhdfs* as the interface to HDFS. Documentation for compiling and running Fuse-DFS is located in the *src/contrib/fuse-dfs* directory of the Hadoop distribution.

The Java Interface

In this section, we dig into the Hadoop's `FileSystem` class: the API for interacting with one of Hadoop's filesystems.[5] Although we focus mainly on the HDFS implementation, `DistributedFileSystem`, in general you should strive to write your code against the `FileSystem` abstract class, to retain portability across filesystems. This is very useful when testing your program, for example, because you can rapidly run tests using data stored on the local filesystem.

Reading Data from a Hadoop URL

One of the simplest ways to read a file from a Hadoop filesystem is by using a `java.net.URL` object to open a stream to read the data from. The general idiom is:

```
InputStream in = null;
try {
```

---

5. In releases after 1.x, there is a new filesystem interface called `FileContext` with better handling of multiple filesystems (so a single `FileContext` can resolve multiple filesystem schemes, for example) and a cleaner, more consistent interface.

```
    in = new URL("hdfs://host/path").openStream();
    // process in
  } finally {
    IOUtils.closeStream(in);
  }
```

There's a little bit more work required to make Java recognize Hadoop's hdfs URL
scheme. This is achieved by calling the setURLStreamHandlerFactory method on URL
with an instance of FsUrlStreamHandlerFactory. This method can be called only once
per JVM, so it is typically executed in a static block. This limitation means that if some
other part of your program—perhaps a third-party component outside your control—
sets a URLStreamHandlerFactory, you won't be able to use this approach for reading data
from Hadoop. The next section discusses an alternative.

Example 3-1 shows a program for displaying files from Hadoop filesystems on standard
output, like the Unix cat command.

*Example 3-1. Displaying files from a Hadoop filesystem on standard output using a
URLStreamHandler*

```java
public class URLCat {

  static {
    URL.setURLStreamHandlerFactory(new FsUrlStreamHandlerFactory());
  }

  public static void main(String[] args) throws Exception {
    InputStream in = null;
    try {
      in = new URL(args[0]).openStream();
      IOUtils.copyBytes(in, System.out, 4096, false);
    } finally {
      IOUtils.closeStream(in);
    }
  }
}
```

We make use of the handy IOUtils class that comes with Hadoop for closing the stream
in the finally clause, and also for copying bytes between the input stream and the
output stream (System.out in this case). The last two arguments to the copyBytes
method are the buffer size used for copying and whether to close the streams when the
copy is complete. We close the input stream ourselves, and System.out doesn't need to
be closed.

Here's a sample run:[6]

```
% hadoop URLCat hdfs://localhost/user/tom/quangle.txt
On the top of the Crumpetty Tree
The Quangle Wangle sat,
But his face you could not see,
On account of his Beaver Hat.
```

Reading Data Using the FileSystem API

As the previous section explained, sometimes it is impossible to set a URLStreamHand
lerFactory for your application. In this case, you will need to use the FileSystem API
to open an input stream for a file.

A file in a Hadoop filesystem is represented by a Hadoop Path object (and not
a java.io.File object, since its semantics are too closely tied to the local filesystem).
You can think of a Path as a Hadoop filesystem URI, such as *hdfs://localhost/user/tom/
quangle.txt*.

FileSystem is a general filesystem API, so the first step is to retrieve an instance for the
filesystem we want to use—HDFS in this case. There are several static factory methods
for getting a FileSystem instance:

```
public static FileSystem get(Configuration conf) throws IOException
public static FileSystem get(URI uri, Configuration conf) throws IOException
public static FileSystem get(URI uri, Configuration conf, String user)
   throws IOException
```

A Configuration object encapsulates a client or server's configuration, which is set using
configuration files read from the classpath, such as *conf/core-site.xml*. The first method
returns the default filesystem (as specified in the file *conf/core-site.xml*, or the default
local filesystem if not specified there). The second uses the given URI's scheme and
authority to determine the filesystem to use, falling back to the default filesystem if no
scheme is specified in the given URI. The third retrieves the filesystem as the given user,
which is important in the context of security (see "Security" on page 325).

In some cases, you may want to retrieve a local filesystem instance, in which case you
can use the convenience method, getLocal():

```
public static LocalFileSystem getLocal(Configuration conf) throws IOException
```

With a FileSystem instance in hand, we invoke an open() method to get the input stream
for a file:

```
public FSDataInputStream open(Path f) throws IOException
public abstract FSDataInputStream open(Path f, int bufferSize) throws IOException
```

The first method uses a default buffer size of 4 KB.

Putting this together, we can rewrite Example 3-1 as shown in Example 3-2.

---

6. The text is from *The Quangle Wangle's Hat* by Edward Lear.

Example 3-2. Displaying files from a Hadoop filesystem on standard output by using the FileSystem directly

```
public class FileSystemCat {

  public static void main(String[] args) throws Exception {
    String uri = args[0];
    Configuration conf = new Configuration();
    FileSystem fs = FileSystem.get(URI.create(uri), conf);
    InputStream in = null;
    try {
      in = fs.open(new Path(uri));
      IOUtils.copyBytes(in, System.out, 4096, false);
    } finally {
      IOUtils.closeStream(in);
    }
  }
}
```

The program runs as follows:

```
% hadoop FileSystemCat hdfs://localhost/user/tom/quangle.txt
On the top of the Crumpetty Tree
The Quangle Wangle sat,
But his face you could not see,
On account of his Beaver Hat.
```

FSDataInputStream

The open() method on FileSystem actually returns a FSDataInputStream rather than a standard java.io class. This class is a specialization of java.io.DataInputStream with support for random access, so you can read from any part of the stream:

```
package org.apache.hadoop.fs;

public class FSDataInputStream extends DataInputStream
    implements Seekable, PositionedReadable {
  // implementation elided
}
```

The Seekable interface permits seeking to a position in the file and a query method for the current offset from the start of the file (getPos()):

```
public interface Seekable {
  void seek(long pos) throws IOException;
  long getPos() throws IOException;
}
```

Calling seek() with a position that is greater than the length of the file will result in an IOException. Unlike the skip() method of java.io.InputStream, which positions the stream at a point later than the current position, seek() can move to an arbitrary, absolute position in the file.

Example 3-3 is a simple extension of Example 3-2 that writes a file to standard out twice: after writing it once, it seeks to the start of the file and streams through it once again.

Example 3-3. Displaying files from a Hadoop filesystem on standard output twice, by using seek

```java
public class FileSystemDoubleCat {

  public static void main(String[] args) throws Exception {
    String uri = args[0];
    Configuration conf = new Configuration();
    FileSystem fs = FileSystem.get(URI.create(uri), conf);
    FSDataInputStream in = null;
    try {
      in = fs.open(new Path(uri));
      IOUtils.copyBytes(in, System.out, 4096, false);
      in.seek(0); // go back to the start of the file
      IOUtils.copyBytes(in, System.out, 4096, false);
    } finally {
      IOUtils.closeStream(in);
    }
  }
}
```

Here's the result of running it on a small file:

```
% hadoop FileSystemDoubleCat hdfs://localhost/user/tom/quangle.txt
On the top of the Crumpetty Tree
The Quangle Wangle sat,
But his face you could not see,
On account of his Beaver Hat.
On the top of the Crumpetty Tree
The Quangle Wangle sat,
But his face you could not see,
On account of his Beaver Hat.
```

FSDataInputStream also implements the PositionedReadable interface for reading parts of a file at a given offset:

```java
public interface PositionedReadable {

  public int read(long position, byte[] buffer, int offset, int length)
    throws IOException;

  public void readFully(long position, byte[] buffer, int offset, int length)
    throws IOException;

  public void readFully(long position, byte[] buffer) throws IOException;
}
```

The read() method reads up to length bytes from the given position in the file into the buffer at the given offset in the buffer. The return value is the number of bytes actually read; callers should check this value, as it may be less than length. The readFully() methods will read length bytes into the buffer (or buffer.length bytes for the version that just takes a byte array buffer), unless the end of the file is reached, in which case an EOFException is thrown.

All of these methods preserve the current offset in the file and are thread-safe (although FSDataInputStream is not designed for concurrent access, therefore, it's better to create multiple instances), so they provide a convenient way to access another part of the file —metadata perhaps—while reading the main body of the file.

Finally, bear in mind that calling seek() is a relatively expensive operation and should be used sparingly. You should structure your application access patterns to rely on streaming data (by using MapReduce, for example) rather than performing a large number of seeks.

Writing Data

The FileSystem class has a number of methods for creating a file. The simplest is the method that takes a Path object for the file to be created and returns an output stream to write to:

```
public FSDataOutputStream create(Path f) throws IOException
```

There are overloaded versions of this method that allow you to specify whether to forcibly overwrite existing files, the replication factor of the file, the buffer size to use when writing the file, the block size for the file, and file permissions.

 The create() methods create any parent directories of the file to be written that don't already exist. Though convenient, this behavior may be unexpected. If you want the write to fail when the parent directory doesn't exist, you should check for the existence of the parent directory first by calling the exists() method.

There's also an overloaded method for passing a callback interface, Progressable, so your application can be notified of the progress of the data being written to the datanodes:

```
package org.apache.hadoop.util;

public interface Progressable {
  public void progress();
}
```

As an alternative to creating a new file, you can append to an existing file using the append() method (there are also some other overloaded versions):

```
public FSDataOutputStream append(Path f) throws IOException
```

The append operation allows a single writer to modify an already written file by opening it and writing data from the final offset in the file. With this API, applications that produce unbounded files, such as logfiles, can write to an existing file after having closed it. The append operation is optional and not implemented by all Hadoop file-systems. For example, HDFS supports append,[7] but S3 filesystems don't.

Example 3-4 shows how to copy a local file to a Hadoop filesystem. We illustrate progress by printing a period every time the progress() method is called by Hadoop, which is after each 64 KB packet of data is written to the datanode pipeline. (Note that this particular behavior is not specified by the API, so it is subject to change in later versions of Hadoop. The API merely allows you to infer that "something is happening.")

Example 3-4. Copying a local file to a Hadoop filesystem

```java
public class FileCopyWithProgress {
  public static void main(String[] args) throws Exception {
    String localSrc = args[0];
    String dst = args[1];

    InputStream in = new BufferedInputStream(new FileInputStream(localSrc));

    Configuration conf = new Configuration();
    FileSystem fs = FileSystem.get(URI.create(dst), conf);
    OutputStream out = fs.create(new Path(dst), new Progressable() {
      public void progress() {
        System.out.print(".");
      }
    });

    IOUtils.copyBytes(in, out, 4096, true);
  }
}
```

Typical usage:

```
% hadoop FileCopyWithProgress input/docs/1400-8.txt hdfs://localhost/user/tom/
    1400-8.txt
...............
```

Currently, none of the other Hadoop filesystems call progress() during writes. Progress is important in MapReduce applications, as you will see in later chapters.

FSDataOutputStream

The create() method on FileSystem returns an FSDataOutputStream, which, like FSDataInputStream, has a method for querying the current position in the file:

```java
package org.apache.hadoop.fs;

public class FSDataOutputStream extends DataOutputStream implements Syncable {

  public long getPos() throws IOException {
```

---

7. There have been reliability problems with the append implementation in Hadoop 1.x, so it is generally recommended to use append only in the releases after 1.x, which contain a new, rewritten implementation.

```
    // implementation elided
  }

  // implementation elided

}
```

However, unlike FSDataInputStream, FSDataOutputStream does not permit seeking. This is because HDFS allows only sequential writes to an open file or appends to an already written file. In other words, there is no support for writing to anywhere other than the end of the file, so there is no value in being able to seek while writing.

Directories

FileSystem provides a method to create a directory:

```
public boolean mkdirs(Path f) throws IOException
```

This method creates all of the necessary parent directories if they don't already exist, just like the java.io.File's mkdirs() method. It returns true if the directory (and all parent directories) was (were) successfully created.

Often, you don't need to explicitly create a directory, because writing a file by calling create() will automatically create any parent directories.

Querying the Filesystem

File metadata: FileStatus

An important feature of any filesystem is the ability to navigate its directory structure and retrieve information about the files and directories that it stores. The FileStatus class encapsulates filesystem metadata for files and directories, including file length, block size, replication, modification time, ownership, and permission information.

The method getFileStatus() on FileSystem provides a way of getting a FileStatus object for a single file or directory. Example 3-5 shows an example of its use.

Example 3-5. Demonstrating file status information

```
public class ShowFileStatusTest {

  private MiniDFSCluster cluster; // use an in-process HDFS cluster for testing
  private FileSystem fs;

  @Before
  public void setUp() throws IOException {
    Configuration conf = new Configuration();
    if (System.getProperty("test.build.data") == null) {
      System.setProperty("test.build.data", "/tmp");
    }
    cluster = new MiniDFSCluster(conf, 1, true, null);
    fs = cluster.getFileSystem();
```

```
    OutputStream out = fs.create(new Path("/dir/file"));
    out.write("content".getBytes("UTF-8"));
    out.close();
  }

  @After
  public void tearDown() throws IOException {
    if (fs != null) { fs.close(); }
    if (cluster != null) { cluster.shutdown(); }
  }

  @Test(expected = FileNotFoundException.class)
  public void throwsFileNotFoundForNonExistentFile() throws IOException {
    fs.getFileStatus(new Path("no-such-file"));
  }

  @Test
  public void fileStatusForFile() throws IOException {
    Path file = new Path("/dir/file");
    FileStatus stat = fs.getFileStatus(file);
    assertThat(stat.getPath().toUri().getPath(), is("/dir/file"));
    assertThat(stat.isDir(), is(false));
    assertThat(stat.getLen(), is(7L));
    assertThat(stat.getModificationTime(),
        is(lessThanOrEqualTo(System.currentTimeMillis())));
    assertThat(stat.getReplication(), is((short) 1));
    assertThat(stat.getBlockSize(), is(64 * 1024 * 1024L));
    assertThat(stat.getOwner(), is("tom"));
    assertThat(stat.getGroup(), is("supergroup"));
    assertThat(stat.getPermission().toString(), is("rw-r--r--"));
  }

  @Test
  public void fileStatusForDirectory() throws IOException {
    Path dir = new Path("/dir");
    FileStatus stat = fs.getFileStatus(dir);
    assertThat(stat.getPath().toUri().getPath(), is("/dir"));
    assertThat(stat.isDir(), is(true));
    assertThat(stat.getLen(), is(0L));
    assertThat(stat.getModificationTime(),
        is(lessThanOrEqualTo(System.currentTimeMillis())));
    assertThat(stat.getReplication(), is((short) 0));
    assertThat(stat.getBlockSize(), is(0L));
    assertThat(stat.getOwner(), is("tom"));
    assertThat(stat.getGroup(), is("supergroup"));
    assertThat(stat.getPermission().toString(), is("rwxr-xr-x"));
  }

}
```

If no file or directory exists, a FileNotFoundException is thrown. However, if you are interested only in the existence of a file or directory, the exists() method on FileSystem is more convenient:

```
    public boolean exists(Path f) throws IOException
```

Listing files

Finding information on a single file or directory is useful, but you also often need to be able to list the contents of a directory. That's what FileSystem's listStatus() methods are for:

```
public FileStatus[] listStatus(Path f) throws IOException
public FileStatus[] listStatus(Path f, PathFilter filter) throws IOException
public FileStatus[] listStatus(Path[] files) throws IOException
public FileStatus[] listStatus(Path[] files, PathFilter filter) throws IOException
```

When the argument is a file, the simplest variant returns an array of FileStatus objects of length 1. When the argument is a directory, it returns zero or more FileStatus objects representing the files and directories contained in the directory.

Overloaded variants allow a PathFilter to be supplied to restrict the files and directories to match. You will see an example of this in the section "PathFilter" on page 66. Finally, if you specify an array of paths, the result is a shortcut for calling the equivalent single-path listStatus method for each path in turn and accumulating the FileStatus object arrays in a single array. This can be useful for building up lists of input files to process from distinct parts of the filesystem tree. Example 3-6 is a simple demonstration of this idea. Note the use of stat2Paths() in FileUtil for turning an array of FileStatus objects to an array of Path objects.

Example 3-6. Showing the file statuses for a collection of paths in a Hadoop filesystem

```java
public class ListStatus {

  public static void main(String[] args) throws Exception {
    String uri = args[0];
    Configuration conf = new Configuration();
    FileSystem fs = FileSystem.get(URI.create(uri), conf);

    Path[] paths = new Path[args.length];
    for (int i = 0; i < paths.length; i++) {
      paths[i] = new Path(args[i]);
    }

    FileStatus[] status = fs.listStatus(paths);
    Path[] listedPaths = FileUtil.stat2Paths(status);
    for (Path p : listedPaths) {
      System.out.println(p);
    }
  }
}
```

We can use this program to find the union of directory listings for a collection of paths:

```
% hadoop ListStatus hdfs://localhost/ hdfs://localhost/user/tom
hdfs://localhost/user
hdfs://localhost/user/tom/books
hdfs://localhost/user/tom/quangle.txt
```

File patterns

It is a common requirement to process sets of files in a single operation. For example, a MapReduce job for log processing might analyze a month's worth of files contained in a number of directories. Rather than having to enumerate each file and directory to specify the input, it is convenient to use wildcard characters to match multiple files with a single expression, an operation that is known as *globbing*. Hadoop provides two FileSystem method for processing globs:

```
public FileStatus[] globStatus(Path pathPattern) throws IOException
public FileStatus[] globStatus(Path pathPattern, PathFilter filter) throws
    IOException
```

The globStatus() method returns an array of FileStatus objects whose paths match the supplied pattern, sorted by path. An optional PathFilter can be specified to restrict the matches further.

Hadoop supports the same set of glob characters as Unix *bash* (see Table 3-2).

Table 3-2. Glob characters and their meanings

Glob	Name	Matches
*	asterisk	Matches zero or more characters
?	question mark	Matches a single character
[ab]	character class	Matches a single character in the set {a, b}
[^ab]	negated character class	Matches a single character that is not in the set {a, b}
[a-b]	character range	Matches a single character in the (closed) range [a, b], where a is lexicographically less than or equal to b
[^a-b]	negated character range	Matches a single character that is not in the (closed) range [a, b], where a is lexicographically less than or equal to b
{a,b}	alternation	Matches either expression a or b
\c	escaped character	Matches character c when it is a metacharacter

Imagine that logfiles are stored in a directory structure organized hierarchically by date. So, for example, logfiles for the last day of 2007 would go in a directory named */2007/12/31*. Suppose that the full file listing is:

```
/
├── 2007/
│   └── 12/
│       ├── 30/
│       └── 31/
└── 2008/
    └── 01/
        ├── 01/
        └── 02/
```

Here are some file globs and their expansions:

Glob	Expansion
/*	/2007 /2008
/*/*	/2007/12 /2008/01
/*/12/*	/2007/12/30 /2007/12/31
/200?	/2007 /2008
/200[78]	/2007 /2008
/200[7-8]	/2007 /2008
/200[^01234569]	/2007 /2008
/*/*/{31,01}	/2007/12/31 /2008/01/01
/*/*/3{0,1}	/2007/12/30 /2007/12/31
/*/{12/31,01/01}	/2007/12/31 /2008/01/01

PathFilter

Glob patterns are not always powerful enough to describe a set of files you want to access. For example, it is not generally possible to exclude a particular file using a glob pattern. The listStatus() and globStatus() methods of FileSystem take an optional PathFilter, which allows programmatic control over matching:

```
package org.apache.hadoop.fs;

public interface PathFilter {
  boolean accept(Path path);
}
```

PathFilter is the equivalent of java.io.FileFilter for Path objects rather than File objects.

Example 3-7 shows a PathFilter for excluding paths that match a regular expression.

Example 3-7. A PathFilter for excluding paths that match a regular expression

```
public class RegexExcludePathFilter implements PathFilter {

  private final String regex;

  public RegexExcludePathFilter(String regex) {
    this.regex = regex;
  }

  public boolean accept(Path path) {
    return !path.toString().matches(regex);
  }
}
```

The filter passes only those files that *don't* match the regular expression. After the glob picks out an initial set of files to include, the filter is used to refine the results. For example:

```
fs.globStatus(new Path("/2007/*/*"), new RegexExcludeFilter("^.*/2007/12/31$"))
```

will expand to */2007/12/30*.

Filters can act only on a file's name, as represented by a `Path`. They can't use a file's properties, such as creation time, as the basis of the filter. Nevertheless, they can perform matching that neither glob patterns nor regular expressions can achieve. For example, if you store files in a directory structure that is laid out by date (like in the previous section), you can write a `PathFilter` to pick out files that fall in a given date range.

Deleting Data

Use the `delete()` method on `FileSystem` to permanently remove files or directories:

```
public boolean delete(Path f, boolean recursive) throws IOException
```

If `f` is a file or an empty directory, the value of `recursive` is ignored. A nonempty directory is deleted, along with its contents, only if `recursive` is `true` (otherwise, an `IOException` is thrown).

Data Flow

Anatomy of a File Read

To get an idea of how data flows between the client interacting with HDFS, the namenode, and the datanodes, consider Figure 3-2, which shows the main sequence of events when reading a file.

The client opens the file it wishes to read by calling `open()` on the `FileSystem` object, which for HDFS is an instance of `DistributedFileSystem` (step 1 in Figure 3-2). `DistributedFileSystem` calls the namenode, using RPC, to determine the locations of the blocks for the first few blocks in the file (step 2). For each block, the namenode returns the addresses of the datanodes that have a copy of that block. Furthermore, the datanodes are sorted according to their proximity to the client (according to the topology of the cluster's network; see "Network Topology and Hadoop" on page 69). If the client is itself a datanode (in the case of a MapReduce task, for instance), the client will read from the local datanode if that datanode hosts a copy of the block (see also Figure 2-2).

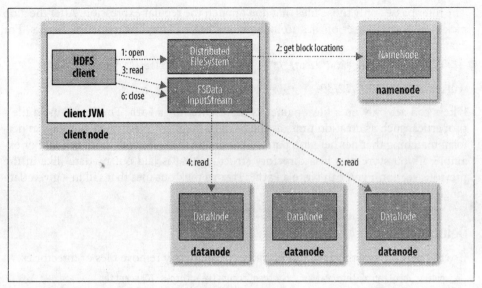

Figure 3-2. A client reading data from HDFS

The DistributedFileSystem returns an FSDataInputStream (an input stream that supports file seeks) to the client for it to read data from. FSDataInputStream in turn wraps a DFSInputStream, which manages the datanode and namenode I/O.

The client then calls read() on the stream (step 3). DFSInputStream, which has stored the datanode addresses for the first few blocks in the file, then connects to the first (closest) datanode for the first block in the file. Data is streamed from the datanode back to the client, which calls read() repeatedly on the stream (step 4). When the end of the block is reached, DFSInputStream will close the connection to the datanode, then find the best datanode for the next block (step 5). This happens transparently to the client, which from its point of view is just reading a continuous stream.

Blocks are read in order, with the DFSInputStream opening new connections to datanodes as the client reads through the stream. It will also call the namenode to retrieve the datanode locations for the next batch of blocks as needed. When the client has finished reading, it calls close() on the FSDataInputStream (step 6).

During reading, if the DFSInputStream encounters an error while communicating with a datanode, it will try the next closest one for that block. It will also remember datanodes that have failed so that it doesn't needlessly retry them for later blocks. The DFSInputStream also verifies checksums for the data transferred to it from the datanode. If a corrupted block is found, it is reported to the namenode before the DFSInput Stream attempts to read a replica of the block from another datanode.

One important aspect of this design is that the client contacts datanodes directly to retrieve data and is guided by the namenode to the best datanode for each block. This design allows HDFS to scale to a large number of concurrent clients because the data traffic is spread across all the datanodes in the cluster. Meanwhile, the namenode merely has to service block location requests (which it stores in memory, making them very efficient) and does not, for example, serve data, which would quickly become a bottleneck as the number of clients grew.

Network Topology and Hadoop

What does it mean for two nodes in a local network to be "close" to each other? In the context of high-volume data processing, the limiting factor is the rate at which we can transfer data between nodes—bandwidth is a scarce commodity. The idea is to use the bandwidth between two nodes as a measure of distance.

Rather than measuring bandwidth between nodes, which can be difficult to do in practice (it requires a quiet cluster, and the number of pairs of nodes in a cluster grows as the square of the number of nodes), Hadoop takes a simple approach in which the network is represented as a tree and the distance between two nodes is the sum of their distances to their closest common ancestor. Levels in the tree are not predefined, but it is common to have levels that correspond to the data center, the rack, and the node that a process is running on. The idea is that the bandwidth available for each of the following scenarios becomes progressively less:

- Processes on the same node
- Different nodes on the same rack
- Nodes on different racks in the same data center
- Nodes in different data centers[8]

For example, imagine a node *n1* on rack *r1* in data center *d1*. This can be represented as */d1/r1/n1*. Using this notation, here are the distances for the four scenarios:

- *distance(/d1/r1/n1, /d1/r1/n1)* = 0 (processes on the same node)
- *distance(/d1/r1/n1, /d1/r1/n2)* = 2 (different nodes on the same rack)
- *distance(/d1/r1/n1, /d1/r2/n3)* = 4 (nodes on different racks in the same data center)
- *distance(/d1/r1/n1, /d2/r3/n4)* = 6 (nodes in different data centers)

This is illustrated schematically in Figure 3-3. (Mathematically inclined readers will notice that this is an example of a distance metric.)

Finally, it is important to realize that Hadoop cannot divine your network topology for you. It needs some help, we'll cover how to configure topology in "Network Topology" on page 299. By default, though, it assumes that the network is flat—a single-level hierarchy—or in other words, that all nodes are on a single rack in a single data center. For small clusters, this may actually be the case, and no further configuration is required.

---

8. At the time of this writing, Hadoop is not suited for running across data centers.

Figure 3-3. Network distance in Hadoop

Anatomy of a File Write

Next we'll look at how files are written to HDFS. Although quite detailed, it is instructive to understand the data flow because it clarifies HDFS's coherency model.

We're going to consider the case of creating a new file, writing data to it, then closing the file. See Figure 3-4.

The client creates the file by calling create() on DistributedFileSystem (step 1 in Figure 3-4). DistributedFileSystem makes an RPC call to the namenode to create a new file in the filesystem's namespace, with no blocks associated with it (step 2). The namenode performs various checks to make sure the file doesn't already exist and that the client has the right permissions to create the file. If these checks pass, the namenode makes a record of the new file; otherwise, file creation fails and the client is thrown an IOException. The DistributedFileSystem returns an FSDataOutputStream for the client to start writing data to. Just as in the read case, FSDataOutputStream wraps a DFSOutput Stream, which handles communication with the datanodes and namenode.

As the client writes data (step 3), DFSOutputStream splits it into packets, which it writes to an internal queue, called the *data queue*. The data queue is consumed by the Data Streamer, which is responsible for asking the namenode to allocate new blocks by picking a list of suitable datanodes to store the replicas. The list of datanodes forms a pipeline, and here we'll assume the replication level is three, so there are three nodes in the pipeline. The DataStreamer streams the packets to the first datanode in the pipeline, which stores the packet and forwards it to the second datanode in the pipeline.

Similarly, the second datanode stores the packet and forwards it to the third (and last) datanode in the pipeline (step 4).

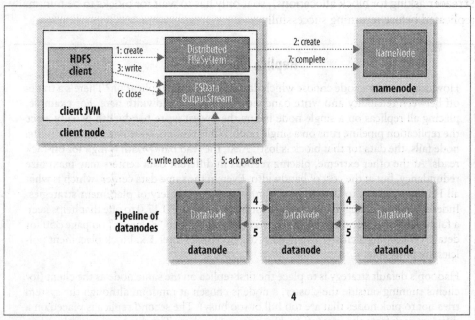

Figure 3-4. A client writing data to HDFS

DFSOutputStream also maintains an internal queue of packets that are waiting to be acknowledged by datanodes, called the *ack queue*. A packet is removed from the ack queue only when it has been acknowledged by all the datanodes in the pipeline (step 5).

If a datanode fails while data is being written to it, then the following actions are taken, which are transparent to the client writing the data. First, the pipeline is closed, and any packets in the ack queue are added to the front of the data queue so that datanodes that are downstream from the failed node will not miss any packets. The current block on the good datanodes is given a new identity, which is communicated to the namenode, so that the partial block on the failed datanode will be deleted if the failed datanode recovers later on. The failed datanode is removed from the pipeline, and the remainder of the block's data is written to the two good datanodes in the pipeline. The namenode notices that the block is under-replicated, and it arranges for a further replica to be created on another node. Subsequent blocks are then treated as normal.

It's possible, but unlikely, that multiple datanodes fail while a block is being written. As long as dfs.replication.min replicas (which default to one) are written, the write will succeed, and the block will be asynchronously replicated across the cluster until its target replication factor is reached (dfs.replication, which defaults to three).

When the client has finished writing data, it calls close() on the stream (step 6). This action flushes all the remaining packets to the datanode pipeline and waits for acknowledgments before contacting the namenode to signal that the file is complete (step 7). The namenode already knows which blocks the file is made up of (via Data Streamer asking for block allocations), so it only has to wait for blocks to be minimally replicated before returning successfully.

Replica Placement

How does the namenode choose which datanodes to store replicas on? There's a trade-off between reliability and write bandwidth and read bandwidth here. For example, placing all replicas on a single node incurs the lowest write bandwidth penalty since the replication pipeline runs on a single node, but this offers no real redundancy (if the node fails, the data for that block is lost). Also, the read bandwidth is high for off-rack reads. At the other extreme, placing replicas in different data centers may maximize redundancy, but at the cost of bandwidth. Even in the same data center (which is what all Hadoop clusters to date have run in), there are a variety of placement strategies. Indeed, Hadoop changed its placement strategy in release 0.17.0 to one that helps keep a fairly even distribution of blocks across the cluster. (See "Balancer" on page 350 for details on keeping a cluster balanced.) And in releases after 1.x, block placement policies are pluggable.

Hadoop's default strategy is to place the first replica on the same node as the client (for clients running outside the cluster, a node is chosen at random, although the system tries not to pick nodes that are too full or too busy). The second replica is placed on a different rack from the first (off-rack), chosen at random. The third replica is placed on the same rack as the second, but on a different node chosen at random. Further replicas are placed on random nodes on the cluster, although the system tries to avoid placing too many replicas on the same rack.

Once the replica locations have been chosen, a pipeline is built, taking network topology into account. For a replication factor of 3, the pipeline might look like Figure 3-5.

Overall, this strategy gives a good balance among reliability (blocks are stored on two racks), write bandwidth (writes only have to traverse a single network switch), read performance (there's a choice of two racks to read from), and block distribution across the cluster (clients only write a single block on the local rack).

Coherency Model

A coherency model for a filesystem describes the data visibility of reads and writes for a file. HDFS trades off some POSIX requirements for performance, so some operations may behave differently than you expect them to.

After creating a file, it is visible in the filesystem namespace, as expected:

```
Path p = new Path("p");
fs.create(p);
assertThat(fs.exists(p), is(true));
```

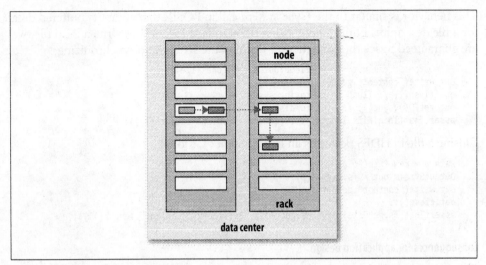

Figure 3-5. A typical replica pipeline

However, any content written to the file is not guaranteed to be visible, even if the stream is flushed. So the file appears to have a length of zero:

```
Path p = new Path("p");
OutputStream out = fs.create(p);
out.write("content".getBytes("UTF-8"));
out.flush();
assertThat(fs.getFileStatus(p).getLen(), is(0L));
```

Once more than a block's worth of data has been written, the first block will be visible to new readers. This is true of subsequent blocks, too: it is always the current block being written that is not visible to other readers.

HDFS provides a method for forcing all buffers to be synchronized to the datanodes via the `sync()` method on `FSDataOutputStream`. After a successful return from `sync()`, HDFS guarantees that the data written up to that point in the file has reached all the datanodes in the write pipeline and is visible to all new readers:[9]

```
Path p = new Path("p");
FSDataOutputStream out = fs.create(p);
out.write("content".getBytes("UTF-8"));
out.flush();
out.sync();
assertThat(fs.getFileStatus(p).getLen(), is(((long) "content".length()))));
```

9. Post Hadoop 1.x, sync() is deprecated in favor of the equivalent hflush() method. Another method, hsync(), has also been added that makes a stronger guarantee that the operating system has flushed the data to the datanodes' disks (like POSIX fsync). However, at the time of this writing, this has not been implemented and merely calls hflush().

This behavior is similar to the `fsync` system call in POSIX that commits buffered data for a file descriptor. For example, using the standard Java API to write a local file, we are guaranteed to see the content after flushing the stream and synchronizing:

```
FileOutputStream out = new FileOutputStream(localFile);
out.write("content".getBytes("UTF-8"));
out.flush(); // flush to operating system
out.getFD().sync(); // sync to disk
assertThat(localFile.length(), is(((long) "content".length())));
```

Closing a file in HDFS performs an implicit `sync()`, too:

```
Path p = new Path("p");
OutputStream out = fs.create(p);
out.write("content".getBytes("UTF-8"));
out.close();
assertThat(fs.getFileStatus(p).getLen(), is(((long) "content".length())));
```

Consequences for application design

This coherency model has implications for the way you design applications. With no calls to `sync()`, you should be prepared to lose up to a block of data in the event of client or system failure. For many applications, this is unacceptable, so you should call `sync()` at suitable points, such as after writing a certain number of records or number of bytes. Though the `sync()` operation is designed to not unduly tax HDFS, it does have some overhead, so there is a trade-off between data robustness and throughput. What constitutes an acceptable trade-off is application-dependent, and suitable values can be selected after measuring your application's performance with different `sync()` frequencies.

Data Ingest with Flume and Sqoop

Rather than writing an application to move data into HDFS, it's worth considering some of the existing tools for ingesting data because they cover many of the common requirements.

Apache Flume (*http://incubator.apache.org/flume/*) is a system for moving large quantities of streaming data into HDFS. A very common use case is collecting log data from one system—a bank of web servers, for example—and aggregating it in HDFS for later analysis. Flume supports a large variety of sources; some of the more commonly used ones include `tail` (which pipes data from a local file being written to into Flume, just like Unix `tail`), syslog, and Apache log4j (allowing Java applications to write events to files in HDFS via Flume).

Flume nodes can be arranged in arbitrary topologies. Typically there is a node running on each source machine (each web server, for example), with tiers of aggregating nodes that the data flows through on its way to HDFS.

Flume offers different levels of delivery reliability, from *best-effort* delivery, which doesn't tolerate any Flume node failures, to *end-to-end*, which guarantees delivery even in the event of multiple Flume node failures between the source and HDFS.

Apache Sqoop (*http://sqoop.apache.org/*), on the other hand, is designed for performing bulk imports of data into HDFS from structured data stores, such as relational databases. An example of a Sqoop use case is an organization that runs a nightly Sqoop import to load the day's data from a production database into a Hive data warehouse for analysis. Sqoop is covered in Chapter 15.

Parallel Copying with distcp

The HDFS access patterns that we have seen so far focus on single-threaded access. It's possible to act on a collection of files—by specifying file globs, for example—but for efficient parallel processing of these files, you would have to write a program yourself. Hadoop comes with a useful program called *distcp* for copying large amounts of data to and from Hadoop filesystems in parallel.

The canonical use case for *distcp* is for transferring data between two HDFS clusters. If the clusters are running identical versions of Hadoop, the *hdfs* scheme is appropriate:

```
% hadoop distcp hdfs://namenode1/foo hdfs://namenode2/bar
```

This will copy the */foo* directory (and its contents) from the first cluster to the */bar* directory on the second cluster, so the second cluster ends up with the directory structure */bar/foo*. If */bar* doesn't exist, it will be created first. You can specify multiple source paths, and all will be copied to the destination. Source paths must be absolute.

By default, *distcp* will skip files that already exist in the destination, but they can be overwritten by supplying the -overwrite option. You can also update only the files that have changed using the -update option.

 Using either (or both) -overwrite or -update changes how the source and destination paths are interpreted. This is best shown with an example. If we changed a file in the */foo* subtree on the first cluster from the previous example, we could synchronize the change with the second cluster by running:

```
% hadoop distcp -update hdfs://namenode1/foo hdfs://namenode2/bar/foo
```

The extra trailing */foo* subdirectory is needed on the destination, because now the *contents* of the source directory are copied to the *contents* of the destination directory. (If you are familiar with *rsync*, you can think of the -overwrite or -update options as adding an implicit trailing slash to the source.)

If you are unsure of the effect of a *distcp* operation, it is a good idea to try it out on a small test directory tree first.

There are more options to control the behavior of *distcp*, including ones to preserve file attributes, ignore failures, and limit the number of files or total data copied. Run it with no options to see the usage instructions.

distcp is implemented as a MapReduce job where the work of copying is done by the maps that run in parallel across the cluster. There are no reducers. Each file is copied by a single map, and *distcp* tries to give each map approximately the same amount of data by bucketing files into roughly equal allocations.

The number of maps is decided as follows. Because it's a good idea to get each map to copy a reasonable amount of data to minimize overheads in task setup, each map copies at least 256 MB (unless the total size of the input is less, in which case one map handles it all). For example, 1 GB of files will be given four map tasks. When the data size is very large, it becomes necessary to limit the number of maps in order to limit bandwidth and cluster utilization. By default, the maximum number of maps is 20 per (tasktracker) cluster node. For example, copying 1,000 GB of files to a 100-node cluster will allocate 2,000 maps (20 per node), so each will copy 512 MB on average. This can be reduced by specifying the -m argument to *distcp*. For example, -m 1000 would allocate 1,000 maps, each copying 1 GB on average.

When you try to use *distcp* between two HDFS clusters that are running different versions, the copy will fail if you use the *hdfs* protocol because the RPC systems are incompatible. To remedy this, you can use the read-only HTTP-based HFTP filesystem to read from the source. The job must run on the destination cluster so that the HDFS RPC versions are compatible. To repeat the previous example using HFTP:

```
% hadoop distcp hftp://namenode1:50070/foo hdfs://namenode2/bar
```

Note that you need to specify the namenode's web port in the source URI. This is determined by the dfs.http.address property, which defaults to 50070.

Using the newer *webhdfs* protocol (which replaces *hftp*), it is possible to use HTTP for both the source and destination clusters without hitting any wire incompatibility problems.

```
% hadoop distcp webhdfs://namenode1:50070/foo webhdfs://namenode2:50070/bar
```

Another variant is to use an HDFS HTTP proxy as the *distcp* source or destination, which has the advantage of being able to set firewall and bandwidth controls (see "HTTP" on page 53).

Keeping an HDFS Cluster Balanced

When copying data into HDFS, it's important to consider cluster balance. HDFS works best when the file blocks are evenly spread across the cluster, so you want to ensure that *distcp* doesn't disrupt this. Going back to the 1,000 GB example, by specifying -m 1, a single map would do the copy, which—apart from being slow and not using the cluster resources efficiently—would mean that the first replica of each block would reside on the node running the map (until the disk filled up). The second and third replicas would be spread across the cluster, but this one node would be unbalanced. By having more maps than nodes in the cluster, this problem is avoided. For this reason, it's best to start by running *distcp* with the default of 20 maps per node.

However, it's not always possible to prevent a cluster from becoming unbalanced. Perhaps you want to limit the number of maps so that some of the nodes can be used by other jobs. In this case, you can use the *balancer* tool (see "Balancer" on page 350) to subsequently even out the block distribution across the cluster.

Hadoop Archives

HDFS stores small files inefficiently, since each file is stored in a block, and block metadata is held in memory by the namenode. Thus, a large number of small files can eat up a lot of memory on the namenode. (Note, however, that small files do not take up any more disk space than is required to store the raw contents of the file. For example, a 1 MB file stored with a block size of 128 MB uses 1 MB of disk space, not 128 MB.)

Hadoop Archives, or HAR files, are a file archiving facility that packs files into HDFS blocks more efficiently, thereby reducing namenode memory usage while still allowing transparent access to files. In particular, Hadoop Archives can be used as input to MapReduce.

Using Hadoop Archives

A Hadoop Archive is created from a collection of files using the *archive* tool. The tool runs a MapReduce job to process the input files in parallel, so to run it, you need a running MapReduce cluster to use it. Here are some files in HDFS that we would like to archive:

```
% hadoop fs -lsr /my/files
-rw-r--r--   1 tom supergroup          1 2009-04-09 19:13 /my/files/a
drwxr-xr-x   - tom supergroup          0 2009-04-09 19:13 /my/files/dir
-rw-r--r--   1 tom supergroup          1 2009-04-09 19:13 /my/files/dir/b
```

Now we can run the `archive` command:

```
% hadoop archive -archiveName files.har /my/files /my
```

The first option is the name of the archive, here *files.har*. HAR files always have a *.har* extension, which is mandatory for reasons we shall see later. Next come the files to put in the archive. Here we are archiving only one source tree, the files in */my/files* in HDFS, but the tool accepts multiple source trees. The final argument is the output directory for the HAR file. Let's see what the archive has created:

```
% hadoop fs -ls /my
Found 2 items
drwxr-xr-x   - tom supergroup          0 2009-04-09 19:13 /my/files
```

```
drwxr-xr-x   - tom supergroup          0 2009-04-09 19:13 /my/files.har
% hadoop fs -ls /my/files.har
Found 3 items
-rw-r--r--  10 tom supergroup        165 2009-04-09 19:13 /my/files.har/_index
-rw-r--r--  10 tom supergroup         23 2009-04-09 19:13 /my/files.har/_masterindex
-rw-r--r--   1 tom supergroup          2 2009-04-09 19:13 /my/files.har/part-0
```

The directory listing shows what a HAR file is made of: two index files and a collection of part files (this example has just one of the latter). The part files contain the contents of a number of the original files concatenated together, and the indexes make it possible to look up the part file that an archived file is contained in, as well as its offset and length. All these details are hidden from the application, however, which uses the *har* URI scheme to interact with HAR files, using a HAR filesystem that is layered on top of the underlying filesystem (HDFS in this case). The following command recursively lists the files in the archive:

```
% hadoop fs -lsr har:///my/files.har
drw-r--r--   - tom supergroup          0 2009-04-09 19:13 /my/files.har/my
drw-r--r--   - tom supergroup          0 2009-04-09 19:13 /my/files.har/my/files
-rw-r--r--  10 tom supergroup          1 2009-04-09 19:13 /my/files.har/my/files/a
drw-r--r--   - tom supergroup          0 2009-04-09 19:13 /my/files.har/my/files/dir
-rw-r--r--  10 tom supergroup          1 2009-04-09 19:13 /my/files.har/my/files/dir/b
```

This is quite straightforward when the filesystem that the HAR file is on is the default filesystem. On the other hand, if you want to refer to a HAR file on a different filesystem, you need to use a different form of the path URI. These two commands have the same effect, for example:

```
% hadoop fs -lsr har:///my/files.har/my/files/dir
% hadoop fs -lsr har://hdfs-localhost:8020/my/files.har/my/files/dir
```

Notice in the second form that the scheme is still *har* to signify a HAR filesystem, but the authority is *hdfs* to specify the underlying filesystem's scheme, followed by a dash and the HDFS host (localhost) and port (8020). We can now see why HAR files must have a *.har* extension. The HAR filesystem translates the *har* URI into a URI for the underlying filesystem by looking at the authority and path up to and including the component with the *.har* extension. In this case, it is *hdfs://localhost:8020/my/files .har*. The remaining part of the path is the path of the file in the archive: */my/files/dir*.

To delete a HAR file, you need to use the recursive form of delete because from the underlying filesystem's point of view, the HAR file is a directory:

```
% hadoop fs -rmr /my/files.har
```

Limitations

There are a few limitations to be aware of with HAR files. Creating an archive creates a copy of the original files, so you need as much disk space as the files you are archiving to create the archive (although you can delete the originals once you have created the archive). There is currently no support for archive compression, although the files that go into the archive can be compressed (HAR files are like *tar* files in this respect).

Archives are immutable once they have been created. To add or remove files, you must re-create the archive. In practice, this is not a problem for files that don't change after being written, since they can be archived in batches on a regular basis, such as daily or weekly.

As noted earlier, HAR files can be used as input to MapReduce. However, there is no archive-aware `InputFormat` that can pack multiple files into a single MapReduce split, so processing lots of small files, even in a HAR file, can still be inefficient. "Small files and CombineFileInputFormat" on page 239 discusses another approach to this problem.

Finally, if you are hitting namenode memory limits even after taking steps to minimize the number of small files in the system, consider using HDFS Federation to scale the namespace (see "HDFS Federation" on page 47).

Hadoop I/O

Hadoop comes with a set of primitives for data I/O. Some of these are techniques that are more general than Hadoop, such as data integrity and compression, but deserve special consideration when dealing with multiterabyte datasets. Others are Hadoop tools or APIs that form the building blocks for developing distributed systems, such as serialization frameworks and on-disk data structures.

Data Integrity

Users of Hadoop rightly expect that no data will be lost or corrupted during storage or processing. However, because every I/O operation on the disk or network carries with it a small chance of introducing errors into the data that it is reading or writing, when the volumes of data flowing through the system are as large as the ones Hadoop is capable of handling, the chance of data corruption occurring is high.

The usual way of detecting corrupted data is by computing a *checksum* for the data when it first enters the system, and again whenever it is transmitted across a channel that is unreliable and hence capable of corrupting the data. The data is deemed to be corrupt if the newly generated checksum doesn't exactly match the original. This technique doesn't offer any way to fix the data—it is merely error detection. (And this is a reason for not using low-end hardware; in particular, be sure to use ECC memory.) Note that it is possible that it's the checksum that is corrupt, not the data, but this is very unlikely, because the checksum is much smaller than the data.

A commonly used error-detecting code is CRC-32 (cyclic redundancy check), which computes a 32-bit integer checksum for input of any size.

Data Integrity in HDFS

HDFS transparently checksums all data written to it and by default verifies checksums when reading data. A separate checksum is created for every io.bytes.per.checksum bytes of data. The default is 512 bytes, and because a CRC-32 checksum is 4 bytes long, the storage overhead is less than 1%.

Datanodes are responsible for verifying the data they receive before storing the data and its checksum. This applies to data that they receive from clients and from other datanodes during replication. A client writing data sends it to a pipeline of datanodes (as explained in Chapter 3), and the last datanode in the pipeline verifies the checksum. If it detects an error, the client receives a ChecksumException, a subclass of IOException, which it should handle in an application-specific manner; for example, by retrying the operation.

When clients read data from datanodes, they verify checksums as well, comparing them with the ones stored at the datanode. Each datanode keeps a persistent log of checksum verifications, so it knows the last time each of its blocks was verified. When a client successfully verifies a block, it tells the datanode, which updates its log. Keeping statistics such as these is valuable in detecting bad disks.

Aside from block verification on client reads, each datanode runs a DataBlockScanner in a background thread that periodically verifies all the blocks stored on the datanode. This is to guard against corruption due to "bit rot" in the physical storage media. See "Datanode block scanner" on page 349 for details on how to access the scanner reports.

Because HDFS stores replicas of blocks, it can "heal" corrupted blocks by copying one of the good replicas to produce a new, uncorrupt replica. The way this works is that if a client detects an error when reading a block, it reports the bad block and the datanode it was trying to read from to the namenode before throwing a ChecksumException. The namenode marks the block replica as corrupt so it doesn't direct clients to it or try to copy this replica to another datanode. It then schedules a copy of the block to be replicated on another datanode, so its replication factor is back at the expected level. Once this has happened, the corrupt replica is deleted.

It is possible to disable verification of checksums by passing false to the setVerifyChecksum() method on FileSystem before using the open() method to read a file. The same effect is possible from the shell by using the -ignoreCrc option with the -get or the equivalent -copyToLocal command. This feature is useful if you have a corrupt file that you want to inspect so you can decide what to do with it. For example, you might want to see whether it can be salvaged before you delete it.

LocalFileSystem

The Hadoop LocalFileSystem performs client-side checksumming. This means that when you write a file called *filename*, the filesystem client transparently creates a hidden file, *.filename.crc*, in the same directory containing the checksums for each chunk of the file. Like HDFS, the chunk size is controlled by the io.bytes.per.checksum property, which defaults to 512 bytes. The chunk size is stored as metadata in the *.crc* file, so the file can be read back correctly even if the setting for the chunk size has changed. Checksums are verified when the file is read, and if an error is detected, LocalFileSystem throws a ChecksumException.

Checksums are fairly cheap to compute (in Java, they are implemented in native code), typically adding a few percent overhead to the time to read or write a file.For most applications, this is an acceptable price to pay for data integrity. It is, however, possible to disable checksums, typically when the underlying filesystem supports checksums natively. This is accomplished by using RawLocalFileSystem in place of Local FileSystem. To do this globally in an application, it suffices to remap the implementation for *file* URIs by setting the property fs.file.impl to the value org.apache.hadoop.fs.RawLocalFileSystem. Alternatively, you can directly create a RawLocalFile System instance, which may be useful if you want to disable checksum verification for only some reads, for example:

```
Configuration conf = ...
FileSystem fs = new RawLocalFileSystem();
fs.initialize(null, conf);
```

ChecksumFileSystem

LocalFileSystem uses ChecksumFileSystem to do its work, and this class makes it easy to add checksumming to other (nonchecksummed) filesystems, as Checksum FileSystem is just a wrapper around FileSystem. The general idiom is as follows:

```
FileSystem rawFs = ...
FileSystem checksummedFs = new ChecksumFileSystem(rawFs);
```

The underlying filesystem is called the *raw* filesystem, and may be retrieved using the getRawFileSystem() method on ChecksumFileSystem. ChecksumFileSystem has a few more useful methods for working with checksums, such as getChecksumFile() for getting the path of a checksum file for any file. Check the documentation for the others.

If an error is detected by ChecksumFileSystem when reading a file, it will call its reportChecksumFailure() method. The default implementation does nothing, but LocalFileSystem moves the offending file and its checksum to a side directory on the same device called *bad_files*. Administrators should periodically check for these bad files and take action on them.

Compression

File compression brings two major benefits: it reduces the space needed to store files, and it speeds up data transfer across the network or to or from disk. When dealing with large volumes of data, both of these savings can be significant, so it pays to carefully consider how to use compression in Hadoop.

There are many different compression formats, tools and algorithms, each with different characteristics. Table 4-1 lists some of the more common ones that can be used with Hadoop.

Table 4-1. A summary of compression formats

Compression format	Tool	Algorithm	Filename extension	Splittable?
DEFLATE[a]	N/A	DEFLATE	.deflate	No
gzip	gzip	DEFLATE	.gz	No
bzip2	bzip2	bzip2	.bz2	Yes
LZO	lzop	LZO	.lzo	No[b]
LZ4	N/A	LZ4	.lz4	No
Snappy	N/A	Snappy	.snappy	No

[a] DEFLATE is a compression algorithm whose standard implementation is zlib. There is no commonly available command-line tool for producing files in DEFLATE format, as gzip is normally used. (Note that the gzip file format is DEFLATE with extra headers and a footer.) The .deflate filename extension is a Hadoop convention.

[b] However, LZO files are splittable if they have been indexed in a preprocessing step. See page 89.

All compression algorithms exhibit a space/time trade-off: faster compression and decompression speeds usually come at the expense of smaller space savings. The tools listed in Table 4-1 typically give some control over this trade-off at compression time by offering nine different options: -1 means optimize for speed, and -9 means optimize for space. For example, the following command creates a compressed file *file.gz* using the fastest compression method:

```
gzip -1 file
```

The different tools have very different compression characteristics. Gzip is a general-purpose compressor and sits in the middle of the space/time trade-off. Bzip2 compresses more effectively than gzip, but is slower. Bzip2's decompression speed is faster than its compression speed, but it is still slower than the other formats. LZO, LZ4. and Snappy, on the other hand, all optimize for speed and are around an order of magnitude faster than gzip, but compress less effectively. Snappy and LZ4 are also significantly faster than LZO for decompression.[1]

The "Splittable" column in Table 4-1 indicates whether the compression format supports splitting, that is, whether you can seek to any point in the stream and start reading from some point further on. Splittable compression formats are especially suitable for MapReduce; see "Compression and Input Splits" on page 89 for further discussion.

---

1. For a comprehensive set of compression benchmarks, *https://github.com/ning/jvm-compressor -benchmark* is a good reference for JVM-compatible libraries (includes some native libraries). For command-line tools, see Jeff Gilchrist's Archive Comparison Test at *http://compression.ca/act/act -summary.html*.

Codecs

A *codec* is the implementation of a compression-decompression algorithm. In Hadoop, a codec is represented by an implementation of the CompressionCodec interface. So, for example, GzipCodec encapsulates the compression and decompression algorithm for gzip. Table 4-2 lists the codecs that are available for Hadoop.

Table 4-2. Hadoop compression codecs

Compression format	Hadoop CompressionCodec
DEFLATE	org.apache.hadoop.io.compress.DefaultCodec
gzip	org.apache.hadoop.io.compress.GzipCodec
bzip2	org.apache.hadoop.io.compress.BZip2Codec
LZO	com.hadoop.compression.lzo.LzopCodec
LZ4	org.apache.hadoop.io.compress.Lz4Codec
Snappy	org.apache.hadoop.io.compress.SnappyCodec

The LZO libraries are GPL-licensed and may not be included in Apache distributions, so for this reason the Hadoop codecs must be downloaded separately from *http://code .google.com/p/hadoop-gpl-compression/* (or *http://github.com/kevinweil/hadoop-lzo*, which includes bug fixes and more tools). The LzopCodec is compatible with the lzop tool, which is essentially the LZO format with extra headers, and is the one you normally want. There is also a LzoCodec for the pure LZO format, which uses the *.lzo_deflate* filename extension (by analogy with DEFLATE, which is gzip without the headers).

Compressing and decompressing streams with CompressionCodec

CompressionCodec has two methods that allow you to easily compress or decompress data. To compress data being written to an output stream, use the createOutput Stream(OutputStream out) method to create a CompressionOutputStream to which you write your uncompressed data to have it written in compressed form to the underlying stream. Conversely, to decompress data being read from an input stream, call createInputStream(InputStream in) to obtain a CompressionInputStream, which allows you to read uncompressed data from the underlying stream.

CompressionOutputStream and CompressionInputStream are similar to java.util. zip.DeflaterOutputStream and java.util.zip.DeflaterInputStream, except that both of the former provide the ability to reset their underlying compressor or decompressor, which is important for applications that compress sections of the data stream as separate blocks, such as SequenceFile, described in "SequenceFile" on page 130.

Example 4-1 illustrates how to use the API to compress data read from standard input and write it to standard output.

Example 4-1. A program to compress data read from standard input and write it to standard output

```java
public class StreamCompressor {

  public static void main(String[] args) throws Exception {
    String codecClassname = args[0];
    Class<?> codecClass = Class.forName(codecClassname);
    Configuration conf = new Configuration();
    CompressionCodec codec = (CompressionCodec)
      ReflectionUtils.newInstance(codecClass, conf);

    CompressionOutputStream out = codec.createOutputStream(System.out);
    IOUtils.copyBytes(System.in, out, 4096, false);
    out.finish();
  }
}
```

The application expects the fully qualified name of the CompressionCodec implementation as the first command-line argument. We use ReflectionUtils to construct a new instance of the codec, then obtain a compression wrapper around System.out. Then we call the utility method copyBytes() on IOUtils to copy the input to the output, which is compressed by the CompressionOutputStream. Finally, we call finish() on CompressionOutputStream, which tells the compressor to finish writing to the compressed stream, but doesn't close the stream. We can try it out with the following command line, which compresses the string "Text" using the StreamCompressor program with the GzipCodec, then decompresses it from standard input using *gunzip*:

```
% echo "Text" | hadoop StreamCompressor org.apache.hadoop.io.compress.GzipCodec \
  | gunzip -
Text
```

Inferring CompressionCodecs using CompressionCodecFactory

If you are reading a compressed file, normally you can infer which codec to use by looking at its filename extension. A file ending in *.gz* can be read with GzipCodec, and so on. The extension for each compression format is listed in Table 4-1.

CompressionCodecFactory provides a way of mapping a filename extension to a CompressionCodec using its getCodec() method, which takes a Path object for the file in question. Example 4-2 shows an application that uses this feature to decompress files.

Example 4-2. A program to decompress a compressed file using a codec inferred from the file's extension

```java
public class FileDecompressor {

  public static void main(String[] args) throws Exception {
    String uri = args[0];
    Configuration conf = new Configuration();
    FileSystem fs = FileSystem.get(URI.create(uri), conf);

    Path inputPath = new Path(uri);
    CompressionCodecFactory factory = new CompressionCodecFactory(conf);
```

```
CompressionCodec codec = factory.getCodec(inputPath);
if (codec == null) {
  System.err.println("No codec found for " + uri);
  System.exit(1);
}

String outputUri =
  CompressionCodecFactory.removeSuffix(uri, codec.getDefaultExtension());

InputStream in = null;
OutputStream out = null;
try {
  in = codec.createInputStream(fs.open(inputPath));
  out = fs.create(new Path(outputUri));
  IOUtils.copyBytes(in, out, conf);
} finally {
  IOUtils.closeStream(in);
  IOUtils.closeStream(out);
  }
 }
}
```

Once the codec has been found, it is used to strip off the file suffix to form the output filename (via the removeSuffix() static method of CompressionCodecFactory). In this way, a file named *file.gz* is decompressed to *file* by invoking the program as follows:

```
% hadoop FileDecompressor file.gz
```

CompressionCodecFactory finds codecs from a list defined by the io.compression. codecs configuration property. By default, this lists all the codecs provided by Hadoop (see Table 4-3), so you would need to alter it only if you have a custom codec that you wish to register (such as the externally hosted LZO codecs). Each codec knows its default filename extension, thus permitting CompressionCodecFactory to search through the registered codecs to find a match for a given extension (if any).

Table 4-3. Compression codec properties

Property name	Type	Default value	Description
io.compression.codecs	Comma-separated Class names	org.apache.hadoop.io. compress.DefaultCodec, org.apache.hadoop.io. compress.GzipCodec, org.apache.hadoop.io. compress.BZip2Codec	A list of the CompressionCodec classes for compression/ decompression

Native libraries

For performance, it is preferable to use a native library for compression and decompression. For example, in one test, using the native gzip libraries reduced decompression times by up to 50% and compression times by around 10% (compared to the built-in Java implementation). Table 4-4 shows the availability of Java and native implementations for each compression format. Not all formats have native implementations (bzip2, for example), whereas others are available only as a native implementation (LZO, for example).

Table 4-4. Compression library implementations

Compression format	Java implementation?	Native implementation?
DEFLATE	Yes	Yes
gzip	Yes	Yes
bzip2	Yes	No
LZO	No	Yes
LZ4	No	Yes
Snappy	No	Yes

Hadoop comes with prebuilt native compression libraries for 32- and 64-bit Linux, which you can find in the *lib/native* directory. For other platforms, you will need to compile the libraries yourself, following the instructions on the Hadoop wiki at *http://wiki.apache.org/hadoop/NativeHadoop*.

The native libraries are picked up using the Java system property `java.library.path`. The *hadoop* script in the *bin* directory sets this property for you, but if you don't use this script, you will need to set the property in your application.

By default, Hadoop looks for native libraries for the platform it is running on, and loads them automatically if they are found. This means you don't have to change any configuration settings to use the native libraries. In some circumstances, however, you may wish to disable use of native libraries, such as when you are debugging a compression-related problem. You can achieve this by setting the property `hadoop.native.lib` to `false`, which ensures that the built-in Java equivalents will be used (if they are available).

CodecPool. If you are using a native library and you are doing a lot of compression or decompression in your application, consider using `CodecPool`, which allows you to reuse compressors and decompressors, thereby amortizing the cost of creating these objects.

The code in Example 4-3 shows the API, although in this program, which creates only a single `Compressor`, there is really no need to use a pool.

Example 4-3. A program to compress data read from standard input and write it to standard output using a pooled compressor

```
public class PooledStreamCompressor {

  public static void main(String[] args) throws Exception {
    String codecClassname = args[0];
    Class<?> codecClass = Class.forName(codecClassname);
    Configuration conf = new Configuration();
    CompressionCodec codec = (CompressionCodec)
```

```
    ReflectionUtils.newInstance(codecClass, conf);
  Compressor compressor = null;
  try {
    compressor = CodecPool.getCompressor(codec);
    CompressionOutputStream out =
      codec.createOutputStream(System.out, compressor);
    IOUtils.copyBytes(System.in, out, 4096, false);
    out.finish();
  } finally {
    CodecPool.returnCompressor(compressor);
  }
 }
}
```

We retrieve a `Compressor` instance from the pool for a given `CompressionCodec`, which we use in the codec's overloaded `createOutputStream()` method. By using a `finally` block, we ensure that the compressor is returned to the pool even if there is an `IOException` while copying the bytes between the streams.

Compression and Input Splits

When considering how to compress data that will be processed by MapReduce, it is important to understand whether the compression format supports splitting. Consider an uncompressed file stored in HDFS whose size is 1 GB. With an HDFS block size of 64 MB, the file will be stored as 16 blocks, and a MapReduce job using this file as input will create 16 input splits, each processed independently as input to a separate map task.

Imagine now that the file is a gzip-compressed file whose compressed size is 1 GB. As before, HDFS will store the file as 16 blocks. However, creating a split for each block won't work, because it is impossible to start reading at an arbitrary point in the gzip stream and therefore impossible for a map task to read its split independently of the others. The gzip format uses DEFLATE to store the compressed data, and DEFLATE stores data as a series of compressed blocks. The problem is that the start of each block is not distinguished in any way that would allow a reader positioned at an arbitrary point in the stream to advance to the beginning of the next block, thereby synchronizing itself with the stream. For this reason, gzip does not support splitting.

In this case, MapReduce will do the right thing and not try to split the gzipped file, since it knows that the input is gzip-compressed (by looking at the filename extension) and that gzip does not support splitting. This will work, but at the expense of locality: a single map will process the 16 HDFS blocks, most of which will not be local to the map. Also, with fewer maps, the job is less granular and so may take longer to run.

If the file in our hypothetical example were an LZO file, we would have the same problem because the underlying compression format does not provide a way for a reader to synchronize itself with the stream. However, it is possible to preprocess LZO files using an indexer tool that comes with the Hadoop LZO libraries, which you can obtain from the sites listed in "Codecs" on page 85. The tool builds an index of split points, effectively making them splittable when the appropriate MapReduce input format is used.

A bzip2 file, on the other hand, does provide a synchronization marker between blocks (a 48-bit approximation of pi), so it does support splitting. (Table 4-1 lists whether each compression format supports splitting.)

Which Compression Format Should I Use?

Hadoop applications process large datasets, so you should strive to take advantage of compression. Which compression format you use depends on such considerations as file size, format, and the tools you are using for processing. Here are some suggestions, arranged roughly in order of most to least effective:

- Use a container file format such as Sequence File (page 130), RCFile (page 438), or Avro datafile (page 117), all of which support both compression and splitting. A fast compressor such as LZO, LZ4, or Snappy is generally a good choice.

- Use a compression format that supports splitting, such as bzip2 (although bzip2 is fairly slow), or one that can be indexed to support splitting, such as LZO.

- Split the file into chunks in the application, and compress each chunk separately using any supported compression format (it doesn't matter whether it is splittable). In this case, you should choose the chunk size so that the compressed chunks are approximately the size of an HDFS block.

- Store the files uncompressed.

For large files, you should *not* use a compression format that does not support splitting on the whole file, because you lose locality and make MapReduce applications very inefficient.

Using Compression in MapReduce

As described in "Inferring CompressionCodecs using CompressionCodecFactory" on page 86, if your input files are compressed, they will be decompressed automatically as they are read by MapReduce, using the filename extension to determine which codec to use.

To compress the output of a MapReduce job, in the job configuration, set the `mapred.output.compress` property to `true` and the `mapred.output.compression.codec` property to the classname of the compression codec you want to use. Alternatively, you can use the static convenience methods on `FileOutputFormat` to set these properties as shown in Example 4-4.

Example 4-4. Application to run the maximum temperature job producing compressed output

```
public class MaxTemperatureWithCompression {

  public static void main(String[] args) throws Exception {
```

```
    if (args.length != 2) {
      System.err.println("Usage: MaxTemperatureWithCompression <input path> " +
        "<output path>");
      System.exit(-1);
    }

    Job job = new Job();
    job.setJarByClass(MaxTemperature.class);

    FileInputFormat.addInputPath(job, new Path(args[0]));
    FileOutputFormat.setOutputPath(job, new Path(args[1]));

    job.setOutputKeyClass(Text.class);
    job.setOutputValueClass(IntWritable.class);

    FileOutputFormat.setCompressOutput(job, true);
    FileOutputFormat.setOutputCompressorClass(job, GzipCodec.class);

    job.setMapperClass(MaxTemperatureMapper.class);
    job.setCombinerClass(MaxTemperatureReducer.class);
    job.setReducerClass(MaxTemperatureReducer.class);

    System.exit(job.waitForCompletion(true) ? 0 : 1);
  }
}
```

We run the program over compressed input (which doesn't have to use the same compression format as the output, although it does in this example) as follows:

```
% hadoop MaxTemperatureWithCompression input/ncdc/sample.txt.gz output
```

Each part of the final output is compressed; in this case, there is a single part:

```
% gunzip -c output/part-r-00000.gz
1949    111
1950    22
```

If you are emitting sequence files for your output, you can set the mapred.output.com
pression.type property to control the type of compression to use. The default is
RECORD, which compresses individual records. Changing this to BLOCK, which
compresses groups of records, is recommended because it compresses better (see "The
SequenceFile format" on page 136).

There is also a static convenience method on SequenceFileOutputFormat called setOut
putCompressionType() to set this property.

The configuration properties to set compression for MapReduce job outputs are summarized in Table 4-5. If your MapReduce driver uses the Tool interface (described in
"GenericOptionsParser, Tool, and ToolRunner" on page 150), you can pass any of
these properties to the program on the command line, which may be more convenient
than modifying your program to hardcode the compression properties.

Table 4-5. MapReduce compression properties

Property name	Type	Default value	Description
mapred.output.com press	boolean	false	Compress outputs
mapred.output.com pression. codec	Class name	org.apache.hadoop.io. compress.DefaultCodec	The compression codec to use for out-puts
mapred.output.com pression. type	String	RECORD	The type of compression to use for Se-quenceFile outputs: NONE, RECORD, or BLOCK

Compressing map output

Even if your MapReduce application reads and writes uncompressed data, it may ben-efit from compressing the intermediate output of the map phase. Since the map output is written to disk and transferred across the network to the reducer nodes, by using a fast compressor such as LZO, LZ4, or Snappy, you can get performance gains simply because the volume of data to transfer is reduced. The configuration properties to en-able compression for map outputs and to set the compression format are shown in Table 4-6.

Table 4-6. Map output compression properties

Property name	Type	Default value	Description
mapred.compress.map.output	boolean	false	Compress map outputs
mapred.map.output. compression.codec	Class	org.apache.hadoop.io. compress.DefaultCodec	The compression codec to use for map outputs

Here are the lines to add to enable gzip map output compression in your job (using the new API):

```
Configuration conf = new Configuration();
conf.setBoolean("mapred.compress.map.output", true);
conf.setClass("mapred.map.output.compression.codec", GzipCodec.class,
    CompressionCodec.class);
Job job = new Job(conf);
```

In the old API, there are convenience methods on the JobConf object for doing the same thing:

```
conf.setCompressMapOutput(true);
conf.setMapOutputCompressorClass(GzipCodec.class);
```

Serialization

Serialization is the process of turning structured objects into a byte stream for transmission over a network or for writing to persistent storage. *Deserialization* is the reverse process of turning a byte stream back into a series of structured objects.

Serialization appears in two quite distinct areas of distributed data processing: for interprocess communication and for persistent storage.

In Hadoop, interprocess communication between nodes in the system is implemented using *remote procedure calls* (RPCs). The RPC protocol uses serialization to render the message into a binary stream to be sent to the remote node, which then deserializes the binary stream into the original message. In general, it is desirable that an RPC serialization format is:

Compact
> A compact format makes the best use of network bandwidth, which is the most scarce resource in a data center.

Fast
> Interprocess communication forms the backbone for a distributed system, so it is essential that there is as little performance overhead as possible for the serialization and deserialization process.

Extensible
> Protocols change over time to meet new requirements, so it should be straightforward to evolve the protocol in a controlled manner for clients and servers. For example, it should be possible to add a new argument to a method call and have the new servers accept messages in the old format (without the new argument) from old clients.

Interoperable
> For some systems, it is desirable to be able to support clients that are written in different languages to the server, so the format needs to be designed to make this possible.

On the face of it, the data format chosen for persistent storage would have different requirements from a serialization framework. After all, the lifespan of an RPC is less than a second, whereas persistent data may be read years after it was written. As it turns out, the four desirable properties of an RPC's serialization format are also crucial for a persistent storage format. We want the storage format to be compact (to make efficient use of storage space), fast (so the overhead in reading or writing terabytes of data is minimal), extensible (so we can transparently read data written in an older format), and interoperable (so we can read or write persistent data using different languages).

Hadoop uses its own serialization format, Writables, which is certainly compact and fast, but not so easy to extend or use from languages other than Java. Because Writables are central to Hadoop (most MapReduce programs use them for their key and value types), we look at them in some depth in the next three sections, before looking at serialization frameworks in general and then Avro (a serialization system that was designed to overcome some of the limitations of Writables) in more detail.

The Writable Interface

The Writable interface defines two methods: one for writing its state to a DataOutput binary stream and one for reading its state from a DataInput binary stream.

```
package org.apache.hadoop.io;

import java.io.DataOutput;
import java.io.DataInput;
import java.io.IOException;

public interface Writable {
  void write(DataOutput out) throws IOException;
  void readFields(DataInput in) throws IOException;
}
```

Let's look at a particular Writable to see what we can do with it. We will use IntWritable, a wrapper for a Java int. We can create one and set its value using the set() method:

```
IntWritable writable = new IntWritable();
writable.set(163);
```

Equivalently, we can use the constructor that takes the integer value:

```
IntWritable writable = new IntWritable(163);
```

To examine the serialized form of the IntWritable, we write a small helper method that wraps a java.io.ByteArrayOutputStream in a java.io.DataOutputStream (an implementation of java.io.DataOutput) to capture the bytes in the serialized stream:

```
public static byte[] serialize(Writable writable) throws IOException {
  ByteArrayOutputStream out = new ByteArrayOutputStream();
  DataOutputStream dataOut = new DataOutputStream(out);
  writable.write(dataOut);
  dataOut.close();
  return out.toByteArray();
}
```

An integer is written using four bytes (as we see using JUnit 4 assertions):

```
byte[] bytes = serialize(writable);
assertThat(bytes.length, is(4));
```

The bytes are written in big-endian order (so the most significant byte is written to the stream first, which is dictated by the java.io.DataOutput interface), and we can see their hexadecimal representation by using a method on Hadoop's StringUtils:

```
assertThat(StringUtils.byteToHexString(bytes), is("000000a3"));
```

Let's try deserialization. Again, we create a helper method to read a `Writable` object from a byte array:

```
public static byte[] deserialize(Writable writable, byte[] bytes)
    throws IOException {
  ByteArrayInputStream in = new ByteArrayInputStream(bytes);
  DataInputStream dataIn = new DataInputStream(in);
  writable.readFields(dataIn);
  dataIn.close();
  return bytes;
}
```

We construct a new, value-less `IntWritable`, and then call `deserialize()` to read from the output data that we just wrote. Then we check that its value, retrieved using the `get()` method, is the original value, 163:

```
IntWritable newWritable = new IntWritable();
deserialize(newWritable, bytes);
assertThat(newWritable.get(), is(163));
```

WritableComparable and comparators

`IntWritable` implements the `WritableComparable` interface, which is just a subinterface of the `Writable` and `java.lang.Comparable` interfaces:

```
package org.apache.hadoop.io;

public interface WritableComparable<T> extends Writable, Comparable<T> {
}
```

Comparison of types is crucial for MapReduce, where there is a sorting phase during which keys are compared with one another. One optimization that Hadoop provides is the `RawComparator` extension of Java's `Comparator`:

```
package org.apache.hadoop.io;

import java.util.Comparator;

public interface RawComparator<T> extends Comparator<T> {

  public int compare(byte[] b1, int s1, int l1, byte[] b2, int s2, int l2);

}
```

This interface permits implementors to compare records read from a stream without deserializing them into objects, thereby avoiding any overhead of object creation. For example, the comparator for `IntWritables` implements the raw `compare()` method by reading an integer from each of the byte arrays `b1` and `b2` and comparing them directly from the given start positions (`s1` and `s2`) and lengths (`l1` and `l2`).

`WritableComparator` is a general-purpose implementation of `RawComparator` for `WritableComparable` classes. It provides two main functions. First, it provides a default implementation of the raw `compare()` method that deserializes the objects to be compared from the stream and invokes the object `compare()` method. Second, it acts as a factory for RawComparator instances (that Writable implementations have registered). For example, to obtain a comparator for IntWritable, we just use:

```
RawComparator<IntWritable> comparator = WritableComparator.get(IntWritable.class);
```

The comparator can be used to compare two IntWritable objects:

```
IntWritable w1 = new IntWritable(163);
IntWritable w2 = new IntWritable(67);
assertThat(comparator.compare(w1, w2), greaterThan(0));
```

or their serialized representations:

```
byte[] b1 = serialize(w1);
byte[] b2 = serialize(w2);
assertThat(comparator.compare(b1, 0, b1.length, b2, 0, b2.length),
    greaterThan(0));
```

Writable Classes

Hadoop comes with a large selection of Writable classes in the org.apache.hadoop.io package. They form the class hierarchy shown in Figure 4-1.

Writable wrappers for Java primitives

There are Writable wrappers for all the Java primitive types (see Table 4-7) except char (which can be stored in an IntWritable). All have a get() and set() method for retrieving and storing the wrapped value.

Table 4-7. Writable wrapper classes for Java primitives

Java primitive	Writable implementation	Serialized size (bytes)
boolean	BooleanWritable	1
byte	ByteWritable	1
short	ShortWritable	2
int	IntWritable	4
	VIntWritable	1–5
float	FloatWritable	4
long	LongWritable	8
	VLongWritable	1–9
double	DoubleWritable	8

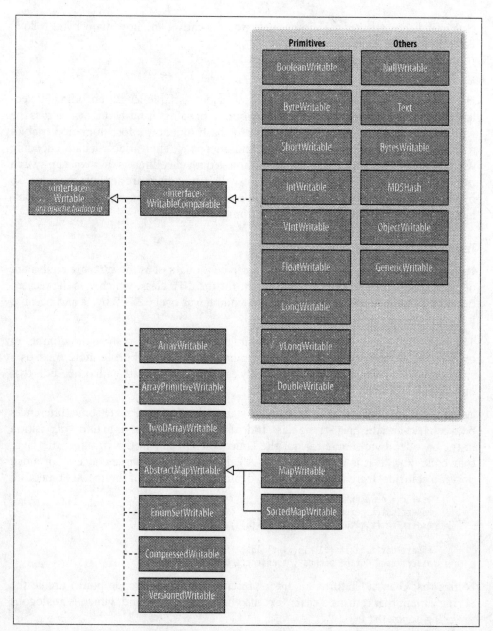

Figure 4-1. Writable class hierarchy

When it comes to encoding integers, there is a choice between the fixed-length formats (IntWritable and LongWritable) and the variable-length formats (VIntWritable and VLongWritable). The variable-length formats use only a single byte to encode the value if it is small enough (between −112 and 127, inclusive); otherwise, they use the first byte to indicate whether the value is positive or negative, and how many bytes follow. For example, 163 requires two bytes:

```
byte[] data = serialize(new VIntWritable(163));
assertThat(StringUtils.byteToHexString(data), is("8fa3"));
```

How do you choose between a fixed-length and a variable-length encoding? Fixed-length encodings are good when the distribution of values is fairly uniform across the whole value space, such as a (well-designed) hash function. Most numeric variables tend to have nonuniform distributions, and on average the variable-length encoding will save space. Another advantage of variable-length encodings is that you can switch from VIntWritable to VLongWritable, because their encodings are actually the same. So by choosing a variable-length representation, you have room to grow without committing to an 8-byte long representation from the beginning.

Text

Text is a Writable for UTF-8 sequences. It can be thought of as the Writable equivalent of java.lang.String. Text is a replacement for the UTF8 class, which was deprecated because it didn't support strings whose encoding was over 32,767 bytes and because it used Java's modified UTF-8.

The Text class uses an int (with a variable-length encoding) to store the number of bytes in the string encoding, so the maximum value is 2 GB. Furthermore, Text uses standard UTF-8, which makes it potentially easier to interoperate with other tools that understand UTF-8.

Indexing. Because of its emphasis on using standard UTF-8, there are some differences between Text and the Java String class. Indexing for the Text class is in terms of position in the encoded byte sequence, not the Unicode character in the string or the Java char code unit (as it is for String). For ASCII strings, these three concepts of index position coincide. Here is an example to demonstrate the use of the charAt() method:

```
Text t = new Text("hadoop");
assertThat(t.getLength(), is(6));
assertThat(t.getBytes().length, is(6));

assertThat(t.charAt(2), is((int) 'd'));
assertThat("Out of bounds", t.charAt(100), is(-1));
```

Notice that charAt() returns an int representing a Unicode code point, unlike the String variant that returns a char. Text also has a find() method, which is analogous to String's indexOf():

```
Text t = new Text("hadoop");
assertThat("Find a substring", t.find("do"), is(2));
assertThat("Finds first 'o'", t.find("o"), is(3));
assertThat("Finds 'o' from position 4 or later", t.find("o", 4), is(4));
assertThat("No match", t.find("pig"), is(-1));
```

Unicode. When we start using characters that are encoded with more than a single byte, the differences between Text and String become clear. Consider the Unicode characters shown in Table 4-8.[2]

Table 4-8. Unicode characters

Unicode code point	U+0041	U+00DF	U+6771	U+10400
Name	LATIN CAPITAL LETTER A	LATIN SMALL LETTER SHARP S	N/A (a unified Han ideograph)	DESERET CAPITAL LETTER LONG I
UTF-8 code units	41	c3 9f	e6 9d b1	f0 90 90 80
Java representation	\u0041	\u00DF	\u6771	\uuD801\uDC00

All but the last character in the table, U+10400, can be expressed using a single Java char. U+10400 is a supplementary character and is represented by two Java chars, known as a surrogate pair. The tests in Example 4-5 show the differences between String and Text when processing a string of the four characters from Table 4-8.

Example 4-5. Tests showing the differences between the String and Text classes

```java
public class StringTextComparisonTest {

    @Test
    public void string() throws UnsupportedEncodingException {

        String s = "\u0041\u00DF\u6771\uD801\uDC00";
        assertThat(s.length(), is(5));
        assertThat(s.getBytes("UTF-8").length, is(10));

        assertThat(s.indexOf("\u0041"), is(0));
        assertThat(s.indexOf("\u00DF"), is(1));
        assertThat(s.indexOf("\u6771"), is(2));
        assertThat(s.indexOf("\uD801\uDC00"), is(3));

        assertThat(s.charAt(0), is('\u0041'));
        assertThat(s.charAt(1), is('\u00DF'));
        assertThat(s.charAt(2), is('\u6771'));
        assertThat(s.charAt(3), is('\uD801'));
        assertThat(s.charAt(4), is('\uDC00'));

        assertThat(s.codePointAt(0), is(0x0041));
        assertThat(s.codePointAt(1), is(0x00DF));
        assertThat(s.codePointAt(2), is(0x6771));
        assertThat(s.codePointAt(3), is(0x10400));
    }

    @Test
    public void text() {
```

---

2. This example is based on one from the article "Supplementary Characters in the Java Platform." (*http:// java.sun.com/developer/technicalArticles/Intl/Supplementary/*)

```
    Text t = new Text("\u0041\u00DF\u6771\uD801\uDC00");
    assertThat(t.getLength(), is(10));

    assertThat(t.find("\u0041"), is(0));
    assertThat(t.find("\u00DF"), is(1));
    assertThat(t.find("\u6771"), is(3));
    assertThat(t.find("\uD801\uDC00"), is(6));

    assertThat(t.charAt(0), is(0x0041));
    assertThat(t.charAt(1), is(0x00DF));
    assertThat(t.charAt(3), is(0x6771));
    assertThat(t.charAt(6), is(0x10400));
  }
}
```

The test confirms that the length of a String is the number of char code units it contains (5, made up of one from each of the first three characters in the string and a surrogate pair from the last), whereas the length of a Text object is the number of bytes in its UTF-8 encoding (10 = 1+2+3+4). Similarly, the indexOf() method in String returns an index in char code units, and find() for Text is a byte offset.

The charAt() method in String returns the char code unit for the given index, which in the case of a surrogate pair will not represent a whole Unicode character. The code PointAt() method, indexed by char code unit, is needed to retrieve a single Unicode character represented as an int. In fact, the charAt() method in Text is more like the codePointAt() method than its namesake in String. The only difference is that it is indexed by byte offset.

Iteration. Iterating over the Unicode characters in Text is complicated by the use of byte offsets for indexing, since you can't just increment the index. The idiom for iteration is a little obscure (see Example 4-6): turn the Text object into a java.nio.ByteBuffer, then repeatedly call the bytesToCodePoint() static method on Text with the buffer. This method extracts the next code point as an int and updates the position in the buffer. The end of the string is detected when bytesToCodePoint() returns −1.

Example 4-6. Iterating over the characters in a Text object

```
public class TextIterator {

  public static void main(String[] args) {
    Text t = new Text("\u0041\u00DF\u6771\uD801\uDC00");

    ByteBuffer buf = ByteBuffer.wrap(t.getBytes(), 0, t.getLength());
    int cp;
    while (buf.hasRemaining() && (cp = Text.bytesToCodePoint(buf)) != -1) {
      System.out.println(Integer.toHexString(cp));
    }
  }
}
```

Running the program prints the code points for the four characters in the string:

```
% hadoop TextIterator
41
df
6771
10400
```

Mutability. Another difference with `String` is that `Text` is mutable (like all `Writable` implementations in Hadoop, except `NullWritable`, which is a singleton). You can reuse a `Text` instance by calling one of the `set()` methods on it. For example:

```
Text t = new Text("hadoop");
t.set("pig");
assertThat(t.getLength(), is(3));
assertThat(t.getBytes().length, is(3));
```

 In some situations, the byte array returned by the `getBytes()` method may be longer than the length returned by `getLength()`:

```
Text t = new Text("hadoop");
t.set(new Text("pig"));
assertThat(t.getLength(), is(3));
assertThat("Byte length not shortened", t.getBytes().length,
  is(6));
```

This shows why it is imperative that you always call `getLength()` when calling `getBytes()`, so you know how much of the byte array is valid data.

Resorting to String. `Text` doesn't have as rich an API for manipulating strings as `java.lang.String`, so in many cases, you need to convert the `Text` object to a `String`. This is done in the usual way, using the `toString()` method:

```
assertThat(new Text("hadoop").toString(), is("hadoop"));
```

BytesWritable

`BytesWritable` is a wrapper for an array of binary data. Its serialized format is an integer field (4 bytes) that specifies the number of bytes to follow, followed by the bytes themselves. For example, the byte array of length two with values 3 and 5 is serialized as a 4-byte integer (00000002) followed by the two bytes from the array (03 and 05):

```
BytesWritable b = new BytesWritable(new byte[] { 3, 5 });
byte[] bytes = serialize(b);
assertThat(StringUtils.byteToHexString(bytes), is("000000020305"));
```

`BytesWritable` is mutable, and its value may be changed by calling its `set()` method. As with `Text`, the size of the byte array returned from the `getBytes()` method for `Byte sWritable`—the capacity—may not reflect the actual size of the data stored in the `BytesWritable`. You can determine the size of the `BytesWritable` by calling get `Length()`. To demonstrate:

```
b.setCapacity(11);
assertThat(b.getLength(), is(2));
assertThat(b.getBytes().length, is(11));
```

NullWritable

NullWritable is a special type of Writable, as it has a zero-length serialization. No bytes are written to or read from the stream. It is used as a placeholder; for example, in MapReduce, a key or a value can be declared as a NullWritable when you don't need to use that position, effectively storing a constant empty value. NullWritable can also be useful as a key in SequenceFile when you want to store a list of values, as opposed to key-value pairs. It is an immutable singleton, and the instance can be retrieved by calling NullWritable.get().

ObjectWritable and GenericWritable

ObjectWritable is a general-purpose wrapper for the following: Java primitives, String, enum, Writable, null, or arrays of any of these types. It is used in Hadoop RPC to marshal and unmarshal method arguments and return types.

ObjectWritable is useful when a field can be of more than one type. For example, if the values in a SequenceFile have multiple types, you can declare the value type as an ObjectWritable and wrap each type in an ObjectWritable. Being a general-purpose mechanism, it wasted a fair amount of space because it writes the classname of the wrapped type every time it is serialized. In cases where the number of types is small and known ahead of time, this can be improved by having a static array of types and using the index into the array as the serialized reference to the type. This is the approach that GenericWritable takes, and you have to subclass it to specify which types to support.

Writable collections

There are six Writable collection types in the org.apache.hadoop.io package: Array Writable, ArrayPrimitiveWritable, TwoDArrayWritable, MapWritable, SortedMapWritable, and EnumSetWritable.

ArrayWritable and TwoDArrayWritable are Writable implementations for arrays and two-dimensional arrays (array of arrays) of Writable instances. All the elements of an ArrayWritable or a TwoDArrayWritable must be instances of the same class, which is specified at construction as follows:

```
ArrayWritable writable = new ArrayWritable(Text.class);
```

In contexts where the Writable is defined by type, such as in SequenceFile keys or values or as input to MapReduce in general, you need to subclass ArrayWritable (or TwoDArrayWritable, as appropriate) to set the type statically. For example:

```
public class TextArrayWritable extends ArrayWritable {
  public TextArrayWritable() {
    super(Text.class);
  }
}
```

`ArrayWritable` and `TwoDArrayWritable` both have `get()` and `set()` methods, as well as a `toArray()` method, which creates a shallow copy of the array (or 2D array).

`ArrayPrimitiveWritable` is a wrapper for arrays of Java primitives. The component type is detected when you call `set()`, so there is no need to subclass to set the type.

`MapWritable` and `SortedMapWritable` are implementations of `java.util.Map<Writable, Writable>` and `java.util.SortedMap<WritableComparable, Writable>`, respectively. The type of each key and value field is a part of the serialization format for that field. The type is stored as a single byte that acts as an index into an array of types. The array is populated with the standard types in the `org.apache.hadoop.io` package, but custom `Writable` types are accommodated, too, by writing a header that encodes the type array for nonstandard types. As they are implemented, `MapWritable` and `SortedMapWritable` use positive `byte` values for custom types, so a maximum of 127 distinct nonstandard `Writable` classes can be used in any particular `MapWritable` or `SortedMapWritable` instance. Here's a demonstration of using a `MapWritable` with different types for keys and values:

```
MapWritable src = new MapWritable();
src.put(new IntWritable(1), new Text("cat"));
src.put(new VIntWritable(2), new LongWritable(163));

MapWritable dest = new MapWritable();
WritableUtils.cloneInto(dest, src);
assertThat((Text) dest.get(new IntWritable(1)), is(new Text("cat")));
assertThat((LongWritable) dest.get(new VIntWritable(2)), is(new
  LongWritable(163)));
```

Conspicuous by their absence are `Writable` collection implementations for sets and lists. A general set can be emulated by using a `MapWritable` (or a `SortedMapWritable` for a sorted set) with `NullWritable` values. There is also `EnumSetWritable` for sets of enum types. For lists of a single type of `Writable`, `ArrayWritable` is adequate, but to store different types of `Writable` in a single list, you can use `GenericWritable` to wrap the elements in an `ArrayWritable`. Alternatively, you could write a general `ListWritable` using the ideas from `MapWritable`.

Implementing a Custom Writable

Hadoop comes with a useful set of `Writable` implementations that serve most purposes; however, on occasion, you may need to write your own custom implementation. With a custom `Writable`, you have full control over the binary representation and the sort order. Because `Writable`s are at the heart of the MapReduce data path, tuning the binary representation can have a significant effect on performance. The stock `Writable` implementations that come with Hadoop are well-tuned, but for more elaborate structures, it is often better to create a new `Writable` type rather than compose the stock types.

To demonstrate how to create a custom `Writable`, we shall write an implementation that represents a pair of strings, called `TextPair`. The basic implementation is shown in Example 4-7.

Example 4-7. A Writable implementation that stores a pair of Text objects

```java
import java.io.*;

import org.apache.hadoop.io.*;

public class TextPair implements WritableComparable<TextPair> {

  private Text first;
  private Text second;

  public TextPair() {
    set(new Text(), new Text());
  }

  public TextPair(String first, String second) {
    set(new Text(first), new Text(second));
  }

  public TextPair(Text first, Text second) {
    set(first, second);
  }

  public void set(Text first, Text second) {
    this.first = first;
    this.second = second;
  }

  public Text getFirst() {
    return first;
  }

  public Text getSecond() {
    return second;
  }

  @Override
  public void write(DataOutput out) throws IOException {
    first.write(out);
    second.write(out);
  }

  @Override
  public void readFields(DataInput in) throws IOException {
    first.readFields(in);
    second.readFields(in);
  }

  @Override
  public int hashCode() {
    return first.hashCode() * 163 + second.hashCode();
```

```
  }

  @Override
  public boolean equals(Object o) {
    if (o instanceof TextPair) {
      TextPair tp = (TextPair) o;
      return first.equals(tp.first) && second.equals(tp.second);
    }
    return false;
  }

  @Override
  public String toString() {
    return first + "\t" + second;
  }

  @Override
  public int compareTo(TextPair tp) {
    int cmp = first.compareTo(tp.first);
    if (cmp != 0) {
      return cmp;
    }
    return second.compareTo(tp.second);
  }
}
```

The first part of the implementation is straightforward: there are two Text instance variables, first and second, and associated constructors, getters, and setters. All Writable implementations must have a default constructor so that the MapReduce framework can instantiate them, then populate their fields by calling readFields(). Writable instances are mutable and often reused, so you should take care to avoid allocating objects in the write() or readFields() methods.

TextPair's write() method serializes each Text object in turn to the output stream by delegating to the Text objects themselves. Similarly, readFields() deserializes the bytes from the input stream by delegating to each Text object. The DataOutput and DataInput interfaces have a rich set of methods for serializing and deserializing Java primitives, so, in general, you have complete control over the wire format of your Writable object.

Just as you would for any value object you write in Java, you should override the hashCode(), equals(), and toString() methods from java.lang.Object. The hash Code() method is used by the HashPartitioner (the default partitioner in MapReduce) to choose a reduce partition, so you should make sure that you write a good hash function that mixes well to ensure reduce partitions are of a similar size.

 If you ever plan to use your custom Writable with TextOutputFormat, then you must implement its toString() method. TextOutputFormat calls toString() on keys and values for their output representation. For Text Pair, we write the underlying Text objects as strings separated by a tab character.

`TextPair` is an implementation of `WritableComparable`, so it provides an implementation of the `compareTo()` method that imposes the ordering you would expect: it sorts by the first string followed by the second. Notice that `TextPair` differs from `TextArrayWrita ble` from the previous section (apart from the number of `Text` objects it can store), since `TextArrayWritable` is only a `Writable`, not a `WritableComparable`.

Implementing a RawComparator for speed

The code for `TextPair` in Example 4-7 will work as it stands; however, there is a further optimization we can make. As explained in "WritableComparable and comparators" on page 95, when `TextPair` is being used as a key in MapReduce, it will have to be deserialized into an object for the `compareTo()` method to be invoked. What if it were possible to compare two `TextPair` objects just by looking at their serialized representations?

It turns out that we can do this because `TextPair` is the concatenation of two `Text` objects, and the binary representation of a `Text` object is a variable-length integer containing the number of bytes in the UTF-8 representation of the string, followed by the UTF-8 bytes themselves. The trick is to read the initial length so we know how long the first `Text` object's byte representation is; then we can delegate to `Text`'s `RawCompara tor` and invoke it with the appropriate offsets for the first or second string. Example 4-8 gives the details (note that this code is nested in the `TextPair` class).

Example 4-8. A RawComparator for comparing TextPair byte representations

```
public static class Comparator extends WritableComparator {

  private static final Text.Comparator TEXT_COMPARATOR = new Text.Comparator();

  public Comparator() {
    super(TextPair.class);
  }

  @Override
  public int compare(byte[] b1, int s1, int l1,
                     byte[] b2, int s2, int l2) {

    try {
      int firstL1 = WritableUtils.decodeVIntSize(b1[s1]) + readVInt(b1, s1);
      int firstL2 = WritableUtils.decodeVIntSize(b2[s2]) + readVInt(b2, s2);
      int cmp = TEXT_COMPARATOR.compare(b1, s1, firstL1, b2, s2, firstL2);
      if (cmp != 0) {
        return cmp;
      }
      return TEXT_COMPARATOR.compare(b1, s1 + firstL1, l1 - firstL1,
                                     b2, s2 + firstL2, l2 - firstL2);
    } catch (IOException e) {
      throw new IllegalArgumentException(e);
    }
  }
}
```

```
static {
  WritableComparator.define(TextPair.class, new Comparator());
}
```

We actually subclass `WritableComparator` rather than implement `RawComparator` directly, since it provides some convenience methods and default implementations. The subtle part of this code is calculating `firstL1` and `firstL2`, the lengths of the first `Text` field in each byte stream. Each is made up of the length of the variable-length integer (returned by `decodeVIntSize()` on `WritableUtils`) and the value it is encoding (returned by `readVInt()`).

The static block registers the raw comparator so that whenever MapReduce sees the `TextPair` class, it knows to use the raw comparator as its default comparator.

Custom comparators

As we can see with `TextPair`, writing raw comparators takes some care because you have to deal with details at the byte level. It is worth looking at some of the implementations of `Writable` in the `org.apache.hadoop.io` package for further ideas if you need to write your own. The utility methods on `WritableUtils` are very handy, too.

Custom comparators should also be written to be `RawComparators`, if possible. These are comparators that implement a different sort order from the natural sort order defined by the default comparator. Example 4-9 shows a comparator for `TextPair`, called `FirstComparator`, that considers only the first string of the pair. Note that we override the `compare()` method that takes objects so both `compare()` methods have the same semantics.

We will make use of this comparator in Chapter 8, when we look at joins and secondary sorting in MapReduce (see "Joins" on page 283).

Example 4-9. A custom RawComparator for comparing the first field of TextPair byte representations

```
public static class FirstComparator extends WritableComparator {

  private static final Text.Comparator TEXT_COMPARATOR = new Text.Comparator();

  public FirstComparator() {
    super(TextPair.class);
  }

  @Override
  public int compare(byte[] b1, int s1, int l1,
                     byte[] b2, int s2, int l2) {

    try {
      int firstL1 = WritableUtils.decodeVIntSize(b1[s1]) + readVInt(b1, s1);
      int firstL2 = WritableUtils.decodeVIntSize(b2[s2]) + readVInt(b2, s2);
      return TEXT_COMPARATOR.compare(b1, s1, firstL1, b2, s2, firstL2);
    } catch (IOException e) {
      throw new IllegalArgumentException(e);
```

```
    }
  }

  @Override
  public int compare(WritableComparable a, WritableComparable b) {
    if (a instanceof TextPair && b instanceof TextPair) {
      return ((TextPair) a).first.compareTo(((TextPair) b).first);
    }
    return super.compare(a, b);
  }
}
```

Serialization Frameworks

Although most MapReduce programs use `Writable` key and value types, this isn't man-
dated by the MapReduce API. In fact, any type can be used; the only requirement is a
mechanism that translates to and from a binary representation of each type.

To support this, Hadoop has an API for pluggable serialization frameworks. A serialization framework is represented by an implementation of `Serialization` (in the
`org.apache.hadoop.io.serializer` package). `WritableSerialization`, for example, is
the implementation of `Serialization` for `Writable` types.

A `Serialization` defines a mapping from types to `Serializer` instances (for turning an
object into a byte stream) and `Deserializer` instances (for turning a byte stream into
an object).

Set the `io.serializations` property to a comma-separated list of classnames to register
`Serialization` implementations. Its default value includes `org.apache.hadoop.io.seri
alizer.WritableSerialization` and the Avro-specific and reflect serializations, which
means that only `Writable` or Avro objects can be serialized or deserialized out of the box.

Hadoop includes a class called `JavaSerialization` that uses Java Object Serialization.
Although it makes it convenient to be able to use standard Java types such as `Integer`
or `String` in MapReduce programs, Java Object Serialization is not as efficient as Writables, so it's not worth making this trade-off (see the sidebar "Why Not Use Java Object
Serialization?" on page 108).

Why Not Use Java Object Serialization?

Java comes with its own serialization mechanism, called Java Object Serialization (often
referred to simply as "Java Serialization"), that is tightly integrated with the language,
so it's natural to ask why this wasn't used in Hadoop. Here's what Doug Cutting said
in response to that question:

> Why didn't I use Serialization when we first started Hadoop? Because it looked
> big and hairy and I thought we needed something lean and mean, where we had
> precise control over exactly how objects are written and read, since that is central
> to Hadoop. With Serialization you can get some control, but you have to fight for
> it.

The logic for not using RMI was similar. Effective, high-performance inter-process communications are critical to Hadoop. I felt like we'd need to precisely control how things like connections, timeouts and buffers are handled, and RMI gives you little control over those.

The problem is that Java Serialization doesn't meet the criteria for a serialization format listed earlier: compact, fast, extensible, and interoperable.

Java Serialization is not compact. Classes that implement `java.io.Serializable` or `java.io.Externalizable` write their classname and the object representation to the stream. Subsequent instances of the same class write a reference handle to the first occurrence, which occupies only 5 bytes. However, reference handles don't work well with random access, because the referent class may occur at any point in the preceding stream—that is, there is state stored in the stream. Even worse, reference handles play havoc with sorting records in a serialized stream, since the first record of a particular class is distinguished and must be treated as a special case.

All these problems are avoided by not writing the classname to the stream at all, which is the approach that Writable takes. This makes the assumption that the client knows the expected type. The result is that the format is considerably more compact than Java Serialization, and random access and sorting work as expected because each record is independent of the others (so there is no stream state).

Java Serialization is a general-purpose mechanism for serializing graphs of objects, so it necessarily has some overhead for serialization and deserialization operations. What's more, the deserialization procedure creates a new instance for each object deserialized from the stream. Writable objects, on the other hand, can be (and often are) reused. For example, for a MapReduce job, which at its core serializes and deserializes billions of records of just a handful of different types, the savings gained by not having to allocate new objects are significant.

In terms of extensibility, Java Serialization has some support for evolving a type, but it is brittle and hard to use effectively (Writables have no support; the programmer has to manage them himself).

In principle, other languages could interpret the Java Serialization stream protocol (defined by the Java Object Serialization Specification), but in practice there are no widely used implementations in other languages, so it is a Java-only solution. The situation is the same for Writables.

Serialization IDL

There are a number of other serialization frameworks that approach the problem in a different way: rather than defining types through code, you define them in a language-neutral, declarative fashion, using an *interface description language* (IDL). The system can then generate types for different languages, which is good for interoperability. They also typically define versioning schemes that make type evolution straightforward.

Hadoop's own Record I/O (found in the `org.apache.hadoop.record` package) has an IDL that is compiled into Writable objects, which makes it convenient for generating types that are compatible with MapReduce. For whatever reason, however, Record I/O was not widely used, and has been deprecated in favor of Avro.

Apache Thrift (*http://incubator.apache.org/thrift/*) and Google Protocol Buffers (*http://code.google.com/p/protobuf/*) are both popular serialization frameworks, and they are commonly used as a format for persistent binary data. There is limited support for these as MapReduce formats;[3] however, they are used internally in parts of Hadoop for RPC and data exchange.

In the next section, we look at Avro, an IDL-based serialization framework designed to work well with large-scale data processing in Hadoop.

Avro

Apache Avro (*http://avro.apache.org/*)[4] is a language-neutral data serialization system. The project was created by Doug Cutting (the creator of Hadoop) to address the major downside of Hadoop Writables: lack of language portability. Having a data format that can be processed by many languages (currently C, C++, C#, Java, PHP, Python, and Ruby) makes it easier to share datasets with a wider audience than one tied to a single language. It is also more future-proof, allowing data to potentially outlive the language used to read and write it.

But why a new data serialization system? Avro has a set of features that, taken together, differentiate it from other systems such as Apache Thrift or Google's Protocol Buffers.[5] Like these systems and others, Avro data is described using a language-independent *schema*. However, unlike some other systems, code generation is optional in Avro, which means you can read and write data that conforms to a given schema even if your code has not seen that particular schema before. To achieve this, Avro assumes that the schema is always present—at both read and write time—which makes for a very compact encoding, since encoded values do not need to be tagged with a field identifier.

Avro schemas are usually written in JSON, and data is usually encoded using a binary format, but there are other options, too. There is a higher-level language called Avro IDL for writing schemas in a C-like language that is more familiar to developers. There is also a JSON-based data encoder, which, being human-readable, is useful for prototyping and debugging Avro data.

The *Avro specification (http://avro.apache.org/docs/current/spec.html)* precisely defines the binary format that all implementations must support. It also specifies many of the

---

3. Twitter's Elephant Bird project (*http://github.com/kevinweil/elephant-bird*) includes tools for working with Thrift and Protocol Buffers in Hadoop.

4. Named after the British aircraft manufacturer from the 20th century.

5. Avro also performs favorably compared to other serialization libraries, as the benchmarks at *http://code.google.com/p/thrift-protobuf-compare/* demonstrate.

other features of Avro that implementations should support. One area that the specification does not rule on, however, is APIs: implementations have complete latitude in the API they expose for working with Avro data, since each one is necessarily language-specific. The fact that there is only one binary format is significant, because it means the barrier for implementing a new language binding is lower and avoids the problem of a combinatorial explosion of languages and formats, which would harm interoperability.

Avro has rich *schema resolution* capabilities. Within certain carefully defined constraints, the schema used to read data need not be identical to the schema that was used to write the data. This is the mechanism by which Avro supports schema evolution. For example, a new, optional field may be added to a record by declaring it in the schema used to read the old data. New and old clients alike will be able to read the old data, while new clients can write new data that uses the new field. Conversely, if an old client sees newly encoded data, it will gracefully ignore the new field and carry on processing as it would have done with old data.

Avro specifies an *object container format* for sequences of objects—similar to Hadoop's sequence file. An *Avro datafile* has a metadata section where the schema is stored, which makes the file self-describing. Avro datafiles support compression and are splittable, which is crucial for a MapReduce data input format. Furthermore, since Avro was designed with MapReduce in mind, in the future it will be possible to use Avro to bring first-class MapReduce APIs (that is, ones that are richer than Streaming, such as the Java API or C++ Pipes) to languages that speak Avro.

Avro can be used for RPC, too, although this isn't covered here. More information is in the specification.

Avro Data Types and Schemas

Avro defines a small number of primitive data types, which can be used to build application-specific data structures by writing schemas. For interoperability, implementations must support all Avro types.

Avro's primitive types are listed in Table 4-9. Each primitive type may also be specified using a more verbose form by using the type attribute, such as:

    { "type": "null" }

Table 4-9. Avro primitive types

Type	Description	Schema
null	The absence of a value	"null"
boolean	A binary value	"boolean"
int	32-bit signed integer	"int"
long	64-bit signed integer	"long"

Type	Description	Schema
float	Single-precision (32-bit) IEEE 754 floating-point number	"float"
double	Double-precision (64-bit) IEEE 754 floating-point number	"double"
bytes	Sequence of 8-bit unsigned bytes	"bytes"
string	Sequence of Unicode characters	"string"

Avro also defines the complex types listed in Table 4-10, along with a representative example of a schema of each type.

Table 4-10. Avro complex types

Type	Description	Schema example

array	An ordered collection of objects. All objects in a particular array must have the same schema.	`{`
		`  "type": "array",`
		`  "items": "long"`
		`}`

map	An unordered collection of key-value pairs. Keys must be strings and values may be any type, although within a particular map, all values must have the same schema.	`{`
		`  "type": "map",`
		`  "values": "string"`
		`}`

record	A collection of named fields of any type.	`{`
		`  "type": "record",`
		`  "name": "WeatherRecord",`
		`  "doc": "A weather reading.",`
		`  "fields": [`
		`    {"name": "year", "type": "int"},`
		`    {"name": "temperature", "type": "int"},`
		`    {"name": "stationId", "type": "string"}`
		`  ]`
		`}`

enum	A set of named values.	`{`
		`  "type": "enum",`
		`  "name": "Cutlery",`
		`  "doc": "An eating utensil.",`
		`  "symbols": ["KNIFE", "FORK", "SPOON"]`
		`}`

fixed	A fixed number of 8-bit unsigned bytes.	`{`
		`  "type": "fixed",`
		`  "name": "Md5Hash",`
		`  "size": 16`
		`}`

union	A union of schemas. A union is represented by a JSON array, where each element in the array is a schema. Data represented by a union must match one of the schemas in the union.	`[`
		`  "null",`
		`  "string",`
		`  {"type": "map", "values": "string"}`
		`]`

Each Avro language API has a representation for each Avro type that is specific to the language. For example, Avro's double type is represented in C, C++, and Java by a double, in Python by a float, and in Ruby by a Float.

What's more, there may be more than one representation, or mapping, for a language. All languages support a dynamic mapping, which can be used even when the schema is not known ahead of runtime. Java calls this the *generic* mapping.

In addition, the Java and C++ implementations can generate code to represent the data for an Avro schema. Code generation, which is called the *specific* mapping in Java, is an optimization that is useful when you have a copy of the schema before you read or write data. Generated classes also provide a more domain-oriented API for user code than generic ones.

Java has a third mapping, the *reflect* mapping, which maps Avro types onto preexisting Java types using reflection. It is slower than the generic and specific mappings, and is generally not recommended for new applications.

Java's type mappings are shown in Table 4-11. As the table shows, the specific mapping is the same as the generic one unless otherwise noted (and the reflect one is the same as the specific one unless noted). The specific mapping differs from the generic one only for record, enum, and fixed, all of which have generated classes (the name of which is controlled by the name and optional namespace attribute).

Avro string can be represented by either Java String or the Avro Utf8 Java type. The reason to use Utf8 is efficiency: because it is mutable, a single Utf8 instance may be reused for reading or writing a series of values. Also, Java String decodes UTF-8 at object construction time, whereas Avro Utf8 does it lazily, which can increase performance in some cases.

Utf8 implements Java's java.lang.CharSequence interface, which allows some interoperability with Java libraries. In other cases it may be necessary to convert Utf8 instances to String objects by calling its toString() method.

From Avro 1.6.0 onward, there is an option to have Avro always perform the conversion to String. There are a couple of ways to achieve this. The first is to set the avro.java.string property in the schema to String:

```
{ "type": "string", "avro.java.string": "String" }
```

Alternatively, for the specific mapping, you can generate classes that have String-based getters and setters. When using the Avro Maven plugin, this is done by setting the configuration property stringType to String (the example code that accompanies the book has a demonstration of this).

Finally, note that the Java reflect mapping always uses String objects, since it is designed for Java compatibility, not performance.

Table 4-11. Avro Java type mappings

Avro type	Generic Java mapping	Specific Java mapping	Reflect Java mapping
null	null type		
boolean	boolean		
int	int		short or int
long	long		
float	float		
double	double		
bytes	java.nio.ByteBuffer		Array of byte
string	org.apache.avro. util.Utf8 or java.lang.String		java.lang.String
array	org.apache.avro. generic.GenericArray		Array or java.util.Collection
map	java.util.Map		
record	org.apache.avro. generic.Generic Record	Generated class implementing org.apache.avro. specific.Specific Record.	Arbitrary user class with a zero-argument constructor. All inherited nontransient instance fields are used.
enum	java.lang.String	Generated Java enum.	Arbitrary Java enum.
fixed	org.apache.avro. generic.GenericFixed	Generated class implementing org.apache.avro. specific.SpecificFixed.	org.apache.avro. generic.GenericFixed
union	java.lang.Object		

In-Memory Serialization and Deserialization

Avro provides APIs for serialization and deserialization, which are useful when you want to integrate Avro with an existing system, such as a messaging system where the framing format is already defined. In other cases, consider using Avro's datafile format.

Let's write a Java program to read and write Avro data to and from streams. We'll start with a simple Avro schema for representing a pair of strings as a record:

```
{
  "type": "record",
  "name": "StringPair",
  "doc": "A pair of strings.",
  "fields": [
    {"name": "left", "type": "string"},
    {"name": "right", "type": "string"}
  ]
}
```

If this schema is saved in a file on the classpath called *StringPair.avsc* (.avsc is the conventional extension for an Avro schema), we can load it using the following two lines of code:

```
Schema.Parser parser = new Schema.Parser();
Schema schema = parser.parse(getClass().getResourceAsStream("StringPair.avsc"));
```

We can create an instance of an Avro record using the generic API as follows:

```
GenericRecord datum = new GenericData.Record(schema);
datum.put("left", "L");
datum.put("right", "R");
```

Next, we serialize the record to an output stream:

```
ByteArrayOutputStream out = new ByteArrayOutputStream();
DatumWriter<GenericRecord> writer = new GenericDatumWriter<GenericRecord>(schema);
Encoder encoder = EncoderFactory.get().binaryEncoder(out, null);
writer.write(datum, encoder);
encoder.flush();
out.close();
```

There are two important objects here: the DatumWriter and the Encoder. A DatumWriter translates data objects into the types understood by an Encoder, which the latter writes to the output stream. Here we are using a GenericDatumWriter, which passes the fields of GenericRecord to the Encoder. We pass a null to the encoder factory because we are not reusing a previously constructed encoder here.

In this example only one object is written to the stream, but we could call write() with more objects before closing the stream if we wanted to.

The GenericDatumWriter needs to be passed the schema because it follows the schema to determine which values from the data objects to write out. After we have called the writer's write() method, we flush the encoder, then close the output stream.

We can reverse the process and read the object back from the byte buffer:

```
DatumReader<GenericRecord> reader = new GenericDatumReader<GenericRecord>(schema);
Decoder decoder = DecoderFactory.get().binaryDecoder(out.toByteArray(), null);
GenericRecord result = reader.read(null, decoder);
assertThat(result.get("left").toString(), is("L"));
assertThat(result.get("right").toString(), is("R"));
```

We pass null to the calls to binaryDecoder() and read() because we are not reusing objects here (the decoder or the record, respectively).

The objects returned by result.get("left") and result.get("left") are of type Utf8, so we convert them into Java String objects by calling their toString() methods.

The specific API

Let's look now at the equivalent code using the specific API. We can generate the StringPair class from the schema file by using Avro's Maven plug-in for compiling schemas. The following is the relevant part of the Maven Project Object Model (POM):

```
<project>
    ...
  <build>
    <plugins>
      <plugin>
        <groupId>org.apache.avro</groupId>
        <artifactId>avro-maven-plugin</artifactId>
        <version>${avro.version}</version>
        <executions>
          <execution>
            <id>schemas</id>
            <phase>generate-sources</phase>
            <goals>
              <goal>schema</goal>
            </goals>
            <configuration>
              <includes>
                <include>StringPair.avsc</include>
              </includes>
              <sourceDirectory>src/main/resources</sourceDirectory>
              <outputDirectory>${project.build.directory}/generated-sources/java
              </outputDirectory>
            </configuration>
          </execution>
        </executions>
      </plugin>
    </plugins>
  </build>
    ...
</project>
```

As an alternative to Maven, you can use Avro's Ant task, `org.apache.avro.spe`
`cific.SchemaTask`, or the Avro command-line tools[6] to generate Java code for a schema.

In the code for serializing and deserializing, instead of a `GenericRecord` we construct a
`StringPair` instance, which we write to the stream using a `SpecificDatumWriter` and
read back using a `SpecificDatumReader`:

```
StringPair datum = new StringPair();
datum.left = "L";
datum.right = "R";

ByteArrayOutputStream out = new ByteArrayOutputStream();
DatumWriter<StringPair> writer =
  new SpecificDatumWriter<StringPair>(StringPair.class);
Encoder encoder = EncoderFactory.get().binaryEncoder(out, null);
writer.write(datum, encoder);
encoder.flush();
out.close();

DatumReader<StringPair> reader =
  new SpecificDatumReader<StringPair>(StringPair.class);
```

---

6. Avro can be downloaded in both source and binary forms from *http://avro.apache.org/releases.html*. Get
usage instructions for the Avro tools by typing `java -jar avro-tools-*.jar`.

```
Decoder decoder = DecoderFactory.get().binaryDecoder(out.toByteArray(), null);
StringPair result = reader.read(null, decoder);
assertThat(result.left.toString(), is("L"));
assertThat(result.right.toString(), is("R"));
```

From Avro 1.6.0, the generated Java code has getters and setters, so you can instead write datum.setLeft("L") and result.getLeft().

Avro Datafiles

Avro's object container file format is for storing sequences of Avro objects. It is very similar in design to Hadoop's sequence files, which are described in "Sequence-File" on page 130. The main difference is that Avro datafiles are designed to be portable across languages, so, for example, you can write a file in Python and read it in C (we will do exactly this in the next section).

A datafile has a header containing metadata, including the Avro schema and a *sync marker*, followed by a series of (optionally compressed) blocks containing the serialized Avro objects. Blocks are separated by a sync marker that is unique to the file (the marker for a particular file is found in the header) and that permits rapid resynchronization with a block boundary after seeking to an arbitrary point in the file, such as an HDFS block boundary. Thus, Avro datafiles are splittable, which makes them amenable to efficient MapReduce processing.

Writing Avro objects to a datafile is similar to writing to a stream. We use a DatumWriter as before, but instead of using an Encoder, we create a DataFileWriter instance with the DatumWriter. Then we can create a new datafile (which, by convention, has a .avro extension) and append objects to it:

```
File file = new File("data.avro");
DatumWriter<GenericRecord> writer = new GenericDatumWriter<GenericRecord>(schema);
DataFileWriter<GenericRecord> dataFileWriter =
  new DataFileWriter<GenericRecord>(writer);
dataFileWriter.create(schema, file);
dataFileWriter.append(datum);
dataFileWriter.close();
```

The objects that we write to the datafile must conform to the file's schema; otherwise, an exception will be thrown when we call append().

This example demonstrates writing to a local file (java.io.File in the previous snippet), but we can write to any java.io.OutputStream by using the overloaded create() method on DataFileWriter. To write a file to HDFS, for example, get an OutputStream by calling create() on FileSystem (see "Writing Data" on page 60).

Reading back objects from a datafile is similar to the earlier case of reading objects from an in-memory stream, with one important difference: we don't have to specify a schema, since it is read from the file metadata. Indeed, we can get the schema from the DataFileReader instance, using getSchema(), and verify that it is the same as the one we used to write the original object:

```
DatumReader<GenericRecord> reader = new GenericDatumReader<GenericRecord>();
DataFileReader<GenericRecord> dataFileReader =
  new DataFileReader<GenericRecord>(file, reader);
assertThat("Schema is the same", schema, is(dataFileReader.getSchema()));
```

DataFileReader is a regular Java iterator, so we can iterate through its data objects by calling its **hasNext()** and **next()** methods. The following snippet checks that there is only one record and that it has the expected field values:

```
assertThat(dataFileReader.hasNext(), is(true));
GenericRecord result = dataFileReader.next();
assertThat(result.get("left").toString(), is("L"));
assertThat(result.get("right").toString(), is("R"));
assertThat(dataFileReader.hasNext(), is(false));
```

Rather than using the usual **next()** method, however, it is preferable to use the over-loaded form that takes an instance of the object to be returned (in this case, **GenericRecord**), since it will reuse the object and save allocation and garbage collection costs for files containing many objects. The following is idiomatic:

```
GenericRecord record = null;
while (dataFileReader.hasNext()) {
  record = dataFileReader.next(record);
  // process record
}
```

If object reuse is not important, you can use this shorter form:

```
for (GenericRecord record : dataFileReader) {
  // process record
}
```

For the general case of reading a file on a Hadoop filesystem, use Avro's **FsInput** to specify the input file using a Hadoop **Path** object. **DataFileReader** actually offers random access to Avro datafiles (via its **seek()** and **sync()** methods); however, in many cases, sequential streaming access is sufficient, for which **DataFileStream** should be used. **DataFileStream** can read from any Java **InputStream**.

Interoperability

To demonstrate Avro's language interoperability, let's write a datafile using one language (Python) and read it back with another (C).

Python API

The program in Example 4-10 reads comma-separated strings from standard input and writes them as **StringPair** records to an Avro datafile. Like the Java code for writing a datafile, we create a **DatumWriter** and a **DataFileWriter** object. Notice that we have embedded the Avro schema in the code, although we could equally well have read it from a file.

Python represents Avro records as dictionaries; each line that is read from standard in is turned into a dict object and appended to the DataFileWriter.

Example 4-10. A Python program for writing Avro record pairs to a datafile

```python
import os
import string
import sys

from avro import schema
from avro import io
from avro import datafile

if __name__ == '__main__':
  if len(sys.argv) != 2:
    sys.exit('Usage: %s <data_file>' % sys.argv[0])
  avro_file = sys.argv[1]
  writer = open(avro_file, 'wb')
  datum_writer = io.DatumWriter()
  schema_object = schema.parse("\
{ "type": "record",
  "name": "StringPair",
  "doc": "A pair of strings.",
  "fields": [
    {"name": "left", "type": "string"},
    {"name": "right", "type": "string"}
  ]
}")
  dfw = datafile.DataFileWriter(writer, datum_writer, schema_object)
  for line in sys.stdin.readlines():
    (left, right) = string.split(line.strip(), ',')
    dfw.append({'left':left, 'right':right});
  dfw.close()
```

Before we can run the program, we need to install Avro for Python:

```
% easy_install avro
```

To run the program, we specify the name of the file to write output to (*pairs.avro*) and send input pairs over standard in, marking the end of file by typing Ctrl-D:

```
% python avro/src/main/py/write_pairs.py pairs.avro
a,1
c,2
b,3
b,2
^D
```

C API

Next we'll turn to the C API and write a program to display the contents of *pairs.avro*; see Example 4-11.[7]

Example 4-11. A C program for reading Avro record pairs from a datafile

```c
#include <avro.h>
#include <stdio.h>
#include <stdlib.h>

int main(int argc, char *argv[]) {
  if (argc != 2) {
    fprintf(stderr, "Usage: dump_pairs <data_file>\n");
    exit(EXIT_FAILURE);
  }

  const char *avrofile = argv[1];
  avro_schema_error_t error;
  avro_file_reader_t filereader;
  avro_datum_t pair;
  avro_datum_t left;
  avro_datum_t right;
  int rval;
  char *p;

  avro_file_reader(avrofile, &filereader);
  while (1) {
    rval = avro_file_reader_read(filereader, NULL, &pair);
    if (rval) break;
    if (avro_record_get(pair, "left", &left) == 0) {
      avro_string_get(left, &p);
      fprintf(stdout, "%s,", p);
    }
    if (avro_record_get(pair, "right", &right) == 0) {
      avro_string_get(right, &p);
      fprintf(stdout, "%s\n", p);
    }
  }
  avro_file_reader_close(filereader);
  return 0;
}
```

The core of the program does three things:

1. Opens a file reader of type `avro_file_reader_t` by calling Avro's `avro_file_reader` function[8]

---

7. For the general case, the Avro tools JAR file has a `tojson` command that dumps the contents of a Avro datafile as JSON.

8. Avro functions and types have a `avro_` prefix and are defined in the *avro.h* header file.

---

2. Reads Avro data from the file reader with the `avro_file_reader_read` function in a while loop until there are no pairs left (as determined by the return value `rval`)

3. Closes the file reader with `avro_file_reader_close`

The `avro_file_reader_read` function accepts a schema as its second argument to support the case where the schema for reading is different from the one used when the file was written (this is explained in the next section), but we simply pass in `NULL`, which tells Avro to use the datafile's schema. The third argument is a pointer to a `avro_datum_t` object, which is populated with the contents of the next record read from the file. We unpack the pair structure into its fields by calling `avro_record_get`, and then we extract the value of these fields as strings using `avro_string_get`, which we print to the console.

Running the program using the output of the Python program prints the original input:

```
% ./dump_pairs pairs.avro
a,1
c,2
b,3
b,2
```

We have successfully exchanged complex data between two Avro implementations.

Schema Resolution

We can choose to use a different schema for reading the data back (the *reader's schema*) from the one we used to write it (the *writer's schema*). This is a powerful tool because it enables schema evolution. To illustrate, consider a new schema for string pairs with an added `description` field:

```
{
  "type": "record",
  "name": "StringPair",
  "doc": "A pair of strings with an added field.",
  "fields": [
    {"name": "left", "type": "string"},
    {"name": "right", "type": "string"},
    {"name": "description", "type": "string", "default": ""}
  ]
}
```

We can use this schema to read the data we serialized earlier because crucially, we have given the `description` field a default value (the empty string),[9] which Avro will use when there is no field defined in the records it is reading. Had we omitted the `default` attribute, we would get an error when trying to read the old data.

---

9. Default values for fields are encoded using JSON. See the Avro specification for a description of this encoding for each data type.

To make the default value `null` rather than the empty string, we would instead define the description field using a union with the `null` Avro type:

```
{"name": "description", "type": ["null", "string"], "default": null}
```

When the reader's schema is different from the writer's, we use the constructor for `GenericDatumReader` that takes two schema objects, the writer's and the reader's, in that order:

```
DatumReader<GenericRecord> reader =
  new GenericDatumReader<GenericRecord>(schema, newSchema);
Decoder decoder = DecoderFactory.get().binaryDecoder(out.toByteArray(), null);
GenericRecord result = reader.read(null, decoder);
assertThat(result.get("left").toString(), is("L"));
assertThat(result.get("right").toString(), is("R"));
assertThat(result.get("description").toString(), is(""));
```

For datafiles, which have the writer's schema stored in the metadata, we only need to specify the readers's schema explicitly, which we can do by passing `null` for the writer's schema:

```
DatumReader<GenericRecord> reader =
  new GenericDatumReader<GenericRecord>(null, newSchema);
```

Another common use of a different reader's schema is to drop fields in a record, an operation called *projection*. This is useful when you have records with a large number of fields and you want to read only some of them. For example, this schema can be used to get only the `right` field of a `StringPair`:

```
{
  "type": "record",
  "name": "StringPair",
  "doc": "The right field of a pair of strings.",
  "fields": [
    {"name": "right", "type": "string"}
  ]
}
```

The rules for schema resolution have a direct bearing on how schemas may evolve from one version to the next, and are spelled out in the Avro specification for all Avro types. A summary of the rules for record evolution from the point of view of readers and writers (or servers and clients) is presented in Table 4-12.

Table 4-12. Schema resolution of records

New schema	Writer	Reader	Action
Added field	Old	New	The reader uses the default value of the new field, since it is not written by the writer.
	New	Old	The reader does not know about the new field written by the writer, so it is ignored (projection).
Removed field	Old	New	The reader ignores the removed field (projection).

New schema	Writer	Reader	Action
	New	Old	The removed field is not written by the writer. If the old schema had a default defined for the field, the reader uses this; otherwise, it gets an error. In this case, it is best to update the reader's schema, either at the same time as or before the writer's.

Another useful technique for evolving Avro schemas is the use of name *aliases*. Aliases allow you to use different names in the schema used to read the Avro data than in the schema originally used to write the data. For example, the following reader's schema can be used to read StringPair data with the new field names first and second instead of left and right (which is what it was written with).

```
{
    "type": "record",
    "name": "StringPair",
    "doc": "A pair of strings with aliased field names.",
    "fields": [
        {"name": "first", "type": "string", "aliases": ["left"]},
        {"name": "second", "type": "string", "aliases": ["right"]}
    ]
}
```

Note that the aliases are used to translate (at read time) the writer's schema into the reader's, but the alias names are not available to the reader. In this example, the reader cannot use the field names left and right, because they have already been translated to first and second.

Sort Order

Avro defines a sort order for objects. For most Avro types, the order is the natural one you would expect—for example, numeric types are ordered by ascending numeric value. Others are a little more subtle. For instance, enums are compared by the order in which the symbol is defined and not by the value of the symbol string.

All types except record have preordained rules for their sort order, as described in the Avro specification, that cannot be overridden by the user. For records, however, you can control the sort order by specifying the order attribute for a field. It takes one of three values: ascending (the default), descending (to reverse the order), or ignore (so the field is skipped for comparison purposes).

For example, the following schema (*SortedStringPair.avsc*) defines an ordering of StringPair records by the right field in descending order. The left field is ignored for the purposes of ordering, but it is still present in the projection:

```
{
    "type": "record",
    "name": "StringPair",
    "doc": "A pair of strings, sorted by right field descending.",
    "fields": [
        {"name": "left", "type": "string", "order": "ignore"},
```

```
        {"name": "right", "type": "string", "order": "descending"}
    ]
}
```

The record's fields are compared pairwise in the document order of the reader's schema. Thus, by specifying an appropriate reader's schema, you can impose an arbitrary ordering on data records. This schema (*SwitchedStringPair.avsc*) defines a sort order by the right field, then the left:

```
{
    "type": "record",
    "name": "StringPair",
    "doc": "A pair of strings, sorted by right then left.",
    "fields": [
        {"name": "right", "type": "string"},
        {"name": "left", "type": "string"}
    ]
}
```

Avro implements efficient binary comparisons. That is to say, Avro does not have to deserialize a binary data into objects to perform the comparison, because it can instead work directly on the byte streams.[10] In the case of the original StringPair schema (with no order attributes), for example, Avro implements the binary comparison as follows.

The first field, left, is a UTF-8-encoded string, for which Avro can compare the bytes lexicographically. If they differ, the order is determined, and Avro can stop the comparison there. Otherwise, if the two-byte sequences are the same, it compares the second two (right) fields, again lexicographically at the byte level because the field is another UTF-8 string.

Notice that this description of a comparison function has exactly the same logic as the binary comparator we wrote for Writables in "Implementing a RawComparator for speed" on page 106. The great thing is that Avro provides the comparator for us, so we don't have to write and maintain this code. It's also easy to change the sort order just by changing the reader's schema. For the *SortedStringPair.avsc* or *SwitchedString-Pair.avsc* schemas, the comparison function Avro uses is essentially the same as the one just described. The differences are which fields are considered, the order in which they are considered, and whether the sort order is ascending or descending.

Later in the chapter we'll use Avro's sorting logic in conjunction with MapReduce to sort Avro datafiles in parallel.

Avro MapReduce

Avro provides a number of classes for making it easy to run MapReduce programs on Avro data. For example, AvroMapper and AvroReducer in the org.apache.avro.mapred

---

10. A useful consequence of this property is that you can compute an Avro datum's hash code from either the object or the binary representation (the latter by using the static hashCode() method on BinaryData) and get the same result in both cases.

---

package are specializations of Hadoop's (old-style) `Mapper` and `Reducer` classes. They eliminate the key-value distinction for inputs and outputs, since Avro datafiles are just a sequence of values. However, intermediate data is still divided into key-value pairs for the shuffle.

Let's rework the MapReduce program for finding the maximum temperature for each year in the weather dataset, this time using the Avro MapReduce API. We will represent weather records using the following schema:

```
{
    "type": "record",
    "name": "WeatherRecord",
    "doc": "A weather reading.",
    "fields": [
      {"name": "year", "type": "int"},
      {"name": "temperature", "type": "int"},
      {"name": "stationId", "type": "string"}
    ]
}
```

The program in Example 4-12 reads text input (in the format we saw in earlier chapters) and writes Avro datafiles containing weather records as output.

Example 4-12. MapReduce program to find the maximum temperature, creating Avro output

```
public class AvroGenericMaxTemperature extends Configured implements Tool {

  private static final Schema SCHEMA = new Schema.Parser().parse(
    "{" +
    "  \"type\": \"record\"," +
    "  \"name\": \"WeatherRecord\"," +
    "  \"doc\": \"A weather reading.\"," +
    "  \"fields\": [" +
    "    {\"name\": \"year\", \"type\": \"int\"}," +
    "    {\"name\": \"temperature\", \"type\": \"int\"}," +
    "    {\"name\": \"stationId\", \"type\": \"string\"}" +
    "  ]" +
    "}"
  );

  public static class MaxTemperatureMapper
      extends AvroMapper<Utf8, Pair<Integer, GenericRecord>> {
    private NcdcRecordParser parser = new NcdcRecordParser();
    private GenericRecord record = new GenericData.Record(SCHEMA);
    @Override
    public void map(Utf8 line,
        AvroCollector<Pair<Integer, GenericRecord>> collector,
        Reporter reporter) throws IOException {
      parser.parse(line.toString());
      if (parser.isValidTemperature()) {
        record.put("year", parser.getYearInt());
        record.put("temperature", parser.getAirTemperature());
        record.put("stationId", parser.getStationId());
        collector.collect(
            new Pair<Integer, GenericRecord>(parser.getYearInt(), record));
```

```
      }
    }
  }

  public static class MaxTemperatureReducer
      extends AvroReducer<Integer, GenericRecord, GenericRecord> {

    @Override
    public void reduce(Integer key, Iterable<GenericRecord> values,
        AvroCollector<GenericRecord> collector, Reporter reporter)
        throws IOException {
      GenericRecord max = null;
      for (GenericRecord value : values) {
        if (max == null ||
            (Integer) value.get("temperature") > (Integer) max.get("temperature")) {
          max = newWeatherRecord(value);
        }
      }
      collector.collect(max);
    }
    private GenericRecord newWeatherRecord(GenericRecord value) {
      GenericRecord record = new GenericData.Record(SCHEMA);
      record.put("year", value.get("year"));
      record.put("temperature", value.get("temperature"));
      record.put("stationId", value.get("stationId"));
      return record;
    }
  }

  @Override
  public int run(String[] args) throws Exception {
    if (args.length != 2) {
      System.err.printf("Usage: %s [generic options] <input> <output>\n",
          getClass().getSimpleName());
      ToolRunner.printGenericCommandUsage(System.err);
      return -1;
    }

    JobConf conf = new JobConf(getConf(), getClass());
    conf.setJobName("Max temperature");

    FileInputFormat.addInputPath(conf, new Path(args[0]));
    FileOutputFormat.setOutputPath(conf, new Path(args[1]));

    AvroJob.setInputSchema(conf, Schema.create(Schema.Type.STRING));
    AvroJob.setMapOutputSchema(conf,
        Pair.getPairSchema(Schema.create(Schema.Type.INT), SCHEMA));
    AvroJob.setOutputSchema(conf, SCHEMA);

    conf.setInputFormat(AvroUtf8InputFormat.class);

    AvroJob.setMapperClass(conf, MaxTemperatureMapper.class);
    AvroJob.setReducerClass(conf, MaxTemperatureReducer.class);

    JobClient.runJob(conf);
```

```
    return 0;
  }

  public static void main(String[] args) throws Exception {
    int exitCode = ToolRunner.run(new AvroGenericMaxTemperature(), args);
    System.exit(exitCode);
  }
}
```

This program uses the generic Avro mapping. This frees us from generating code to represent records, at the expense of type safety (field names are referred to by string value, such as "temperature").[11] The schema for weather records is inlined in the code for convenience (and read into the SCHEMA constant), although in practice it might be more maintainable to read the schema from a local file in the driver code and pass it to the mapper and reducer via the Hadoop job configuration. (Techniques for achieving this are discussed in "Side Data Distribution" on page 288.)

There are a couple of differences from the regular Hadoop MapReduce API. The first is the use of a org.apache.avro.mapred.Pair to wrap the map output key and value in MaxTemperatureMapper. (The reason that the org.apache.avro.mapred.AvroMapper doesn't have a fixed output key and value is so that map-only jobs can emit just values to Avro datafiles.) For this MapReduce program, the key is the year (an integer), and the value is the weather record, which is represented by Avro's GenericRecord.

Avro MapReduce does preserve the notion of key-value pairs for the input to the reducer, however, because this is what comes out of the shuffle, and it unwraps the Pair before invoking the org.apache.avro.mapred.AvroReducer. The MaxTemperatureReducer iterates through the records for each key (year) and finds the one with the maximum temperature. It is necessary to make a copy of the record with the highest temperature found so far, since the iterator reuses the instance for reasons of efficiency (and only the fields are updated).

The second major difference from regular MapReduce is the use of AvroJob for configuring the job. AvroJob is a convenience class for specifying the Avro schemas for the input, map output, and final output data. In this program the input schema is an Avro string because we are reading from a text file, and the input format is set correspondingly, to AvroUtf8InputFormat. The map output schema is a pair schema whose key schema is an Avro int and whose value schema is the weather record schema. The final output schema is the weather record schema, and the output format is the default, AvroOutputFormat, which writes to Avro datafiles.

The following command line shows how to run the program on a small sample dataset:

```
% hadoop jar avro-examples.jar AvroGenericMaxTemperature \
    input/ncdc/sample.txt output
```

---

11. For an example that uses the specific mapping with generated classes, see the AvroSpecificMaxTemperature class in the example code.

On completion we can look at the output using the Avro tools JAR to render the Avro datafile as JSON, one record per line:

```
% java -jar $AVRO_HOME/avro-tools-*.jar tojson output/part-00000.avro
{"year":1949,"temperature":111,"stationId":"012650-99999"}
{"year":1950,"temperature":22,"stationId":"011990-99999"}
```

In this example, we used an `AvroMapper` and an `AvroReducer`, but the API supports a mixture of regular MapReduce mappers and reducers with Avro-specific ones, which is useful for converting between Avro formats and other formats, such as SequenceFiles. See the documentation for the Avro MapReduce package for details.

Sorting Using Avro MapReduce

In this section we use Avro's sort capabilities and combine them with MapReduce to write a program to sort an Avro datafile (Example 4-13).

Example 4-13. A MapReduce program to sort an Avro datafile

```java
public class AvroSort extends Configured implements Tool {

  static class SortMapper<K> extends AvroMapper<K, Pair<K, K>> {
    public void map(K datum, AvroCollector<Pair<K, K>> collector,
        Reporter reporter) throws IOException {
      collector.collect(new Pair<K, K>(datum, null, datum, null));
    }
  }

  static class SortReducer<K> extends AvroReducer<K, K, K> {
    public void reduce(K key, Iterable<K> values,
        AvroCollector<K> collector,
        Reporter reporter) throws IOException {
      for (K value : values) {
        collector.collect(value);
      }
    }
  }

  @Override
  public int run(String[] args) throws Exception {

    if (args.length != 3) {
      System.err.printf(
        "Usage: %s [generic options] <input> <output> <schema-file>\n",
        getClass().getSimpleName());
      ToolRunner.printGenericCommandUsage(System.err);
      return -1;
    }

    String input = args[0];
    String output = args[1];
    String schemaFile = args[2];

    JobConf conf = new JobConf(getConf(), getClass());
```

```
    conf.setJobName("Avro sort");

    FileInputFormat.addInputPath(conf, new Path(input));
    FileOutputFormat.setOutputPath(conf, new Path(output));

    Schema schema = new Schema.Parser().parse(new File(schemaFile));
    AvroJob.setInputSchema(conf, schema);
    Schema intermediateSchema = Pair.getPairSchema(schema, schema);
    AvroJob.setMapOutputSchema(conf, intermediateSchema);
    AvroJob.setOutputSchema(conf, schema);

    AvroJob.setMapperClass(conf, SortMapper.class);
    AvroJob.setReducerClass(conf, SortReducer.class);

    JobClient.runJob(conf);
    return 0;
  }

  public static void main(String[] args) throws Exception {
    int exitCode = ToolRunner.run(new AvroSort(), args);
    System.exit(exitCode);
  }
}
```

This program (which uses the generic Avro mapping and hence does not require any code generation) can sort Avro records of any type, represented in Java by the generic type parameter K. We choose a value that is the same as the key, so that when the values are grouped by key we can emit all of the values in the case that more than one of them share the same key (according to the sorting function), thereby not losing any records.[12] The mapper simply emits an org.apache.avro.mapred.Pair object with this key and value. The reducer acts as an identity, passing the values through to the (single-valued) output, which will get written to an Avro datafile.

The sorting happens in the MapReduce shuffle, and the sort function is determined by the Avro schema that is passed to the program. Let's use the program to sort the *pairs.avro* file created earlier, using the *SortedStringPair.avsc* schema to sort by the right field in descending order. First, we inspect the input using the Avro tools JAR:

```
% java -jar $AVRO_HOME/avro-tools-*.jar tojson input/avro/pairs.avro
{"left":"a","right":"1"}
{"left":"c","right":"2"}
{"left":"b","right":"3"}
{"left":"b","right":"2"}
```

Then we run the sort:

```
% hadoop jar avro-examples.jar AvroSort input/avro/pairs.avro output \
  ch04-avro/src/main/resources/SortedStringPair.avsc
```

Finally, we inspect the output and see that it is sorted correctly.

---

12. We encounter this idea of duplicating information from the key in the value object again in "Secondary Sort" on page 277.

```
% java -jar $AVRO_HOME/avro-tools-*.jar tojson output/part-00000.avro
{"left":"b","right":"3"}
{"left":"c","right":"2"}
{"left":"b","right":"2"}
{"left":"a","right":"1"}
```

Avro MapReduce in Other Languages

For languages other than Java, there are a few choices for working with Avro data.

AvroAsTextInputFormat is designed to allow Hadoop Streaming programs to read Avro datafiles. Each datum in the file is converted to a string, which is the JSON representation of the datum, or just to the raw bytes if the type is Avro bytes. Going the other way, you can specify AvroTextOutputFormat as the output format of a Streaming job to create Avro datafiles with a bytes schema, where each datum is the tab-delimited key-value pair written from the Streaming output. Both of these classes can be found in the org.apache.avro.mapred package.

For a richer interface than Streaming, Avro provides a connector framework (in the org.apache.avro.mapred.tether package), which is the Avro analog of Hadoop Pipes. At the time of this writing, there are no bindings for other languages, but a Python implementation will be available in a future release.

It's also worth considering Pig and Hive for doing Avro processing, since both can read and write Avro datafiles by specifying the appropriate storage formats.

File-Based Data Structures

For some applications, you need a specialized data structure to hold your data. For doing MapReduce-based processing, putting each blob of binary data into its own file doesn't scale, so Hadoop developed a number of higher-level containers for these situations.

SequenceFile

Imagine a logfile where each log record is a new line of text. If you want to log binary types, plain text isn't a suitable format. Hadoop's SequenceFile class fits the bill in this situation, providing a persistent data structure for binary key-value pairs. To use it as a logfile format, you would choose a key, such as timestamp represented by a LongWritable, and the value would be Writable that represents the quantity being logged.

SequenceFiles also work well as containers for smaller files. HDFS and MapReduce are optimized for large files, so packing files into a SequenceFile makes storing and processing the smaller files more efficient. ("Processing a whole file as a record" on page 242 contains a program to pack files into a SequenceFile).[13]

Writing a SequenceFile

To create a SequenceFile, use one of its createWriter() static methods, which return a SequenceFile.Writer instance. There are several overloaded versions, but they all require you to specify a stream to write to (either an FSDataOutputStream or a FileSystem and Path pairing), a Configuration object, and the key and value types. Optional arguments include the compression type and codec, a Progressable callback to be informed of write progress, and a Metadata instance to be stored in the Sequence File header.

The keys and values stored in a SequenceFile do not necessarily need to be Writable. Any types that can be serialized and deserialized by a Serialization may be used.

Once you have a SequenceFile.Writer, you then write key-value pairs using the append() method. When you've finished, you call the close() method (Sequence File.Writer implements java.io.Closeable).

Example 4-14 shows a short program to write some key-value pairs to a SequenceFile using the API just described.

Example 4-14. Writing a SequenceFile

```
public class SequenceFileWriteDemo {

  private static final String[] DATA = {
    "One, two, buckle my shoe",
    "Three, four, shut the door",
    "Five, six, pick up sticks",
    "Seven, eight, lay them straight",
    "Nine, ten, a big fat hen"
  };

  public static void main(String[] args) throws IOException {
    String uri = args[0];
    Configuration conf = new Configuration();
    FileSystem fs = FileSystem.get(URI.create(uri), conf);
    Path path = new Path(uri);

    IntWritable key = new IntWritable();
    Text value = new Text();
    SequenceFile.Writer writer = null;
    try {
      writer = SequenceFile.createWriter(fs, conf, path,
```

---

13. In a similar vein, the blog post "A Million Little Files" by Stuart Sierra includes code for converting a *tar* file into a SequenceFile ((((*http://stuartsierra.com/2008/04/24/a-million-little-files*)).

```
        key.getClass(), value.getClass());

    for (int i = 0; i < 100; i++) {
      key.set(100 - i);
      value.set(DATA[i % DATA.length]);
      System.out.printf("[%s]\t%s\t%s\n", writer.getLength(), key, value);
      writer.append(key, value);
    }
  } finally {
    IOUtils.closeStream(writer);
  }
}
}
```

The keys in the sequence file are integers counting down from 100 to 1, represented as
IntWritable objects. The values are Text objects. Before each record is appended to the
SequenceFile.Writer, we call the getLength() method to discover the current position
in the file. (We will use this information about record boundaries in the next section
when we read the file nonsequentially.) We write the position out to the console, along
with the key and value pairs. The result of running it is shown here:

```
% hadoop SequenceFileWriteDemo numbers.seq
[128]   100     One, two, buckle my shoe
[173]   99      Three, four, shut the door
[220]   98      Five, six, pick up sticks
[264]   97      Seven, eight, lay them straight
[314]   96      Nine, ten, a big fat hen
[359]   95      One, two, buckle my shoe
[404]   94      Three, four, shut the door
[451]   93      Five, six, pick up sticks
[495]   92      Seven, eight, lay them straight
[545]   91      Nine, ten, a big fat hen
...
[1976]  60      One, two, buckle my shoe
[2021]  59      Three, four, shut the door
[2088]  58      Five, six, pick up sticks
[2132]  57      Seven, eight, lay them straight
[2182]  56      Nine, ten, a big fat hen
...
[4557]  5       One, two, buckle my shoe
[4602]  4       Three, four, shut the door
[4649]  3       Five, six, pick up sticks
[4693]  2       Seven, eight, lay them straight
[4743]  1       Nine, ten, a big fat hen
```

Reading a SequenceFile

Reading sequence files from beginning to end is a matter of creating an instance of
SequenceFile.Reader and iterating over records by repeatedly invoking one of the
next() methods. Which one you use depends on the serialization framework you are
using. If you are using Writable types, you can use the next() method that takes a key

and a value argument and reads the next key and value in the stream into these variables:

```
public boolean next(Writable key, Writable val)
```

The return value is true if a key-value pair was read and false if the end of the file has been reached.

For other, non-Writable serialization frameworks (such as Apache Thrift), you should use these two methods:

```
public Object next(Object key) throws IOException
public Object getCurrentValue(Object val) throws IOException
```

In this case, you need to make sure that the serialization you want to use has been set in the io.serializations property; see "Serialization Frameworks" on page 108.

If the next() method returns a non-null object, a key-value pair was read from the stream, and the value can be retrieved using the getCurrentValue() method. Otherwise, if next() returns null, the end of the file has been reached.

The program in Example 4-15 demonstrates how to read a sequence file that has Writable keys and values. Note how the types are discovered from the Sequence File.Reader via calls to getKeyClass() and getValueClass(), and then ReflectionU tils is used to create an instance for the key and an instance for the value. By using this technique, the program can be used with any sequence file that has Writable keys and values.

Example 4-15. Reading a SequenceFile

```
public class SequenceFileReadDemo {

  public static void main(String[] args) throws IOException {
    String uri = args[0];
    Configuration conf = new Configuration();
    FileSystem fs = FileSystem.get(URI.create(uri), conf);
    Path path = new Path(uri);

    SequenceFile.Reader reader = null;
    try {
      reader = new SequenceFile.Reader(fs, path, conf);
      Writable key = (Writable)
        ReflectionUtils.newInstance(reader.getKeyClass(), conf);
      Writable value = (Writable)
        ReflectionUtils.newInstance(reader.getValueClass(), conf);
      long position = reader.getPosition();
      while (reader.next(key, value)) {
        String syncSeen = reader.syncSeen() ? "*" : "";
        System.out.printf("[%s%s]\t%s\t%s\n", position, syncSeen, key, value);
        position = reader.getPosition(); // beginning of next record
      }
    } finally {
      IOUtils.closeStream(reader);
    }
```

```
      }
}
```

Another feature of the program is that it displays the position of the *sync points* in the sequence file. A sync point is a point in the stream that can be used to resynchronize with a record boundary if the reader is "lost"—for example, after seeking to an arbitrary position in the stream. Sync points are recorded by SequenceFile.Writer, which inserts a special entry to mark the sync point every few records as a sequence file is being written. Such entries are small enough to incur only a modest storage overhead—less than 1%. Sync points always align with record boundaries.

Running the program in Example 4-15 shows the sync points in the sequence file as asterisks. The first one occurs at position 2021 (the second one occurs at position 4075, but is not shown in the output):

```
% hadoop SequenceFileReadDemo numbers.seq
[128]   100   One, two, buckle my shoe
[173]    99   Three, four, shut the door
[220]    98   Five, six, pick up sticks
[264]    97   Seven, eight, lay them straight
[314]    96   Nine, ten, a big fat hen
[359]    95   One, two, buckle my shoe
[404]    94   Three, four, shut the door
[451]    93   Five, six, pick up sticks
[495]    92   Seven, eight, lay them straight
[545]    91   Nine, ten, a big fat hen
[590]    90   One, two, buckle my shoe
...
[1976]   60   One, two, buckle my shoe
[2021*]  59   Three, four, shut the door
[2088]   58   Five, six, pick up sticks
[2132]   57   Seven, eight, lay them straight
[2182]   56   Nine, ten, a big fat hen
...
[4557]    5   One, two, buckle my shoe
[4602]    4   Three, four, shut the door
[4649]    3   Five, six, pick up sticks
[4693]    2   Seven, eight, lay them straight
[4743]    1   Nine, ten, a big fat hen
```

There are two ways to seek to a given position in a sequence file. The first is the seek() method, which positions the reader at the given point in the file. For example, seeking to a record boundary works as expected:

```
reader.seek(359);
assertThat(reader.next(key, value), is(true));
assertThat(((IntWritable) key).get(), is(95));
```

But if the position in the file is not at a record boundary, the reader fails when the next() method is called:

```
reader.seek(360);
reader.next(key, value); // fails with IOException
```

The second way to find a record boundary makes use of sync points. The sync(long position) method on SequenceFile.Reader positions the reader at the next sync point after position. (If there are no sync points in the file after this position, then the reader will be positioned at the end of the file.) Thus, we can call sync() with any position in the stream—a nonrecord boundary, for example—and the reader will reestablish itself at the next sync point so reading can continue:

```
reader.sync(360);
assertThat(reader.getPosition(), is(2021L));
assertThat(reader.next(key, value), is(true));
assertThat(((IntWritable) key).get(), is(59));
```

 SequenceFile.Writer has a method called sync() for inserting a sync point at the current position in the stream. This is not to be confused with the identically named but otherwise unrelated sync() method defined by the Syncable interface for synchronizing buffers to the underlying device.

Sync points come into their own when using sequence files as input to MapReduce, since they permit the file to be split and different portions of it can be processed independently by separate map tasks. See "SequenceFileInputFormat" on page 249.

Displaying a SequenceFile with the command-line interface

The hadoop fs command has a -text option to display sequence files in textual form. It looks at a file's magic number so that it can attempt to detect the type of the file and appropriately convert it to text. It can recognize gzipped files and sequence files; otherwise, it assumes the input is plain text.

For sequence files, this command is really useful only if the keys and values have a meaningful string representation (as defined by the toString() method). Also, if you have your own key or value classes, you will need to make sure they are on Hadoop's classpath.

Running it on the sequence file we created in the previous section gives the following output:

```
% hadoop fs -text numbers.seq | head
100    One, two, buckle my shoe
99     Three, four, shut the door
98     Five, six, pick up sticks
97     Seven, eight, lay them straight
96     Nine, ten, a big fat hen
95     One, two, buckle my shoe
94     Three, four, shut the door
93     Five, six, pick up sticks
92     Seven, eight, lay them straight
91     Nine, ten, a big fat hen
```

Sorting and merging SequenceFiles

The most powerful way of sorting (and merging) one or more sequence files is to use MapReduce. MapReduce is inherently parallel and will let you specify the number of reducers to use, which determines the number of output partitions. For example, by specifying one reducer, you get a single output file. We can use the sort example that comes with Hadoop by specifying that the input and output are sequence files and by setting the key and value types:

```
% hadoop jar $HADOOP_INSTALL/hadoop-*-examples.jar sort -r 1 \
  -inFormat org.apache.hadoop.mapred.SequenceFileInputFormat \
  -outFormat org.apache.hadoop.mapred.SequenceFileOutputFormat \
  -outKey org.apache.hadoop.io.IntWritable \
  -outValue org.apache.hadoop.io.Text \
  numbers.seq sorted
% hadoop fs -text sorted/part-00000 | head
1       Nine, ten, a big fat hen
2       Seven, eight, lay them straight
3       Five, six, pick up sticks
4       Three, four, shut the door
5       One, two, buckle my shoe
6       Nine, ten, a big fat hen
7       Seven, eight, lay them straight
8       Five, six, pick up sticks
9       Three, four, shut the door
10      One, two, buckle my shoe
```

Sorting is covered in more detail in "Sorting" on page 268.

As an alternative to using MapReduce for sort/merge, there is a SequenceFile.Sorter class that has a number of sort() and merge() methods. These functions predate MapReduce and are lower-level functions than MapReduce (for example, to get parallelism, you need to partition your data manually), so in general MapReduce is the preferred approach to sort and merge sequence files.

The SequenceFile format

A sequence file consists of a header followed by one or more records (see Figure 4-2). The first three bytes of a sequence file are the bytes SEQ, which acts as a magic number, followed by a single byte representing the version number. The header contains other fields, including the names of the key and value classes, compression details, user-defined metadata, and the sync marker.[14] Recall that the sync marker is used to allow a reader to synchronize to a record boundary from any position in the file. Each file has a randomly generated sync marker, whose value is stored in the header. Sync markers appear between records in the sequence file. They are designed to incur less than a 1% storage overhead, so they don't necessarily appear between every pair of records (such is the case for short records).

---

14. Full details of the format of these fields may be found in SequenceFile's documentation (*http://hadoop .apache.org/common/docs/current/api/org/apache/hadoop/io/SequenceFile.html*) and source code.

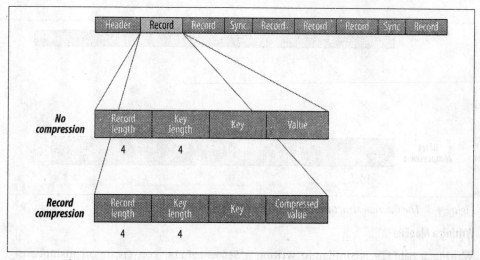

Figure 4-2. The internal structure of a sequence file with no compression and with record compression

The internal format of the records depends on whether compression is enabled, and if it is, whether it is record compression or block compression.

If no compression is enabled (the default), each record is made up of the record length (in bytes), the key length, the key, and then the value. The length fields are written as four-byte integers adhering to the contract of the writeInt() method of java.io.Data Output. Keys and values are serialized using the Serialization defined for the class being written to the sequence file.

The format for record compression is almost identical to no compression, except the value bytes are compressed using the codec defined in the header. Note that keys are not compressed.

Block compression compresses multiple records at once; it is therefore more compact than and should generally be preferred over record compression because it has the opportunity to take advantage of similarities between records. (See Figure 4-3.) Records are added to a block until it reaches a minimum size in bytes, defined by the io.seqfile.compress.blocksize property; the default is 1 million bytes. A sync marker is written before the start of every block. The format of a block is a field indicating the number of records in the block, followed by four compressed fields: the key lengths, the keys, the value lengths, and the values.

MapFile

A MapFile is a sorted SequenceFile with an index to permit lookups by key. MapFile can be thought of as a persistent form of java.util.Map (although it doesn't implement this interface), which is able to grow beyond the size of a Map that is kept in memory.

Block
compression

1-5

Figure 4-3. The internal structure of a sequence file with block compression

Writing a MapFile

Writing a MapFile is similar to writing a SequenceFile: you create an instance of MapFile.Writer, then call the append() method to add entries in order. (Attempting to add entries out of order will result in an IOException.) Keys must be instances of WritableComparable, and values must be Writable. Contrast this to SequenceFile, which can use any serialization framework for its entries.

The program in Example 4-16 creates a MapFile and writes some entries to it. It is very similar to the program in Example 4-14 for creating a SequenceFile.

Example 4-16. Writing a MapFile

```
public class MapFileWriteDemo {

  private static final String[] DATA = {
    "One, two, buckle my shoe",
    "Three, four, shut the door",
    "Five, six, pick up sticks",
    "Seven, eight, lay them straight",
    "Nine, ten, a big fat hen"
  };

  public static void main(String[] args) throws IOException {
    String uri = args[0];
    Configuration conf = new Configuration();
    FileSystem fs = FileSystem.get(URI.create(uri), conf);

    IntWritable key = new IntWritable();
    Text value = new Text();
    MapFile.Writer writer = null;
    try {
      writer = new MapFile.Writer(conf, fs, uri,
          key.getClass(), value.getClass());

      for (int i = 0; i < 1024; i++) {
        key.set(i + 1);
        value.set(DATA[i % DATA.length]);
```

```
        writer.append(key, value);
    }
  } finally {
    IOUtils.closeStream(writer);
  }
 }
}
```

Let's use this program to build a MapFile:

```
% hadoop MapFileWriteDemo numbers.map
```

If we look at the MapFile, we see it's actually a directory containing two files called *data* and *index*:

```
% ls -l numbers.map
total 104
-rw-r--r--   1 tom  tom  47898 Jul 29 22:06 data
-rw-r--r--   1 tom  tom    251 Jul 29 22:06 index
```

Both files are SequenceFiles. The *data* file contains all of the entries, in order:

```
% hadoop fs -text numbers.map/data | head
1       One, two, buckle my shoe
2       Three, four, shut the door
3       Five, six, pick up sticks
4       Seven, eight, lay them straight
5       Nine, ten, a big fat hen
6       One, two, buckle my shoe
7       Three, four, shut the door
8       Five, six, pick up sticks
9       Seven, eight, lay them straight
10      Nine, ten, a big fat hen
```

The *index* file contains a fraction of the keys and contains a mapping from the key to that key's offset in the *data* file:

```
% hadoop fs -text numbers.map/index
1       128
129     6079
257     12054
385     18030
513     24002
641     29976
769     35947
897     41922
```

As we can see from the output, by default only every 128th key is included in the index, although you can change this value either by setting the io.map.index.interval property or by calling the setIndexInterval() method on the MapFile.Writer instance. A reason to increase the index interval would be to decrease the amount of memory that the MapFile needs to store the index. Conversely, you might decrease the interval to improve the time for random selection (since fewer records need to be skipped on average) at the expense of memory usage.

Because the index is only a partial index of keys, `MapFile` is not able to provide methods to enumerate, or even count, all the keys it contains. The only way to perform these operations is to read the whole file.

Reading a MapFile

Iterating through the entries in order in a `MapFile` is similar to the procedure for a `SequenceFile`: you create a `MapFile.Reader`, then call the `next()` method until it returns `false`, signifying that no entry was read because the end of the file was reached:

```
public boolean next(WritableComparable key, Writable val) throws IOException
```

A random access lookup can be performed by calling the `get()` method:

```
public Writable get(WritableComparable key, Writable val) throws IOException
```

The return value is used to determine whether an entry was found in the `MapFile`; if it's `null`, no value exists for the given key. If key was found, the value for that key is read into `val`, as well as being returned from the method call.

It might be helpful to understand how this is implemented. Here is a snippet of code that retrieves an entry for the `MapFile` we created in the previous section:

```
Text value = new Text();
reader.get(new IntWritable(496), value);
assertThat(value.toString(), is("One, two, buckle my shoe"));
```

For this operation, the `MapFile.Reader` reads the *index* file into memory (this is cached so that subsequent random access calls will use the same in-memory index). The reader then performs a binary search on the in-memory index to find the key in the index that is less than or equal to the search key, 496. In this example, the index key found is 385, with value 18030, which is the offset in the *data* file. Next, the reader seeks to this offset in the *data* file and reads entries until the key is greater than or equal to the search key (496). In this case, a match is found and the value is read from the *data* file. Overall, a lookup takes a single disk seek and a scan through up to 128 entries on disk. For a random-access read, this is actually very efficient.

The `getClosest()` method is like `get()`, except it returns the "closest" match to the specified key rather than returning `null` on no match. More precisely, if the `MapFile` contains the specified key, then that is the entry returned; otherwise, the key in the `MapFile` that is immediately after (or before, according to a `boolean` argument) the specified key is returned.

A very large `MapFile`'s index can take up a lot of memory. Rather than reindex to change the index interval, it is possible to load only a fraction of the index keys into memory when reading the `MapFile` by setting the `io.map.index.skip` property. This property is normally 0, which means no index keys are skipped; a value of 1 means skip one key for every key in the index (so every other key ends up in the index), 2 means skip two keys for every key in the index (so one third of the keys end up in the index), and so on. Larger skip values save memory but at the expense of lookup time, since on average, more entries have to be scanned on disk.

MapFile variants

Hadoop comes with a few variants on the general key-value MapFile interface:

- SetFile is a specialization of MapFile for storing a set of Writable keys. The keys must be added in sorted order.
- ArrayFile is a MapFile where the key is an integer representing the index of the element in the array and the value is a Writable value.
- BloomMapFile is a MapFile that offers a fast version of the get() method, especially for sparsely populated files. The implementation uses a dynamic bloom filter for testing whether a given key is in the map. The test is very fast because it is in-memory, but it has a nonzero probability of false positives, in which case the regular get() method is called.

  There are two tuning parameters: io.mapfile.bloom.size for the (approximate) number of entries in the map (default 1,048,576) and io.map file.bloom.error.rate for the desired maximum error rate (default 0.005, which is 0.5%).

Converting a SequenceFile to a MapFile

One way of looking at a MapFile is as an indexed and sorted SequenceFile. So it's quite natural to want to be able to convert a SequenceFile into a MapFile. We covered how to sort a SequenceFile in "Sorting and merging SequenceFiles" on page 136, so here we look at how to create an index for a SequenceFile. The program in Example 4-17 hinges around the static utility method fix() on MapFile, which re-creates the index for a MapFile.

Example 4-17. Re-creating the index for a MapFile

```
public class MapFileFixer {

  public static void main(String[] args) throws Exception {
    String mapUri = args[0];

    Configuration conf = new Configuration();

    FileSystem fs = FileSystem.get(URI.create(mapUri), conf);
    Path map = new Path(mapUri);
    Path mapData = new Path(map, MapFile.DATA_FILE_NAME);

    // Get key and value types from data sequence file
    SequenceFile.Reader reader = new SequenceFile.Reader(fs, mapData, conf);
    Class keyClass = reader.getKeyClass();
    Class valueClass = reader.getValueClass();
    reader.close();
```

```
    // Create the map file index file
    long entries = MapFile.fix(fs, map, keyClass, valueClass, false, conf);
    System.out.printf("Created MapFile %s with %d entries\n", map, entries);
  }
}
```

The fix() method is usually used for recreating corrupted indexes, but because it creates a new index from scratch, it's exactly what we need here. The recipe is as follows:

1. Sort the sequence file *numbers.seq* into a new directory called *number.map* that will become the MapFile (if the sequence file is already sorted, you can skip this step; instead, copy it to a file *number.map/data*, and go to step 3):

   ```
   % hadoop jar $HADOOP_INSTALL/hadoop-*-examples.jar sort -r 1 \
     -inFormat org.apache.hadoop.mapred.SequenceFileInputFormat \
     -outFormat org.apache.hadoop.mapred.SequenceFileOutputFormat \
     -outKey org.apache.hadoop.io.IntWritable \
     -outValue org.apache.hadoop.io.Text \
     numbers.seq numbers.map
   ```

2. Rename the MapReduce output to be the *data* file:

   ```
   % hadoop fs -mv numbers.map/part-00000 numbers.map/data
   ```

3. Create the *index* file:

   ```
   % hadoop MapFileFixer numbers.map
   Created MapFile numbers.map with 100 entries
   ```

The MapFile *numbers.map* now exists and can be used.

Developing a MapReduce Application

In Chapter 2, we introduced the MapReduce model. In this chapter, we look at the practical aspects of developing a MapReduce application in Hadoop.

Writing a program in MapReduce follows a certain pattern. You start by writing your map and reduce functions, ideally with unit tests to make sure they do what you expect. Then you write a driver program to run a job, which can run from your IDE using a small subset of the data to check that it is working. If it fails, you can use your IDE's debugger to find the source of the problem. With this information, you can expand your unit tests to cover this case and improve your mapper or reducer as appropriate to handle such input correctly.

When the program runs as expected against the small dataset, you are ready to unleash it on a cluster. Running against the full dataset is likely to expose some more issues, which you can fix as before, by expanding your tests and mapper or reducer to handle the new cases. Debugging failing programs in the cluster is a challenge, so we look at some common techniques to make it easier.

After the program is working, you may wish to do some tuning, first by running through some standard checks for making MapReduce programs faster and then by doing task profiling. Profiling distributed programs is not easy, but Hadoop has hooks to aid the process.

Before we start writing a MapReduce program, we need to set up and configure the development environment. And to do that, we need to learn a bit about how Hadoop does configuration.

The Configuration API

Components in Hadoop are configured using Hadoop's own configuration API. An instance of the Configuration class (found in the org.apache.hadoop.conf package) represents a collection of configuration *properties* and their values. Each property is named by a String, and the type of a value may be one of several types, including Java primitives such as boolean, int, long, and float, other useful types such as String, Class, and java.io.File, and collections of Strings.

Configurations read their properties from *resources*—XML files with a simple structure for defining name-value pairs. See Example 5-1.

Example 5-1. A simple configuration file, configuration-1.xml

```xml
<?xml version="1.0"?>
<configuration>
  <property>
    <name>color</name>
    <value>yellow</value>
    <description>Color</description>
  </property>

  <property>
    <name>size</name>
    <value>10</value>
    <description>Size</description>
  </property>

  <property>
    <name>weight</name>
    <value>heavy</value>
    <final>true</final>
    <description>Weight</description>
  </property>

  <property>
    <name>size-weight</name>
    <value>${size},${weight}</value>
    <description>Size and weight</description>
  </property>
</configuration>
```

Assuming this configuration file is in a file called *configuration-1.xml*, we can access its properties using a piece of code like this:

```java
Configuration conf = new Configuration();
conf.addResource("configuration-1.xml");
assertThat(conf.get("color"), is("yellow"));
assertThat(conf.getInt("size", 0), is(10));
assertThat(conf.get("breadth", "wide"), is("wide"));
```

There are a couple of things to note: type information is not stored in the XML file; instead, properties can be interpreted as a given type when they are read. Also, the get() methods allow you to specify a default value, which is used if the property is not defined in the XML file, as in the case of breadth here.

Combining Resources

Things get interesting when more than one resource is used to define a configuration. This is used in Hadoop to separate out the default properties for the system, defined internally in a file called *core-default.xml*, from the site-specific overrides in *core-site.xml*. The file in Example 5-2 defines the size and weight properties.

Example 5-2. A second configuration file, configuration-2.xml

```xml
<?xml version="1.0"?>
<configuration>
  <property>
    <name>size</name>
    <value>12</value>
  </property>

  <property>
    <name>weight</name>
    <value>light</value>
  </property>
</configuration>
```

Resources are added to a Configuration in order:

```
Configuration conf = new Configuration();
conf.addResource("configuration-1.xml");
conf.addResource("configuration-2.xml");
```

Properties defined in resources that are added later override the earlier definitions. So the size property takes its value from the second configuration file, *configuration-2.xml*:

```
assertThat(conf.getInt("size", 0), is(12));
```

However, properties that are marked as final cannot be overridden in later definitions. The weight property is final in the first configuration file, so the attempt to override it in the second fails, and it takes the value from the first:

```
assertThat(conf.get("weight"), is("heavy"));
```

Attempting to override final properties usually indicates a configuration error, so this results in a warning message being logged to aid diagnosis. Administrators mark properties as final in the daemon's site files that they don't want users to change in their client-side configuration files or job submission parameters.

Variable Expansion

Configuration properties can be defined in terms of other properties, or system properties. For example, the property `size-weight` in the first configuration file is defined as `${size},${weight}`, and these properties are expanded using the values found in the configuration:

```
assertThat(conf.get("size-weight"), is("12,heavy"));
```

System properties take priority over properties defined in resource files:

```
System.setProperty("size", "14");
assertThat(conf.get("size-weight"), is("14,heavy"));
```

This feature is useful for overriding properties on the command line by using -D*property=value* JVM arguments.

Note that although configuration properties can be defined in terms of system properties, unless system properties are redefined using configuration properties, they are *not* accessible through the configuration API. Hence:

```
System.setProperty("length", "2");
assertThat(conf.get("length"), is((String) null));
```

Setting Up the Development Environment

The first step is to create a project so you can build MapReduce programs and run them in local (standalone) mode from the command line or within your IDE. The Maven POM in Example 5-3 shows the dependencies needed for building and testing MapReduce programs.

Example 5-3. A Maven POM for building and testing a MapReduce application

```
<project>
  <modelVersion>4.0.0</modelVersion>
  <groupId>com.hadoopbook</groupId>
  <artifactId>hadoop-book-mr-dev</artifactId>
  <version>3.0</version>
  <properties>
    <project.build.sourceEncoding>UTF-8</project.build.sourceEncoding>
    <project.reporting.outputEncoding>UTF-8</project.reporting.outputEncoding>
  </properties>
  <dependencies>
    <!-- Hadoop main artifact -->
    <dependency>
      <groupId>org.apache.hadoop</groupId>
      <artifactId>hadoop-core</artifactId>
      <version>1.0.0</version>
    </dependency>
    <!-- Unit test artifacts -->
    <dependency>
      <groupId>junit</groupId>
      <artifactId>junit</artifactId>
```

```xml
        <version>4.10</version>
        <scope>test</scope>
    </dependency>
    <dependency>
        <groupId>org.hamcrest</groupId>
        <artifactId>hamcrest-all</artifactId>
        <version>1.1</version>
        <scope>test</scope>
    </dependency>
    <dependency>
        <groupId>org.apache.mrunit</groupId>
        <artifactId>mrunit</artifactId>
        <version>0.8.0-incubating</version>
        <scope>test</scope>
    </dependency>
    <!-- Hadoop test artifacts for running mini clusters -->
    <dependency>
        <groupId>org.apache.hadoop</groupId>
        <artifactId>hadoop-test</artifactId>
        <version>1.0.0</version>
        <scope>test</scope>
    </dependency>
    <!-- Missing dependency for running mini clusters -->
    <dependency>
        <groupId>com.sun.jersey</groupId>
        <artifactId>jersey-core</artifactId>
        <version>1.8</version>
        <scope>test</scope>
    </dependency>
</dependencies>
<build>
    <finalName>hadoop-examples</finalName>
    <plugins>
        <plugin>
            <groupId>org.apache.maven.plugins</groupId>
            <artifactId>maven-compiler-plugin</artifactId>
            <version>2.3.2</version>
            <configuration>
                <source>1.6</source>
                <target>1.6</target>
            </configuration>
        </plugin>
        <plugin>
            <groupId>org.apache.maven.plugins</groupId>
            <artifactId>maven-jar-plugin</artifactId>
            <version>2.4</version>
            <configuration>
                <outputDirectory>${basedir}</outputDirectory>
            </configuration>
        </plugin>
    </plugins>
</build>
</project>
```

The dependencies section is the interesting part of the POM. (It is straightforward to use another build tool, such as Gradle or Ant with Ivy, as long as you use the same set of dependencies defined here.) For building MapReduce jobs you only need to have the hadoop-core dependency, which contains all the Hadoop classes. For running unit tests we use junit, as well as a couple of helper libraries: hamcrest-all provides useful matchers for writing test assertions, and mrunit is used for writing MapReduce tests. The hadoop-test library contains the "mini-" clusters that are useful for testing with Hadoop clusters running in a single JVM (we also pull in jersey-core because it is missing from the Hadoop POM).

 The JAR packaging has changed in releases after 1.x, so unfortunately you can't just change the version number of the hadoop-core dependency and expect it to work. The example code on the book's website contains up-to-date dependency declarations for different Hadoop releases.

Many IDEs can read Maven POMs directly, so you can just point them at the directory containing the *pom.xml* file and start writing code.[1] Alternatively, you can use Maven to generate configuration files for your IDE. For example, the following creates Eclipse configuration files so you can import the project into Eclipse:

```
% mvn eclipse:eclipse -DdownloadSources=true -DdownloadJavadocs=true
```

Managing Configuration

When developing Hadoop applications, it is common to switch between running the application locally and running it on a cluster. In fact, you may have several clusters you work with, or you may have a local "pseudodistributed" cluster that you like to test on (a pseudodistributed cluster is one whose daemons all run on the local machine; setting up this mode is covered in Appendix A, too).

One way to accommodate these variations is to have Hadoop configuration files containing the connection settings for each cluster you run against and specify which one you are using when you run Hadoop applications or tools. As a matter of best practice, it's recommended to keep these files outside Hadoop's installation directory tree, as this makes it easy to switch between Hadoop versions without duplicating or losing settings.

For the purposes of this book, we assume the existence of a directory called *conf* that contains three configuration files: *hadoop-local.xml*, *hadoop-localhost.xml*, and *hadoop-cluster.xml* (these are available in the example code for this book). Note that there is nothing special about the names of these files; they are just convenient ways to package up some configuration settings. (Compare this to Table A-1 in Appendix A, which sets out the equivalent server-side configurations.)

---

1. Karmasphere (*http://www.karmasphere.com/*) also provides Eclipse and NetBeans plug-ins for developing and running MapReduce jobs and browsing Hadoop clusters.

The *hadoop-local.xml* file contains the default Hadoop configuration for the default filesystem and the jobtracker:

```xml
<?xml version="1.0"?>
<configuration>

  <property>
    <name>fs.default.name</name>
    <value>file:///</value>
  </property>

  <property>
    <name>mapred.job.tracker</name>
    <value>local</value>
  </property>

</configuration>
```

The settings in *hadoop-localhost.xml* point to a namenode and a jobtracker both running on localhost:

```xml
<?xml version="1.0"?>
<configuration>

  <property>
    <name>fs.default.name</name>
    <value>hdfs://localhost/</value>
  </property>

  <property>
    <name>mapred.job.tracker</name>
    <value>localhost:8021</value>
  </property>

</configuration>
```

Finally, *hadoop-cluster.xml* contains details of the cluster's namenode and jobtracker addresses. In practice, you would name the file after the name of the cluster, rather than "cluster" as we have here:

```xml
<?xml version="1.0"?>
<configuration>

  <property>
    <name>fs.default.name</name>
    <value>hdfs://namenode/</value>
  </property>

  <property>
    <name>mapred.job.tracker</name>
    <value>jobtracker:8021</value>
  </property>

</configuration>
```

You can add other configuration properties to these files as needed. For example, if you wanted to set your Hadoop username for a particular cluster, you could do it in the appropriate file.

Setting User Identity

The user identity that Hadoop uses for permissions in HDFS is determined by running the whoami command on the client system. Similarly, the group names are derived from the output of running groups.

If, however, your Hadoop user identity is different from the name of your user account on your client machine, you can explicitly set your Hadoop username and group names by setting the hadoop.job.ugi property. The username and group names are specified as a comma-separated list of strings (e.g., preston,directors,inventors would set the username to preston and the group names to directors and inventors).

You can set the user identity that the HDFS web interface runs as by setting dfs.web.ugi using the same syntax. By default, it is webuser,webgroup, which is not a super user, so system files are not accessible through the web interface.

Notice that, by default, there is no authentication with this system. See "Security" on page 325 for how to use Kerberos authentication with Hadoop.

With this setup, it is easy to use any configuration with the -conf command-line switch. For example, the following command shows a directory listing on the HDFS server running in pseudodistributed mode on localhost:

```
% hadoop fs -conf conf/hadoop-localhost.xml -ls .
Found 2 items
drwxr-xr-x   - tom supergroup          0 2009-04-08 10:32 /user/tom/input
drwxr-xr-x   - tom supergroup          0 2009-04-08 13:09 /user/tom/output
```

If you omit the -conf option, you pick up the Hadoop configuration in the *conf* subdirectory under $HADOOP_INSTALL. Depending on how you set this up, this may be for a standalone setup or a pseudodistributed cluster.

Tools that come with Hadoop support the -conf option, but it's also straightforward to make your programs (such as programs that run MapReduce jobs) support it, too, using the Tool interface.

GenericOptionsParser, Tool, and ToolRunner

Hadoop comes with a few helper classes for making it easier to run jobs from the command line. GenericOptionsParser is a class that interprets common Hadoop command-line options and sets them on a Configuration object for your application to use as desired. You don't usually use GenericOptionsParser directly, as it's more convenient to implement the Tool interface and run your application with the ToolRunner, which uses GenericOptionsParser internally:

```
public interface Tool extends Configurable {
  int run(String [] args) throws Exception;
}
```

Example 5-4 shows a very simple implementation of Tool that prints the keys and values of all the properties in the Tool's Configuration object.

Example 5-4. An example Tool implementation for printing the properties in a Configuration

```
public class ConfigurationPrinter extends Configured implements Tool {

  static {
    Configuration.addDefaultResource("hdfs-default.xml");
    Configuration.addDefaultResource("hdfs-site.xml");
    Configuration.addDefaultResource("mapred-default.xml");
    Configuration.addDefaultResource("mapred-site.xml");
  }

  @Override
  public int run(String[] args) throws Exception {
    Configuration conf = getConf();
    for (Entry<String, String> entry: conf) {
      System.out.printf("%s=%s\n", entry.getKey(), entry.getValue());
    }
    return 0;
  }

  public static void main(String[] args) throws Exception {
    int exitCode = ToolRunner.run(new ConfigurationPrinter(), args);
    System.exit(exitCode);
  }
}
```

We make ConfigurationPrinter a subclass of Configured, which is an implementation of the Configurable interface. All implementations of Tool need to implement Configurable (since Tool extends it), and subclassing Configured is often the easiest way to achieve this. The run() method obtains the Configuration using Configurable's getConf() method and then iterates over it, printing each property to standard output.

The static block makes sure that the HDFS and MapReduce configurations are picked up in addition to the core ones (which Configuration knows about already).

ConfigurationPrinter's main() method does not invoke its own run() method directly. Instead, we call ToolRunner's static run() method, which takes care of creating a Configuration object for the Tool before calling its run() method. ToolRunner also uses a GenericOptionsParser to pick up any standard options specified on the command line and to set them on the Configuration instance. We can see the effect of picking up the properties specified in *conf/hadoop-localhost.xml* by running the following command:

```
% mvn compile
% export HADOOP_CLASSPATH=target/classes/
% hadoop ConfigurationPrinter -conf conf/hadoop-localhost.xml \
```

```
| grep mapred.job.tracker=
mapred.job.tracker=localhost:8021
```

Which Properties Can I Set?

ConfigurationPrinter is a useful tool for discovering what a property is set to in your environment.

You can also see the default settings for all the public properties in Hadoop by looking in the *docs* directory of your Hadoop installation for HTML files called *core-default.html*, *hdfs-default.html*, and *mapred-default.html*. Each property has a description that explains what it is for and what values it can be set to.

The default settings documentation files can be found online at URLs of the form *http://hadoop.apache.org/common/docs/r<version>/<component>-default.html*; for example, the HDFS defaults for release 1.0.0 are at *http://hadoop.apache.org/common/docs/r1.0.0/hdfs-default.html*.

Be aware that some properties have no effect when set in the client configuration. For example, if you set mapred.tasktracker.map.tasks.maximum in your job submission with the expectation that it would change the number of task slots for the tasktrackers running your job, you would be disappointed, because this property is honored only if set in the tasktracker's *mapred-site.xml* file. In general, you can tell the component where a property should be set by its name, so the fact that mapred.tasktracker.map.tasks.maximum starts with mapred.tasktracker gives you a clue that it can be set only for the tasktracker daemon. This is not a hard and fast rule, however, so in some cases you may need to resort to trial and error, or even to reading the source.

We discuss many of Hadoop's most important configuration properties throughout this book.

GenericOptionsParser also allows you to set individual properties. For example:

```
% hadoop ConfigurationPrinter -D color=yellow | grep color
color=yellow
```

The -D option is used to set the configuration property with key color to the value yellow. Options specified with -D take priority over properties from the configuration files. This is very useful because you put defaults into configuration files and then override them with the -D option as needed. A common example of this is setting the number of reducers for a MapReduce job via -D mapred.reduce.tasks=*n*. This will override the number of reducers set on the cluster or set in any client-side configuration files.

The other options that GenericOptionsParser and ToolRunner support are listed in Table 5-1. You can find more on Hadoop's configuration API in "The Configuration API" on page 144.

Do not confuse setting Hadoop properties using the -D *property=value* option to GenericOptionsParser (and ToolRunner) with setting JVM system properties using the -D*property=value* option to the java command. The syntax for JVM system properties does not allow any whitespace between the D and the property name, whereas GenericOptionsParser does allow whitespace.

JVM system properties are retrieved from the java.lang.System class, whereas Hadoop properties are accessible only from a Configuration object. So, the following command will print nothing, even though the color system property has been set (via HADOOP_OPTS), because the System class is not used by ConfigurationPrinter:

```
% HADOOP_OPTS='-Dcolor=yellow' \
hadoop ConfigurationPrinter | grep color
```

If you want to be able to set configuration through system properties, you need to mirror the system properties of interest in the configuration file. See "Variable Expansion" on page 146 for further discussion.

Table 5-1. GenericOptionsParser and ToolRunner options

Option	Description
-D *property=value*	Sets the given Hadoop configuration property to the given value. Overrides any default or site properties in the configuration and any properties set via the -conf option.
-conf *filename* ...	Adds the given files to the list of resources in the configuration. This is a convenient way to set site properties or to set a number of properties at once.
-fs *uri*	Sets the default filesystem to the given URI. Shortcut for -D fs.default.name=*uri*
-jt *host:port*	Sets the jobtracker to the given host and port. Shortcut for -D mapred.job.tracker=*host:port*
-files *file1,file2,...*	Copies the specified files from the local filesystem (or any filesystem if a scheme is specified) to the shared filesystem used by the jobtracker (usually HDFS) and makes them available to MapReduce programs in the task's working directory. (See "Distributed Cache" on page 289 for more on the distributed cache mechanism for copying files to tasktracker machines.)
-archives *archive1,archive2,...*	Copies the specified archives from the local filesystem (or any filesystem if a scheme is specified) to the shared filesystem used by the jobtracker (usually HDFS), unarchives them, and makes them available to MapReduce programs in the task's working directory.
-libjars *jar1,jar2,...*	Copies the specified JAR files from the local filesystem (or any filesystem if a scheme is specified) to the shared filesystem used by the jobtracker (usually HDFS), and adds them to the MapReduce task's classpath. This option is a useful way of shipping JAR files that a job is dependent on.

Writing a Unit Test with MRUnit

The map and reduce functions in MapReduce are easy to test in isolation, which is a consequence of their functional style. MRUnit (*http://incubator.apache.org/mrunit/*) is a testing library that makes it easy to pass known inputs to a mapper or a reducer and check that the outputs are as expected. MRUnit is used in conjunction with a standard test execution framework, such as JUnit, so you can run the tests for MapReduce jobs as a part of your normal development environment. For example, all of the tests described here can be run from within an IDE by following the instructions from earlier in this chapter in "Setting Up the Development Environment" on page 146.

Mapper

The test for the mapper is shown in Example 5-5.

Example 5-5. Unit test for MaxTemperatureMapper

```
import java.io.IOException;
import org.apache.hadoop.io.*;
import org.apache.hadoop.mrunit.mapreduce.MapDriver;
import org.junit.*;

public class MaxTemperatureMapperTest {

  @Test
  public void processesValidRecord() throws IOException, InterruptedException {
    Text value = new Text("0043011990999991950051518004+68750+023550FM-12+0382" +
                                        // Year ^^^^
      "99999V0203201N00261220001CN9999999N9-00111+99999999999");
                                        // Temperature ^^^^^
    new MapDriver<LongWritable, Text, Text, IntWritable>()
      .withMapper(new MaxTemperatureMapper())
      .withInputValue(value)
      .withOutput(new Text("1950"), new IntWritable(-11))
      .runTest();
  }
}
```

The idea of the test is very simple: pass a weather record as input to the mapper, and check that the output is the year and temperature reading.

Since we are testing the mapper, we use MRUnit's `MapDriver`, which we configure with the mapper under test (`MaxTemperatureMapper`), the input value, and the expected output key (a `Text` object representing the year, 1950) and expected output value (an `IntWritable` representing the temperature, -1.1°C), before finally calling the `runTest()` method to execute the test. If the expected output values are not emitted by the mapper, MRUnit will fail the test. Notice that we didn't set the input key because our mapper ignores it.

Proceeding in a test-driven fashion, we create a `Mapper` implementation that passes the test (see Example 5-6). Because we will be evolving the classes in this chapter, each is put in a different package indicating its version for ease of exposition. For example, `v1.MaxTemperatureMapper` is version 1 of `MaxTemperatureMapper`. In reality, of course, you would evolve classes without repackaging them.

Example 5-6. First version of a Mapper that passes MaxTemperatureMapperTest

```java
public class MaxTemperatureMapper
  extends Mapper<LongWritable, Text, Text, IntWritable> {

  @Override
  public void map(LongWritable key, Text value, Context context)
      throws IOException, InterruptedException {

    String line = value.toString();
    String year = line.substring(15, 19);
    int airTemperature = Integer.parseInt(line.substring(87, 92));
    context.write(new Text(year), new IntWritable(airTemperature));
  }
}
```

This is a very simple implementation that pulls the year and temperature fields from the line and writes them to the `Context`. Let's add a test for missing values, which in the raw data are represented by a temperature of +9999:

```java
    @Test
    public void ignoresMissingTemperatureRecord() throws IOException,
        InterruptedException {
      Text value = new Text("0043011990999991950051518004+68750+023550FM-12+0382" +
                                    // Year ^^^^
        "99999V0203201N00261220001CN9999999N9+99991+99999999999");
                                    // Temperature ^^^^^
      new MapDriver<LongWritable, Text, Text, IntWritable>()
        .withMapper(new MaxTemperatureMapper())
        .withInputValue(value)
        .runTest();
    }
```

A `MapDriver` can be used to check for zero, one, or more output records, according to the number of times that `withOutput()` is called. In our application, since records with missing temperatures should be filtered out, this test asserts that no output is produced for this particular input value.

The existing test fails with a `NumberFormatException`, as `parseInt()` cannot parse integers with a leading plus sign, so we fix up the implementation (version 2) to handle missing values:

```java
    @Override
    public void map(LongWritable key, Text value, Context context)
        throws IOException, InterruptedException {

      String line = value.toString();
```

```
        String year = line.substring(15, 19);
        String temp = line.substring(87, 92);
        if (!missing(temp)) {
            int airTemperature = Integer.parseInt(temp);
            context.write(new Text(year), new IntWritable(airTemperature));
        }
    }

    private boolean missing(String temp) {
        return temp.equals("+9999");
    }
}
```

With the test for the mapper passing, we move on to writing the reducer.

Reducer

The reducer has to find the maximum value for a given key. Here's a simple test for this feature, which uses a ReduceDriver:

```
@Test
public void returnsMaximumIntegerInValues() throws IOException,
    InterruptedException {
    new ReduceDriver<Text, IntWritable, Text, IntWritable>()
        .withReducer(new MaxTemperatureReducer())
        .withInputKey(new Text("1950"))
        .withInputValues(Arrays.asList(new IntWritable(10), new IntWritable(5)))
        .withOutput(new Text("1950"), new IntWritable(10))
        .runTest();
}
```

We construct a list of some IntWritable values and then verify that MaxTemperatureReducer picks the largest. The code in Example 5-7 is for an implementation of MaxTemperatureReducer that passes the test.

Example 5-7. Reducer for the maximum temperature example

```
public class MaxTemperatureReducer
    extends Reducer<Text, IntWritable, Text, IntWritable> {

    @Override
    public void reduce(Text key, Iterable<IntWritable> values,
        Context context)
        throws IOException, InterruptedException {

        int maxValue = Integer.MIN_VALUE;
        for (IntWritable value : values) {
            maxValue = Math.max(maxValue, value.get());
        }
        context.write(key, new IntWritable(maxValue));
    }
}
```

Running Locally on Test Data

Now that we have the mapper and reducer working on controlled inputs, the next step is to write a job driver and run it on some test data on a development machine.

Running a Job in a Local Job Runner

Using the `Tool` interface introduced earlier in the chapter, it's easy to write a driver to run our MapReduce job for finding the maximum temperature by year (see `MaxTemperatureDriver` in Example 5-8).

Example 5-8. Application to find the maximum temperature

```
public class MaxTemperatureDriver extends Configured implements Tool {

  @Override
  public int run(String[] args) throws Exception {
    if (args.length != 2) {
      System.err.printf("Usage: %s [generic options] <input> <output>\n",
          getClass().getSimpleName());
      ToolRunner.printGenericCommandUsage(System.err);
      return -1;
    }

    Job job = new Job(getConf(), "Max temperature");
    job.setJarByClass(getClass());

    FileInputFormat.addInputPath(job, new Path(args[0]));
    FileOutputFormat.setOutputPath(job, new Path(args[1]));

    job.setMapperClass(MaxTemperatureMapper.class);
    job.setCombinerClass(MaxTemperatureReducer.class);
    job.setReducerClass(MaxTemperatureReducer.class);

    job.setOutputKeyClass(Text.class);
    job.setOutputValueClass(IntWritable.class);

    return job.waitForCompletion(true) ? 0 : 1;
  }

  public static void main(String[] args) throws Exception {
    int exitCode = ToolRunner.run(new MaxTemperatureDriver(), args);
    System.exit(exitCode);
  }
}
```

`MaxTemperatureDriver` implements the `Tool` interface, so we get the benefit of being able to set the options that `GenericOptionsParser` supports. The `run()` method constructs a `Job` object based on the tool's configuration, which it uses to launch a job. Among the possible job configuration parameters, we set the input and output file paths, the mapper, reducer, and combiner classes, and the output types (the input types are determined by the input format, which defaults to `TextInputFormat` and has `LongWritable` keys and `Text` values). It's also a good idea to set a name for the job (Max temperature) so that you can pick it out in the job list during execution and after it has completed. By default, the name is the name of the JAR file, which normally is not particularly descriptive.

Now we can run this application against some local files. Hadoop comes with a local job runner, a cut-down version of the MapReduce execution engine for running MapReduce jobs in a single JVM. It's designed for testing and is very convenient for use in an IDE, since you can run it in a debugger to step through the code in your mapper and reducer.

> The local job runner is designed only for simple testing of MapReduce programs, so inevitably it differs from the full MapReduce implementation. The biggest difference is that it can't run more than one reducer. (It can support the zero reducer case, too.) Normally, this is not a problem, as most applications can work with one reducer, although on a cluster you would choose a larger number to take advantage of parallelism. The thing to watch out for is that even if you set the number of reducers to a value over one, the local runner will silently ignore the setting and use a single reducer.
>
> This limitation may be removed in a future version of Hadoop.

The local job runner is enabled by a configuration setting. Normally, `mapred.job.tracker` is a *host:port* pair to specify the address of the jobtracker, but when it has the special value of `local` (which is actually the default), the job is run in-process without accessing an external jobtracker.

In MapReduce 2 (covered in "YARN (MapReduce 2)" on page 196), the equivalent setting is `mapreduce.framework.name`, which must be set to `local` (again the default).

From the command line, we can run the driver by typing:

```
% mvn compile
% export HADOOP_CLASSPATH=target/classes/
% hadoop v2.MaxTemperatureDriver -conf conf/hadoop-local.xml \
    input/ncdc/micro output
```

Equivalently, we could use the `-fs` and `-jt` options provided by `GenericOptionsParser`:

```
% hadoop v2.MaxTemperatureDriver -fs file:/// -jt local input/ncdc/micro output
```

This command executes `MaxTemperatureDriver` using input from the local *input/ncdc/micro* directory, producing output in the local *output* directory. Note that although we've set `-fs` so we use the local filesystem (`file:///`), the local job runner will actually work fine against any filesystem, including HDFS (and it can be handy to do this if you have a few files that are on HDFS).

When we run the program, it fails and prints the following exception:

```
java.lang.NumberFormatException: For input string: "+0000"
```

Fixing the mapper

This exception shows that the map method still can't parse positive temperatures. (If the stack trace hadn't given us enough information to diagnose the fault, we could run the test in a local debugger, since it runs in a single JVM.) Earlier, we made it handle the special case of a missing temperature, +9999, but not the general case of any positive temperature. With more logic going into the mapper, it makes sense to factor out a parser class to encapsulate the parsing logic; see Example 5-9 (now on version 3).

Example 5-9. A class for parsing weather records in NCDC format

```
public class NcdcRecordParser {

  private static final int MISSING_TEMPERATURE = 9999;

  private String year;
  private int airTemperature;
  private String quality;

  public void parse(String record) {
    year = record.substring(15, 19);
    String airTemperatureString;
    // Remove leading plus sign as parseInt doesn't like them
    if (record.charAt(87) == '+') {
      airTemperatureString = record.substring(88, 92);
    } else {
      airTemperatureString = record.substring(87, 92);
    }
    airTemperature = Integer.parseInt(airTemperatureString);
    quality = record.substring(92, 93);
  }

  public void parse(Text record) {
    parse(record.toString());
  }

  public boolean isValidTemperature() {
    return airTemperature != MISSING_TEMPERATURE && quality.matches("[01459]");
  }

  public String getYear() {
    return year;
  }

  public int getAirTemperature() {
    return airTemperature;
  }
}
```

The resulting mapper is much simpler (see Example 5-10). It just calls the parser's parse() method, which parses the fields of interest from a line of input, checks whether a valid temperature was found using the isValidTemperature() query method, and if it was, retrieves the year and the temperature using the getter methods on the parser. Notice that we also check the quality status field as well as missing temperatures in isValidTemperature() to filter out poor temperature readings.

Another benefit of creating a parser class is that it makes it easy to write related mappers for similar jobs without duplicating code. It also gives us the opportunity to write unit tests directly against the parser, for more targeted testing.

Example 5-10. A Mapper that uses a utility class to parse records

```java
public class MaxTemperatureMapper
  extends Mapper<LongWritable, Text, Text, IntWritable> {

  private NcdcRecordParser parser = new NcdcRecordParser();

  @Override
  public void map(LongWritable key, Text value, Context context)
      throws IOException, InterruptedException {

    parser.parse(value);
    if (parser.isValidTemperature()) {
      context.write(new Text(parser.getYear()),
          new IntWritable(parser.getAirTemperature()));
    }
  }
}
```

With these changes, the test passes.

Testing the Driver

Apart from the flexible configuration options offered by making your application implement Tool, you also make it more testable because it allows you to inject an arbitrary Configuration. You can take advantage of this to write a test that uses a local job runner to run a job against known input data, which checks that the output is as expected.

There are two approaches to doing this. The first is to use the local job runner and run the job against a test file on the local filesystem. The code in Example 5-11 gives an idea of how to do this.

Example 5-11. A test for MaxTemperatureDriver that uses a local, in-process job runner

```java
@Test
public void test() throws Exception {
  Configuration conf = new Configuration();
  conf.set("fs.default.name", "file:///");
  conf.set("mapred.job.tracker", "local");

  Path input = new Path("input/ncdc/micro");
  Path output = new Path("output");
```

```
    FileSystem fs = FileSystem.getLocal(conf);
    fs.delete(output, true); // delete old output

    MaxTemperatureDriver driver = new MaxTemperatureDriver();
    driver.setConf(conf);

    int exitCode = driver.run(new String[] {
        input.toString(), output.toString() });
    assertThat(exitCode, is(0));

    checkOutput(conf, output);
  }
```

The test explicitly sets `fs.default.name` and `mapred.job.tracker` so it uses the local filesystem and the local job runner. It then runs the `MaxTemperatureDriver` via its `Tool` interface against a small amount of known data. At the end of the test, the `checkOutput()` method is called to compare the actual output with the expected output, line by line.

The second way of testing the driver is to run it using a "mini-" cluster. Hadoop has a set of testing classes, called `MiniDFSCluster`, `MiniMRCluster`, and `MiniYARNCluster`, that provide a programmatic way of creating in-process clusters. Unlike the local job runner, these allow testing against the full HDFS and MapReduce machinery. Bear in mind, too, that tasktrackers in a mini-cluster launch separate JVMs to run tasks in, which can make debugging more difficult.

Mini-clusters are used extensively in Hadoop's own automated test suite, but they can be used for testing user code, too. Hadoop's `ClusterMapReduceTestCase` abstract class provides a useful base for writing such a test, handles the details of starting and stopping the in-process HDFS and MapReduce clusters in its `setUp()` and `tearDown()` methods, and generates a suitable configuration object that is set up to work with them. Subclasses need only populate data in HDFS (perhaps by copying from a local file), run a MapReduce job, and confirm the output is as expected. Refer to the `MaxTemperature DriverMiniTest` class in the example code that comes with this book for the listing.

Tests like this serve as regression tests, and are a useful repository of input edge cases and their expected results. As you encounter more test cases, you can simply add them to the input file and update the file of expected output accordingly.

Running on a Cluster

Now that we are happy with the program running on a small test dataset, we are ready to try it on the full dataset on a Hadoop cluster. Chapter 9 covers how to set up a fully distributed cluster, although you can also work through this section on a pseudo-distributed cluster.

Packaging a Job

The local job runner uses a single JVM to run a job, so as long as all the classes that your job needs are on its classpath, then things will just work.

In a distributed setting, things are a little more complex. For a start, a job's classes must be packaged into a *job JAR file* to send to the cluster. Hadoop will find the job JAR automatically by searching for the JAR on the driver's classpath that contains the class set in the setJarByClass() method (on JobConf or Job). Alternatively, if you want to set an explicit JAR file by its file path, you can use the setJar() method.

Creating a job JAR file is conveniently achieved using a build tool such as Ant or Maven. The following Maven command, for example, will create a JAR file called *hadoop-examples.jar* in the project directory containing all of the compiled classes:

```
% mvn package -DskipTests
```

If you have a single job per JAR, you can specify the main class to run in the JAR file's manifest. If the main class is not in the manifest, it must be specified on the command line (as we will see shortly when we run the job).

Any dependent JAR files can be packaged in a *lib* subdirectory in the job JAR file, although there are other ways to include dependencies, discussed later. Similarly, resource files can be packaged in a *classes* subdirectory. (This is analogous to a Java *Web application archive*, or WAR file, except in that case the JAR files go in a *WEB-INF/ lib* subdirectory and classes go in a *WEB-INF/classes* subdirectory in the WAR file.)

The client classpath

The user's client-side classpath set by hadoop jar <*jar*> is made up of:

- The job JAR file
- Any JAR files in the *lib* directory of the job JAR file, and the *classes* directory (if present)
- The classpath defined by HADOOP_CLASSPATH, if set

Incidentally, this explains why you have to set HADOOP_CLASSPATH to point to dependent classes and libraries if you are running using the local job runner without a job JAR (hadoop *CLASSNAME*).

The task classpath

On a cluster (and this includes pseudodistributed mode), map and reduce tasks run in separate JVMs, and their classpaths are *not* controlled by HADOOP_CLASSPATH. HADOOP_CLASSPATH is a client-side setting and only sets the classpath for the driver JVM, which submits the job.

Instead, the user's task classpath is comprised of the following:

- The job JAR file
- Any JAR files contained in the *lib* directory of the job JAR file, and the *classes* directory (if present)
- Any files added to the distributed cache, using the `-libjars` option (see Table 5-1), or the `addFileToClassPath()` method on `DistributedCache` (old API), or `Job` (new API)

Packaging dependencies

Given these different ways of controlling what is on the client and task classpaths, there are corresponding options for including library dependencies for a job.

- Unpack the libraries and repackage them in the job JAR.
- Package the libraries in the *lib* directory of the job JAR.
- Keep the libraries separate from the job JAR, and add them to the client classpath via `HADOOP_CLASSPATH` and to the task classpath via `-libjars`.

The last option, using the distributed cache, is simplest from a build point of view because dependencies don't need rebundling in the job JAR. Also, the distributed cache can mean fewer transfers of JAR files around the cluster, since files may be cached on a node between tasks. (You can read more about the distributed cache on page 289.)

Task classpath precedence

User JAR files are added to the end of both the client classpath and the task classpath, which in some cases can cause a dependency conflict with Hadoop's built-in libraries if Hadoop uses a different, incompatible version of a library that your code uses. Sometimes you need to be able to control the task classpath order so that your classes are picked up first. On the client side, you can force Hadoop to put the user classpath first in the search order by setting the `HADOOP_USER_CLASSPATH_FIRST` environment variable to true. For the task classpath, you can set `mapreduce.task.classpath.first` to true. Note that by setting these options you change the class loading for Hadoop framework dependencies (but only in your job), which could potentially cause the job submission or task to fail, so use these options with caution.

Launching a Job

To launch the job, we need to run the driver, specifying the cluster that we want to run the job on with the `-conf` option (we equally could have used the `-fs` and `-jt` options):

```
% unset HADOOP_CLASSPATH
% hadoop jar hadoop-examples.jar v3.MaxTemperatureDriver \
  -conf conf/hadoop-cluster.xml input/ncdc/all max-temp
```

We unset the HADOOP_CLASSPATH environment variable because we don't have any third-party dependencies for this job. If it were left set to target/classes/ (from earlier in the chapter), Hadoop wouldn't be able to find the job JAR if it loaded the MaxTemperatureDriver class from *target/classes* rather than the JAR, and the job would fail.

The waitForCompletion() method on Job launches the job and polls for progress, writing a line summarizing the map and reduce's progress whenever either changes. Here's the output (some lines have been removed for clarity):

```
09/04/11 08:15:52 INFO mapred.FileInputFormat: Total input paths to process : 101
09/04/11 08:15:53 INFO mapred.JobClient: Running job: job_200904110811_0002
09/04/11 08:15:54 INFO mapred.JobClient:  map 0% reduce 0%
09/04/11 08:16:06 INFO mapred.JobClient:  map 28% reduce 0%
09/04/11 08:16:07 INFO mapred.JobClient:  map 30% reduce 0%
...
09/04/11 08:21:36 INFO mapred.JobClient:  map 100% reduce 100%
09/04/11 08:21:38 INFO mapred.JobClient: Job complete: job_200904110811_0002
09/04/11 08:21:38 INFO mapred.JobClient: Counters: 19
09/04/11 08:21:38 INFO mapred.JobClient:   Job Counters
09/04/11 08:21:38 INFO mapred.JobClient:     Launched reduce tasks=32
09/04/11 08:21:38 INFO mapred.JobClient:     Rack-local map tasks=82
09/04/11 08:21:38 INFO mapred.JobClient:     Launched map tasks=127
09/04/11 08:21:38 INFO mapred.JobClient:     Data-local map tasks=45
09/04/11 08:21:38 INFO mapred.JobClient:   FileSystemCounters
09/04/11 08:21:38 INFO mapred.JobClient:     FILE_BYTES_READ=12667214
09/04/11 08:21:38 INFO mapred.JobClient:     HDFS_BYTES_READ=33485841275
09/04/11 08:21:38 INFO mapred.JobClient:     FILE_BYTES_WRITTEN=989397
09/04/11 08:21:38 INFO mapred.JobClient:     HDFS_BYTES_WRITTEN=904
09/04/11 08:21:38 INFO mapred.JobClient:   Map-Reduce Framework
09/04/11 08:21:38 INFO mapred.JobClient:     Reduce input groups=100
09/04/11 08:21:38 INFO mapred.JobClient:     Combine output records=4489
09/04/11 08:21:38 INFO mapred.JobClient:     Map input records=1209901509
09/04/11 08:21:38 INFO mapred.JobClient:     Reduce shuffle bytes=19140
09/04/11 08:21:38 INFO mapred.JobClient:     Reduce output records=100
09/04/11 08:21:38 INFO mapred.JobClient:     Spilled Records=9481
09/04/11 08:21:38 INFO mapred.JobClient:     Map output bytes=10282306995
09/04/11 08:21:38 INFO mapred.JobClient:     Map input bytes=274600205558
09/04/11 08:21:38 INFO mapred.JobClient:     Combine input records=1142482941
09/04/11 08:21:38 INFO mapred.JobClient:     Map output records=1142478555
09/04/11 08:21:38 INFO mapred.JobClient:     Reduce input records=103
```

The output includes more useful information. Before the job starts, its ID is printed; this is needed whenever you want to refer to the job—in logfiles, for example—or when interrogating it via the hadoop job command. When the job is complete, its statistics (known as counters) are printed out. These are very useful for confirming that the job did what you expected. For example, for this job we can see that around 275 GB of input data was analyzed (Map input bytes), read from around 34 GB of compressed files on HDFS (HDFS_BYTES_READ). The input was broken into 101 gzipped files of reasonable size, so there was no problem with not being able to split them.

Job, Task, and Task Attempt IDs

The format of a job ID is composed of the time that the jobtracker (not the job) started and an incrementing counter maintained by the jobtracker to uniquely identify the job to that instance of the jobtracker. So the job with this ID:

```
job_200904110811_0002
```

is the second (0002; job IDs are 1-based) job run by the jobtracker, which started at 08:11 on April 11, 2009. The counter is formatted with leading zeros to make job IDs sort nicely—in directory listings, for example. However, when the counter reaches 10000, it is *not* reset, resulting in longer job IDs (which don't sort so well).

Tasks belong to a job, and their IDs are formed by replacing the `job` prefix of a job ID with a `task` prefix and adding a suffix to identify the task within the job. For example:

```
task_200904110811_0002_m_000003
```

is the fourth (000003, task IDs are 0-based) map (m) task of the job with ID `job_200904110811_0002`. The task IDs are created for a job when it is initialized, so they do not necessarily dictate the order in which the tasks will be executed.

Tasks may be executed more than once, due to failure (see "Task failure" on page 202) or speculative execution (see "Speculative Execution" on page 215), so to identify different instances of a task execution, task attempts are given unique IDs on the jobtracker. For example:

```
attempt_200904110811_0002_m_000003_0
```

is the first (0; attempt IDs are 0-based) attempt at running task `task_200904110811_0002_m_000003`. Task attempts are allocated during the job run as needed, so their ordering represents the order in which they were created for tasktrackers to run.

The final count in the task attempt ID is incremented by 1,000 if the job is restarted after the jobtracker is restarted and recovers its running jobs (although this behavior is disabled by default; see "Jobtracker failure" on page 204).

The MapReduce Web UI

Hadoop comes with a web UI for viewing information about your jobs. It is useful for following a job's progress while it is running, as well as finding job statistics and logs after the job has completed. You can find the UI at *http://jobtracker-host:50030/*.

The jobtracker page

A screenshot of the home page is shown in Figure 5-1. The first section of the page gives details of the Hadoop installation, such as the version number and when it was compiled, and the current state of the jobtracker (in this case, running) and when it was started.

Next is a summary of the cluster, which has measures of cluster capacity and utilization. This shows the number of maps and reduces currently running on the cluster, the total number of job submissions, the number of tasktracker nodes currently available, and the cluster's capacity, in terms of the number of map and reduce slots available across the cluster ("Map Task Capacity" and "Reduce Task Capacity") and the number of available slots per node, on average. The number of tasktrackers that have been blacklisted by the jobtracker is listed as well (blacklisting is discussed in "Tasktracker failure" on page 204).

Below the summary, there is a section about the job scheduler that is running (here, the default). You can click through to see job queues.

Further down, we see sections for running, (successfully) completed, and failed jobs. Each of these sections has a table of jobs, with a row per job that shows the job's ID, owner, name (as set in the Job constructor or setJobName() method, both of which internally set the mapred.job.name property), and progress information.

Finally, at the foot of the page, there are links to the jobtracker's logs and the jobtracker's history, which contains information on all the jobs that the jobtracker has run. The main view displays only 100 jobs (configurable via the mapred.jobtracker.completeuserjobs.maximum property) before consigning them to the history page. Note also that the job history is persistent, so you can find jobs here from previous runs of the jobtracker.

Figure 5-1. Screenshot of the jobtracker page

Job History

Job history refers to the events and configuration for a completed job. It is retained regardless of whether the job was successful, in an attempt to provide interesting information for the user running a job.

Job history files are stored on the local filesystem of the jobtracker in a *history* subdirectory of the *logs* directory. It is possible to set the location to an arbitrary Hadoop filesystem via the hadoop.job.history.location property. The jobtracker's history files are kept for 30 days before being deleted by the system.

A second copy is also stored for the user in the *_logs/history* subdirectory of the job's output directory. This location may be overridden by setting hadoop.job.history.user.location. By setting it to the special value none, no user job history is saved, although job history is still saved centrally. A user's job history files are never deleted by the system.

The history log includes job, task, and attempt events, all of which are stored in a plain-text file. The history for a particular job may be viewed through the web UI or via the command line using `hadoop job -history` (which you point at the job's output directory).

The job page

Clicking on a job ID brings you to a page for the job, illustrated in Figure 5-2. At the top of the page is a summary of the job, with basic information such as job owner and name and how long the job has been running for. The job file is the consolidated configuration file for the job, containing all the properties and their values that were in effect during the job run. If you are unsure of what a particular property was set to, you can click through to inspect the file.

While the job is running, you can monitor its progress on this page, which periodically updates itself. Below the summary is a table that shows the map progress and the reduce progress. "Num Tasks" shows the total number of map and reduce tasks for this job (a row for each). The other columns then show the state of these tasks: "Pending" (waiting to run), "Running," "Complete" (successfully run), or "Killed" (tasks that have failed; this column would be more accurately labeled "Failed"). The final column shows the total number of failed and killed task attempts for all the map or reduce tasks for the job (task attempts may be marked as killed if they are a speculative execution duplicate, if the tasktracker they are running on dies, or if they are killed by a user). See "Task failure" on page 202 for background on task failure.

Farther down the page, you can find completion graphs for each task that show their progress graphically. The reduce completion graph is divided into the three phases of the reduce task: copy (when the map outputs are being transferred to the reduce's tasktracker), sort (when the reduce inputs are being merged), and reduce (when the reduce function is being run to produce the final output). The phases are described in more detail in "Shuffle and Sort" on page 208.

In the middle of the page is a table of job counters. These are dynamically updated during the job run and provide another useful window into the job's progress and general health. There is more information about what these counters mean in "Built-in Counters" on page 259.

Retrieving the Results

Once the job is finished, there are various ways to retrieve the results. Each reducer produces one output file, so there are 30 part files named *part-r-00000* to *part-r-00029* in the *max-temp* directory.

Hadoop job_200904110811_0002 on ip-10-250-110-47

User: root
Job Name: Max temperature
Job File: hdfs://ip-10-250-110-47.ec2.internal/mnt/hadoop/mapred/system/job_200904110811_0002/job.xml
Job Setup: Successful
Status: Running
Started at: Sat Apr 11 08:15:53 EDT 2009
Running for: 5mins, 38sec
Job Cleanup: Pending

Kind	% Complete	Num Tasks	Pending	Running	Complete	Killed	Failed/Killed Task Attempts
map	100.00%	101	0	0	101	0	0 / 26
reduce	70.74%	30	0	13	17	0	0 / 0

	Counter	Map	Reduce	Total
Job Counters	Launched reduce tasks	0	0	32
	Rack-local map tasks	0	0	82
	Launched map tasks	0	0	127
	Data-local map tasks	0	0	45
FileSystemCounters	FILE_BYTES_READ	12,665,901	564	12,666,465
	HDFS_BYTES_READ	33,485,841,275	0	33,485,841,275
	FILE_BYTES_WRITTEN	988,084	564	988,648
	HDFS_BYTES_WRITTEN	0	360	360
Map-Reduce Framework	Reduce input groups	0	40	40
	Combine output records	4,489	0	4,489
	Map input records	1,209,901,509	0	1,209,901,509
	Reduce shuffle bytes	0	18,397	18,397
	Reduce output records	0	40	40
	Spilled Records	9,378	42	9,420
	Map output bytes	10,282,306,995	0	10,282,306,995
	Map input bytes	274,600,205,558	0	274,600,205,558
	Map output records	1,142,478,555	0	1,142,478,555
	Combine input records	1,142,482,941	0	1,142,482,941
	Reduce input records	0	42	42

Map Completion Graph - close

Reduce Completion Graph - close

Go back to JobTracker

Hadoop, 2009.

Figure 5-2. Screenshot of the job page

As their names suggest, a good way to think of these "part" files is as parts of the *max-temp* "file."

If the output is large (which it isn't in this case), it is important to have multiple parts so that more than one reducer can work in parallel. Usually, if a file is in this partitioned form, it can still be used easily enough —as the input to another MapReduce job, for example. In some cases, you can exploit the structure of multiple partitions to do a map-side join, for example (see "Map-Side Joins" on page 284), or a MapFile lookup (see "An application: Partitioned MapFile lookups" on page 271).

This job produces a very small amount of output, so it is convenient to copy it from HDFS to our development machine. The -getmerge option to the hadoop fs command is useful here, as it gets all the files in the directory specified in the source pattern and merges them into a single file on the local filesystem:

```
% hadoop fs -getmerge max-temp max-temp-local
% sort max-temp-local | tail
1991    607
1992    605
1993    567
1994    568
1995    567
1996    561
1997    565
1998    568
1999    568
2000    558
```

We sorted the output, as the reduce output partitions are unordered (owing to the hash partition function). Doing a bit of postprocessing of data from MapReduce is very common, as is feeding it into analysis tools such as R, a spreadsheet, or even a relational database.

Another way of retrieving the output if it is small is to use the -cat option to print the output files to the console:

```
% hadoop fs -cat max-temp/*
```

On closer inspection, we see that some of the results don't look plausible. For instance, the maximum temperature for 1951 (not shown here) is 590°C! How do we find out what's causing this? Is it corrupt input data or a bug in the program?

Debugging a Job

The time-honored way of debugging programs is via print statements, and this is certainly possible in Hadoop. However, there are complications to consider: with programs running on tens, hundreds, or thousands of nodes, how do we find and examine the output of the debug statements, which may be scattered across these nodes? For this particular case, where we are looking for (what we think is) an unusual case, we can use a debug statement to log to standard error, in conjunction with a message to update the task's status message to prompt us to look in the error log. The web UI makes this easy, as we will see.

We also create a custom counter to count the total number of records with implausible temperatures in the whole dataset. This gives us valuable information about how to deal with the condition. If it turns out to be a common occurrence, we might need to learn more about the condition and how to extract the temperature in these cases, rather than simply dropping the record. In fact, when trying to debug a job, you should always ask yourself if you can use a counter to get the information you need to find out what's happening. Even if you need to use logging or a status message, it may be useful to use a counter to gauge the extent of the problem. (There is more on counters in "Counters" on page 259.)

If the amount of log data you produce in the course of debugging is large, you have a couple of options. The first is to write the information to the map's output, rather than to standard error, for analysis and aggregation by the reduce. This approach usually necessitates structural changes to your program, so start with the other techniques first. Alternatively, you can write a program (in MapReduce, of course) to analyze the logs produced by your job.

We add our debugging to the mapper (version 4), as opposed to the reducer, as we want to find out what the source data causing the anomalous output looks like:

```
public class MaxTemperatureMapper
    extends Mapper<LongWritable, Text, Text, IntWritable> {

  enum Temperature {
    OVER_100
  }

  private NcdcRecordParser parser = new NcdcRecordParser();

  @Override
  public void map(LongWritable key, Text value, Context context)
      throws IOException, InterruptedException {

    parser.parse(value);
    if (parser.isValidTemperature()) {
      int airTemperature = parser.getAirTemperature();
      if (airTemperature > 1000) {
        System.err.println("Temperature over 100 degrees for input: " + value);
        context.setStatus("Detected possibly corrupt record: see logs.");
        context.getCounter(Temperature.OVER_100).increment(1);
      }
      context.write(new Text(parser.getYear()), new IntWritable(airTemperature));
    }
  }
}
```

If the temperature is over 100°C (represented by 1000, because temperatures are in tenths of a degree), we print a line to standard error with the suspect line, as well as update the map's status message using the setStatus() method on Context directing us to look in the log. We also increment a counter, which in Java is represented by a field of an enum type. In this program, we have defined a single field OVER_100 as a way to count the number of records with a temperature of over 100°C.

With this modification, we recompile the code, re-create the JAR file, then rerun the job, and while it's running, go to the tasks page.

The tasks page

The job page has a number of links for viewing the tasks in a job in more detail. For example, by clicking on the "map" link, you are brought to a page that lists information for all of the map tasks on one page. You can also see just the completed tasks. The screenshot in Figure 5-3 shows a portion of this page for the job run with our debugging statements. Each row in the table is a task, and it provides such information as the start and end times for each task, any errors reported back from the tasktracker, and a link to view the counters for an individual task.

The "Status" column can be helpful for debugging because it shows a task's latest status message. Before a task starts, it shows its status as "initializing," and then once it starts reading records, it shows the split information for the split it is reading as a filename with a byte offset and length. You can see the status we set for debugging for task task_200904110811_0003_m_000044, so let's click through to the logs page to find the associated debug message. (Notice, too, that there is an extra counter for this task because our user counter has a nonzero count for this task.)

The task details page

From the tasks page, you can click on any task to get more information about it. The task details page, shown in Figure 5-4, shows each task attempt. In this case, there was one task attempt, which completed successfully. The table provides further useful data, such as the node the task attempt ran on and links to task logfiles and counters.

The "Actions" column contains links for killing a task attempt. By default, this is disabled, making the web UI a read-only interface. Set webinterface.private.actions to true to enable the actions links.

Hadoop map task list for job_200904110811_0003 on ip-10-250-110-47

Completed Tasks

Task	Complete	Status	Start Time	Finish Time	Errors	Counters
task_200904110811_0003_m_000043	100.00%	hdfs://ip-10-250-110-47.ec2.internal /user/root/input/ncdc/all /1949.gz:0+220338475	11-Apr-2009 09:00:06	11-Apr-2009 09:01:25 (1mins, 18sec)		10
task_200904110811_0003_m_000044	100.00%	Detected possibly corrupt record: see logs.	11-Apr-2009 09:00:06	11-Apr-2009 09:01:28 (1mins, 21sec)		11
task_200904110811_0003_m_000045	100.00%	hdfs://ip-10-250-110-47.ec2.internal /user/root/input/ncdc/all /1970.gz:0+208374610	11-Apr-2009 09:00:06	11-Apr-2009 09:01:28 (1mins, 21sec)		10

Figure 5-3. Screenshot of the tasks page

Job job_200904110811_0003

All Task Attempts

Task Attempts	Machine	Status	Progress	Start Time	Finish Time	Errors	Task Logs	Counters	Actions
attempt_200904110811_0003_m_000044_0	/default-rack/ip-10-250-163-143.ec2.internal	SUCCEEDED	100.00%	11-Apr-2009 09:00:06	11-Apr-2009 09:01:25 (1mins, 19sec)		Last 4KB Last 8KB All	11	

Input Split Locations

/default-rack/10.250.202.127
/default-rack/10.250.123.223
/default-rack/10.250.115.79

Go back to the job
Go back to JobTracker

Hadoop, 2009.

Figure 5-4. Screenshot of the task details page

 By setting webinterface.private.actions to true, you also allow anyone with access to the HDFS web interface to delete files. The dfs.web.ugi property determines the user that the HDFS web UI runs as, thus controlling which files may be viewed and deleted.

For map tasks, there is also a section showing which nodes the input split was located on.

By following one of the links to the logfiles for the successful task attempt (you can see the last 4 KB or 8 KB of each logfile, or the entire file), we can find the suspect input record that we logged (the line is wrapped and truncated to fit on the page):

```
Temperature over 100 degrees for input:
0335999999433181957042302005+37950+139117SA0   +0004RJSN V020113590031500703569999994
3320195701010005+35317+139650SA0  +000899999V02002359002650076249N004000599+0067...
```

This record seems to be in a different format from the others. For one thing, there are spaces in the line, which are not described in the specification.

When the job has finished, we can look at the value of the counter we defined to see how many records over 100°C there are in the whole dataset. Counters are accessible via the web UI or the command line:

```
% hadoop job -counter job_200904110811_0003 'v4.MaxTemperatureMapper$Temperature' \
    OVER_100
3
```

The -counter option takes the job ID, counter group name (which is the fully qualified classname here), and the counter name (the enum name). There are only three malformed records in the entire dataset of over a billion records. Throwing out bad records is standard for many big data problems, although we need to be careful in this case because we are looking for an extreme value—the maximum temperature rather than an aggregate measure. Still, throwing away three records is probably not going to change the result.

Handling malformed data

Capturing input data that causes a problem is valuable, as we can use it in a test to check that the mapper does the right thing. In this MRUnit test, we check that the counter is updated for the malformed input:

```
@Test
public void parsesMalformedTemperature() throws IOException,
    InterruptedException {
  Text value = new Text("0335999999433181957042302005+37950+139117SA0  +0004" +
                              // Year ^^^^
      "RJSN V02011359003150070356999994433201957010100005+353");
                              // Temperature ^^^^^
  Counters counters = new Counters();
  new MapDriver<LongWritable, Text, Text, IntWritable>()
    .withMapper(new MaxTemperatureMapper())
    .withInputValue(value)
    .withCounters(counters)
    .runTest();
  Counter c = counters.findCounter(MaxTemperatureMapper.Temperature.MALFORMED);
  assertThat(c.getValue(), is(1L));
}
```

The record that was causing the problem is of a different format from the other lines we've seen. Example 5-12 shows a modified program (version 5) using a parser that ignores each line with a temperature field that does not have a leading sign (plus or minus). We've also introduced a counter to measure the number of records that we are ignoring for this reason.

Example 5-12. Mapper for the maximum temperature example

```java
public class MaxTemperatureMapper
  extends Mapper<LongWritable, Text, Text, IntWritable> {

  enum Temperature {
    MALFORMED
  }

  private NcdcRecordParser parser = new NcdcRecordParser();

  @Override
  public void map(LongWritable key, Text value, Context context)
      throws IOException, InterruptedException {

    parser.parse(value);
    if (parser.isValidTemperature()) {
      int airTemperature = parser.getAirTemperature();
      context.write(new Text(parser.getYear()), new IntWritable(airTemperature));
    } else if (parser.isMalformedTemperature()) {
      System.err.println("Ignoring possibly corrupt input: " + value);
      context.getCounter(Temperature.MALFORMED).increment(1);
    }
  }
}
```

Hadoop Logs

Hadoop produces logs in various places, and for various audiences. These are summarized in Table 5-2.

Table 5-2. Types of Hadoop logs

Logs	Primary audience	Description	Further information
System daemon logs	Administrators	Each Hadoop daemon produces a logfile (using log4j) and another file that combines standard out and error. Written in the directory defined by the HADOOP_LOG_DIR environment variable.	"System log-files" on page 309 and "Logging" on page 352
HDFS audit logs	Administrators	A log of all HDFS requests, turned off by default. Written to the namenode's log, although this is configurable.	"Audit Logging" on page 346
MapReduce job history logs	Users	A log of the events (such as task completion) that occur in the course of running a job. Saved centrally on the jobtracker and in the job's output directory in a _logs/history subdirectory.	"Job History" on page 167
MapReduce task logs	Users	Each tasktracker child process produces a logfile using log4j (called *syslog*), a file for data sent to standard out (*stdout*), and a file for standard error (*stderr*). Written in the	This section

Logs	Primary audience	Description	Further information
		userlogs subdirectory of the directory defined by the HADOOP_LOG_DIR environment variable.	

As we have seen in the previous section, MapReduce task logs are accessible through the web UI, which is the most convenient way to view them. You can also find the logfiles on the local filesystem of the tasktracker that ran the task attempt, located in a directory named by the task attempt. If task JVM reuse is enabled (see "Task JVM Reuse" on page 219), each logfile accumulates the logs for the entire JVM run, so multiple task attempts will be found in each logfile. The web UI hides this by showing only the portion that is relevant for the task attempt being viewed.

It is straightforward to write to these logfiles. Anything written to standard output or standard error is directed to the relevant logfile. (Of course, in Streaming, standard output is used for the map or reduce output, so it will not show up in the standard output log.)

In Java, you can write to the task's *syslog* file if you wish by using the Apache Commons Logging API. This is shown in Example 5-13.

Example 5-13. An identity mapper that writes to standard output and also uses the Apache Commons Logging API

```
import org.apache.commons.logging.Log;
import org.apache.commons.logging.LogFactory;
import org.apache.hadoop.mapreduce.Mapper;

public class LoggingIdentityMapper<KEYIN, VALUEIN, KEYOUT, VALUEOUT>
  extends Mapper<KEYIN, VALUEIN, KEYOUT, VALUEOUT> {

  private static final Log LOG = LogFactory.getLog(LoggingIdentityMapper.class);

  @Override
  public void map(KEYIN key, VALUEIN value, Context context)
      throws IOException, InterruptedException {
    // Log to stdout file
    System.out.println("Map key: " + key);

    // Log to syslog file
    LOG.info("Map key: " + key);
    if (LOG.isDebugEnabled()) {
      LOG.debug("Map value: " + value);
    }
    context.write((KEYOUT) key, (VALUEOUT) value);
  }
}
```

The default log level is INFO, so DEBUG level messages do not appear in the *syslog* task logfile. However, sometimes you want to see these messages. To do this, set mapred.map.child.log.level or mapred.reduce.child.log.level, as appropriate (from

0.22). For example, in this case we could set it for the mapper to see the map values in the log as follows:

```
% hadoop jar hadoop-examples.jar LoggingDriver -conf conf/hadoop-cluster.xml \
   -D mapred.map.child.log.level=DEBUG input/ncdc/sample.txt logging-out
```

There are some controls for managing the retention and size of task logs. By default, logs are deleted after a minimum of 24 hours (set this using the `mapred.user log.retain.hours` property). You can also set a cap on the maximum size of each logfile using the `mapred.userlog.limit.kb` property, which is 0 by default, meaning there is no cap.

 Sometimes you may need to debug a problem that you suspect is occurring in the JVM running a Hadoop command, rather than on the cluster. You can send `DEBUG` level logs to the console by using an invocation like this:

```
% HADOOP_ROOT_LOGGER=DEBUG,console hadoop fs -text /foo/bar
```

Remote Debugging

When a task fails and there is not enough information logged to diagnose the error, you may want to resort to running a debugger for that task. This is hard to arrange when running the job on a cluster, as you don't know which node is going to process which part of the input, so you can't set up your debugger ahead of the failure. However, there are a few other options available:

Reproduce the failure locally
Often the failing task fails consistently on a particular input. You can try to reproduce the problem locally by downloading the file that the task is failing on and running the job locally, possibly using a debugger such as Java's VisualVM.

Use JVM debugging options
A common cause of failure is a Java out of memory error in the task JVM. You can set `mapred.child.java.opts` to include `-XX:-HeapDumpOnOutOfMemoryError -XX:Heap DumpPath=`*/path/to/dumps*. This setting produces a heap dump that can be examined afterward with tools such as *jhat* or the Eclipse Memory Analyzer. Note that the JVM options should be added to the existing memory settings specified by `mapred.child.java.opts`. These are explained in more detail in "Memory" on page 307.

Use task profiling
Java profilers give a lot of insight into the JVM, and Hadoop provides a mechanism to profile a subset of the tasks in a job. See "Profiling Tasks" on page 179.

Use `IsolationRunner`
Older versions of Hadoop provided a special task runner called `IsolationRunner` that could rerun failed tasks in situ on the cluster. Unfortunately, it is no longer

available in recent versions, but you can track its replacement at *https://issues .apache.org/jira/browse/MAPREDUCE-2637*.

In some cases it's useful to keep the intermediate files for a failed task attempt for later inspection, particularly if supplementary dump or profile files are created in the task's working directory. You can set `keep.failed.task.files` to `true` to keep a failed task's files.

You can keep the intermediate files for successful tasks, too, which may be handy if you want to examine a task that isn't failing. In this case, set the property `keep.task.files.pattern` to a regular expression that matches the IDs of the tasks you want to keep.

To examine the intermediate files, log into the node that the task failed on and look for the directory for that task attempt. It will be under one of the local MapReduce directories, as set by the `mapred.local.dir` property (covered in more detail in "Important Hadoop Daemon Properties" on page 311). If this property is a comma-separated list of directories (to spread load across the physical disks on a machine), you may need to look in all of the directories before you find the directory for that particular task attempt. The task attempt directory is in the following location:

```
mapred.local.dir/taskTracker/jobcache/job-ID/task-attempt-ID
```

Tuning a Job

After a job is working, the question many developers ask is, "Can I make it run faster?"

There are a few Hadoop-specific "usual suspects" that are worth checking to see whether they are responsible for a performance problem. You should run through the checklist in Table 5-3 before you start trying to profile or optimize at the task level.

Table 5-3. Tuning checklist

Area	Best practice	Further information
Number of mappers	How long are your mappers running for? If they are only running for a few seconds on average, you should see whether there's a way to have fewer mappers and make them all run longer, a minute or so, as a rule of thumb. The extent to which this is possible depends on the input format you are using.	"Small files and CombineFileInputFormat" on page 239
Number of reducers	For maximum performance, the number of reducers should be slightly less than the number of reduce slots in the cluster. This allows the reducers to finish in one wave and fully utilizes the cluster during the reduce phase.	"Choosing the Number of Reducers" on page 231
Combiners	Check whether your job can take advantage of a combiner to reduce the amount of data passing through the shuffle.	"Combiner Functions" on page 33
Intermediate compression	Job execution time can almost always benefit from enabling map output compression.	"Compressing map output" on page 92

Area	Best practice	Further information
Custom serialization	If you are using your own custom `Writable` objects or custom comparators, make sure you have implemented RawComparator.	"Implementing a RawComparator for speed" on page 106
Shuffle tweaks	The MapReduce shuffle exposes around a dozen tuning parameters for memory management, which may help you wring out the last bit of performance.	"Configuration Tuning" on page 211

Profiling Tasks

Like debugging, profiling a job running on a distributed system such as MapReduce presents some challenges. Hadoop allows you to profile a fraction of the tasks in a job, and as each task completes, pulls down the profile information to your machine for later analysis with standard profiling tools.

Of course, it's possible, and somewhat easier, to profile a job running in the local job runner. And provided you can run with enough input data to exercise the map and reduce tasks, this can be a valuable way of improving the performance of your mappers and reducers. There are a couple of caveats, however. The local job runner is a very different environment from a cluster, and the data flow patterns are very different. Optimizing the CPU performance of your code may be pointless if your MapReduce job is I/O-bound (as many jobs are). To be sure that any tuning is effective, you should compare the new execution time with the old one running on a real cluster. Even this is easier said than done, since job execution times can vary due to resource contention with other jobs and the decisions the scheduler makes regarding task placement. To get a good idea of job execution time under these circumstances, perform a series of runs (with and without the change) and check whether any improvement is statistically significant.

It's unfortunately true that some problems (such as excessive memory use) can be reproduced only on the cluster, and in these cases the ability to profile in situ is indispensable.

The HPROF profiler

There are a number of configuration properties to control profiling, which are also exposed via convenience methods on `JobConf`. The following modification to `MaxTemperatureDriver` (version 6) will enable remote HPROF profiling. HPROF is a profiling tool that comes with the JDK that, although basic, can give valuable information about a program's CPU and heap usage:[2]

---

2. HPROF uses byte code insertion to profile your code, so you do not need to recompile your application with special options to use it. For more information on HPROF, see "HPROF: A Heap/CPU Profiling Tool in J2SE 5.0" by Kelly O'Hair at *http://java.sun.com/developer/technicalArticles/Programming/ HPROF.html*.

```
Configuration conf = getConf();
conf.setBoolean("mapred.task.profile", true);
conf.set("mapred.task.profile.params", "-agentlib:hprof=cpu=samples," +
    "heap=sites,depth=6,force=n,thread=y,verbose=n,file=%s");
conf.set("mapred.task.profile.maps", "0-2");
conf.set("mapred.task.profile.reduces", ""); // no reduces
Job job = new Job(conf, "Max temperature");
```

The first line enables profiling, which by default is turned off. (In the new API, you can use the JobContext.TASK_PROFILE constant instead of using mapred.task.profile.)

Next we set the profile parameters, which are the extra command-line arguments to pass to the task's JVM. (When profiling is enabled, a new JVM is allocated for each task, even if JVM reuse is turned on; see "Task JVM Reuse" on page 219.) The default parameters specify the HPROF profiler; here we set an extra HPROF option, depth=6, to give more stack trace depth than the HPROF default. (Using JobContext.TASK_PRO FILE_PARAMS is equivalent to setting the mapred.task.profile.params property.)

Finally, we specify which tasks we want to profile. We normally want profile information from only a few tasks, so we use the properties mapred.task.profile.maps and mapred.task.profile.reduces to specify the range of (map or reduce) task IDs that we want profile information for. We've set the maps property to 0-2 (which is actually the default), which means map tasks with IDs 0, 1, and 2 are profiled. A set of ranges is permitted, using a notation that allows open ranges. For example, 0-1,4,6- would specify all tasks except those with IDs 2, 3, and 5. The tasks to profile can also be controlled using the JobContext.NUM_MAP_PROFILES constant for map tasks and JobCon text.NUM_REDUCE_PROFILES for reduce tasks.

When we run a job with the modified driver, the profile output turns up at the end of the job in the directory from which we launched the job. Because we are profiling only a few tasks, we can run the job on a subset of the dataset.

Here's a snippet of one of the mapper's profile files, which shows the CPU sampling information:

```
CPU SAMPLES BEGIN (total = 1002) Sat Apr 11 11:17:52 2009
rank   self  accum   count trace method
   1  3.49%  3.49%      35 307969 java.lang.Object.<init>
   2  3.39%  6.89%      34 307954 java.lang.Object.<init>
   3  3.19% 10.08%      32 307945 java.util.regex.Matcher.<init>
   4  3.19% 13.27%      32 307963 java.lang.Object.<init>
   5  3.19% 16.47%      32 307973 java.lang.Object.<init>
```

Cross-referencing the trace number 307973 gives us the stacktrace from the same file:

```
TRACE 307973: (thread=200001)
    java.lang.Object.<init>(Object.java:20)
    org.apache.hadoop.io.IntWritable.<init>(IntWritable.java:29)
    v5.MaxTemperatureMapper.map(MaxTemperatureMapper.java:30)
    v5.MaxTemperatureMapper.map(MaxTemperatureMapper.java:14)
    org.apache.hadoop.mapred.MapRunner.run(MapRunner.java:50)
    org.apache.hadoop.mapred.MapTask.runOldMapper(MapTask.java:356)
```

So it looks like the mapper is spending 3% of its time constructing `IntWritable` objects. This observation might lead us to try reusing the `Writable` instances being output to see whether there is any performance gain on our particular cluster and dataset. In one experiment, I changed the mapper to store the `Writable` objects as instance variables. When I ran the modified program on an 11-node cluster, I did not see a statistically significant difference in overall job execution time. Of course, your results may vary.

Other profilers

The mechanism for retrieving profile output is HPROF-specific, so if you use another profiler, you will need to manually retrieve the profiler's output from tasktrackers for analysis.

If the profiler is not installed on all the tasktracker machines, consider using the Distributed Cache (see "Distributed Cache" on page 289) to make the profiler binary available on the required machines.

MapReduce Workflows

So far in this chapter, you have seen the mechanics of writing a program using MapReduce. We haven't yet considered how to turn a data processing problem into the MapReduce model.

The data processing you have seen so far in this book is to solve a fairly simple problem: finding the maximum recorded temperature for given years. When the processing gets more complex, this complexity is generally manifested by having more MapReduce jobs, rather than having more complex map and reduce functions. In other words, as a rule of thumb, think about adding *more* jobs, rather than adding complexity *to* jobs.

For more complex problems, it is worth considering a higher-level language than MapReduce, such as Pig, Hive, Cascading, Cascalog, or Crunch. One immediate benefit is that it frees you from having to do the translation into MapReduce jobs, allowing you to concentrate on the analysis you are performing.

Finally, the book *Data-Intensive Text Processing with MapReduce* by Jimmy Lin and Chris Dyer (Morgan & Claypool Publishers, 2010, *http://mapreduce.me/*) is a great resource for learning more about MapReduce algorithm design and is highly recommended.

Decomposing a Problem into MapReduce Jobs

Let's look at an example of a more complex problem that we want to translate into a MapReduce workflow.

Imagine that we want to find the mean maximum recorded temperature for every day of the year and every weather station. In concrete terms, to calculate the mean maximum daily temperature recorded by station 029070-99999, say, on January 1, we take the mean of the maximum daily temperatures for this station for January 1, 1901; January 1, 1902; and so on, up to January 1, 2000.

How can we compute this using MapReduce? The computation decomposes most naturally into two stages:

1. Compute the maximum daily temperature for every station-date pair.

   The MapReduce program in this case is a variant of the maximum temperature program, except that the keys in this case are a composite station-date pair, rather than just the year.

2. Compute the mean of the maximum daily temperatures for every station-day-month key.

   The mapper takes the output from the previous job (station-date, maximum temperature) records and projects it into (station-day-month, maximum temperature) records by dropping the year component. The reduce function then takes the mean of the maximum temperatures for each station-day-month key.

The output from the first stage looks like this for the station we are interested in (the *mean_max_daily_temp.sh* script in the examples provides an implementation in Hadoop Streaming):

```
029070-99999    19010101   0
029070-99999    19020101   -94
...
```

The first two fields form the key, and the final column is the maximum temperature from all the readings for the given station and date. The second stage averages these daily maxima over years to yield:

```
029070-99999    0101    -68
```

which is interpreted as saying the mean maximum daily temperature on January 1 for station 029070-99999 over the century is –6.8°C.

It's possible to do this computation in one MapReduce stage, but it takes more work on the part of the programmer.[3]

The arguments for having more (but simpler) MapReduce stages are that doing so leads to more composable and more maintainable mappers and reducers. The case studies in Chapter 16 cover a wide range of real-world problems that were solved using Map-Reduce, and in each case, the data processing task is implemented using two or more MapReduce jobs. The details in that chapter are invaluable for getting a better idea of how to decompose a processing problem into a MapReduce workflow.

It's possible to make map and reduce functions even more composable than we have done. A mapper commonly performs input format parsing, projection (selecting the relevant fields), and filtering (removing records that are not of interest). In the mappers

---

3. It's an interesting exercise to do this. Hint: use "Secondary Sort" on page 277.

---

you have seen so far, we have implemented all of these functions in a single mapper. However, there is a case for splitting these into distinct mappers and chaining them into a single mapper using the `ChainMapper` library class that comes with Hadoop. Combined with a `ChainReducer`, you can run a chain of mappers, followed by a reducer and another chain of mappers, in a single MapReduce job.

JobControl

When there is more than one job in a MapReduce workflow, the question arises: how do you manage the jobs so they are executed in order? There are several approaches, and the main consideration is whether you have a linear chain of jobs or a more complex directed acyclic graph (DAG) of jobs.

For a linear chain, the simplest approach is to run each job one after another, waiting until a job completes successfully before running the next:

```
JobClient.runJob(conf1);
JobClient.runJob(conf2);
```

If a job fails, the `runJob()` method will throw an `IOException`, so later jobs in the pipeline don't get executed. Depending on your application, you might want to catch the exception and clean up any intermediate data that was produced by any previous jobs.

The approach is similar with the new MapReduce API, except you need to examine the Boolean return value of the `waitForCompletion()` method on `Job`: `true` means the job succeeded, and `false` means it failed.

For anything more complex than a linear chain, there are libraries that can help orchestrate your workflow (although they are also suited to linear chains, or even one-off jobs). The simplest is in the `org.apache.hadoop.mapreduce.jobcontrol` package: the `JobControl` class. (There is an equivalent class in the `org.apache.hadoop.mapred.jobcontrol` package too.) An instance of `JobControl` represents a graph of jobs to be run. You add the job configurations, then tell the `JobControl` instance the dependencies between jobs. You run the `JobControl` in a thread, and it runs the jobs in dependency order. You can poll for progress, and when the jobs have finished, you can query for all the jobs' statuses and the associated errors for any failures. If a job fails, `JobControl` won't run its dependencies.

Apache Oozie

Apache Oozie is a system for running workflows of dependent jobs. It is composed of two main parts: a *workflow engine* that stores and runs workflows composed of different types of Hadoop jobs (MapReduce, Pig, Hive, and so on), and a *coordinator engine* that runs workflow jobs based on predefined schedules and data availability. Oozie has been designed to scale, and it can manage the timely execution of thousands of workflows in a Hadoop cluster, each composed of possibly dozens of constituent jobs.

Oozie makes rerunning failed workflows more tractable, since no time is wasted running successful parts of a workflow. Anyone who has managed a complex batch system knows how difficult it can be to catch up from jobs missed due to downtime or failure, and will appreciate this feature. (Furthermore, coordinator applications representing a single data pipeline may be packaged into a *bundle* and run together as a unit.)

Unlike JobControl, which runs on the client machine submitting the jobs, Oozie runs as a service in the cluster, and clients submit workflow definitions for immediate or later execution. In Oozie parlance, a workflow is a DAG of *action nodes* and *control-flow nodes*.

An action node performs a workflow task, such as moving files in HDFS, running a MapReduce, Streaming, Pig, or Hive job, performing a Sqoop import, or running an arbitrary shell script or Java program. A control-flow node governs the workflow execution between actions by allowing such constructs as conditional logic (so different execution branches may be followed depending on the result of an earlier action node) or parallel execution. When the workflow completes, Oozie can make an HTTP callback to the client to inform it of the workflow status. It is also possible to receive callbacks every time the workflow enters or exits an action node.

Defining an Oozie workflow

Workflow definitions are written in XML using the Hadoop Process Definition Language, the specification for which can be found on the Oozie website (*http://incubator.apache.org/oozie/*). Example 5-14 shows a simple Oozie workflow definition for running a single MapReduce job.

Example 5-14. Oozie workflow definition to run the maximum temperature MapReduce job

```
<workflow-app xmlns="uri:oozie:workflow:0.1" name="max-temp-workflow">
  <start to="max-temp-mr"/>
  <action name="max-temp-mr">
    <map-reduce>
      <job-tracker>${jobTracker}</job-tracker>
      <name-node>${nameNode}</name-node>
      <prepare>
        <delete path="${nameNode}/user/${wf:user()}/output"/>
      </prepare>
      <configuration>
        <property>
          <name>mapred.mapper.class</name>
          <value>OldMaxTemperature$OldMaxTemperatureMapper</value>
        </property>
        <property>
          <name>mapred.combiner.class</name>
          <value>OldMaxTemperature$OldMaxTemperatureReducer</value>
        </property>
        <property>
          <name>mapred.reducer.class</name>
          <value>OldMaxTemperature$OldMaxTemperatureReducer</value>
        </property>
```

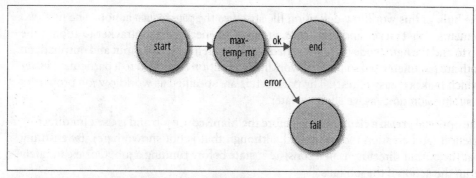

Figure 5-5. Transition diagram of an Oozie workflow

```
        <property>
            <name>mapred.output.key.class</name>
            <value>org.apache.hadoop.io.Text</value>
        </property>
        <property>
            <name>mapred.output.value.class</name>
            <value>org.apache.hadoop.io.IntWritable</value>
        </property>
        <property>
            <name>mapred.input.dir</name>
            <value>/user/${wf:user()}/input/ncdc/micro</value>
        </property>
        <property>
            <name>mapred.output.dir</name>
            <value>/user/${wf:user()}/output</value>
        </property>
      </configuration>
    </map-reduce>
    <ok to="end"/>
    <error to="fail"/>
  </action>
  <kill name="fail">
    <message>MapReduce failed, error message[${wf:errorMessage(wf:lastErrorNode())}]
    </message>
  </kill>
  <end name="end"/>
</workflow-app>
```

This workflow has three control-flow nodes and one action node: a start control node, a map-reduce action node, a kill control node, and an end control node. The nodes and allowed transitions between them are shown in Figure 5-5.

All workflows must have one start and one end node. When the workflow job starts, it transitions to the node specified by the start node (the max-temp-mr action in this example). A workflow job succeeds when it transitions to the end node. However, if the workflow job transitions to a kill node, it is considered to have failed and reports the appropriate error message specified by the message element in the workflow definition.

The bulk of this workflow definition file specifies the `map-reduce` action. The first two elements, `job-tracker` and `name-node`, are used to specify the jobtracker to submit the job to and the namenode (actually a Hadoop filesystem URI) for input and output data. Both are parameterized so that the workflow definition is not tied to a particular cluster (which makes it easy to test). The parameters are specified as workflow job properties at submission time, as we shall see later.

The optional `prepare` element runs before the MapReduce job and is used for directory deletion (and creation too, if needed, although that is not shown here). By ensuring that the output directory is in a consistent state before running a job, Oozie can safely rerun the action if the job fails.

The MapReduce job to run is specified in the `configuration` element using nested elements for specifying the Hadoop configuration name-value pairs. You can view the MapReduce configuration section as a declarative replacement for the driver classes that we have used elsewhere in this book for running MapReduce programs (such as Example 2-6).

There are two nonstandard Hadoop properties, `mapred.input.dir` and `mapred.out put.dir`, which are used to set the `FileInputFormat` input paths and `FileOutputFormat` output path, respectively.

We have taken advantage of JSP Expression Language (EL) syntax in several places in the workflow definition. Oozie provides a set of functions for interacting with the workflow. For example, `${wf:user()}` returns the name of the user who started the current workflow job, and we use it to specify the correct filesystem path. The Oozie specification lists all the EL functions that Oozie supports.

Packaging and deploying an Oozie workflow application

A workflow application is made up of the workflow definition plus all the associated resources (such as MapReduce JAR files, Pig scripts, and so on) needed to run it. Applications must adhere to a simple directory structure, and are deployed to HDFS so that they can be accessed by Oozie. For this workflow application, we'll put all of the files in a base directory called *max-temp-workflow*, as shown diagrammatically here:

```
max-temp-workflow/
├── lib/
│   └── hadoop-examples.jar
└── workflow.xml
```

The workflow definition file *workflow.xml* must appear in the top level of this directory. JAR files containing the application's MapReduce classes are placed in the *lib* directory.

Workflow applications that conform to this layout can be built with any suitable build tool, such as Ant or Maven; you can find an example in the code that accompanies this book. Once an application has been built, it should be copied to HDFS using regular Hadoop tools. Here is the appropriate command for this application:

```
% hadoop fs -put hadoop-examples/target/max-temp-workflow max-temp-workflow
```

Running an Oozie workflow job

Next, let's see how to run a workflow job for the application we just uploaded. For this we use the oozie command-line tool, a client program for communicating with an Oozie server. For convenience we export the OOZIE_URL environment variable to tell the oozie command which Oozie server to use (here we're using one running locally):

```
% export OOZIE_URL="http://localhost:11000/oozie"
```

There are lots of subcommands for the oozie tool (type oozie help to get a list), but we're going to call the job subcommand with the -run option to run the workflow job:

```
% oozie job -config ch05/src/main/resources/max-temp-workflow.properties -run
job: 0000009-120119174508294-oozie-tom-W
```

The -config option specifies a local Java properties file containing definitions for the parameters in the workflow XML file (in this case, nameNode and jobTracker), as well as oozie.wf.application.path, which tells Oozie the location of the workflow application in HDFS. Here are the contents of the properties file:

```
nameNode=hdfs://localhost:8020
jobTracker=localhost:8021
oozie.wf.application.path=${nameNode}/user/${user.name}/max-temp-workflow
```

To get information about the status of the workflow job, we use the -info option, specifying the job ID that was printed by the run command earlier (type oozie job to get a list of all jobs):

```
% oozie job -info 0000009-120119174508294-oozie-tom-W
```

The output shows the status: RUNNING, KILLED, or SUCCEEDED. You can find all this information via Oozie's web UI too, available at *http://localhost:11000/oozie*.

When the job has succeeded, we can inspect the results in the usual way:

```
% hadoop fs -cat output/part-*
1949    111
1950    22
```

This example only scratched the surface of writing Oozie workflows. The documentation on Oozie's website has information about creating more complex workflows, as well as writing and running coordinator jobs.

How MapReduce Works

In this chapter, we look at how MapReduce in Hadoop works in detail. This knowledge provides a good foundation for writing more advanced MapReduce programs, which we will cover in the following two chapters.

Anatomy of a MapReduce Job Run

You can run a MapReduce job with a single method call: `submit()` on a `Job` object (note that you can also call `waitForCompletion()`, which submits the job if it hasn't been submitted already, then waits for it to finish).[1] This method call conceals a great deal of processing behind the scenes. This section uncovers the steps Hadoop takes to run a job.

We saw in Chapter 5 that the way Hadoop executes a MapReduce program depends on a couple of configuration settings.

In versions of Hadoop up to and including the 0.20 release series, `mapred.job.tracker` determines the means of execution. If this configuration property is set to `local` (the default), the local job runner is used. This runner runs the whole job in a single JVM. It's designed for testing and for running MapReduce programs on small datasets.

Alternatively, if `mapred.job.tracker` is set to a colon-separated host and port pair, then the property is interpreted as a jobtracker address, and the runner submits the job to the jobtracker at that address. The whole process is described in detail in the next section.

In Hadoop 2.0, a new MapReduce implementation was introduced. The new implementation (called MapReduce 2) is built on a system called YARN, described in "YARN (MapReduce 2)" on page 196. For now, just note that the framework that is used for execution is set by the `mapreduce.framework.name` property, which takes the values

---

1. In the old MapReduce API, you can call `JobClient.submitJob(conf)` or `JobClient.runJob(conf)`.

local (for the local job runner), classic (for the "classic" MapReduce framework, also called MapReduce 1, which uses a jobtracker and tasktrackers), and yarn (for the new framework).

 It's important to realize that the old and new MapReduce APIs are not the same thing as the classic and YARN-based MapReduce implementations (MapReduce 1 and 2, respectively). The APIs are user-facing client-side features and determine how you write MapReduce programs, whereas the implementations are just different ways of running MapReduce programs. All four combinations are supported: both the old and new API run on both MapReduce 1 and 2. Table 1-2 lists which of these combinations are supported in the different Hadoop releases.

Classic MapReduce (MapReduce 1)

A job run in classic MapReduce is illustrated in Figure 6-1. At the highest level, there are four independent entities:

- The client, which submits the MapReduce job.
- The jobtracker, which coordinates the job run. The jobtracker is a Java application whose main class is JobTracker.
- The tasktrackers, which run the tasks that the job has been split into. Tasktrackers are Java applications whose main class is TaskTracker.
- The distributed filesystem (normally HDFS, covered in Chapter 3), which is used for sharing job files between the other entities.

Job submission

The submit() method on Job creates an internal JobSummitter instance and calls submitJobInternal() on it (step 1 in Figure 6-1). Having submitted the job, waitForCompletion() polls the job's progress once per second and reports the progress to the console if it has changed since the last report. When the job completes successfully, the job counters are displayed. Otherwise, the error that caused the job to fail is logged to the console.

The job submission process implemented by JobSummitter does the following:

- Asks the jobtracker for a new job ID (by calling getNewJobId() on JobTracker) (step 2).
- Checks the output specification of the job. For example, if the output directory has not been specified or it already exists, the job is not submitted and an error is thrown to the MapReduce program.
- Computes the input splits for the job. If the splits cannot be computed (because the input paths don't exist, for example), the job is not submitted and an error is thrown to the MapReduce program.

Figure 6-1. How Hadoop runs a MapReduce job using the classic framework

- Copies the resources needed to run the job, including the job JAR file, the configuration file, and the computed input splits, to the jobtracker's filesystem in a directory named after the job ID. The job JAR is copied with a high replication factor (controlled by the `mapred.submit.replication` property, which defaults to 10) so that there are lots of copies across the cluster for the tasktrackers to access when they run tasks for the job (step 3).

- Tells the jobtracker that the job is ready for execution by calling `submitJob()` on `JobTracker` (step 4).

Job initialization

When the `JobTracker` receives a call to its `submitJob()` method, it puts it into an internal queue from where the job scheduler will pick it up and initialize it. Initialization involves creating an object to represent the job being run, which encapsulates its tasks, and bookkeeping information to keep track of the status and progress of its tasks (step 5).

To create the list of tasks to run, the job scheduler first retrieves the input splits computed by the client from the shared filesystem (step 6). It then creates one map task for each split. The number of reduce tasks to create is determined by the `mapred.reduce.tasks` property in the `Job`, which is set by the `setNumReduceTasks()` method, and the scheduler simply creates this number of reduce tasks to be run. Tasks are given IDs at this point.

In addition to the map and reduce tasks, two further tasks are created: a job setup task and a job cleanup task. These are run by tasktrackers and are used to run code to set up the job before any map tasks run, and to cleanup after all the reduce tasks are complete. The `OutputCommitter` that is configured for the job determines the code to be run, and by default this is a `FileOutputCommitter`. For the job setup task it will create the final output directory for the job and the temporary working space for the task output, and for the job cleanup task it will delete the temporary working space for the task output. The commit protocol is described in more detail in "Output Committers" on page 217.

Task assignment

Tasktrackers run a simple loop that periodically sends heartbeat method calls to the jobtracker. Heartbeats tell the jobtracker that a tasktracker is alive, but they also double as a channel for messages. As a part of the heartbeat, a tasktracker will indicate whether it is ready to run a new task, and if it is, the jobtracker will allocate it a task, which it communicates to the tasktracker using the heartbeat return value (step 7).

Before it can choose a task for the tasktracker, the jobtracker must choose a job to select the task from. There are various scheduling algorithms, as explained later in this chapter (see "Job Scheduling" on page 206), but the default one simply maintains a priority list of jobs. Having chosen a job, the jobtracker now chooses a task for the job.

Tasktrackers have a fixed number of slots for map tasks and for reduce tasks, and these are set independently. For example, a tasktracker may be configured to run two map tasks and two reduce tasks simultaneously. (The precise number depends on the number of cores and the amount of memory on the tasktracker; see "Memory" on page 307.) In the context of a given job, the default scheduler fills empty map task slots before reduce task slots. So if the tasktracker has at least one empty map task slot, the jobtracker will select a map task; otherwise, it will select a reduce task.

To choose a reduce task, the jobtracker simply takes the next in its list of yet-to-be-run reduce tasks, since there are no data locality considerations. For a map task, however, it takes into account the tasktracker's network location and picks a task whose input split is as close as possible to the tasktracker. In the optimal case, the task is *data-local*, that is, running on the same node that the split resides on. Alternatively, the task may be *rack-local*: on the same rack, but not the same node, as the split. Some tasks are neither data-local nor rack-local and retrieve their data from a different rack than the one they are running on. You can tell the proportion of each type of task by looking at a job's counters (see "Built-in Counters" on page 259).

Task execution

Now that the tasktracker has been assigned a task, the next step is for it to run the task. First, it localizes the job JAR by copying it from the shared filesystem to the tasktracker's filesystem. It also copies any files needed from the distributed cache by the application to the local disk; see "Distributed Cache" on page 289 (step 8). Second, it creates a local working directory for the task and "un-jars" the contents of the JAR into this directory. Third, it creates an instance of `TaskRunner` to run the task.

`TaskRunner` launches a new Java Virtual Machine (JVM, step 9) to run each task in (step 10), so that any bugs in the user-defined map and reduce functions don't affect the tasktracker (by causing it to crash or hang, for example). However, it is possible to reuse the JVM between tasks; see "Task JVM Reuse" on page 219.

The child process communicates with its parent through the *umbilical* interface. It informs the parent of the task's progress every few seconds until the task is complete.

Each task can perform setup and cleanup actions, which are run in the same JVM as the task itself and are determined by the `OutputCommitter` for the job (see "Output Committers" on page 217). The cleanup action is used to commit the task, which in the case of file-based jobs means that its output is written to the final location for that task. The commit protocol ensures that when speculative execution is enabled (see "Speculative Execution" on page 215), only one of the duplicate tasks is committed and the other is aborted.

Streaming and pipes. Both Streaming and Pipes run special map and reduce tasks for the purpose of launching the user-supplied executable and communicating with it (Figure 6-2).

In the case of Streaming, the Streaming task communicates with the process (which may be written in any language) using standard input and output streams. The Pipes task, on the other hand, listens on a socket and passes the C++ process a port number in its environment so that on startup, the C++ process can establish a persistent socket connection back to the parent Java Pipes task.

In both cases, during execution of the task, the Java process passes input key-value pairs to the external process, which runs it through the user-defined map or reduce function and passes the output key-value pairs back to the Java process. From the tasktracker's point of view, it is as if the tasktracker child process ran the map or reduce code itself.

Progress and status updates

MapReduce jobs are long-running batch jobs, taking anything from minutes to hours to run. Because this is a significant length of time, it's important for the user to get feedback on how the job is progressing. A job and each of its tasks have a *status*, which includes such things as the state of the job or task (e.g., running, successfully completed, failed), the progress of maps and reduces, the values of the job's counters, and a status message or description (which may be set by user code). These statuses change over the course of the job, so how do they get communicated back to the client?

When a task is running, it keeps track of its *progress*, that is, the proportion of the task completed. For map tasks, this is the proportion of the input that has been processed. For reduce tasks, it's a little more complex, but the system can still estimate the proportion of the reduce input processed. It does this by dividing the total progress into three parts, corresponding to the three phases of the shuffle (see "Shuffle and Sort" on page 208). For example, if the task has run the reducer on half its input, the task's progress is 5/6, since it has completed the copy and sort phases (1/3 each) and is halfway through the reduce phase (1/6).

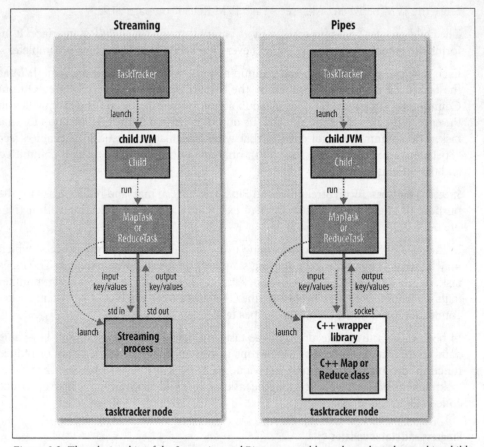

Figure 6-2. The relationship of the Streaming and Pipes executable to the tasktracker and its child

Tasks also have a set of counters that count various events as the task runs (we saw an example in "A test run" on page 25), which are either those built into the framework, such as the number of map output records written, or defined by users.

If a task reports progress, it sets a flag to indicate that the status change should be sent to the tasktracker. The flag is checked in a separate thread every three seconds, and if set, it notifies the tasktracker of the current task status. Meanwhile, the tasktracker is sending heartbeats to the jobtracker every five seconds (this is a minimum, as the heartbeat interval is actually dependent on the size of the cluster; for larger clusters, the interval is longer), and the status of all the tasks being run by the tasktracker is sent in the call. Counters are sent less frequently than every five seconds because they can be relatively high-bandwidth.

The jobtracker combines these updates to produce a global view of the status of all the jobs being run and their constituent tasks. Finally, as mentioned earlier, the Job receives the latest status by polling the jobtracker every second. Clients can also use Job's getStatus() method to obtain a JobStatus instance, which contains all of the status information for the job.

The method calls are illustrated in Figure 6-3.

Job completion

When the jobtracker receives a notification that the last task for a job is complete (this will be the special job cleanup task), it changes the status for the job to "successful." Then, when the Job polls for status, it learns that the job has completed successfully, so it prints a message to tell the user and then returns from the waitForCompletion() method. Job statistics and counters are printed to the console at this point.

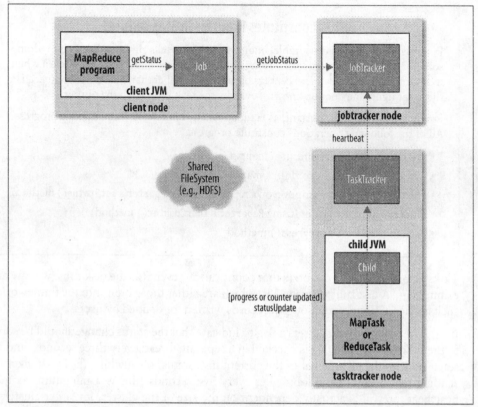

Figure 6-3. How status updates are propagated through the MapReduce 1 system

The jobtracker also sends an HTTP job notification if it is configured to do so. This can be configured by clients wishing to receive callbacks, via the `job.end.notifica tion.url` property.

Finally, the jobtracker cleans up its working state for the job and instructs tasktrackers to do the same (so intermediate output is deleted, for example).

YARN (MapReduce 2)

For very large clusters in the region of 4,000 nodes and higher, the MapReduce system described in the previous section begins to hit scalability bottlenecks, so in 2010 a group at Yahoo! began to design the next generation of MapReduce. The result was *YARN*, short for Yet Another Resource Negotiator (or if you prefer recursive acronyms, YARN Application Resource Negotiator).[2]

---

2. You can read more about the motivation for and development of YARN in Arun C. Murthy's post titled "The Next Generation of Apache Hadoop MapReduce (*http://developer.yahoo.com/blogs/hadoop/posts/ 2011/02/mapreduce-nextgen/*)."

YARN remedies the scalability shortcomings of "classic" MapReduce by splitting the responsibilities of the jobtracker into separate entities. The jobtracker takes care of both job scheduling (matching tasks with tasktrackers) and task progress monitoring (keeping track of tasks, restarting failed or slow tasks, and doing task bookkeeping, such as maintaining counter totals).

YARN separates these two roles into two independent daemons: a *resource manager* to manage the use of resources across the cluster and an *application master* to manage the lifecycle of applications running on the cluster. The idea is that an application master negotiates with the resource manager for cluster resources—described in terms of a number of *containers,* each with a certain memory limit—and then runs application-specific processes in those containers. The containers are overseen by *node managers* running on cluster nodes, which ensure that the application does not use more resources than it has been allocated.[3]

In contrast to the jobtracker, each instance of an application—here a MapReduce job —has a dedicated application master, which runs for the duration of the application. This model is actually closer to the original Google MapReduce paper, which describes how a master process is started to coordinate map and reduce tasks running on a set of workers.

As described, YARN is more general than MapReduce, and in fact MapReduce is just one type of YARN application. There are a few other YARN applications, such as a distributed shell that can run a script on a set of nodes in the cluster, and others are actively being developed (some are listed at *http://wiki.apache.org/hadoop/Powered ByYarn*). The beauty of YARN's design is that different YARN applications can coexist on the same cluster—so a MapReduce application can run at the same time as an MPI application, for example—which brings great benefits for manageability and cluster utilization.

Furthermore, it is even possible for users to run different versions of MapReduce on the same YARN cluster, which makes the process of upgrading MapReduce more manageable. (Note that some parts of MapReduce, such as the job history server and the shuffle handler, as well as YARN itself, still need to be upgraded across the cluster.)

MapReduce on YARN involves more entities than classic MapReduce. They are:[4]

- The client, which submits the MapReduce job.
- The YARN resource manager, which coordinates the allocation of compute resources on the cluster.

---

3. At the time of this writing, memory is the only resource that is managed, and node managers will kill any container that exceeds its allocated memory limits.

4. Not discussed in this section are the job history server daemon (for retaining job history data) and the shuffle handler auxiliary service (for serving map outputs to reduce tasks), which are a part of the jobtracker and the tasktracker (respectively) in classic MapReduce, but are independent entities in YARN.

- The YARN node managers, which launch and monitor the compute containers on machines in the cluster.
- The MapReduce application master, which coordinates the tasks running the MapReduce job. The application master and the MapReduce tasks run in containers that are scheduled by the resource manager and managed by the node managers.
- The distributed filesystem (normally HDFS, covered in Chapter 3), which is used for sharing job files between the other entities.

The process of running a job is shown in Figure 6-4 and described in the following sections.

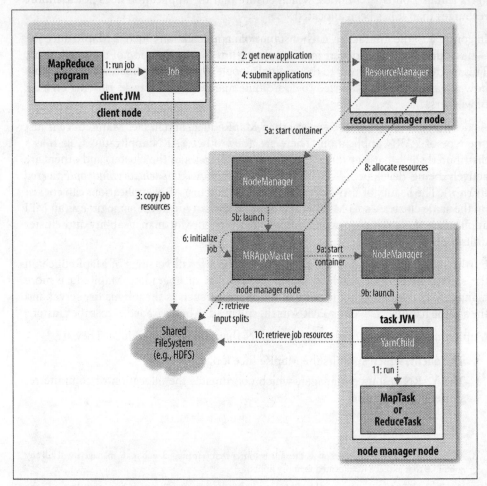

Figure 6-4. How Hadoop runs a MapReduce job using YARN

Job submission

Jobs are submitted in MapReduce 2 using the same user API as MapReduce 1 (step 1). MapReduce 2 has an implementation of `ClientProtocol` that is activated when `mapre duce.framework.name` is set to `yarn`. The submission process is very similar to the classic implementation. The new job ID is retrieved from the resource manager (rather than the jobtracker), although in the nomenclature of YARN, it is an application ID (step 2). The job client checks the output specification of the job; computes input splits (although there is an option to generate them on the cluster, `yarn.app.mapreduce.am.com pute-splits-in-cluster`, which can be beneficial for jobs with many splits); and copies job resources (including the job JAR, configuration, and split information) to HDFS (step 3). Finally, the job is submitted by calling `submitApplication()` on the resource manager (step 4).

Job initialization

When the resource manager receives a call to its `submitApplication()`, it hands off the request to the scheduler. The scheduler allocates a container, and the resource manager then launches the application master's process there, under the node manager's management (steps 5a and 5b).

The application master for MapReduce jobs is a Java application whose main class is `MRAppMaster`. It initializes the job by creating a number of bookkeeping objects to keep track of the job's progress, as it will receive progress and completion reports from the tasks (step 6). Next, it retrieves the input splits computed in the client from the shared filesystem (step 7). It then creates a map task object for each split, as well as a number of reduce task objects determined by the `mapreduce.job.reduces` property.

The next thing the application master does is decide how to run the tasks that make up the MapReduce job. If the job is small, the application master may choose to run the tasks in the same JVM as itself. This happens when it judges the overhead of allocating and running tasks in new containers outweighs the gain to be had in running them in parallel, compared to running them sequentially on one node. (This is different from MapReduce 1, where small jobs are never run on a single tasktracker.) Such a job is said to be *uberized*, or run as an *uber task*.

What qualifies as a small job? By default, a small job is one that has less than 10 mappers, only one reducer, and an input size that is less than the size of one HDFS block. (These values may be changed for a job by setting `mapreduce.job.ubertask.maxmaps`, `mapreduce.job.ubertask.maxreduces`, and `mapreduce.job.ubertask.maxbytes`.) It's also possible to disable uber tasks entirely (by setting `mapreduce.job.ubertask.enable` to `false`).

Before any tasks can be run, the job setup method is called (for the job's `OutputCommit ter`) to create the job's output directory. In contrast to MapReduce 1, where it is called in a special task that is run by the tasktracker, in the YARN implementation the method is called directly by the application master.

Task assignment

If the job does not qualify for running as an uber task, then the application master requests containers for all the map and reduce tasks in the job from the resource manager (step 8). All requests, which are piggybacked on heartbeat calls, includes information about each map task's data locality, in particular the hosts and corresponding racks that the input split resides on. The scheduler uses this information to make scheduling decisions (just like a jobtracker's scheduler does). It attempts to place tasks on data-local nodes in the ideal case, but if this is not possible, the scheduler prefers rack-local placement to nonlocal placement.

Requests also specify memory requirements for tasks. By default, both map and reduce tasks are allocated 1024 MB of memory, but this is configurable by setting `mapre duce.map.memory.mb` and `mapreduce.reduce.memory.mb`.

The way memory is allocated is different from MapReduce 1, where tasktrackers have a fixed number of "slots," set at cluster configuration time, and each task runs in a single slot. Slots have a maximum memory allowance, which again is fixed for a cluster, leading to both problems of underutilization when tasks use less memory (because other waiting tasks are not able to take advantage of the unused memory) and problems of job failure when a task can't complete since it can't get enough memory to run correctly and therefore can't complete.

In YARN, resources are more fine-grained, so both of these problems can be avoided. In particular, applications may request a memory capability that is anywhere between the minimum allocation and a maximum allocation, and that must be a multiple of the minimum allocation. Default memory allocations are scheduler-specific, and for the capacity scheduler, the default minimum is 1024 MB (set by `yarn.scheduler.capacity .minimum-allocation-mb`) and the default maximum is 10240 MB (set by `yarn.schedu ler.capacity.maximum-allocation-mb`). Thus, tasks can request any memory allocation between 1 and 10 GB (inclusive), in multiples of 1 GB (the scheduler will round up to the nearest multiple if needed), by setting `mapreduce.map.memory.mb` and `mapre duce.reduce.memory.mb` appropriately.

Task execution

Once a task has been assigned a container by the resource manager's scheduler, the application master starts the container by contacting the node manager (steps 9a and 9b). The task is executed by a Java application whose main class is `YarnChild`. Before it can run the task it localizes the resources that the task needs, including the job configuration and JAR file, and any files from the distributed cache (step 10). Finally, it runs the map or reduce task (step 11).

The `YarnChild` runs in a dedicated JVM, for the same reason that tasktrackers spawn new JVMs for tasks in MapReduce 1: to isolate user code from long-running system daemons. Unlike MapReduce 1, however, YARN does not support JVM reuse, so each task runs in a new JVM.

Streaming and Pipes programs work in the same way as MapReduce 1. The Yarn Child launches the Streaming or Pipes process and communicates with it using standard input/output or a socket (respectively), as shown in Figure 6-2 (except the child and subprocesses run on node managers, not tasktrackers).

Progress and status updates

When running under YARN, the task reports its progress and status (including counters) back to its application master, which has an aggregate view of the job, every three seconds over the umbilical interface. The process is illustrated in Figure 6-5. Contrast this to MapReduce 1, where progress updates flow from the child through the tasktracker to the jobtracker for aggregation.

The client polls the application master every second (set via `mapreduce.client.progressmonitor.pollinterval`) to receive progress updates, which are usually displayed to the user.

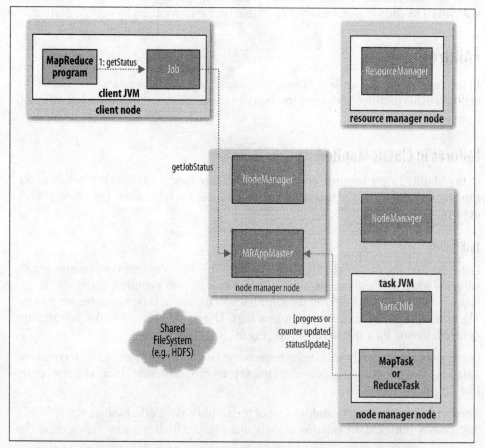

Figure 6-5. How status updates are propagated through the MapReduce 2 system

In MapReduce 1, the job tracker web UI has a list of running jobs and their progress. In YARN, the resource manager web UI displays all the running applications with links to the web UIs of their respective application masters, each of which displays further details on the MapReduce job, including its progress.

Job completion

As well as polling the application master for progress, every five seconds the client checks whether the job has completed by calling the `waitForCompletion()` method on `Job`. The polling interval can be set via the `mapreduce.client.comple` `tion.pollinterval` configuration property.

Notification of job completion via an HTTP callback is also supported, as it is in MapReduce 1. In MapReduce 2, however, the application master initiates the callback.

On job completion, the application master and the task containers clean up their working state, and the `OutputCommitter`'s job cleanup method is called. Job information is archived by the job history server to enable later interrogation by users if desired.

Failures

In the real world, user code is buggy, processes crash, and machines fail. One of the major benefits of using Hadoop is its ability to handle such failures and allow your job to complete.

Failures in Classic MapReduce

In the MapReduce 1 runtime, there are three failure modes to consider: failure of the running task, failure of the tasktracker, and failure of the jobtracker. Let's look at each in turn.

Task failure

Consider first the case of the child task failing. The most common occurrence of this failure is when user code in the map or reduce task throws a runtime exception. If this happens, the child JVM reports the error back to its parent tasktracker before it exits. The error ultimately makes it into the user logs. The tasktracker marks the task attempt as *failed*, freeing up a slot to run another task.

For Streaming tasks, if the Streaming process exits with a nonzero exit code, it is marked as failed. This behavior is governed by the `stream.non.zero.exit.is.failure` property (the default is `true`).

Another failure mode is the sudden exit of the child JVM—perhaps there is a JVM bug that causes the JVM to exit for a particular set of circumstances exposed by the

MapReduce user code. In this case, the tasktracker notices that the process has exited and marks the attempt as failed.

Hanging tasks are dealt with differently. The tasktracker notices that it hasn't received a progress update for a while and proceeds to mark the task as failed. The child JVM process will be killed automatically after this period.[5] The timeout period after which tasks are considered failed is normally 10 minutes and can be configured on a per-job basis (or a cluster basis) by setting the `mapred.task.timeout` property to a value in milliseconds.

Setting the timeout to a value of zero disables the timeout, so long-running tasks are never marked as failed. In this case, a hanging task will never free up its slot, and over time there may be cluster slowdown as a result. This approach should therefore be avoided, and making sure that a task is reporting progress periodically will suffice (see "What Constitutes Progress in MapReduce?" on page 195).

When the jobtracker is notified of a task attempt that has failed (by the tasktracker's heartbeat call), it will reschedule execution of the task. The jobtracker will try to avoid rescheduling the task on a tasktracker where it has previously failed. Furthermore, if a task fails four times (or more), it will not be retried again. This value is configurable. The maximum number of attempts to run a task is controlled by the `mapred.map.max.attempts` property for map tasks and `mapred.reduce.max.attempts` for reduce tasks. By default, if any task fails four times (or whatever the maximum number of attempts is configured to), the whole job fails.

For some applications, it is undesirable to abort the job when a few tasks fail, as it may be possible to use the results of the job despite some failures. In this case, the maximum percentage of tasks that are allowed to fail without triggering job failure can be set for the job. Map tasks and reduce tasks are controlled independently, using the `mapred.max.map.failures.percent` and `mapred.max.reduce.failures.percent` properties.

A task attempt may also be *killed*, which is different from failing. A task attempt may be killed because it is a speculative duplicate (for more information, see "Speculative Execution" on page 215), or because the tasktracker it was running on failed and the jobtracker marked all the task attempts running on it as killed. Killed task attempts do not count against the number of attempts to run the task (as set by `mapred.map.max.attempts` and `mapred.reduce.max.attempts`), because it wasn't the task's fault that an attempt was killed.

---

5. If a Streaming or Pipes process hangs, the tasktracker will kill it (along with the JVM that launched it) only in the following circumstances: either `mapred.task.tracker.task-controller` is set to `org.apache.hadoop.mapred.LinuxTaskController`, or the default task controller is being used (`org.apache.hadoop.mapred.DefaultTaskController`) and the `setsid` command is available on the system (so that the child JVM and any processes it launches are in the same process group). In any other case, orphaned Streaming or Pipes processes will accumulate on the system, which will impact utilization over time.

Users may also kill or fail task attempts using the web UI or the command line (type hadoop job to see the options). Jobs may also be killed by the same mechanisms.

Tasktracker failure

Failure of a tasktracker is another failure mode. If a tasktracker fails by crashing or running very slowly, it will stop sending heartbeats to the jobtracker (or send them very infrequently). The jobtracker will notice a tasktracker that has stopped sending heartbeats if it hasn't received one for 10 minutes (configured via the mapred.task tracker.expiry.interval property, in milliseconds) and remove it from its pool of tasktrackers to schedule tasks on. The jobtracker arranges for map tasks that were run and completed successfully on that tasktracker to be rerun if they belong to incomplete jobs, since their intermediate output residing on the failed tasktracker's local filesystem may not be accessible to the reduce task. Any tasks in progress are also rescheduled.

A tasktracker can also be *blacklisted* by the jobtracker, even if the tasktracker has not failed. If more than four tasks from the same job fail on a particular tasktracker (set by mapred.max.tracker.failures), the jobtracker records this as a fault. A tasktracker is blacklisted if the number of faults is over some minimum threshold (the default is four, set by mapred.max.tracker.blacklists) and is significantly higher than the average number of faults for tasktrackers in the cluster.

Blacklisted tasktrackers are not assigned tasks, but they continue to communicate with the jobtracker. Faults expire over time (at the rate of one per day), so tasktrackers get the chance to run jobs again simply by continuing to run. Alternatively, if there is an underlying fault that can be fixed (by replacing hardware, for example), the tasktracker will be removed from the jobtracker's blacklist after it restarts and rejoins the cluster.

Jobtracker failure

Failure of the jobtracker is the most serious failure mode. Hadoop has no mechanism for dealing with jobtracker failure—it is a single point of failure—so in this case all running jobs fail. However, this failure mode is unlikely because the chance of a particular machine failing is low. The good news is that the situation is improved with YARN, since one of its design goals is to eliminate single points of failure in MapReduce.

After restarting a jobtracker, any jobs that were running at the time it was stopped will need to be resubmitted. There is a configuration option that attempts to recover any running jobs (mapred.jobtracker.restart.recover, turned off by default), but it is known not to work reliably, so should not be used.

Failures in YARN

For MapReduce programs running on YARN, we need to consider the failure of any of the following entities: the task, the application master, the node manager, and the resource manager.

Task failure

Failure of the running task is similar to the classic case. Runtime exceptions and sudden exits of the JVM are propagated back to the application master, and the task attempt is marked as failed. Likewise, hanging tasks are noticed by the application master through the absence of a ping over the umbilical channel (the timeout is set by `mapreduce.task.timeout`), and again the task attempt is marked as failed.

The configuration properties for determining when a task has failed are the same as the classic case: a task is marked as failed after four attempts (set by `mapreduce.map.maxattempts` for map tasks and `mapreduce.reduce.maxattempts` for reducer tasks). A job will be failed if more than `mapreduce.map.failures.maxpercent` percent of the map tasks in the job fail or more than `mapreduce.reduce.failures.maxpercent` percent of the reduce tasks fail.

Application master failure

Just like MapReduce tasks are given several attempts to succeed (in the face of hardware or network failures), applications in YARN are tried multiple times in the event of failure. By default, applications are marked as failed if they fail once, but this can be increased by setting the property `yarn.resourcemanager.am.max-retries`.

An application master sends periodic heartbeats to the resource manager, and in the event of application master failure, the resource manager will detect the failure and start a new instance of the master running in a new container (managed by a node manager) . In the case of the MapReduce application master, it can recover the state of the tasks that were already run by the (failed) application so they don't have to be rerun. Recovery is not enabled by default, so failed application masters will rerun all their tasks, but you can turn this on by setting `yarn.app.mapreduce.am.job.recovery.enable` to true.

The client polls the application master for progress reports; if its application master fails, the client needs to locate the new instance. During job initialization, the client asks the resource manager for the application master's address, and then caches it so it doesn't overload the resource manager with a request every time it needs to poll the application master. If the application master fails, however, the client will experience a timeout when it issues a status update, at which point the client will go back to the resource manager to ask for the new application master's address.

Node manager failure

If a node manager fails, it will stop sending heartbeats to the resource manager, and the node manager will be removed from the resource manager's pool of available nodes. The property `yarn.resourcemanager.nm.liveness-monitor.expiry-interval-ms`, which defaults to 600000 (10 minutes), determines the time the resource manager waits before considering a node manager that has sent no heartbeat during that period as failed.

Any task or application master running on the failed node manager will be recovered using the mechanisms described in the previous two sections.

Node managers may be blacklisted if the number of failures for the application is high. Blacklisting is done by the application master, and for MapReduce the application master will try to reschedule tasks on different nodes if more than three tasks fail on a node manager. The user may set the threshold with the `mapreduce.job.maxtaskfai lures.per.tracker`.

 Note that the resource manager does not do blacklisting (at the time of this writing), so tasks from new jobs may be scheduled on bad nodes, even if they have been blacklisted by an application master running an earlier job.

Resource manager failure

Failure of the resource manager is serious, because without it, neither jobs nor task containers can be launched. The resource manager was designed from the outset to be able to recover from crashes by using a checkpointing mechanism to save its state to persistent storage, although at the time of this writing, the latest release did not have a complete implementation.

After a crash, a new resource manager instance is brought up (by an administrator), and it recovers from the saved state. The state consists of the node managers in the system as well as the running applications. (Note that tasks are not part of the resource manager's state, since they are managed by the application master. Thus the amount of state to be stored is much more manageable than that of the jobtracker.)

The storage used by the resource manager is configurable via the `yarn.resourceman ager.store.class` property. The default is `org.apache.hadoop.yarn.server.resource manager.recovery.MemStore`, which keeps the store in memory and therefore is not highly available. However, there is a ZooKeeper-based store in the works that will support reliable recovery from resource manager failures in the future.

Job Scheduling

Early versions of Hadoop had a very simple approach to scheduling users' jobs: they ran in order of submission, using a FIFO scheduler. Typically, each job would use the whole cluster, so jobs had to wait their turn. Although a shared cluster offers great potential for offering large resources to many users, the problem of sharing resources fairly between users requires a better scheduler. Production jobs need to complete in a timely manner, while allowing users who are making smaller ad hoc queries to get results back in a reasonable time.

Later on, the ability to set a job's priority was added, via the `mapred.job.priority` property or the `setJobPriority()` method on `JobClient` (both of which take one of the values `VERY_HIGH`, `HIGH`, `NORMAL`, `LOW`, or `VERY_LOW`). When the job scheduler is choosing the next job to run, it selects one with the highest priority. However, with the FIFO scheduler, priorities do not support *preemption*, so a high-priority job can still be blocked by a long-running, low-priority job that started before the high-priority job was scheduled.

MapReduce in Hadoop comes with a choice of schedulers. The default in MapReduce 1 is the original FIFO queue-based scheduler, and there are also multiuser schedulers called the Fair Scheduler and the Capacity Scheduler.

The Fair Scheduler

The Fair Scheduler aims to give every user a fair share of the cluster capacity over time. If a single job is running, it gets all of the cluster. As more jobs are submitted, free task slots are given to the jobs in such a way as to give each user a fair share of the cluster. A short job belonging to one user will complete in a reasonable time even while another user's long job is running, and the long job will still make progress.

Jobs are placed in pools, and by default, each user gets her own pool. A user who submits more jobs than a second user will not get any more cluster resources than the second, on average. It is also possible to define custom pools with guaranteed minimum capacities specified in terms of the number of map and reduce slots, and to set weightings for each pool.

The Fair Scheduler supports preemption, so if a pool has not received its fair share for a certain period of time, the scheduler will kill tasks in pools running over capacity in order to give more slots to the pool running under capacity.

The Fair Scheduler is a "contrib" module. To enable it, place its JAR file on Hadoop's classpath by copying it from Hadoop's *contrib/fairscheduler* directory to the *lib* directory. Then set the `mapred.jobtracker.taskScheduler` property to:

```
org.apache.hadoop.mapred.FairScheduler
```

The Fair Scheduler will work without further configuration, but to take full advantage of its features and learn how to configure it (including its web interface), refer to the *README* file in the *src/contrib/fairscheduler* directory of the distribution.

The Capacity Scheduler

The Capacity Scheduler takes a slightly different approach to multiuser scheduling. A cluster is made up of a number of queues (like the Fair Scheduler's pools), which may be hierarchical (so a queue may be the child of another queue), and each queue has an allocated capacity. This is like the Fair Scheduler, except that within each queue, jobs are scheduled using FIFO scheduling (with priorities). In effect, the Capacity Scheduler allows users or organizations (defined using queues) to simulate a separate MapReduce cluster with FIFO scheduling for each user or organization. In contrast, the Fair Scheduler (which actually also supports FIFO job scheduling within pools as an option, making it like the Capacity Scheduler) enforces fair sharing within each pool, so running jobs share the pool's resources.

Shuffle and Sort

MapReduce makes the guarantee that the input to every reducer is sorted by key. The process by which the system performs the sort—and transfers the map outputs to the reducers as inputs—is known as the *shuffle*.[6] In this section, we look at how the shuffle works, as a basic understanding would be helpful, should you need to optimize a MapReduce program. The shuffle is an area of the codebase where refinements and improvements are continually being made, so the following description necessarily conceals many details (and may change over time; this is for version 0.20). In many ways, the shuffle is the heart of MapReduce and is where the "magic" happens.

The Map Side

When the map function starts producing output, it is not simply written to disk. The process is more involved, and takes advantage of buffering writes in memory and doing some presorting for efficiency reasons. Figure 6-6 shows what happens.

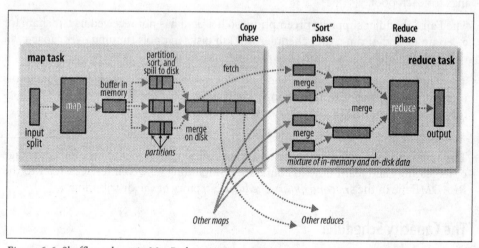

Figure 6-6. Shuffle and sort in MapReduce

6. The term *shuffle* is actually imprecise, since in some contexts it refers to only the part of the process where map outputs are fetched by reduce tasks. In this section, we take it to mean the whole process, from the point where a map produces output to where a reduce consumes input.

Each map task has a circular memory buffer that it writes the output to. The buffer is 100 MB by default, a size that can be tuned by changing the io.sort.mb property. When the contents of the buffer reaches a certain threshold size (io.sort.spill.percent, which has the default 0.80, or 80%), a background thread will start to *spill* the contents to disk. Map outputs will continue to be written to the buffer while the spill takes place, but if the buffer fills up during this time, the map will block until the spill is complete.

Spills are written in round-robin fashion to the directories specified by the mapred.local.dir property, in a job-specific subdirectory.

Before it writes to disk, the thread first divides the data into partitions corresponding to the reducers that they will ultimately be sent to. Within each partition, the background thread performs an in-memory sort by key, and if there is a combiner function, it is run on the output of the sort. Running the combiner function makes for a more compact map output, so there is less data to write to local disk and to transfer to the reducer.

Each time the memory buffer reaches the spill threshold, a new spill file is created, so after the map task has written its last output record, there could be several spill files. Before the task is finished, the spill files are merged into a single partitioned and sorted output file. The configuration property io.sort.factor controls the maximum number of streams to merge at once; the default is 10.

If there are at least three spill files (set by the min.num.spills.for.combine property), the combiner is run again before the output file is written. Recall that combiners may be run repeatedly over the input without affecting the final result. If there are only one or two spills, the potential reduction in map output size is not worth the overhead in invoking the combiner, so it is not run again for this map output.

It is often a good idea to compress the map output as it is written to disk because doing so makes it faster to write to disk, saves disk space, and reduces the amount of data to transfer to the reducer. By default, the output is not compressed, but it is easy to enable this by setting mapred.compress.map.output to true. The compression library to use is specified by mapred.map.output.compression.codec; see "Compression" on page 83 for more on compression formats.

The output file's partitions are made available to the reducers over HTTP. The maximum number of worker threads used to serve the file partitions is controlled by the tasktracker.http.threads property; this setting is per tasktracker, not per map task slot. The default of 40 may need to be increased for large clusters running large jobs. In MapReduce 2, this property is not applicable because the maximum number of threads used is set automatically based on the number of processors on the machine. (MapReduce 2 uses Netty, which by default allows up to twice as many threads as there are processors.)

The Reduce Side

Let's turn now to the reduce part of the process. The map output file is sitting on the local disk of the machine that ran the map task (note that although map outputs always get written to local disk, reduce outputs may not be), but now it is needed by the machine that is about to run the reduce task for the partition. Furthermore, the reduce task needs the map output for its particular partition from several map tasks across the cluster. The map tasks may finish at different times, so the reduce task starts copying their outputs as soon as each completes. This is known as the *copy phase* of the reduce task. The reduce task has a small number of copier threads so that it can fetch map outputs in parallel. The default is five threads, but this number can be changed by setting the `mapred.reduce.parallel.copies` property.

> How do reducers know which machines to fetch map output from?
>
> As map tasks complete successfully, they notify their parent tasktracker of the status update, which in turn notifies the jobtracker. (In MapReduce 2, the tasks notify their application master directly.) These notifications are transmitted over the heartbeat communication mechanism described earlier. Therefore, for a given job, the jobtracker (or application master) knows the mapping between map outputs and hosts. A thread in the reducer periodically asks the master for map output hosts until it has retrieved them all.
>
> Hosts do not delete map outputs from disk as soon as the first reducer has retrieved them, as the reducer may subsequently fail. Instead, they wait until they are told to delete them by the jobtracker (or application master), which is after the job has completed.

The map outputs are copied to the reduce task JVM's memory if they are small enough (the buffer's size is controlled by `mapred.job.shuffle.input.buffer.percent`, which specifies the proportion of the heap to use for this purpose); otherwise, they are copied to disk. When the in-memory buffer reaches a threshold size (controlled by `mapred.job.shuffle.merge.percent`) or reaches a threshold number of map outputs (`mapred.inmem.merge.threshold`), it is merged and spilled to disk. If a combiner is specified, it will be run during the merge to reduce the amount of data written to disk.

As the copies accumulate on disk, a background thread merges them into larger, sorted files. This saves some time merging later on. Note that any map outputs that were compressed (by the map task) have to be decompressed in memory in order to perform a merge on them.

When all the map outputs have been copied, the reduce task moves into the *sort phase* (which should properly be called the *merge* phase, as the sorting was carried out on the map side), which merges the map outputs, maintaining their sort ordering. This is done in rounds. For example, if there were 50 map outputs and the *merge factor* was 10 (the default, controlled by the `io.sort.factor` property, just like in the map's merge), there would be five rounds. Each round would merge 10 files into one, so at the end there would be five intermediate files.

Rather than have a final round that merges these five files into a single sorted file, the merge saves a trip to disk by directly feeding the reduce function in what is the last phase: the *reduce phase*. This final merge can come from a mixture of in-memory and on-disk segments.

> The number of files merged in each round is actually more subtle than this example suggests. The goal is to merge the minimum number of files to get to the merge factor for the final round. So if there were 40 files, the merge would not merge 10 files in each of the four rounds to get 4 files. Instead, the first round would merge only 4 files, and the subsequent three rounds would merge the full 10 files. The 4 merged files and the 6 (as yet unmerged) files make a total of 10 files for the final round. The process is illustrated in Figure 6-7.
>
> Note that this does not change the number of rounds; it's just an optimization to minimize the amount of data that is written to disk, since the final round always merges directly into the reduce.

During the reduce phase, the reduce function is invoked for each key in the sorted output. The output of this phase is written directly to the output filesystem, typically HDFS. In the case of HDFS, because the tasktracker node (or node manager) is also running a datanode, the first block replica will be written to the local disk.

Configuration Tuning

We are now in a better position to understand how to tune the shuffle to improve MapReduce performance. The relevant settings, which can be used on a per-job basis (except where noted), are summarized in Tables 6-1 and 6-2, along with the defaults, which are good for general-purpose jobs.

The general principle is to give the shuffle as much memory as possible. However, there is a trade-off, in that you need to make sure that your map and reduce functions get enough memory to operate. This is why it is best to write your map and reduce functions to use as little memory as possible—certainly they should not use an unbounded amount of memory (by avoiding accumulating values in a map, for example).

The amount of memory given to the JVMs in which the map and reduce tasks run is set by the `mapred.child.java.opts` property. You should try to make this as large as possible for the amount of memory on your task nodes; the discussion in "Memory" on page 307 goes through the constraints to consider.

On the map side, the best performance can be obtained by avoiding multiple spills to disk; one is optimal. If you can estimate the size of your map outputs, you can set the `io.sort.*` properties appropriately to minimize the number of spills. In particular, you

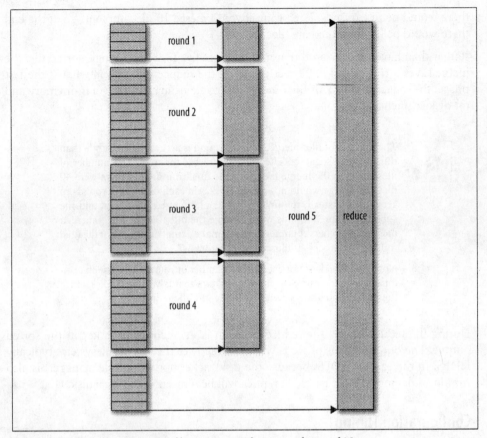

Figure 6-7. Efficiently merging 40 file segments with a merge factor of 10

should increase io.sort.mb if you can. There is a MapReduce counter ("Spilled records"; see "Counters" on page 259) that counts the total number of records that were spilled to disk over the course of a job, which can be useful for tuning. Note that the counter includes both map- and reduce-side spills.

On the reduce side, the best performance is obtained when the intermediate data can reside entirely in memory. This does not happen by default, since for the general case all the memory is reserved for the reduce function. But if your reduce function has light memory requirements, setting the mapred.inmem.merge.threshold to 0 and the mapred.job.reduce.input.buffer.percent to 1.0 (or a lower value; see Table 6-2) may bring a performance boost.

More generally, Hadoop uses a buffer size of 4 KB by default, which is low, so you should increase this across the cluster (by setting io.file.buffer.size; see also "Other Hadoop Properties" on page 317).

In April 2008, Hadoop won the general-purpose terabyte sort benchmark (described in "TeraByte Sort on Apache Hadoop" on page 603), and one of the optimizations used was keeping the intermediate data in memory on the reduce side.

Table 6-1. Map-side tuning properties

Property name	Type	Default value	Description
io.sort.mb	int	100	The size, in megabytes, of the memory buffer to use while sorting map output.
io.sort.record.percent	float	0.05	The proportion of io.sort.mb reserved for storing record boundaries of the map outputs. The remaining space is used for the map output records themselves. This property was removed in releases after 1.x, as the shuffle code was improved to do a better job of using all the available memory for map output and accounting information.
io.sort.spill.percent	float	0.80	The threshold usage proportion for both the map output memory buffer and the record boundaries index to start the process of spilling to disk.
io.sort.factor	int	10	The maximum number of streams to merge at once when sorting files. This property is also used in the reduce. It's fairly common to increase this to 100.
min.num.spills.for. combine	int	3	The minimum number of spill files needed for the combiner to run (if a combiner is specified).
mapred.compress.map. output	boolean	false	Compress map outputs.
mapred.map.output. compression.codec	Class name	org.apache.hadoop.io. compress.DefaultCodec	The compression codec to use for map outputs.
task tracker.http.threads	int	40	The number of worker threads per tasktracker for serving the map outputs to reducers. This is a cluster-wide setting and cannot be set by individual jobs. Not applicable in MapReduce 2.

Table 6-2. Reduce-side tuning properties

Property name	Type	Default value	Description
mapred.reduce.parallel.copies	int	5	The number of threads used to copy map outputs to the reducer.
mapred.reduce.copy.backoff	int	300	The maximum amount of time, in seconds, to spend retrieving one map output for a reducer before declaring it as failed. The reducer may repeatedly reattempt a transfer within this time if it fails (using exponential backoff).
io.sort.factor	int	10	The maximum number of streams to merge at once when sorting files. This property is also used in the map.
mapred.job.shuffle.input.buffer.percent	float	0.70	The proportion of total heap size to be allocated to the map outputs buffer during the copy phase of the shuffle.
mapred.job.shuffle.merge.percent	float	0.66	The threshold usage proportion for the map outputs buffer (defined by mapred.job.shuffle.input.buffer.percent) for starting the process of merging the outputs and spilling to disk.
mapred.inmem.merge.threshold	int	1000	The threshold number of map outputs for starting the process of merging the outputs and spilling to disk. A value of 0 or less means there is no threshold, and the spill behavior is governed solely by mapred.job.shuffle.merge.percent.
mapred.job.reduce.input.buffer.percent	float	0.0	The proportion of total heap size to be used for retaining map outputs in memory during the reduce. For the reduce phase to begin, the size of map outputs in memory must be no more than this size. By default, all map outputs are merged to disk before the reduce begins, to give the reducers as much memory as possible. However, if your reducers require less memory, this value may be increased to minimize the number of trips to disk.

Task Execution

We saw how the MapReduce system executes tasks in the context of the overall job at the beginning of this chapter in "Anatomy of a MapReduce Job Run" on page 189. In this section, we'll look at some more controls that MapReduce users have over task execution.

The Task Execution Environment

Hadoop provides information to a map or reduce task about the environment in which it is running. For example, a map task can discover the name of the file it is processing (see "File information in the mapper" on page 241), and a map or reduce task can find out the attempt number of the task. The properties in Table 6-3 can be accessed from the job's configuration, obtained in the old MapReduce API by providing an implementation of the `configure()` method for `Mapper` or `Reducer`, where the configuration is passed in as an argument. In the new API, these properties can be accessed from the context object passed to all methods of the `Mapper` or `Reducer`.

Table 6-3. Task environment properties

Property name	Type	Description	Example
mapred.job.id	String	The job ID (see "Job, Task, and Task Attempt IDs" on page 165 for a description of the format)	job_200811201130_0004
mapred.tip.id	String	The task ID	task_200811201130_0004_m_000003
mapred.task.id	String	The task attempt ID (*not* the task ID)	attempt_200811201130_0004_m_000003_0
mapred.task. partition	int	The index of the task within the job	3
mapred.task.is.map	boolean	Whether this task is a map task	true

Streaming environment variables

Hadoop sets job configuration parameters as environment variables for Streaming programs. However, it replaces nonalphanumeric characters with underscores to make sure they are valid names. The following Python expression illustrates how you can retrieve the value of the `mapred.job.id` property from within a Python Streaming script:

```
os.environ["mapred_job_id"]
```

You can also set environment variables for the Streaming processes launched by MapReduce by supplying the `-cmdenv` option to the Streaming launcher program (once for each variable you wish to set). For example, the following sets the `MAGIC_PARAMETER` environment variable:

```
-cmdenv MAGIC_PARAMETER=abracadabra
```

Speculative Execution

The MapReduce model is to break jobs into tasks and run the tasks in parallel to make the overall job execution time smaller than it would be if the tasks ran sequentially.

This makes the job execution time sensitive to slow-running tasks, as it takes only one slow task to make the whole job take significantly longer than it would have done otherwise. When a job consists of hundreds or thousands of tasks, the possibility of a few straggling tasks is very real.

Tasks may be slow for various reasons, including hardware degradation or software misconfiguration, but the causes may be hard to detect because the tasks still complete successfully, albeit after a longer time than expected. Hadoop doesn't try to diagnose and fix slow-running tasks; instead, it tries to detect when a task is running slower than expected and launches another equivalent task as a backup. This is termed *speculative execution* of tasks.

It's important to understand that speculative execution does not work by launching two duplicate tasks at about the same time so they can race each other. This would be wasteful of cluster resources. Rather, a speculative task is launched only after all the tasks for a job have been launched, and then only for tasks that have been running for some time (at least a minute) and have failed to make as much progress, on average, as the other tasks from the job. When a task completes successfully, any duplicate tasks that are running are killed since they are no longer needed. So if the original task completes before the speculative task, the speculative task is killed; on the other hand, if the speculative task finishes first, the original is killed.

Speculative execution is an optimization, and not a feature to make jobs run more reliably. If there are bugs that sometimes cause a task to hang or slow down, relying on speculative execution to avoid these problems is unwise and won't work reliably, since the same bugs are likely to affect the speculative task. You should fix the bug so that the task doesn't hang or slow down.

Speculative execution is turned on by default. It can be enabled or disabled independently for map tasks and reduce tasks, on a cluster-wide basis, or on a per-job basis. The relevant properties are shown in Table 6-4.

Table 6-4. Speculative execution properties

Property name	Type	Default value	Description
mapred.map.tasks.specula tive.execution	boolean	true	Whether extra instances of map tasks may be launched if a task is making slow progress
mapred.reduce.tasks.specula tive. execution	boolean	true	Whether extra instances of reduce tasks may be launched if a task is making slow progress
yarn.app.mapreduce.am.job. speculator.class	Class	org.apache.hadoop.mapre duce.v2. app.speculate.DefaultSpe culator	The Speculator class implementing the speculative execution policy (MapReduce 2 only)

Property name	Type	Default value	Description
yarn.app.mapreduce.am.job.task.estimator.class	Class	org.apache.hadoop.mapreduce.v2.app.speculate.LegacyTaskRuntimeEstimator	An implementation of TaskRuntimeEstimator used by Speculator instances that provides estimates for task runtimes (MapReduce 2 only)

Why would you ever want to turn off speculative execution? The goal of speculative execution is to reduce job execution time, but this comes at the cost of cluster efficiency. On a busy cluster, speculative execution can reduce overall throughput, since redundant tasks are being executed in an attempt to bring down the execution time for a single job. For this reason, some cluster administrators prefer to turn it off on the cluster and have users explicitly turn it on for individual jobs. This was especially relevant for older versions of Hadoop, when speculative execution could be overly aggressive in scheduling speculative tasks.

There is a good case for turning off speculative execution for reduce tasks, since any duplicate reduce tasks have to fetch the same map outputs as the original task, and this can significantly increase network traffic on the cluster.

Another reason for turning off speculative execution is for tasks that are not idempotent. However, in many cases it is possible to write tasks to be idempotent and use an OutputCommitter to promote the output to its final location when the task succeeds. This technique is explained in more detail in the next section.

Output Committers

Hadoop MapReduce uses a commit protocol to ensure that jobs and tasks either succeed or fail cleanly. The behavior is implemented by the OutputCommitter in use for the job, and this is set in the old MapReduce API by calling the setOutputCommitter() on JobConf or by setting mapred.output.committer.class in the configuration. In the new MapReduce API, the OutputCommitter is determined by the OutputFormat, via its getOutputCommitter() method. The default is FileOutputCommitter, which is appropriate for file-based MapReduce. You can customize an existing OutputCommitter or even write a new implementation if you need to do special setup or cleanup for jobs or tasks.

The OutputCommitter API is as follows (in both old and new MapReduce APIs):

```
public abstract class OutputCommitter {

  public abstract void setupJob(JobContext jobContext) throws IOException;
  public void commitJob(JobContext jobContext) throws IOException { }
  public void abortJob(JobContext jobContext, JobStatus.State state)
    throws IOException { }

  public abstract void setupTask(TaskAttemptContext taskContext)
```

```
    throws IOException;
  public abstract boolean needsTaskCommit(TaskAttemptContext taskContext)
    throws IOException;
  public abstract void commitTask(TaskAttemptContext taskContext)
    throws IOException;
  public abstract void abortTask(TaskAttemptContext taskContext)
    throws IOException;

  }
}
```

The setupJob() method is called before the job is run, and is typically used to perform initialization. For FileOutputCommitter, the method creates the final output directory, ${mapred.output.dir}, and a temporary working space for task output, ${mapred.output.dir}/_temporary.

If the job succeeds, the commitJob() method is called, which in the default file-based implementation deletes the temporary working space and creates a hidden empty marker file in the output directory called _SUCCESS to indicate to filesystem clients that the job completed successfully. If the job did not succeed, abortJob() is called with a state object indicating whether the job failed or was killed (by a user, for example). In the default implementation, this will delete the job's temporary working space.

The operations are similar at the task level. The setupTask() method is called before the task is run, and the default implementation doesn't do anything, because temporary directories named for task outputs are created when the task outputs are written.

The commit phase for tasks is optional and may be disabled by returning false from needsTaskCommit(). This saves the framework from having to run the distributed commit protocol for the task, and neither commitTask() nor abortTask() is called. FileOutputCommitter will skip the commit phase when no output has been written by a task.

If a task succeeds, commitTask() is called, which in the default implementation moves the temporary task output directory (which has the task attempt ID in its name to avoid conflicts between task attempts) to the final output path, ${mapred.output.dir}. Otherwise, the framework calls abortTask(), which deletes the temporary task output directory.

The framework ensures that in the event of multiple task attempts for a particular task, only one will be committed; the others will be aborted. This situation may arise because the first attempt failed for some reason—in which case it would be aborted, and a later, successful attempt would be committed. Another case is if two task attempts were running concurrently as speculative duplicates; in this instance, the one that finished first would be committed, and the other would be aborted.

Task side-effect files

The usual way of writing output from map and reduce tasks is by using the OutputCollector to collect key-value pairs. Some applications need more flexibility than a single key-value pair model, so these applications write output files directly from the map or reduce task to a distributed filesystem, such as HDFS. (There are other ways to produce multiple outputs, too, as described in "Multiple Outputs" on page 253.)

Care needs to be taken to ensure that multiple instances of the same task don't try to write to the same file. As we saw in the previous section, the OutputCommitter protocol solves this problem. If applications write side files in their tasks' working directories, the side files for tasks that successfully complete will be promoted to the output directory automatically, whereas failed tasks will have their side files deleted.

A task may find its working directory by retrieving the value of the mapred.work.out put.dir property from its configuration file. Alternatively, a MapReduce program using the Java API may call the getWorkOutputPath() static method on FileOutputFormat to get the Path object representing the working directory. The framework creates the working directory before executing the task, so you don't need to create it.

To take a simple example, imagine a program for converting image files from one format to another. One way to do this is to have a map-only job, where each map is given a set of images to convert (perhaps using NLineInputFormat; see "NLineInputFormat" on page 247). If a map task writes the converted images into its working directory, they will be promoted to the output directory when the task successfully finishes.

Task JVM Reuse

Hadoop runs tasks in their own Java Virtual Machine to isolate them from other running tasks. Starting a new JVM for each task can take around a second, which for jobs that run for a minute or so is insignificant. However, jobs that have a large number of very short-lived tasks (these are usually map tasks) or that have a lengthy initialization can see performance gains when the JVM is reused for subsequent tasks.[7]

Note that with task JVM reuse enabled, tasks are *not* run concurrently in a single JVM; rather, the JVM runs tasks sequentially. Tasktrackers can, however, run more than one task at a time, but this is always done in separate JVMs. The properties for controlling the number of map task slots and reduce task slots per tasktracker are discussed in "Memory" on page 307.

The property for controlling task JVM reuse is mapred.job.reuse.jvm.num.tasks. This property specifies the maximum number of tasks to run for a given job for each JVM launched; the default is 1 (see Table 6-5). No distinction is made between map or reduce tasks; however, tasks from different jobs are always run in separate JVMs. The method setNumTasksToExecutePerJvm() on JobConf can also be used to configure this property.

---

7. JVM reuse is not currently supported in MapReduce 2.

Table 6-5. Task JVM reuse properties

Property name	Type	Default value	Description
mapred.job.reuse.jvm.num.tasks	int	1	The maximum number of tasks to run for a given job for each JVM on a tasktracker. A value of −1 indicates no limit, which means the same JVM may be used for all tasks for a job.

Tasks that are CPU-bound may also benefit from task JVM reuse by taking advantage of runtime optimizations applied by the HotSpot JVM. After running for a while, the HotSpot JVM builds up enough information to detect performance-critical sections in the code and dynamically translates the Java byte codes of these hot spots into native machine code. This works well for long-running processes, but JVMs that run for seconds or a few minutes may not gain the full benefit of HotSpot. In these cases, consider enabling task JVM reuse.

Skipping Bad Records

Large datasets are messy. They often have corrupt records. They often have records that are in a different format. They often have missing fields. In an ideal world, your code would cope gracefully with all of these conditions. In practice, it is often expedient to ignore the offending records. Depending on the analysis being performed, if only a small percentage of records are affected, then skipping them may not significantly affect the result. However, if a task trips up when it encounters a bad record—by throwing a runtime exception—then the task fails. Failing tasks are retried (since the failure may be due to hardware failure or some other reason outside the task's control), but if a task fails four times, the whole job is marked as failed (see "Task failure" on page 202). If it is the data that is causing the task to throw an exception, rerunning the task won't help, since it will fail in exactly the same way each time.

> If you are using TextInputFormat ("TextInputFormat" on page 246), you can set a maximum expected line length to safeguard against corrupted files. Corruption in a file can manifest itself as a very long line, which can cause out-of-memory errors and then task failure. By setting mapred.linerecordreader.maxlength to a value in bytes that fits in memory (and is comfortably greater than the length of lines in your input data), the record reader will skip the (long) corrupt lines without the task failing.

The best way to handle corrupt records is in your mapper or reducer code. You can detect the bad record and ignore it, or you can abort the job by throwing an exception. You can also count the total number of bad records in the job using counters to see how widespread the problem is.

In rare cases, though, you can't handle the problem because there is a bug in a third-party library that you can't work around in your mapper or reducer. In these cases, you can use Hadoop's optional *skipping mode* for automatically skipping bad records.[8]

When skipping mode is enabled, tasks report the records being processed back to the tasktracker. When the task fails, the tasktracker retries the task, skipping the records that caused the failure. Because of the extra network traffic and bookkeeping to maintain the failed record ranges, skipping mode is turned on for a task only after it has failed twice.

Thus, for a task consistently failing on a bad record, the tasktracker runs the following task attempts with these outcomes:

1. Task fails.
2. Task fails.
3. Skipping mode is enabled. Task fails, but the failed record is stored by the task-tracker.
4. Skipping mode is still enabled. Task succeeds by skipping the bad record that failed in the previous attempt.

Skipping mode is off by default; you enable it independently for map and reduce tasks using the `SkipBadRecords` class. It's important to note that skipping mode can detect only one bad record per task attempt, so this mechanism is appropriate only for detecting occasional bad records (a few per task, say). You may need to increase the maximum number of task attempts (via `mapred.map.max.attempts` and `mapred.reduce.max.attempts`) to give skipping mode enough attempts to detect and skip all the bad records in an input split.

Bad records that have been detected by Hadoop are saved as sequence files in the job's output directory under the *_logs/skip* subdirectory. These can be inspected for diagnostic purposes after the job has completed (using `hadoop fs -text`, for example).

8. Skipping mode is not supported in the new MapReduce API.

MapReduce Types and Formats

MapReduce has a simple model of data processing: inputs and outputs for the map and reduce functions are key-value pairs. This chapter looks at the MapReduce model in detail and, in particular, how data in various formats, from simple text to structured binary objects, can be used with this model.

MapReduce Types

The map and reduce functions in Hadoop MapReduce have the following general form:

```
map: (K1, V1) → list(K2, V2)
reduce: (K2, list(V2)) → list(K3, V3)
```

In general, the map input key and value types (K1 and V1) are different from the map output types (K2 and V2). However, the reduce input must have the same types as the map output, although the reduce output types may be different again (K3 and V3). The Java API mirrors this general form:

```
public class Mapper<KEYIN, VALUEIN, KEYOUT, VALUEOUT> {

  public class Context extends MapContext<KEYIN, VALUEIN, KEYOUT, VALUEOUT> {
    // ...
  }

  protected void map(KEYIN key, VALUEIN value,
                     Context context) throws IOException, InterruptedException {
    // ...
  }
}

public class Reducer<KEYIN, VALUEIN, KEYOUT, VALUEOUT> {

  public class Context extends ReducerContext<KEYIN, VALUEIN, KEYOUT, VALUEOUT> {
    // ...
  }
```

```
protected void reduce(KEYIN key, Iterable<VALUEIN> values,
                       Context context) throws IOException,
   InterruptedException {
   // ...
   }
}
```

The context objects are used for emitting key-value pairs, and so they are parameterized by the output types so that the signature of the write() method is:

```
public void write(KEYOUT key, VALUEOUT value)
     throws IOException, InterruptedException
```

Since Mapper and Reducer are separate classes, the type parameters have different scopes, and the actual type argument of KEYIN (say) in the Mapper may be different from the type of the type parameter of the same name (KEYIN) in the Reducer. For instance, in the maximum temperature example from earlier chapters, KEYIN is replaced by LongWrita ble for the Mapper and by Text for the Reducer.

Similarly, even though the map output types and the reduce input types must match, this is not enforced by the Java compiler.

The type parameters are named differently from the abstract types (KEYIN versus K1, and so on), but the form is the same.

If a combine function is used, then it is the same form as the reduce function (and is an implementation of Reducer), except its output types are the intermediate key and value types (K2 and V2), so they can feed the reduce function:

```
map:     (K1, V1)       → list(K2, V2)
combine: (K2, list(V2)) → list(K2, V2)
reduce:  (K2, list(V2)) → list(K3, V3)
```

Often the combine and reduce functions are the same, in which case K3 is the same as K2, and V3 is the same as V2.

The partition function operates on the intermediate key and value types (K2 and V2) and returns the partition index. In practice, the partition is determined solely by the key (the value is ignored):

```
partition: (K2, V2) → integer
```

Or in Java:

```
public abstract class Partitioner<KEY, VALUE> {

  public abstract int getPartition(KEY key, VALUE value, int numPartitions);
}
```

So much for the theory. How does this help configure MapReduce jobs? Table 7-1 summarizes the configuration options for the new API (and Table 7-2 does the same for the old API). It is divided into the properties that determine the types and those that have to be compatible with the configured types.

Input types are set by the input format. So, for instance, a TextInputFormat generates keys of type LongWritable and values of type Text. The other types are set explicitly by calling the methods on the Job (or JobConf in the old API). If not set explicitly, the intermediate types default to the (final) output types, which default to LongWritable and Text. So if K2 and K3 are the same, you don't need to call setMapOutputKeyClass(), because it falls back to the type set by calling setOutputKeyClass(). Similarly, if V2 and V3 are the same, you only need to use setOutputValueClass().

It may seem strange that these methods for setting the intermediate and final output types exist at all. After all, why can't the types be determined from a combination of the mapper and the reducer? The answer has to do with a limitation in Java generics: type erasure means that the type information isn't always present at runtime, so Hadoop has to be given it explicitly. This also means that it's possible to configure a MapReduce job with incompatible types, because the configuration isn't checked at compile time. The settings that have to be compatible with the MapReduce types are listed in the lower part of Table 7-1. Type conflicts are detected at runtime during job execution, and for this reason, it is wise to run a test job using a small amount of data to flush out and fix any type incompatibilities.

Table 7-1. Configuration of MapReduce types in the new API

Property	Job setter method	Input types		Intermediate types		Output types	
		K1	V1	K2	V2	K3	V3
Properties for configuring types:							
mapreduce.job.inputformat.class	setInputFormatClass()	•	•				
mapreduce.map.output.key.class	setMapOutputKeyClass()			•			
mapreduce.map.output.value.class	setMapOutputValueClass()				•		
mapreduce.job.output.key.class	setOutputKeyClass()					•	
mapreduce.job.output.value.class	setOutputValueClass()						•
Properties that must be consistent with the types:							
mapreduce.job.map.class	setMapperClass()	•	•	•	•		
mapreduce.job.combine.class	setCombinerClass()			•	•		
mapreduce.job.partitioner.class	setPartitionerClass()			•	•		
mapreduce.job.output.key.comparator.class	setSortComparatorClass()			•			
mapreduce.job.output.group.comparator.class	setGroupingComparatorClass()			•			
mapreduce.job.reduce.class	setReducerClass()			•	•	•	•
mapreduce.job.outputformat.class	setOutputFormatClass()					•	•

Table 7-2. *Configuration of MapReduce types in the old API*

Property	JobConf setter method	Input types		Intermediate types		Output types	
		K1	V1	K2	V2	K3	V3
Properties for configuring types:							
mapred.input.format.class	setInputFormat()	•	•				
mapred.mapoutput.key.class	setMapOutputKeyClass()			•			
mapred.mapoutput.value.class	setMapOutputValueClass()				•		
mapred.output.key.class	setOutputKeyClass()					•	
mapred.output.value.class	setOutputValueClass()						•
Properties that must be consistent with the types:							
mapred.mapper.class	setMapperClass()	•	•	•	•		
mapred.map.runner.class	setMapRunnerClass()	•	•	•	•		
mapred.combiner.class	setCombinerClass()			•	•		
mapred.partitioner.class	setPartitionerClass()			•	•		
mapred.output.key.comparator.class	setOutputKeyComparatorClass()			•			
mapred.output.value.groupfn.class	setOutputValueGroupingComparator()			•			
mapred.reducer.class	setReducerClass()			•	•	•	•
mapred.output.format.class	setOutputFormat()					•	•

The Default MapReduce Job

What happens when you run MapReduce without setting a mapper or a reducer? Let's try it by running this minimal MapReduce program:

```
public class MinimalMapReduce extends Configured implements Tool {

  @Override
  public int run(String[] args) throws Exception {
    if (args.length != 2) {
      System.err.printf("Usage: %s [generic options] <input> <output>\n",
          getClass().getSimpleName());
      ToolRunner.printGenericCommandUsage(System.err);
      return -1;
    }

    Job job = new Job(getConf());
    job.setJarByClass(getClass());
    FileInputFormat.addInputPath(job, new Path(args[0]));
    FileOutputFormat.setOutputPath(job, new Path(args[1]));
    return job.waitForCompletion(true) ? 0 : 1;
  }

  public static void main(String[] args) throws Exception {
    int exitCode = ToolRunner.run(new MinimalMapReduce(), args);
    System.exit(exitCode);
  }
}
```

The only configuration that we set is an input path and an output path. We run it over a subset of our weather data with the following:

```
% hadoop MinimalMapReduce "input/ncdc/all/190{1,2}.gz" output
```

We do get some output: one file named *part-r-00000* in the output directory. Here's what the first few lines look like (truncated to fit the page):

```
0→0029029070999991901010106004+64333+023450FM-12+000599999V0202701N01591...
0→0035029070999991902010106004+64333+023450FM-12+000599999V0201401N01181...
135→0029029070999991901010113004+64333+023450FM-12+000599999V0202901N00821...
141→0035029070999991902010113004+64333+023450FM-12+000599999V0201401N01181...
270→0029029070999991901010120004+64333+023450FM-12+000599999V0209991C00001...
282→0035029070999991902010120004+64333+023450FM-12+000599999V0201401N01391...
```

Each line is an integer followed by a tab character, followed by the original weather data record. Admittedly, it's not a very useful program, but understanding how it produces its output does provide some insight into the defaults that Hadoop uses when running MapReduce jobs. Example 7-1 shows a program that has exactly the same effect as MinimalMapReduce, but explicitly sets the job settings to their defaults.

Example 7-1. A minimal MapReduce driver, with the defaults explicitly set

```
public class MinimalMapReduceWithDefaults extends Configured implements Tool {

  @Override
  public int run(String[] args) throws Exception {
    Job job = JobBuilder.parseInputAndOutput(this, getConf(), args);
    if (job == null) {
      return -1;
    }

    job.setInputFormatClass(TextInputFormat.class);

    job.setMapperClass(Mapper.class);

    job.setMapOutputKeyClass(LongWritable.class);
    job.setMapOutputValueClass(Text.class);

    job.setPartitionerClass(HashPartitioner.class);

    job.setNumReduceTasks(1);
    job.setReducerClass(Reducer.class);

    job.setOutputKeyClass(LongWritable.class);
    job.setOutputValueClass(Text.class);

    job.setOutputFormatClass(TextOutputFormat.class);

    return job.waitForCompletion(true) ? 0 : 1;
  }

  public static void main(String[] args) throws Exception {
    int exitCode = ToolRunner.run(new MinimalMapReduceWithDefaults(), args);
    System.exit(exitCode);
  }
}
```

We've simplified the first few lines of the run() method by extracting the logic for printing usage and setting the input and output paths into a helper method. Almost all MapReduce drivers take these two arguments (input and output), so reducing the boilerplate code here is a good thing. Here are the relevant methods in the JobBuilder class for reference:

```
    public static Job parseInputAndOutput(Tool tool, Configuration conf,
        String[] args) throws IOException {

      if (args.length != 2) {
        printUsage(tool, "<input> <output>");
        return null;
      }
      Job job = new Job(conf);
      job.setJarByClass(tool.getClass());
      FileInputFormat.addInputPath(job, new Path(args[0]));
      FileOutputFormat.setOutputPath(job, new Path(args[1]));
      return job;
```

```
  }

  public static void printUsage(Tool tool, String extraArgsUsage) {
    System.err.printf("Usage: %s [genericOptions] %s\n\n",
        tool.getClass().getSimpleName(), extraArgsUsage);
    GenericOptionsParser.printGenericCommandUsage(System.err);
  }
```

Going back to `MinimalMapReduceWithDefaults` in Example 7-1, although there are many other default job settings, the ones highlighted are those most central to running a job. Let's go through them in turn.

The default input format is `TextInputFormat`, which produces keys of type `LongWrita ble` (the offset of the beginning of the line in the file) and values of type `Text` (the line of text). This explains where the integers in the final output come from: they are the line offsets.

The default mapper is just the `Mapper` class, which writes the input key and value unchanged to the output:

```
public class Mapper<KEYIN, VALUEIN, KEYOUT, VALUEOUT> {

  protected void map(KEYIN key, VALUEIN value,
                     Context context) throws IOException, InterruptedException {
    context.write((KEYOUT) key, (VALUEOUT) value);
  }
}
```

`Mapper` is a generic type, which allows it to work with any key or value types. In this case, the map input and output key is of type `LongWritable`, and the map input and output value is of type `Text`.

The default partitioner is `HashPartitioner`, which hashes a record's key to determine which partition the record belongs in. Each partition is processed by a reduce task, so the number of partitions is equal to the number of reduce tasks for the job:

```
public class HashPartitioner<K, V> extends Partitioner<K, V> {

  public int getPartition(K key, V value,
                          int numReduceTasks) {
    return (key.hashCode() & Integer.MAX_VALUE) % numReduceTasks;
  }
}
```

The key's hash code is turned into a nonnegative integer by bitwise ANDing it with the largest integer value. It is then reduced modulo the number of partitions to find the index of the partition that the record belongs in.

By default, there is a single reducer, and therefore a single partition, so the action of the partitioner is irrelevant in this case since everything goes into one partition. However, it is important to understand the behavior of `HashPartitioner` when you have more than one reduce task. Assuming the key's hash function is a good one, the records

---

will be allocated evenly across reduce tasks, with all records that share the same key being processed by the same reduce task.

You may have noticed that we didn't set the number of map tasks. The reason for this is that the number is equal to the number of splits that the input is turned into, which is driven by the size of the input and the file's block size (if the file is in HDFS). The options for controlling split size are discussed in "FileInputFormat input splits" on page 238.

Choosing the Number of Reducers

The single reducer default is something of a gotcha for new users to Hadoop. Almost all real-world jobs should set this to a larger number; otherwise, the job will be very slow since all the intermediate data flows through a single reduce task. (Note that when running under the local job runner, only zero or one reducers are supported.)

The optimal number of reducers is related to the total number of available reducer slots in your cluster. The total number of slots is found by multiplying the number of nodes in the cluster and the number of slots per node (which is determined by the value of the `mapred.tasktracker.reduce.tasks.maximum` property, described in "Environment Settings" on page 307).

One common setting is to have slightly fewer reducers than total slots, which gives one wave of reduce tasks (and tolerates a few failures, without extending job execution time). If your reduce tasks are very big, it makes sense to have a larger number of reducers (resulting in two waves, for example) so that the tasks are more fine-grained and failure doesn't affect job execution time significantly.

The default reducer is Reducer, again a generic type, which simply writes all its input to its output:

```
public class Reducer<KEYIN, VALUEIN, KEYOUT, VALUEOUT> {

  protected void reduce(KEYIN key, Iterable<VALUEIN> values, Context context
                        Context context) throws IOException, InterruptedException {
    for (VALUEIN value: values) {
      context.write((KEYOUT) key, (VALUEOUT) value);
    }
  }
}
```

For this job, the output key is LongWritable and the output value is Text. In fact, all the keys for this MapReduce program are LongWritable, and all the values are Text, since these are the input keys and values, and the map and reduce functions are both identity functions, which by definition preserve type. Most MapReduce programs, however, don't use the same key or value types throughout, so you need to configure the job to declare the types you are using, as described in the previous section.

Records are sorted by the MapReduce system before being presented to the reducer. In this case, the keys are sorted numerically, which has the effect of interleaving the lines from the input files into one combined output file.

The default output format is TextOutputFormat, which writes out records, one per line, by converting keys and values to strings and separating them with a tab character. This is why the output is tab-separated: it is a feature of TextOutputFormat.

The default Streaming job

In Streaming, the default job is similar, but not identical, to the Java equivalent. The minimal form is:

```
% hadoop jar $HADOOP_INSTALL/contrib/streaming/hadoop-*-streaming.jar \
  -input input/ncdc/sample.txt \
  -output output \
  -mapper /bin/cat
```

Notice that you have to supply a mapper; the default identity mapper will not work. The reason has to do with the default input format, TextInputFormat, which generates LongWritable keys and Text values. However, Streaming output keys and values (including the map keys and values) are always both of type Text.[1] The identity mapper cannot change LongWritable keys to Text keys, so it fails.

When we specify a non-Java mapper and the input format is TextInputFormat, Streaming does something special. It doesn't pass the key to the mapper process; it just passes the value. (For other input formats, the same effect can be achieved by setting stream.map.input.ignoreKey to true.) This is actually very useful because the key is just the line offset in the file and the value is the line, which is all most applications are interested in. The overall effect of this job is to perform a sort of the input.

With more of the defaults spelled out, the command looks like this (notice that Streaming uses the old MapReduce API classes):

```
% hadoop jar $HADOOP_INSTALL/contrib/streaming/hadoop-*-streaming.jar \
  -input input/ncdc/sample.txt \
  -output output \
  -inputformat org.apache.hadoop.mapred.TextInputFormat \
  -mapper /bin/cat \
  -partitioner org.apache.hadoop.mapred.lib.HashPartitioner \
  -numReduceTasks 1 \
  -reducer org.apache.hadoop.mapred.lib.IdentityReducer \
  -outputformat org.apache.hadoop.mapred.TextOutputFormat
```

The mapper and reducer arguments take a command or a Java class. A combiner may optionally be specified using the -combiner argument.

---

1. Except when used in binary mode (not available in 1.x) via the -io rawbytes or -io typedbytes options. Text mode (-io text) is the default.

Keys and values in Streaming

A Streaming application can control the separator that is used when a key-value pair is turned into a series of bytes and sent to the map or reduce process over standard input. The default is a tab character, but it is useful to be able to change it in the case that the keys or values themselves contain tab characters.

Similarly, when the map or reduce writes out key-value pairs, they may be separated by a configurable separator. Furthermore, the key from the output can be composed of more than the first field: it can be made up of the first n fields (defined by `stream.num.map.output.key.fields` or `stream.num.reduce.output.key.fields`), with the value being the remaining fields. For example, if the output from a Streaming process were a,b,c (with a comma as the separator,) and n were two, the key would be parsed as a,b and the value as c.

Separators may be configured independently for maps and reduces. The properties are listed in Table 7-3 and shown in a diagram of the data flow path in Figure 7-1.

These settings do not have any bearing on the input and output formats. For example, if `stream.reduce.output.field.separator` were set to be a colon, say, and the reduce stream process wrote the line a:b to standard out, the Streaming reducer would know to extract the key as a and the value as b. With the standard `TextOutputFormat`, this record would be written to the output file with a tab separating a and b. You can change the separator that `TextOutputFormat` uses by setting `mapred.textoutputfor mat.separator`.

A list of Streaming configuration parameters can be found on the Hadoop website at *http://hadoop.apache.org/mapreduce/docs/current/streaming.html#Configurable+pa rameters*.

Table 7-3. Streaming separator properties

Property name	Type	Default value	Description
`stream.map.input.field. separator`	String	\t	The separator to use when passing the input key and value strings to the stream map process as a stream of bytes
`stream.map.output.field. separator`	String	\t	The separator to use when splitting the output from the stream map process into key and value strings for the map output
`stream.num.map. output.key.fields`	int	1	The number of fields separated by `stream.map.output.field.separator` to treat as the map output key
`stream.reduce.input.field. separator`	String	\t	The separator to use when passing the input key and value strings to the stream reduce process as a stream of bytes

Property name	Type	Default value	Description
stream.reduce.output.field.separator	String	\t	The separator to use when splitting the output from the stream reduce process into key and value strings for the final reduce output
stream.num.reduce.output.key.fields	int	1	The number of fields separated by `stream.reduce.output.field.separator` to treat as the reduce output key

Figure 7-1. *Where separators are used in a Streaming MapReduce job*

Input Formats

Hadoop can process many different types of data formats, from flat text files to databases. In this section, we explore the different formats available.

Input Splits and Records

As we saw in Chapter 2, an input split is a chunk of the input that is processed by a single map. Each map processes a single split. Each split is divided into records, and the map processes each record—a key-value pair—in turn. Splits and records are logical: there is nothing that requires them to be tied to files, for example, although in their most common incarnations, they are. In a database context, a split might correspond to a range of rows from a table and a record to a row in that range (this is precisely what `DBInputFormat` does, which is an input format for reading data from a relational database).

Input splits are represented by the Java class `InputSplit` (which, like all of the classes mentioned in this section, is in the `org.apache.hadoop.mapreduce` package):[2]

```
public abstract class InputSplit {
    public abstract long getLength() throws IOException, InterruptedException;
```

---

2. But see the classes in `org.apache.hadoop.mapred` for the old MapReduce API counterparts.

```
    public abstract String[] getLocations() throws IOException,
        InterruptedException;
}
```

An InputSplit has a length in bytes and a set of storage locations, which are just host-name strings. Notice that a split doesn't contain the input data; it is just a reference to the data. The storage locations are used by the MapReduce system to place map tasks as close to the split's data as possible, and the size is used to order the splits so that the largest get processed first, in an attempt to minimize the job runtime (this is an instance of a greedy approximation algorithm).

As a MapReduce application writer, you don't need to deal with InputSplits directly, as they are created by an InputFormat. An InputFormat is responsible for creating the input splits and dividing them into records. Before we see some concrete examples of InputFormat, let's briefly examine how it is used in MapReduce. Here's the interface:

```
public abstract class InputFormat<K, V> {
    public abstract List<InputSplit> getSplits(JobContext context)
        throws IOException, InterruptedException;

    public abstract RecordReader<K, V>
        createRecordReader(InputSplit split,
                    TaskAttemptContext context) throws IOException,
                                        InterruptedException;
}
```

The client running the job calculates the splits for the job by calling getSplits(), then sends them to the jobtracker, which uses their storage locations to schedule map tasks that will process them on the tasktrackers. On a tasktracker, the map task passes the split to the createRecordReader() method on InputFormat to obtain a RecordReader for that split. A RecordReader is little more than an iterator over records, and the map task uses one to generate record key-value pairs, which it passes to the map function. We can see this by looking at the Mapper's run() method:

```
public void run(Context context) throws IOException, InterruptedException {
    setup(context);
    while (context.nextKeyValue()) {
        map(context.getCurrentKey(), context.getCurrentValue(), context);
    }
    cleanup(context);
}
```

After running setup(), the nextKeyValue() is called repeatedly on the Context (which delegates to the identically-named method on the RecordReader) to populate the key and value objects for the mapper. The key and value are retrieved from the Record Reader by way of the Context and are passed to the map() method for it to do its work. When the reader gets to the end of the stream, the nextKeyValue() method returns false, and the map task runs its cleanup() method and then completes.

It's not shown in the code snippet, but for reasons of efficiency Record Reader implementations will return the *same* key and value objects on each call to getCurrentKey() and getCurrentValue(). Only the contents of these objects are changed by the reader's nextKeyValue() method. This can be a surprise to users, who might expect keys and values to be immutable, and not to be reused. This causes problems when a reference to a key or value object is retained outside the map() method, as its value can change without warning. If you need to do this, make a copy of the object you want to hold on to. For example, for a Text object, you can use its copy constructor: new Text(value).

The situation is similar with reducers. In this case, the value objects in the reducer's iterator are reused, so you need to copy any that you need to retain between calls to the iterator (see Example 8-14).

Finally, note that the Mapper's run() method is public and may be customized by users. MultithreadedMapper is an implementation that runs mappers concurrently in a configurable number of threads (set by mapreduce.mapper.multithreadedmapper.threads). For most data processing tasks, it confers no advantage over the default implementation. However, for mappers that spend a long time processing each record—because they contact external servers, for example—it allows multiple mappers to run in one JVM with little contention. See "Fetcher: A multithreaded MapRunner in action" on page 577 for an example of an application that uses the multithreaded version (using the old API).

FileInputFormat

FileInputFormat is the base class for all implementations of InputFormat that use files as their data source (see Figure 7-2). It provides two things: a place to define which files are included as the input to a job, and an implementation for generating splits for the input files. The job of dividing splits into records is performed by subclasses.

FileInputFormat input paths

The input to a job is specified as a collection of paths, which offers great flexibility in constraining the input to a job. FileInputFormat offers four static convenience methods for setting a Job's input paths:

```
public static void addInputPath(Job job, Path path)
public static void addInputPaths(Job job, String commaSeparatedPaths)
public static void setInputPaths(Job job, Path... inputPaths)
public static void setInputPaths(Job job, String commaSeparatedPaths)
```

The addInputPath() and addInputPaths() methods add a path or paths to the list of inputs. You can call these methods repeatedly to build the list of paths. The setInput Paths() methods set the entire list of paths in one go (replacing any paths set on the Job in previous calls).

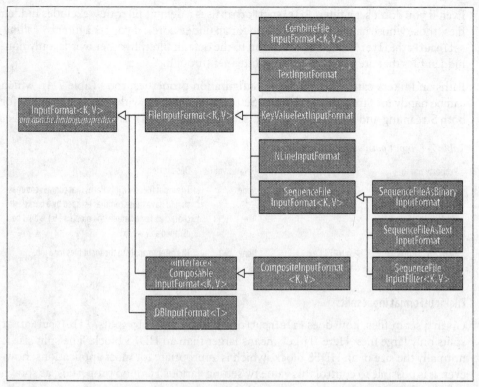

Figure 7-2. InputFormat class hierarchy

A path may represent a file, a directory, or, by using a glob, a collection of files and directories. A path representing a directory includes all the files in the directory as input to the job. See "File patterns" on page 65 for more on using globs.

 The contents of a directory specified as an input path are not processed recursively. In fact, the directory should only contain files. If the directory contains a subdirectory, it will be interpreted as a file, which will cause an error. The way to handle this case is to use a file glob or a filter to select only the files in the directory based on a name pattern. Alternatively, set `mapred.input.dir.recursive` to `true` to force the input directory to be read recursively.

The add and set methods allow files to be specified by inclusion only. To exclude certain files from the input, you can set a filter using the `setInputPathFilter()` method on `FileInputFormat`:

```
public static void setInputPathFilter(Job job, Class<? extends PathFilter> filter)
```

Filters are discussed in more detail in "PathFilter" on page 66.

Even if you don't set a filter, `FileInputFormat` uses a default filter that excludes hidden files (those whose names begin with a dot or an underscore). If you set a filter by calling `setInputPathFilter()`, it acts in addition to the default filter. In other words, only non-hidden files that are accepted by your filter get through.

Paths and filters can be set through configuration properties, too (Table 7-4), which can be handy for Streaming and Pipes. Setting paths is done with the `-input` option for both Streaming and Pipes interfaces, so setting paths directly usually is not needed.

Table 7-4. Input path and filter properties

Property name	Type	Default value	Description
mapred.input.dir	Comma-separated paths	None	The input files for a job. Paths that contain commas should have those commas escaped by a backslash character. For example, the glob {a,b} would be escaped as {a\,b}.
mapred.input. pathFilter.class	PathFilter classname	None	The filter to apply to the input files for a job.

FileInputFormat input splits

Given a set of files, how does `FileInputFormat` turn them into splits? `FileInputFormat` splits only large files. Here "large" means larger than an HDFS block. The split size is normally the size of an HDFS block, which is appropriate for most applications; however, it is possible to control this value by setting various Hadoop properties, as shown in Table 7-5.

Table 7-5. Properties for controlling split size

Property name	Type	Default value	Description
mapred.min.split.size	int	1	The smallest valid size in bytes for a file split
mapred.max.split.size [a]	long	Long.MAX_VALUE, that is, 9223372036854775807	The largest valid size in bytes for a file split
dfs.block.size	long	64 MB, that is,67108864	The size of a block in HDFS in bytes

[a] This property is not present in the old MapReduce API (with the exception of `CombineFileInputFormat`). Instead, it is calculated indirectly as the size of the total input for the job, divided by the guide number of map tasks specified by `mapred.map.tasks` (or the `setNumMapTasks()` method on `JobConf`). Because `mapred.map.tasks` defaults to 1, this makes the maximum split size the size of the input.

The minimum split size is usually 1 byte, although some formats have a lower bound on the split size. (For example, sequence files insert sync entries every so often in the stream, so the minimum split size has to be large enough to ensure that every split has a sync point to allow the reader to resynchronize with a record boundary.)

Applications may impose a minimum split size. By setting this to a value larger than the block size, they can force splits to be larger than a block. There is no good reason for doing this when using HDFS, because doing so will increase the number of blocks that are not local to a map task.

The maximum split size defaults to the maximum value that can be represented by a Java `long` type. It has an effect only when it is less than the block size, forcing splits to be smaller than a block.

The split size is calculated by the formula (see the `computeSplitSize()` method in `FileInputFormat`):

    max(minimumSize, min(maximumSize, blockSize))

and by default:

    minimumSize < blockSize < maximumSize

so the split size is `blockSize`. Various settings for these parameters and how they affect the final split size are illustrated in Table 7-6.

Table 7-6. Examples of how to control the split size

Minimum split size	Maximum split size	Block size	Split size	Comment
1 (default)	Long.MAX_VALUE (default)	64 MB (default)	64 MB	By default, the split size is the same as the default block size.
1 (default)	Long.MAX_VALUE (default)	128 MB	128 MB	The most natural way to increase the split size is to have larger blocks in HDFS, either by setting dfs.block size or on a per-file basis at file construction time.
128 MB	Long.MAX_VALUE (default)	64 MB (default)	128 MB	Making the minimum split size greater than the block size increases the split size, but at the cost of locality.
1 (default)	32 MB	64 MB (default)	32 MB	Making the maximum split size less than the block size decreases the split size.

Small files and CombineFileInputFormat

Hadoop works better with a small number of large files than a large number of small files. One reason for this is that `FileInputFormat` generates splits in such a way that each split is all or part of a single file. If the file is very small ("small" means significantly smaller than an HDFS block) and there are a lot of them, each map task will process very little input, and there will be a lot of them (one per file), each of which imposes extra bookkeeping overhead. Compare a 1 GB file broken into sixteen 64 MB blocks and 10,000 or so 100 KB files. The 10,000 files use one map each, and the job time can be tens or hundreds of times slower than the equivalent one with a single input file and 16 map tasks.

The situation is alleviated somewhat by CombineFileInputFormat, which was designed to work well with small files. Where FileInputFormat creates a split per file, CombineFileInputFormat packs many files into each split so that each mapper has more to process. Crucially, CombineFileInputFormat takes node and rack locality into account when deciding which blocks to place in the same split, so it does not compromise the speed at which it can process the input in a typical MapReduce job.

Of course, if possible, it is still a good idea to avoid the many small files case because MapReduce works best when it can operate at the transfer rate of the disks in the cluster, and processing many small files increases the number of seeks that are needed to run a job. Also, storing large numbers of small files in HDFS is wasteful of the namenode's memory. One technique for avoiding the many small files case is to merge small files into larger files by using a SequenceFile; with this approach, the keys can act as file-names (or a constant such as NullWritable, if not needed) and the values as file contents. See Example 7-4. But if you already have a large number of small files in HDFS, CombineFileInputFormat is worth trying.

CombineFileInputFormat isn't just good for small files; it can bring benefits when processing large files, too. Essentially, CombineFileInputFormat decouples the amount of data that a mapper consumes from the block size of the files in HDFS.

If your mappers can process each block in a matter of seconds, you could use CombineFileInputFormat with the maximum split size set to a small multiple of the number of blocks (by setting the mapred.max.split.size property in bytes) so that each mapper processes more than one block. In return, the overall processing time falls, since proportionally fewer mappers run, which reduces the overhead in task bookkeeping and startup time associated with a large number of short-lived mappers.

Because CombineFileInputFormat is an abstract class without any concrete classes (unlike FileInputFormat), you need to do a bit more work to use it. (Hopefully, common implementations will be added to the library over time.) For example, to have the CombineFileInputFormat equivalent of TextInputFormat, you would create a concrete subclass of CombineFileInputFormat and implement the getRecordReader() method.

Preventing splitting

Some applications don't want files to be split, as this allows a single mapper to process each input file in its entirety. For example, a simple way to check if all the records in a file are sorted is to go through the records in order, checking whether each record is not less than the preceding one. Implemented as a map task, this algorithm will work only if one map processes the whole file.[3]

There are a couple of ways to ensure that an existing file is not split. The first (quick and dirty) way is to increase the minimum split size to be larger than the largest file in your system. Setting it to its maximum value, Long.MAX_VALUE, has this effect. The second is to subclass the concrete subclass of FileInputFormat that you want to use, to override the isSplitable() method[4] to return false. For example, here's a nonsplittable TextInputFormat:

```
import org.apache.hadoop.fs.Path;
import org.apache.hadoop.mapreduce.JobContext;
import org.apache.hadoop.mapreduce.lib.input.TextInputFormat;

public class NonSplittableTextInputFormat extends TextInputFormat {
  @Override
  protected boolean isSplitable(JobContext context, Path file) {
    return false;
  }
}
```

File information in the mapper

A mapper processing a file input split can find information about the split by calling the getInputSplit() method on the Mapper's Context object. When the input format derives from FileInputFormat, the InputSplit returned by this method can be cast to a FileSplit to access the file information listed in Table 7-7.

In the old MapReduce API, Streaming, and Pipes, the same file split information is made available through properties that can be read from the mapper's configuration. (In the old MapReduce API this is achieved by implementing configure() in your Mapper implementation to get access to the JobConf object.)

In addition to the properties in Table 7-7, all mappers and reducers have access to the properties listed in "The Task Execution Environment" on page 215.

Table 7-7. File split properties

FileSplit method	Property name	Type	Description
getPath()	map.input.file	Path/String	The path of the input file being processed

---

3. This is how the mapper in SortValidator.RecordStatsChecker is implemented.

4. In the method name isSplitable(), "splitable" has a single "t." It is usually spelled "splittable," which is the spelling I have used in this book.

FileSplit method	Property name	Type	Description
getStart()	map.input.start	long	The byte offset of the start of the split from the beginning of the file
getLength()	map.input.length	long	The length of the split in bytes

In the next section, you shall see how to use a `FileSplit` when we need to access the split's filename.

Processing a whole file as a record

A related requirement that sometimes crops up is for mappers to have access to the full contents of a file. Not splitting the file gets you part of the way there, but you also need to have a RecordReader that delivers the file contents as the value of the record. The listing for `WholeFileInputFormat` in Example 7-2 shows a way of doing this.

Example 7-2. An InputFormat for reading a whole file as a record

```java
public class WholeFileInputFormat
    extends FileInputFormat<NullWritable, BytesWritable> {

  @Override
  protected boolean isSplitable(JobContext context, Path file) {
    return false;
  }

  @Override
  public RecordReader<NullWritable, BytesWritable> createRecordReader(
      InputSplit split, TaskAttemptContext context) throws IOException,
      InterruptedException {
    WholeFileRecordReader reader = new WholeFileRecordReader();
    reader.initialize(split, context);
    return reader;
  }
}
```

`WholeFileInputFormat` defines a format where the keys are not used, represented by `NullWritable`, and the values are the file contents, represented by `BytesWritable` instances. It defines two methods. First, the format is careful to specify that input files should never be split, by overriding `isSplitable()` to return `false`. Second, we implement `createRecordReader()` to return a custom implementation of `Record Reader`, which appears in Example 7-3.

Example 7-3. The RecordReader used by WholeFileInputFormat for reading a whole file as a record

```java
class WholeFileRecordReader extends RecordReader<NullWritable, BytesWritable> {

  private FileSplit fileSplit;
  private Configuration conf;
  private BytesWritable value = new BytesWritable();
  private boolean processed = false;
```

```java
  @Override
  public void initialize(InputSplit split, TaskAttemptContext context)
      throws IOException, InterruptedException {
    this.fileSplit = (FileSplit) split;
    this.conf = context.getConfiguration();
  }

  @Override
  public boolean nextKeyValue() throws IOException, InterruptedException {
    if (!processed) {
      byte[] contents = new byte[(int) fileSplit.getLength()];
      Path file = fileSplit.getPath();
      FileSystem fs = file.getFileSystem(conf);
      FSDataInputStream in = null;
      try {
        in = fs.open(file);
        IOUtils.readFully(in, contents, 0, contents.length);
        value.set(contents, 0, contents.length);
      } finally {
        IOUtils.closeStream(in);
      }
      processed = true;
      return true;
    }
    return false;
  }

  @Override
  public NullWritable getCurrentKey() throws IOException, InterruptedException {
    return NullWritable.get();
  }

  @Override
  public BytesWritable getCurrentValue() throws IOException,
      InterruptedException {
    return value;
  }

  @Override
  public float getProgress() throws IOException {
    return processed ? 1.0f : 0.0f;
  }

  @Override
  public void close() throws IOException {
    // do nothing
  }
}
```

WholeFileRecordReader is responsible for taking a FileSplit and converting it into a single record, with a null key and a value containing the bytes of the file. Because there is only a single record, WholeFileRecordReader has either processed it or not, so it maintains a Boolean called processed. If the file has not been processed when the nextKey

Value() method is called, then we open the file, create a byte array whose length is the length of the file, and use the Hadoop IOUtils class to slurp the file into the byte array. Then we set the array on the BytesWritable instance that was passed into the next() method, and return true to signal that a record has been read.

The other methods are straightforward bookkeeping methods for accessing the current key and value types, getting the progress of the reader, and a close() method, which is invoked by the MapReduce framework when the reader is done.

To demonstrate how WholeFileInputFormat can be used, consider a MapReduce job for packaging small files into sequence files, where the key is the original filename and the value is the content of the file. The listing is in Example 7-4.

Example 7-4. A MapReduce program for packaging a collection of small files as a single SequenceFile

```java
public class SmallFilesToSequenceFileConverter extends Configured
    implements Tool {

  static class SequenceFileMapper
      extends Mapper<NullWritable, BytesWritable, Text, BytesWritable> {

    private Text filenameKey;

    @Override
    protected void setup(Context context) throws IOException,
        InterruptedException {
      InputSplit split = context.getInputSplit();
      Path path = ((FileSplit) split).getPath();
      filenameKey = new Text(path.toString());
    }

    @Override
    protected void map(NullWritable key, BytesWritable value, Context context)
        throws IOException, InterruptedException {
      context.write(filenameKey, value);
    }

  }

  @Override
  public int run(String[] args) throws Exception {
    Job job = JobBuilder.parseInputAndOutput(this, getConf(), args);
    if (job == null) {
      return -1;
    }

    job.setInputFormatClass(WholeFileInputFormat.class);
    job.setOutputFormatClass(SequenceFileOutputFormat.class);

    job.setOutputKeyClass(Text.class);
    job.setOutputValueClass(BytesWritable.class);

    job.setMapperClass(SequenceFileMapper.class);
```

```
    return job.waitForCompletion(true) ? 0 : 1;
  }

  public static void main(String[] args) throws Exception {
    int exitCode = ToolRunner.run(new SmallFilesToSequenceFileConverter(), args);
    System.exit(exitCode);
  }
}
```

Because the input format is a `WholeFileInputFormat`, the mapper only has to find the filename for the input file split. It does this by casting the `InputSplit` from the context to a `FileSplit`, which has a method to retrieve the file path. The path is stored in a `Text` object for the key. The reducer is the identity (not explicitly set), and the output format is a `SequenceFileOutputFormat`.

Here's a run on a few small files. We've chosen to use two reducers, so we get two output sequence files:

```
% hadoop jar hadoop-examples.jar SmallFilesToSequenceFileConverter \
  -conf conf/hadoop-localhost.xml -D mapred.reduce.tasks=2 input/smallfiles output
```

Two part files are created, each of which is a sequence file. We can inspect these with the -text option to the filesystem shell:

```
% hadoop fs -conf conf/hadoop-localhost.xml -text output/part-r-00000
hdfs://localhost/user/tom/input/smallfiles/a   61 61 61 61 61 61 61 61 61 61
hdfs://localhost/user/tom/input/smallfiles/c   63 63 63 63 63 63 63 63 63 63
hdfs://localhost/user/tom/input/smallfiles/e
% hadoop fs -conf conf/hadoop-localhost.xml -text output/part-r-00001
hdfs://localhost/user/tom/input/smallfiles/b   62 62 62 62 62 62 62 62 62 62
hdfs://localhost/user/tom/input/smallfiles/d   64 64 64 64 64 64 64 64 64 64
hdfs://localhost/user/tom/input/smallfiles/f   66 66 66 66 66 66 66 66 66 66
```

The input files were named *a*, *b*, *c*, *d*, *e*, and *f*, and each contained 10 characters of the corresponding letter (so, for example, *a* contained 10 "a" characters), except *e*, which was empty. We can see this in the textual rendering of the sequence files, which prints the filename followed by the hex representation of the file.

There's at least one way we could improve this program. As mentioned earlier, having one mapper per file is inefficient, so subclassing `CombineFileInputFormat` instead of `FileInputFormat` would be a better approach. Also, for a related technique of packing files into a Hadoop Archive rather than a sequence file, see the section "Hadoop Archives" on page 77.

Text Input

Hadoop excels at processing unstructured text. In this section, we discuss the different InputFormats that Hadoop provides to process text.

TextInputFormat

TextInputFormat is the default InputFormat. Each record is a line of input. The key, a LongWritable, is the byte offset within the file of the beginning of the line. The value is the contents of the line, excluding any line terminators (e.g., newline or carriage return), and is packaged as a Text object. So a file containing the following text:

```
On the top of the Crumpetty Tree
The Quangle Wangle sat,
But his face you could not see,
On account of his Beaver Hat.
```

is divided into one split of four records. The records are interpreted as the following key-value pairs:

```
(0, On the top of the Crumpetty Tree)
(33, The Quangle Wangle sat,)
(57, But his face you could not see,)
(89, On account of his Beaver Hat.)
```

Clearly, the keys are *not* line numbers. This would be impossible to implement in general, in that a file is broken into splits at byte, not line, boundaries. Splits are processed independently. Line numbers are really a sequential notion. You have to keep a count of lines as you consume them, so knowing the line number within a split would be possible, but not within the file.

However, the offset within the file of each line is known by each split independently of the other splits, since each split knows the size of the preceding splits and just adds this onto the offsets within the split to produce a global file offset. The offset is usually sufficient for applications that need a unique identifier for each line. Combined with the file's name, it is unique within the filesystem. Of course, if all the lines are a fixed width, calculating the line number is simply a matter of dividing the offset by the width.

The Relationship Between Input Splits and HDFS Blocks

The logical records that FileInputFormats define usually do not fit neatly into HDFS blocks. For example, a TextInputFormat's logical records are lines, which will cross HDFS boundaries more often than not. This has no bearing on the functioning of your program—lines are not missed or broken, for example—but it's worth knowing about because it does mean that data-local maps (that is, maps that are running on the same host as their input data) will perform some remote reads. The slight overhead this causes is not normally significant.

Figure 7-3 shows an example. A single file is broken into lines, and the line boundaries do not correspond with the HDFS block boundaries. Splits honor logical record boundaries, in this case lines, so we see that the first split contains line 5, even though it spans the first and second block. The second split starts at line 6.

Figure 7-3. Logical records and HDFS blocks for TextInputFormat

KeyValueTextInputFormat

TextInputFormat's keys, being simply the offset within the file, are not normally very useful. It is common for each line in a file to be a key-value pair, separated by a delimiter such as a tab character. For example, this is the output produced by TextOutputFormat, Hadoop's default OutputFormat. To interpret such files correctly, KeyValueTextInputFormat is appropriate.

You can specify the separator via the mapreduce.input.keyvaluelinerecordreader.key.value.separator property (or key.value.separator.in.input.line in the old API). It is a tab character by default. Consider the following input file, where → represents a (horizontal) tab character:

```
line1→On the top of the Crumpetty Tree
line2→The Quangle Wangle sat,
line3→But his face you could not see,
line4→On account of his Beaver Hat.
```

Like in the TextInputFormat case, the input is in a single split comprising four records, although this time the keys are the Text sequences before the tab in each line:

```
(line1, On the top of the Crumpetty Tree)
(line2, The Quangle Wangle sat,)
(line3, But his face you could not see,)
(line4, On account of his Beaver Hat.)
```

NLineInputFormat

With TextInputFormat and KeyValueTextInputFormat, each mapper receives a variable number of lines of input. The number depends on the size of the split and the length of the lines. If you want your mappers to receive a fixed number of lines of input, then NLineInputFormat is the InputFormat to use. Like TextInputFormat, the keys are the byte offsets within the file and the values are the lines themselves.

N refers to the number of lines of input that each mapper receives. With N set to one (the default), each mapper receives exactly one line of input. The mapreduce.input.lineinputformat.linespermap property (the mapred.line.input.format.linespermap property in the old API) controls the value of N. By way of example, consider these four lines again:

```
On the top of the Crumpetty Tree
The Quangle Wangle sat,
But his face you could not see,
On account of his Beaver Hat.
```

If, for example, N is two, then each split contains two lines. One mapper will receive the first two key-value pairs:

```
(0, On the top of the Crumpetty Tree)
(33, The Quangle Wangle sat,)
```

And another mapper will receive the second two key-value pairs:

```
(57, But his face you could not see,)
(89, On account of his Beaver Hat.)
```

The keys and values are the same as those that TextInputFormat produces. The difference is in the way the splits are constructed.

Usually, having a map task for a small number of lines of input is inefficient (due to the overhead in task setup), but there are applications that take a small amount of input data and run an extensive (that is, CPU-intensive) computation for it, then emit their output. Simulations are a good example. By creating an input file that specifies input parameters, one per line, you can perform a *parameter sweep*: run a set of simulations in parallel to find how a model varies as the parameter changes.

 If you have long-running simulations, you may fall afoul of task time-outs. When a task doesn't report progress for more than 10 minutes, the tasktracker assumes it has failed and aborts the process (see "Task failure" on page 202).

The best way to guard against this is to report progress periodically, by writing a status message or incrementing a counter, for example. See "What Constitutes Progress in MapReduce?" on page 195.

Another example is using Hadoop to bootstrap data loading from multiple data sources, such as databases. You create a "seed" input file that lists the data sources, one per line. Then each mapper is allocated a single data source, and it loads the data from that source into HDFS. The job doesn't need the reduce phase, so the number of reducers should be set to zero (by calling setNumReduceTasks() on Job). Furthermore, MapReduce jobs can be run to process the data loaded into HDFS. See Appendix C for an example.

XML

Most XML parsers operate on whole XML documents, so if a large XML document is made up of multiple input splits, it is a challenge to parse these individually. Of course, you can process the entire XML document in one mapper (if it is not too large) using the technique in "Processing a whole file as a record" on page 242.

Large XML documents that are composed of a series of "records" (XML document fragments) can be broken into these records using simple string or regular-expression matching to find the start and end tags of records. This alleviates the problem when the document is split by the framework because the next start tag of a record is easy to find by simply scanning from the start of the split, just like `TextInputFormat` finds new-line boundaries.

Hadoop comes with a class for this purpose called `StreamXmlRecordReader` (which is in the `org.apache.hadoop.streaming` package, although it can be used outside of Streaming). You can use it by setting your input format to `StreamInputFormat` and setting the `stream.recordreader.class` property to `org.apache.hadoop.streaming.StreamXml RecordReader`. The reader is configured by setting job configuration properties to tell it the patterns for the start and end tags (see the class documentation for details).[5]

To take an example, Wikipedia provides dumps of its content in XML form, which are appropriate for processing in parallel with MapReduce using this approach. The data is contained in one large XML wrapper document, which contains a series of elements, such as `page` elements that contain a page's content and associated metadata. Using `StreamXmlRecordReader`, the `page` elements can be interpreted as records for processing by a mapper.

Binary Input

Hadoop MapReduce is not restricted to processing textual data. It has support for binary formats, too.

SequenceFileInputFormat

Hadoop's sequence file format stores sequences of binary key-value pairs. Sequence files are well suited as a format for MapReduce data because they are splittable (they have sync points so that readers can synchronize with record boundaries from an arbitrary point in the file, such as the start of a split), they support compression as a part of the format, and they can store arbitrary types using a variety of serialization frameworks. (These topics are covered in "SequenceFile" on page 130.)

To use data from sequence files as the input to MapReduce, you use `SequenceFileIn putFormat`. The keys and values are determined by the sequence file, and you need to make sure that your map input types correspond. For example, if your sequence file has `IntWritable` keys and `Text` values, like the one created in Chapter 4, then the map signature would be `Mapper<IntWritable, Text, K, V>`, where `K` and `V` are the types of the map's output keys and values.

---

5. See Mahout's `XmlInputFormat` (available from *http://mahout.apache.org/*) for an improved XML input format.

Although its name doesn't give it away, `SequenceFileInputFormat` can read MapFiles as well as sequence files. If it finds a directory where it was expecting a sequence file, `SequenceFileInputFormat` assumes that it is reading a MapFile and uses its datafile. This is why there is no `MapFileInputFormat` class.

SequenceFileAsTextInputFormat

`SequenceFileAsTextInputFormat` is a variant of `SequenceFileInputFormat` that converts the sequence file's keys and values to `Text` objects. The conversion is performed by calling `toString()` on the keys and values. This format makes sequence files suitable input for Streaming.

SequenceFileAsBinaryInputFormat

`SequenceFileAsBinaryInputFormat` is a variant of `SequenceFileInputFormat` that retrieves the sequence file's keys and values as opaque binary objects. They are encapsulated as `BytesWritable` objects, and the application is free to interpret the underlying byte array as it pleases. Combined with a process that creates sequence files with `Sequence File.Writer`'s `appendRaw()` method or `SequenceFileAsBinaryOutputFormat`, this provides a way to use any binary data types with MapReduce (packaged as a sequence file), although plugging into Hadoop's serialization mechanism is normally a cleaner alternative (see "Serialization Frameworks" on page 108).

Multiple Inputs

Although the input to a MapReduce job may consist of multiple input files (constructed by a combination of file globs, filters, and plain paths), all of the input is interpreted by a single `InputFormat` and a single `Mapper`. What often happens, however, is that the data format evolves over time, so you have to write your mapper to cope with all of your legacy formats. Or you have data sources that provide the same type of data but in different formats. This arises in the case of performing joins of different datasets; see "Reduce-Side Joins" on page 285. For instance, one might be tab-separated plain text, and the other a binary sequence file. Even if they are in the same format, they may have different representations and, therefore, need to be parsed differently.

These cases are handled elegantly by using the `MultipleInputs` class, which allows you to specify which `InputFormat` and `Mapper` to use on a per-path basis. For example, if we had weather data from the UK Met Office[6] that we wanted to combine with the NCDC data for our maximum temperature analysis, we might set up the input as follows:

---

6. Met Office data is generally available only to the research and academic community. However, there is a small amount of monthly weather station data available at *http://www.metoffice.gov.uk/climate/uk/ stationdata/*.

```
MultipleInputs.addInputPath(job, ncdcInputPath,
    TextInputFormat.class, MaxTemperatureMapper.class);
MultipleInputs.addInputPath(job, metOfficeInputPath,
    TextInputFormat.class, MetOfficeMaxTemperatureMapper.class);
```

This code replaces the usual calls to FileInputFormat.addInputPath() and job.setMap
perClass(). Both the Met Office and NCDC data is text-based, so we use TextInput
Format for each. But the line format of the two data sources is different, so we use two
different mappers. The MaxTemperatureMapper reads NCDC input data and extracts the
year and temperature fields. The MetOfficeMaxTemperatureMapper reads Met Office input data and extracts the year and temperature fields. The important thing is that the
map outputs have the same types, since the reducers (which are all of the same type)
see the aggregated map outputs and are not aware of the different mappers used to
produce them.

The MultipleInputs class has an overloaded version of addInputPath() that doesn't take
a mapper:

```
public static void addInputPath(Job job, Path path,
                        Class<? extends InputFormat> inputFormatClass)
```

This is useful when you only have one mapper (set using the Job's setMapperClass()
method) but multiple input formats.

Database Input (and Output)

DBInputFormat is an input format for reading data from a relational database, using
JDBC. Because it doesn't have any sharding capabilities, you need to be careful not to
overwhelm the database from which you are reading by running too many mappers.
For this reason, it is best used for loading relatively small datasets, perhaps for joining
with larger datasets from HDFS using MultipleInputs. The corresponding output format is DBOutputFormat, which is useful for dumping job outputs (of modest size) into a
database.[7]

For an alternative way of moving data between relational databases and HDFS, consider
using Sqoop, which is described in Chapter 15.

HBase's TableInputFormat is designed to allow a MapReduce program to operate on
data stored in an HBase table. TableOutputFormat is for writing MapReduce outputs
into an HBase table.

Output Formats

Hadoop has output data formats that correspond to the input formats covered in the
previous section. The OutputFormat class hierarchy appears in Figure 7-4.

---

7. Instructions for how to use these formats are provided in "Database Access with Hadoop" (*http://www
.cloudera.com/blog/2009/03/06/database-access-with-hadoop/*) by Aaron Kimball.

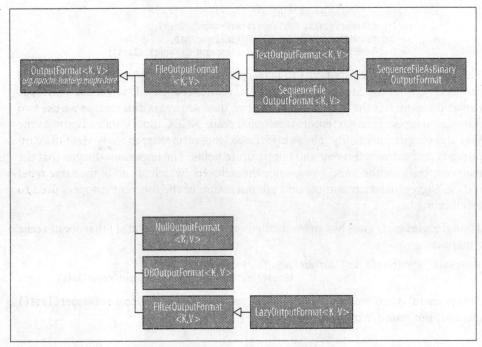

Figure 7-4. OutputFormat class hierarchy

Text Output

The default output format, TextOutputFormat, writes records as lines of text. Its keys and values may be of any type, since TextOutputFormat turns them to strings by calling toString() on them. Each key-value pair is separated by a tab character, although that may be changed using the mapreduce.output.textoutputformat.separator property (mapred.textoutputformat.separator in the old API). The counterpart to TextOutput Format for reading in this case is KeyValueTextInputFormat, since it breaks lines into key-value pairs based on a configurable separator (see "KeyValueTextInputFormat" on page 247).

You can suppress the key or the value (or both, making this output format equivalent to NullOutputFormat, which emits nothing) from the output using a NullWritable type. This also causes no separator to be written, which makes the output suitable for reading in using TextInputFormat.

Binary Output

SequenceFileOutputFormat

As the name indicates, `SequenceFileOutputFormat` writes sequence files for its output. This is a good choice of output if it forms the input to a further MapReduce job, since it is compact and is readily compressed. Compression is controlled via the static methods on `SequenceFileOutputFormat`, as described in "Using Compression in Map-Reduce" on page 90. For an example of how to use `SequenceFileOutputFormat`, see "Sorting" on page 268.

SequenceFileAsBinaryOutputFormat

`SequenceFileAsBinaryOutputFormat` is the counterpart to `SequenceFileAsBinaryInputFormat`, and it writes keys and values in raw binary format into a SequenceFile container.

MapFileOutputFormat

`MapFileOutputFormat` writes MapFiles as output. The keys in a MapFile must be added in order, so you need to ensure that your reducers emit keys in sorted order.

> The reduce *input* keys are guaranteed to be sorted, but the output keys are under the control of the reduce function, and there is nothing in the general MapReduce contract that states that the reduce *output* keys have to be ordered in any way. The extra constraint of sorted reduce output keys is just needed for `MapFileOutputFormat`.

Multiple Outputs

`FileOutputFormat` and its subclasses generate a set of files in the output directory. There is one file per reducer, and files are named by the partition number: *part-r-00000*, *part-r-00001*, etc. Sometimes there is a need to have more control over the naming of the files or to produce multiple files per reducer. MapReduce comes with the `MultipleOut` puts class to help you do this.[8]

---

8. In the old MapReduce API, there are two classes for producing multiple outputs: `MultipleOutputFormat` and `MultipleOutputs`. In a nutshell, `MultipleOutputs` is more fully featured, but `MultipleOutputFormat` has more control over the output directory structure and file naming. `MultipleOutputs` in the new API combines the best features of the two multiple output classes in the old API. The code on this book's website includes old API equivalents of the examples in this section using both `MultipleOutputs` and `MultipleOutputFormat`.

An example: Partitioning data

Consider the problem of partitioning the weather dataset by weather station. We would like to run a job whose output is one file per station, with each file containing all the records for that station.

One way of doing this is to have a reducer for each weather station. To arrange this, we need to do two things. First, write a partitioner that puts records from the same weather station into the same partition. Second, set the number of reducers on the job to be the number of weather stations. The partitioner would look like this:

```java
public class StationPartitioner extends Partitioner<LongWritable, Text> {

  private NcdcRecordParser parser = new NcdcRecordParser();

  @Override
  public int getPartition(LongWritable key, Text value, int numPartitions) {
    parser.parse(value);
    return getPartition(parser.getStationId());
  }

  private int getPartition(String stationId) {
    ...
  }

}
```

The getPartition(String) method, whose implementation is not shown, turns the station ID into a partition index. To do this, it needs a list of all the station IDs and then just returns the index of the station ID in the list.

There are two drawbacks to this approach. The first is that since the number of partitions needs to be known before the job is run, so does the number of weather stations. Although the NCDC provides metadata about its stations, there is no guarantee that the IDs encountered in the data match those in the metadata. A station that appears in the metadata but not in the data wastes a reducer slot. Worse, a station that appears in the data but not in the metadata doesn't get a reducer slot; it has to be thrown away. One way of mitigating this problem would be to write a job to extract the unique station IDs, but it's a shame that we need an extra job to do this.

The second drawback is more subtle. It is generally a bad idea to allow the number of partitions to be rigidly fixed by the application, since this can lead to small or uneven-sized partitions. Having many reducers doing a small amount of work isn't an efficient way of organizing a job; it's much better to get reducers to do more work and have fewer of them, as the overhead in running a task is then reduced. Uneven-sized partitions can be difficult to avoid, too. Different weather stations will have gathered a widely varying amount of data; for example, compare a station that opened one year ago to one that has been gathering data for one century. If a few reduce tasks take significantly longer than the others, they will dominate the job execution time and cause it to be longer than it needs to be.

There are two special cases when it does make sense to allow the application to set the number of partitions (or equivalently, the number of reducers):

Zero reducers
> This is a vacuous case: there are no partitions, as the application needs to run only map tasks.

One reducer
> It can be convenient to run small jobs to combine the output of previous jobs into a single file. This should be attempted only when the amount of data is small enough to be processed comfortably by one reducer.

It is much better to let the cluster drive the number of partitions for a job, the idea being that the more cluster reduce slots are available, the faster the job can complete. This is why the default `HashPartitioner` works so well, as it works with any number of partitions and ensures each partition has a good mix of keys, leading to more even-sized partitions.

If we go back to using `HashPartitioner`, each partition will contain multiple stations, so to create a file per station, we need to arrange for each reducer to write multiple files, which is where `MultipleOutputs` comes in.

MultipleOutputs

`MultipleOutputs` allows you to write data to files whose names are derived from the output keys and values, or in fact from an arbitrary string. This allows each reducer (or mapper in a map-only job) to create more than a single file. Filenames are of the form *name-m-nnnnn* for map outputs and *name-r-nnnnn* for reduce outputs, where *name* is an arbitrary name that is set by the program, and *nnnnn* is an integer designating the part number, starting from zero. The part number ensures that outputs written from different partitions (mappers or reducers) do not collide in the case of the same name.

The program in Example 7-5 shows how to use `MultipleOutputs` to partition the dataset by station.

Example 7-5. Partitioning whole dataset into files named by the station ID using MultipleOutputs

```
public class PartitionByStationUsingMultipleOutputs extends Configured
  implements Tool {

  static class StationMapper
    extends Mapper<LongWritable, Text, Text, Text> {

    private NcdcRecordParser parser = new NcdcRecordParser();

    @Override
    protected void map(LongWritable key, Text value, Context context)
        throws IOException, InterruptedException {
```

```java
      parser.parse(value);
      context.write(new Text(parser.getStationId()), value);
    }
  }

  static class MultipleOutputsReducer
      extends Reducer<Text, Text, NullWritable, Text> {

    private MultipleOutputs<NullWritable, Text> multipleOutputs;

    @Override
    protected void setup(Context context)
        throws IOException, InterruptedException {
      multipleOutputs = new MultipleOutputs<NullWritable, Text>(context);
    }

    @Override
    protected void reduce(Text key, Iterable<Text> values, Context context)
        throws IOException, InterruptedException {
      for (Text value : values) {
        multipleOutputs.write(NullWritable.get(), value, key.toString());
      }
    }

    @Override
    protected void cleanup(Context context)
        throws IOException, InterruptedException {
      multipleOutputs.close();
    }
  }

  @Override
  public int run(String[] args) throws Exception {
    Job job = JobBuilder.parseInputAndOutput(this, getConf(), args);
    if (job == null) {
      return -1;
    }

    job.setMapperClass(StationMapper.class);
    job.setMapOutputKeyClass(Text.class);
    job.setReducerClass(MultipleOutputsReducer.class);
    job.setOutputKeyClass(NullWritable.class);

    return job.waitForCompletion(true) ? 0 : 1;
  }
  public static void main(String[] args) throws Exception {
    int exitCode = ToolRunner.run(new PartitionByStationUsingMultipleOutputs(),
        args);
    System.exit(exitCode);
  }
}
```

In the reducer, which is where we generate the output, we construct an instance of MultipleOutputs in the setup() method and assign it to an instance variable. We then use the MultipleOutputs instance in the reduce() method to write to the output, in place of the context. The write() method takes the key and value, as well as a name. We use the station identifier for the name, so the overall effect is to produce output files with the naming scheme *station_identifier-r-nnnnn*.

In one run, the first few output files were named as follows:

```
output/010010-99999-r-00027
output/010050-99999-r-00013
output/010100-99999-r-00015
output/010280-99999-r-00014
output/010550-99999-r-00000
output/010980-99999-r-00011
output/011060-99999-r-00025
output/012030-99999-r-00029
output/012350-99999-r-00018
output/012620-99999-r-00004
```

The base path specified in the write() method of MultipleOutputs is interpreted relative to the output directory, and because it may contain file path separator characters (/), it's possible to create subdirectories of arbitrary depth. For example, the following modification partitions the data by station and year so that each year's data is contained in a directory named by the station ID (such as *029070-99999/1901/part-r-00000*):

```
@Override
protected void reduce(Text key, Iterable<Text> values, Context context)
    throws IOException, InterruptedException {
  for (Text value : values) {
    parser.parse(value);
    String basePath = String.format("%s/%s/part",
        parser.getStationId(), parser.getYear());
    multipleOutputs.write(NullWritable.get(), value, basePath);
  }
}
```

MultipleOutputs delegates to the mapper's OutputFormat, which in this example is a TextOutputFormat, but more complex setups are possible. For example, you can create named outputs, each with its own OutputFormat and key and value types (which may differ from the output types of the mapper or reducer). Furthermore, the mapper or reducer (or both) may write to multiple output files for each record processed. Consult the Java documentation for more information.

Lazy Output

FileOutputFormat subclasses will create output (*part-r-nnnnn*) files, even if they are empty. Some applications prefer that empty files not be created, which is where Lazy OutputFormat helps. It is a wrapper output format that ensures that the output file is created only when the first record is emitted for a given partition. To use it, call its setOutputFormatClass() method with the JobConf and the underlying output format.

Streaming and Pipes support a -lazyOutput option to enable LazyOutputFormat.

Database Output

The output formats for writing to relational databases and to HBase are mentioned in "Database Input (and Output)" on page 251.

MapReduce Features

This chapter looks at some of the more advanced features of MapReduce, including counters and sorting and joining datasets.

Counters

There are often things you would like to know about the data you are analyzing but that are peripheral to the analysis you are performing. For example, if you were counting invalid records and discovered that the proportion of invalid records in the whole dataset was very high, you might be prompted to check why so many records were being marked as invalid—perhaps there is a bug in the part of the program that detects invalid records? Or if the data were of poor quality and genuinely did have very many invalid records, after discovering this, you might decide to increase the size of the dataset so that the number of good records was large enough for meaningful analysis.

Counters are a useful channel for gathering statistics about the job: for quality control or for application-level statistics. They are also useful for problem diagnosis. If you are tempted to put a log message into your map or reduce task, it is often better to see whether you can use a counter instead to record that a particular condition occurred. In addition to counter values being much easier to retrieve than log output for large distributed jobs, you get a record of the number of times that condition occurred, which is more work to obtain from a set of logfiles.

Built-in Counters

Hadoop maintains some built-in counters for every job, and these report various metrics. For example, there are counters for the number of bytes and records processed, which allows you to confirm that the expected amount of input was consumed and the expected amount of output was produced.

Counters are divided into groups, and there are several groups for the built-in counters, listed in Table 8-1.

Table 8-1. Built-in counter groups

Group	Name/Enum	Reference
MapReduce task counters	`org.apache.hadoop.mapred.Task$Counter` (1.x) `org.apache.hadoop.mapreduce.TaskCounter` (post-1.x)	Table 8-2
Filesystem counters	`FileSystemCounters` (1.x) `org.apache.hadoop.mapreduce.FileSystemCounter` (post 1.x)	Table 8-3
FileInput-Format counters	`org.apache.hadoop.mapred.FileInputFormat$Counter` (1.x) `org.apache.hadoop.mapreduce.lib.input.FileInputFormatCounter` (post-1.x)	Table 8-4
FileOutput-Format counters	`org.apache.hadoop.mapred.FileOutputFormat$Counter` (1.x) `org.apache.hadoop.mapreduce.lib.output.FileOutputFormatCounter` (post-1.x)	Table 8-5
Job counters	`org.apache.hadoop.mapred.JobInProgress$Counter` (1.x) `org.apache.hadoop.mapreduce.JobCounter` (post-1.x)	Table 8-6

Each group either contains *task counters* (which are updated as a task progresses) or *job counters* (which are updated as a job progresses). We look at both types in the following sections.

Task counters

Task counters gather information about tasks over the course of their execution, and the results are aggregated over all the tasks in a job. For example, the `MAP_INPUT_RECORDS` counter counts the input records read by each map task and aggregates over all map tasks in a job, so that the final figure is the total number of input records for the whole job.

Task counters are maintained by each task attempt, and periodically sent to the tasktracker and then to the jobtracker so they can be globally aggregated. (This is described in "Progress and status updates" on page 193. Note that the information flow is different in YARN; see "YARN (MapReduce 2)" on page 196.) Task counters are sent in full every time, rather than sending the counts since the last transmission, since this guards against errors due to lost messages. Furthermore, during a job run, counters may go down if a task fails.

Counter values are definitive only once a job has successfully completed. However, some counters provide useful diagnostic information as a task is progressing, and it can be useful to monitor them with the web UI. For example, `PHYSICAL_MEMORY_BYTES`, `VIRTUAL_MEMORY_BYTES`, and `COMMITTED_HEAP_BYTES` provide an indication of how memory usage varies over the course of a particular task attempt.

The built-in task counters include those in the MapReduce task counters group (Table 8-2) and those in the file-related counters groups (Table 8-3, Table 8-4, and Table 8-5).

Table 8-2. Built-in MapReduce task counters

Counter	Description
Map input records (MAP_INPUT_RECORDS)	The number of input records consumed by all the maps in the job. Incremented every time a record is read from a RecordReader and passed to the map's map() method by the framework.
Map skipped records (MAP_SKIPPED_RECORDS)	The number of input records skipped by all the maps in the job. See "Skipping Bad Records" on page 220.
Map input bytes (MAP_INPUT_BYTES)	The number of bytes of uncompressed input consumed by all the maps in the job. Incremented every time a record is read from a RecordReader and passed to the map's map() method by the framework.
Split raw bytes (SPLIT_RAW_BYTES)	The number of bytes of input-split objects read by maps. These objects represent the split metadata (that is, the offset and length within a file) rather than the split data itself, so the total size should be small.
Map output records (MAP_OUTPUT_RECORDS)	The number of map output records produced by all the maps in the job. Incremented every time the collect() method is called on a map's OutputCollector.
Map output bytes (MAP_OUTPUT_BYTES)	The number of bytes of uncompressed output produced by all the maps in the job. Incremented every time the collect() method is called on a map's OutputCollector.
Map output materialized bytes (MAP_OUTPUT_MATERIALIZED_BYTES)	The number of bytes of map output actually written to disk. If map output compression is enabled, this is reflected in the counter value.
Combine input records (COMBINE_INPUT_RECORDS)	The number of input records consumed by all the combiners (if any) in the job. Incremented every time a value is read from the combiner's iterator over values. Note that this count is the number of values consumed by the combiner, not the number of distinct key groups (which would not be a useful metric, since there is not necessarily one group per key for a combiner; see "Combiner Functions" on page 33, and also "Shuffle and Sort" on page 208).
Combine output records (COMBINE_OUTPUT_RECORDS)	The number of output records produced by all the combiners (if any) in the job. Incremented every time the collect() method is called on a combiner's OutputCollector.
Reduce input groups (REDUCE_INPUT_GROUPS)	The number of distinct key groups consumed by all the reducers in the job. Incremented every time the reducer's reduce() method is called by the framework.
Reduce input records (REDUCE_INPUT_RECORDS)	The number of input records consumed by all the reducers in the job. Incremented every time a value is read from the reducer's iterator over values. If reducers consume all of their inputs, this count should be the same as the count for map output records.
Reduce output records (REDUCE_OUTPUT_RECORDS)	The number of reduce output records produced by all the maps in the job. Incremented every time the collect() method is called on a reducer's OutputCollector.
Reduce skipped groups (REDUCE_SKIPPED_GROUPS)	The number of distinct key groups skipped by all the reducers in the job. See "Skipping Bad Records" on page 220.
Reduce skipped records	The number of input records skipped by all the reducers in the job.

Counter	Description
(REDUCE_SKIPPED_RECORDS)	
Reduce shuffle bytes (REDUCE_SHUFFLE_BYTES)	The number of bytes of map output copied by the shuffle to reducers.
Spilled records (SPILLED_RECORDS)	The number of records spilled to disk in all map and reduce tasks in the job.
CPU milliseconds (CPU_MILLISECONDS)	The cumulative CPU time for a task in milliseconds, as reported by /proc/cpuinfo.
Physical memory bytes (PHYSICAL_MEMORY_BYTES)	The physical memory being used by a task in bytes, as reported by /proc/meminfo.
Virtual memory bytes (VIRTUAL_MEMORY_BYTES)	The virtual memory being used by a task in bytes, as reported by /proc/meminfo.
Committed heap bytes (COMMITTED_HEAP_BYTES)	The total amount of memory available in the JVM in bytes, as reported by Runtime.getRuntime().totalMemory().
GC time milliseconds (GC_TIME_MILLIS)	The elapsed time for garbage collection in tasks in milliseconds, as reported by GarbageCollectorMXBean.getCollectionTime(). (Not available in 1.x.)
Shuffled maps (SHUFFLED_MAPS)	The number of map output files transferred to reducers by the shuffle (See "Shuffle and Sort" on page 208.) (Not available in 1.x.)
Failed shuffle (FAILED_SHUFFLE)	The number of map output copy failures during the shuffle. (Not available in 1.x.)
Merged map outputs (MERGED_MAP_OUTPUTS)	The number of map outputs that have been merged on the reduce side of the shuffle. (Not available in 1.x.)

Table 8-3. Built-in filesystem task counters

Counter	Description
Filesystem bytes read (BYTES_READ)	The number of bytes read by each filesystem by map and reduce tasks. There is a counter for each filesystem, and *Filesystem*, which may be Local, HDFS, S3, KFS, etc.
Filesystem bytes written (BYTES_WRITTEN)	The number of bytes written by each filesystem by map and reduce tasks.

Table 8-4. Built-in FileInputFormat task counters

Counter	Description
Bytes read (BYTES_READ)	The number of bytes read by map tasks via the FileInputFormat.

Table 8-5. Built-in FileOutputFormat task counters

Counter	Description
Bytes written (BYTES_WRITTEN)	The number of bytes written by map tasks (for map-only jobs) or reduce tasks via the FileOutputFormat.

Job counters

Job counters (Table 8-6) are maintained by the jobtracker (or application master in YARN), so they don't need to be sent across the network, unlike all other counters, including user-defined ones. They measure job-level statistics, not values that change while a task is running. For example, TOTAL_LAUNCHED_MAPS counts the number of map tasks that were launched over the course of a job (including tasks that failed).

Table 8-6. Built-in job counters

Counter	Description
Launched map tasks (TOTAL_LAUNCHED_MAPS)	The number of map tasks that were launched. Includes tasks that were started speculatively.
Launched reduce tasks (TOTAL_LAUNCHED_REDUCES)	The number of reduce tasks that were launched. Includes tasks that were started speculatively.
Launched uber tasks (TOTAL_LAUNCHED_UBERTASKS)	The number of uber tasks (see "YARN (MapReduce 2)" on page 196) that were launched. (Only in YARN-based MapReduce.)
Maps in uber tasks (NUM_UBER_SUBMAPS)	The number of maps in uber tasks. (Only in YARN-based MapReduce.)
Reduces in uber tasks (NUM_UBER_SUBREDUCES)	The number of reduces in uber tasks. (Only in YARN-based MapReduce.)
Failed map tasks (NUM_FAILED_MAPS)	The number of map tasks that failed. See "Task failure" on page 202 for potential causes.
Failed reduce tasks (NUM_FAILED_REDUCES)	The number of reduce tasks that failed.
Failed uber tasks (NUM_FAILED_UBERTASKS)	The number of uber tasks that failed. (Only in YARN-based MapReduce.)
Data-local map tasks (DATA_LOCAL_MAPS)	The number of map tasks that ran on the same node as their input data.
Rack-local map tasks (RACK_LOCAL_MAPS)	The number of map tasks that ran on a node in the same rack as their input data, but that are not data-local.
Other local map tasks (OTHER_LOCAL_MAPS)	The number of map tasks that ran on a node in a different rack to their input data. Inter-rack bandwidth is scarce, and Hadoop tries to place map tasks close to their input data, so this count should be low. See Figure 2-2.
Total time in map tasks (SLOTS_MILLIS_MAPS)	The total time taken running map tasks in milliseconds. Includes tasks that were started speculatively.
Total time in reduce tasks (SLOTS_MILLIS_REDUCES)	The total time taken running reduce tasks in milliseconds. Includes tasks that were started speculatively.
Total time in map tasks waiting after reserving slots (FALLOW_SLOTS_MILLIS_MAPS)	The total time in milliseconds spent waiting after reserving slots for map tasks. Slot reservation is a Capacity Scheduler feature for high-memory jobs; see "Task memory limits" on page 318. Not used by YARN-based MapReduce.

Counter	Description
Total time in reduce tasks waiting after reserving slots (FALLOW_SLOTS_MILLIS_REDUCES)	The total time in milliseconds spent waiting after reserving slots for reduce tasks. Slot reservation is a Capacity Scheduler feature for high-memory jobs; see "Task memory limits" on page 318. Not used by YARN-based MapReduce.

User-Defined Java Counters

MapReduce allows user code to define a set of counters, which are then incremented as desired in the mapper or reducer. Counters are defined by a Java enum, which serves to group related counters. A job may define an arbitrary number of enums, each with an arbitrary number of fields. The name of the enum is the group name, and the enum's fields are the counter names. Counters are global: the MapReduce framework aggregates them across all maps and reduces to produce a grand total at the end of the job.

We created some counters in Chapter 5 for counting malformed records in the weather dataset. The program in Example 8-1 extends that example to count the number of missing records and the distribution of temperature quality codes.

Example 8-1. Application to run the maximum temperature job, including counting missing and malformed fields and quality codes

```
public class MaxTemperatureWithCounters extends Configured implements Tool {

  enum Temperature {
    MISSING,
    MALFORMED
  }

  static class MaxTemperatureMapperWithCounters
    extends Mapper<LongWritable, Text, Text, IntWritable> {

    private NcdcRecordParser parser = new NcdcRecordParser();

    @Override
    protected void map(LongWritable key, Text value, Context context)
        throws IOException, InterruptedException {

      parser.parse(value);
      if (parser.isValidTemperature()) {
        int airTemperature = parser.getAirTemperature();
        context.write(new Text(parser.getYear()),
            new IntWritable(airTemperature));
      } else if (parser.isMalformedTemperature()) {
        System.err.println("Ignoring possibly corrupt input: " + value);
        context.getCounter(Temperature.MALFORMED).increment(1);
      } else if (parser.isMissingTemperature()) {
        context.getCounter(Temperature.MISSING).increment(1);
      }

      // dynamic counter
      context.getCounter("TemperatureQuality", parser.getQuality()).increment(1);
```

```
    }
  }

  @Override
  public int run(String[] args) throws Exception {
    Job job = JobBuilder.parseInputAndOutput(this, getConf(), args);
    if (job == null) {
      return -1;
    }

    job.setOutputKeyClass(Text.class);
    job.setOutputValueClass(IntWritable.class);

    job.setMapperClass(MaxTemperatureMapperWithCounters.class);
    job.setCombinerClass(MaxTemperatureReducer.class);
    job.setReducerClass(MaxTemperatureReducer.class);

    return job.waitForCompletion(true) ? 0 : 1;
  }

  public static void main(String[] args) throws Exception {
    int exitCode = ToolRunner.run(new MaxTemperatureWithCounters(), args);
    System.exit(exitCode);
  }
}
```

The best way to see what this program does is to run it over the complete dataset:

```
% hadoop jar hadoop-examples.jar MaxTemperatureWithCounters \
    input/ncdc/all output-counters
```

When the job has successfully completed, it prints out the counters at the end (this is done by the job client). Here are the ones we are interested in:

```
12/02/04 19:46:38 INFO mapred.JobClient:     TemperatureQuality
12/02/04 19:46:38 INFO mapred.JobClient:       2=1246032
12/02/04 19:46:38 INFO mapred.JobClient:       1=973422173
12/02/04 19:46:38 INFO mapred.JobClient:       0=1
12/02/04 19:46:38 INFO mapred.JobClient:       6=40066
12/02/04 19:46:38 INFO mapred.JobClient:       5=158291879
12/02/04 19:46:38 INFO mapred.JobClient:       4=10764500
12/02/04 19:46:38 INFO mapred.JobClient:       9=66136858
12/02/04 19:46:38 INFO mapred.JobClient:     Air Temperature Records
12/02/04 19:46:38 INFO mapred.JobClient:       Malformed=3
12/02/04 19:46:38 INFO mapred.JobClient:       Missing=66136856
```

Dynamic counters

The code makes use of a dynamic counter—one that isn't defined by a Java enum. Because a Java enum's fields are defined at compile time, you can't create new counters on the fly using enums. Here we want to count the distribution of temperature quality codes, and though the format specification defines the values that the temperature quality code can take, it is more convenient to use a dynamic counter to emit the values that it actually takes. The method we use on the `Reporter` object takes a group and counter name using `String` names:

```
public void incrCounter(String group, String counter, long amount)
```

The two ways of creating and accessing counters—using enums and using strings— are actually equivalent because Hadoop turns enums into strings to send counters over RPC. Enums are slightly easier to work with, provide type safety, and are suitable for most jobs. For the odd occasion when you need to create counters dynamically, you can use the `String` interface.

Readable counter names

By default, a counter's name is the enum's fully qualified Java classname. These names are not very readable when they appear on the web UI or in the console, so Hadoop provides a way to change the display names using resource bundles. We've done this here, so we see "Air Temperature Records" instead of "Temperature$MISSING." For dynamic counters, the group and counter names are used for the display names, so normally this is not an issue.

The recipe to provide readable names is as follows. Create a properties file named after the enum, using an underscore as a separator for nested classes. The properties file should be in the same directory as the top-level class containing the enum. The file is named *MaxTemperatureWithCounters_Temperature.properties* for the counters in Example 8-1.

The properties file should contain a single property named `CounterGroupName`, whose value is the display name for the whole group. Then each field in the enum should have a corresponding property defined for it, whose name is the name of the field suffixed with `.name` and whose value is the display name for the counter. Here are the contents of *MaxTemperatureWithCounters_Temperature.properties*:

```
CounterGroupName=Air Temperature Records
MISSING.name=Missing
MALFORMED.name=Malformed
```

Hadoop uses the standard Java localization mechanisms to load the correct properties for the locale you are running in. So, for example, you can create a Chinese version of the properties in a file named *MaxTemperatureWithCounters_Temperature_zh_CN.properties*, and they will be used when running in the zh_CN locale. Refer to the documentation for `java.util.PropertyResourceBundle` for more information.

Retrieving counters

In addition to being available via the web UI and the command line (using `hadoop job -counter`), you can retrieve counter values using the Java API. You can do this while the job is running, although it is more usual to get counters at the end of a job run, when they are stable. Example 8-2 shows a program that calculates the proportion of records that have missing temperature fields.

Example 8-2. Application to calculate the proportion of records with missing temperature fields

```
import org.apache.hadoop.conf.Configured;
import org.apache.hadoop.mapred.*;
import org.apache.hadoop.util.*;

public class MissingTemperatureFields extends Configured implements Tool {

  @Override
  public int run(String[] args) throws Exception {
    if (args.length != 1) {
      JobBuilder.printUsage(this, "<job ID>");
      return -1;
    }
    String jobID = args[0];
    JobClient jobClient = new JobClient(new JobConf(getConf()));
    RunningJob job = jobClient.getJob(JobID.forName(jobID));
    if (job == null) {
      System.err.printf("No job with ID %s found.\n", jobID);
      return -1;
    }
    if (!job.isComplete()) {
      System.err.printf("Job %s is not complete.\n", jobID);
      return -1;
    }

    Counters counters = job.getCounters();
    long missing = counters.getCounter(
        MaxTemperatureWithCounters.Temperature.MISSING);

    long total = counters.getCounter(Task.Counter.MAP_INPUT_RECORDS);

    System.out.printf("Records with missing temperature fields: %.2f%%\n",
        100.0 * missing / total);
    return 0;
  }
  public static void main(String[] args) throws Exception {
    int exitCode = ToolRunner.run(new MissingTemperatureFields(), args);
    System.exit(exitCode);
  }
}
```

First we retrieve a RunningJob object from a JobClient by calling the getJob() method with the job ID. We check whether there is actually a job with the given ID. There may not be, either because the ID was incorrectly specified or because the jobtracker no longer has a reference to the job (only the last 100 jobs are kept in memory, controlled by mapred.jobtracker.completeuserjobs.maximum, and all are cleared out if the jobtracker is restarted).

After confirming that the job has completed, we call the RunningJob's getCounters() method, which returns a Counters object, encapsulating all the counters for a job. The Counters class provides various methods for finding the names and values of counters. We use the getCounter() method, which takes an enum to find the number of records that had a missing temperature field and also the total number of records processed (from a built-in counter).

Finally, we print the proportion of records that had a missing temperature field. Here's what we get for the whole weather dataset:

```
% hadoop jar hadoop-examples.jar MissingTemperatureFields job_201202040938_0012
Records with missing temperature fields: 5.47%
```

Using the new MapReduce API. We used the old API in this example because the new equivalent for retrieving counters after a job has finished is not available in Hadoop 1.x. (Note that it is possible to retrieve the counters from a job that ran using the new API with retrieval code that uses the old API.) The main difference is the use of a `Cluster` object to retrieve a `Job` (rather than a `RunningJob`), and then calling its `getCounters()` method:

```
Cluster cluster = new Cluster(getConf());
Job job = cluster.getJob(JobID.forName(jobID));
Counters counters = job.getCounters();
long missing = counters.findCounter(
    MaxTemperatureWithCounters.Temperature.MISSING).getValue();
long total = counters.findCounter(TaskCounter.MAP_INPUT_RECORDS).getValue();
```

Another difference is the use of the `org.apache.hadoop.mapreduce.TaskCounter` enum in the new API, rather than `org.apache.hadoop.mapred.Task.Counter` from the old API.

User-Defined Streaming Counters

A Streaming MapReduce program can increment counters by sending a specially formatted line to the standard error stream, which is co-opted as a control channel in this case. The line must have the following format:

```
reporter:counter:group,counter,amount
```

This snippet in Python shows how to increment the "Missing" counter in the "Temperature" group by one:

```
sys.stderr.write("reporter:counter:Temperature,Missing,1\n")
```

In a similar way, a status message may be sent with a line formatted like this:

```
reporter:status:message
```

Sorting

The ability to sort data is at the heart of MapReduce. Even if your application isn't concerned with sorting per se, it may be able to use the sorting stage that MapReduce provides to organize its data. In this section, we examine different ways of sorting datasets and how you can control the sort order in MapReduce. Sorting Avro data is covered separately in "Sorting Using Avro MapReduce" on page 128.

Preparation

We are going to sort the weather dataset by temperature. Storing temperatures as Text objects doesn't work for sorting purposes, because signed integers don't sort lexicographically.[1] Instead, we are going to store the data using sequence files whose IntWritable keys represent the temperature (and sort correctly) and whose Text values are the lines of data.

The MapReduce job in Example 8-3 is a map-only job that also filters the input to remove records that don't have a valid temperature reading. Each map creates a single block-compressed sequence file as output. It is invoked with the following command:

```
% hadoop jar hadoop-examples.jar SortDataPreprocessor input/ncdc/all \
    input/ncdc/all-seq
```

Example 8-3. A MapReduce program for transforming the weather data into SequenceFile format

```java
public class SortDataPreprocessor extends Configured implements Tool {

  static class CleanerMapper
    extends Mapper<LongWritable, Text, IntWritable, Text> {

    private NcdcRecordParser parser = new NcdcRecordParser();

    @Override
    protected void map(LongWritable key, Text value, Context context)
        throws IOException, InterruptedException {

      parser.parse(value);
      if (parser.isValidTemperature()) {
        context.write(new IntWritable(parser.getAirTemperature()), value);
      }
    }
  }

  @Override
  public int run(String[] args) throws Exception {
    Job job = JobBuilder.parseInputAndOutput(this, getConf(), args);
    if (job == null) {
      return -1;
    }

    job.setMapperClass(CleanerMapper.class);
    job.setOutputKeyClass(IntWritable.class);
    job.setOutputValueClass(Text.class);
    job.setNumReduceTasks(0);
    job.setOutputFormatClass(SequenceFileOutputFormat.class);
    SequenceFileOutputFormat.setCompressOutput(job, true);
    SequenceFileOutputFormat.setOutputCompressorClass(job, GzipCodec.class);
```

---

1. One commonly used workaround for this problem—particularly in text-based Streaming applications—is to add an offset to eliminate all negative numbers and to left pad with zeros so all numbers are the same number of characters. However, see "Streaming" on page 281 for another approach.

```
        SequenceFileOutputFormat.setOutputCompressionType(job,
            CompressionType.BLOCK);

        return job.waitForCompletion(true) ? 0 : 1;
    }
    public static void main(String[] args) throws Exception {
        int exitCode = ToolRunner.run(new SortDataPreprocessor(), args);
        System.exit(exitCode);
    }
}
```

Partial Sort

In "The Default MapReduce Job" on page 228, we saw that, by default, MapReduce
will sort input records by their keys. Example 8-4 is a variation for sorting sequence
files with IntWritable keys.

*Example 8-4. A MapReduce program for sorting a SequenceFile with IntWritable keys using the
default HashPartitioner*

```
public class SortByTemperatureUsingHashPartitioner extends Configured
    implements Tool {

    @Override
    public int run(String[] args) throws Exception {
        Job job = JobBuilder.parseInputAndOutput(this, getConf(), args);
        if (job == null) {
            return -1;
        }

        job.setInputFormatClass(SequenceFileInputFormat.class);
        job.setOutputKeyClass(IntWritable.class);
        job.setOutputFormatClass(SequenceFileOutputFormat.class);
        SequenceFileOutputFormat.setCompressOutput(job, true);
        SequenceFileOutputFormat.setOutputCompressorClass(job, GzipCodec.class);
        SequenceFileOutputFormat.setOutputCompressionType(job,
            CompressionType.BLOCK);

        return job.waitForCompletion(true) ? 0 : 1;
    }

    public static void main(String[] args) throws Exception {
        int exitCode = ToolRunner.run(new SortByTemperatureUsingHashPartitioner(),
            args);
        System.exit(exitCode);
    }
}
```

Suppose we run this program using 30 reducers:[2]

```
% hadoop jar hadoop-examples.jar SortByTemperatureUsingHashPartitioner \
    -D mapred.reduce.tasks=30 input/ncdc/all-seq output-hashsort
```

This command produces 30 output files, each of which is sorted. However, there is no easy way to combine the files (by concatenation, for example, in the case of plain-text files) to produce a globally sorted file. For many applications, this doesn't matter. For example, having a partially sorted set of files is fine when you want to do lookups.

An application: Partitioned MapFile lookups

To perform lookups by key, for instance, having multiple files works well. If we change the output format to be a MapFileOutputFormat, as shown in Example 8-5, the output is 30 map files, against which we can perform lookups.[3]

Example 8-5. A MapReduce program for sorting a SequenceFile and producing MapFiles as output

```
public class SortByTemperatureToMapFile extends Configured implements Tool {

  @Override
  public int run(String[] args) throws Exception {
    Job job = JobBuilder.parseInputAndOutput(this, getConf(), args);
    if (job == null) {
```

---

2. See "Sorting and merging SequenceFiles" on page 136 for how to do the same thing using the sort program example that comes with Hadoop.

3. The new API version of MapFileOutputFormat is not available in the Hadoop 1.x release series at the time of this writing. Equivalent old API code for the examples in this section can be found on this book's website.

```
      return -1;
    }

    job.setInputFormatClass(SequenceFileInputFormat.class);
    job.setOutputKeyClass(IntWritable.class);
    job.setOutputFormatClass(MapFileOutputFormat.class);
    SequenceFileOutputFormat.setCompressOutput(job, true);
    SequenceFileOutputFormat.setOutputCompressorClass(job, GzipCodec.class);
    SequenceFileOutputFormat.setOutputCompressionType(job,
        CompressionType.BLOCK);

    return job.waitForCompletion(true) ? 0 : 1;
  }

  public static void main(String[] args) throws Exception {
    int exitCode = ToolRunner.run(new SortByTemperatureToMapFile(), args);
    System.exit(exitCode);
  }
}
```

MapFileOutputFormat provides a pair of convenience static methods for performing lookups against MapReduce output; their use is shown in Example 8-6.

Example 8-6. Retrieve the first entry with a given key from a collection of MapFiles

```
public class LookupRecordByTemperature extends Configured implements Tool {

  @Override
  public int run(String[] args) throws Exception {
    if (args.length != 2) {
      JobBuilder.printUsage(this, "<path> <key>");
      return -1;
    }
    Path path = new Path(args[0]);
    IntWritable key = new IntWritable(Integer.parseInt(args[1]));

    Reader[] readers = MapFileOutputFormat.getReaders(path, getConf());
    Partitioner<IntWritable, Text> partitioner =
      new HashPartitioner<IntWritable, Text>();
    Text val = new Text();
    Writable entry =
      MapFileOutputFormat.getEntry(readers, partitioner, key, val);
    if (entry == null) {
      System.err.println("Key not found: " + key);
      return -1;
    }
    NcdcRecordParser parser = new NcdcRecordParser();
    parser.parse(val.toString());
    System.out.printf("%s\t%s\n", parser.getStationId(), parser.getYear());
    return 0;
  }

  public static void main(String[] args) throws Exception {
    int exitCode = ToolRunner.run(new LookupRecordByTemperature(), args);
    System.exit(exitCode);
```

```
      }
}
```

The getReaders() method opens a MapFile.Reader for each of the output files created by the MapReduce job. The getEntry() method then uses the partitioner to choose the reader for the key and finds the value for that key by calling Reader's get() method. If getEntry() returns null, it means no matching key was found. Otherwise, it returns the value, which we translate into a station ID and year.

To see this in action, let's find the first entry for a temperature of −10°C (remember that temperatures are stored as integers representing tenths of a degree, which is why we ask for a temperature of -100):

```
% hadoop jar hadoop-examples.jar LookupRecordByTemperature output-hashmapsort -100
357460-99999    1956
```

We can also use the readers directly to get all the records for a given key. The array of readers that is returned is ordered by partition, so that the reader for a given key may be found using the same partitioner that was used in the MapReduce job:

```
Reader reader = readers[partitioner.getPartition(key, val, readers.length)];
```

Once we have the reader, we get the first key using MapFile's get() method, then repeatedly call next() to retrieve the next key and value until the key changes. A program to do this is shown in Example 8-7.

Example 8-7. Retrieve all entries with a given key from a collection of MapFiles

```
public class LookupRecordsByTemperature extends Configured implements Tool {

  @Override
  public int run(String[] args) throws Exception {
    if (args.length != 2) {
      JobBuilder.printUsage(this, "<path> <key>");
      return -1;
    }
    Path path = new Path(args[0]);
    IntWritable key = new IntWritable(Integer.parseInt(args[1]));

    Reader[] readers = MapFileOutputFormat.getReaders(path, getConf());
    Partitioner<IntWritable, Text> partitioner =
      new HashPartitioner<IntWritable, Text>();
    Text val = new Text();

    Reader reader = readers[partitioner.getPartition(key, val, readers.length)];
    Writable entry = reader.get(key, val);
    if (entry == null) {
      System.err.println("Key not found: " + key);
      return -1;
    }
    NcdcRecordParser parser = new NcdcRecordParser();
    IntWritable nextKey = new IntWritable();
    do {
      parser.parse(val.toString());
```

```
      System.out.printf("%s\t%s\n", parser.getStationId(), parser.getYear());
    } while(reader.next(nextKey, val) && key.equals(nextKey));
    return 0;
  }

  public static void main(String[] args) throws Exception {
    int exitCode = ToolRunner.run(new LookupRecordsByTemperature(), args);
    System.exit(exitCode);
  }
}
```

And here is a sample run to retrieve all readings of −10°C and count them:

```
% hadoop jar hadoop-examples.jar LookupRecordsByTemperature output-hashmapsort -100 \
  2> /dev/null | wc -l
1489272
```

Total Sort

How can you produce a globally sorted file using Hadoop? The naive answer is to use a single partition.[4] But this is incredibly inefficient for large files because one machine has to process all of the output, so you are throwing away the benefits of the parallel architecture that MapReduce provides.

Instead, it is possible to produce a set of sorted files that, if concatenated, would form a globally sorted file. The secret to doing this is to use a partitioner that respects the total order of the output. For example, if we had four partitions, we could put keys for temperatures less than −10°C in the first partition, those between −10°C and 0°C in the second, those between 0°C and 10°C in the third, and those over 10°C in the fourth.

Although this approach works, you have to choose your partition sizes carefully to ensure that they are fairly even, so job times aren't dominated by a single reducer. For the partitioning scheme just described, the relative sizes of the partitions are as follows:

Temperature range	< −10°C	[−10°C, 0°C)	[0°C, 10°C)	>= 10°C
Proportion of records	11%	13%	17%	59%

These partitions are not very even. To construct more even partitions, we need to have a better understanding of the temperature distribution for the whole dataset. It's fairly easy to write a MapReduce job to count the number of records that fall into a collection of temperature buckets. For example, Figure 8-1 shows the distribution for buckets of size 1°C, where each point on the plot corresponds to one bucket.

---

4. A better answer is to use Pig ("Sorting Data" on page 407) or Hive ("Sorting and Aggregating" on page 444), both of which can sort with a single command.

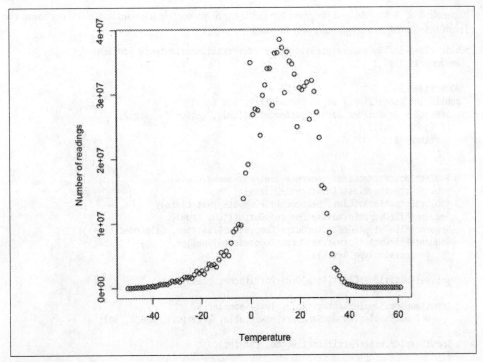

Figure 8-1. Temperature distribution for the weather dataset

Although we could use this information to construct a very even set of partitions, the fact that we needed to run a job that used the entire dataset to construct them is not ideal. It's possible to get a fairly even set of partitions by *sampling* the key space. The idea behind sampling is that you look at a small subset of the keys to approximate the key distribution, which is then used to construct partitions. Luckily, we don't have to write the code to do this ourselves, as Hadoop comes with a selection of samplers.

The `InputSampler` class defines a nested `Sampler` interface whose implementations return a sample of keys given an `InputFormat` and `Job`:

```
public interface Sampler<K, V> {
  K[] getSample(InputFormat<K, V> inf, Job job)
      throws IOException, InterruptedException;
}
```

This interface usually is not called directly by clients. Instead, the `writePartition File()` static method on `InputSampler` is used, which creates a sequence file to store the keys that define the partitions:

```
public static <K, V> void writePartitionFile(Job job, Sampler<K, V> sampler)
      throws IOException, ClassNotFoundException, InterruptedException
```

The sequence file is used by `TotalOrderPartitioner` to create partitions for the sort job. Example 8-8 puts it all together.

Example 8-8. A MapReduce program for sorting a SequenceFile with IntWritable keys using the TotalOrderPartitioner to globally sort the data

```java
public class SortByTemperatureUsingTotalOrderPartitioner extends Configured
  implements Tool {

  @Override
  public int run(String[] args) throws Exception {
    Job job = JobBuilder.parseInputAndOutput(this, getConf(), args);
    if (job == null) {
      return -1;
    }

    job.setInputFormatClass(SequenceFileInputFormat.class);
    job.setOutputKeyClass(IntWritable.class);
    job.setOutputFormatClass(SequenceFileOutputFormat.class);
    SequenceFileOutputFormat.setCompressOutput(job, true);
    SequenceFileOutputFormat.setOutputCompressorClass(job, GzipCodec.class);
    SequenceFileOutputFormat.setOutputCompressionType(job,
        CompressionType.BLOCK);

    job.setPartitionerClass(TotalOrderPartitioner.class);

    InputSampler.Sampler<IntWritable, Text> sampler =
      new InputSampler.RandomSampler<IntWritable, Text>(0.1, 10000, 10);

    InputSampler.writePartitionFile(job, sampler);

    // Add to DistributedCache
    Configuration conf = job.getConfiguration();
    String partitionFile =TotalOrderPartitioner.getPartitionFile(conf);
    URI partitionUri = new URI(partitionFile + "#" +
        TotalOrderPartitioner.DEFAULT_PATH);
    DistributedCache.addCacheFile(partitionUri, conf);
    DistributedCache.createSymlink(conf);

    return job.waitForCompletion(true) ? 0 : 1;
  }

  public static void main(String[] args) throws Exception {
    int exitCode = ToolRunner.run(
        new SortByTemperatureUsingTotalOrderPartitioner(), args);
    System.exit(exitCode);
  }
}
```

We use a `RandomSampler`, which chooses keys with a uniform probability—here, 0.1. There are also parameters for the maximum number of samples to take and the maximum number of splits to sample (here, 10,000 and 10, respectively; these settings are the defaults when `InputSampler` is run as an application), and the sampler stops when the first of these limits is met. Samplers run on the client, making it important to limit the number of splits that are downloaded so the sampler runs quickly. In practice, the time taken to run the sampler is a small fraction of the overall job time.

The InputSampler writes a partition file that we need to share with the tasks running on the cluster by adding it to the distributed cache (see "Distributed Cache" on page 289).

On one run, the sampler chose –5.6°C, 13.9°C, and 22.0°C as partition boundaries (for four partitions), which translates into more even partition sizes than the earlier choice:

Temperature range	< –5.6°C	[–5.6°C, 13.9°C)	[13.9°C, 22.0°C)	>= 22.0°C
Proportion of records	29%	24%	23%	24%

Your input data determines the best sampler to use. For example, SplitSampler, which samples only the first *n* records in a split, is not so good for sorted data,[5] because it doesn't select keys from throughout the split.

On the other hand, IntervalSampler chooses keys at regular intervals through the split and makes a better choice for sorted data. RandomSampler is a good general-purpose sampler. If none of these suits your application (and remember that the point of sampling is to produce partitions that are *approximately* equal in size), you can write your own implementation of the Sampler interface.

One of the nice properties of InputSampler and TotalOrderPartitioner is that you are free to choose the number of partitions. This choice is normally driven by the number of reducer slots in your cluster (choose a number slightly fewer than the total, to allow for failures). However, TotalOrderPartitioner will work only if the partition boundaries are distinct. One problem with choosing a high number is that you may get collisions if you have a small key space.

Here's how we run it:

```
% hadoop jar hadoop-examples.jar SortByTemperatureUsingTotalOrderPartitioner \
    -D mapred.reduce.tasks=30 input/ncdc/all-seq output-totalsort
```

The program produces 30 output partitions, each of which is internally sorted; in addition, for these partitions, all the keys in partition *i* are less than the keys in partition *i* + 1.

Secondary Sort

The MapReduce framework sorts the records by key before they reach the reducers. For any particular key, however, the values are *not* sorted. The order in which the values appear is not even stable from one run to the next, because they come from different map tasks, which may finish at different times from run to run. Generally speaking, most MapReduce programs are written so as not to depend on the order in which the

5. In some applications, it's common for some of the input to already be sorted, or at least partially sorted. For example, the weather dataset is ordered by time, which may introduce certain biases, making the RandomSampler a safer choice.

values appear to the reduce function. However, it is possible to impose an order on the values by sorting and grouping the keys in a particular way.

To illustrate the idea, consider the MapReduce program for calculating the maximum temperature for each year. If we arranged for the values (temperatures) to be sorted in descending order, we wouldn't have to iterate through them to find the maximum; instead, we could take the first for each year and ignore the rest. (This approach isn't the most efficient way to solve this particular problem, but it illustrates how secondary sort works in general.)

To achieve this, we change our keys to be composite: a combination of year and temperature. We want the sort order for keys to be by year (ascending) and then by temperature (descending):

```
1900  35°C
1900  34°C
1900  34°C
...
1901  36°C
1901  35°C
```

If all we did was change the key, this wouldn't help, because then records for the same year would have different keys and therefore would not (in general) go to the same reducer. For example, (1900, 35°C) and (1900, 34°C) could go to different reducers. By setting a partitioner to partition by the year part of the key, we can guarantee that records for the same year go to the same reducer. This still isn't enough to achieve our goal, however. A partitioner ensures only that one reducer receives all the records for a year; it doesn't change the fact that the reducer groups by key within the partition:

```
          Partition  Group
1900 35°C     |        |
1900 34°C     |        |
1900 34°C     |        |
    ...
1901 36°C     |        |
1901 35°C     |        |
```

The final piece of the puzzle is the setting to control the grouping. If we group values in the reducer by the year part of the key, we will see all the records for the same year in one reduce group. And because they are sorted by temperature in descending order, the first is the maximum temperature:

```
          Partition  Group
1900 35°C     |        |
1900 34°C     |        |
1900 34°C     |        |
    ...
1901 36°C     |        |
1901 35°C     |        |
```

To summarize, there is a recipe here to get the effect of sorting by value:

- Make the key a composite of the natural key and the natural value.
- The sort comparator should order by the composite key, that is, the natural key *and* natural value.
- The partitioner and grouping comparator for the composite key should consider only the natural key for partitioning and grouping.

Java code

Putting this all together results in the code in Example 8-9. This program uses the plaintext input again.

Example 8-9. Application to find the maximum temperature by sorting temperatures in the key

```
public class MaxTemperatureUsingSecondarySort
  extends Configured implements Tool {

  static class MaxTemperatureMapper
    extends Mapper<LongWritable, Text, IntPair, NullWritable> {

    private NcdcRecordParser parser = new NcdcRecordParser();

    @Override
    protected void map(LongWritable key, Text value,
        Context context) throws IOException, InterruptedException {

      parser.parse(value);
      if (parser.isValidTemperature()) {
        context.write(new IntPair(parser.getYearInt(),
            parser.getAirTemperature()), NullWritable.get());
      }
    }
  }

  static class MaxTemperatureReducer
    extends Reducer<IntPair, NullWritable, IntPair, NullWritable> {

    @Override
    protected void reduce(IntPair key, Iterable<NullWritable> values,
        Context context) throws IOException, InterruptedException {

      context.write(key, NullWritable.get());
    }
  }

  public static class FirstPartitioner
    extends Partitioner<IntPair, NullWritable> {

    @Override
    public int getPartition(IntPair key, NullWritable value, int numPartitions) {
      // multiply by 127 to perform some mixing
      return Math.abs(key.getFirst() * 127) % numPartitions;
```

```java
      }
    }

    public static class KeyComparator extends WritableComparator {
      protected KeyComparator() {
        super(IntPair.class, true);
      }
      @Override
      public int compare(WritableComparable w1, WritableComparable w2) {
        IntPair ip1 = (IntPair) w1;
        IntPair ip2 = (IntPair) w2;
        int cmp = IntPair.compare(ip1.getFirst(), ip2.getFirst());
        if (cmp != 0) {
          return cmp;
        }
        return -IntPair.compare(ip1.getSecond(), ip2.getSecond()); //reverse
      }
    }

    public static class GroupComparator extends WritableComparator {
      protected GroupComparator() {
        super(IntPair.class, true);
      }
      @Override
      public int compare(WritableComparable w1, WritableComparable w2) {
        IntPair ip1 = (IntPair) w1;
        IntPair ip2 = (IntPair) w2;
        return IntPair.compare(ip1.getFirst(), ip2.getFirst());
      }
    }

    @Override
    public int run(String[] args) throws Exception {
      Job job = JobBuilder.parseInputAndOutput(this, getConf(), args);
      if (job == null) {
        return -1;
      }

      job.setMapperClass(MaxTemperatureMapper.class);
      job.setPartitionerClass(FirstPartitioner.class);
      job.setSortComparatorClass(KeyComparator.class);
      job.setGroupingComparatorClass(GroupComparator.class);
      job.setReducerClass(MaxTemperatureReducer.class);
      job.setOutputKeyClass(IntPair.class);
      job.setOutputValueClass(NullWritable.class);

      return job.waitForCompletion(true) ? 0 : 1;
    }

    public static void main(String[] args) throws Exception {
      int exitCode = ToolRunner.run(new MaxTemperatureUsingSecondarySort(), args);
      System.exit(exitCode);
    }
  }
```

In the mapper, we create a key representing the year and temperature, using an IntPair Writable implementation. (IntPair is like the TextPair class we developed in "Implementing a Custom Writable" on page 103.) We don't need to carry any information in the value, because we can get the first (maximum) temperature in the reducer from the key, so we use a NullWritable. The reducer emits the first key, which due to the secondary sorting, is an IntPair for the year and its maximum temperature. IntPair's toString() method creates a tab-separated string, so the output is a set of tab-separated year-temperature pairs.

> Many applications need to access all the sorted values, not just the first value as we have provided here. To do this, you need to populate the value fields since in the reducer you can retrieve only the first key. This necessitates some unavoidable duplication of information between key and value.

We set the partitioner to partition by the first field of the key (the year) using a custom partitioner called FirstPartitioner. To sort keys by year (ascending) and temperature (descending), we use a custom sort comparator, using setSortComparatorClass(), that extracts the fields and performs the appropriate comparisons. Similarly, to group keys by year, we set a custom comparator, using setGroupingComparatorClass(), to extract the first field of the key for comparison.[6]

Running this program gives the maximum temperatures for each year:

```
% hadoop jar hadoop-examples.jar MaxTemperatureUsingSecondarySort input/ncdc/all \
> output-secondarysort
% hadoop fs -cat output-secondarysort/part-* | sort | head
1901    317
1902    244
1903    289
1904    256
1905    283
1906    294
1907    283
1908    289
1909    278
1910    294
```

Streaming

To do a secondary sort in Streaming, we can take advantage of a couple of library classes that Hadoop provides. Here's the driver that we can use to do a secondary sort:

```
hadoop jar $HADOOP_INSTALL/contrib/streaming/hadoop-*-streaming.jar \
    -D stream.num.map.output.key.fields=2 \
    -D mapred.text.key.partitioner.options=-k1,1 \
```

6. For simplicity, these custom comparators as shown are not optimized; see "Implementing a RawComparator for speed" on page 106 for the steps we would need to take to make them faster.

```
  -D mapred.output.key.comparator.class=\
org.apache.hadoop.mapred.lib.KeyFieldBasedComparator \
  -D mapred.text.key.comparator.options="-k1n -k2nr" \
  -input input/ncdc/all \
  -output output_secondarysort_streaming \
  -mapper ch08/src/main/python/secondary_sort_map.py \
  -partitioner org.apache.hadoop.mapred.lib.KeyFieldBasedPartitioner \
  -reducer ch08/src/main/python/secondary_sort_reduce.py \
  -file ch08/src/main/python/secondary_sort_map.py \
  -file ch08/src/main/python/secondary_sort_reduce.py
```

Our map function (Example 8-10) emits records with year and temperature fields. We want to treat the combination of both of these fields as the key, so we set `stream.num.map.output.key.fields` to 2. This means that values will be empty, just like in the Java case.

Example 8-10. Map function for secondary sort in Python

```python
#!/usr/bin/env python

import re
import sys

for line in sys.stdin:
  val = line.strip()
  (year, temp, q) = (val[15:19], int(val[87:92]), val[92:93])
  if temp == 9999:
    sys.stderr.write("reporter:counter:Temperature,Missing,1\n")
  elif re.match("[01459]", q):
    print "%s\t%s" % (year, temp)
```

However, we don't want to partition by the entire key, so we use the `KeyFieldBased Partitioner` partitioner, which allows us to partition by a part of the key. The specification `mapred.text.key.partitioner.options` configures the partitioner. The value `-k1,1` instructs the partitioner to use only the first field of the key, where fields are assumed to be separated by a string defined by the `map.output.key.field.separator` property (a tab character by default).

Next, we want a comparator that sorts the year field in ascending order and the temperature field in descending order, so that the reduce function can simply return the first record in each group. Hadoop provides `KeyFieldBasedComparator`, which is ideal for this purpose. The comparison order is defined by a specification that is like the one used for GNU *sort*. It is set using the `mapred.text.key.comparator.options` property. The value `-k1n -k2nr` used in this example means "sort by the first field in numerical order, then by the second field in reverse numerical order." Like its partitioner cousin, `KeyFieldBasedPartitioner`, it uses the separator defined by the `map.output. key.field.separator` to split a key into fields.

In the Java version, we had to set the grouping comparator; however, in Streaming, groups are not demarcated in any way, so in the reduce function we have to detect the group boundaries ourselves by looking for when the year changes (Example 8-11).

Example 8-11. Reducer function for secondary sort in Python

```
#!/usr/bin/env python

import sys

last_group = None
for line in sys.stdin:
  val = line.strip()
  (year, temp) = val.split("\t")
  group = year
  if last_group != group:
    print val
    last_group = group
```

When we run the Streaming program, we get the same output as the Java version.

Finally, note that KeyFieldBasedPartitioner and KeyFieldBasedComparator are not confined to use in Streaming programs; they are applicable to Java MapReduce programs, too.

Joins

MapReduce can perform joins between large datasets, but writing the code to do joins from scratch is fairly involved. Rather than writing MapReduce programs, you might consider using a higher-level framework such as Pig, Hive, or Cascading, in which join operations are a core part of the implementation.

Let's briefly consider the problem we are trying to solve. We have two datasets—for example, the weather stations database and the weather records—and we want to reconcile the two. Let's say we want to see each station's history, with the station's metadata inlined in each output row. This is illustrated in Figure 8-2.

How we implement the join depends on how large the datasets are and how they are partitioned. If one dataset is large (the weather records) but the other one is small enough to be distributed to each node in the cluster (as the station metadata is), the join can be effected by a MapReduce job that brings the records for each station together (a partial sort on station ID, for example). The mapper or reducer uses the smaller dataset to look up the station metadata for a station ID, so it can be written out with each record. See "Side Data Distribution" on page 288 for a discussion of this approach, where we focus on the mechanics of distributing the data to tasktrackers.

If the join is performed by the mapper, it is called a *map-side join*, whereas if it is performed by the reducer it is called a *reduce-side join*.

If both datasets are too large for either to be copied to each node in the cluster, we can still join them using MapReduce with a map-side or reduce-side join, depending on how the data is structured. One common example of this case is a user database and a log of some user activity (such as access logs). For a popular service, it is not feasible to distribute the user database (or the logs) to all the MapReduce nodes.

Map-Side Joins

A map-side join between large inputs works by performing the join before the data reaches the map function. For this to work, though, the inputs to each map must be partitioned and sorted in a particular way. Each input dataset must be divided into the same number of partitions, and it must be sorted by the same key (the join key) in each source. All the records for a particular key must reside in the same partition. This may sound like a strict requirement (and it is), but it actually fits the description of the output of a MapReduce job.

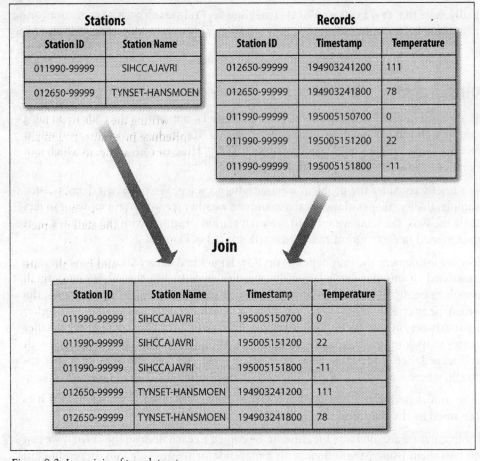

Figure 8-2. Inner join of two datasets

A map-side join can be used to join the outputs of several jobs that had the same number of reducers, the same keys, and output files that are not splittable (by being smaller than an HDFS block or by virtue of being gzip compressed, for example). In the context of the weather example, if we ran a partial sort on the stations file by station ID, and another, identical sort on the records, again by station ID and with the same number of reducers, then the two outputs would satisfy the conditions for running a map-side join.

Use a `CompositeInputFormat` from the `org.apache.hadoop.mapreduce.join` package to run a map-side join. The input sources and join type (inner or outer) for `CompositeInputFormat` are configured through a join expression that is written according to a simple grammar. The package documentation has details and examples.

The `org.apache.hadoop.examples.Join` example is a general-purpose command-line program for running a map-side join, since it allows you to run a MapReduce job for any specified mapper and reducer over multiple inputs that are joined with a given join operation.

Reduce-Side Joins

A reduce-side join is more general than a map-side join, in that the input datasets don't have to be structured in any particular way, but it is less efficient because both datasets have to go through the MapReduce shuffle. The basic idea is that the mapper tags each record with its source and uses the join key as the map output key, so that the records with the same key are brought together in the reducer. We use several ingredients to make this work in practice:

Multiple inputs

The input sources for the datasets generally have different formats, so it is very convenient to use the `MultipleInputs` class (see "Multiple Inputs" on page 250) to separate the logic for parsing and tagging each source.

Secondary sort

As described, the reducer will see the records from both sources that have the same key, but they are not guaranteed to be in any particular order. However, to perform the join, it is important to have the data from one source before another. For the weather data join, the station record must be the first of the values seen for each key, so the reducer can fill in the weather records with the station name and emit them straightaway. Of course, it would be possible to receive the records in any order if we buffered them in memory, but this should be avoided because the number of records in any group may be very large and exceed the amount of memory available to the reducer.[7]

---

7. The `data_join` package in the *contrib* directory implements reduce-side joins by buffering records in memory, so it suffers from this limitation.

We saw in "Secondary Sort" on page 277 how to impose an order on the values for each key that the reducers see, so we use this technique here.

To tag each record, we use TextPair from Chapter 4 for the keys (to store the station ID) and the tag. The only requirement for the tag values is that they sort in such a way that the station records come before the weather records. This can be achieved by tagging station records as 0 and weather records as 1. The mapper classes to do this are shown in Examples 8-12 and 8-13.

Example 8-12. Mapper for tagging station records for a reduce-side join

```
public class JoinStationMapper
    extends Mapper<LongWritable, Text, TextPair, Text> {
  private NcdcStationMetadataParser parser = new NcdcStationMetadataParser();

  @Override
  protected void map(LongWritable key, Text value, Context context)
      throws IOException, InterruptedException {
    if (parser.parse(value)) {
      context.write(new TextPair(parser.getStationId(), "0"),
          new Text(parser.getStationName()));
    }
  }
}
```

Example 8-13. Mapper for tagging weather records for a reduce-side join

```
public class JoinRecordMapper
    extends Mapper<LongWritable, Text, TextPair, Text> {
  private NcdcRecordParser parser = new NcdcRecordParser();

  @Override
  protected void map(LongWritable key, Text value, Context context)
      throws IOException, InterruptedException {
    parser.parse(value);
    context.write(new TextPair(parser.getStationId(), "1"), value);
  }

}
```

The reducer knows that it will receive the station record first, so it extracts its name from the value and writes it out as a part of every output record (Example 8-14).

Example 8-14. Reducer for joining tagged station records with tagged weather records

```
public class JoinReducer extends Reducer<TextPair, Text, Text, Text> {

  @Override
  protected void reduce(TextPair key, Iterable<Text> values, Context context)
      throws IOException, InterruptedException {
    Iterator<Text> iter = values.iterator();
    Text stationName = new Text(iter.next());
    while (iter.hasNext()) {
      Text record = iter.next();
```

```
      Text outValue = new Text(stationName.toString() + "\t" + record.toString());
      context.write(key.getFirst(), outValue);
    }
  }
}
```

The code assumes that every station ID in the weather records has exactly one matching record in the station dataset. If this were not the case, we would need to generalize the code to put the tag into the value objects, by using another TextPair. The reduce() method would then be able to tell which entries were station names and detect (and handle) missing or duplicate entries before processing the weather records.

 Because objects in the reducer's values iterator are reused (for efficiency purposes), it is vital that the code makes a copy of the first Text object from the values iterator:

```
Text stationName = new Text(iter.next());
```

If the copy is not made, the stationName reference will refer to the value just read when it is turned into a string, which is a bug.

Tying the job together is the driver class, shown in Example 8-15. The essential point is that we partition and group on the first part of the key, the station ID, which we do with a custom Partitioner (KeyPartitioner) and a custom group comparator, First Comparator (from TextPair).

Example 8-15. Application to join weather records with station names

```
public class JoinRecordWithStationName extends Configured implements Tool {

  public static class KeyPartitioner extends Partitioner<TextPair, Text> {
    @Override
    public int getPartition(TextPair key, Text value, int numPartitions) {
      return (key.getFirst().hashCode() & Integer.MAX_VALUE) % numPartitions;
    }
  }

  @Override
  public int run(String[] args) throws Exception {
    if (args.length != 3) {
      JobBuilder.printUsage(this, "<ncdc input> <station input> <output>");
      return -1;
    }

    Job job = new Job(getConf(), "Join weather records with station names");
    job.setJarByClass(getClass());

    Path ncdcInputPath = new Path(args[0]);
    Path stationInputPath = new Path(args[1]);
    Path outputPath = new Path(args[2]);

    MultipleInputs.addInputPath(job, ncdcInputPath,
        TextInputFormat.class, JoinRecordMapper.class);
```

```
MultipleInputs.addInputPath(job, stationInputPath,
    TextInputFormat.class, JoinStationMapper.class);
FileOutputFormat.setOutputPath(job, outputPath);

job.setPartitionerClass(KeyPartitioner.class);
job.setGroupingComparatorClass(TextPair.FirstComparator.class);

job.setMapOutputKeyClass(TextPair.class);

job.setReducerClass(JoinReducer.class);

job.setOutputKeyClass(Text.class);

return job.waitForCompletion(true) ? 0 : 1;
}

public static void main(String[] args) throws Exception {
  int exitCode = ToolRunner.run(new JoinRecordWithStationName(), args);
  System.exit(exitCode);
}
}
```

Running the program on the sample data yields the following output:

```
011990-99999    SIHCCAJAVRI          0067011990999991950051507004+68750...
011990-99999    SIHCCAJAVRI          0043011990999991950051512004+68750...
011990-99999    SIHCCAJAVRI          0043011990999991950051518004+68750...
012650-99999    TYNSET-HANSMOEN      0043012650999991949032412004+62300...
012650-99999    TYNSET-HANSMOEN      0043012650999991949032418004+62300...
```

Side Data Distribution

Side data can be defined as extra read-only data needed by a job to process the main dataset. The challenge is to make side data available to all the map or reduce tasks (which are spread across the cluster) in a convenient and efficient fashion.

Using the Job Configuration

You can set arbitrary key-value pairs in the job configuration using the various setter methods on Configuration (or JobConf in the old MapReduce API). This is very useful when you need to pass a small piece of metadata to your tasks.

In the task you can retrieve the data from the configuration returned by Context's getConfiguration() method. (In the old API, it's a little more involved: override the configure() method in the Mapper or Reducer and use a getter method on the JobConf object passed in to retrieve the data. It's very common to store the data in an instance field so it can be used in the map() or reduce() method.)

Usually a primitive type is sufficient to encode your metadata, but for arbitrary objects you can either handle the serialization yourself (if you have an existing mechanism for turning objects to strings and back) or use Hadoop's Stringifier class. The

`DefaultStringifier` uses Hadoop's serialization framework to serialize objects (see "Serialization" on page 93).

You shouldn't use this mechanism for transferring more than a few kilobytes of data, because it can put pressure on the memory usage in the Hadoop daemons, particularly in a system running hundreds of jobs. The job configuration is read by the jobtracker, the tasktracker, and the child JVM, and each time the configuration is read, all of its entries are read into memory, even if they are not used. User properties are not used by the jobtracker or the tasktracker, so they just waste time and memory.

Distributed Cache

Rather than serializing side data in the job configuration, it is preferable to distribute datasets using Hadoop's distributed cache mechanism. This provides a service for copying files and archives to the task nodes in time for the tasks to use them when they run. To save network bandwidth, files are normally copied to any particular node once per job.

Usage

For tools that use `GenericOptionsParser` (this includes many of the programs in this book; see "GenericOptionsParser, Tool, and ToolRunner" on page 150), you can specify the files to be distributed as a comma-separated list of URIs as the argument to the -`files` option. Files can be on the local filesystem, on HDFS, or on another Hadoop-readable filesystem (such as S3). If no scheme is supplied, then the files are assumed to be local. (This is true even when the default filesystem is not the local filesystem.)

You can also copy archive files (JAR files, ZIP files, tar files, and gzipped tar files) to your tasks using the -`archives` option; these are unarchived on the task node. The -`libjars` option will add JAR files to the classpath of the mapper and reducer tasks. This is useful if you haven't bundled library JAR files in your job JAR file.

> Streaming doesn't use the distributed cache for copying the streaming scripts across the cluster. You specify a file to be copied using the -`file` option (note the singular), which should be repeated for each file to be copied. Furthermore, files specified using the -`file` option must be file paths only, not URIs, so they must be accessible from the local filesystem of the client launching the Streaming job.
>
> Streaming also accepts the -`files` and -`archives` options for copying files into the distributed cache for use by your Streaming scripts.

Let's see how to use the distributed cache to share a metadata file for station names. The command we will run is:

```
% hadoop jar hadoop-examples.jar MaxTemperatureByStationNameUsingDistributedCacheFile \
  -files input/ncdc/metadata/stations-fixed-width.txt input/ncdc/all output
```

This command will copy the local file *stations-fixed-width.txt* (no scheme is supplied, so the path is automatically interpreted as a local file) to the task nodes, so we can use it to look up station names. The listing for MaxTemperatureByStationNameUsingDistri butedCacheFile appears in Example 8-16.

Example 8-16. Application to find the maximum temperature by station, showing station names from a lookup table passed as a distributed cache file

```java
public class MaxTemperatureByStationNameUsingDistributedCacheFile
  extends Configured implements Tool {

  static class StationTemperatureMapper
    extends Mapper<LongWritable, Text, Text, IntWritable> {

    private NcdcRecordParser parser = new NcdcRecordParser();

    @Override
    protected void map(LongWritable key, Text value, Context context)
        throws IOException, InterruptedException {

      parser.parse(value);
      if (parser.isValidTemperature()) {
        context.write(new Text(parser.getStationId()),
            new IntWritable(parser.getAirTemperature()));
      }
    }
  }

  static class MaxTemperatureReducerWithStationLookup
    extends Reducer<Text, IntWritable, Text, IntWritable> {

    private NcdcStationMetadata metadata;

    @Override
    protected void setup(Context context)
        throws IOException, InterruptedException {
      metadata = new NcdcStationMetadata();
      metadata.initialize(new File("stations-fixed-width.txt"));
    }

    @Override
    protected void reduce(Text key, Iterable<IntWritable> values,
        Context context) throws IOException, InterruptedException {

      String stationName = metadata.getStationName(key.toString());

      int maxValue = Integer.MIN_VALUE;
      for (IntWritable value : values) {
        maxValue = Math.max(maxValue, value.get());
      }
      context.write(new Text(stationName), new IntWritable(maxValue));
    }
  }
```

```
@Override
public int run(String[] args) throws Exception {
  Job job = JobBuilder.parseInputAndOutput(this, getConf(), args);
  if (job == null) {
    return -1;
  }

  job.setOutputKeyClass(Text.class);
  job.setOutputValueClass(IntWritable.class);

  job.setMapperClass(StationTemperatureMapper.class);
  job.setCombinerClass(MaxTemperatureReducer.class);
  job.setReducerClass(MaxTemperatureReducerWithStationLookup.class);

  return job.waitForCompletion(true) ? 0 : 1;
}

public static void main(String[] args) throws Exception {
  int exitCode = ToolRunner.run(
      new MaxTemperatureByStationNameUsingDistributedCacheFile(), args);
  System.exit(exitCode);
}
}
```

The program finds the maximum temperature by weather station, so the mapper (StationTemperatureMapper) simply emits (station ID, temperature) pairs. For the combiner, we reuse MaxTemperatureReducer (from Chapters 2 and 5) to pick the maximum temperature for any given group of map outputs on the map side. The reducer (MaxTemperatureReducerWithStationLookup) is different from the combiner, since in addition to finding the maximum temperature, it uses the cache file to look up the station name.

We use the reducer's setup() method to retrieve the cache file using its original name, relative to the working directory of the task.

 You can use the distributed cache for copying files that do not fit in memory. MapFiles are very useful in this regard, since they serve as an on-disk lookup format (see "MapFile" on page 137). Because MapFiles are a collection of files with a defined directory structure, you should put them into an archive format (JAR, ZIP, TAR, or gzipped TAR) and add them to the cache using the -archives option.

Here's a snippet of the output, showing some maximum temperatures for a few weather stations:

```
PEATS RIDGE WARATAH      372
STRATHALBYN RACECOU      410
SHEOAKS AWS              399
WANGARATTA AERO          409
MOOGARA                  334
MACKAY AERO              331
```

How it works

When you launch a job, Hadoop copies the files specified by the `-files`, `-archives`, and `-libjars` options to the distributed filesystem (normally HDFS). Then, before a task is run, the tasktracker copies the files from the distributed filesystem to a local disk —the cache—so the task can access the files. The files are said to be *localized* at this point. From the task's point of view, the files are just there (and it doesn't care that they came from HDFS). In addition, files specified by `-libjars` are added to the task's classpath before it is launched.

The tasktracker also maintains a reference count for the number of tasks using each file in the cache. Before the task has run, the file's reference count is incremented by one; then, after the task has run, the count is decreased by one. Only when the count reaches zero is it eligible for deletion, since no tasks are using it. Files are deleted to make room for a new file when the cache exceeds a certain size—10 GB by default. The cache size may be changed by setting the configuration property `local.cache.size`, which is measured in bytes.

Although this design doesn't guarantee that subsequent tasks from the same job running on the same tasktracker will find the file in the cache, it is very likely that they will, since tasks from a job are usually scheduled to run at around the same time, so there isn't the opportunity for enough other jobs to run and cause the original task's file to be deleted from the cache.

Files are localized under the *${mapred.local.dir}/taskTracker/archive* directory on the tasktrackers. Applications don't have to know this, however, because the files are symbolically linked from the task's working directory.

The distributed cache API

Most applications don't need to use the distributed cache API, because they can use the cache via `GenericOptionsParser`, as we saw in Example 8-16. However, some applications may need to use more advanced features of the distributed cache, and for this they can use its API directly. The API is in two parts: methods for putting data into the cache (found in `Job`) and methods for retrieving data from the cache (found in `JobContext`).[8] Here are the pertinent methods in `Job` for putting data into the cache:

```
public void addCacheFile(URI uri)
public void addCacheArchive(URI uri)
public void setCacheFiles(URI[] files)
public void setCacheArchives(URI[] archives)
public void addFileToClassPath(Path file)
public void addArchiveToClassPath(Path archive)
public void createSymlink()
```

---

8. If you are using the old MapReduce API, the same methods can be found in `org.apache.hadoop.file` `cache.DistributedCache`.

Recall that there are two types of objects that can be placed in the cache: files and archives. Files are left intact on the task node, whereas archives are unarchived on the task node. For each type of object, there are three methods: an addCacheXXXX() method to add the file or archive to the distributed cache, a setCacheXXXXs() method to set the entire list of files or archives to be added to the cache in a single call (replacing those set in any previous calls), and an addXXXXToClassPath() to add the file or archive to the MapReduce task's classpath. Table Table 8-7 compares these API methods to the GenericOptionsParser options described in Table 5-1.

Table 8-7. Distributed cache API

Job API method	GenericOptionsParser equivalent	Description
addCacheFile(URI uri) setCacheFiles(URI[] files)	-files file1,file2,...	Add files to the distributed cache to be copied to the task node.
addCacheArchive(URI uri) setCacheArchives(URI[] files)	-archives archive1,archive2,...	Add archives to the distributed cache to be copied to the task node and unarchived there.
addFileToClassPath(Path file)	-libjars jar1,jar2,...	Add files to the distributed cache to be added to the MapReduce task's classpath. The files are not unarchived, so this is a useful way to add JAR files to the classpath.
addArchiveToClassPath(Path archive)	None	Add archives to the distributed cache to be unarchived and added to the MapReduce task's classpath. This can be useful when you want to add a directory of files to the classpath, since you can create an archive containing the files. Alternatively, you could create a JAR file and use addFileToClassPath(), which works equally well.

The URIs referenced in the add() or set() methods must be files in a shared filesystem that exist when the job is run. On the other hand, the files specified as a GenericOptionsParser option (e.g., -files) may refer to a local file, in which case they get copied to the default shared filesystem (normally HDFS) on your behalf.

This is the key difference between using the Java API directly and using GenericOptionsParser: the Java API does *not* copy the file specified in the add() or set() method to the shared filesystem, whereas the GenericOptionsParser does.

The remaining distributed cache API method on Job is createSymlink(), which creates symbolic links for all the files for the current job when they are localized on the task node. The symbolic link name is set by the fragment identifier of the file's URI. For example, the file specified by the URI *hdfs://namenode/foo/bar#myfile* is symlinked as *myfile* in the task's working directory. (There's an example of using this API in Example 8-8.) If there is no fragment identifier, then no symbolic link is created. Files added to the distributed cache using GenericOptionsParser are automatically symlinked.

 Symbolic links are not created for files in the distributed cache when using the local job runner, so for this reason you may choose to use the getLocalCacheFiles() and getLocalCacheArchives() methods (discussed next) if you want your jobs to work both locally and on a cluster.

The second part of the distributed cache API is found on JobContext, and it is used from the map or reduce task code when you want to access files from the distributed cache.

```
public Path[] getLocalCacheFiles() throws IOException;
public Path[] getLocalCacheArchives() throws IOException;
public Path[] getFileClassPaths();
public Path[] getArchiveClassPaths();
```

If the files from the distributed cache have symbolic links in the task's working directory, you can access the localized file directly by name, as we did in Example 8-16. It's also possible to get a reference to files and archives in the cache using the getLocalCacheFiles() and getLocalCacheArchives() methods. In the case of archives, the paths returned are to the directory containing the unarchived files. (For completeness, you can also retrieve the files and archives added to the task classpath via getFileClassPaths() and getArchiveClassPaths().)

Note that files are returned as *local* Path objects. To read the files, you can use a Hadoop local FileSystem instance, retrieved using its getLocal() method. Alternatively, you can use the java.io.File API, as shown in this updated setup() method for MaxTemperatureReducerWithStationLookup:

```
@Override
protected void setup(Context context)
    throws IOException, InterruptedException {
  metadata = new NcdcStationMetadata();
  Path[] localPaths = context.getLocalCacheFiles();
  if (localPaths.length == 0) {
    throw new FileNotFoundException("Distributed cache file not found.");
  }
  File localFile = new File(localPaths[0].toString());
  metadata.initialize(localFile);
}
```

When using the old MapReduce API, we use the static method on DistributedCache instead, as follows:

```
@Override
public void configure(JobConf conf) {
```

```
metadata = new NcdcStationMetadata();
try {
  Path[] localPaths = DistributedCache.getLocalCacheFiles(conf);
  if (localPaths.length == 0) {
    throw new FileNotFoundException("Distributed cache file not found.");
  }
  File localFile = new File(localPaths[0].toString());
  metadata.initialize(localFile);
} catch (IOException e) {
  throw new RuntimeException(e);
}
}
```

MapReduce Library Classes

Hadoop comes with a library of mappers and reducers for commonly used functions. They are listed with brief descriptions in Table 8-8. For further information on how to use them, please consult their Java documentation.

Table 8-8. MapReduce library classes

Classes	Description
ChainMapper, ChainReducer	Runs a chain of mappers in a single mapper, and runs a reducer followed by a chain of mappers in a single reducer. (Symbolically, M+RM*, where M is a mapper and R is a reducer.) This can substantially reduce the amount of disk I/O incurred compared to running multiple MapReduce jobs.
FieldSelectionMapReduce (old API) FieldSelectionMapper and FieldSelectionReducer (new API)	A mapper and a reducer that can select fields (like the Unix cut command) from the input keys and values and emit them as output keys and values.
IntSumReducer, LongSumReducer	Reducers that sum integer values to produce a total for every key.
InverseMapper	A mapper that swaps keys and values.
MultithreadedMapRunner (old API) MultithreadedMapper (new API)	A mapper (or map runner in the old API) that runs mappers concurrently in separate threads. Useful for mappers that are not CPU-bound.
TokenCounterMapper	A mapper that tokenizes the input value into words (using Java's StringTokenizer) and emits each word along with a count of one.
RegexMapper	A mapper that finds matches of a regular expression in the input value and emits the matches along with a count of one.

Setting Up a Hadoop Cluster

This chapter explains how to set up Hadoop to run on a cluster of machines. Running HDFS and MapReduce on a single machine is great for learning about these systems, but to do useful work they need to run on multiple nodes.

There are a few options when it comes to getting a Hadoop cluster, from building your own, to running on rented hardware or using an offering that provides Hadoop as a service in the cloud. This chapter and the next give you enough information to set up and operate your own cluster, but even if you are using a Hadoop service in which a lot of the routine maintenance is done for you, these chapters still offer valuable information about how Hadoop works from an operations point of view.

Cluster Specification

Hadoop is designed to run on commodity hardware. That means that you are not tied to expensive, proprietary offerings from a single vendor; rather, you can choose standardized, commonly available hardware from any of a large range of vendors to build your cluster.

"Commodity" does not mean "low-end." Low-end machines often have cheap components, which have higher failure rates than more expensive (but still commodity-class) machines. When you are operating tens, hundreds, or thousands of machines, cheap components turn out to be a false economy, as the higher failure rate incurs a greater maintenance cost. On the other hand, large database-class machines are not recommended either, since they don't score well on the price/performance curve. And even though you would need fewer of them to build a cluster of comparable performance than one built of mid-range commodity hardware, when one did fail, it would have a bigger impact on the cluster because a larger proportion of the cluster hardware would be unavailable.

Hardware specifications rapidly become obsolete, but for the sake of illustration, a typical choice of machine for running a Hadoop datanode and tasktracker in mid-2010 would have the following specifications:

Processor
  Two quad-core 2-2.5 GHz CPUs

Memory
  16-24 GB ECC RAM[1]

Storage
  Four 1 TB SATA disks

Network
  Gigabit Ethernet

Although the hardware specification for your cluster will assuredly be different, Hadoop is designed to use multiple cores and disks, so it will be able to take full advantage of more powerful hardware.

Why Not Use RAID?

HDFS clusters do not benefit from using RAID (Redundant Array of Independent Disks) for datanode storage (although RAID is recommended for the namenode's disks, to protect against corruption of its metadata). The redundancy that RAID provides is not needed, since HDFS handles it by replication between nodes.

Furthermore, RAID striping (RAID 0), which is commonly used to increase performance, turns out to be *slower* than the JBOD (Just a Bunch Of Disks) configuration used by HDFS, which round-robins HDFS blocks between all disks. This is because RAID 0 read and write operations are limited by the speed of the slowest disk in the RAID array. In JBOD, disk operations are independent, so the average speed of operations is greater than that of the slowest disk. Disk performance often shows considerable variation in practice, even for disks of the same model. In some benchmarking carried out on a Yahoo! cluster (*http://markmail.org/message/xmzc45zi25htr7ry*), JBOD performed 10% faster than RAID 0 in one test (Gridmix) and 30% better in another (HDFS write throughput).

Finally, if a disk fails in a JBOD configuration, HDFS can continue to operate without the failed disk, whereas with RAID, failure of a single disk causes the whole array (and hence the node) to become unavailable.

The bulk of Hadoop is written in Java and can therefore run on any platform with a JVM, although there are enough parts that harbor Unix assumptions (the control scripts, for example) to make it unwise to run on a non-Unix platform in production.

---

1. ECC memory is strongly recommended, as several Hadoop users have reported seeing many checksum errors when using non-ECC memory on Hadoop clusters.

In fact, Windows operating systems are not supported production platforms (although they can be used with Cygwin as a development platform; see Appendix A).

How large should your cluster be? There isn't an exact answer to this question, but the beauty of Hadoop is that you can start with a small cluster (say, 10 nodes) and grow it as your storage and computational needs grow. In many ways, a better question is this: how fast does my cluster need to grow? You can get a good feel for this by considering storage capacity.

For example, if your data grows by 1 TB a week and you have three-way HDFS replication, you need an additional 3 TB of raw storage per week. Allow some room for intermediate files and logfiles (around 30%, say), and this works out at about one (2010-vintage) machine per week, on average. In practice, you wouldn't buy a new machine each week and add it to the cluster. The value of doing a back-of-the-envelope calculation like this is that it gives you a feel for how big your cluster should be. In this example, a cluster that holds two years of data needs 100 machines.

For a small cluster (on the order of 10 nodes), it is usually acceptable to run the namenode and the jobtracker on a single master machine (as long as at least one copy of the namenode's metadata is stored on a remote filesystem). As the cluster and the number of files stored in HDFS grow, the namenode needs more memory, so the namenode and jobtracker should be moved onto separate machines.

The secondary namenode can be run on the same machine as the namenode, but again for reasons of memory usage (the secondary has the same memory requirements as the primary), it is best to run it on a separate piece of hardware, especially for larger clusters. (This topic is discussed in more detail in "Master node scenarios" on page 306.) Machines running the namenodes should typically run on 64-bit hardware to avoid the 3 GB limit on Java heap size in 32-bit architectures.[2]

Network Topology

A common Hadoop cluster architecture consists of a two-level network topology, as illustrated in Figure 9-1. Typically there are 30 to 40 servers per rack, with a 1 GB switch for the rack (only three are shown in the diagram) and an uplink to a core switch or router (which is normally 1 GB or better). The salient point is that the aggregate bandwidth between nodes on the same rack is much greater than that between nodes on different racks.

---

2. The traditional advice says other machines in the cluster (jobtracker, datanodes/tasktrackers) should be 32-bit to avoid the memory overhead of larger pointers. Sun's Java 6 update 14 features "compressed ordinary object pointers," which eliminates much of this overhead, so there's now no real downside to running on 64-bit hardware.

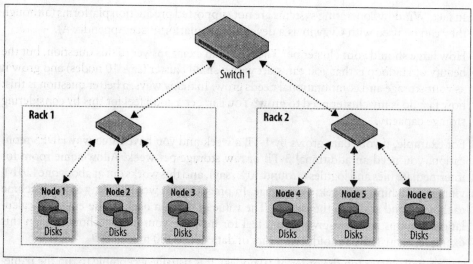

Figure 9-1. Typical two-level network architecture for a Hadoop cluster

Rack awareness

To get maximum performance out of Hadoop, it is important to configure Hadoop so that it knows the topology of your network. If your cluster runs on a single rack, then there is nothing more to do, since this is the default. However, for multirack clusters, you need to map nodes to racks. By doing this, Hadoop will prefer within-rack transfers (where there is more bandwidth available) to off-rack transfers when placing MapReduce tasks on nodes. HDFS will be able to place replicas more intelligently to trade off performance and resilience.

Network locations such as nodes and racks are represented in a tree, which reflects the network "distance" between locations. The namenode uses the network location when determining where to place block replicas (see "Network Topology and Hadoop" on page 69); the MapReduce scheduler uses network location to determine where the closest replica is as input to a map task.

For the network in Figure 9-1, the rack topology is described by two network locations, say, */switch1/rack1* and */switch1/rack2*. Because there is only one top-level switch in this cluster, the locations can be simplified to */rack1* and */rack2*.

The Hadoop configuration must specify a map between node addresses and network locations. The map is described by a Java interface, `DNSToSwitchMapping`, whose signature is:

```
public interface DNSToSwitchMapping {
  public List<String> resolve(List<String> names);
}
```

The `names` parameter is a list of IP addresses, and the return value is a list of corresponding network location strings. The `topology.node.switch.mapping.impl` configuration property defines an implementation of the `DNSToSwitchMapping` interface that the namenode and the jobtracker use to resolve worker node network locations.

For the network in our example, we would map *node1*, *node2*, and *node3* to */rack1*, and *node4*, *node5*, and *node6* to */rack2*.

Most installations don't need to implement the interface themselves, however, since the default implementation is `ScriptBasedMapping`, which runs a user-defined script to determine the mapping. The script's location is controlled by the property `topology.script.file.name`. The script must accept a variable number of arguments that are the hostnames or IP addresses to be mapped, and it must emit the corresponding network locations to standard output, separated by whitespace. The Hadoop wiki has an example at *http://wiki.apache.org/hadoop/topology_rack_awareness_scripts*.

If no script location is specified, the default behavior is to map all nodes to a single network location, called */default-rack*.

Cluster Setup and Installation

Your hardware has arrived. The next steps are to get it racked up and install the software needed to run Hadoop.

There are various ways to install and configure Hadoop. This chapter describes how to do it from scratch using the Apache Hadoop distribution and provides background information on the things you need to think about when setting up Hadoop. Alternatively, if you would like to use RPMs or Debian packages for managing your Hadoop installation, then you might want to start with Cloudera's Distribution, described in Appendix B.

To ease the burden of installing and maintaining the same software on each node, it is normal to use an automated installation method such as Red Hat Linux's Kickstart or Debian's Fully Automatic Installation. These tools allow you to automate the operating system installation by recording the answers to questions that are asked during the installation process (such as the disk partition layout), as well as which packages to install. Crucially, they also provide hooks to run scripts at the end of the process, which are invaluable for doing the final system tweaks and customization that are not covered by the standard installer.

The following sections describe the customizations that are needed to run Hadoop. These should all be added to the installation script.

Installing Java

Java 6 or later is required to run Hadoop. The latest stable Sun JDK is the preferred option, although Java distributions from other vendors may work, too. The following command confirms that Java was installed correctly:

```
% java -version
java version "1.6.0_12"
Java(TM) SE Runtime Environment (build 1.6.0_12-b04)
Java HotSpot(TM) 64-Bit Server VM (build 11.2-b01, mixed mode)
```

Creating a Hadoop User

It's good practice to create a dedicated Hadoop user account to separate the Hadoop installation from other services running on the same machine.

For small clusters, some administrators choose to make this user's home directory an NFS-mounted drive, to aid with SSH key distribution (see the following discussion). The NFS server is typically outside the Hadoop cluster. If you use NFS, it is worth considering autofs, which allows you to mount the NFS filesystem on demand when the system accesses it. Autofs provides some protection against the NFS server failing and allows you to use replicated filesystems for failover. There are other NFS gotchas to watch out for, such as synchronizing UIDs and GIDs. For help setting up NFS on Linux, refer to the HOWTO at *http://nfs.sourceforge.net/nfs-howto/index.html*.

Installing Hadoop

Download Hadoop from the Apache Hadoop releases page (*http://hadoop.apache.org/core/releases.html*), and unpack the contents of the distribution in a sensible location, such as */usr/local* (*/opt* is another standard choice). Note that Hadoop is *not* installed in the hadoop user's home directory, as that may be an NFS-mounted directory:

```
% cd /usr/local
% sudo tar xzf hadoop-x.y.z.tar.gz
```

We also need to change the owner of the Hadoop files to be the hadoop user and group:

```
% sudo chown -R hadoop:hadoop hadoop-x.y.z
```

Some administrators like to install HDFS and MapReduce in separate locations on the same system. At the time of this writing, only HDFS and MapReduce from the same Hadoop release are compatible with one another; however, in future releases, the compatibility requirements will be loosened. When this happens, having independent installations makes sense, as it gives more upgrade options (for more, see "Upgrades" on page 362). For example, it is convenient to be able to upgrade MapReduce—perhaps to patch a bug—while leaving HDFS running.

Note that separate installations of HDFS and MapReduce can still share configuration by using the `--config` option (when starting daemons) to refer to a common configuration directory. They can also log to the same directory because the logfiles they produce are named in such a way as to avoid clashes.

Testing the Installation

Once you've created an installation script, you are ready to test it by installing it on the machines in your cluster. This will probably take a few iterations as you discover kinks in the install. When it's working, you can proceed to configure Hadoop and give it a test run. This process is documented in the following sections.

SSH Configuration

The Hadoop control scripts (but not the daemons) rely on SSH to perform cluster-wide operations. For example, there is a script for stopping and starting all the daemons in the cluster. Note that the control scripts are optional—cluster-wide operations can be performed by other mechanisms, too (such as a distributed shell).

To work seamlessly, SSH needs to be set up to allow password-less login for the hadoop user from machines in the cluster. The simplest way to achieve this is to generate a public/private key pair and place it in an NFS location that is shared across the cluster.

First, generate an RSA key pair by typing the following in the hadoop user account:

```
% ssh-keygen -t rsa -f ~/.ssh/id_rsa
```

Even though we want password-less logins, keys without passphrases are not considered good practice (it's OK to have an empty passphrase when running a local pseudo-distributed cluster, as described in Appendix A), so we specify a passphrase when prompted for one. We use *ssh-agent* to avoid the need to enter a password for each connection.

The private key is in the file specified by the -f option, *~/.ssh/id_rsa*, and the public key is stored in a file with the same name but with *.pub* appended, *~/.ssh/id_rsa.pub*.

Next we need to make sure that the public key is in the ~/.ssh/authorized_keys file on all the machines in the cluster that we want to connect to. If the hadoop user's home directory is an NFS filesystem, as described earlier, the keys can be shared across the cluster by typing:

```
% cat ~/.ssh/id_rsa.pub >> ~/.ssh/authorized_keys
```

If the home directory is not shared using NFS, the public keys will need to be shared by some other means (such as *ssh-copy-id*).

Test that you can SSH from the master to a worker machine by making sure *ssh-agent* is running,[3] and then run *ssh-add* to store your passphrase. You should be able to *ssh* to a worker without entering the passphrase again.

Hadoop Configuration

There are a handful of files for controlling the configuration of a Hadoop installation; the most important ones are listed in Table 9-1. This section covers MapReduce 1, which employs the jobtracker and tasktracker daemons. Running MapReduce 2 is substantially different and is covered in "YARN Configuration" on page 320.

Table 9-1. Hadoop configuration files

Filename	Format	Description
hadoop-env.sh	Bash script	Environment variables that are used in the scripts to run Hadoop
core-site.xml	Hadoop configuration XML	Configuration settings for Hadoop Core, such as I/O settings that are common to HDFS and MapReduce
hdfs-site.xml	Hadoop configuration XML	Configuration settings for HDFS daemons: the namenode, the secondary namenode, and the datanodes
mapred-site.xml	Hadoop configuration XML	Configuration settings for MapReduce daemons: the jobtracker, and the tasktrackers
masters	Plain text	A list of machines (one per line) that each run a secondary namenode
slaves	Plain text	A list of machines (one per line) that each run a datanode and a tasktracker
hadoop-metrics .properties	Java Properties	Properties for controlling how metrics are published in Hadoop (see "Metrics" on page 352)
log4j.properties	Java Properties	Properties for system logfiles, the namenode audit log, and the task log for the tasktracker child process ("Hadoop Logs" on page 175)

These files are all found in the *conf* directory of the Hadoop distribution. The configuration directory can be relocated to another part of the filesystem (outside the Hadoop

---

3. See its main page for instructions on how to start *ssh-agent*.

installation, which makes upgrades marginally easier) as long as daemons are started with the --config option specifying the location of this directory on the local filesystem.

Configuration Management

Hadoop does not have a single, global location for configuration information. Instead, each Hadoop node in the cluster has its own set of configuration files, and it is up to administrators to ensure that they are kept in sync across the system. Hadoop provides a rudimentary facility for synchronizing configuration using *rsync* (see the upcoming discussion); alternatively, there are parallel shell tools that can help do this, such as *dsh* or *pdsh*.

Hadoop is designed so that it is possible to have a single set of configuration files that are used for all master and worker machines. The great advantage of this is simplicity, both conceptually (since there is only one configuration to deal with) and operationally (as the Hadoop scripts are sufficient to manage a single configuration setup).

For some clusters, the one-size-fits-all configuration model breaks down. For example, if you expand the cluster with new machines that have a different hardware specification from the existing ones, you need a different configuration for the new machines to take advantage of their extra resources.

In these cases, you need to have the concept of a *class* of machine and maintain a separate configuration for each class. Hadoop doesn't provide tools to do this, but there are several excellent tools for doing precisely this type of configuration management, such as Chef, Puppet, cfengine, and bcfg2.

For a cluster of any size, it can be a challenge to keep all of the machines in sync: consider what happens if the machine is unavailable when you push out an update. Who ensures it gets the update when it becomes available? This is a big problem and can lead to divergent installations, so even if you use the Hadoop control scripts for managing Hadoop, it may be a good idea to use configuration management tools for maintaining the cluster. These tools are also excellent for doing regular maintenance, such as patching security holes and updating system packages.

Control scripts

Hadoop comes with scripts for running commands and starting and stopping daemons across the whole cluster. To use these scripts (which can be found in the *bin* directory), you need to tell Hadoop which machines are in the cluster. There are two files for this purpose, called *masters* and *slaves*, each of which contains a list of the machine hostnames or IP addresses, one per line. The *masters* file is actually a misleading name, in that it determines which machine or machines should run a secondary namenode. The *slaves* file lists the machines that the datanodes and tasktrackers should run on. Both *masters* and *slaves* files reside in the configuration directory, although the *slaves* file may be placed elsewhere (and given another name) by changing the HADOOP_SLAVES setting in *hadoop-env.sh*. Also, these files do not need to be distributed to worker nodes, since they are used only by the control scripts running on the namenode or jobtracker.

You don't need to specify which machine (or machines) the namenode and jobtracker run on in the *masters* file, as this is determined by the machine the scripts are run on. (In fact, specifying these in the *masters* file would cause a secondary namenode to run there, which isn't always what you want.) For example, the *start-dfs.sh* script, which starts all the HDFS daemons in the cluster, runs the namenode on the machine that the script is run on. In slightly more detail, it:

1. Starts a namenode on the local machine (the machine that the script is run on)
2. Starts a datanode on each machine listed in the *slaves* file
3. Starts a secondary namenode on each machine listed in the *masters* file

There is a similar script called *start-mapred.sh*, which starts all the MapReduce daemons in the cluster. More specifically, it:

1. Starts a jobtracker on the local machine
2. Starts a tasktracker on each machine listed in the *slaves* file

Note that *masters* is not used by the MapReduce control scripts.

Also provided are *stop-dfs.sh* and *stop-mapred.sh* scripts to stop the daemons started by the corresponding start script.

These scripts start and stop Hadoop daemons using the *hadoop-daemon.sh* script. If you use the aforementioned scripts, you shouldn't call *hadoop-daemon.sh* directly. But if you need to control Hadoop daemons from another system or from your own scripts, the *hadoop-daemon.sh* script is a good integration point. Likewise, *hadoop-daemons.sh* (with an "s") is handy for starting the same daemon on a set of hosts.

Master node scenarios

Depending on the size of the cluster, there are various configurations for running the master daemons: the namenode, secondary namenode, and jobtracker. On a small cluster (a few tens of nodes), it is convenient to put them on a single machine; however, as the cluster gets larger, there are good reasons to separate them.

The namenode has high memory requirements, as it holds file and block metadata for the entire namespace in memory. The secondary namenode, although idle most of the time, has a comparable memory footprint to the primary when it creates a checkpoint. (This is explained in detail in "The filesystem image and edit log" on page 340.) For filesystems with a large number of files, there may not be enough physical memory on one machine to run both the primary and secondary namenode.

The secondary namenode keeps a copy of the latest checkpoint of the filesystem metadata that it creates. Keeping this (stale) backup on a different node from the namenode allows recovery in the event of loss (or corruption) of all the namenode's metadata files. (This is discussed further in Chapter 10.)

On a busy cluster running lots of MapReduce jobs, the jobtracker uses considerable memory and CPU resources, so it should run on a dedicated node.

Whether the master daemons run on one or more nodes, the following instructions apply:

- Run the HDFS control scripts from the namenode machine. The *masters* file should contain the address of the secondary namenode.
- Run the MapReduce control scripts from the jobtracker machine.

When the namenode and jobtracker are on separate nodes, their *slaves* files need to be kept in sync, since each node in the cluster should run a datanode and a tasktracker.

Environment Settings

In this section, we consider how to set the variables in *hadoop-env.sh*.

Memory

By default, Hadoop allocates 1,000 MB (1 GB) of memory to each daemon it runs. This is controlled by the HADOOP_HEAPSIZE setting in *hadoop-env.sh*. In addition, the task tracker launches separate child JVMs to run map and reduce tasks in, so we need to factor these into the total memory footprint of a worker machine.

The maximum number of map tasks that can run on a tasktracker at one time is controlled by the mapred.tasktracker.map.tasks.maximum property, which defaults to two tasks. There is a corresponding property for reduce tasks, mapred.task tracker.reduce.tasks.maximum, which also defaults to two tasks. The tasktracker is said to have two *map slots* and two *reduce slots*.

The memory given to each child JVM running a task can be changed by setting the mapred.child.java.opts property. The default setting is -Xmx200m, which gives each task 200 MB of memory. (Incidentally, you can provide extra JVM options here, too. For example, you might enable verbose GC logging to debug GC.) The default configuration therefore uses 2,800 MB of memory for a worker machine (see Table 9-2).

Table 9-2. Worker node memory calculation

JVM	Default memory used (MB)	Memory used for eight processors, 400 MB per child (MB)
Datanode	1,000	1,000
Tasktracker	1,000	1,000
Tasktracker child map task	2 × 200	7 × 400
Tasktracker child reduce task	2 × 200	7 × 400
Total	2,800	7,600

The number of tasks that can be run simultaneously on a tasktracker is related to the number of processors available on the machine. Because MapReduce jobs are normally I/O-bound, it makes sense to have more tasks than processors to get better utilization. The amount of oversubscription depends on the CPU utilization of jobs you run, but a good rule of thumb is to have a factor of between one and two more tasks (counting both map and reduce tasks) than processors.

For example, if you had eight processors and you wanted to run two processes on each processor, you could set both `mapred.tasktracker.map.tasks.maximum` and `mapred.task tracker.reduce.tasks.maximum` to 7 (not 8, because the datanode and the tasktracker each take one slot). If you also increased the memory available to each child task to 400 MB, the total memory usage would be 7,600 MB (see Table 9-2).

Whether this Java memory allocation will fit into 8 GB of physical memory depends on the other processes that are running on the machine. If you are running Streaming or Pipes programs, this allocation will probably be inappropriate (and the memory allocated to the child should be dialed down), since it doesn't allow enough memory for users' (Streaming or Pipes) processes to run. The thing to avoid is processes being swapped out, as this leads to severe performance degradation. The precise memory settings are necessarily very cluster-dependent and can be optimized over time with experience gained from monitoring the memory usage across the cluster. Tools such as Ganglia ("GangliaContext" on page 354) are good for gathering this information. See "Task memory limits" on page 318 for more on how to enforce task memory limits.

Hadoop also provides settings to control how much memory is used for MapReduce operations. These can be set on a per-job basis and are covered in the section on "Shuffle and Sort" on page 208.

For the master nodes, each of the namenode, secondary namenode, and jobtracker daemons uses 1,000 MB by default, for a total of 3,000 MB.

How Much Memory Does a Namenode Need?

A namenode can eat up memory, since a reference to every block of every file is maintained in memory. It's difficult to give a precise formula because memory usage depends on the number of blocks per file, the filename length, and the number of directories in the filesystem; plus, it can change from one Hadoop release to another.

The default of 1,000 MB of namenode memory is normally enough for a few million files, but as a rule of thumb for sizing purposes, you can conservatively allow 1,000 MB per million blocks of storage.

For example, a 200-node cluster with 4 TB of disk space per node, a block size of 128 MB, and a replication factor of 3 has room for about 2 million blocks (or more): 200 × 4,000,000 MB / (128 MB × 3). So in this case, setting the namenode memory to 2,000 MB would be a good starting point.

You can increase the namenode's memory without changing the memory allocated to other Hadoop daemons by setting HADOOP_NAMENODE_OPTS in *hadoop-env.sh* to include a

---

JVM option for setting the memory size. HADOOP_NAMENODE_OPTS allows you to pass extra options to the namenode's JVM. So, for example, if you were using a Sun JVM, -Xmx2000m would specify that 2,000 MB of memory should be allocated to the namenode.

If you change the namenode's memory allocation, don't forget to do the same for the secondary namenode (using the HADOOP_SECONDARYNAMENODE_OPTS variable), since its memory requirements are comparable to the primary namenode's. You probably also want to run the secondary namenode on a different machine in this case.

There are corresponding environment variables for the other Hadoop daemons, so you can customize their memory allocations, if desired. See *hadoop-env.sh* for details.

Java

The location of the Java implementation to use is determined by the JAVA_HOME setting in *hadoop-env.sh* or from the JAVA_HOME shell environment variable, if not set in *hadoop-env.sh*. It's a good idea to set the value in *hadoop-env.sh*, so that it is clearly defined in one place and to ensure that the whole cluster is using the same version of Java.

System logfiles

System logfiles produced by Hadoop are stored in *$HADOOP_INSTALL/logs* by default. This can be changed using the HADOOP_LOG_DIR setting in *hadoop-env.sh*. It's a good idea to change this so that logfiles are kept out of the directory that Hadoop is installed in. Changing this keeps logfiles in one place, even after the installation directory changes due to an upgrade. A common choice is */var/log/hadoop*, set by including the following line in *hadoop-env.sh*:

```
export HADOOP_LOG_DIR=/var/log/hadoop
```

The log director will be created if it doesn't already exist. (If it does not exist, confirm that the Hadoop user has permission to create it.) Each Hadoop daemon running on a machine produces two logfiles. The first is the log output written via log4j. This file, which ends in *.log*, should be the first port of call when diagnosing problems because most application log messages are written here. The standard Hadoop log4j configuration uses a Daily Rolling File Appender to rotate logfiles. Old logfiles are never deleted, so you should arrange for them to be periodically deleted or archived, so as to not run out of disk space on the local node.

The second logfile is the combined standard output and standard error log. This logfile, which ends in *.out*, usually contains little or no output, since Hadoop uses log4j for logging. It is rotated only when the daemon is restarted, and only the last five logs are retained. Old logfiles are suffixed with a number between 1 and 5, with 5 being the oldest file.

Logfile names (of both types) are a combination of the name of the user running the daemon, the daemon name, and the machine hostname. For example, *hadoop-tom-datanode-sturges.local.log.2008-07-04* is the name of a logfile after it has been rotated.

This naming structure makes it possible to archive logs from all machines in the cluster in a single directory, if needed, since the filenames are unique.

The username in the logfile name is actually the default for the HADOOP_IDENT_STRING setting in *hadoop-env.sh*. If you wish to give the Hadoop instance a different identity for the purposes of naming the logfiles, change HADOOP_IDENT_STRING to be the identifier you want.

SSH settings

The control scripts allow you to run commands on (remote) worker nodes from the master node using SSH. It can be useful to customize the SSH settings, for various reasons. For example, you may want to reduce the connection timeout (using the ConnectTimeout option) so the control scripts don't hang around waiting to see whether a dead node is going to respond. Obviously, this can be taken too far. If the timeout is too low, then busy nodes will be skipped, which is bad.

Another useful SSH setting is StrictHostKeyChecking, which can be set to no to automatically add new host keys to the known hosts files. The default, ask, prompts the user to confirm that he has verified the key fingerprint, which is not a suitable setting in a large cluster environment.[4]

To pass extra options to SSH, define the HADOOP_SSH_OPTS environment variable in *hadoop-env.sh*. See the ssh and ssh_config manual pages for more SSH settings.

The Hadoop control scripts can distribute configuration files to all nodes of the cluster using rsync. This is not enabled by default, but by defining the HADOOP_MASTER setting in *hadoop-env.sh*, worker daemons will rsync the tree rooted at HADOOP_MASTER to the local node's HADOOP_INSTALL whenever the daemon starts up.

What if you have two masters—a namenode and a jobtracker—on separate machines? You can pick one as the source and the other can rsync from it, along with all the workers. In fact, you could use any machine, even one outside the Hadoop cluster, to rsync from.

Because HADOOP_MASTER is unset by default, there is a bootstrapping problem: how do we make sure *hadoop-env.sh* with HADOOP_MASTER set is present on worker nodes? For small clusters, it is easy to write a small script to copy *hadoop-env.sh* from the master to all of the worker nodes. For larger clusters, tools such as *dsh* can do the copies in parallel. Alternatively, a suitable *hadoop-env.sh* can be created as a part of the automated installation script (such as Kickstart).

When starting a large cluster with rsyncing enabled, the worker nodes start at around the same time and can overwhelm the master node with rsync requests. To avoid this, set the HADOOP_SLAVE_SLEEP setting to a small number of seconds, such as 0.1 for one-

---

4. For more discussion on the security implications of SSH Host Keys, consult the article "SSH Host Key Protection" by Brian Hatch at *http://www.securityfocus.com/infocus/1806*.

tenth of a second. When running commands on all nodes of the cluster, the master will sleep for this period between invoking the command on each worker machine in turn.

Important Hadoop Daemon Properties

Hadoop has a bewildering number of configuration properties. In this section, we address the ones that you need to define (or at least understand why the default is appropriate) for any real-world working cluster. These properties are set in the Hadoop site files: *core-site.xml*, *hdfs-site.xml*, and *mapred-site.xml*. Typical examples of these files are shown in Example 9-1, Example 9-2, and Example 9-3. Notice that most properties are marked as final in order to prevent them from being overridden by job configurations. You can learn more about how to write Hadoop's configuration files in "The Configuration API" on page 144.

Example 9-1. A typical core-site.xml configuration file

```
<?xml version="1.0"?>
<!-- core-site.xml -->
<configuration>
  <property>
    <name>fs.default.name</name>
    <value>hdfs://namenode/</value>
    <final>true</final>
  </property>
</configuration>
```

Example 9-2. A typical hdfs-site.xml configuration file

```
<?xml version="1.0"?>
<!-- hdfs-site.xml -->
<configuration>
  <property>
    <name>dfs.name.dir</name>
    <value>/disk1/hdfs/name,/remote/hdfs/name</value>
    <final>true</final>
  </property>

  <property>
    <name>dfs.data.dir</name>
    <value>/disk1/hdfs/data,/disk2/hdfs/data</value>
    <final>true</final>
  </property>

  <property>
    <name>fs.checkpoint.dir</name>
    <value>/disk1/hdfs/namesecondary,/disk2/hdfs/namesecondary</value>
    <final>true</final>
  </property>
</configuration>
```

Example 9-3. A typical mapred-site.xml configuration file

```xml
<?xml version="1.0"?>
<!-- mapred-site.xml -->
<configuration>
  <property>
    <name>mapred.job.tracker</name>
    <value>jobtracker:8021</value>
    <final>true</final>
  </property>

  <property>
    <name>mapred.local.dir</name>
    <value>/disk1/mapred/local,/disk2/mapred/local</value>
    <final>true</final>
  </property>

  <property>
    <name>mapred.system.dir</name>
    <value>/tmp/hadoop/mapred/system</value>
    <final>true</final>
  </property>

  <property>
    <name>mapred.tasktracker.map.tasks.maximum</name>
    <value>7</value>
    <final>true</final>
  </property>

  <property>
    <name>mapred.tasktracker.reduce.tasks.maximum</name>
    <value>7</value>
    <final>true</final>
  </property>

  <property>
    <name>mapred.child.java.opts</name>
    <value>-Xmx400m</value>
    <!-- Not marked as final so jobs can include JVM debugging options -->
  </property>
</configuration>
```

HDFS

To run HDFS, you need to designate one machine as a namenode. In this case, the property fs.default.name is an HDFS filesystem URI whose host is the namenode's hostname or IP address and whose port is the port that the namenode will listen on for RPCs. If no port is specified, the default of 8020 is used.

> The *masters* file that is used by the control scripts is not used by the HDFS (or MapReduce) daemons to determine hostnames. In fact, because the *masters* file is used only by the scripts, you can ignore it if you don't use them.

The `fs.default.name` property also doubles as specifying the default filesystem. The default filesystem is used to resolve relative paths, which are handy to use because they save typing (and avoid hardcoding knowledge of a particular namenode's address). For example, with the default filesystem defined in Example 9-1, the relative URI */a/b* is resolved to *hdfs://namenode/a/b*.

> If you are running HDFS, the fact that `fs.default.name` is used to specify both the HDFS namenode *and* the default filesystem means HDFS has to be the default filesystem in the server configuration. Bear in mind, however, that it is possible to specify a different filesystem as the default in the client configuration, for convenience.
>
> For example, if you use both HDFS and S3 filesystems, then you have a choice of specifying either as the default in the client configuration, which allows you to refer to the default with a relative URI and the other with an absolute URI.

There are a few other configuration properties you should set for HDFS: those that set the storage directories for the namenode and for datanodes. The property `dfs.name.dir` specifies a list of directories where the namenode stores persistent filesystem metadata (the edit log and the filesystem image). A copy of each metadata file is stored in each directory for redundancy. It's common to configure `dfs.name.dir` so that the namenode metadata is written to one or two local disks, as well as a remote disk, such as an NFS-mounted directory. Such a setup guards against failure of a local disk and failure of the entire namenode, since in both cases the files can be recovered and used to start a new namenode. (The secondary namenode takes only periodic checkpoints of the namenode, so it does not provide an up-to-date backup of the namenode.)

You should also set the `dfs.data.dir` property, which specifies a list of directories for a datanode to store its blocks. Unlike the namenode, which uses multiple directories for redundancy, a datanode round-robins writes between its storage directories, so for performance you should specify a storage directory for each local disk. Read performance also benefits from having multiple disks for storage, because blocks will be spread across them and concurrent reads for distinct blocks will be correspondingly spread across disks.

> For maximum performance, you should mount storage disks with the `noatime` option. This setting means that last-accessed time information is not written on file reads, which gives significant performance gains.

Finally, you should configure where the secondary namenode stores its checkpoints of the filesystem. The `fs.checkpoint.dir` property specifies a list of directories where the checkpoints are kept. Like the storage directories for the namenode, which keep redundant copies of the namenode metadata, the checkpointed filesystem image is stored in each checkpoint directory for redundancy.

Table 9-3 summarizes the important configuration properties for HDFS.

Table 9-3. Important HDFS daemon properties

Property name	Type	Default value	Description
fs.default.name	URI	file:///	The default filesystem. The URI defines the hostname and port that the namenode's RPC server runs on. The default port is 8020. This property is set in *core-site.xml*.
dfs.name.dir	Comma-separated directory names	${hadoop.tmp.dir}/dfs/name	The list of directories where the namenode stores its persistent metadata. The namenode stores a copy of the metadata in each directory in the list.
dfs.data.dir	Comma-separated directory names	${hadoop.tmp.dir}/dfs/data	A list of directories where the datanode stores blocks. Each block is stored in only one of these directories.
fs.checkpoint.dir	Comma-separated directory names	${hadoop.tmp.dir}/dfs/namesecondary	A list of directories where the secondary namenode stores checkpoints. It stores a copy of the checkpoint in each directory in the list.

Note that the storage directories for HDFS are under Hadoop's temporary directory by default (the hadoop.tmp.dir property, whose default is /tmp/hadoop-${user.name}). Therefore, it is critical that these properties are set so that data is not lost by the system when it clears out temporary directories.

MapReduce

To run MapReduce, you need to designate one machine as a jobtracker, which on small clusters may be the same machine as the namenode. To do this, set the mapred.job.tracker property to the hostname or IP address and port that the jobtracker will listen on. Note that this property is not a URI, but instead a host-port pair, separated by a colon. The port number 8021 is a common choice.

During a MapReduce job, intermediate data and working files are written to temporary local files. Because this data includes the potentially very large output of map tasks, you need to ensure that the mapred.local.dir property, which controls the location of local temporary storage, is configured to use disk partitions that are large enough. The mapred.local.dir property takes a comma-separated list of directory names, and you should use all available local disks to spread disk I/O. Typically, you will use the same disks and partitions (but different directories) for MapReduce temporary data as you use for datanode block storage, as governed by the `dfs.data.dir` property, which was discussed earlier.

MapReduce uses a distributed filesystem to share files (such as the job JAR file) with the tasktrackers that run the MapReduce tasks. The `mapred.system.dir` property is used to specify a directory where these files can be stored. This directory is resolved relative to the default filesystem (configured in `fs.default.name`), which is usually HDFS.

Finally, you should set the `mapred.tasktracker.map.tasks.maximum` and `mapred.task tracker.reduce.tasks.maximum` properties to reflect the number of available cores on the tasktracker machines and `mapred.child.java.opts` to reflect the amount of memory available for the tasktracker child JVMs. See the discussion in "Memory" on page 307.

Table 9-4 summarizes the important configuration properties for MapReduce.

Table 9-4. Important MapReduce daemon properties

Property name	Type	Default value	Description
mapred.job.tracker	Hostname and port	local	The hostname and port that the job-tracker's RPC server runs on. If set to the default value of `local`, the job-tracker is run in-process on demand when you run a MapReduce job (you don't need to start the jobtracker in this case, and in fact you will get an error if you try to start it in this mode).
mapred.local.dir	Comma-separated directory names	${hadoop.tmp.dir} /mapred/local	A list of directories where MapReduce stores intermediate data for jobs. The data is cleared out when the job ends.
mapred.system.dir	URI	${hadoop.tmp.dir} /mapred/system	The directory relative to `fs.default.name` where shared files are stored during a job run.
mapred.tasktracker. map.tasks.maximum	int	2	The number of map tasks that may be run on a tasktracker at any one time.
mapred.tasktracker. reduce.tasks.maximum	int	2	The number of reduce tasks that may be run on a tasktracker at any one time.
mapred.child.java.opts	String	-Xmx200m	The JVM options used to launch the tasktracker child process that runs map and reduce tasks. This property can be set on a per-job basis, which can be useful for setting JVM properties for debugging, for example.

Property name	Type	Default value	Description
mapreduce.map. java.opts	String	-Xmx200m	The JVM options used for the child process that runs map tasks. (Not available in 1.x.)
mapreduce.reduce. java.opts	String	-Xmx200m	The JVM options used for the child process that runs reduce tasks. (Not available in 1.x.)

Hadoop Daemon Addresses and Ports

Hadoop daemons generally run both an RPC server (Table 9-5) for communication between daemons and an HTTP server to provide web pages for human consumption (Table 9-6). Each server is configured by setting the network address and port number to listen on. By specifying the network address as 0.0.0.0, Hadoop will bind to all addresses on the machine. Alternatively, you can specify a single address to bind to. A port number of 0 instructs the server to start on a free port, but this is generally discouraged because it is incompatible with setting cluster-wide firewall policies.

Table 9-5. RPC server properties

Property name	Default value	Description
fs.default.name	file:///	When set to an HDFS URI, this property determines the namenode's RPC server address and port. The default port is 8020 if not specified.
dfs.datanode.ipc.address	0.0.0.0:50020	The datanode's RPC server address and port.
mapred.job.tracker	local	When set to a hostname and port, this property specifies the jobtracker's RPC server address and port. A commonly used port is 8021.
mapred.task.tracker.report.address	127.0.0.1:0	The tasktracker's RPC server address and port. This is used by the tasktracker's child JVM to communicate with the tasktracker. Using any free port is acceptable in this case, as the server only binds to the loopback address. You should change this setting only if the machine has no loopback address.

In addition to an RPC server, datanodes run a TCP/IP server for block transfers. The server address and port is set by the dfs.datanode.address property and has a default value of 0.0.0.0:50010.

Table 9-6. HTTP server properties

Property name	Default value	Description
mapred.job.tracker.http.address	0.0.0.0:50030	The jobtracker's HTTP server address and port
mapred.task.tracker.http.address	0.0.0.0:50060	The tasktracker's HTTP server address and port

Property name	Default value	Description
dfs.http.address	0.0.0.0:50070	The namenode's HTTP server address and port
dfs.datanode.http.address	0.0.0.0:50075	The datanode's HTTP server address and port
dfs.secondary.http.address	0.0.0.0:50090	The secondary namenode's HTTP server address and port

There are also settings for controlling which network interfaces the datanodes and tasktrackers report as their IP addresses (for HTTP and RPC servers). The relevant properties are dfs.datanode.dns.interface and mapred.tasktracker.dns.interface, both of which are set to default, which will use the default network interface. You can set this explicitly to report the address of a particular interface (eth0, for example).

Other Hadoop Properties

This section discusses some other properties that you might consider setting.

Cluster membership

To aid the addition and removal of nodes in the future, you can specify a file containing a list of authorized machines that may join the cluster as datanodes or tasktrackers. The file is specified using the dfs.hosts and mapred.hosts properties (for datanodes and tasktrackers, respectively), as well as the corresponding dfs.hosts.exclude and mapred.hosts.exclude files used for decommissioning. See "Commissioning and Decommissioning Nodes" on page 359 for further discussion.

Buffer size

Hadoop uses a buffer size of 4 KB (4,096 bytes) for its I/O operations. This is a conservative setting, and with modern hardware and operating systems, you will likely see performance benefits by increasing it; 128 KB (131,072 bytes) is a common choice. Set this using the io.file.buffer.size property in *core-site.xml*.

HDFS block size

The HDFS block size is 64 MB by default, but many clusters use 128 MB (134,217,728 bytes) or even 256 MB (268,435,456 bytes) to ease memory pressure on the namenode and to give mappers more data to work on. Set this using the dfs.block.size property in *hdfs-site.xml*.

Reserved storage space

By default, datanodes will try to use all of the space available in their storage directories. If you want to reserve some space on the storage volumes for non-HDFS use, you can set dfs.datanode.du.reserved to the amount, in bytes, of space to reserve.

Trash

Hadoop filesystems have a trash facility, in which deleted files are not actually deleted, but rather are moved to a trash folder, where they remain for a minimum period before being permanently deleted by the system. The minimum period in minutes that a file will remain in the trash is set using the `fs.trash.interval` configuration property in *core-site.xml*. By default, the trash interval is zero, which disables trash.

Like in many operating systems, Hadoop's trash facility is a user-level feature, meaning that only files that are deleted using the filesystem shell are put in the trash. Files deleted programmatically are deleted immediately. It is possible to use the trash programmatically, however, by constructing a `Trash` instance, then calling its `moveToTrash()` method with the `Path` of the file intended for deletion. The method returns a value indicating success; a value of `false` means either that trash is not enabled or that the file is already in the trash.

When trash is enabled, each user has her own trash directory called *.Trash* in her home directory. File recovery is simple: you look for the file in a subdirectory of *.Trash* and move it out of the trash subtree.

HDFS will automatically delete files in trash folders, but other filesystems will not, so you have to arrange for this to be done periodically. You can *expunge* the trash, which will delete files that have been in the trash longer than their minimum period, using the filesystem shell:

```
% hadoop fs -expunge
```

The `Trash` class exposes an `expunge()` method that has the same effect.

Job scheduler

Particularly in a multiuser MapReduce setting, consider changing the default FIFO job scheduler to one of the more fully featured alternatives. See "Job Scheduling" on page 206.

Reduce slow start

By default, schedulers wait until 5% of the map tasks in a job have completed before scheduling reduce tasks for the same job. For large jobs this can cause problems with cluster utilization, since they take up reduce slots while waiting for the map tasks to complete. Setting `mapred.reduce.slowstart.completed.maps` to a higher value, such as 0.80 (80%), can help improve throughput.

Task memory limits

On a shared cluster, it shouldn't be possible for one user's errant MapReduce program to bring down nodes in the cluster. This can happen if the map or reduce task has a memory leak, for example, because the machine on which the tasktracker is running will run out of memory and may affect the other running processes.

Or consider the case where a user sets `mapred.child.java.opts` to a large value and causes memory pressure on other running tasks, causing them to swap. Marking this property as final on the cluster would prevent it from being changed by users in their jobs, but there are legitimate reasons to allow some jobs to use more memory, so this is not always an acceptable solution. Furthermore, even locking down `mapred.child.java.opts` does not solve the problem, because tasks can spawn new processes that are not constrained in their memory usage. Streaming and Pipes jobs do exactly that, for example.

To prevent cases like these, some way of enforcing a limit on a task's memory usage is needed. Hadoop provides two mechanisms for this. The simplest is via the Linux *ulimit* command, which can be done at the operating-system level (in the *limits.conf* file, typically found in */etc/security*) or by setting `mapred.child.ulimit` in the Hadoop configuration. The value is specified in kilobytes, and should be comfortably larger than the memory of the JVM set by `mapred.child.java.opts`; otherwise, the child JVM might not start.

The second mechanism is Hadoop's *task memory monitoring* feature.[5] The idea is that an administrator sets a range of allowed virtual memory limits for tasks on the cluster, and users specify the maximum memory requirements for their jobs in the job configuration. If a user doesn't set memory requirements for his job, then the defaults are used (`mapred.job.map.memory.mb` and `mapred.job.reduce.memory.mb`).

This approach has a couple of advantages over the *ulimit* approach. First, it enforces the memory usage of the whole task process tree, including spawned processes. Second, it enables memory-aware scheduling, where tasks are scheduled on tasktrackers that have enough free memory to run them. The Capacity Scheduler, for example, will account for slot usage based on the memory settings, so if a job's `mapred.job.map.memory.mb` setting exceeds `mapred.cluster.map.memory.mb`, the scheduler will allocate more than one slot on a tasktracker to run each map task for that job.

To enable task memory monitoring, you need to set all six of the properties in Table 9-7. The default values are all `-1`, which means the feature is disabled.

Table 9-7. MapReduce task memory monitoring properties

Property name	Type	Default value	Description
`mapred.cluster.map.mem ory.mb`	int	-1	The amount of virtual memory, in MB, that defines a map slot. Map tasks that require more than this amount of memory will use more than one map slot.
`mapred.cluster.reduce.mem ory.mb`	int	-1	The amount of virtual memory, in MB, that defines a reduce slot. Reduce tasks that require more than this amount of memory will use more than one reduce slot.

---

5. YARN uses a different memory model to the one described here, and the configuration options are different. See "Memory" on page 323.

Property name	Type	Default value	Description
mapred.job.map.memory.mb	int	-1	The amount of virtual memory, in MB, that a map task requires to run. If a map task exceeds this limit, it may be terminated and marked as failed.
mapred.job.reduce.mem ory.mb	int	-1	The amount of virtual memory, in MB, that a reduce task requires to run. If a reduce task exceeds this limit, it may be terminated and marked as failed.
mapred.clus ter.max.map.memory.mb	int	-1	The maximum limit that users can set mapred.job.map.memory.mb to.
mapred.clus ter.max.reduce.memory.mb	int	-1	The maximum limit that users can set mapred.job.reduce.memory.mb to.

User Account Creation

Once you have a Hadoop cluster up and running, you need to give users access to it. This involves creating a home directory for each user and setting ownership permissions on it:

```
% hadoop fs -mkdir /user/username
% hadoop fs -chown username:username /user/username
```

This is a good time to set space limits on the directory. The following sets a 1 TB limit on the given user directory:

```
% hadoop dfsadmin -setSpaceQuota 1t /user/username
```

YARN Configuration

YARN is the next-generation architecture for running MapReduce (and is described in "YARN (MapReduce 2)" on page 196). It has a different set of daemons and configuration options than classic MapReduce (also called MapReduce 1), and in this section we look at these differences and discuss how to run MapReduce on YARN.

Under YARN, you no longer run a jobtracker or tasktrackers. Instead, there is a single resource manager running on the same machine as the HDFS namenode (for small clusters) or on a dedicated machine, and node managers running on each worker node in the cluster.

The YARN *start-yarn.sh* script (in the *sbin* directory) starts the YARN daemons in the cluster. This script will start a resource manager (on the machine the script is run on) and a node manager on each machine listed in the *slaves* file.

YARN also has a job history server daemon that provides users with details of past job runs, and a web app proxy server for providing a secure way for users to access the UI provided by YARN applications. In the case of MapReduce, the web UI served by the proxy provides information about the current job you are running, similar to the one described in "The MapReduce Web UI" on page 165. By default, the web app proxy server runs in the same process as the resource manager, but it may be configured to run as a standalone daemon.

YARN has its own set of configuration files, listed in Table 9-8; these are used in addition to those in Table 9-1.

Table 9-8. YARN configuration files

Filename	Format	Description
yarn-env.sh	Bash script	Environment variables that are used in the scripts to run YARN
yarn-site.xml	Hadoop configuration XML	Configuration settings for YARN daemons: the resource manager, the job history server, the webapp proxy server, and the node managers

Important YARN Daemon Properties

When running MapReduce on YARN, the *mapred-site.xml* file is still used for general MapReduce properties, although the jobtracker- and tasktracker-related properties are not used. None of the properties in Table 9-4 are applicable to YARN, except for `mapred.child.java.opts` (and the related properties `mapreduce.map.java.opts` and `map reduce.reduce.java.opts`, which apply only to map or reduce tasks, respectively). The JVM options specified in this way are used to launch the YARN child process that runs map or reduce tasks.

The configuration files in Example 9-4 show some of the important configuration properties for running MapReduce on YARN.

Example 9-4. An example set of site configuration files for running MapReduce on YARN

```
<?xml version="1.0"?>
<!-- mapred-site.xml -->
<configuration>
  <property>
    <name>mapred.child.java.opts</name>
    <value>-Xmx400m</value>
    <!-- Not marked as final so jobs can include JVM debugging options -->
  </property>
</configuration>

<?xml version="1.0"?>
<!-- yarn-site.xml -->
<configuration>
  <property>
    <name>yarn.resourcemanager.address</name>
    <value>resourcemanager:8032</value>
  </property>
  <property>
    <name>yarn.nodemanager.local-dirs</name>
    <value>/disk1/nm-local-dir,/disk2/nm-local-dir</value>
    <final>true</final>
  </property>
```

```
<property>
  <name>yarn.nodemanager.aux-services</name>
  <value>mapreduce.shuffle</value>
</property>
<property>
  <name>yarn.nodemanager.resource.memory-mb</name>
  <value>8192</value>
</property>
</configuration>
```

The YARN resource manager address is controlled via `yarn.resourceman ager.address`, which takes the form of a host-port pair. In a client configuration, this property is used to connect to the resource manager (using RPC), and in addition, the `mapreduce.framework.name` property must be set to `yarn` for the client to use YARN rather than the local job runner.

Although YARN does not honor `mapred.local.dir`, it has an equivalent property called `yarn.nodemanager.local-dirs`, which allows you to specify the local disks to store intermediate data on. It is specified by a comma-separated list of local directory paths, which are used in a round-robin fashion.

YARN doesn't have tasktrackers to serve map outputs to reduce tasks, so for this function it relies on shuffle handlers, which are long-running auxiliary services running in node managers. Because YARN is a general-purpose service, the MapReduce shuffle handlers need to be enabled explicitly in *yarn-site.xml* by setting the `yarn.nodeman ager.aux-services` property to `mapreduce.shuffle`.

Table 9-9 summarizes the important configuration properties for YARN.

Table 9-9. Important YARN daemon properties

Property name	Type	Default value	Description
yarn.resourceman ager.address	Hostname and port	0.0.0.0:8032	The hostname and port that the resource manager's RPC server runs on.
yarn.nodeman ager.local-dirs	Comma-separated directory names	/tmp/nm-local-dir	A list of directories where node managers allow containers to store intermediate data. The data is cleared out when the application ends.
yarn.nodeman ager.aux-services	Comma-separated service names		A list of auxiliary services run by the node manager. A service is implemented by the class defined by the property `yarn.nodemanager.aux-serv ices.service-name.class`. By default, no auxiliary services are specified.
yarn.nodeman ager.resource.mem ory-mb	int	8192	The amount of physical memory (in MB) that may be allocated to containers being run by the node manager.

Property name	Type	Default value	Description
yarn.nodeman ager.vmem-pmem-ratio	float	2.1	The ratio of virtual to physical memory for containers. Virtual memory usage may exceed the allocation by this amount.

Memory

YARN treats memory in a more fine-grained manner than the slot-based model used in the classic implementation of MapReduce. Rather than specifying a fixed maximum number of map and reduce slots that may run on a tasktracker node at once, YARN allows applications to request an arbitrary amount of memory (within limits) for a task. In the YARN model, node managers allocate memory from a pool, so the number of tasks that are running on a particular node depends on the sum of their memory requirements, and not simply on a fixed number of slots.

The slot-based model can lead to cluster underutilization, since the proportion of map slots to reduce slots is fixed as a cluster-wide configuration. However, the number of map versus reduce slots that are *in demand* changes over time: at the beginning of a job only map slots are needed, whereas at the end of the job only reduce slots are needed. On larger clusters with many concurrent jobs, the variation in demand for a particular type of slot may be less pronounced, but there is still wastage. YARN avoids this problem by not distinguishing between the two types of slots.

The considerations for how much memory to dedicate to a node manager for running containers are similar to the those discussed in "Memory" on page 307. Each Hadoop daemon uses 1,000 MB, so for a datanode and a node manager, the total is 2,000 MB. Set aside enough for other processes that are running on the machine, and the remainder can be dedicated to the node manager's containers by setting the configuration property yarn.nodemanager.resource.memory-mb to the total allocation in MB. (The default is 8,192 MB.)

The next step is to determine how to set memory options for individual jobs. There are two controls: mapred.child.java.opts, which allows you to set the JVM heap size of the map or reduce task; and mapreduce.map.memory.mb (or mapreduce.reduce.memory.mb), which is used to specify how much memory you need for map (or reduce) task containers. The latter setting is used by the application master when negotiating for resources in the cluster, and also by the node manager, which runs and monitors the task containers.

For example, suppose that mapred.child.java.opts is set to -Xmx800m and mapreduce.map.memory.mb is left at its default value of 1,024 MB. When a map task is run, the node manager will allocate a 1,024 MB container (decreasing the size of its pool by that amount for the duration of the task) and will launch the task JVM configured with an 800 MB maximum heap size. Note that the JVM process will have a larger memory footprint than the heap size, and the overhead will depend on such things as the native libraries that are in use, the size of the permanent generation space, and so on. The important thing is that the physical memory used by the JVM process, including any processes that it spawns, such as Streaming or Pipes processes, does not exceed its allocation (1,024 MB). If a container uses more memory than it has been allocated, then it may be terminated by the node manager and marked as failed.

Schedulers may impose a minimum or maximum on memory allocations. For example, for the Capacity Scheduler, the default minimum is 1024 MB (set by yarn.scheduler.capacity.minimum-allocation-mb), and the default maximum is 10240 MB (set by yarn.scheduler.capacity.maximum-allocation-mb).

There are also virtual memory constraints that a container must meet. If a container's virtual memory usage exceeds a given multiple of the allocated physical memory, the node manager may terminate the process. The multiple is expressed by the yarn.node manager.vmem-pmem-ratio property, which defaults to 2.1. In the example used earlier, the virtual memory threshold above which the task may be terminated is 2,150 MB, which is 2.1 × 1,024 MB.

When configuring memory parameters it's very useful to be able to monitor a task's actual memory usage during a job run, and this is possible via MapReduce task counters. The counters PHYSICAL_MEMORY_BYTES, VIRTUAL_MEMORY_BYTES, and COMMITTED _HEAP_BYTES (described in Table 8-2) provide snapshot values of memory usage and are therefore suitable for observation during the course of a task attempt.

YARN Daemon Addresses and Ports

YARN daemons run one or more RPC and HTTP servers, details of which are covered in Table 9-10 and Table 9-11.

Table 9-10. YARN RPC server properties

Property name	Default value	Description
yarn.resourceman ager.address	0.0.0.0:8032	The resource manager's RPC server address and port. This is used by the client (typically outside the cluster) to communicate with the resource manager.
yarn.resourceman ager.admin.address	0.0.0.0:8033	The resource manager's admin RPC server address and port. This is used by the admin client (invoked with yarn rmadmin, typically run outside the cluster) to communicate with the resource manager.
yarn.resourceman ager.scheduler.address	0.0.0.0:8030	The resource manager scheduler's RPC server address and port. This is used by (in-cluster) application masters to communicate with the resource manager.
yarn.resourceman ager.resource- tracker.address	0.0.0.0:8031	The resource manager resource tracker's RPC server address and port. This is used by the (in-cluster) node managers to communicate with the resource manager.

Property name	Default value	Description
yarn.nodeman ager.address	0.0.0.0:0	The node manager's RPC server address and port. This is used by (in-cluster) application masters to communicate with node managers.
yarn.nodemanager.local izer.address	0.0.0.0:8040	The node manager localizer's RPC server address and port.
mapreduce.jobhis tory.address	0.0.0.0:10020	The job history server's RPC server address and port. This is used by the client (typically outside the cluster) to query job history. This property is set in *mapred-site.xml*.

Table 9-11. YARN HTTP server properties

Property name	Default value	Description
yarn.resourceman ager.webapp.address	0.0.0.0:8088	The resource manager's HTTP server address and port.
yarn.nodeman ager.webapp.address	0.0.0.0:8042	The node manager's HTTP server address and port.
yarn.web-proxy.address		The web app proxy server's HTTP server address and port. If not set (the default), then the web app proxy server will run in the resource manager process.
mapreduce.jobhis tory.webapp.address	0.0.0.0:19888	The job history server's HTTP server address and port. This property is set in *mapred-site.xml*.
mapreduce.shuffle.port	8080	The shuffle handler's HTTP port number. This is used for serving map outputs, and is not a user-accessible web UI. This property is set in *mapred-site.xml*.

Security

Early versions of Hadoop assumed that HDFS and MapReduce clusters would be used by a group of cooperating users within a secure environment. The measures for restricting access were designed to prevent accidental data loss, rather than to prevent unauthorized access to data. For example, the file permissions system in HDFS prevents one user from accidentally wiping out the whole filesystem from a bug in a program, or by mistakenly typing hadoop fs -rmr /, but it doesn't prevent a malicious user from assuming root's identity (see "Setting User Identity" on page 150) to access or delete any data in the cluster.

In security parlance, what was missing was a secure *authentication* mechanism to assure Hadoop that the user seeking to perform an operation on the cluster is who she claims to be and therefore can be trusted. HDFS file permissions provide only a mechanism for *authorization*, which controls what a particular user can do to a particular file. For example, a file may be readable only by a certain group of users, so anyone not in that group is not authorized to read it. However, authorization is not enough by itself, because the system is still open to abuse via spoofing by a malicious user who can gain network access to the cluster.

It's common to restrict access to data that contains personally identifiable information (such as an end user's full name or IP address) to a small set of users (of the cluster) within the organization who are authorized to access such information. Less sensitive (or anonymized) data may be made available to a larger set of users. It is convenient to host a mix of datasets with different security levels on the same cluster (not least because it means the datasets with lower security levels can be shared). However, to meet regulatory requirements for data protection, secure authentication must be in place for shared clusters.

This is the situation that Yahoo! faced in 2009, which led a team of engineers there to implement secure authentication for Hadoop. In their design, Hadoop itself does not manage user credentials; instead, it relies on Kerberos, a mature open-source network authentication protocol, to authenticate the user. In turn, Kerberos doesn't manage permissions. Kerberos says that a user is who he says he is; it's Hadoop's job to determine whether that user has permission to perform a given action. There's a lot to Kerberos, so here we only cover enough to use it in the context of Hadoop, referring readers who want more background to *Kerberos: The Definitive Guide (http://oreilly.com/cata log/9780596004033/)* by Jason Garman (O'Reilly, 2003).

Which Versions of Hadoop Support Kerberos Authentication?

Kerberos for authentication was first added in the 0.20.20x series of Apache Hadoop releases. See Table 1-2 for which recent release series support this feature.

Kerberos and Hadoop

At a high level, there are three steps that a client must take to access a service when using Kerberos, each of which involves a message exchange with a server:

1. *Authentication.* The client authenticates itself to the Authentication Server and receives a timestamped Ticket-Granting Ticket (TGT).

2. *Authorization.* The client uses the TGT to request a service ticket from the Ticket Granting Server.

3. *Service request.* The client uses the service ticket to authenticate itself to the server that is providing the service the client is using. In the case of Hadoop, this might be the namenode or the jobtracker.

Together, the Authentication Server and the Ticket Granting Server form the *Key Distribution Center* (KDC). The process is shown graphically in Figure 9-2.

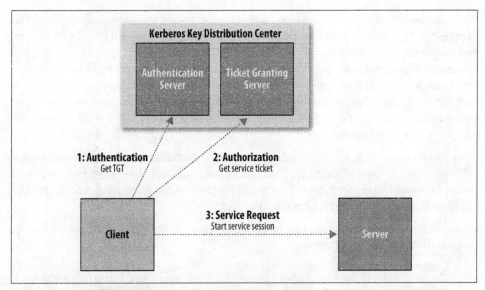

Figure 9-2. The three-step Kerberos ticket exchange protocol

The authorization and service request steps are not user-level actions; the client performs these steps on the user's behalf. The authentication step, however, is normally carried out explicitly by the user using the kinit command, which will prompt for a password. However, this doesn't mean you need to enter your password every time you run a job or access HDFS, since TGTs last for 10 hours by default (and can be renewed for up to a week). It's common to automate authentication at operating system login time, thereby providing *single sign-on* to Hadoop.

In cases where you don't want to be prompted for a password (for running an unattended MapReduce job, for example), you can create a Kerberos *keytab* file using the ktutil command. A keytab is a file that stores passwords and may be supplied to kinit with the -t option.

An example

Let's look at an example of the process in action. The first step is to enable Kerberos authentication by setting the hadoop.security.authentication property in *core-site.xml* to kerberos.[6] The default setting is simple, which signifies that the old backwards-compatible (but insecure) behavior of using the operating system user name to determine identity should be employed.

---

6. To use Kerberos authentication with Hadoop, you need to install, configure, and run a KDC (Hadoop does not come with one). Your organization may already have a KDC you can use (an Active Directory installation, for example); if not, you can set up an MIT Kerberos 5 KDC using the instructions in the *Linux Security Cookbook (http://oreilly.com/catalog/9780596003913/)* (O'Reilly, 2003).

We also need to enable service-level authorization by setting hadoop.security.author
ization to true in the same file. You may configure Access Control Lists (ACLs) in the
hadoop-policy.xml configuration file to control which users and groups have permission
to connect to each Hadoop service. Services are defined at the protocol level, so there
are ones for MapReduce job submission, namenode communication, and so on. By
default, all ACLs are set to *, which means that all users have permission to access each
service, but on a real cluster you should lock the ACLs down to only those users and
groups that should have access.

The format for an ACL is a comma-separated list of usernames, followed by whitespace,
followed by a comma-separated list of group names. For example, the ACL
preston,howard directors,inventors would authorize access to users named preston
or howard, or in groups directors or inventors.

With Kerberos authentication turned on, let's see what happens when we try to copy
a local file to HDFS:

```
% hadoop fs -put quangle.txt .
10/07/03 15:44:58 WARN ipc.Client: Exception encountered while connecting to the
server: javax.security.sasl.SaslException: GSS initiate failed [Caused by GSSEx
ception: No valid credentials provided (Mechanism level: Failed to find any Ker
beros tgt)]
Bad connection to FS. command aborted. exception: Call to localhost/127.0.0.1:80
20 failed on local exception: java.io.IOException: javax.security.sasl.SaslExcep
tion: GSS initiate failed [Caused by GSSException: No valid credentials provided
(Mechanism level: Failed to find any Kerberos tgt)]
```

The operation fails because we don't have a Kerberos ticket. We can get one by au-
thenticating to the KDC, using kinit:

```
% kinit
Password for hadoop-user@LOCALDOMAIN: password
% hadoop fs -put quangle.txt .
% hadoop fs -stat %n quangle.txt
quangle.txt
```

And we see that the file is successfully written to HDFS. Notice that even though we
carried out two filesystem commands, we only needed to call kinit once, since the
Kerberos ticket is valid for 10 hours (use the klist command to see the expiry time of
your tickets and kdestroy to invalidate your tickets). After we get a ticket, everything
works just as it normally would.

Delegation Tokens

In a distributed system such as HDFS or MapReduce, there are many client-server
interactions, each of which must be authenticated. For example, an HDFS read operation will involve multiple calls to the namenode and calls to one or more datanodes.
Instead of using the three-step Kerberos ticket exchange protocol to authenticate each
call, which would present a high load on the KDC on a busy cluster, Hadoop uses
delegation tokens to allow later authenticated access without having to contact the KDC

again. Delegation tokens are created and used transparently by Hadoop on behalf of users, so there's no action you need to take as a user beyond using `kinit` to sign in, but it's useful to have a basic idea of how they are used.

A delegation token is generated by the server (the namenode in this case) and can be thought of as a shared secret between the client and the server. On the first RPC call to the namenode, the client has no delegation token, so it uses Kerberos to authenticate, and as a part of the response it gets a delegation token from the namenode. In subsequent calls, it presents the delegation token, which the namenode can verify (since it generated it using a secret key), and hence the client is authenticated to the server.

When it wants to perform operations on HDFS blocks, the client uses a special kind of delegation token, called a *block access token*, that the namenode passes to the client in response to a metadata request. The client uses the block access token to authenticate itself to datanodes. This is possible only because the namenode shares its secret key used to generate the block access token with datanodes (which it sends in heartbeat messages), so that they can verify block access tokens. Thus, an HDFS block may be accessed only by a client with a valid block access token from a namenode. This closes the security hole in unsecured Hadoop where only the block ID was needed to gain access to a block. This property is enabled by setting `dfs.block.access.token.enable` to `true`.

In MapReduce, job resources and metadata (such as JAR files, input splits, and configuration files) are shared in HDFS for the jobtracker to access, and user code runs on the tasktrackers and accesses files on HDFS (the process is explained in "Anatomy of a MapReduce Job Run" on page 189). Delegation tokens are used by the jobtracker and tasktrackers to access HDFS during the course of the job. When the job has finished, the delegation tokens are invalidated.

Delegation tokens are automatically obtained for the default HDFS instance, but if your job needs to access other HDFS clusters, you can load the delegation tokens for these by setting the `mapreduce.job.hdfs-servers` job property to a comma-separated list of HDFS URIs.

Other Security Enhancements

Security has been tightened throughout HDFS and MapReduce to protect against unauthorized access to resources.[7] The more notable changes are listed here:

- Tasks can be run using the operating system account for the user who submitted the job, rather than the user running the tasktracker. This means that the operating system is used to isolate running tasks, so they can't send signals to each other (to

---

7. At the time of this writing, other projects, such as HBase and Hive, had not been integrated with this security model.

kill another user's tasks, for example) and so local information, such as task data, is kept private via local filesystem permissions.

This feature is enabled by setting `mapred.task.tracker.task-controller` to `org.apache.hadoop.mapred.LinuxTaskController`.[8] In addition, administrators need to ensure that each user is given an account on every node in the cluster (typically using LDAP).

- When tasks are run as the user who submitted the job, the distributed cache ("Distributed Cache" on page 289) is secure. Files that are world-readable are put in a shared cache (the insecure default); otherwise, they go in a private cache, readable only by the owner.

- Users can view and modify only their own jobs, not others. This is enabled by setting `mapred.acls.enabled` to `true`. There are two job configuration properties, `mapreduce.job.acl-view-job` and `mapreduce.job.acl-modify-job`, which may be set to a comma-separated list of users to control who may view or modify a particular job.

- The shuffle is secure, preventing a malicious user from requesting another user's map outputs. However, the shuffle is not encrypted, so it is subject to malicious sniffing.

- When appropriately configured, it's no longer possible for a malicious user to run a rogue secondary namenode, datanode, or tasktracker that can join the cluster and potentially compromise data stored in the cluster. This is enforced by requiring daemons to authenticate with the master node they are connecting to.

  To enable this feature, you first need to configure Hadoop to use a keytab previously generated with the `ktutil` command. For a datanode, for example, you would set the `dfs.datanode.keytab.file` property to the keytab filename and `dfs.datanode.kerberos.principal` to the username to use for the datanode. Finally, the ACL for the `DataNodeProtocol` (which is used by datanodes to communicate with the namenode) must be set in *hadoop-policy.xml*, by restricting `security.datanode.protocol.acl` to the datanode's username.

- A datanode may be run on a privileged port (one lower than 1024), so a client may be reasonably sure that it was started securely.

- A task may communicate only with its parent tasktracker, thus preventing an attacker from obtaining MapReduce data from another user's job.

One area that hasn't yet been addressed in the security work is encryption: neither RPC nor block transfers are encrypted. HDFS blocks are not stored in an encrypted form either. These features are planned for a future release, and in fact, encrypting the data stored in HDFS could be carried out in existing versions of Hadoop by the application itself (by writing an encryption `CompressionCodec`, for example).

---

8. `LinuxTaskController` uses a setuid executable called *task-controller*, found in the *bin* directory. You should ensure that this binary is owned by root and has the setuid bit set (with `chmod +s`).

Benchmarking a Hadoop Cluster

Is the cluster set up correctly? The best way to answer this question is empirically: run some jobs and confirm that you get the expected results. Benchmarks make good tests because you also get numbers that you can compare with other clusters as a sanity check on whether your new cluster is performing roughly as expected. And you can tune a cluster using benchmark results to squeeze the best performance out of it. This is often done with monitoring systems in place (see "Monitoring" on page 351), so you can see how resources are being used across the cluster.

To get the best results, you should run benchmarks on a cluster that is not being used by others. In practice, this is just before it is put into service and users start relying on it. Once users have scheduled periodic jobs on a cluster, it is generally impossible to find a time when the cluster is not being used (unless you arrange downtime with users), so you should run benchmarks to your satisfaction before this happens.

Experience has shown that most hardware failures for new systems are hard drive failures. By running I/O-intensive benchmarks—such as the ones described next—you can "burn in" the cluster before it goes live.

Hadoop Benchmarks

Hadoop comes with several benchmarks that you can run very easily with minimal setup cost. Benchmarks are packaged in the test JAR file, and you can get a list of them, with descriptions, by invoking the JAR file with no arguments:

```
% hadoop jar $HADOOP_INSTALL/hadoop-*-test.jar
```

Most of the benchmarks show usage instructions when invoked with no arguments. For example:

```
% hadoop jar $HADOOP_INSTALL/hadoop-*-test.jar TestDFSIO
TestFDSIO.0.0.4
Usage: TestFDSIO -read | -write | -clean [-nrFiles N] [-fileSize MB] [-resFile
resultFileName] [-bufferSize Bytes]
```

Benchmarking HDFS with TestDFSIO

TestDFSIO tests the I/O performance of HDFS. It does this by using a MapReduce job as a convenient way to read or write files in parallel. Each file is read or written in a separate map task, and the output of the map is used for collecting statistics related to the file just processed. The statistics are accumulated in the reduce to produce a summary.

The following command writes 10 files of 1,000 MB each:

```
% hadoop jar $HADOOP_INSTALL/hadoop-*-test.jar TestDFSIO -write -nrFiles 10
-fileSize 1000
```

At the end of the run, the results are written to the console and also recorded in a local file (which is appended to, so you can rerun the benchmark and not lose old results):

```
% cat TestDFSIO_results.log
----- TestDFSIO ----- : write
           Date & time: Sun Apr 12 07:14:09 EDT 2009
       Number of files: 10
 Total MBytes processed: 10000
      Throughput mb/sec: 7.796340865378244
 Average IO rate mb/sec: 7.8862199783325195
  IO rate std deviation: 0.9101254683525547
     Test exec time sec: 163.387
```

The files are written under the */benchmarks/TestDFSIO* directory by default (this can be changed by setting the test.build.data system property), in a directory called *io_data*.

To run a read benchmark, use the -read argument. Note that these files must already exist (having been written by TestDFSIO -write):

```
% hadoop jar $HADOOP_INSTALL/hadoop-*-test.jar TestDFSIO -read -nrFiles 10
-fileSize 1000
```

Here are the results for a real run:

```
----- TestDFSIO ----- : read
           Date & time: Sun Apr 12 07:24:28 EDT 2009
       Number of files: 10
 Total MBytes processed: 10000
      Throughput mb/sec: 80.25553361904304
 Average IO rate mb/sec: 98.6801528930664
  IO rate std deviation: 36.63507598174921
     Test exec time sec: 47.624
```

When you've finished benchmarking, you can delete all the generated files from HDFS using the -clean argument:

```
% hadoop jar $HADOOP_INSTALL/hadoop-*-test.jar TestDFSIO -clean
```

Benchmarking MapReduce with Sort

Hadoop comes with a MapReduce program that does a partial sort of its input. It is very useful for benchmarking the whole MapReduce system, as the full input dataset is transferred through the shuffle. The three steps are: generate some random data, perform the sort, then validate the results.

First, we generate some random data using RandomWriter. It runs a MapReduce job with 10 maps per node, and each map generates (approximately) 1 GB of random binary data, with keys and values of various sizes. You can change these values if you like by setting the properties test.randomwriter.maps_per_host and test.random write.bytes_per_map. There are also settings for the size ranges of the keys and values; see RandomWriter for details.

Here's how to invoke `RandomWriter` (found in the example JAR file, not the test one) to write its output to a directory called *random-data*:

```
% hadoop jar $HADOOP_INSTALL/hadoop-*-examples.jar randomwriter random-data
```

Next, we can run the Sort program:

```
% hadoop jar $HADOOP_INSTALL/hadoop-*-examples.jar sort random-data sorted-data
```

The overall execution time of the sort is the metric we are interested in, but it's instructive to watch the job's progress via the web UI (*http://jobtracker-host:50030/*), where you can get a feel for how long each phase of the job takes. Adjusting the parameters mentioned in "Tuning a Job" on page 178 is a useful exercise, too.

As a final sanity check, we validate that the data in *sorted-data* is, in fact, correctly sorted:

```
% hadoop jar $HADOOP_INSTALL/hadoop-*-test.jar testmapredsort -sortInput random-data \
  -sortOutput sorted-data
```

This command runs the `SortValidator` program, which performs a series of checks on the unsorted and sorted data to check whether the sort is accurate. It reports the outcome to the console at the end of its run:

```
SUCCESS! Validated the MapReduce framework's 'sort' successfully.
```

Other benchmarks

There are many more Hadoop benchmarks, but the following are widely used:

- `MRBench` (invoked with `mrbench`) runs a small job a number of times. It acts as a good counterpoint to sort, as it checks whether small job runs are responsive.

- `NNBench` (invoked with `nnbench`) is useful for load-testing namenode hardware.

- *Gridmix* is a suite of benchmarks designed to model a realistic cluster workload by mimicking a variety of data-access patterns seen in practice. See the documentation in the distribution for how to run Gridmix, and the blog post at *http://developer .yahoo.net/blogs/hadoop/2010/04/gridmix3_emulating_production.html* for more background.[9]

User Jobs

For tuning, it is best to include a few jobs that are representative of the jobs that your users run, so your cluster is tuned for these and not just for the standard benchmarks. If this is your first Hadoop cluster and you don't have any user jobs yet, then Gridmix is a good substitute.

---

9. In a similar vein, *PigMix* is a set of benchmarks for Pig, available at *https://cwiki.apache.org/confluence/ display/PIG/PigMix*.

When running your own jobs as benchmarks, you should select a dataset for your user jobs and use it each time you run the benchmarks to allow comparisons between runs. When you set up a new cluster or upgrade a cluster, you will be able to use the same dataset to compare the performance with previous runs.

Hadoop in the Cloud

Although many organizations choose to run Hadoop in-house, it is also popular to run Hadoop in the cloud on rented hardware or as a service. For instance, Cloudera offers tools for running Hadoop in a public or private cloud (see Appendix B), and Amazon has a Hadoop cloud service called Elastic MapReduce.

In this section, we look at running Hadoop on Amazon EC2, which is a great way to try out your own Hadoop cluster on a low-commitment trial basis.

Apache Whirr

Amazon Elastic Compute Cloud (EC2) is a computing service that allows customers to rent computers (*instances*) on which they can run their own applications. A customer can launch and terminate instances on demand, paying by the hour for active instances.

The Apache Whirr project (*http://whirr.apache.org/*) provides a Java API and a set of scripts that make it easy to run Hadoop on EC2 and other cloud providers.[10] The scripts allow you to perform such operations as launching or terminating a cluster, or listing the running instances in a cluster.

Running Hadoop on EC2 is especially appropriate for certain workflows. For example, if you store data on Amazon S3, you can run a cluster on EC2 and run MapReduce jobs that read the S3 data and write output back to S3 before shutting down the cluster. If you're working with longer-lived clusters, you might copy S3 data onto HDFS running on EC2 for more efficient processing, as HDFS can take advantage of data locality, but S3 cannot (since S3 storage is not collocated with EC2 nodes).

Setup

First, install Whirr by downloading a recent release tarball and unpacking it on the machine you want to launch the cluster from, as follows:

```
% tar xzf whirr-x.y.z.tar.gz
```

Whirr uses SSH to communicate with machines running in the cloud, so it's a good idea to generate an SSH keypair for exclusive use with Whirr. Here we create an RSA keypair with an empty passphrase, stored in a file called *id_rsa_whirr* in the current user's *.ssh* directory:

---

10. There are also bash scripts in the *src/contrib/ec2* subdirectory of the Hadoop distribution, but these are deprecated in favor of Whirr.

```
% ssh-keygen -t rsa -P '' -f ~/.ssh/id_rsa_whirr
```

 Do not confuse the Whirr SSH keypair with any certificates, private keys, or SSH keypairs associated with your Amazon Web Services account. Whirr is designed to work with many cloud providers, and it must have access to both the public and private SSH key of a passphraseless keypair that's read from the local filesystem. In practice, it's simplest to generate a new keypair for Whirr, as we did here.

We need to tell Whirr our cloud provider credentials. We can export them as environment variables as follows, although you can alternatively specify them on the command line or in the configuration file for the service.

```
% export AWS_ACCESS_KEY_ID='...'
% export AWS_SECRET_ACCESS_KEY='...'
```

Launching a cluster

We are now ready to launch a cluster. Whirr comes with several recipes files for launching common service configurations, and here we use the recipe to run Hadoop on EC2:

```
% bin/whirr launch-cluster --config recipes/hadoop-ec2.properties \
    --private-key-file ~/.ssh/id_rsa_whirr
```

The launch-cluster command provisions the cloud instances and starts the services running on them before returning control to the user.

Configuration

Before we start using the cluster, let's look at Whirr configuration in more detail. Configuration parameters are passed to Whirr commands as bundles in a configuration file specified by the --config option, or individually using command-line arguments, like the --private-key-file argument we used to indicate the location of the SSH private key file.

The recipe file is actually just a Java properties file that defines a number of Whirr properties. Let's step through the salient properties from *hadoop-ec2.properties*, starting with the two properties that define the cluster and the services running on it:

```
whirr.cluster-name=hadoop
whirr.instance-templates=1 hadoop-namenode+hadoop-jobtracker,5 hadoop-datanode+
hadoop-tasktracker
```

Every cluster has a name, specified by whirr.cluster-name, which serves to identify the cluster so you can perform operations on it, such as listing all running instances or terminating the cluster. The name must be unique within the cloud account that the cluster is running in.

The whirr.instance-templates property defines the services that run on a cluster. An instance template specifies a cardinality and a set of roles that run on each instance of that type. Thus, we have one instance running in both the hadoop-namenode role and the hadoop-jobtracker role. There are also 5 instances running a hadoop-datanode and a hadoop-tasktracker. With whirr.instance-templates, you can define the precise composition of your cluster. There are plenty of other services you can run in addition to Hadoop, and you can discover them by running *bin/whirr* with no arguments.

The next group of properties specify cloud credentials:

```
whirr.provider=aws-ec2
whirr.identity=${env:AWS_ACCESS_KEY_ID}
whirr.credential=${env:AWS_SECRET_ACCESS_KEY}
```

The whirr.provider property defines the cloud provider, here EC2 (other supported providers are listed in the Whirr documentation). The whirr.identity and whirr.credential properties are the cloud-specific credentials—roughly speaking, the username and password, although the terminology varies from provider to provider.

The final three parameters offer control over the cluster hardware (instance capabilities, such as memory, disk, CPU, and network speed), the machine image (operating system), and geographic location (data center). These are all provider-dependent, but if you omit them, Whirr will try to pick good defaults.

```
whirr.hardware-id=c1.xlarge
whirr.image-id=us-east-1/ami-da0cf8b3
whirr.location-id=us-east-1
```

Properties in the file are prefixed with whirr., but if they are passed as arguments on the command line, the prefix is dropped. So, for example, you could set the cluster name by adding --cluster-name hadoop on the command line, and this would take precedence over any value set in the properties file. Conversely, we could have set the private key file in the properties file by adding a line like:

```
whirr.private-key-file=/user/tom/.ssh/id_rsa_whirr
```

There are also properties for specifying the version of Hadoop to run on the cluster and for setting Hadoop configuration properties across the cluster (details are in the recipe file).

Running a proxy

To use the cluster, network traffic from the client needs to be proxied through the master node of the cluster using an SSH tunnel, which we can set up using the following command:

```
% . ~/.whirr/hadoop/hadoop-proxy.sh
```

You should keep the proxy running as long as the cluster is running. When you have finished with the cluster, stop the proxy with Ctrl-C.

Running a MapReduce job

You can run MapReduce jobs either from within the cluster or from an external machine. Here we show how to run a job from the machine we launched the cluster on. Note that the Hadoop version that has been installed locally must be the same as the one running on the cluster.

When we launched the cluster, Hadoop site configuration files were created in the directory ~/.whirr/hadoop. We can use this to connect to the cluster by setting the HADOOP_CONF_DIR environment variable as follows:

```
% export HADOOP_CONF_DIR=~/.whirr/hadoop
```

The cluster's filesystem is empty, so before we run a job, we need to populate it with data. Doing a parallel copy from S3 (see "Hadoop Filesystems" on page 52 for more on the S3 filesystems in Hadoop) using Hadoop's *distcp* tool is an efficient way to transfer data into HDFS:

```
% hadoop distcp \
  -Dfs.s3n.awsAccessKeyId='...' \
  -Dfs.s3n.awsSecretAccessKey='...' \
  s3n://hadoopbook/ncdc/all input/ncdc/all
```

> The permissions on the files in the *hadoopbook* S3 bucket allow copying only to the US East EC2 region, which means you should run the *distcp* command from within that region. The easiest way to achieve that is to log into the master node (its address is printed to the console during launch) with:
>
> ```
> % ssh -i ~/.ssh/id_rsa_whirr master_host
> ```

After the data has been copied, we can run a job in the usual way:

```
% hadoop jar hadoop-examples.jar MaxTemperatureWithCombiner \
  /user/$USER/input/ncdc/all /user/$USER/output
```

Alternatively, we could have specified the output to be on S3, as follows:

```
% hadoop jar hadoop-examples.jar MaxTemperatureWithCombiner \
  /user/$USER/input/ncdc/all s3n://mybucket/output
```

You can track the progress of the job using the jobtracker's web UI, found at *http:// master_host:50030/*. To access web pages running on worker nodes, you need to set up a proxy auto-config (PAC) file in your browser. See the Whirr documentation for details on how to do this.

Shutting down a cluster

To shut down the cluster, issue the `destroy-cluster` command:

```
% bin/whirr destroy-cluster --config recipes/hadoop-ec2.properties
```

This will terminate all the running instances in the cluster and delete all the data stored in the cluster.

Administering Hadoop

The previous chapter was devoted to setting up a Hadoop cluster. In this chapter, we look at the procedures to keep a cluster running smoothly.

HDFS

Persistent Data Structures

As an administrator, it is invaluable to have a basic understanding of how the components of HDFS—the namenode, the secondary namenode, and the datanodes—organize their persistent data on disk. Knowing which files are which can help you diagnose problems or spot that something is awry.

Namenode directory structure

A newly formatted namenode creates the following directory structure:

```
${dfs.name.dir}/
└── current/
    ├── VERSION
    ├── edits
    ├── fsimage
    └── fstime
```

Recall from Chapter 9 that the dfs.name.dir property is a list of directories, with the same contents mirrored in each directory. This mechanism provides resilience, particularly if one of the directories is an NFS mount, as is recommended.

The *VERSION* file is a Java properties file that contains information about the version of HDFS that is running. Here are the contents of a typical file:

```
#Tue Mar 10 19:21:36 GMT 2009
namespaceID=134368441
cTime=0
```

```
storageType=NAME_NODE
layoutVersion=-18
```

The layoutVersion is a negative integer that defines the version of HDFS's persistent data structures. This version number has no relation to the release number of the Hadoop distribution. Whenever the layout changes, the version number is decremented (for example, the version after –18 is –19). When this happens, HDFS needs to be upgraded, since a newer namenode (or datanode) will not operate if its storage layout is an older version. Upgrading HDFS is covered in "Upgrades" on page 362.

The namespaceID is a unique identifier for the filesystem, which is created when the filesystem is first formatted. The namenode uses it to identify new datanodes, since they will not know the namespaceID until they have registered with the namenode.

The cTime property marks the creation time of the namenode's storage. For newly formatted storage, the value is always zero, but it is updated to a timestamp whenever the filesystem is upgraded.

The storageType indicates that this storage directory contains data structures for a namenode.

The other files in the namenode's storage directory are *edits*, *fsimage*, and *fstime*. These are all binary files that use Hadoop Writable objects as their serialization format (see "Serialization" on page 93). To understand what these files are for, we need to dig into the workings of the namenode a little more.

The filesystem image and edit log

When a filesystem client performs a write operation (such as creating or moving a file), it is first recorded in the edit log. The namenode also has an in-memory representation of the filesystem metadata, which it updates after the edit log has been modified. The in-memory metadata is used to serve read requests.

The edit log is flushed and synced after every write before a success code is returned to the client. For namenodes that write to multiple directories, the write must be flushed and synced to every copy before returning successfully. This ensures that no operation is lost due to machine failure.

The *fsimage* file is a persistent checkpoint of the filesystem metadata. However, it is *not* updated for every filesystem write operation, because writing out the *fsimage* file, which can grow to be gigabytes in size, would be very slow. This does not compromise resilience, however, because if the namenode fails, then the latest state of its metadata can be reconstructed by loading the *fsimage* from disk into memory, and then applying each of the operations in the edit log. In fact, this is precisely what the namenode does when it starts up (see "Safe Mode" on page 344).

The *fsimage* file contains a serialized form of all the directory and file inodes in the filesystem. Each inode is an internal representation of a file or directory's metadata and contains such information as the file's replication level, modification and access times, access permissions, block size, and the blocks a file is made up of. For directories, the modification time, permissions, and quota metadata is stored.

The *fsimage* file does *not* record the datanodes on which the blocks are stored. Instead, the namenode keeps this mapping in memory, which it constructs by asking the datanodes for their block lists when they join the cluster and periodically afterward to ensure the namenode's block mapping is up-to-date.

As described, the *edits* file would grow without bound. Though this state of affairs would have no impact on the system while the namenode is running, if the namenode were restarted, it would take a long time to apply each of the operations in its (very long) edit log. During this time, the filesystem would be offline, which is generally undesirable.

The solution is to run the secondary namenode, whose purpose is to produce checkpoints of the primary's in-memory filesystem metadata.[1] The checkpointing process proceeds as follows (and is shown schematically in Figure 10-1):

1. The secondary asks the primary to roll its *edits* file, so new edits go to a new file.

2. The secondary retrieves *fsimage* and *edits* from the primary (using HTTP GET).

3. The secondary loads *fsimage* into memory, applies each operation from *edits*, then creates a new consolidated *fsimage* file.

4. The secondary sends the new *fsimage* back to the primary (using HTTP POST).

5. The primary replaces the old *fsimage* with the new one from the secondary and the old *edits* file with the new one it started in step 1. It also updates the *fstime* file to record the time that the checkpoint was taken.

At the end of the process, the primary has an up-to-date *fsimage* file and a shorter *edits* file (it is not necessarily empty, as it may have received some edits while the checkpoint was being taken). It is possible for an administrator to run this process manually while the namenode is in safe mode, using the `hadoop dfsadmin -saveNamespace` command.

---

1. From Hadoop version 0.22.0 onward you can start a namenode with the `-checkpoint` option so that it runs the checkpointing process against another (primary) namenode. This is functionally equivalent to running a secondary namenode, but at the time of this writing offers no advantages over the secondary namenode (and indeed the secondary namenode is the most tried and tested option). When running in a high-availability environment (see "HDFS High-Availability" on page 48), it will be possible for the standby node to do checkpointing.

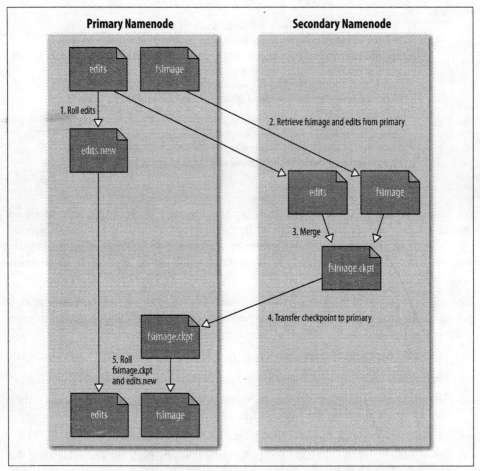

Figure 10-1. The checkpointing process

This procedure makes it clear why the secondary has similar memory requirements to the primary (since it loads the *fsimage* into memory), which is the reason that the secondary needs a dedicated machine on large clusters.

The schedule for checkpointing is controlled by two configuration parameters. The secondary namenode checkpoints every hour (`fs.checkpoint.period` in seconds) or sooner if the edit log has reached 64 MB (`fs.checkpoint.size` in bytes), which it checks every five minutes.

Secondary namenode directory structure

A useful side effect of the checkpointing process is that the secondary has a checkpoint at the end of the process, which can be found in a subdirectory called *previous.checkpoint*. This can be used as a source for making (stale) backups of the namenode's metadata:

```
${fs.checkpoint.dir}/
├── current/
│   ├── VERSION
│   ├── edits
│   ├── fsimage
│   └── fstime
└── previous.checkpoint/
    ├── VERSION
    ├── edits
    ├── fsimage
    └── fstime
```

The layout of this directory and of the secondary's *current* directory is identical to the namenode's. This is by design, since in the event of total namenode failure (when there are no recoverable backups, even from NFS), it allows recovery from a secondary namenode. This can be achieved either by copying the relevant storage directory to a new namenode or, if the secondary is taking over as the new primary namenode, by using the -importCheckpoint option when starting the namenode daemon. The -importCheckpoint option will load the namenode metadata from the latest checkpoint in the directory defined by the fs.checkpoint.dir property, but only if there is no metadata in the dfs.name.dir directory, to ensure that there is no risk of overwriting precious metadata.

Datanode directory structure

Unlike namenodes, datanodes do not need to be explicitly formatted, because they create their storage directories automatically on startup. Here are the key files and directories:

```
${dfs.data.dir}/
└── current/
    ├── VERSION
    ├── blk_<id_1>
    ├── blk_<id_1>.meta
    ├── blk_<id_2>
    ├── blk_<id_2>.meta
    ├── ...
    ├── blk_<id_64>
    ├── blk_<id_64>.meta
    ├── subdir0/
    ├── subdir1/
    ├── ...
    └── subdir63/
```

A datanode's *VERSION* file is very similar to the namenode's:

```
#Tue Mar 10 21:32:31 GMT 2009
namespaceID=134368441
storageID=DS-547717739-172.16.85.1-50010-1236720751627
```

```
cTime=0
storageType=DATA_NODE
layoutVersion=-18
```

The namespaceID, cTime, and layoutVersion are all the same as the values in the name-node (in fact, the namespaceID is retrieved from the namenode when the datanode first connects). The storageID is unique to the datanode (it is the same across all storage directories) and is used by the namenode to uniquely identify the datanode. The storageType identifies this directory as a datanode storage directory.

The other files in the datanode's *current* storage directory are the files with the *blk_* prefix. There are two types: the HDFS blocks themselves (which just consist of the file's raw bytes) and the metadata for a block (with a *.meta* suffix). A block file just consists of the raw bytes of a portion of the file being stored; the metadata file is made up of a header with version and type information, followed by a series of checksums for sections of the block.

When the number of blocks in a directory grows to a certain size, the datanode creates a new subdirectory in which to place new blocks and their accompanying metadata. It creates a new subdirectory every time the number of blocks in a directory reaches 64 (set by the dfs.datanode.numblocks configuration property). The effect is to have a tree with high fan-out, so even for systems with a very large number of blocks, the directories will be only a few levels deep. By taking this measure, the datanode ensures that there is a manageable number of files per directory, which avoids the problems that most operating systems encounter when there are a large number of files (tens or hundreds of thousands) in a single directory.

If the configuration property dfs.data.dir specifies multiple directories on different drives, blocks are written to each in a round-robin fashion. Note that blocks are *not* replicated on each drive on a single datanode; instead, block replication is across distinct datanodes.

Safe Mode

When the namenode starts, the first thing it does is load its image file (*fsimage*) into memory and apply the edits from the edit log (*edits*). Once it has reconstructed a consistent in-memory image of the filesystem metadata, it creates a new *fsimage* file (effectively doing the checkpoint itself, without recourse to the secondary namenode) and an empty edit log. Only at this point does the namenode start listening for RPC and HTTP requests. However, the namenode is running in *safe mode*, which means that it offers only a read-only view of the filesystem to clients.

 Strictly speaking, in safe mode, only filesystem operations that access the filesystem metadata (such as producing a directory listing) are guaranteed to work. Reading a file will work only when the blocks are available on the current set of datanodes in the cluster, and file modifications (writes, deletes, or renames) will always fail.

Recall that the locations of blocks in the system are not persisted by the namenode; this information resides with the datanodes, in the form of a list of the blocks it is storing. During normal operation of the system, the namenode has a map of block locations stored in memory. Safe mode is needed to give the datanodes time to check in to the namenode with their block lists, so the namenode can be informed of enough block locations to run the filesystem effectively. If the namenode didn't wait for enough datanodes to check in, then it would start the process of replicating blocks to new datanodes, which would be unnecessary in most cases (because it only needed to wait for the extra datanodes to check in) and would put a great strain on the cluster's resources. Indeed, while in safe mode, the namenode does not issue any block-replication or deletion instructions to datanodes.

Safe mode is exited when the *minimal replication condition* is reached, plus an extension time of 30 seconds. The minimal replication condition is when 99.9% of the blocks in the whole filesystem meet their minimum replication level (which defaults to one and is set by `dfs.replication.min`; see Table 10-1).

When you are starting a newly formatted HDFS cluster, the namenode does not go into safe mode, since there are no blocks in the system.

Table 10-1. Safe mode properties

Property name	Type	Default value	Description
dfs.replication.min	int	1	The minimum number of replicas that have to be written for a write to be successful.
dfs.safemode.threshold.pct	float	0.999	The proportion of blocks in the system that must meet the minimum replication level defined by dfs.replication.min before the namenode will exit safe mode. Setting this value to 0 or less forces the namenode not to start in safe mode. Setting this value to more than 1 means the namenode never exits safe mode.
dfs.safemode.extension	int	30,000	The time, in milliseconds, to extend safe mode after the minimum replication condition defined by dfs.safemode.threshold.pct has been satisfied. For small clusters (tens of nodes), it can be set to 0.

Entering and leaving safe mode

To see whether the namenode is in safe mode, you can use the `dfsadmin` command:

```
% hadoop dfsadmin -safemode get
Safe mode is ON
```

The front page of the HDFS web UI provides another indication of whether the namenode is in safe mode.

Sometimes you want to wait for the namenode to exit safe mode before carrying out a command, particularly in scripts. The `wait` option achieves this:

```
hadoop dfsadmin -safemode wait
# command to read or write a file
```

An administrator has the ability to make the namenode enter or leave safe mode at any time. It is sometimes necessary to do this when carrying out maintenance on the cluster or after upgrading a cluster to confirm that data is still readable. To enter safe mode, use the following command:

```
% hadoop dfsadmin -safemode enter
Safe mode is ON
```

You can use this command when the namenode is still in safe mode while starting up to ensure that it never leaves safe mode. Another way of making sure that the namenode stays in safe mode indefinitely is to set the property `dfs.safemode.threshold.pct` to a value over one.

You can make the namenode leave safe mode by using:

```
% hadoop dfsadmin -safemode leave
Safe mode is OFF
```

Audit Logging

HDFS can log all filesystem access requests, a feature that some organizations require for auditing purposes. Audit logging is implemented using log4j logging at the INFO level. In the default configuration it is disabled, as the log threshold is set to WARN in *log4j.properties*:

```
log4j.logger.org.apache.hadoop.hdfs.server.namenode.FSNamesystem.audit=WARN
```

You can enable audit logging by replacing WARN with INFO, and the result will be a log line written to the namenode's log for every HDFS event. Here's an example for a list status request on */user/tom*:

```
2009-03-13 07:11:22,982 INFO org.apache.hadoop.hdfs.server.namenode.FSNamesystem.
 audit: ugi=tom,staff,admin ip=/127.0.0.1 cmd=listStatus src=/user/tom dst=null
 perm=null
```

It is a good idea to configure log4j so that the audit log is written to a separate file and isn't mixed up with the namenode's other log entries. An example of how to do this can be found on the Hadoop wiki at *http://wiki.apache.org/hadoop/HowToConfigure*.

Tools

dfsadmin

The *dfsadmin* tool is a multipurpose tool for finding information about the state of HDFS, as well as for performing administration operations on HDFS. It is invoked as hadoop dfsadmin and requires superuser privileges.

Some of the available commands to *dfsadmin* are described in Table 10-2. Use the -help command to get more information.

Table 10-2. *dfsadmin commands*

Command	Description
-help	Shows help for a given command, or all commands if no command is specified.
-report	Shows filesystem statistics (similar to those shown in the web UI) and information on connected datanodes.
-metasave	Dumps information to a file in Hadoop's log directory about blocks that are being replicated or deleted, as well as a list of connected datanodes.
-safemode	Changes or queries the state of safe mode. See "Safe Mode" on page 344.
-saveNamespace	Saves the current in-memory filesystem image to a new *fsimage* file and resets the *edits* file. This operation may be performed only in safe mode.
-refreshNodes	Updates the set of datanodes that are permitted to connect to the namenode. See "Commissioning and Decommissioning Nodes" on page 359.
-upgradeProgress	Gets information on the progress of an HDFS upgrade or forces an upgrade to proceed. See "Upgrades" on page 362.
-finalizeUpgrade	Removes the previous version of the namenode and datanode storage directories. Used after an upgrade has been applied and the cluster is running successfully on the new version. See "Upgrades" on page 362.
-setQuota	Sets directory quotas. Directory quotas set a limit on the number of names (files or directories) in the directory tree. Directory quotas are useful for preventing users from creating large numbers of small files, a measure that helps preserve the namenode's memory (recall that accounting information for every file, directory, and block in the filesystem is stored in memory).
-clrQuota	Clears specified directory quotas.
-setSpaceQuota	Sets space quotas on directories. Space quotas set a limit on the size of files that may be stored in a directory tree. They are useful for giving users a limited amount of storage.
-clrSpaceQuota	Clears specified space quotas.
-refreshServiceAcl	Refreshes the namenode's service-level authorization policy file.

Filesystem check (fsck)

Hadoop provides an *fsck* utility for checking the health of files in HDFS. The tool looks for blocks that are missing from all datanodes, as well as under- or over-replicated blocks. Here is an example of checking the whole filesystem for a small cluster:

```
% hadoop fsck /
......................Status: HEALTHY
 Total size:    511799225 B
 Total dirs:    10
 Total files:   22
 Total blocks (validated):    22 (avg. block size 23263601 B)
 Minimally replicated blocks:    22 (100.0 %)
 Over-replicated blocks:    0 (0.0 %)
 Under-replicated blocks:    0 (0.0 %)
 Mis-replicated blocks:    0 (0.0 %)
 Default replication factor:    3
 Average block replication:    3.0
 Corrupt blocks:    0
 Missing replicas:    0 (0.0 %)
 Number of data-nodes:    4
 Number of racks:    1


The filesystem under path '/' is HEALTHY
```

fsck recursively walks the filesystem namespace, starting at the given path (here the filesystem root), and checks the files it finds. It prints a dot for every file it checks. To check a file, *fsck* retrieves the metadata for the file's blocks and looks for problems or inconsistencies. Note that *fsck* retrieves all of its information from the namenode; it does not communicate with any datanodes to actually retrieve any block data.

Most of the output from *fsck* is self-explanatory, but here are some of the conditions it looks for:

Over-replicated blocks

These are blocks that exceed their target replication for the file they belong to. Normally, over-replication is not a problem, and HDFS will automatically delete excess replicas.

Under-replicated blocks

These are blocks that do not meet their target replication for the file they belong to. HDFS will automatically create new replicas of under-replicated blocks until they meet the target replication. You can get information about the blocks being replicated (or waiting to be replicated) using hadoop dfsadmin -metasave.

Misreplicated blocks

These are blocks that do not satisfy the block replica placement policy (see "Replica Placement" on page 72). For example, for a replication level of three in a multirack cluster, if all three replicas of a block are on the same rack, then the block is mis-replicated because the replicas should be spread across at least two racks for resilience. HDFS will automatically re-replicate misreplicated blocks so that they satisfy the rack placement policy.

Corrupt blocks

These are blocks whose replicas are all corrupt. Blocks with at least one noncorrupt replica are not reported as corrupt; the namenode will replicate the noncorrupt replica until the target replication is met.

Missing replicas

These are blocks with no replicas anywhere in the cluster.

Corrupt or missing blocks are the biggest cause for concern, as it means data has been lost. By default, *fsck* leaves files with corrupt or missing blocks, but you can tell it to perform one of the following actions on them:

- *Move* the affected files to the */lost+found* directory in HDFS, using the -move option. Files are broken into chains of contiguous blocks to aid any salvaging efforts you may attempt.

- *Delete* the affected files, using the -delete option. Files cannot be recovered after being deleted.

Finding the blocks for a file. The *fsck* tool provides an easy way to find out which blocks are in any particular file. For example:

```
% hadoop fsck /user/tom/part-00007 -files -blocks -racks
/user/tom/part-00007 25582428 bytes, 1 block(s):  OK
0. blk_-3724870485760122836_1035 len=25582428 repl=3 [/default-rack/10.251.43.2:50010,
/default-rack/10.251.27.178:50010, /default-rack/10.251.123.163:50010]
```

This says that the file */user/tom/part-00007* is made up of one block and shows the datanodes where the blocks are located. The *fsck* options used are as follows:

- The -files option shows the line with the filename, size, number of blocks, and its health (whether there are any missing blocks).

- The -blocks option shows information about each block in the file, one line per block.

- The -racks option displays the rack location and the datanode addresses for each block.

Running hadoop fsck without any arguments displays full usage instructions.

Datanode block scanner

Every datanode runs a block scanner, which periodically verifies all the blocks stored on the datanode. This allows bad blocks to be detected and fixed before they are read by clients. The DataBlockScanner maintains a list of blocks to verify and scans them one by one for checksum errors. The scanner employs a throttling mechanism to preserve disk bandwidth on the datanode.

Blocks are periodically verified every three weeks to guard against disk errors over time (this is controlled by the dfs.datanode.scan.period.hours property, which defaults to 504 hours). Corrupt blocks are reported to the namenode to be fixed.

You can get a block verification report for a datanode by visiting the datanode's web interface at *http://datanode:50075/blockScannerReport*. Here's an example of a report, which should be self-explanatory:

```
Total Blocks                  :  21131
Verified in last hour         :     70
Verified in last day          :   1767
Verified in last week         :   7360
Verified in last four weeks   :  20057
Verified in SCAN_PERIOD       :  20057
Not yet verified              :   1074
Verified since restart        :  35912
Scans since restart           :   6541
Scan errors since restart     :      0
Transient scan errors         :      0
Current scan rate limit KBps  :   1024
Progress this period          :    109%
Time left in cur period       :  53.08%
```

By specifying the `listblocks` parameter, *http://datanode:50075/blockScannerReport ?listblocks*, the report is preceded by a list of all the blocks on the datanode along with their latest verification status. Here is a snippet of the block list (lines are split to fit the page):

```
blk_6035596358209321442    : status : ok     type : none   scan time : 0
    not yet verified
blk_3065580480714947643    : status : ok     type : remote scan time : 1215755306400
    2008-07-11 05:48:26,400
blk_8729669677359108508    : status : ok     type : local  scan time : 1215755727345
    2008-07-11 05:55:27,345
```

The first column is the block ID, followed by some key-value pairs. The status can be one of `failed` or `ok` according to whether the last scan of the block detected a checksum error. The type of scan is `local` if it was performed by the background thread, `remote` if it was performed by a client or a remote datanode, or `none` if a scan of this block has yet to be made. The last piece of information is the scan time, which is displayed as the number of milliseconds since midnight of January 1, 1970, and also as a more readable value.

Balancer

Over time, the distribution of blocks across datanodes can become unbalanced. An unbalanced cluster can affect locality for MapReduce, and it puts a greater strain on the highly utilized datanodes, so it's best avoided.

The *balancer* program is a Hadoop daemon that redistributes blocks by moving them from overutilized datanodes to underutilized datanodes, while adhering to the block replica placement policy that makes data loss unlikely by placing block replicas on different racks (see "Replica Placement" on page 72). It moves blocks until the cluster is deemed to be balanced, which means that the utilization of every datanode (ratio of used space on the node to total capacity of the node) differs from the utilization of the cluster (ratio of used space on the cluster to total capacity of the cluster) by no more than a given threshold percentage. You can start the balancer with:

```
% start-balancer.sh
```

The -threshold argument specifies the threshold percentage that defines what it means for the cluster to be balanced. The flag is optional, in which case the threshold is 10%. At any one time, only one balancer may be running on the cluster.

The balancer runs until the cluster is balanced; it cannot move any more blocks, or it loses contact with the namenode. It produces a logfile in the standard log directory, where it writes a line for every iteration of redistribution that it carries out. Here is the output from a short run on a small cluster:

```
Time Stamp        Iteration# Bytes Already Moved  Bytes Left To Move  Bytes Being Moved
Mar 18, 2009 5:23:42 PM  0               0 KB            219.21 MB           150.29 MB
Mar 18, 2009 5:27:14 PM  1          195.24 MB             22.45 MB           150.29 MB
The cluster is balanced. Exiting...
Balancing took 6.072933333333333 minutes
```

The balancer is designed to run in the background without unduly taxing the cluster or interfering with other clients using the cluster. It limits the bandwidth that it uses to copy a block from one node to another. The default is a modest 1 MB/s, but this can be changed by setting the dfs.balance.bandwidthPerSec property in *hdfs-site.xml*, specified in bytes.

Monitoring

Monitoring is an important part of system administration. In this section, we look at the monitoring facilities in Hadoop and how they can hook into external monitoring systems.

The purpose of monitoring is to detect when the cluster is not providing the expected level of service. The master daemons are the most important to monitor: the namenodes (primary and secondary) and the jobtracker. Failure of datanodes and tasktrackers is to be expected, particularly on larger clusters, so you should provide extra capacity so that the cluster can tolerate having a small percentage of dead nodes at any time.

In addition to the facilities described next, some administrators run test jobs on a periodic basis as a test of the cluster's health.

Though it is not covered here, there is a lot of work going on to add more monitoring capabilities to Hadoop. For example, Chukwa (*http://hadoop.apache.org/chukwa*), a data collection and monitoring system built on HDFS and MapReduce, excels at mining log data for finding large-scale trends.

Logging

All Hadoop daemons produce logfiles that can be very useful for finding out what is happening in the system. "System logfiles" on page 309 explains how to configure these files.

Setting log levels

When debugging a problem, it is very convenient to be able to change the log level temporarily for a particular component in the system.

Hadoop daemons have a web page for changing the log level for any log4j log name, which can be found at */logLevel* in the daemon's web UI. By convention, log names in Hadoop correspond to the classname doing the logging, although there are exceptions to this rule, so you should consult the source code to find log names.

For example, to enable debug logging for the JobTracker class, we would visit the job-tracker's web UI at *http://jobtracker-host:50030/logLevel* and set the log name org.apache.hadoop.mapred.JobTracker to level DEBUG.

The same thing can be achieved from the command line as follows:

```
% hadoop daemonlog -setlevel jobtracker-host:50030 \
    org.apache.hadoop.mapred.JobTracker DEBUG
```

Log levels changed in this way are reset when the daemon restarts, which is usually what you want. However, to make a persistent change to a log level, simply change the *log4j.properties* file in the configuration directory. In this case, the line to add is:

```
log4j.logger.org.apache.hadoop.mapred.JobTracker=DEBUG
```

Getting stack traces

Hadoop daemons expose a web page (*/stacks* in the web UI) that produces a thread dump for all running threads in the daemon's JVM. For example, you can get a thread dump for a jobtracker from *http://jobtracker-host:50030/stacks*.

Metrics

The HDFS and MapReduce daemons collect information about events and measurements that are collectively known as *metrics*. For example, datanodes collect the following metrics (and many more): the number of bytes written, the number of blocks replicated, and the number of read requests from clients (both local and remote).

Metrics belong to a *context*, and Hadoop currently uses "dfs", "mapred", "rpc", and "jvm" contexts. Hadoop daemons usually collect metrics under several contexts. For example, datanodes collect metrics for the "dfs", "rpc", and "jvm" contexts.

A context defines the unit of publication; you can choose to publish the "dfs" context, but not the "jvm" context, for instance. Metrics are configured in the *conf/hadoop-metrics.properties* file, and by default, all contexts are configured so they do not publish their metrics. This is the contents of the default configuration file (minus the comments):

```
dfs.class=org.apache.hadoop.metrics.spi.NullContext
mapred.class=org.apache.hadoop.metrics.spi.NullContext
jvm.class=org.apache.hadoop.metrics.spi.NullContext
rpc.class=org.apache.hadoop.metrics.spi.NullContext
```

Each line in this file configures a different context and specifies the class that handles the metrics for that context. The class must be an implementation of the MetricsContext interface; and, as the name suggests, the NullContext class neither publishes nor updates metrics.[2]

The other implementations of MetricsContext are covered in the following sections.

You can view raw metrics gathered by a particular Hadoop daemon by connecting to its */metrics* web page. This is handy for debugging. For example, you can view jobtracker metrics in plain text at *http://jobtracker-host:50030/metrics*. To retrieve metrics in JSON format, you would use *http://jobtracker-host:50030/metrics?format=json*.

FileContext

FileContext writes metrics to a local file. It exposes two configuration properties: fileName, which specifies the absolute name of the file to write to, and period, for the

---

2. The term "context" is (perhaps unfortunately) overloaded here, since it can refer to either a collection of metrics (the "dfs" context, for example) or the class that publishes metrics (the NullContext, for example).

time interval (in seconds) between file updates. Both properties are optional; if not set, the metrics will be written to standard output every five seconds.

Configuration properties apply to a context name and are specified by appending the property name to the context name (separated by a dot). For example, to dump the "jvm" context to a file, we alter its configuration to be the following:

```
jvm.class=org.apache.hadoop.metrics.file.FileContext
jvm.fileName=/tmp/jvm_metrics.log
```

In the first line, we have changed the "jvm" context to use a FileContext, and in the second, we have set the "jvm" context's fileName property to be a temporary file. Here are two lines of output from the logfile, split over several lines to fit the page:

```
jvm.metrics: hostName=ip-10-250-59-159, processName=NameNode, sessionId=, ↵
gcCount=46, gcTimeMillis=394, logError=0, logFatal=0, logInfo=59, logWarn=1, ↵
memHeapCommittedM=4.9375, memHeapUsedM=2.5322647, memNonHeapCommittedM=18.25, ↵
memNonHeapUsedM=11.330269, threadsBlocked=0, threadsNew=0, threadsRunnable=6, ↵
threadsTerminated=0, threadsTimedWaiting=8, threadsWaiting=13
jvm.metrics: hostName=ip-10-250-59-159, processName=SecondaryNameNode, sessionId=, ↵
gcCount=36, gcTimeMillis=261, logError=0, logFatal=0, logInfo=18, logWarn=4, ↵
memHeapCommittedM=5.4414062, memHeapUsedM=4.46756, memNonHeapCommittedM=18.25, ↵
memNonHeapUsedM=10.624519, threadsBlocked=0, threadsNew=0, threadsRunnable=5, ↵
threadsTerminated=0, threadsTimedWaiting=4, threadsWaiting=2
```

FileContext can be useful on a local system for debugging purposes, but is unsuitable on a larger cluster because the output files are spread across the cluster, which makes analyzing them difficult.

GangliaContext

Ganglia (*http://ganglia.info/*) is an open source distributed monitoring system for very large clusters. It is designed to impose very low resource overheads on each node in the cluster. Ganglia itself collects metrics, such as CPU and memory usage, and by using GangliaContext, you can inject Hadoop metrics into Ganglia.

GangliaContext has one required property, **servers**, which takes a space- and/or comma-separated list of Ganglia server host-port pairs. Further details on configuring this context can be found on the Hadoop wiki (*http://wiki.apache.org/hadoop/Ganglia Metrics*).

For a flavor of the kind of information you can get out of Ganglia, see Figure 10-2, which shows how the number of tasks in the jobtracker's queue varies over time.

NullContextWithUpdateThread

Both FileContext and a GangliaContext push metrics to an external system. However, some monitoring systems—notably JMX—need to pull metrics from Hadoop. Null ContextWithUpdateThread is designed for this. Like NullContext, it doesn't publish any metrics, but in addition it runs a timer that periodically updates the metrics stored in

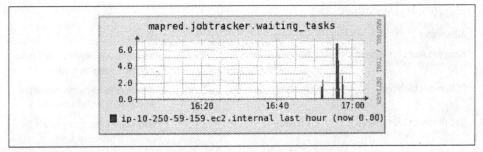

Figure 10-2. Ganglia plot of the number of tasks in the jobtracker queue

memory. This ensures that the metrics are up-to-date when they are fetched by another system.

All implementations of `MetricsContext`, except `NullContext`, perform this updating function (and they all expose a `period` property that defaults to five seconds), so you need to use `NullContextWithUpdateThread` only if you are not collecting metrics using another output. If you were using `GangliaContext`, for example, then it would ensure the metrics are updated, so you would be able to use JMX in addition with no further configuration of the metrics system. JMX is discussed in more detail shortly.

CompositeContext

`CompositeContext` allows you to output the same set of metrics to multiple contexts, such as a `FileContext` and a `GangliaContext`. The configuration is slightly tricky and is best shown by an example:

```
jvm.class=org.apache.hadoop.metrics.spi.CompositeContext
jvm.arity=2
jvm.sub1.class=org.apache.hadoop.metrics.file.FileContext
jvm.fileName=/tmp/jvm_metrics.log
jvm.sub2.class=org.apache.hadoop.metrics.ganglia.GangliaContext
jvm.servers=ip-10-250-59-159.ec2.internal:8649
```

The `arity` property is used to specify the number of subcontexts; in this case, there are two. The property names for each subcontext are modified to have a part specifying the subcontext number, hence `jvm.sub1.class` and `jvm.sub2.class`.

Java Management Extensions

Java Management Extensions (JMX) is a standard Java API for monitoring and managing applications. Hadoop includes several managed beans (MBeans), which expose Hadoop metrics to JMX-aware applications. There are MBeans that expose the metrics in the "dfs" and "rpc" contexts, but none for the "mapred" context (at the time of this writing) or the "jvm" context (as the JVM itself exposes a richer set of JVM metrics). These MBeans are listed in Table 10-3.

Table 10-3. Hadoop MBeans

MBean class	Daemons	Metrics
NameNodeActivityMBean	Namenode	Namenode activity metrics, such as the number of create file operations
FSNamesystemMBean	Namenode	Namenode status metrics, such as the number of connected datanodes
DataNodeActivityMBean	Datanode	Datanode activity metrics, such as the number of bytes read
FSDatasetMBean	Datanode	Datanode storage metrics, such as capacity and free storage space
RpcActivityMBean	All daemons that use RPC: namenode, datanode, jobtracker, and tasktracker	RPC statistics, such as average processing time

The JDK comes with a tool called JConsole for viewing MBeans in a running JVM. It's useful for browsing Hadoop metrics, as demonstrated in Figure 10-3.

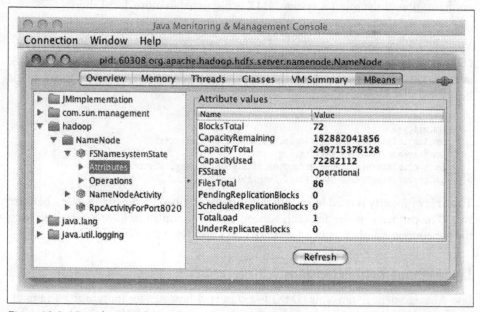

Figure 10-3. JConsole view of a locally running namenode, showing metrics for the filesystem state

Although you can see Hadoop metrics via JMX using the default metrics configuration, they will not be updated unless you change the MetricsContext implementation to something other than NullContext. For example, NullContextWithUpdateThread is appropriate if JMX is the only way you will be monitoring metrics.

Many third-party monitoring and alerting systems (such as Nagios or Hyperic) can query MBeans, making JMX the natural way to monitor your Hadoop cluster from an existing monitoring system. You will need to enable remote access to JMX, however, and choose a level of security that is appropriate for your cluster. The options here include password authentication, SSL connections, and SSL client-authentication. See the official Java documentation[3] for an in-depth guide on configuring these options.

All the options for enabling remote access to JMX involve setting Java system properties, which we do for Hadoop by editing the *conf/hadoop-env.sh* file. The following configuration settings show how to enable password-authenticated remote access to JMX on the namenode (with SSL disabled). The process is very similar for other Hadoop daemons:

```
export HADOOP_NAMENODE_OPTS="-Dcom.sun.management.jmxremote
 -Dcom.sun.management.jmxremote.ssl=false
 -Dcom.sun.management.jmxremote.password.file=$HADOOP_CONF_DIR/jmxremote.password
 -Dcom.sun.management.jmxremote.port=8004 $HADOOP_NAMENODE_OPTS"
```

The *jmxremote.password* file lists the usernames and their passwords in plain text; the JMX documentation has further details on the format of this file.

With this configuration, we can use JConsole to browse MBeans on a remote namenode. Alternatively, we can use one of the many JMX tools to retrieve MBean attribute values. Here is an example of using the "jmxquery" command-line tool (and Nagios plug-in, available from *http://code.google.com/p/jmxquery/*) to retrieve the number of under-replicated blocks:

```
% ./check_jmx -U service:jmx:rmi:///jndi/rmi://namenode-host:8004/jmxrmi -O \
hadoop:service=NameNode,name=FSNamesystemState -A UnderReplicatedBlocks \
-w 100 -c 1000 -username monitorRole -password secret
JMX OK - UnderReplicatedBlocks is 0
```

This command establishes a JMX RMI connection to the host *namenode-host* on port 8004 and authenticates using the given username and password. It reads the attribute UnderReplicatedBlocks of the object named hadoop:service=NameNode,name=FSNamesys temState and prints out its value on the console. The -w and -c options specify warning and critical levels for the value. The appropriate values for these are normally determined after operating a cluster for a while.

It's common to use Ganglia in conjunction with an alerting system such as Nagios for monitoring a Hadoop cluster. Ganglia is good for efficiently collecting a large number of metrics and graphing them, whereas Nagios and similar systems are good at sending alerts when a critical threshold is reached in any of a smaller set of metrics.

---

3. *http://java.sun.com/javase/6/docs/technotes/guides/management/agent.html*

Maintenance

Routine Administration Procedures

Metadata backups

If the namenode's persistent metadata is lost or damaged, the entire filesystem is rendered unusable, so it is critical that backups are made of these files. You should keep multiple copies of different ages (one hour, one day, one week, and one month, say) to protect against corruption, either in the copies themselves or in the live files running on the namenode.

A straightforward way to make backups is to write a script to periodically archive the secondary namenode's *previous.checkpoint* subdirectory (under the directory defined by the fs.checkpoint.dir property) to an offsite location. The script should additionally test the integrity of the copy. This can be done by starting a local namenode daemon and verifying that it has successfully read the *fsimage* and *edits* files into memory (by scanning the namenode log for the appropriate success message, for example).[4]

Data backups

Although HDFS is designed to store data reliably, data loss can occur, just like in any storage system, and thus a backup strategy is essential. With the large data volumes that Hadoop can store, deciding what data to back up and where to store it is a challenge. The key here is to prioritize your data. The highest priority is the data that cannot be regenerated and that is critical to the business; however, data that is either straightforward to regenerate or essentially disposable because it is of limited business value is the lowest priority, and you may choose not to make backups of this low-priority data.

Do not make the mistake of thinking that HDFS replication is a substitute for making backups. Bugs in HDFS can cause replicas to be lost, and so can hardware failures. Although Hadoop is expressly designed so that hardware failure is very unlikely to result in data loss, the possibility can never be completely ruled out, particularly when combined with software bugs or human error.

When it comes to backups, think of HDFS in the same way as you would RAID. Although the data will survive the loss of an individual RAID disk, it may not if the RAID controller fails or is buggy (perhaps overwriting some data), or the entire array is damaged.

---

4. Hadoop 2.0 comes with an Offline Image Viewer and Offline Edits Viewer, which can be used to check the integrity of the *fsimage* and *edits* files. Note that both viewers support older formats of these files, so you can use them to diagnose problems in these files generated by previous releases of Hadoop. Type hdfs oiv and hdfs oev to invoke these tools.

It's common to have a policy for user directories in HDFS. For example, they may have space quotas and be backed up nightly. Whatever the policy, make sure your users know what it is, so they know what to expect.

The *distcp* tool is ideal for making backups to other HDFS clusters (preferably running on a different version of the software, to guard against loss due to bugs in HDFS) or other Hadoop filesystems (such as S3 or KFS) because it can copy files in parallel. Alternatively, you can employ an entirely different storage system for backups, using one of the methods for exporting data from HDFS described in "Hadoop Filesystems" on page 52.

Filesystem check (fsck)

It is advisable to run HDFS's *fsck* tool regularly (for example, daily) on the whole filesystem to proactively look for missing or corrupt blocks. See "Filesystem check (fsck)" on page 347.

Filesystem balancer

Run the balancer tool (see "Balancer" on page 350) regularly to keep the filesystem datanodes evenly balanced.

Commissioning and Decommissioning Nodes

As an administrator of a Hadoop cluster, you will need to add or remove nodes from time to time. For example, to grow the storage available to a cluster, you commission new nodes. Conversely, sometimes you may wish to shrink a cluster, and to do so, you decommission nodes. Sometimes it is necessary to decommission a node if it is misbehaving, perhaps because it is failing more often than it should or its performance is noticeably slow.

Nodes normally run both a datanode and a tasktracker, and both are typically commissioned or decommissioned in tandem.

Commissioning new nodes

Although commissioning a new node can be as simple as configuring the *hdfs-site.xml* file to point to the namenode, configuring the *mapred-site.xml* file to point to the jobtracker, and starting the datanode and jobtracker daemons, it is generally best to have a list of authorized nodes.

It is a potential security risk to allow any machine to connect to the namenode and act as a datanode, because the machine may gain access to data that it is not authorized to see. Furthermore, because such a machine is not a real datanode, it is not under your control and may stop at any time, causing potential data loss. (Imagine what would happen if a number of such nodes were connected and a block of data was present only on the "alien" nodes?) This scenario is a risk even inside a firewall, due to the possibility of misconfiguration, so datanodes (and tasktrackers) should be explicitly managed on all production clusters.

Datanodes that are permitted to connect to the namenode are specified in a file whose name is specified by the `dfs.hosts` property. The file resides on the namenode's local filesystem, and it contains a line for each datanode, specified by network address (as reported by the datanode; you can see what this is by looking at the namenode's web UI). If you need to specify multiple network addresses for a datanode, put them on one line, separated by whitespace.

Similarly, tasktrackers that may connect to the jobtracker are specified in a file whose name is specified by the `mapred.hosts` property. In most cases, there is one shared file, referred to as the *include file*, that both `dfs.hosts` and `mapred.hosts` refer to, since nodes in the cluster run both datanode and tasktracker daemons.

 The file (or files) specified by the `dfs.hosts` and `mapred.hosts` properties is different from the *slaves* file. The former is used by the namenode and jobtracker to determine which worker nodes may connect. The *slaves* file is used by the Hadoop control scripts to perform cluster-wide operations, such as cluster restarts. It is never used by the Hadoop daemons.

To add new nodes to the cluster:

1. Add the network addresses of the new nodes to the include file.
2. Update the namenode with the new set of permitted datanodes using this command:

   ```
   % hadoop dfsadmin -refreshNodes
   ```

3. Update the jobtracker with the new set of permitted tasktrackers using:

   ```
   % hadoop mradmin -refreshNodes
   ```

4. Update the *slaves* file with the new nodes, so that they are included in future operations performed by the Hadoop control scripts.
5. Start the new datanodes and tasktrackers.
6. Check that the new datanodes and tasktrackers appear in the web UI.

HDFS will not move blocks from old datanodes to new datanodes to balance the cluster. To do this, you should run the balancer described in "Balancer" on page 350.

Decommissioning old nodes

Although HDFS is designed to tolerate datanode failures, this does not mean you can just terminate datanodes en masse with no ill effect. With a replication level of three, for example, the chances are very high that you will lose data by simultaneously shutting down three datanodes if they are on different racks. The way to decommission datanodes is to inform the namenode of the nodes that you wish to take out of circulation, so that it can replicate the blocks to other datanodes before the datanodes are shut down.

With tasktrackers, Hadoop is more forgiving. If you shut down a tasktracker that is running tasks, the jobtracker will notice the failure and reschedule the tasks on other tasktrackers.

The decommissioning process is controlled by an *exclude file*, which for HDFS is set by the dfs.hosts.exclude property and for MapReduce by the mapred.hosts.exclude property. It is often the case that these properties refer to the same file. The exclude file lists the nodes that are not permitted to connect to the cluster.

The rules for whether a tasktracker may connect to the jobtracker are simple: a tasktracker may connect only if it appears in the include file and does *not* appear in the exclude file. An unspecified or empty include file is taken to mean that all nodes are in the include file.

For HDFS, the rules are slightly different. If a datanode appears in both the include and the exclude file, then it may connect, but only to be decommissioned. Table 10-4 summarizes the different combinations for datanodes. As for tasktrackers, an unspecified or empty include file means all nodes are included.

Table 10-4. HDFS include and exclude file precedence

Node appears in include file	Node appears in exclude file	Interpretation
No	No	Node may not connect.
No	Yes	Node may not connect.
Yes	No	Node may connect.
Yes	Yes	Node may connect and will be decommissioned.

To remove nodes from the cluster:

1. Add the network addresses of the nodes to be decommissioned to the exclude file. Do not update the include file at this point.

2. Update the namenode with the new set of permitted datanodes, using this command:

   ```
   % hadoop dfsadmin -refreshNodes
   ```

3. Update the jobtracker with the new set of permitted tasktrackers using:

   ```
   % hadoop mradmin -refreshNodes
   ```

4. Go to the web UI and check whether the admin state has changed to "Decommission In Progress" for the datanodes being decommissioned. They will start copying their blocks to other datanodes in the cluster.

5. When all the datanodes report their state as "Decommissioned," all the blocks have been replicated. Shut down the decommissioned nodes.

6. Remove the nodes from the include file, and run:

```
% hadoop dfsadmin -refreshNodes
% hadoop mradmin -refreshNodes
```

7. Remove the nodes from the *slaves* file.

Upgrades

Upgrading an HDFS and MapReduce cluster requires careful planning. The most important consideration is the HDFS upgrade. If the layout version of the filesystem has changed, then the upgrade will automatically migrate the filesystem data and metadata to a format that is compatible with the new version. As with any procedure that involves data migration, there is a risk of data loss, so you should be sure that both your data and metadata is backed up (see "Routine Administration Procedures" on page 358).

Part of the planning process should include a trial run on a small test cluster with a copy of data that you can afford to lose. A trial run will allow you to familiarize yourself with the process, customize it to your particular cluster configuration and toolset, and iron out any snags before running the upgrade procedure on a production cluster. A test cluster also has the benefit of being available to test client upgrades on. You can read about general compatibility concerns for clients in "Compatibility" on page 15.

Upgrading a cluster when the filesystem layout has not changed is fairly straightforward: install the new versions of HDFS and MapReduce on the cluster (and on clients at the same time), shut down the old daemons, update configuration files, and then start up the new daemons and switch clients to use the new libraries. This process is reversible, so rolling back an upgrade is also straightforward.

After every successful upgrade, you should perform a couple of final cleanup steps:

• Remove the old installation and configuration files from the cluster.

• Fix any deprecation warnings in your code and configuration.

HDFS data and metadata upgrades

If you use the procedure just described to upgrade to a new version of HDFS and it expects a different layout version, then the namenode will refuse to run. A message like the following will appear in its log:

```
File system image contains an old layout version -16.
An upgrade to version -18 is required.
Please restart NameNode with -upgrade option.
```

The most reliable way of finding out whether you need to upgrade the filesystem is by performing a trial on a test cluster.

An upgrade of HDFS makes a copy of the previous version's metadata and data. Doing an upgrade does not double the storage requirements of the cluster, as the datanodes use hard links to keep two references (for the current and previous version) to the same block of data. This design makes it straightforward to roll back to the previous version of the filesystem, if you need to. You should understand that any changes made to the data on the upgraded system will be lost after the rollback completes.

You can keep only the previous version of the filesystem, which means you can't roll back several versions. Therefore, to carry out another upgrade to HDFS data and metadata, you will need to delete the previous version, a process called *finalizing the upgrade*. Once an upgrade is finalized, there is no procedure for rolling back to a previous version.

In general, you can skip releases when upgrading (for example, you can upgrade from release 0.18.3 to 0.20.0 without having to upgrade to a 0.19.x release first), but in some cases, you may have to go through intermediate releases. The release notes make it clear when this is required.

You should only attempt to upgrade a healthy filesystem. Before running the upgrade, do a full *fsck* (see "Filesystem check (fsck)" on page 347). As an extra precaution, you can keep a copy of the *fsck* output that lists all the files and blocks in the system, so you can compare it with the output of running *fsck* after the upgrade.

It's also worth clearing out temporary files before doing the upgrade, both from the MapReduce system directory on HDFS and local temporary files.

With these preliminaries out of the way, here is the high-level procedure for upgrading a cluster when the filesystem layout needs to be migrated:

1. Make sure that any previous upgrade is finalized before proceeding with another upgrade.
2. Shut down MapReduce, and kill any orphaned task processes on the tasktrackers.
3. Shut down HDFS, and back up the namenode directories.
4. Install new versions of Hadoop HDFS and MapReduce on the cluster and on clients.
5. Start HDFS with the -upgrade option.
6. Wait until the upgrade is complete.
7. Perform some sanity checks on HDFS.
8. Start MapReduce.
9. Roll back or finalize the upgrade (optional).

While running the upgrade procedure, it is a good idea to remove the Hadoop scripts from your PATH environment variable. This forces you to be explicit about which version of the scripts you are running. It can be convenient to define two environment variables for the new installation directories; in the following instructions, we have defined OLD_HADOOP_INSTALL and NEW_HADOOP_INSTALL.

Start the upgrade. To perform the upgrade, run the following command (this is step 5 in the high-level upgrade procedure):

```
% $NEW_HADOOP_INSTALL/bin/start-dfs.sh -upgrade
```

This causes the namenode to upgrade its metadata, placing the previous version in a new directory called *previous*:

```
${dfs.name.dir}/current/VERSION
                      /edits
                      /fsimage
                      /fstime
              /previous/VERSION
                      /edits
                      /fsimage
                      /fstime
```

Similarly, datanodes upgrade their storage directories, preserving the old copy in a directory called *previous*.

Wait until the upgrade is complete. The upgrade process is not instantaneous, but you can check the progress of an upgrade using *dfsadmin* (step 6; upgrade events also appear in the daemons' logfiles):

```
% $NEW_HADOOP_INSTALL/bin/hadoop dfsadmin -upgradeProgress status
Upgrade for version -18 has been completed.
Upgrade is not finalized.
```

Check the upgrade. This shows that the upgrade is complete. At this stage, you should run some sanity checks (step 7) on the filesystem (e.g., check files and blocks using *fsck*, test basic file operations). You might choose to put HDFS into safe mode while you are running some of these checks (the ones that are read-only) to prevent others from making changes.

Roll back the upgrade (optional). If you find that the new version is not working correctly, you may choose to roll back to the previous version (step 9). This is possible only if you have not finalized the upgrade.

A rollback reverts the filesystem state to before the upgrade was performed, so any changes made in the meantime will be lost. In other words, it rolls back to the previous state of the filesystem, rather than downgrading the current state of the filesystem to a former version.

First, shut down the new daemons:

```
% $NEW_HADOOP_INSTALL/bin/stop-dfs.sh
```

Then start up the old version of HDFS with the -rollback option:

```
% $OLD_HADOOP_INSTALL/bin/start-dfs.sh -rollback
```

This command gets the namenode and datanodes to replace their current storage directories with their previous copies. The filesystem will be returned to its previous state.

Finalize the upgrade (optional). When you are happy with the new version of HDFS, you can finalize the upgrade (step 9) to remove the previous storage directories.

 After an upgrade has been finalized, there is no way to roll back to the previous version.

This step is required before performing another upgrade:

```
% $NEW_HADOOP_INSTALL/bin/hadoop dfsadmin -finalizeUpgrade
% $NEW_HADOOP_INSTALL/bin/hadoop dfsadmin -upgradeProgress status
There are no upgrades in progress.
```

HDFS is now fully upgraded to the new version.

Pig

Pig raises the level of abstraction for processing large datasets. MapReduce allows you, as the programmer, to specify a map function followed by a reduce function, but working out how to fit your data processing into this pattern, which often requires multiple MapReduce stages, can be a challenge. With Pig, the data structures are much richer, typically being multivalued and nested, and the set of transformations you can apply to the data are much more powerful. They include joins, for example, which are not for the faint of heart in MapReduce.

Pig is made up of two pieces:

- The language used to express data flows, called *Pig Latin*.
- The execution environment to run Pig Latin programs. There are currently two environments: local execution in a single JVM and distributed execution on a Hadoop cluster.

A Pig Latin program is made up of a series of operations, or transformations, that are applied to the input data to produce output. Taken as a whole, the operations describe a data flow, which the Pig execution environment translates into an executable representation and then runs. Under the covers, Pig turns the transformations into a series of MapReduce jobs, but as a programmer you are mostly unaware of this, which allows you to focus on the data rather than the nature of the execution.

Pig is a scripting language for exploring large datasets. One criticism of MapReduce is that the development cycle is very long. Writing the mappers and reducers, compiling and packaging the code, submitting the job(s), and retrieving the results is a time-consuming business, and even with Streaming, which removes the compile and package step, the experience is still involved. Pig's sweet spot is its ability to process terabytes of data simply by issuing a half-dozen lines of Pig Latin from the console. Indeed, it was created at Yahoo! to make it easier for researchers and engineers to mine the huge datasets there. Pig is very supportive of a programmer writing a query, since it provides several commands for introspecting the data structures in your program as it is written. Even more useful, it can perform a sample run on a representative subset of your input data, so you can see whether there are errors in the processing before unleashing it on the full dataset.

Pig was designed to be extensible. Virtually all parts of the processing path are customizable: loading, storing, filtering, grouping, and joining can all be altered by user-defined functions (UDFs). These functions operate on Pig's nested data model, so they can integrate very deeply with Pig's operators. As another benefit, UDFs tend to be more reusable than the libraries developed for writing MapReduce programs.

Pig isn't suitable for all data processing tasks, however. Like MapReduce, it is designed for batch processing of data. If you want to perform a query that touches only a small amount of data in a large dataset, then Pig will not perform well, because it is set up to scan the whole dataset, or at least large portions of it.

In some cases, Pig doesn't perform as well as programs written in MapReduce. However, the gap is narrowing with each release, as the Pig team implements sophisticated algorithms for applying Pig's relational operators. It's fair to say that unless you are willing to invest a lot of effort optimizing Java MapReduce code, writing queries in Pig Latin will save you time.

This chapter provides a basic introduction to using Pig. For a more detailed guide, see *Programming Pig (http://shop.oreilly.com/product/0636920018087.do)* by Alan Gates (O'Reilly, 2011).

Installing and Running Pig

Pig runs as a client-side application. Even if you want to run Pig on a Hadoop cluster, there is nothing extra to install on the cluster: Pig launches jobs and interacts with HDFS (or other Hadoop filesystems) from your workstation.

Installation is straightforward. Java 6 is a prerequisite (and on Windows, you will need Cygwin). Download a stable release from *http://pig.apache.org/releases.html*, and unpack the tarball in a suitable place on your workstation:

```
% tar xzf pig-x.y.z.tar.gz
```

It's convenient to add Pig's binary directory to your command-line path. For example:

```
% export PIG_INSTALL=/home/tom/pig-x.y.z
% export PATH=$PATH:$PIG_INSTALL/bin
```

You also need to set the JAVA_HOME environment variable to point to a suitable Java installation.

Try typing pig -help to get usage instructions.

Execution Types

Pig has two execution types or modes: local mode and MapReduce mode.

Local mode

In local mode, Pig runs in a single JVM and accesses the local filesystem. This mode is suitable only for small datasets and when trying out Pig.

The execution type is set using the `-x` or `-exectype` option. To run in local mode, set the option to `local`:

```
% pig -x local
grunt>
```

This starts Grunt, the Pig interactive shell, which is discussed in more detail shortly.

MapReduce mode

In MapReduce mode, Pig translates queries into MapReduce jobs and runs them on a Hadoop cluster. The cluster may be a pseudo- or fully distributed cluster. MapReduce mode (with a fully distributed cluster) is what you use when you want to run Pig on large datasets.

To use MapReduce mode, you first need to check that the version of Pig you downloaded is compatible with the version of Hadoop you are using. Pig releases will only work against particular versions of Hadoop; this is documented in the release notes.

Pig honors the `HADOOP_HOME` environment variable for finding which Hadoop client to run. However, if it is not set, Pig will use a bundled copy of the Hadoop libraries. Note that these may not match the version of Hadoop running on your cluster, so it is best to explicitly set `HADOOP_HOME`.

Next, you need to point Pig at the cluster's namenode and jobtracker. If the installation of Hadoop at `HADOOP_HOME` is already configured for this, then there is nothing more to do. Otherwise, you can set `HADOOP_CONF_DIR` to a directory containing the Hadoop site file (or files) that define `fs.default.name` and `mapred.job.tracker`.

Alternatively, you can set these two properties in the *pig.properties* file in Pig's *conf* directory (or the directory specified by `PIG_CONF_DIR`). Here's an example for a pseudo-distributed setup:

```
fs.default.name=hdfs://localhost/
mapred.job.tracker=localhost:8021
```

Once you have configured Pig to connect to a Hadoop cluster, you can launch Pig, setting the `-x` option to `mapreduce` or omitting it entirely, as MapReduce mode is the default:

```
% pig
2012-01-18 20:23:05,764 [main] INFO  org.apache.pig.Main - Logging error message
s to: /private/tmp/pig_1326946985762.log
2012-01-18 20:23:06,009 [main] INFO  org.apache.pig.backend.hadoop.executionengi
ne.HExecutionEngine - Connecting to hadoop file system at: hdfs://localhost/
2012-01-18 20:23:06,274 [main] INFO  org.apache.pig.backend.hadoop.executionengi
ne.HExecutionEngine - Connecting to map-reduce job tracker at: localhost:8021
grunt>
```

As you can see from the output, Pig reports the filesystem and jobtracker that it has connected to.

Running Pig Programs

There are three ways of executing Pig programs, all of which work in both local and MapReduce mode:

Script

> Pig can run a script file that contains Pig commands. For example, `pig script.pig` runs the commands in the local file *script.pig*. Alternatively, for very short scripts, you can use the `-e` option to run a script specified as a string on the command line.

Grunt

> Grunt is an interactive shell for running Pig commands. Grunt is started when no file is specified for Pig to run and the `-e` option is not used. It is also possible to run Pig scripts from within Grunt using `run` and `exec`.

Embedded

> You can run Pig programs from Java using the `PigServer` class, much like you can use JDBC to run SQL programs from Java. For programmatic access to Grunt, use `PigRunner`.

Grunt

Grunt has line-editing facilities like those found in GNU Readline (used in the bash shell and many other command-line applications). For instance, the Ctrl-E key combination will move the cursor to the end of the line. Grunt remembers command history, too,[1] and you can recall lines in the history buffer using Ctrl-P or Ctrl-N (for previous and next) or, equivalently, the up or down cursor keys.

Another handy feature is Grunt's completion mechanism, which will try to complete Pig Latin keywords and functions when you press the Tab key. For example, consider the following incomplete line:

```
grunt> a = foreach b ge
```

If you press the Tab key at this point, `ge` will expand to `generate`, a Pig Latin keyword:

```
grunt> a = foreach b generate
```

You can customize the completion tokens by creating a file named *autocomplete* and placing it on Pig's classpath (such as in the *conf* directory in Pig's *install* directory) or in the directory you invoked Grunt from. The file should have one token per line, and tokens must not contain any whitespace. Matching is case-sensitive. It can be very

---

1. History is stored in a file called *.pig_history* in your home directory.

handy to add commonly used file paths (especially because Pig does not perform file-name completion) or the names of any user-defined functions you have created.

You can get a list of commands using the help command. When you've finished your Grunt session, you can exit with the quit command.

Pig Latin Editors

PigPen is an Eclipse plug-in that provides an environment for developing Pig programs. It includes a Pig script text editor, an example generator (equivalent to the ILLUS-TRATE command), and a button for running the script on a Hadoop cluster. There is also an operator graph window, which shows a script in graph form, for visualizing the data flow. For full installation and usage instructions, refer to the Pig wiki at *https:// cwiki.apache.org/confluence/display/PIG/PigTools*.

There are also Pig Latin syntax highlighters for other editors, including Vim and Text-Mate. Details are available on the Pig wiki.

An Example

Let's look at a simple example by writing the program to calculate the maximum recorded temperature by year for the weather dataset in Pig Latin (just like we did using MapReduce in Chapter 2). The complete program is only a few lines long:

```
-- max_temp.pig: Finds the maximum temperature by year
records = LOAD 'input/ncdc/micro-tab/sample.txt'
  AS (year:chararray, temperature:int, quality:int);
filtered_records = FILTER records BY temperature != 9999 AND
  (quality == 0 OR quality == 1 OR quality == 4 OR quality == 5 OR quality == 9);
grouped_records = GROUP filtered_records BY year;
max_temp = FOREACH grouped_records GENERATE group,
  MAX(filtered_records.temperature);
DUMP max_temp;
```

To explore what's going on, we'll use Pig's Grunt interpreter, which allows us to enter lines and interact with the program to understand what it's doing. Start up Grunt in local mode, and then enter the first line of the Pig script:

```
grunt> records = LOAD 'input/ncdc/micro-tab/sample.txt'
>>   AS (year:chararray, temperature:int, quality:int);
```

For simplicity, the program assumes that the input is tab-delimited text, with each line having just year, temperature, and quality fields. (Pig actually has more flexibility than this with regard to the input formats it accepts, as you'll see later.) This line describes the input data we want to process. The year:chararray notation describes the field's name and type; chararray is like a Java string, and an int is like a Java int. The LOAD operator takes a URI argument; here we are just using a local file, but we could refer to an HDFS URI. The AS clause (which is optional) gives the fields names to make it convenient to refer to them in subsequent statements.

The result of the LOAD operator, and indeed any operator in Pig Latin, is a *relation*, which is just a set of tuples. A *tuple* is just like a row of data in a database table, with multiple fields in a particular order. In this example, the LOAD function produces a set of (year, temperature, quality) tuples that are present in the input file. We write a relation with one tuple per line, where tuples are represented as comma-separated items in parentheses:

```
(1950,0,1)
(1950,22,1)
(1950,-11,1)
(1949,111,1)
```

Relations are given names, or *aliases*, so they can be referred to. This relation is given the records alias. We can examine the contents of an alias using the DUMP operator:

```
grunt> DUMP records;
(1950,0,1)
(1950,22,1)
(1950,-11,1)
(1949,111,1)
(1949,78,1)
```

We can also see the structure of a relation—the relation's *schema*—using the DESCRIBE operator on the relation's alias:

```
grunt> DESCRIBE records;
records: {year: chararray,temperature: int,quality: int}
```

This tells us that records has three fields, with aliases year, temperature, and quality, which are the names we gave them in the AS clause. The fields have the types given to them in the AS clause, too. We examine types in Pig in more detail later.

The second statement removes records that have a missing temperature (indicated by a value of 9999) or an unsatisfactory quality reading. For this small dataset, no records are filtered out:

```
grunt> filtered_records = FILTER records BY temperature != 9999 AND
>>    (quality == 0 OR quality == 1 OR quality == 4 OR quality == 5 OR quality == 9);
grunt> DUMP filtered_records;
(1950,0,1)
(1950,22,1)
(1950,-11,1)
(1949,111,1)
(1949,78,1)
```

The third statement uses the GROUP function to group the records relation by the year field. Let's use DUMP to see what it produces:

```
grunt> grouped_records = GROUP filtered_records BY year;
grunt> DUMP grouped_records;
(1949,{(1949,111,1),(1949,78,1)})
(1950,{(1950,0,1),(1950,22,1),(1950,-11,1)})
```

We now have two rows, or tuples, one for each year in the input data. The first field in each tuple is the field being grouped by (the year), and the second field is a bag of tuples for that year. A *bag* is just an unordered collection of tuples, which in Pig Latin is represented using curly braces.

By grouping the data in this way, we have created a row per year, so now all that remains is to find the maximum temperature for the tuples in each bag. Before we do this, let's understand the structure of the grouped_records relation:

```
grunt> DESCRIBE grouped_records;
grouped_records: {group: chararray,filtered_records: {year: chararray,
temperature: int,quality: int}}
```

This tells us that the grouping field is given the alias group by Pig, and the second field is the same structure as the filtered_records relation that was being grouped. With this information, we can try the fourth transformation:

```
grunt> max_temp = FOREACH grouped_records GENERATE group,
>>    MAX(filtered_records.temperature);
```

FOREACH processes every row to generate a derived set of rows, using a GENERATE clause to define the fields in each derived row. In this example, the first field is group, which is just the year. The second field is a little more complex. The filtered_records.temperature reference is to the temperature field of the filtered_records bag in the grouped_records relation. MAX is a built-in function for calculating the maximum value of fields in a bag. In this case, it calculates the maximum temperature for the fields in each filtered_records bag. Let's check the result:

```
grunt> DUMP max_temp;
(1949,111)
(1950,22)
```

So we've successfully calculated the maximum temperature for each year.

Generating Examples

In this example, we've used a small sample dataset with just a handful of rows to make it easier to follow the data flow and aid debugging. Creating a cut-down dataset is an art, as ideally it should be rich enough to cover all the cases to exercise your queries (the *completeness* property), yet small enough to make sense to the programmer (the *conciseness* property). Using a random sample doesn't work well in general because join and filter operations tend to remove all random data, leaving an empty result, which is not illustrative of the general data flow.

With the ILLUSTRATE operator, Pig provides a tool for generating a reasonably complete and concise sample dataset. Here is the output from running ILLUSTRATE (slightly reformatted to fit the page):

```
grunt> ILLUSTRATE max_temp;
```

records	year:chararray	temperature:int	quality:int	
	1949	78	1	
	1949	111	1	
	1949	9999	1	

filtered_records	year:chararray	temperature:int	quality:int	
	1949	78	1	
	1949	111	1	

grouped_records	group:chararray	filtered_records:bag{:tuple(year:chararray, temperature:int,quality:int)}
	1949	{(1949, 78, 1), (1949, 111, 1)}

max_temp	group:chararray	:int
	1949	111

Notice that Pig used some of the original data (this is important to keep the generated dataset realistic), as well as creating some new data. It noticed the special value 9999 in the query and created a tuple containing this value to exercise the FILTER statement.

In summary, the output of the ILLUSTRATE is easy to follow and can help you understand what your query is doing.

Comparison with Databases

Having seen Pig in action, it might seem that Pig Latin is similar to SQL. The presence of such operators as GROUP BY and DESCRIBE reinforces this impression. However, there are several differences between the two languages, and between Pig and relational database management systems (RDBMSs) in general.

The most significant difference is that Pig Latin is a data flow programming language, whereas SQL is a declarative programming language. In other words, a Pig Latin program is a step-by-step set of operations on an input relation, in which each step is a single transformation. By contrast, SQL statements are a set of constraints that, taken together, define the output. In many ways, programming in Pig Latin is like working at the level of an RDBMS query planner, which figures out how to turn a declarative statement into a system of steps.

RDBMSs store data in tables, with tightly predefined schemas. Pig is more relaxed about the data that it processes: you can define a schema at runtime, but it's optional. Essentially, it will operate on any source of tuples (although the source should support being read in parallel, by being in multiple files, for example), where a UDF is used to read the tuples from their raw representation.[2] The most common representation is a text file with tab-separated fields, and Pig provides a built-in load function for this format. Unlike a traditional database, there is no data import process to load the data into the RDBMS. The data is loaded from the filesystem (usually HDFS) as the first step in the processing.

Pig's support for complex, nested data structures differentiates it from SQL, which operates on flatter data structures. Also, Pig's ability to use UDFs and streaming operators that are tightly integrated with the language and Pig's nested data structures makes Pig Latin more customizable than most SQL dialects.

RDBMSs have several features to support online, low-latency queries, such as transactions and indexes, that are absent in Pig. As mentioned earlier, Pig does not support random reads or queries in the order of tens of milliseconds. Nor does it support random writes to update small portions of data; all writes are bulk streaming writes, just like MapReduce.

Hive (covered in Chapter 12) sits between Pig and conventional RDBMSs. Like Pig, Hive is designed to use HDFS for storage, but otherwise there are some significant differences. Its query language, HiveQL, is based on SQL, and anyone who is familiar with SQL would have little trouble writing queries in HiveQL. Like RDBMSs, Hive mandates that all data be stored in tables, with a schema under its management; however, it can associate a schema with preexisting data in HDFS, so the load step is optional. Hive does not support low-latency queries, a characteristic it shares with Pig.

Pig Latin

This section gives an informal description of the syntax and semantics of the Pig Latin programming language.[3] It is not meant to offer a complete reference to the language,[4] but there should be enough here for you to get a good understanding of Pig Latin's constructs.

---

2. Or as the Pig Philosophy (*http://pig.apache.org/philosophy.html*) has it, "Pigs eat anything."

3. Not to be confused with Pig Latin, the language game. English words are translated into Pig Latin by moving the initial consonant sound to the end of the word and adding an "ay" sound. For example, "pig" becomes "ig-pay," and "Hadoop" becomes "Adoop-hay."

4. Pig Latin does not have a formal language definition as such, but there is a comprehensive guide to the language that you can find through a link on the Pig website at *http://pig.apache.org/*.

Structure

A Pig Latin program consists of a collection of statements. A statement can be thought of as an operation or a command.[5] For example, a GROUP operation is a type of statement:

```
grouped_records = GROUP records BY year;
```

The command to list the files in a Hadoop filesystem is another example of a statement:

```
ls /
```

Statements are usually terminated with a semicolon, as in the example of the GROUP statement. In fact, this is an example of a statement that must be terminated with a semicolon; it is a syntax error to omit it. The ls command, on the other hand, does not have to be terminated with a semicolon. As a general guideline, statements or commands for interactive use in Grunt do not need the terminating semicolon. This group includes the interactive Hadoop commands, as well as the diagnostic operators such as DESCRIBE. It's never an error to add a terminating semicolon, so if in doubt, it's simplest to add one.

Statements that have to be terminated with a semicolon can be split across multiple lines for readability:

```
records = LOAD 'input/ncdc/micro-tab/sample.txt'
  AS (year:chararray, temperature:int, quality:int);
```

Pig Latin has two forms of comments. Double hyphens are single-line comments. Everything from the first hyphen to the end of the line is ignored by the Pig Latin interpreter:

```
-- My program
DUMP A; -- What's in A?
```

C-style comments are more flexible since they delimit the beginning and end of the comment block with /* and */ markers. They can span lines or be embedded in a single line:

```
/*
 * Description of my program spanning
 * multiple lines.
 */
A = LOAD 'input/pig/join/A';
B = LOAD 'input/pig/join/B';
C = JOIN A BY $0, /* ignored */ B BY $1;
DUMP C;
```

Pig Latin has a list of keywords that have a special meaning in the language and cannot be used as identifiers. These include the operators (LOAD, ILLUSTRATE), commands

---

5. You sometimes see these terms being used interchangeably in documentation on Pig Latin, for example, "GROUP command, " "GROUP operation," "GROUP statement."

(cat, ls), expressions (matches, FLATTEN), and functions (DIFF, MAX)—all of which are covered in the following sections.

Pig Latin has mixed rules on case sensitivity. Operators and commands are not case-sensitive (to make interactive use more forgiving); however, aliases and function names are case-sensitive.

Statements

As a Pig Latin program is executed, each statement is parsed in turn. If there are syntax errors or other (semantic) problems, such as undefined aliases, the interpreter will halt and display an error message. The interpreter builds a *logical plan* for every relational operation, which forms the core of a Pig Latin program. The logical plan for the statement is added to the logical plan for the program so far, and then the interpreter moves on to the next statement.

It's important to note that no data processing takes place while the logical plan of the program is being constructed. For example, consider again the Pig Latin program from the first example:

```
-- max_temp.pig: Finds the maximum temperature by year
records = LOAD 'input/ncdc/micro-tab/sample.txt'
  AS (year:chararray, temperature:int, quality:int);
filtered_records = FILTER records BY temperature != 9999 AND
  (quality == 0 OR quality == 1 OR quality == 4 OR quality == 5 OR quality == 9);
grouped_records = GROUP filtered_records BY year;
max_temp = FOREACH grouped_records GENERATE group,
  MAX(filtered_records.temperature);
DUMP max_temp;
```

When the Pig Latin interpreter sees the first line containing the LOAD statement, it confirms that it is syntactically and semantically correct, and adds it to the logical plan, but it does *not* load the data from the file (or even check whether the file exists). Indeed, where would it load it? Into memory? Even if it did fit into memory, what would it do with the data? Perhaps not all the input data is needed (because later statements filter it, for example), so it would be pointless to load it. The point is that it makes no sense to start any processing until the whole flow is defined. Similarly, Pig validates the GROUP and FOREACH...GENERATE statements, and adds them to the logical plan without executing them. The trigger for Pig to start execution is the DUMP statement. At that point, the logical plan is compiled into a physical plan and executed.

Multiquery Execution

Because DUMP is a diagnostic tool, it will always trigger execution. However, the STORE command is different. In interactive mode, STORE acts like DUMP and will always trigger execution (this includes the run command), but in batch mode it will not (this includes the exec command). The reason for this is efficiency. In batch mode, Pig will parse the whole script to see whether there are any optimizations that could be

---

made to limit the amount of data to be written to or read from disk. Consider the following simple example:

```
A = LOAD 'input/pig/multiquery/A';
B = FILTER A BY $1 == 'banana';
C = FILTER A BY $1 != 'banana';
STORE B INTO 'output/b';
STORE C INTO 'output/c';
```

Relations B and C are both derived from A, so to save reading A twice, Pig can run this script as a single MapReduce job by reading A once and writing two output files from the job, one for each of B and C. This feature is called *multiquery execution*.

In previous versions of Pig that did not have multiquery execution, each STORE statement in a script run in batch mode triggered execution, resulting in a job for each STORE statement. It is possible to restore the old behavior by disabling multiquery execution with the -M or -no_multiquery option to pig.

The physical plan that Pig prepares is a series of MapReduce jobs, which in local mode Pig runs in the local JVM, and in MapReduce mode Pig runs on a Hadoop cluster.

You can see the logical and physical plans created by Pig using the EXPLAIN command on a relation (EXPLAIN max_temp; for example).

EXPLAIN will also show the MapReduce plan, which shows how the physical operators are grouped into MapReduce jobs. This is a good way to find out how many MapReduce jobs Pig will run for your query.

The relational operators that can be a part of a logical plan in Pig are summarized in Table 11-1. We go through the operators in more detail in "Data Processing Operators" on page 399.

Table 11-1. Pig Latin relational operators

Category	Operator	Description
Loading and storing	LOAD	Loads data from the filesystem or other storage into a relation
	STORE	Saves a relation to the filesystem or other storage
	DUMP	Prints a relation to the console
Filtering	FILTER	Removes unwanted rows from a relation
	DISTINCT	Removes duplicate rows from a relation
	FOREACH...GENERATE	Adds or removes fields from a relation
	MAPREDUCE	Runs a MapReduce job using a relation as input
	STREAM	Transforms a relation using an external program
	SAMPLE	Selects a random sample of a relation
Grouping and joining	JOIN	Joins two or more relations

Category	Operator	Description
	COGROUP	Groups the data in two or more relations
	GROUP	Groups the data in a single relation
	CROSS	Creates the cross-product of two or more relations
Sorting	ORDER	Sorts a relation by one or more fields
	LIMIT	Limits the size of a relation to a maximum number of tuples
Combining and splitting	UNION	Combines two or more relations into one
	SPLIT	Splits a relation into two or more relations

There are other types of statements that are not added to the logical plan. For example, the diagnostic operators—DESCRIBE, EXPLAIN, and ILLUSTRATE—are provided to allow the user to interact with the logical plan for debugging purposes (see Table 11-2). DUMP is a sort of diagnostic operator, too, since it is used only to allow interactive debugging of small result sets or in combination with LIMIT to retrieve a few rows from a larger relation. The STORE statement should be used when the size of the output is more than a few lines, as it writes to a file rather than to the console.

Table 11-2. Pig Latin diagnostic operators

Operator	Description
DESCRIBE	Prints a relation's schema
EXPLAIN	Prints the logical and physical plans
ILLUSTRATE	Shows a sample execution of the logical plan, using a generated subset of the input

Pig Latin provides three statements—REGISTER, DEFINE, and IMPORT—that make it possible to incorporate macros and user-defined functions into Pig scripts (see Table 11-3).

Table 11-3. Pig Latin macro and UDF statements

Statement	Description
REGISTER	Registers a JAR file with the Pig runtime
DEFINE	Creates an alias for a macro, UDF, streaming script, or command specification
IMPORT	Import macros defined in a separate file into a script

Because they do not process relations, commands are not added to the logical plan; instead, they are executed immediately. Pig provides commands to interact with Hadoop filesystems (which are very handy for moving data around before or after processing with Pig) and MapReduce, as well as a few utility commands (described in Table 11-4).

Table 11-4. Pig Latin commands

Category	Command	Description
Hadoop Filesystem	cat	Prints the contents of one or more files
	cd	Changes the current directory
	copyFromLocal	Copies a local file or directory to a Hadoop filesystem
	copyToLocal	Copies a file or directory on a Hadoop filesystem to the local filesystem
	cp	Copies a file or directory to another directory
	fs	Accesses Hadoop's filesystem shell
	ls	Lists files
	mkdir	Creates a new directory
	mv	Moves a file or directory to another directory
	pwd	Prints the path of the current working directory
	rm	Deletes a file or directory
	rmf	Forcibly deletes a file or directory (does not fail if the file or directory does not exist)
Hadoop MapReduce	kill	Kills a MapReduce job
Utility	exec	Runs a script in a new Grunt shell in batch mode
	help	Shows the available commands and options
	quit	Exits the interpreter
	run	Runs a script within the existing Grunt shell
	set	Sets Pig options and MapReduce job properties
	sh	Run a shell command from within Grunt

The filesystem commands can operate on files or directories in any Hadoop filesystem, and they are very similar to the hadoop fs commands (which is not surprising, as both are simple wrappers around the Hadoop FileSystem interface). You can access all of the Hadoop filesystem shell commands using Pig's fs command. For example, fs -ls will show a file listing, and fs -help will show help on all the available commands.

Precisely which Hadoop filesystem is used is determined by the fs.default.name property in the site file for Hadoop Core. See "The Command-Line Interface" on page 49 for more details on how to configure this property.

These commands are mostly self-explanatory, except set, which is used to set options that control Pig's behavior, including arbitrary MapReduce job properties. The debug option is used to turn debug logging on or off from within a script (you can also control the log level when launching Pig, using the -d or -debug option):

```
grunt>
set debug on
```

Another useful option is the job.name option, which gives a Pig job a meaningful name, making it easier to pick out your Pig MapReduce jobs when running on a shared Hadoop cluster. If Pig is running a script (rather than operating as an interactive query from Grunt), its job name defaults to a value based on the script name.

There are two commands in Table 11-4 for running a Pig script, exec and run. The difference is that exec runs the script in batch mode in a new Grunt shell, so any aliases defined in the script are not accessible to the shell after the script has completed. On the other hand, when running a script with run, it is as if the contents of the script had been entered manually, so the command history of the invoking shell contains all the statements from the script. Multiquery execution, where Pig executes a batch of statements in one go (see "Multiquery Execution" on page 377), is used only by exec, not run.

 By design, Pig Latin lacks native control flow statements. The recommended approach for writing programs that have conditional logic or loop constructs is to embed Pig Latin in another language, such as Python, JavaScript, or Java, and manage the control flow from there. In this model the host script uses a compile-bind-run API to execute Pig scripts and retrieve their status. Consult the Pig documentation for details of the API.

Embedded Pig programs always run in a JVM, so for Python and JavaScript you use the pig command followed by the name of your script, and the appropriate Java scripting engine will be selected (Jython for Python, Rhino for JavaScript).

Expressions

An expression is something that is evaluated to yield a value. Expressions can be used in Pig as a part of a statement containing a relational operator. Pig has a rich variety of expressions, many of which will be familiar from other programming languages. They are listed in Table 11-5, with brief descriptions and examples. We will see examples of many of these expressions throughout the chapter.

Table 11-5. Pig Latin expressions

Category	Expressions	Description	Examples
Constant	Literal	Constant value (see also the "Literal example" column in Table 11-6)	1.0, 'a'
Field (by position)	$n	Field in position n (zero-based)	$0
Field (by name)	f	Field named f	year
Field (disambiguate)	r::f	Field named f from relation r after grouping or joining	A::year

Category	Expressions	Description	Examples
Projection	$c.\$n, c.f$	Field in container c (relation, bag, or tuple) by position, by name	`records.$0,` `records.year`
Map lookup	$m\#k$	Value associated with key k in map m	`items#'Coat'`
Cast	$(t)\ f$	Cast of field f to type t	`(int) year`
Arithmetic	$x + y, x - y$	Addition, subtraction	`$1 + $2,$1 - $2`
	$x * y, x / y$	Multiplication, division	`$1 * $2,$1 / $2`
	$x\ \%\ y$	Modulo, the remainder of x divided by y	`$1 % $2`
	$+x, -x$	Unary positive, negation	`+1,-1`
Conditional	$x\ ?\ y : z$	Bincond/ternary; y if x evaluates to true, z otherwise	`quality == 0 ? 0 : 1`
Comparison	$x == y, x\ != y$	Equals, does not equal	`quality == 0,tempera` `ture != 9999`
	$x > y, x < y$	Greater than, less than	`quality > 0,quality <` `10`
	$x >= y, x <= y$	Greater than or equal to, less than or equal to	`quality >= 1,quality <=` `9`
	x matches y	Pattern matching with regular expression	`quality matches` `'[01459]'`
	x is null	Is null	`temperature is null`
	x is not null	Is not null	`temperature is not null`
Boolean	x or y	Logical or	`q == 0 or q == 1`
	x and y	Logical and	`q == 0 and r == 0`
	not x	Logical negation	`not q matches '[01459]'`
Functional	$fn(f1, f2, ...)$	Invocation of function fn on fields $f1, f2$, etc.	`isGood(quality)`
Flatten	FLATTEN(f)	Removal of a level of nesting from bags and tuples	`FLATTEN(group)`

Types

So far you have seen some of the simple types in Pig, such as int and chararray. Here we will discuss Pig's built-in types in more detail.

Pig has four numeric types: int, long, float, and double, which are identical to their Java counterparts. There is also a bytearray type, like Java's byte array type for representing a blob of binary data, and chararray, which, like java.lang.String, represents textual data in UTF-16 format, although it can be loaded or stored in UTF-8 format. Pig does not have types corresponding to Java's boolean,[6] byte, short, or char primitive types. These are all easily represented using Pig's int type, or chararray for char.

The numeric, textual, and binary types are simple atomic types. Pig Latin also has three complex types for representing nested structures: tuple, bag, and map. All of Pig Latin's types are listed in Table 11-6.

Table 11-6. Pig Latin types

Category	Type	Description	Literal example
Numeric	int	32-bit signed integer	1
	long	64-bit signed integer	1L
	float	32-bit floating-point number	1.0F
	double	64-bit floating-point number	1.0
Text	chararray	Character array in UTF-16 format	'a'
Binary	bytearray	Byte array	Not supported
Complex	tuple	Sequence of fields of any type	(1,'pomegranate')
	bag	An unordered collection of tuples, possibly with duplicates	{(1,'pomegranate'),(2)}
	map	A set of key-value pairs; keys must be character arrays, but values may be any type	['a'#'pomegranate']

The complex types are usually loaded from files or constructed using relational operators. Be aware, however, that the literal form in Table 11-6 is used when a constant value is created from within a Pig Latin program. The raw form in a file is usually different when using the standard PigStorage loader. For example, the representation in a file of the bag in Table 11-6 would be {(1,pomegranate),(2)} (note the lack of quotation marks), and with a suitable schema, this would be loaded as a relation with a single field and row, whose value was the bag.

Pig provides the built-in functions TOTUPLE, TOBAG and TOMAP, which are used for turning expressions into tuples, bags, and maps.

Although relations and bags are conceptually the same (an unordered collection of tuples), in practice Pig treats them slightly differently. A relation is a top-level construct, whereas a bag has to be contained in a relation. Normally you don't have to worry about this, but there are a few restrictions that can trip up the uninitiated. For example, it's not possible to create a relation from a bag literal. So the following statement fails:

6. Although there is no Boolean type for data (until version 0.10.0), Pig has the concept of an expression evaluating to true or false for testing conditions (such as in a FILTER statement). However, Pig does not allow a Boolean expression to be stored in a field.

```
A = {(1,2),(3,4)}; -- Error
```

The simplest workaround in this case is to load the data from a file using the LOAD statement.

As another example, you can't treat a relation like a bag and project a field into a new relation ($0 refers to the first field of A, using the positional notation):

```
B = A.$0;
```

Instead, you have to use a relational operator to turn the relation A into relation B:

```
B = FOREACH A GENERATE $0;
```

It's possible that a future version of Pig Latin will remove these inconsistencies and treat relations and bags in the same way.

Schemas

A relation in Pig may have an associated schema, which gives the fields in the relation names and types. We've seen how an AS clause in a LOAD statement is used to attach a schema to a relation:

```
grunt> records = LOAD 'input/ncdc/micro-tab/sample.txt'
>>    AS (year:int, temperature:int, quality:int);
grunt> DESCRIBE records;
records: {year: int,temperature: int,quality: int}
```

This time we've declared the year to be an integer rather than a chararray, even though the file it is being loaded from is the same. An integer may be more appropriate if we need to manipulate the year arithmetically (to turn it into a timestamp, for example), whereas the chararray representation might be more appropriate when it's being used as a simple identifier. Pig's flexibility in the degree to which schemas are declared contrasts with schemas in traditional SQL databases, which are declared before the data is loaded into to the system. Pig is designed for analyzing plain input files with no associated type information, so it is quite natural to choose types for fields later than you would with an RDBMS.

It's possible to omit type declarations completely, too:

```
grunt> records = LOAD 'input/ncdc/micro-tab/sample.txt'
>>    AS (year, temperature, quality);
grunt> DESCRIBE records;
records: {year: bytearray,temperature: bytearray,quality: bytearray}
```

In this case, we have specified only the names of the fields in the schema: year, temperature, and quality. The types default to bytearray, the most general type, representing a binary string.

You don't need to specify types for every field; you can leave some to default to byte array, as we have done for year in this declaration:

```
grunt> records = LOAD 'input/ncdc/micro-tab/sample.txt'
>>    AS (year, temperature:int, quality:int);
grunt> DESCRIBE records;
records: {year: bytearray,temperature: int,quality: int}
```

However, if you specify a schema in this way, you do need to specify every field. Also, there's no way to specify the type of a field without specifying the name. On the other hand, the schema is entirely optional and can be omitted by not specifying an AS clause:

```
grunt> records = LOAD 'input/ncdc/micro-tab/sample.txt';
grunt> DESCRIBE records;
Schema for records unknown.
```

Fields in a relation with no schema can be referenced using only positional notation: $0 refers to the first field in a relation, $1 to the second, and so on. Their types default to bytearray:

```
grunt> projected_records = FOREACH records GENERATE $0, $1, $2;
grunt> DUMP projected_records;
(1950,0,1)
(1950,22,1)
(1950,-11,1)
(1949,111,1)
(1949,78,1)
grunt> DESCRIBE projected_records;
projected_records: {bytearray,bytearray,bytearray}
```

Although it can be convenient not to assign types to fields (particularly in the first stages of writing a query), doing so can improve the clarity and efficiency of Pig Latin programs and is generally recommended.

> Declaring a schema as a part of the query is flexible but doesn't lend itself to schema reuse. A set of Pig queries over the same input data will often have the same schema repeated in each query. If the query processes a large number of fields, this repetition can become hard to maintain.
>
> The Apache HCatalog project (*http://incubator.apache.org/hcatalog/*) solves this problem by providing a table metadata service, based on Hive's metastore, so that Pig queries can reference schemas by name, rather than specifying them in full each time.

Validation and nulls

An SQL database will enforce the constraints in a table's schema at load time; for example, trying to load a string into a column that is declared to be a numeric type will fail. In Pig, if the value cannot be cast to the type declared in the schema, it will substitute a null value. Let's see how this works when we have the following input for the weather data, which has an "e" character in place of an integer:

```
1950    0    1
1950    22   1
```

```
1950    e    1
1949    111  1
1949    78   1
```

Pig handles the corrupt line by producing a null for the offending value, which is displayed as the absence of a value when dumped to screen (and also when saved using STORE):

```
grunt> records = LOAD 'input/ncdc/micro-tab/sample_corrupt.txt'
>>    AS (year:chararray, temperature:int, quality:int);
grunt> DUMP records;
(1950,0,1)
(1950,22,1)
(1950,,1)
(1949,111,1)
(1949,78,1)
```

Pig produces a warning for the invalid field (not shown here) but does not halt its processing. For large datasets, it is very common to have corrupt, invalid, or merely unexpected data, and it is generally infeasible to incrementally fix every unparsable record. Instead, we can pull out all of the invalid records in one go, so we can take action on them, perhaps by fixing our program (because they indicate that we have made a mistake) or by filtering them out (because the data is genuinely unusable):

```
grunt> corrupt_records = FILTER records BY temperature is null;
grunt> DUMP corrupt_records;
(1950,,1)
```

Note the use of the is null operator, which is analogous to SQL. In practice, we would include more information from the original record, such as an identifier and the value that could not be parsed, to help our analysis of the bad data.

We can find the number of corrupt records using the following idiom for counting the number of rows in a relation:

```
grunt> grouped = GROUP corrupt_records ALL;
grunt> all_grouped = FOREACH grouped GENERATE group, COUNT(corrupt_records);
grunt> DUMP all_grouped;
(all,1)
```

("GROUP" on page 406 explains grouping and the ALL operation in more detail.)

Another useful technique is to use the SPLIT operator to partition the data into "good" and "bad" relations, which can then be analyzed separately:

```
grunt> SPLIT records INTO good_records IF temperature is not null,
>>    bad_records IF temperature is null;
grunt> DUMP good_records;
(1950,0,1)
(1950,22,1)
(1949,111,1)
(1949,78,1)
grunt> DUMP bad_records;
(1950,,1)
```

Going back to the case in which temperature's type was left undeclared, the corrupt data cannot be detected easily, since it doesn't surface as a null:

```
grunt> records = LOAD 'input/ncdc/micro-tab/sample_corrupt.txt'
>>    AS (year:chararray, temperature, quality:int);
grunt> DUMP records;
(1950,0,1)
(1950,22,1)
(1950,e,1)
(1949,111,1)
(1949,78,1)
grunt> filtered_records = FILTER records BY temperature != 9999 AND
>>    (quality == 0 OR quality == 1 OR quality == 4 OR quality == 5 OR quality == 9);
grunt> grouped_records = GROUP filtered_records BY year;
grunt> max_temp = FOREACH grouped_records GENERATE group,
>>    MAX(filtered_records.temperature);
grunt> DUMP max_temp;
(1949,111.0)
(1950,22.0)
```

What happens in this case is that the temperature field is interpreted as a bytearray, so the corrupt field is not detected when the input is loaded. When passed to the MAX function, the temperature field is cast to a double, since MAX works only with numeric types. The corrupt field cannot be represented as a double, so it becomes a null, which MAX silently ignores. The best approach is generally to declare types for your data on loading and look for missing or corrupt values in the relations themselves before you do your main processing.

Sometimes corrupt data shows up as smaller tuples because fields are simply missing. You can filter these out by using the SIZE function as follows:

```
grunt> A = LOAD 'input/pig/corrupt/missing_fields';
grunt> DUMP A;
(2,Tie)
(4,Coat)
(3)
(1,Scarf)
grunt> B = FILTER A BY SIZE(TOTUPLE(*)) > 1;
grunt> DUMP B;
(2,Tie)
(4,Coat)
(1,Scarf)
```

Schema merging

In Pig, you don't declare the schema for every new relation in the data flow. In most cases, Pig can figure out the resulting schema for the output of a relational operation by considering the schema of the input relation.

How are schemas propagated to new relations? Some relational operators don't change the schema, so the relation produced by the LIMIT operator (which restricts a relation to a maximum number of tuples), for example, has the same schema as the relation it operates on. For other operators, the situation is more complicated. UNION, for example, combines two or more relations into one and tries to merge the input relations schemas. If the schemas are incompatible, due to different types or number of fields, then the schema of the result of the UNION is unknown.

You can find out the schema for any relation in the data flow using the DESCRIBE operator. If you want to redefine the schema for a relation, you can use the FOREACH...GENERATE operator with AS clauses to define the schema for some or all of the fields of the input relation.

See "User-Defined Functions" on page 391 for a further discussion of schemas.

Functions

Functions in Pig come in four types:

Eval function

> A function that takes one or more expressions and returns another expression. An example of a built-in eval function is MAX, which returns the maximum value of the entries in a bag. Some eval functions are *aggregate functions*, which means they operate on a bag of data to produce a scalar value; MAX is an example of an aggregate function. Furthermore, many aggregate functions are *algebraic*, which means that the result of the function may be calculated incrementally. In MapReduce terms, algebraic functions make use of the combiner and are much more efficient to calculate (see "Combiner Functions" on page 33). MAX is an algebraic function, whereas a function to calculate the median of a collection of values is an example of a function that is not algebraic.

Filter function

> A special type of eval function that returns a logical Boolean result. As the name suggests, filter functions are used in the FILTER operator to remove unwanted rows. They can also be used in other relational operators that take Boolean conditions and, in general, expressions using Boolean or conditional expressions. An example of a built-in filter function is IsEmpty, which tests whether a bag or a map contains any items.

Load function

> A function that specifies how to load data into a relation from external storage.

Store function

> A function that specifies how to save the contents of a relation to external storage. Often, load and store functions are implemented by the same type. For example, PigStorage, which loads data from delimited text files, can store data in the same format.

Pig comes with a collection of built-in functions, a selection of which are listed in Table 11-7. The complete list of built-in functions, which includes a large number of standard math and string functions, can be found in the documentation for each Pig release.

Table 11-7. A selection of Pig's built-in functions

Category	Function	Description
Eval	AVG	Calculates the average (mean) value of entries in a bag.
	CONCAT	Concatenates byte arrays or character arrays together.
	COUNT	Calculates the number of non-null entries in a bag.
	COUNT_STAR	Calculates the number of entries in a bag, including those that are null.
	DIFF	Calculates the set difference of two bags. If the two arguments are not bags, returns a bag containing both if they are equal; otherwise, returns an empty bag.
	MAX	Calculates the maximum value of entries in a bag.
	MIN	Calculates the minimum value of entries in a bag.
	SIZE	Calculates the size of a type. The size of numeric types is always one; for character arrays, it is the number of characters; for byte arrays, the number of bytes; and for containers (tuple, bag, map), it is the number of entries.
	SUM	Calculates the sum of the values of entries in a bag.
	TOBAG	Converts one or more expressions to individual tuples, which are then put in a bag.
	TOKENIZE	Tokenizes a character array into a bag of its constituent words.
	TOMAP	Converts an even number of expressions to a map of key-value pairs.
	TOP	Calculates the top *n* tuples in a bag.
	TOTUPLE	Converts one or more expressions to a tuple.
Filter	IsEmpty	Tests whether a bag or map is empty.
Load/Store	PigStorage	Loads or stores relations using a field-delimited text format. Each line is broken into fields using a configurable field delimiter (defaults to a tab character) to be stored in the tuple's fields. It is the default storage when none is specified.
	BinStorage	Loads or stores relations from or to binary files in a Pig-specific format that uses Hadoop Writable objects.
	TextLoader	Loads relations from a plain-text format. Each line corresponds to a tuple whose single field is the line of text.
	JsonLoader, JsonStorage	Loads or stores relations from or to a (Pig-defined) JSON format. Each tuple is stored on one line.
	HBaseStorage	Loads or stores relations from or to HBase tables.

If the function you need is not available, you can write your own. Before you do that, however, have a look in the *Piggy Bank*, a repository of Pig functions shared by the Pig community. For example, there are load and store functions in the Piggy Bank for Avro data files, CSV files, Hive RCFiles, SequenceFiles, and XML files. The Pig website has instructions on how to browse and obtain the Piggy Bank functions. If the Piggy Bank doesn't have what you need, you can write your own function (and if it is sufficiently general, you might consider contributing it to the Piggy Bank so that others can benefit from it, too). These are known as *user-defined functions*, or UDFs.

Macros

Macros provide a way to package reusable pieces of Pig Latin code from within Pig Latin itself. For example, we can extract the part of our Pig Latin program that performs grouping on a relation and then finds the maximum value in each group by defining a macro as follows:

```
DEFINE max_by_group(X, group_key, max_field) RETURNS Y {
  A = GROUP $X by $group_key;
  $Y = FOREACH A GENERATE group, MAX($X.$max_field);
};
```

The macro, called `max_by_group`, takes three parameters: a relation, X, and two field names, `group_key` and `max_field`. It returns a single relation, Y. Within the macro body, parameters and return aliases are referenced with a $ prefix, such as $X.

The macro is used as follows:

```
records = LOAD 'input/ncdc/micro-tab/sample.txt'
  AS (year:chararray, temperature:int, quality:int);
filtered_records = FILTER records BY temperature != 9999 AND
  (quality == 0 OR quality == 1 OR quality == 4 OR quality == 5 OR quality == 9);
max_temp = max_by_group(filtered_records, year, temperature);
DUMP max_temp
```

At runtime, Pig will expand the macro using the macro definition. After expansion, the program looks like the following, with the expanded section in bold.

```
records = LOAD 'input/ncdc/micro-tab/sample.txt'
  AS (year:chararray, temperature:int, quality:int);
filtered_records = FILTER records BY temperature != 9999 AND
  (quality == 0 OR quality == 1 OR quality == 4 OR quality == 5 OR quality == 9);
macro_max_by_group_A_0 = GROUP filtered_records by (year);
max_temp = FOREACH macro_max_by_group_A_0 GENERATE group,
  MAX(filtered_records.(temperature));
DUMP max_temp
```

Normally you don't see the expanded form, because Pig creates it internally; however, in some cases it is useful to see it when writing and debugging macros. You can get Pig to perform macro expansion only (without executing the script) by passing the `-dryrun` argument to `pig`.

Notice that the parameters that were passed to the macro (`filtered_records`, `year`, and `temperature`) have been substituted for the names in the macro definition. Aliases in the macro definition that don't have a $ prefix, such as A in this example, are local to the macro definition and are rewritten at expansion time to avoid conflicts with aliases in other parts of the program. In this case, A becomes `macro_max_by_group_A_0` in the expanded form.

To foster reuse, macros can be defined in separate files to Pig scripts, in which case they need to be imported into any script that uses them. An import statement looks like this:

```
IMPORT './ch11/src/main/pig/max_temp.macro';
```

User-Defined Functions

Pig's designers realized that the ability to plug in custom code is crucial for all but the most trivial data processing jobs. For this reason, they made it easy to define and use user-defined functions. We only cover Java UDFs in this section, but be aware that you can write UDFs in Python or JavaScript too, both of which are run using the Java Scripting API.

A Filter UDF

Let's demonstrate by writing a filter function for filtering out weather records that do not have a temperature quality reading of satisfactory (or better). The idea is to change this line:

```
filtered_records = FILTER records BY temperature != 9999 AND
  (quality == 0 OR quality == 1 OR quality == 4 OR quality == 5 OR quality == 9);
```

to:

```
filtered_records = FILTER records BY temperature != 9999 AND isGood(quality);
```

This achieves two things: it makes the Pig script more concise, and it encapsulates the logic in one place so that it can be easily reused in other scripts. If we were just writing an ad hoc query, we probably wouldn't bother to write a UDF. It's when you start doing the same kind of processing over and over again that you see opportunities for reusable UDFs.

Filter UDFs are all subclasses of FilterFunc, which itself is a subclass of EvalFunc. We'll look at EvalFunc in more detail later, but for the moment just note that, in essence, EvalFunc looks like the following class:

```
public abstract class EvalFunc<T> {
  public abstract T exec(Tuple input) throws IOException;
}
```

EvalFunc's only abstract method, exec(), takes a tuple and returns a single value, the (parameterized) type T. The fields in the input tuple consist of the expressions passed to the function—in this case, a single integer. For FilterFunc, T is Boolean, so the method should return true only for those tuples that should not be filtered out.

For the quality filter, we write a class, IsGoodQuality, that extends FilterFunc and implements the exec() method. See Example 11-1. The Tuple class is essentially a list of objects with associated types. Here we are concerned only with the first field (since the function only has a single argument), which we extract by index using the get() method on Tuple. The field is an integer, so if it's not null, we cast it and check whether the value is one that signifies the temperature was a good reading, returning the appropriate value, true or false.

Example 11-1. A FilterFunc UDF to remove records with unsatisfactory temperature quality readings

```java
package com.hadoopbook.pig;

import java.io.IOException;
import java.util.ArrayList;
import java.util.List;

import org.apache.pig.FilterFunc;

import org.apache.pig.backend.executionengine.ExecException;
import org.apache.pig.data.DataType;
import org.apache.pig.data.Tuple;
import org.apache.pig.impl.logicalLayer.FrontendException;

public class IsGoodQuality extends FilterFunc {

  @Override
  public Boolean exec(Tuple tuple) throws IOException {
    if (tuple == null || tuple.size() == 0) {
      return false;
    }
    try {
      Object object = tuple.get(0);
      if (object == null) {
        return false;
      }
      int i = (Integer) object;
      return i == 0 || i == 1 || i == 4 || i == 5 || i == 9;
    } catch (ExecException e) {
      throw new IOException(e);
    }
  }

}
```

To use the new function, we first compile it and package it in a JAR file (the example code that accompanies this book comes with build instructions for how to do this). Then we tell Pig about the JAR file with the REGISTER operator, which is given the local path to the filename (and is *not* enclosed in quotes):

```
grunt> REGISTER pig-examples.jar;
```

Finally, we can invoke the function:

```
grunt> filtered_records = FILTER records BY temperature != 9999 AND
>>    com.hadoopbook.pig.IsGoodQuality(quality);
```

Pig resolves function calls by treating the function's name as a Java classname and attempting to load a class of that name. (This, incidentally, is why function names are case-sensitive: because Java classnames are.) When searching for classes, Pig uses a classloader that includes the JAR files that have been registered. When running in distributed mode, Pig will ensure that your JAR files get shipped to the cluster.

For the UDF in this example, Pig looks for a class with the name `com.hadoop book.pig.IsGoodQuality`, which it finds in the JAR file we registered.

Resolution of built-in functions proceeds in the same way, except for one difference: Pig has a set of built-in package names that it searches, so the function call does not have to be a fully qualified name. For example, the function `MAX` is actually implemented by a class `MAX` in the package `org.apache.pig.builtin`. This is one of the packages that Pig looks in, so we can write `MAX` rather than `org.apache.pig.builtin.MAX` in our Pig programs.

We can add our package name to the search path by invoking Grunt with this command-line argument: `-Dudf.import.list=com.hadoopbook.pig`. Alternatively, we can shorten the function name by defining an alias, using the DEFINE operator:

```
grunt> DEFINE isGood com.hadoopbook.pig.IsGoodQuality();
grunt> filtered_records = FILTER records BY temperature != 9999 AND isGood(quality);
```

Defining an alias is a good idea if you want to use the function several times in the same script. It's also necessary if you want to pass arguments to the constructor of the UDF's implementation class.

Leveraging types

The filter works when the quality field is declared to be of type `int`, but if the type information is absent, the UDF fails! This happens because the field is the default type, `bytearray`, represented by the `DataByteArray` class. Because `DataByteArray` is not an `Integer`, the cast fails.

The obvious way to fix this is to convert the field to an integer in the `exec()` method. However, there is a better way, which is to tell Pig the types of the fields that the function expects. The `getArgToFuncMapping()` method on `EvalFunc` is provided for precisely this reason. We can override it to tell Pig that the first field should be an integer:

```
@Override
public List<FuncSpec> getArgToFuncMapping() throws FrontendException {
  List<FuncSpec> funcSpecs = new ArrayList<FuncSpec>();
  funcSpecs.add(new FuncSpec(this.getClass().getName(),
      new Schema(new Schema.FieldSchema(null, DataType.INTEGER))));

  return funcSpecs;
}
```

This method returns a `FuncSpec` object corresponding to each of the fields of the tuple that are passed to the `exec()` method. Here there is a single field, and we construct an anonymous `FieldSchema` (the name is passed as `null`, since Pig ignores the name when doing type conversion). The type is specified using the `INTEGER` constant on Pig's `DataType` class.

With the amended function, Pig will attempt to convert the argument passed to the function to an integer. If the field cannot be converted, then a null is passed for the field. The exec() method always returns false when the field is null. For this application, this behavior is appropriate, as we want to filter out records whose quality field is unintelligible.

Here's the final program using the new function:

```
-- max_temp_filter_udf.pig
REGISTER pig-examples.jar;
DEFINE isGood com.hadoopbook.pig.IsGoodQuality();
records = LOAD 'input/ncdc/micro-tab/sample.txt'
  AS (year:chararray, temperature:int, quality:int);
filtered_records = FILTER records BY temperature != 9999 AND isGood(quality);
grouped_records = GROUP filtered_records BY year;
max_temp = FOREACH grouped_records GENERATE group,
  MAX(filtered_records.temperature);
DUMP max_temp;
```

An Eval UDF

Writing an eval function is a small step up from writing a filter function. Consider the UDF (in Example 11-2), which trims the leading and trailing whitespace from chararray values, just like the trim() method on java.lang.String. We will use this UDF later in the chapter.

Example 11-2. An EvalFunc UDF to trim leading and trailing whitespace from chararray values

```
public class Trim extends EvalFunc<String> {

  @Override
  public String exec(Tuple input) throws IOException {
    if (input == null || input.size() == 0) {
      return null;
    }
    try {
      Object object = input.get(0);
      if (object == null) {
        return null;
      }
      return ((String) object).trim();
    } catch (ExecException e) {
      throw new IOException(e);
    }
  }

  @Override
  public List<FuncSpec> getArgToFuncMapping() throws FrontendException {
    List<FuncSpec> funcList = new ArrayList<FuncSpec>();
    funcList.add(new FuncSpec(this.getClass().getName(), new Schema(
        new Schema.FieldSchema(null, DataType.CHARARRAY))));

    return funcList;
```

```
  }
}
```

An eval function extends the `EvalFunc` class, parameterized by the type of the return value (which is `String` for the `Trim` UDF).[7] The `exec()` and `getArgToFuncMapping()` methods are straightforward, like the ones in the `IsGoodQuality` UDF.

When you write an eval function, you need to consider what the output's schema looks like. In the following statement, the schema of B is determined by the function `udf`:

```
B = FOREACH A GENERATE udf($0);
```

If `udf` creates tuples with scalar fields, then Pig can determine B's schema through reflection. For complex types such as bags, tuples, or maps, Pig needs more help, and you should implement the `outputSchema()` method to give Pig the information about the output schema.

The `Trim` UDF returns a string, which Pig translates as a `chararray`, as can be seen from the following session:

```
grunt> DUMP A;
( pomegranate)
(banana   )
(apple)
( lychee )
grunt> DESCRIBE A;
A: {fruit: chararray}
grunt> B = FOREACH A GENERATE com.hadoopbook.pig.Trim(fruit);
grunt> DUMP B;
(pomegranate)
(banana)
(apple)
(lychee)
grunt> DESCRIBE B;
B: {chararray}
```

A has `chararray` fields that have leading and trailing spaces. We create B from A by applying the `Trim` function to the first field in A (named `fruit`). B's fields are correctly inferred to be of type `chararray`.

Dynamic invokers

Sometimes you want to use a function that is provided by a Java library, but without going to the effort of writing a UDF. Dynamic invokers allow you to do this by calling Java methods directly from a Pig script. The trade-off is that method calls are made via reflection, which can impose significant overhead when called for every record in a large dataset. So for scripts that are run repeatedly, a dedicated UDF is normally preferred.

---

7. Although not relevant for this example, eval functions that operate on a bag may additionally implement Pig's `Algebraic` or `Accumulator` interfaces for more efficient processing of the bag in chunks.

The following snippet shows how we could define and use a trim UDF that uses the Apache Commons Lang StringUtils class.

```
grunt> DEFINE trim InvokeForString('org.apache.commons.lang.StringUtils.trim', 'String');
grunt> B = FOREACH A GENERATE trim(fruit);
grunt> DUMP B;
(pomegranate)
(banana)
(apple)
(lychee)
```

The InvokeForString invoker is used because the return type of the method is a String. (There are also InvokeForInt, InvokeForLong, InvokeForDouble, and InvokeFor Float invokers.) The first argument to the invoker constructor is the fully qualified method to be invoked. The second is a space-separated list of the method argument classes.

A Load UDF

We'll demonstrate a custom load function that can read plain-text column ranges as fields, very much like the Unix cut command. It is used as follows:

```
grunt> records = LOAD 'input/ncdc/micro/sample.txt'
>>     USING com.hadoopbook.pig.CutLoadFunc('16-19,88-92,93-93')
>>     AS (year:int, temperature:int, quality:int);
grunt> DUMP records;
(1950,0,1)
(1950,22,1)
(1950,-11,1)
(1949,111,1)
(1949,78,1)
```

The string passed to CutLoadFunc is the column specification; each comma-separated range defines a field, which is assigned a name and type in the AS clause. Let's examine the implementation of CutLoadFunc, shown in Example 11-3.

Example 11-3. A LoadFunc UDF to load tuple fields as column ranges

```
public class CutLoadFunc extends LoadFunc {

  private static final Log LOG = LogFactory.getLog(CutLoadFunc.class);

  private final List<Range> ranges;
  private final TupleFactory tupleFactory = TupleFactory.getInstance();
  private RecordReader reader;

  public CutLoadFunc(String cutPattern) {
    ranges = Range.parse(cutPattern);
  }

  @Override
  public void setLocation(String location, Job job)
      throws IOException {
```

```
      FileInputFormat.setInputPaths(job, location);
    }

    @Override
    public InputFormat getInputFormat() {
      return new TextInputFormat();
    }

    @Override
    public void prepareToRead(RecordReader reader, PigSplit split) {
      this.reader = reader;
    }

    @Override
    public Tuple getNext() throws IOException {
      try {
        if (!reader.nextKeyValue()) {
          return null;
        }
        Text value = (Text) reader.getCurrentValue();
        String line = value.toString();
        Tuple tuple = tupleFactory.newTuple(ranges.size());
        for (int i = 0; i < ranges.size(); i++) {
          Range range = ranges.get(i);
          if (range.getEnd() > line.length()) {
            LOG.warn(String.format(
                "Range end (%s) is longer than line length (%s)",
                range.getEnd(), line.length()));
            continue;
          }
          tuple.set(i, new DataByteArray(range.getSubstring(line)));
        }
        return tuple;
      } catch (InterruptedException e) {
        throw new ExecException(e);
      }
    }
  }
}
```

In Pig, like in Hadoop, data loading takes place before the mapper runs, so it is important that the input can be split into portions that are handled independently by each mapper (see "Input Splits and Records" on page 234 for background).

From Pig 0.7.0, the load and store function interfaces have been overhauled to be more closely aligned with Hadoop's InputFormat and OutputFormat classes. Functions written for previous versions of Pig will need rewriting (guidelines for doing so are provided at *http://wiki.apache.org/pig/LoadStoreMigrationGuide*). A LoadFunc will typically use an existing underlying InputFormat to create records, with the LoadFunc providing the logic for turning the records into Pig tuples.

CutLoadFunc is constructed with a string that specifies the column ranges to use for each field. The logic for parsing this string and creating a list of internal Range objects that encapsulates these ranges is contained in the `Range` class, and is not shown here (it is available in the example code that accompanies this book).

Pig calls `setLocation()` on a `LoadFunc` to pass the input location to the loader. Since `CutLoadFunc` uses a `TextInputFormat` to break the input into lines, we just pass the location to set the input path using a static method on `FileInputFormat`.

 Pig uses the new MapReduce API, so we use the input and output formats and associated classes from the `org.apache.hadoop.mapreduce` package.

Next, Pig calls the `getInputFormat()` method to create a `RecordReader` for each split, just like in MapReduce. Pig passes each `RecordReader` to the `prepareToRead()` method of `CutLoadFunc`, which we store a reference to, so we can use it in the `getNext()` method for iterating through the records.

The Pig runtime calls `getNext()` repeatedly, and the load function reads tuples from the reader until the reader reaches the last record in its split. At this point, it returns `null` to signal that there are no more tuples to be read.

It is the responsibility of the `getNext()` implementation to turn lines of the input file into `Tuple` objects. It does this by means of a `TupleFactory`, a Pig class for creating `Tuple` instances. The `newTuple()` method creates a new tuple with the required number of fields, which is just the number of `Range` classes, and the fields are populated using substrings of the line, which are determined by the `Range` objects.

We need to think about what to do when the line is shorter than the range asked for. One option is to throw an exception and stop further processing. This is appropriate if your application cannot tolerate incomplete or corrupt records. In many cases, it is better to return a tuple with `null` fields and let the Pig script handle the incomplete data as it sees fit. This is the approach we take here; by exiting the for loop if the range end is past the end of the line, we leave the current field and any subsequent fields in the tuple with their default value of `null`.

Using a schema

Let's now consider the type of the fields being loaded. If the user has specified a schema, then the fields need to be converted to the relevant types. However, this is performed lazily by Pig, and so the loader should always construct tuples of type `bytearray`, using the `DataByteArray` type. The loader function still has the opportunity to do the conversion, however, by overriding `getLoadCaster()` to return a custom implementation of the `LoadCaster` interface, which provides a collection of conversion methods for this purpose:

```
public interface LoadCaster {
    public Integer bytesToInteger(byte[] b) throws IOException;
```

```
    public Long bytesToLong(byte[] b) throws IOException;
    public Float bytesToFloat(byte[] b) throws IOException;
    public Double bytesToDouble(byte[] b) throws IOException;
    public String bytesToCharArray(byte[] b) throws IOException;
    public Map<String, Object> bytesToMap(byte[] b) throws IOException;
    public Tuple bytesToTuple(byte[] b) throws IOException;
    public DataBag bytesToBag(byte[] b) throws IOException;
}
```

CutLoadFunc doesn't override getLoadCaster() because the default implementation returns Utf8StorageConverter, which provides standard conversions between UTF-8 encoded data and Pig data types.

In some cases, the load function itself can determine the schema. For example, if we were loading self-describing data such as XML or JSON, we could create a schema for Pig by looking at the data. Alternatively, the load function may determine the schema in another way, such as an external file, or by being passed information in its constructor. To support such cases, the load function should implement the LoadMetadata interface (in addition to the LoadFunc interface) so it can supply a schema to the Pig runtime. Note, however, that if a user supplies a schema in the AS clause of LOAD, then it takes precedence over the schema one specified through the LoadMetadata interface.

A load function may additionally implement the LoadPushDown interface as a means for finding out which columns the query is asking for. This can be a useful optimization for column-oriented storage, so that the loader loads only the columns that are needed by the query. There is no obvious way for CutLoadFunc to load only a subset of columns, because it reads the whole line for each tuple, so we don't use this optimization.

Data Processing Operators

Loading and Storing Data

Throughout this chapter, we have seen how to load data from external storage for processing in Pig. Storing the results is straightforward, too. Here's an example of using PigStorage to store tuples as plain-text values separated by a colon character:

```
grunt> STORE A INTO 'out' USING PigStorage(':');
grunt> cat out
Joe:cherry:2
Ali:apple:3
Joe:banana:2
Eve:apple:7
```

Other built-in storage functions were described in Table 11-7.

Filtering Data

Once you have some data loaded into a relation, often the next step is to filter it to remove the data that you are not interested in. By filtering early in the processing pipeline, you minimize the amount of data flowing through the system, which can improve efficiency.

FOREACH...GENERATE

We have already seen how to remove rows from a relation using the FILTER operator with simple expressions and a UDF. The FOREACH...GENERATE operator is used to act on every row in a relation. It can be used to remove fields or to generate new ones. In this example, we do both:

```
grunt> DUMP A;
(Joe,cherry,2)
(Ali,apple,3)
(Joe,banana,2)
(Eve,apple,7)
grunt> B = FOREACH A GENERATE $0, $2+1, 'Constant';
grunt> DUMP B;
(Joe,3,Constant)
(Ali,4,Constant)
(Joe,3,Constant)
(Eve,8,Constant)
```

Here we have created a new relation B with three fields. Its first field is a projection of the first field ($0) of A. B's second field is the third field of A ($2) with one added to it. B's third field is a constant field (every row in B has the same third field) with the chararray value Constant.

The FOREACH...GENERATE operator has a nested form to support more complex processing. In the following example, we compute various statistics for the weather dataset:

```
-- year_stats.pig
REGISTER pig-examples.jar;
DEFINE isGood com.hadoopbook.pig.IsGoodQuality();
records = LOAD 'input/ncdc/all/19{1,2,3,4,5}0*'
  USING com.hadoopbook.pig.CutLoadFunc('5-10,11-15,16-19,88-92,93-93')
  AS (usaf:chararray, wban:chararray, year:int, temperature:int, quality:int);

grouped_records = GROUP records BY year PARALLEL 30;

year_stats = FOREACH grouped_records {
  uniq_stations = DISTINCT records.usaf;
  good_records = FILTER records BY isGood(quality);
  GENERATE FLATTEN(group), COUNT(uniq_stations) AS station_count,
    COUNT(good_records) AS good_record_count, COUNT(records) AS record_count;
}

DUMP year_stats;
```

Using the cut UDF we developed earlier, we load various fields from the input dataset into the records relation. Next, we group records by year. Notice the PARALLEL keyword for setting the number of reducers to use; this is vital when running on a cluster. Then we process each group using a nested FOREACH...GENERATE operator. The first nested statement creates a relation for the distinct USAF identifiers for stations using the DISTINCT operator. The second nested statement creates a relation for the records with "good" readings using the FILTER operator and a UDF. The final nested statement is a GENERATE statement (a nested FOREACH...GENERATE must always have a GENERATE statement as the last nested statement) that generates the summary fields of interest using the grouped records, as well as the relations created in the nested block.

Running it on a few years of data, we get the following:

```
(1920,8L,8595L,8595L)
(1950,1988L,8635452L,8641353L)
(1930,121L,89245L,89262L)
(1910,7L,7650L,7650L)
(1940,732L,1052333L,1052976L)
```

The fields are year, number of unique stations, total number of good readings, and total number of readings. We can see how the number of weather stations and readings grew over time.

STREAM

The STREAM operator allows you to transform data in a relation using an external program or script. It is named by analogy with Hadoop Streaming, which provides a similar capability for MapReduce (see "Hadoop Streaming" on page 36).

STREAM can use built-in commands with arguments. Here is an example that uses the Unix cut command to extract the second field of each tuple in A. Note that the command and its arguments are enclosed in backticks:

```
grunt> C = STREAM A THROUGH `cut -f 2`;
grunt> DUMP C;
(cherry)
(apple)
(banana)
(apple)
```

The STREAM operator uses PigStorage to serialize and deserialize relations to and from the program's standard input and output streams. Tuples in A are converted to tab-delimited lines that are passed to the script. The output of the script is read one line at a time and split on tabs to create new tuples for the output relation C. You can provide a custom serializer and deserializer, which implement PigToStream and StreamToPig, respectively (both in the org.apache.pig package), using the DEFINE operator.

Pig streaming is most powerful when you write custom processing scripts. The following Python script filters out bad weather records:

```
#!/usr/bin/env python

import re
import sys

for line in sys.stdin:
  (year, temp, q) = line.strip().split()
  if (temp != "9999" and re.match("[01459]", q)):
    print "%s\t%s" % (year, temp)
```

To use the script, you need to ship it to the cluster. This is achieved via a DEFINE clause, which also creates an alias for the STREAM command. The STREAM statement can then refer to the alias, as the following Pig script shows:

```
-- max_temp_filter_stream.pig
DEFINE is_good_quality `is_good_quality.py`
  SHIP ('ch11/src/main/python/is_good_quality.py');
records = LOAD 'input/ncdc/micro-tab/sample.txt'
  AS (year:chararray, temperature:int, quality:int);
filtered_records = STREAM records THROUGH is_good_quality
  AS (year:chararray, temperature:int);
grouped_records = GROUP filtered_records BY year;
max_temp = FOREACH grouped_records GENERATE group,
  MAX(filtered_records.temperature);
DUMP max_temp;
```

Grouping and Joining Data

Joining datasets in MapReduce takes some work on the part of the programmer (see "Joins" on page 283), whereas Pig has very good built-in support for join operations, making it much more approachable. Since the large datasets that are suitable for analysis by Pig (and MapReduce in general) are not normalized, joins are used more infrequently in Pig than they are in SQL.

JOIN

Let's look at an example of an inner join. Consider the relations A and B:

```
grunt> DUMP A;
(2,Tie)
(4,Coat)
(3,Hat)
(1,Scarf)
grunt> DUMP B;
(Joe,2)
(Hank,4)
(Ali,0)
(Eve,3)
(Hank,2)
```

We can join the two relations on the numerical (identity) field in each:

```
grunt> C = JOIN A BY $0, B BY $1;
grunt> DUMP C;
```

```
(2,Tie,Joe,2)
(2,Tie,Hank,2)
(3,Hat,Eve,3)
(4,Coat,Hank,4)
```

This is a classic inner join, where each match between the two relations corresponds to a row in the result. (It's actually an equijoin because the join predicate is equality.) The result's fields are made up of all the fields of all the input relations.

You should use the general join operator when all the relations being joined are too large to fit in memory. If one of the relations is small enough to fit in memory, there is a special type of join called a *fragment replicate join*, which is implemented by distributing the small input to all the mappers and performing a map-side join using an in-memory lookup table against the (fragmented) larger relation. There is a special syntax for telling Pig to use a fragment replicate join:[8]

```
grunt> C = JOIN A BY $0, B BY $1 USING "replicated";
```

The first relation must be the large one, followed by one or more small ones (all of which must fit in memory).

Pig also supports outer joins using a syntax that is similar to SQL's (this is covered for Hive in "Outer joins" on page 447). For example:

```
grunt> C = JOIN A BY $0 LEFT OUTER, B BY $1;
grunt> DUMP C;
(1,Scarf,,)
(2,Tie,Joe,2)
(2,Tie,Hank,2)
(3,Hat,Eve,3)
(4,Coat,Hank,4)
```

COGROUP

JOIN always gives a flat structure: a set of tuples. The COGROUP statement is similar to JOIN, but instead creates a nested set of output tuples. This can be useful if you want to exploit the structure in subsequent statements:

```
grunt> D = COGROUP A BY $0, B BY $1;
grunt> DUMP D;
(0,{},{(Ali,0)})
(1,{(1,Scarf)},{})
(2,{(2,Tie)},{(Joe,2),(Hank,2)})
(3,{(3,Hat)},{(Eve,3)})
(4,{(4,Coat)},{(Hank,4)})
```

COGROUP generates a tuple for each unique grouping key. The first field of each tuple is the key, and the remaining fields are bags of tuples from the relations with a matching key. The first bag contains the matching tuples from relation A with the same key.

---

8. There are more keywords that may be used in the USING clause, including "skewed" (for large datasets with a skewed keyspace) and "merge" (to effect a merge join for inputs that are already sorted on the join key). See Pig's documentation for details on how to use these specialized joins.

Similarly, the second bag contains the matching tuples from relation B with the same key.

If for a particular key a relation has no matching key, the bag for that relation is empty. For example, since no one has bought a scarf (with ID 1), the second bag in the tuple for that row is empty. This is an example of an outer join, which is the default type for COGROUP. It can be made explicit using the OUTER keyword, making this COGROUP statement the same as the previous one:

```
D = COGROUP A BY $0 OUTER, B BY $1 OUTER;
```

You can suppress rows with empty bags by using the INNER keyword, which gives the COGROUP inner join semantics. The INNER keyword is applied per relation, so the following suppresses rows only when relation A has no match (dropping the unknown product 0 here):

```
grunt> E = COGROUP A BY $0 INNER, B BY $1;
grunt> DUMP E;
(1,{(1,Scarf)},{})
(2,{(2,Tie)},{(Joe,2),(Hank,2)})
(3,{(3,Hat)},{(Eve,3)})
(4,{(4,Coat)},{(Hank,4)})
```

We can flatten this structure to discover who bought each of the items in relation A:

```
grunt> F = FOREACH E GENERATE FLATTEN(A), B.$0;
grunt> DUMP F;
(1,Scarf,{})
(2,Tie,{(Joe),(Hank)})
(3,Hat,{(Eve)})
(4,Coat,{(Hank)})
```

Using a combination of COGROUP, INNER, and FLATTEN (which removes nesting) it's possible to simulate an (inner) JOIN:

```
grunt> G = COGROUP A BY $0 INNER, B BY $1 INNER;
grunt> H = FOREACH G GENERATE FLATTEN($1), FLATTEN($2);
grunt> DUMP H;
(2,Tie,Joe,2)
(2,Tie,Hank,2)
(3,Hat,Eve,3)
(4,Coat,Hank,4)
```

This gives the same result as JOIN A BY $0, B BY $1.

If the join key is composed of several fields, you can specify them all in the BY clauses of the JOIN or COGROUP statement. Make sure that the number of fields in each BY clause is the same.

Here's another example of a join in Pig, in a script for calculating the maximum temperature for every station over a time period controlled by the input:

```
-- max_temp_station_name.pig
REGISTER pig-examples.jar;
DEFINE isGood com.hadoopbook.pig.IsGoodQuality();
```

```
stations = LOAD 'input/ncdc/metadata/stations-fixed-width.txt'
  USING com.hadoopbook.pig.CutLoadFunc('1-6,8-12,14-42')
  AS (usaf:chararray, wban:chararray, name:chararray);

trimmed_stations = FOREACH stations GENERATE usaf, wban,
  com.hadoopbook.pig.Trim(name);

records = LOAD 'input/ncdc/all/191*'
  USING com.hadoopbook.pig.CutLoadFunc('5-10,11-15,88-92,93-93')
  AS (usaf:chararray, wban:chararray, temperature:int, quality:int);

filtered_records = FILTER records BY temperature != 9999 AND isGood(quality);
grouped_records = GROUP filtered_records BY (usaf, wban) PARALLEL 30;
max_temp = FOREACH grouped_records GENERATE FLATTEN(group),
  MAX(filtered_records.temperature);
max_temp_named = JOIN max_temp BY (usaf, wban), trimmed_stations BY (usaf, wban)
  PARALLEL 30;
max_temp_result = FOREACH max_temp_named GENERATE $0, $1, $5, $2;

STORE max_temp_result INTO 'max_temp_by_station';
```

We use the cut UDF we developed earlier to load one relation holding the station IDs (USAF and WBAN identifiers) and names, and one relation holding all the weather records, keyed by station ID. We group the filtered weather records by station ID and aggregate by maximum temperature before joining with the stations. Finally, we project out the fields we want in the final result: USAF, WBAN, station name, and maximum temperature.

Here are a few results for the 1910s:

```
228020          99999          SORTAVALA       322
029110          99999          VAASA AIRPORT   300
040650          99999          GRIMSEY         378
```

This query could be made more efficient by using a fragment replicate join, as the station metadata is small.

CROSS

Pig Latin includes the cross-product operator (also known as the cartesian product), which joins every tuple in a relation with every tuple in a second relation (and with every tuple in further relations if supplied). The size of the output is the product of the size of the inputs, potentially making the output very large:

```
grunt> I = CROSS A, B;
grunt> DUMP I;
(2,Tie,Joe,2)
(2,Tie,Hank,4)
(2,Tie,Ali,0)
(2,Tie,Eve,3)
(2,Tie,Hank,2)
(4,Coat,Joe,2)
(4,Coat,Hank,4)
```

```
(4,Coat,Ali,0)
(4,Coat,Eve,3)
(4,Coat,Hank,2)
(3,Hat,Joe,2)
(3,Hat,Hank,4)
(3,Hat,Ali,0)
(3,Hat,Eve,3)
(3,Hat,Hank,2)
(1,Scarf,Joe,2)
(1,Scarf,Hank,4)
(1,Scarf,Ali,0)
(1,Scarf,Eve,3)
(1,Scarf,Hank,2)
```

When dealing with large datasets, you should try to avoid operations that generate intermediate representations that are quadratic (or worse) in size. Computing the cross-product of the whole input dataset is rarely needed, if ever.

For example, at first blush one might expect that calculating pairwise document similarity in a corpus of documents would require every document pair to be generated before calculating their similarity. However, if one starts with the insight that most document pairs have a similarity score of zero (that is, they are unrelated), then we can find a way to a better algorithm.

In this case, the key idea is to focus on the entities that we are using to calculate similarity (terms in a document, for example) and make them the center of the algorithm. In practice, we also remove terms that don't help discriminate between documents (stop-words), and this reduces the problem space still further. Using this technique to analyze a set of roughly one million (10^6) documents generates in the order of one billion (10^9) intermediate pairs,[9] rather than the one trillion (10^{12}) produced by the naive approach (generating the cross-product of the input) or the approach with no stopword removal.

GROUP

Although COGROUP groups the data in two or more relations, the GROUP statement groups the data in a single relation. GROUP supports grouping by more than equality of keys: you can use an expression or user-defined function as the group key. For example, consider the following relation A:

```
grunt> DUMP A;
(Joe,cherry)
(Ali,apple)
(Joe,banana)
(Eve,apple)
```

Let's group by the number of characters in the second field:

9. Elsayed, Lin, and Oard. 2008. "Pairwise Document Similarity in Large Collections with MapReduce." *Proceedings of the 46th Annual Meeting of the Association of Computational Linguistics* (ACL 2008): 265-268.

```
grunt> B = GROUP A BY SIZE($1);
grunt> DUMP B;
(5,{(Ali,apple),(Eve,apple)})
(6,{(Joe,cherry),(Joe,banana)})
```

GROUP creates a relation whose first field is the grouping field, which is given the alias group. The second field is a bag containing the grouped fields with the same schema as the original relation (in this case, A).

There are also two special grouping operations: ALL and ANY. ALL groups all the tuples in a relation in a single group, as if the GROUP function were a constant:

```
grunt> C = GROUP A ALL;
grunt> DUMP C;
(all,{(Joe,cherry),(Ali,apple),(Joe,banana),(Eve,apple)})
```

Note that there is no BY in this form of the GROUP statement. The ALL grouping is commonly used to count the number of tuples in a relation, as shown in "Validation and nulls" on page 385.

The ANY keyword is used to group the tuples in a relation randomly, which can be useful for sampling.

Sorting Data

Relations are unordered in Pig. Consider a relation A:

```
grunt> DUMP A;
(2,3)
(1,2)
(2,4)
```

There is no guarantee which order the rows will be processed in. In particular, when retrieving the contents of A using DUMP or STORE, the rows may be written in any order. If you want to impose an order on the output, you can use the ORDER operator to sort a relation by one or more fields. The default sort order compares fields of the same type using the natural ordering, and different types are given an arbitrary, but deterministic, ordering (a tuple is always "less than" a bag, for example).

The following example sorts A by the first field in ascending order and by the second field in descending order:

```
grunt> B = ORDER A BY $0, $1 DESC;
grunt> DUMP B;
(1,2)
(2,4)
(2,3)
```

Any further processing on a sorted relation is not guaranteed to retain its order. For example:

```
grunt> C = FOREACH B GENERATE *;
```

Even though relation C has the same contents as relation B, its tuples may be emitted in any order by a DUMP or a STORE. It is for this reason that it is usual to perform the ORDER operation just before retrieving the output.

The LIMIT statement is useful for limiting the number of results as a quick and dirty way to get a sample of a relation; prototyping (the ILLUSTRATE command) should be preferred for generating more representative samples of the data. It can be used immediately after the ORDER statement to retrieve the first n tuples. Usually, LIMIT will select any n tuples from a relation, but when used immediately after an ORDER statement, the order is retained (in an exception to the rule that processing a relation does not retain its order):

```
grunt> D = LIMIT B 2;
grunt> DUMP D;
(1,2)
(2,4)
```

If the limit is greater than the number of tuples in the relation, all tuples are returned (so LIMIT has no effect).

Using LIMIT can improve the performance of a query because Pig tries to apply the limit as early as possible in the processing pipeline, to minimize the amount of data that needs to be processed. For this reason, you should always use LIMIT if you are not interested in the entire output.

Combining and Splitting Data

Sometimes you have several relations that you would like to combine into one. For this, the UNION statement is used. For example:

```
grunt> DUMP A;
(2,3)
(1,2)
(2,4)
grunt> DUMP B;
(z,x,8)
(w,y,1)
grunt> C = UNION A, B;
grunt> DUMP C;
(2,3)
(1,2)
(2,4)
(z,x,8)
(w,y,1)
```

C is the union of relations A and B, and because relations are unordered, the order of the tuples in C is undefined. Also, it's possible to form the union of two relations with different schemas or with different numbers of fields, as we have done here. Pig attempts to merge the schemas from the relations that UNION is operating on. In this case, they are incompatible, so C has no schema:

```
grunt> DESCRIBE A;
A: {f0: int,f1: int}
grunt> DESCRIBE B;
B: {f0: chararray,f1: chararray,f2: int}
grunt> DESCRIBE C;
Schema for C unknown.
```

If the output relation has no schema, your script needs to be able to handle tuples that vary in the number of fields and/or types.

The SPLIT operator is the opposite of UNION: it partitions a relation into two or more relations. See "Validation and nulls" on page 385 for an example of how to use it.

Pig in Practice

There are some practical techniques that are worth knowing about when you are developing and running Pig programs. This section covers some of them.

Parallelism

When running in MapReduce mode, it's important that the degree of parallelism matches the size of the dataset. By default, Pig will sets the number of reducers by looking at the size of the input and using one reducer per 1 GB of input, up to a maximum of 999 reducers. You can override these parameters by setting `pig.exec.reduc ers.bytes.per.reducer` (the default is 1,000,000,000 bytes) and `pig.exec.reduc ers.max` (the default is 999).

To explicitly set the number of reducers you want for each job, you can use a PARALLEL clause for operators that run in the reduce phase. These include all the grouping and joining operators (GROUP, COGROUP, JOIN, CROSS), as well as DISTINCT and ORDER. The following line sets the number of reducers to 30 for the GROUP:

```
grouped_records = GROUP records BY year PARALLEL 30;
```

Alternatively, you can set the `default_parallel` option, and it will take effect for all subsequent jobs:

```
grunt>
set default_parallel 30
```

A good setting for the number of reduce tasks is slightly fewer than the number of reduce slots in the cluster. See "Choosing the Number of Reducers" on page 231 for further discussion.

The number of map tasks is set by the size of the input (with one map per HDFS block) and is not affected by the PARALLEL clause.

Parameter Substitution

If you have a Pig script that you run on a regular basis, it's quite common to want to be able to run the same script with different parameters. For example, a script that runs daily may use the date to determine which input files it runs over. Pig supports *parameter substitution*, where parameters in the script are substituted with values supplied at runtime. Parameters are denoted by identifiers prefixed with a $ character; for example, $input and $output are used in the following script to specify the input and output paths:

```
-- max_temp_param.pig
records = LOAD '$input' AS (year:chararray, temperature:int, quality:int);
filtered_records = FILTER records BY temperature != 9999 AND
  (quality == 0 OR quality == 1 OR quality == 4 OR quality == 5 OR quality == 9);
grouped_records = GROUP filtered_records BY year;
max_temp = FOREACH grouped_records GENERATE group,
  MAX(filtered_records.temperature);
STORE max_temp into '$output';
```

Parameters can be specified when launching Pig, using the -param option, one for each parameter:

```
% pig -param input=/user/tom/input/ncdc/micro-tab/sample.txt \
>    -param output=/tmp/out \
>    ch11/src/main/pig/max_temp_param.pig
```

You can also put parameters in a file and pass them to Pig using the -param_file option. For example, we can achieve the same result as the previous command by placing the parameter definitions in a file:

```
# Input file
input=/user/tom/input/ncdc/micro-tab/sample.txt
# Output file
output=/tmp/out
```

The *pig* invocation then becomes:

```
% pig -param_file ch11/src/main/pig/max_temp_param.param \
>    ch11/src/main/pig/max_temp_param.pig
```

You can specify multiple parameter files using -param_file repeatedly. You can also use a combination of -param and -param_file options, and if any parameter is defined in both a parameter file and on the command line, the last value on the command line takes precedence.

Dynamic parameters

For parameters that are supplied using the -param option, it is easy to make the value dynamic by running a command or script. Many Unix shells support command substitution for a command enclosed in backticks, and we can use this to make the output directory date-based:

```
% pig -param input=/user/tom/input/ncdc/micro-tab/sample.txt \
>    -param output=/tmp/`date "+%Y-%m-%d"`/out \
>    ch11/src/main/pig/max_temp_param.pig
```

Pig also supports backticks in parameter files by executing the enclosed command in a shell and using the shell output as the substituted value. If the command or scripts exit with a nonzero exit status, then the error message is reported and execution halts. Backtick support in parameter files is a useful feature; it means that parameters can be defined in the same way in a file or on the command line.

Parameter substitution processing

Parameter substitution occurs as a preprocessing step before the script is run. You can see the substitutions that the preprocessor made by executing Pig with the -dryrun option. In dry run mode, Pig performs parameter substitution (and macro expansion) and generates a copy of the original script with substituted values, but does not execute the script. You can inspect the generated script and check that the substitutions look sane (because they are dynamically generated, for example) before running it in normal mode.

At the time of this writing, Grunt does not support parameter substitution.

Hive

In "Information Platforms and the Rise of the Data Scientist,"[1] Jeff Hammerbacher describes Information Platforms as "the locus of their organization's efforts to ingest, process, and generate information," and how they "serve to accelerate the process of learning from empirical data."

One of the biggest ingredients in the Information Platform built by Jeff's team at Facebook was Hive, a framework for data warehousing on top of Hadoop. Hive grew from a need to manage and learn from the huge volumes of data that Facebook was producing every day from its burgeoning social network. After trying a few different systems, the team chose Hadoop for storage and processing, since it was cost-effective and met their scalability needs.[2]

Hive was created to make it possible for analysts with strong SQL skills (but meager Java programming skills) to run queries on the huge volumes of data that Facebook stored in HDFS. Today, Hive is a successful Apache project used by many organizations as a general-purpose, scalable data processing platform.

Of course, SQL isn't ideal for every big data problem—it's not a good fit for building complex machine-learning algorithms, for example—but it's great for many analyses, and it has the huge advantage of being very well known in the industry. What's more, SQL is the *lingua franca* in business intelligence tools (ODBC is a common bridge, for example), so Hive is well placed to integrate with these products.

This chapter is an introduction to using Hive. It assumes that you have working knowledge of SQL and general database architecture; as we go through Hive's features, we'll often compare them to the equivalent in a traditional RDBMS.

1. *Beautiful Data: The Stories Behind Elegant Data Solutions (http://oreilly.com/catalog/9780596157128/)*, by Toby Segaran and Jeff Hammerbacher (O'Reilly, 2009)

2. You can read more about the history of Hadoop at Facebook in "Hadoop and Hive at Facebook" on page 556.

Installing Hive

In normal use, Hive runs on your workstation and converts your SQL query into a series of MapReduce jobs for execution on a Hadoop cluster. Hive organizes data into tables, which provide a means for attaching structure to data stored in HDFS. Metadata—such as table schemas—is stored in a database called the *metastore*.

When starting out with Hive, it is convenient to run the metastore on your local machine. In this configuration, which is the default, the Hive table definitions that you create will be local to your machine, so you can't share them with other users. We'll see how to configure a shared remote metastore, which is the norm in production environments, in "The Metastore" on page 421.

Installation of Hive is straightforward. Java 6 is a prerequisite, and on Windows, you will need Cygwin, too. You also need to have the same version of Hadoop installed locally that your cluster is running.[3] Of course, you may choose to run Hadoop locally, either in standalone or pseudodistributed mode, while getting started with Hive. These options are all covered in Appendix A.

Which Versions of Hadoop Does Hive Work With?

Any given release of Hive is designed to work with multiple versions of Hadoop. Generally, Hive works with the latest stable release of Hadoop, as well as supporting a number of older versions, listed in the release notes. You don't need to do anything special to tell Hive which version of Hadoop you are using, beyond making sure that the *hadoop* executable is on the path or setting the HADOOP_HOME environment variable.

Download a release at *http://hive.apache.org/releases.html*, and unpack the tarball in a suitable place on your workstation:

```
% tar xzf hive-x.y.z.tar.gz
```

It's handy to put Hive on your path to make it easy to launch:

```
% export HIVE_INSTALL=/home/tom/hive-x.y.z-dev
% export PATH=$PATH:$HIVE_INSTALL/bin
```

Now type hive to launch the Hive shell:

```
% hive
hive>
```

---

3. It is assumed that you have network connectivity from your workstation to the Hadoop cluster. You can test this before running Hive by installing Hadoop locally and performing some HDFS operations with the hadoop fs command.

The Hive Shell

The shell is the primary way that we will interact with Hive, by issuing commands in HiveQL. HiveQL is Hive's query language, a dialect of SQL. It is heavily influenced by MySQL, so if you are familiar with MySQL, you should feel at home using Hive.

When starting Hive for the first time, we can check that it is working by listing its tables —there should be none. The command must be terminated with a semicolon to tell Hive to execute it:

```
hive> SHOW TABLES;
OK
Time taken: 10.425 seconds
```

Like SQL, HiveQL is generally case-insensitive (except for string comparisons), so show tables; works equally well here. The Tab key will autocomplete Hive keywords and functions.

For a fresh install, the command takes a few seconds to run as it lazily creates the metastore database on your machine. (The database stores its files in a directory called *metastore_db*, which is relative to the location from which you ran the hive command.)

You can also run the Hive shell in noninteractive mode. The -f option runs the commands in the specified file, which is *script.q* in this example:

```
% hive -f script.q
```

For short scripts, you can use the -e option to specify the commands inline, in which case the final semicolon is not required:

```
% hive -e 'SELECT * FROM dummy'
Hive history file=/tmp/tom/hive_job_log_tom_201005042112_1906486281.txt
OK
X
Time taken: 4.734 seconds
```

 It's useful to have a small table of data to test queries against, such as trying out functions in SELECT expressions using literal data (see "Operators and Functions" on page 428). Here's one way of populating a single-row table:

```
% echo 'X' > /tmp/dummy.txt
% hive -e "CREATE TABLE dummy (value STRING); \
LOAD DATA LOCAL INPATH '/tmp/dummy.txt' \
OVERWRITE INTO TABLE dummy"
```

In both interactive and noninteractive mode, Hive will print information to standard error—such as the time taken to run a query—during the course of operation. You can suppress these messages using the -S option at launch time, which has the effect of showing only the output result for queries:

```
% hive -S -e 'SELECT * FROM dummy'
X
```

Other useful Hive shell features include the ability to run commands on the host operating system by using a ! prefix to the command and the ability to access Hadoop filesystems using the dfs command.

An Example

Let's see how to use Hive to run a query on the weather dataset we explored in earlier chapters. The first step is to load the data into Hive's managed storage. Here we'll have Hive use the local filesystem for storage; later we'll see how to store tables in HDFS.

Just like an RDBMS, Hive organizes its data into tables. We create a table to hold the weather data using the CREATE TABLE statement:

```
CREATE TABLE records (year STRING, temperature INT, quality INT)
ROW FORMAT DELIMITED
   FIELDS TERMINATED BY '\t';
```

The first line declares a records table with three columns: year, temperature, and quality. The type of each column must be specified, too. Here the year is a string, while the other two columns are integers.

So far, the SQL is familiar. The ROW FORMAT clause, however, is particular to HiveQL. This declaration is saying that each row in the data file is tab-delimited text. Hive expects there to be three fields in each row, corresponding to the table columns, with fields separated by tabs and rows by newlines.

Next, we can populate Hive with the data. This is just a small sample, for exploratory purposes:

```
LOAD DATA LOCAL INPATH 'input/ncdc/micro-tab/sample.txt'
OVERWRITE INTO TABLE records;
```

Running this command tells Hive to put the specified local file in its warehouse directory. This is a simple filesystem operation. There is no attempt, for example, to parse the file and store it in an internal database format, because Hive does not mandate any particular file format. Files are stored verbatim; they are not modified by Hive.

In this example, we are storing Hive tables on the local filesystem (fs.default.name is set to its default value of file:///). Tables are stored as directories under Hive's warehouse directory, which is controlled by the hive.metastore.warehouse.dir and defaults to */user/hive/warehouse*.

Thus, the files for the records table are found in the */user/hive/warehouse/records* directory on the local filesystem:

```
% ls /user/hive/warehouse/records/
sample.txt
```

In this case, there is only one file, *sample.txt*, but in general there can be more, and Hive will read all of them when querying the table.

The OVERWRITE keyword in the LOAD DATA statement tells Hive to delete any existing files in the directory for the table. If it is omitted, the new files are simply added to the table's directory (unless they have the same names, in which case they replace the old files).

Now that the data is in Hive, we can run a query against it:

```
hive> SELECT year, MAX(temperature)
    > FROM records
    > WHERE temperature != 9999
    >   AND (quality = 0 OR quality = 1 OR quality = 4 OR quality = 5 OR quality = 9)
    > GROUP BY year;
1949    111
1950    22
```

This SQL query is unremarkable. It is a SELECT statement with a GROUP BY clause for grouping rows into years, which uses the MAX() aggregate function to find the maximum temperature for each year group. But the remarkable thing is that Hive transforms this query into a MapReduce job, which it executes on our behalf, then prints the results to the console. There are some nuances, such as the SQL constructs that Hive supports and the format of the data that we can query—and we explore some of these in this chapter—but it is the ability to execute SQL queries against our raw data that gives Hive its power.

Running Hive

In this section, we look at some more practical aspects of running Hive, including how to set up Hive to run against a Hadoop cluster and a shared metastore. In doing so, we'll see Hive's architecture in some detail.

Configuring Hive

Hive is configured using an XML configuration file like Hadoop's. The file is called *hive-site.xml* and is located in Hive's *conf* directory. This file is where you can set properties that you want to set every time you run Hive. The same directory contains *hive-default.xml*, which documents the properties that Hive exposes and their default values.

You can override the configuration directory that Hive looks for in *hive-site.xml* by passing the --config option to the hive command:

```
% hive --config /Users/tom/dev/hive-conf
```

Note that this option specifies the containing directory, not *hive-site.xml* itself. It can be useful when you have multiple site files—for different clusters, say—that you switch between on a regular basis. Alternatively, you can set the HIVE_CONF_DIR environment variable to the configuration directory for the same effect.

The *hive-site.xml* file is a natural place to put the cluster connection details: you can specify the filesystem and jobtracker using the usual Hadoop properties, `fs.default.name` and `mapred.job.tracker` (see Appendix A for more details on configuring Hadoop). If not set, they default to the local filesystem and the local (in-process) job runner—just like they do in Hadoop—which is very handy when trying out Hive on small trial datasets. Metastore configuration settings (covered in "The Metastore" on page 421) are commonly found in *hive-site.xml*, too.

Hive also permits you to set properties on a per-session basis, by passing the `-hiveconf` option to the `hive` command. For example, the following command sets the cluster (in this case, to a pseudodistributed cluster) for the duration of the session:

```
% hive -hiveconf fs.default.name=localhost -hiveconf mapred.job.tracker=localhost:8021
```

> If you plan to have more than one Hive user sharing a Hadoop cluster, you need to make the directories that Hive uses writable by all users. The following commands will create the directories and set their permissions appropriately:
>
> ```
> % hadoop fs -mkdir /tmp
> % hadoop fs -chmod a+w /tmp
> % hadoop fs -mkdir /user/hive/warehouse
> % hadoop fs -chmod a+w /user/hive/warehouse
> ```
>
> If all users are in the same group, then permissions g+w are sufficient on the warehouse directory.

You can change settings from within a session, too, using the `SET` command. This is useful for changing Hive or MapReduce job settings for a particular query. For example, the following command ensures buckets are populated according to the table definition (see "Buckets" on page 433):

```
hive> SET hive.enforce.bucketing=true;
```

To see the current value of any property, use `SET` with just the property name:

```
hive> SET hive.enforce.bucketing;
hive.enforce.bucketing=true
```

By itself, `SET` will list all the properties (and their values) set by Hive. Note that the list will not include Hadoop defaults, unless they have been explicitly overridden in one of the ways covered in this section. Use `SET -v` to list all the properties in the system, including Hadoop defaults.

There is a precedence hierarchy to setting properties. In the following list, lower numbers take precedence over higher numbers:

1. The Hive `SET` command
2. The command-line `-hiveconf` option
3. *hive-site.xml*
4. *hive-default.xml*

5. *hadoop-site.xml* (or, equivalently, *core-site.xml*, *hdfs-site.xml*, and *mapred-site.xml*)

6. *hadoop-default.xml* (or, equivalently, *core-default.xml*, *hdfs-default.xml*, and *mapred-default.xml*)

Logging

You can find Hive's error log on the local filesystem at */tmp/$USER/hive.log*. It can be very useful when trying to diagnose configuration problems or other types of error. Hadoop's MapReduce task logs are also a useful source for troubleshooting; see "Hadoop Logs" on page 175 for where to find them.

The logging configuration is in *conf/hive-log4j.properties*, and you can edit this file to change log levels and other logging-related settings. However, often it's more convenient to set logging configuration for the session. For example, the following handy invocation will send debug messages to the console:

```
% hive -hiveconf hive.root.logger=DEBUG,console
```

Hive Services

The Hive shell is only one of several services that you can run using the `hive` command. You can specify the service to run using the `--service` option. Type `hive --service help` to get a list of available service names; the most useful are described in the following list.

cli
> The command-line interface to Hive (the shell). This is the default service.

hiveserver
> Runs Hive as a server exposing a Thrift service, enabling access from a range of clients written in different languages. Applications using the Thrift, JDBC, and ODBC connectors need to run a Hive server to communicate with Hive. Set the `HIVE_PORT` environment variable to specify the port the server will listen on (defaults to 10,000).

hwi
> The Hive Web Interface. See "The Hive Web Interface (HWI)" on page 420.

jar
> The Hive equivalent to `hadoop jar`, a convenient way to run Java applications that includes both Hadoop and Hive classes on the classpath.

metastore
> By default, the metastore is run in the same process as the Hive service. Using this service, it is possible to run the metastore as a standalone (remote) process. Set the `METASTORE_PORT` environment variable to specify the port the server will listen on.

Hive clients

If you run Hive as a server (`hive --service hiveserver`), there are a number of different mechanisms for connecting to it from applications. The relationship between Hive clients and Hive services is illustrated in Figure 12-1.

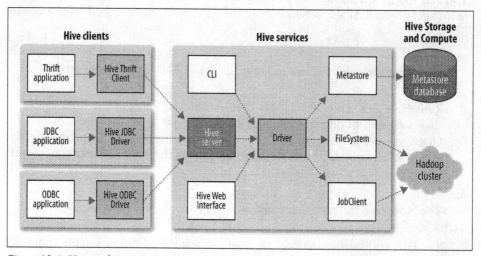

Figure 12-1. Hive architecture

Thrift Client

The Hive Thrift Client makes it easy to run Hive commands from a wide range of programming languages. Thrift bindings for Hive are available for C++, Java, PHP, Python, and Ruby. They can be found in the *src/service/src* subdirectory in the Hive distribution.

JDBC driver

Hive provides a Type 4 (pure Java) JDBC driver, defined in the class `org.apache.hadoop.hive.jdbc.HiveDriver`. When configured with a JDBC URI of the form `jdbc:hive://host:port/dbname`, a Java application will connect to a Hive server running in a separate process at the given host and port. (The driver makes calls to an interface implemented by the Hive Thrift Client using the Java Thrift bindings.)

You may alternatively choose to connect to Hive via JDBC in *embedded mode* using the URI `jdbc:hive://`. In this mode, Hive runs in the same JVM as the application invoking it, so there is no need to launch it as a standalone server, since it does not use the Thrift service or the Hive Thrift Client.

ODBC driver

The Hive ODBC driver allows applications that support the ODBC protocol to connect to Hive. (Like the JDBC driver, the ODBC driver uses Thrift to communicate with the Hive server.) The ODBC driver is still in development, so you should refer to the latest instructions on the Hive wiki for how to build and run it.

There are more details on using these clients on the Hive wiki at *https://cwiki.apache .org/confluence/display/Hive/HiveClient*.

The Metastore

The *metastore* is the central repository of Hive metadata. The metastore is divided into two pieces: a service and the backing store for the data. By default, the metastore service runs in the same JVM as the Hive service and contains an embedded Derby database instance backed by the local disk. This is called the *embedded metastore* configuration (see Figure 12-2).

Using an embedded metastore is a simple way to get started with Hive; however, only one embedded Derby database can access the database files on disk at any one time, which means you can have only one Hive session open at a time that shares the same metastore. Trying to start a second session gives the error:

```
Failed to start database 'metastore_db'
```

when it attempts to open a connection to the metastore.

The solution to supporting multiple sessions (and therefore multiple users) is to use a standalone database. This configuration is referred to as a *local metastore*, since the metastore service still runs in the same process as the Hive service, but connects to a database running in a separate process, either on the same machine or on a remote

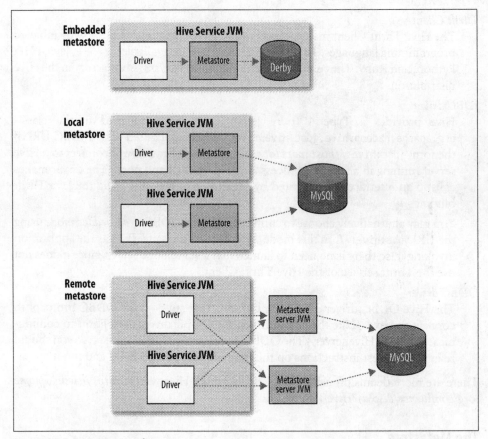

Figure 12-2. Metastore configurations

machine. Any JDBC-compliant database may be used by setting the `javax.jdo.option.*` configuration properties listed in Table 12-1.[4]

MySQL is a popular choice for the standalone metastore. In this case, the `javax.jdo.option.ConnectionURL` is set to `jdbc:mysql://`*host*/*dbname*`?createData baseIfNotExist=true`, and the `javax.jdo.option.ConnectionDriverName` is set to `com.mysql.jdbc.Driver`. (The username and password should be set, too, of course.) The JDBC driver JAR file for MySQL (Connector/J) must be on Hive's classpath, which is simply achieved by placing it in Hive's *lib* directory.

Going a step further, there's another metastore configuration called a *remote metastore*, where one or more metastore servers run in separate processes to the Hive service.

---

4. The properties have the `javax.jdo` prefix because the metastore implementation uses the Java Data Objects (JDO) API for persisting Java objects. Specifically, it uses the DataNucleus implementation of JDO.

This brings better manageability and security because the database tier can be completely firewalled off, and the clients no longer need the database credentials.

A Hive service is configured to use a remote metastore by setting `hive.meta store.local` to `false` and `hive.metastore.uris` to the metastore server URIs, separated by commas if there is more than one. Metastore server URIs are of the form `thrift://host:port`, where the port corresponds to the one set by `METASTORE_PORT` when starting the metastore server (see "Hive Services" on page 419).

Table 12-1. Important metastore configuration properties

Property name	Type	Default value	Description
hive.metastore.warehouse.dir	URI	/user/hive/warehouse	The directory relative to fs.default.name where managed tables are stored.
hive.metastore.local	boolean	true	Whether to use an embedded metastore server (true) or connect to a remote instance (false). If false, then hive.metastore.uris must be set.
hive.metastore.uris	Comma-separated URIs	Not set	The URIs specifying the remote metastore servers to connect to. Clients connect in a round-robin fashion when there are multiple remote servers.
javax.jdo.option.ConnectionURL	URI	jdbc:derby:;databaseName=metastore_db;create=true	The JDBC URL of the metastore database.
javax.jdo.option.ConnectionDriverName	String	org.apache.derby.jdbc.EmbeddedDriver	The JDBC driver classname.
javax.jdo.option.ConnectionUserName	String	APP	The JDBC username.
javax.jdo.option.ConnectionPassword	String	mine	The JDBC password.

Comparison with Traditional Databases

Although Hive resembles a traditional database in many ways (such as supporting an SQL interface), its HDFS and MapReduce underpinnings mean that there are a number of architectural differences that directly influence the features that Hive supports, which in turn affects the uses that Hive can be put to.

Schema on Read Versus Schema on Write

In a traditional database, a table's schema is enforced at data load time. If the data being loaded doesn't conform to the schema, then it is rejected. This design is sometimes called *schema on write* because the data is checked against the schema when it is written into the database.

Hive, on the other hand, doesn't verify the data when it is loaded, but rather when a query is issued. This is called *schema on read*.

There are trade-offs between the two approaches. Schema on read makes for a very fast initial load, since the data does not have to be read, parsed, and serialized to disk in the database's internal format. The load operation is just a file copy or move. It is more flexible, too: consider having two schemas for the same underlying data, depending on the analysis being performed. (This is possible in Hive using external tables; see "Managed Tables and External Tables" on page 429.)

Schema on write makes query time performance faster because the database can index columns and perform compression on the data. The trade-off, however, is that it takes longer to load data into the database. Furthermore, there are many scenarios where the schema is not known at load time, so there are no indexes to apply, because the queries have not been formulated yet. These scenarios are where Hive shines.

Updates, Transactions, and Indexes

Updates, transactions, and indexes are mainstays of traditional databases. Yet, until recently, these features have not been considered a part of Hive's feature set. This is because Hive was built to operate over HDFS data using MapReduce, where full-table scans are the norm and a table update is achieved by transforming the data into a new table. For a data warehousing application that runs over large portions of the dataset, this works well.

Hive doesn't support updates (or deletes), but it does support INSERT INTO, so it is possible to add new rows to an existing table.

With release 0.7.0, Hive introduced indexes, which can speed up queries in certain cases. A query such as SELECT * from t WHERE x = a, for example, can take advantage of an index on column x, since only a small portion of the table's files need to be scanned. There are currently two index types: *compact* and *bitmap*. (The index implementation was designed to be pluggable, so it's expected that a variety of implementations will emerge for different use cases.)

Compact indexes store the HDFS block numbers of each value, rather than each file offset, so they don't take up much disk space but are still effective for the case where values are clustered together in nearby rows. Bitmap indexes use compressed bitsets to efficiently store the rows that a particular value appears in, and they are usually appropriate for low-cardinality columns (such as gender or country).

Release 0.7.0 also saw the introduction of table- and partition-level locking in Hive. Locks prevent, for example, one process from dropping a table while another is reading from it. Locks are managed transparently using ZooKeeper, so the user doesn't have to acquire or release them, although it is possible to get information about which locks are being held via the SHOW LOCKS statement. By default, locks are not enabled.

Change is also coming from another direction: HBase integration. HBase (Chapter 13) has different storage characteristics than HDFS, such as the ability to do row updates and column indexing, so we can expect to see these features used by Hive in future releases. It is already possible to access HBase tables from Hive; you can find out more at *https://cwiki.apache.org/confluence/display/Hive/HBaseIntegration*.

HiveQL

Hive's SQL dialect, called HiveQL, does not support the full SQL-92 specification, since SQL-92 compliance has never been an explicit project goal. Rather, as an open source project, features are added by developers to meet their users' needs, resulting in that Hive's SQL support becoming richer over time. Furthermore, Hive has some extensions that are not in SQL-92, inspired by syntax from other database systems, notably MySQL. In fact, to a first-order approximation, HiveQL most closely resembles MySQL's SQL dialect.

Some of Hive's extensions to SQL-92 were inspired by MapReduce, such as multitable inserts (see "Multitable insert" on page 442) and the TRANSFORM, MAP, and REDUCE clauses (see "MapReduce Scripts" on page 445).

This chapter does not provide a complete reference to HiveQL; for that, see the Hive documentation at *https://cwiki.apache.org/confluence/display/Hive/LanguageManual*. Instead, we focus on commonly used features and pay particular attention to features that diverge from either SQL-92 or popular databases such as MySQL. Table 12-2 provides a high-level comparison of SQL and HiveQL.

Table 12-2. A high-level comparison of SQL and HiveQL

Feature	SQL	HiveQL	References
Updates	UPDATE, INSERT, DELETE	INSERT	"Inserts" on page 441; "Updates, Transactions, and Indexes" on page 424
Transactions	Supported	Supported (table- and partition-level)	
Indexes	Supported	Supported	
Latency	Sub-second	Minutes	
Data types	Integral, floating-point, fixed-point, text and binary strings, temporal	Integral, floating-point, Boolean, text and binary strings, timestamp, array, map, struct	"Data Types" on page 426
Functions	Hundreds of built-in functions	Dozens of built-in functions	"Operators and Functions" on page 428
Multitable inserts	Not supported	Supported	"Multitable insert" on page 442

Feature	SQL	HiveQL	References
Create table as select	Not valid SQL-92, but found in some databases	Supported	"CREATE TABLE...AS SELECT" on page 442
Select	SQL-92	Single table or view in the FROM clause; SORT BY for partial ordering. LIMIT to limit number of rows returned	"Querying Data" on page 444
Joins	SQL-92 or variants (join tables in the FROM clause, join condition in the WHERE clause)	Inner joins, outer joins; semi joins, map joins (SQL-92 syntax, with hinting)	"Joins" on page 446
Subqueries	In any clause (correlated or noncorrelated)	Only in the FROM clause (correlated subqueries not supported)	"Subqueries" on page 449
Views	Updatable (materialized or nonmaterialized)	Read-only (materialized views not supported)	"Views" on page 450
Extension points	User-defined functions. Stored procedures.	User-defined functions, MapReduce scripts.	"User-Defined Functions" on page 451; "MapReduce Scripts" on page 445

Data Types

Hive supports both primitive and complex data types. Primitives include numeric, Boolean, string, and timestamp types. The complex data types include arrays, maps, and structs. Hive's data types are listed in Table 12-3. Note that the literals shown are those used from within HiveQL; they are not the serialized form used in the table's storage format (see "Storage Formats" on page 435).

Table 12-3. Hive data types

Category	Type	Description	Literal examples
Primitive	TINYINT	1-byte (8-bit) signed integer, from -128 to 127	1
	SMALLINT	2-byte (16-bit) signed integer, from -32,768 to 32,767	1
	INT	4-byte (32-bit) signed integer, from -2,147,483,648 to 2,147,483,647	1
	BIGINT	8-byte (64-bit) signed integer, from -9,223,372,036,854,775,808 to 9,223,372,036,854,775,807	1
	FLOAT	4-byte (32-bit) single-precision floating-point number	1.0
	DOUBLE	8-byte (64-bit) double-precision floating-point number	1.0

Category	Type	Description	Literal examples
	BOOLEAN	true/false value	TRUE
	STRING	Character string	'a', "a"
	BINARY	Byte array	Not supported
	TIMESTAMP	Timestamp with nanosecond precision	1325502245000, '2012-01-02 03:04:05.123456789'
Complex	ARRAY	An ordered collection of fields. The fields must all be of the same type.	array(1, 2) [a]
	MAP	An unordered collection of key-value pairs. Keys must be primitives; values may be any type. For a particular map, the keys must be the same type, and the values must be the same type.	map('a', 1, 'b', 2)
	STRUCT	A collection of named fields. The fields may be of different types.	struct('a', 1, 1.0) [b]

[a] The literal forms for arrays, maps, and structs are provided as functions. That is, array(), map(), and struct() are built-in Hive functions.

[b] The columns are named col1, col2, col3, etc.

Primitive types

Hive's primitive types correspond roughly to Java's, although some names are influenced by MySQL's type names (some of which, in turn, overlap with SQL-92). There are four signed integral types: TINYINT, SMALLINT, INT, and BIGINT, which are equivalent to Java's byte, short, int, and long primitive types, respectively; they are 1-byte, 2-byte, 4-byte, and 8-byte signed integers.

Hive's floating-point types, FLOAT and DOUBLE, correspond to Java's float and double, which are 32-bit and 64-bit floating point numbers. Unlike some databases, there is no option to control the number of significant digits or decimal places stored for floating-point values.

Hive supports a BOOLEAN type for storing true and false values.

There is a single Hive data type for storing text, STRING, which is a variable-length character string. Hive's STRING type is like VARCHAR in other databases, although there is no declaration of the maximum number of characters to store with STRING. (The theoretical maximum-size STRING that may be stored is 2GB, although in practice it may be inefficient to materialize such large values. Sqoop has large object support; see "Importing Large Objects" on page 540.)

The BINARY data type is for storing variable-length binary data.

The TIMESTAMP data type stores timestamps with nanosecond precision. Hive comes with UDFs for converting between Hive timestamps, Unix timestamps (seconds since the Unix epoch), and strings, which makes most common date operations tractable.

TIMESTAMP does not encapsulate a timezone; however, the `to_utc_timestamp` and `from_utc_timestamp` functions make it possible to do timezone conversions.

Complex types

Hive has three complex types: ARRAY, MAP, and STRUCT. ARRAY and MAP are like their namesakes in Java, whereas a STRUCT is a record type that encapsulates a set of named fields. Complex types permit an arbitrary level of nesting. Complex type declarations must specify the type of the fields in the collection, using an angled bracket notation, as illustrated in this table definition with three columns, one for each complex type:

```
CREATE TABLE complex (
  col1 ARRAY<INT>,
  col2 MAP<STRING, INT>,
  col3 STRUCT<a:STRING, b:INT, c:DOUBLE>
);
```

If we load the table with one row of data for ARRAY, MAP, and STRUCT as shown in the "Literal examples" column in Table 12-3 (we'll see the file format needed to do this in "Storage Formats" on page 435), the following query demonstrates the field accessor operators for each type:

```
hive> SELECT col1[0], col2['b'], col3.c FROM complex;
1       2      1.0
```

Operators and Functions

The usual set of SQL operators is provided by Hive: relational operators (such as `x = 'a'` for testing equality, `x IS NULL` for testing nullity and `x LIKE 'a%'` for pattern matching), arithmetic operators (such as `x + 1` for addition), and logical operators (such as `x OR y` for logical OR). The operators match those in MySQL, which deviates from SQL-92 because || is logical OR, not string concatenation. Use the `concat` function for the latter in both MySQL and Hive.

Hive comes with a large number of built-in functions—too many to list here—divided into categories that include mathematical and statistical functions, string functions, date functions (for operating on string representations of dates), conditional functions, aggregate functions, and functions for working with XML (using the `xpath` function) and JSON.

You can retrieve a list of functions from the Hive shell by typing SHOW FUNCTIONS.[5] To get brief usage instructions for a particular function, use the DESCRIBE command:

```
hive> DESCRIBE FUNCTION length;
length(str | binary) - Returns the length of str or number of bytes in binary data
```

---

5. Or see the Hive function reference at *https://cwiki.apache.org/confluence/display/Hive/LanguageManual +UDF*.

In the case when there is no built-in function that does what you want, you can write your own; see "User-Defined Functions" on page 451.

Conversions

Primitive types form a hierarchy that dictates the implicit type conversions Hive will perform in function and operator expressions. For example, a TINYINT will be converted to an INT if an expression expects an INT; however, the reverse conversion will not occur, and Hive will return an error unless the CAST operator is used.

The implicit conversion rules can be summarized as follows. Any integral numeric type can be implicitly converted to a wider type. All the integral numeric types, FLOAT, and (perhaps surprisingly) STRING can be implicitly converted to DOUBLE. TINYINT, SMALL INT, and INT can all be converted to FLOAT. BOOLEAN types cannot be converted to any other type, and they cannot be implicitly converted to any other type in expressions. TIMESTAMP can be implicitly converted to STRING.

You can perform explicit type conversion using CAST. For example, CAST('1' AS INT) will convert the string '1' to the integer value 1. If the cast fails—as it does in CAST('X' AS INT), for example—the expression returns NULL.

Tables

A Hive table is logically made up of the data being stored and the associated metadata describing the layout of the data in the table. The data typically resides in HDFS, although it may reside in any Hadoop filesystem, including the local filesystem or S3. Hive stores the metadata in a relational database—and not in HDFS, say (see "The Metastore" on page 421).

In this section, we look in more detail at how to create tables, the different physical storage formats that Hive offers, and how to import data into them.

Multiple Database/Schema Support

Many relational databases have a facility for multiple namespaces, which allow users and applications to be segregated into different databases or schemas. Hive supports the same facility and provides commands such as CREATE DATABASE *dbname*, USE *dbname*, and DROP DATABASE *dbname*. You can fully qualify a table by writing *dbname.tablename*. If no database is specified, tables belong to the default database.

Managed Tables and External Tables

When you create a table in Hive, by default Hive will manage the data, which means that Hive moves the data into its warehouse directory. Alternatively, you may create an *external table*, which tells Hive to refer to the data that is at an existing location outside the warehouse directory.

The difference between the two table types is seen in the LOAD and DROP semantics. Let's consider a managed table first.

When you load data into a managed table, it is moved into Hive's warehouse directory. For example:

```
CREATE TABLE managed_table (dummy STRING);
LOAD DATA INPATH '/user/tom/data.txt' INTO table managed_table;
```

will *move* the file *hdfs://user/tom/data.txt* into Hive's warehouse directory for the managed_table table, which is *hdfs://user/hive/warehouse/managed_table*.[6]

> The load operation is very fast because it is just a move or rename within a filesystem. However, bear in mind that Hive does not check that the files in the table directory conform to the schema declared for the table, even for managed tables. If there is a mismatch, this will become apparent at query time, often by the query returning NULL for a missing field. You can check that the data is being parsed correctly by issuing a simple SELECT statement to retrieve a few rows directly from the table.

If the table is later dropped, using:

```
DROP TABLE managed_table;
```

the table, including its metadata *and its data*, is deleted. It bears repeating that since the initial LOAD performed a move operation, and the DROP performed a delete operation, the data no longer exists anywhere. This is what it means for Hive to manage the data.

An external table behaves differently. You control the creation and deletion of the data. The location of the external data is specified at table creation time:

```
CREATE EXTERNAL TABLE external_table (dummy STRING)
    LOCATION '/user/tom/external_table';
LOAD DATA INPATH '/user/tom/data.txt' INTO TABLE external_table;
```

With the EXTERNAL keyword, Hive knows that it is not managing the data, so it doesn't move it to its warehouse directory. Indeed, it doesn't even check whether the external location exists at the time it is defined. This is a useful feature because it means you can create the data lazily after creating the table.

When you drop an external table, Hive will leave the data untouched and only delete the metadata.

---

6. The move will succeed only if the source and target filesystems are the same. Also, there is a special case when the LOCAL keyword is used, where Hive will *copy* the data from the local filesystem into Hive's warehouse directory (even if it, too, is on the same local filesystem). In all other cases, though, LOAD is a move operation and is best thought of as such.

So how do you choose which type of table to use? In most cases, there is not much difference between the two (except of course for the difference in DROP semantics), so it is a just a matter of preference. As a rule of thumb, if you are doing all your processing with Hive, then use managed tables, but if you wish to use Hive and other tools on the same dataset, then use external tables. A common pattern is to use an external table to access an initial dataset stored in HDFS (created by another process), then use a Hive transform to move the data into a managed Hive table. This works the other way around, too; an external table (not necessarily on HDFS) can be used to export data from Hive for other applications to use.[7]

Another reason for using external tables is when you wish to associate multiple schemas with the same dataset.

Partitions and Buckets

Hive organizes tables into *partitions*, a way of dividing a table into coarse-grained parts based on the value of a *partition column*, such as a date. Using partitions can make it faster to do queries on slices of the data.

Tables or partitions may be subdivided further into *buckets* to give extra structure to the data that may be used for more efficient queries. For example, bucketing by user ID means we can quickly evaluate a user-based query by running it on a randomized sample of the total set of users.

Partitions

To take an example where partitions are commonly used, imagine logfiles where each record includes a timestamp. If we partitioned by date, then records for the same date would be stored in the same partition. The advantage to this scheme is that queries that are restricted to a particular date or set of dates can be answered much more efficiently because they only need to scan the files in the partitions that the query pertains to. Notice that partitioning doesn't preclude more wide-ranging queries: it is still feasible to query the entire dataset across many partitions.

A table may be partitioned in multiple dimensions. For example, in addition to partitioning logs by date, we might also *subpartition* each date partition by country to permit efficient queries by location.

Partitions are defined at table creation time using the PARTITIONED BY clause,[8] which takes a list of column definitions. For the hypothetical logfiles example, we might define a table with records comprising a timestamp and the log line itself:

---

7. You can also use INSERT OVERWRITE DIRECTORY to export data to a Hadoop filesystem, but unlike external tables, you cannot control the output format, which is Control-A-separated text files. Complex data types are serialized using a JSON representation.

8. However, partitions may be added to or removed from a table after creation using an ALTER TABLE statement.

```
CREATE TABLE logs (ts BIGINT, line STRING)
PARTITIONED BY (dt STRING, country STRING);
```

When we load data into a partitioned table, the partition values are specified explicitly:

```
LOAD DATA LOCAL INPATH 'input/hive/partitions/file1'
INTO TABLE logs
PARTITION (dt='2001-01-01', country='GB');
```

At the filesystem level, partitions are simply nested subdirectories of the table directory. After loading a few more files into the logs table, the directory structure might look like this:

```
/user/hive/warehouse/logs
├── dt=2001-01-01/
│   ├── country=GB/
│   │   ├── file1
│   │   └── file2
│   └── country=US/
│       └── file3
└── dt=2001-01-02/
    ├── country=GB/
    │   └── file4
    └── country=US/
        ├── file5
        └── file6
```

The logs table has two date partitions, 2001-01-01 and 2001-01-02, corresponding to subdirectories called *dt=2001-01-01* and *dt=2001-01-02*; and two country subpartitions, GB and US, corresponding to nested subdirectories called *country=GB* and *country=US*. The datafiles reside in the leaf directories.

We can ask Hive for the partitions in a table using SHOW PARTITIONS:

```
hive> SHOW PARTITIONS logs;
dt=2001-01-01/country=GB
dt=2001-01-01/country=US
dt=2001-01-02/country=GB
dt=2001-01-02/country=US
```

One thing to bear in mind is that the column definitions in the PARTITIONED BY clause are full-fledged table columns, called partition columns; however, the datafiles do not contain values for these columns, since they are derived from the directory names.

You can use partition columns in SELECT statements in the usual way. Hive performs *input pruning* to scan only the relevant partitions. For example:

```
SELECT ts, dt, line
FROM logs
WHERE country='GB';
```

will only scan *file1*, *file2*, and *file4*. Notice, too, that the query returns the values of the dt partition column, which Hive reads from the directory names since they are not in the datafiles.

Buckets

There are two reasons why you might want to organize your tables (or partitions) into buckets. The first is to enable more efficient queries. Bucketing imposes extra structure on the table, which Hive can take advantage of when performing certain queries. In particular, a join of two tables that are bucketed on the same columns—which include the join columns—can be efficiently implemented as a map-side join.

The second reason to bucket a table is to make sampling more efficient. When working with large datasets, it is very convenient to try out queries on a fraction of your dataset while you are in the process of developing or refining them. We will see how to do efficient sampling at this end of this section.

First, let's see how to tell Hive that a table should be bucketed. We use the CLUSTERED BY clause to specify the columns to bucket on and the number of buckets:

```
CREATE TABLE bucketed_users (id INT, name STRING)
CLUSTERED BY (id) INTO 4 BUCKETS;
```

Here we are using the user ID to determine the bucket (which Hive does by hashing the value and reducing modulo the number of buckets), so any particular bucket will effectively have a random set of users in it.

In the map-side join case, where the two tables are bucketed in the same way, a mapper processing a bucket of the left table knows that the matching rows in the right table are in its corresponding bucket, so it need only retrieve that bucket (which is a small fraction of all the data stored in the right table) to effect the join. This optimization also works when the number of buckets in the two tables are multiples of each other; they do not have to have exactly the same number of buckets. The HiveQL for joining two bucketed tables is shown in "Map joins" on page 449.

The data within a bucket may additionally be sorted by one or more columns. This allows even more efficient map-side joins, since the join of each bucket becomes an efficient merge-sort. The syntax for declaring that a table has sorted buckets is:

```
CREATE TABLE bucketed_users (id INT, name STRING)
CLUSTERED BY (id) SORTED BY (id ASC) INTO 4 BUCKETS;
```

How can we make sure the data in our table is bucketed? Although it's possible to load data generated outside Hive into a bucketed table, it's often easier to get Hive to do the bucketing, usually from an existing table.

Hive does not check that the buckets in the datafiles on disk are consistent with the buckets in the table definition (either in number or on the basis of bucketing columns). If there is a mismatch, you may get an error or undefined behavior at query time. For this reason, it is advisable to get Hive to perform the bucketing.

Take an unbucketed users table:

```
hive> SELECT * FROM users;
0    Nat
2    Joe
3    Kay
4    Ann
```

To populate the bucketed table, we need to set the hive.enforce.bucketing property to true so that Hive knows to create the number of buckets declared in the table definition. Then it is a matter of just using the INSERT command:

```
INSERT OVERWRITE TABLE bucketed_users
SELECT * FROM users;
```

Physically, each bucket is just a file in the table (or partition) directory. The filename is not important, but bucket *n* is the *n*th file when arranged in lexicographic order. In fact, buckets correspond to MapReduce output file partitions: a job will produce as many buckets (output files) as reduce tasks. We can see this by looking at the layout of the bucketed_users table we just created. Running this command:

```
hive> dfs -ls /user/hive/warehouse/bucketed_users;
```

shows that four files were created, with the following names (the name is generated by Hive):

```
000000_0
000001_0
000002_0
000003_0
```

The first bucket contains the users with IDs 0 and 4, since for an INT the hash is the integer itself, and the value is reduced modulo the number of buckets—4 in this case:[9]

```
hive> dfs -cat /user/hive/warehouse/bucketed_users/000000_0;
0Nat
4Ann
```

We can see the same thing by sampling the table using the TABLESAMPLE clause, which restricts the query to a fraction of the buckets in the table rather than the whole table:

```
hive> SELECT * FROM bucketed_users
    > TABLESAMPLE(BUCKET 1 OUT OF 4 ON id);
0    Nat
4    Ann
```

9. The fields appear to run together when displaying the raw file because the separator character in the output is a nonprinting control character. The control characters used are explained in the next section.

Bucket numbering is 1-based, so this query retrieves all the users from the first of four buckets. For a large, evenly distributed dataset, approximately one quarter of the table's rows would be returned. It's possible to sample a number of buckets by specifying a different proportion (which need not be an exact multiple of the number of buckets, as sampling is not intended to be a precise operation). For example, this query returns half of the buckets:

```
hive> SELECT * FROM bucketed_users
    > TABLESAMPLE(BUCKET 1 OUT OF 2 ON id);
0    Nat
4    Ann
2    Joe
```

Sampling a bucketed table is very efficient because the query only has to read the buckets that match the TABLESAMPLE clause. Contrast this with sampling a nonbucketed table using the rand() function, where the whole input dataset is scanned, even if only a very small sample is needed:

```
hive> SELECT * FROM users
    > TABLESAMPLE(BUCKET 1 OUT OF 4 ON rand());
2    Joe
```

Storage Formats

There are two dimensions that govern table storage in Hive: the *row format* and the *file format*. The row format dictates how rows, and the fields in a particular row, are stored. In Hive parlance, the row format is defined by a *SerDe*, a portmanteau word for a *Serializer-Deserializer*.

When acting as a deserializer, which is the case when querying a table, a SerDe will deserialize a row of data from the bytes in the file to objects used internally by Hive to operate on that row of data. When used as a serializer, which is the case when performing an INSERT or CTAS (see "Importing Data" on page 441), the table's SerDe will serialize Hive's internal representation of a row of data into the bytes that are written to the output file.

The file format dictates the container format for fields in a row. The simplest format is a plain-text file, but there are row-oriented and column-oriented binary formats available, too.

The default storage format: Delimited text

When you create a table with no ROW FORMAT or STORED AS clauses, the default format is delimited text with one row per line.

The default row delimiter is not a tab character, but the Control-A character from the set of ASCII control codes (it has ASCII code 1). The choice of Control-A, sometimes written as ^A in documentation, came about because it is less likely to be a part of the field text than a tab character. There is no means for escaping delimiter characters in Hive, so it is important to choose ones that don't occur in data fields.

The default collection item delimiter is a Control-B character, used to delimit items in an ARRAY or STRUCT, or in key-value pairs in a MAP. The default map key delimiter is a Control-C character, used to delimit the key and value in a MAP. Rows in a table are delimited by a newline character.

The preceding description of delimiters is correct for the usual case of flat data structures, where the complex types contain only primitive types. For nested types, however, this isn't the whole story, and in fact the *level* of the nesting determines the delimiter.

For an array of arrays, for example, the delimiters for the outer array are Control-B characters, as expected, but for the inner array they are Control-C characters, the next delimiter in the list. If you are unsure which delimiters Hive uses for a particular nested structure, you can run a command like:

```
CREATE TABLE nested
AS
SELECT array(array(1, 2), array(3, 4))
FROM dummy;
```

and then use hexdump or something similar to examine the delimiters in the output file.

Hive actually supports eight levels of delimiters, corresponding to ASCII codes 1, 2, ... 8, but you can override only the first three.

Thus, the statement:

```
CREATE TABLE ...;
```

is identical to the more explicit:

```
CREATE TABLE ...
ROW FORMAT DELIMITED
  FIELDS TERMINATED BY '\001'
  COLLECTION ITEMS TERMINATED BY '\002'
  MAP KEYS TERMINATED BY '\003'
  LINES TERMINATED BY '\n'
STORED AS TEXTFILE;
```

Notice that the octal form of the delimiter characters can be used—001 for Control-A, for instance.

Internally, Hive uses a SerDe called LazySimpleSerDe for this delimited format, along with the line-oriented MapReduce text input and output formats we saw in Chapter 7. The "lazy" prefix comes about because it deserializes fields lazily—only as they are accessed. However, it is not a compact format because fields are stored in a verbose textual format, so a Boolean value, for instance, is written as the literal string true or false.

The simplicity of the format has a lot going for it, such as making it easy to process with other tools, including MapReduce programs or Streaming, but there are more compact and performant binary SerDes that you might consider using. Some are listed in Table 12-4.

 Binary SerDes should not be used with the default TEXTFILE format (nor explicitly using a STORED AS TEXTFILE clause). There is always the possibility that a binary row will contain a newline character, which would cause Hive to truncate the row and fail at deserialization time.

Table 12-4. Hive SerDes

SerDe name	Java package	Description
LazySimpleSerDe	org.apache.hadoop.hive.serde2.lazy	The default SerDe. Delimited textual format, with lazy field access.
LazyBinarySerDe	org.apache.hadoop.hive.serde2.lazybinary	A more efficient version of LazySimple SerDe. Binary format with lazy field access. Used internally for such things as temporary tables.
BinarySortableSerDe	org.apache.hadoop.hive.serde2.binarysortable	A binary SerDe like LazyBinarySerDe, but optimized for sorting at the expense of compactness (although it is still significantly more compact than LazySimpleSerDe).
ColumnarSerDe	org.apache.hadoop.hive.serde2.columnar	A variant of LazySimpleSerDe for column-based storage with RCFile.
RegexSerDe	org.apache.hadoop.hive.contrib.serde2	A SerDe for reading textual data where columns are specified by a regular expression. Also writes data using a formatting expression. Useful for reading logfiles, but inefficient, so not suitable for general-purpose storage.
ThriftByteStreamTypedSerDe	org.apache.hadoop.hive.serde2.thrift	A SerDe for reading Thrift-encoded binary data.
HBaseSerDe	org.apache.hadoop.hive.hbase	A SerDe for storing data in an HBase table. HBase storage uses a Hive storage handler, which unifies (and generalizes) the roles of row format and file format. Storage handlers are specified using a STORED BY clause, which replaces the ROW FORMAT and STORED AS clauses. See *https://cwiki.apache.org/confluence/display/Hive/HBaseIntegration*.

Binary storage formats: Sequence files, Avro datafiles and RCFiles

Hadoop's sequence file format (see "SequenceFile" on page 130) is a general-purpose binary format for sequences of records (key-value pairs). You can use sequence files in Hive by using the declaration `STORED AS SEQUENCEFILE` in the `CREATE TABLE` statement.

One of the main benefits of using sequence files is their support for splittable compression. If you have a collection of sequence files that were created outside Hive, then Hive will read them with no extra configuration. If, on the other hand, you want tables populated from Hive to use compressed sequence files for their storage, you need to set a few properties to enable compression (see "Using Compression in MapReduce" on page 90):

```
hive> CREATE TABLE compressed_users (id INT, name STRING)
    > STORED AS SEQUENCEFILE;
hive> SET hive.exec.compress.output=true;
hive> SET mapred.output.compress=true;
hive> SET mapred.output.compression.codec=org.apache.hadoop.io.compress.GzipCodec;
hive> INSERT OVERWRITE TABLE compressed_users
    > SELECT * FROM users;
```

Sequence files are row-oriented. This means that the fields in each row are stored together as the contents of a single sequence-file record.

Avro datafiles are like sequence files (splittable, compressible, row-oriented), except they have support for schema evolution and bindings in multiple languages (see "Avro" on page 110). Hive can read and write Avro datafiles using the *Haivvreo* SerDe, available from *https://github.com/jghoman/haivvreo*.

Hive provides another binary storage format called *RCFile*, short for *Record Columnar File*. RCFiles are similar to sequence files, except that they store data in a column-oriented fashion. RCFile breaks up the table into row splits, then within each split stores the values for each row in the first column, followed by the values for each row in the second column, and so on. This is shown diagrammatically in Figure 12-3.

A column-oriented layout permits columns that are not accessed in a query to be skipped. Consider a query of the table in Figure 12-3 that processes only column 2. With row-oriented storage, like a sequence file, the whole row (stored in a sequence file record) is loaded into memory, even though only the second column is actually read. Lazy deserialization saves some processing cycles by deserializing only the column fields that are accessed, but it can't avoid the cost of reading each row's bytes from disk.

With column-oriented storage, only the column 2 parts of the file (shaded in the figure) need to be read into memory.

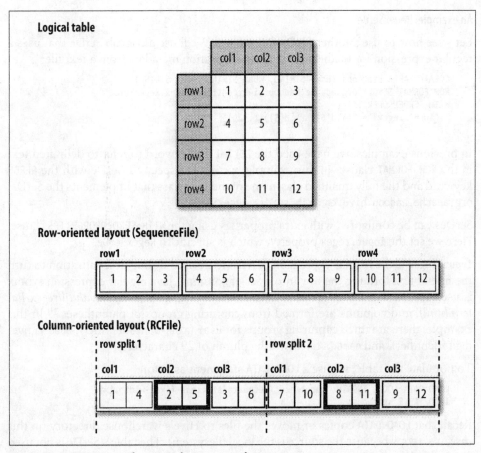

Logical table

	col1	col2	col3
row1	1	2	3
row2	4	5	6
row3	7	8	9
row4	10	11	12

Row-oriented layout (SequenceFile)

row1			row2			row3			row4		
1	2	3	4	5	6	7	8	9	10	11	12

Column-oriented layout (RCFile)

row split 1 / row split 2

col1 | col2 | col3 | col1 | col2 | col3

| 1 | 4 | 2 | 5 | 3 | 6 | 7 | 10 | 8 | 11 | 9 | 12 |

Figure 12-3. Row-oriented versus column-oriented storage

In general, column-oriented formats work well when queries access only a small number of columns in the table. Conversely, row-oriented formats are appropriate when a large number of columns of a single row are needed for processing at the same time. Space permitting, it is relatively straightforward to measure the performance difference between the two formats for your particular workload by creating a copy of a table with a different storage format for comparison, using "CREATE TABLE...AS SE-LECT" on page 442.

Use the following `CREATE TABLE` clauses to enable column-oriented storage in Hive:

```
CREATE TABLE ...
ROW FORMAT SERDE 'org.apache.hadoop.hive.serde2.columnar.ColumnarSerDe'
STORED AS RCFILE;
```

An example: RegexSerDe

Let's see how to use another SerDe for storage. We'll use a contrib SerDe that uses a regular expression for reading the fixed-width station metadata from a text file:

```
CREATE TABLE stations (usaf STRING, wban STRING, name STRING)
ROW FORMAT SERDE 'org.apache.hadoop.hive.contrib.serde2.RegexSerDe'
WITH SERDEPROPERTIES (
  "input.regex" = "(\\d{6}) (\\d{5}) (.{29}) .*"
);
```

In previous examples, we have used the DELIMITED keyword to refer to delimited text in the ROW FORMAT clause. In this example, we instead specify a SerDe with the SERDE keyword and the fully qualified classname of the Java class that implements the SerDe, org.apache.hadoop.hive.contrib.serde2.RegexSerDe.

SerDes can be configured with extra properties using the WITH SERDEPROPERTIES clause. Here we set the input.regex property, which is specific to RegexSerDe.

input.regex is the regular expression pattern to be used during deserialization to turn the line of text forming the row into a set of columns. Java regular expression syntax is used for the matching (see *http://java.sun.com/javase/6/docs/api/java/util/regex/Pattern.html*), and columns are formed from capturing groups of parentheses.[10] In this example, there are three capturing groups for usaf (a six-digit identifier), wban (a five-digit identifier), and name (a fixed-width column of 29 characters).

To populate the table, we use a LOAD DATA statement as before:

```
LOAD DATA LOCAL INPATH "input/ncdc/metadata/stations-fixed-width.txt"
INTO TABLE stations;
```

Recall that LOAD DATA copies or moves the files to Hive's warehouse directory (in this case, it's a copy because the source is the local filesystem). The table's SerDe is not used for the load operation.

When we retrieve data from the table, the SerDe is invoked for deserialization, as we can see from this simple query, which correctly parses the fields for each row:

```
hive> SELECT * FROM stations LIMIT 4;
010000  99999  BOGUS NORWAY
010003  99999  BOGUS NORWAY
010010  99999  JAN MAYEN
010013  99999  ROST
```

---

10. Sometimes you need to use parentheses for regular expression constructs that you don't want to count as a capturing group—for example, the pattern (ab)+ for matching a string of one or more ab characters. The solution is to use a noncapturing group, which has a ? character after the first parenthesis. There are various noncapturing group constructs (see the Java documentation), but in this example we could use (?:ab)+ to avoid capturing the group as a Hive column.

Importing Data

We've already seen how to use the LOAD DATA operation to import data into a Hive table (or partition) by copying or moving files to the table's directory. You can also populate a table with data from another Hive table using an INSERT statement, or at creation time using the *CTAS* construct, which is an abbreviation used to refer to CREATE TABLE...AS SELECT.

If you want to import data from a relational database directly into Hive, have a look at Sqoop, which is covered in "Imported Data and Hive" on page 537.

Inserts

Here's an example of an INSERT statement:

```
INSERT OVERWRITE TABLE target
SELECT col1, col2
  FROM source;
```

For partitioned tables, you can specify the partition to insert into by supplying a PARTITION clause:

```
INSERT OVERWRITE TABLE target
PARTITION (dt='2001-01-01')
SELECT col1, col2
  FROM source;
```

The OVERWRITE keyword means that the contents of the target table (for the first example) or the 2001-01-01 partition (for the second example) are replaced by the results of the SELECT statement. If you want to add records to an already-populated nonpartitioned table or partition, use INSERT INTO TABLE.

You can specify the partition dynamically by determining the partition value from the SELECT statement:

```
INSERT OVERWRITE TABLE target
PARTITION (dt)
SELECT col1, col2, dt
  FROM source;
```

This is known as a *dynamic-partition insert*. This feature is off by default, so you need to enable it by setting hive.exec.dynamic.partition to true first.

> Unlike other databases, Hive does not (currently) support a form of the INSERT statement for inserting a collection of records specified in the query in literal form. That is, statements of the form INSERT INTO...VALUES... are not allowed.

Multitable insert

In HiveQL, you can turn the INSERT statement around and start with the FROM clause for the same effect:

```
FROM source
INSERT OVERWRITE TABLE target
  SELECT col1, col2;
```

The reason for this syntax becomes clear when you see that it's possible to have multiple INSERT clauses in the same query. This so-called *multitable insert* is more efficient than multiple INSERT statements because the source table needs to be scanned only once to produce the multiple, disjoint outputs.

Here's an example that computes various statistics over the weather dataset:

```
FROM records2
INSERT OVERWRITE TABLE stations_by_year
  SELECT year, COUNT(DISTINCT station)
  GROUP BY year
INSERT OVERWRITE TABLE records_by_year
  SELECT year, COUNT(1)
  GROUP BY year
INSERT OVERWRITE TABLE good_records_by_year
  SELECT year, COUNT(1)
  WHERE temperature != 9999
    AND (quality = 0 OR quality = 1 OR quality = 4 OR quality = 5 OR quality = 9)
  GROUP BY year;
```

There is a single source table (records2), but three tables to hold the results from three different queries over the source.

CREATE TABLE...AS SELECT

It's often very convenient to store the output of a Hive query in a new table, perhaps because it is too large to be dumped to the console or because there are further processing steps to carry out on the result.

The new table's column definitions are derived from the columns retrieved by the SELECT clause. In the following query, the target table has two columns named col1 and col2 whose types are the same as the ones in the source table:

```
CREATE TABLE target
AS
SELECT col1, col2
FROM source;
```

A CTAS operation is atomic, so if the SELECT query fails for some reason, the table is not created.

Altering Tables

Because Hive uses the schema on read approach, it's flexible in permitting a table's definition to change after the table has been created. The general caveat, however, is that in many cases, it is up to you to ensure that the data is changed to reflect the new structure.

You can rename a table using the `ALTER TABLE` statement:

```
ALTER TABLE source RENAME TO target;
```

In addition to updating the table metadata, `ALTER TABLE` moves the underlying table directory so that it reflects the new name. In the current example, */user/hive/warehouse/ source* is renamed to */user/hive/warehouse/target*. (An external table's underlying directory is not moved; only the metadata is updated.)

Hive allows you to change the definition for columns, add new columns, or even replace all existing columns in a table with a new set.

For example, consider adding a new column:

```
ALTER TABLE target ADD COLUMNS (col3 STRING);
```

The new column `col3` is added after the existing (nonpartition) columns. The datafiles are not updated, so queries will return `null` for all values of `col3` (unless of course there were extra fields already present in the files). Because Hive does not permit updating existing records, you will need to arrange for the underlying files to be updated by another mechanism. For this reason, it is more common to create a new table that defines new columns and populates them using a `SELECT` statement.

Changing a column's metadata, such as a column's name or data type, is more straightforward, assuming that the old data type can be interpreted as the new data type.

To learn more about how to alter a table's structure, including adding and dropping partitions, changing and replacing columns, and changing table and SerDe properties, see the Hive wiki at *https://cwiki.apache.org/confluence/display/Hive/LanguageManual +DDL*.

Dropping Tables

The `DROP TABLE` statement deletes the data and metadata for a table. In the case of external tables, only the metadata is deleted; the data is left untouched.

If you want to delete all the data in a table but keep the table definition (like `DELETE` or `TRUNCATE` in MySQL), you can simply delete the datafiles. For example:

```
hive>
dfs -rmr /user/hive/warehouse/my_table;
```

Hive treats a lack of files (or indeed no directory for the table) as an empty table.

Another possibility, which achieves a similar effect, is to create a new, empty table that has the same schema as the first, using the LIKE keyword:

```
CREATE TABLE new_table LIKE existing_table;
```

Querying Data

This section discusses how to use various forms of the SELECT statement to retrieve data from Hive.

Sorting and Aggregating

Sorting data in Hive can be achieved by using a standard ORDER BY clause, but there is a catch. ORDER BY produces a result that is totally sorted, as expected, but to do so it sets the number of reducers to one, making it very inefficient for large datasets. (Hopefully, a future release of Hive will employ the techniques described in "Total Sort" on page 274 to support efficient parallel sorting.)

When a globally sorted result is not required—and in many cases it isn't—you can use Hive's nonstandard extension, SORT BY, instead. SORT BY produces a sorted file per reducer.

In some cases, you want to control which reducer a particular row goes to, typically so you can perform some subsequent aggregation. This is what Hive's DISTRIBUTE BY clause does. Here's an example to sort the weather dataset by year and temperature, in such a way to ensure that all the rows for a given year end up in the same reducer partition:[11]

```
hive> FROM records2
    > SELECT year, temperature
    > DISTRIBUTE BY year
    > SORT BY year ASC, temperature DESC;
1949    111
1949    78
1950    22
1950    0
1950    -11
```

A follow-on query (or a query that nests this query as a subquery; see "Subqueries" on page 449) would be able to use the fact that each year's temperatures were grouped and sorted (in descending order) in the same file.

If the columns for SORT BY and DISTRIBUTE BY are the same, you can use CLUSTER BY as a shorthand for specifying both.

---

11. This is a reworking in Hive of the discussion in "Secondary Sort" on page 277.

MapReduce Scripts

Using an approach like Hadoop Streaming, the TRANSFORM, MAP, and REDUCE clauses make it possible to invoke an external script or program from Hive. Suppose we want to use a script to filter out rows that don't meet some condition, such as the script in Example 12-1, which removes poor-quality readings.

Example 12-1. Python script to filter out poor-quality weather records

```python
#!/usr/bin/env python

import re
import sys

for line in sys.stdin:
  (year, temp, q) = line.strip().split()
  if (temp != "9999" and re.match("[01459]", q)):
    print "%s\t%s" % (year, temp)
```

We can use the script as follows in Example 12-2:

Example 12-2. Using the Python script

```
hive> ADD FILE /Users/tom/book-workspace/hadoop-book/ch12/src/main/python/is_good_quality.py;
hive> FROM records2
    > SELECT TRANSFORM(year, temperature, quality)
    > USING 'is_good_quality.py'
    > AS year, temperature;
1950    0
1950    22
1950    -11
1949    111
1949    78
```

Before running the query, we need to register the script with Hive. This is so Hive knows to ship the file to the Hadoop cluster (see "Distributed Cache" on page 289).

The query itself streams the year, temperature, and quality fields as a tab-separated line to the *is_good_quality.py* script, and parses the tab-separated output into year and temperature fields to form the output of the query.

This example has no reducers. If we use a nested form for the query, we can specify a map and a reduce function. This time we use the MAP and REDUCE keywords, but SELECT TRANSFORM in both cases would have the same result. The source for the *max_temperature_reduce.py* script is shown in Example 2-11:

```
FROM (
  FROM records2
  MAP year, temperature, quality
  USING 'is_good_quality.py'
  AS year, temperature) map_output
REDUCE year, temperature
```

```
USING 'max_temperature_reduce.py'
AS year, temperature;
```

Joins

One of the nice things about using Hive, rather than raw MapReduce, is that Hive makes performing commonly used operations very simple. Join operations are a case in point, given how involved they are to implement in MapReduce (see "Joins" on page 283).

Inner joins

The simplest kind of join is the inner join, where each match in the input tables results in a row in the output. Consider two small demonstration tables: sales, which lists the names of people and the ID of the item they bought; and things, which lists the item ID and its name:

```
hive> SELECT * FROM sales;
Joe     2
Hank    4
Ali     0
Eve     3
Hank    2
hive> SELECT * FROM things;
2       Tie
4       Coat
3       Hat
1       Scarf
```

We can perform an inner join on the two tables as follows:

```
hive> SELECT sales.*, things.*
    > FROM sales JOIN things ON (sales.id = things.id);
Joe     2       2       Tie
Hank    2       2       Tie
Eve     3       3       Hat
Hank    4       4       Coat
```

The table in the FROM clause (sales) is joined with the table in the JOIN clause (things), using the predicate in the ON clause. Hive only supports equijoins, which means that only equality can be used in the join predicate, which here matches on the id column in both tables.

Some databases, such as MySQL and Oracle, allow you to list the join tables in the FROM clause and specify the join condition in the WHERE clause of a SELECT statement. However, this syntax is *not* supported in Hive, so the following fails with a parse error:

```
SELECT sales.*, things.*
FROM sales, things
WHERE sales.id = things.id;
```

Hive allows only a single table in the FROM clause, and joins must follow the SQL-92 JOIN clause syntax.

In Hive, you can join on multiple columns in the join predicate by specifying a series of expressions, separated by AND keywords. You can also join more than two tables by supplying additional JOIN...ON... clauses in the query. Hive is intelligent about trying to minimize the number of MapReduce jobs to perform the joins.

A single join is implemented as a single MapReduce job, but multiple joins can be performed in less than one MapReduce job per join if the same column is used in the join condition.[12] You can see how many MapReduce jobs Hive will use for any particular query by prefixing it with the EXPLAIN keyword:

```
EXPLAIN
SELECT sales.*, things.*
FROM sales JOIN things ON (sales.id = things.id);
```

The EXPLAIN output includes many details about the execution plan for the query, including the abstract syntax tree, the dependency graph for the stages that Hive will execute, and information about each stage. Stages may be MapReduce jobs or operations such as file moves. For even more detail, prefix the query with EXPLAIN EXTENDED.

Hive currently uses a rule-based query optimizer for determining how to execute a query, but it's likely that in the future a cost-based optimizer will be added.

Outer joins

Outer joins allow you to find nonmatches in the tables being joined. In the current example, when we performed an inner join, the row for Ali did not appear in the output, because the ID of the item she purchased was not present in the things table. If we change the join type to LEFT OUTER JOIN, the query will return a row for every row in the left table (sales), even if there is no corresponding row in the table it is being joined to (things):

```
hive> SELECT sales.*, things.*
    > FROM sales LEFT OUTER JOIN things ON (sales.id = things.id);
Ali     0    NULL NULL
```

---

12. The order of the tables in the JOIN clauses is significant. It's generally best to have the largest table last, but see *https://cwiki.apache.org/confluence/display/Hive/LanguageManual+Joins* for more details, including how to give hints to the Hive planner.

```
Joe     2   2   Tie
Hank    2   2   Tie
Eve     3   3   Hat
Hank    4   4   Coat
```

Notice that the row for Ali is now returned, and the columns from the things table are NULL because there is no match.

Hive supports right outer joins, which reverses the roles of the tables relative to the left join. In this case, all items from the things table are included, even those that weren't purchased by anyone (a scarf):

```
hive> SELECT sales.*, things.*
    > FROM sales RIGHT OUTER JOIN things ON (sales.id = things.id);
NULL    NULL  1   Scarf
Joe     2     2   Tie
Hank    2     2   Tie
Eve     3     3   Hat
Hank    4     4   Coat
```

Finally, there is a full outer join, where the output has a row for each row from both tables in the join:

```
hive> SELECT sales.*, things.*
    > FROM sales FULL OUTER JOIN things ON (sales.id = things.id);
Ali     0     NULL NULL
NULL    NULL  1    Scarf
Joe     2     2    Tie
Hank    2     2    Tie
Eve     3     3    Hat
Hank    4     4    Coat
```

Semi joins

Hive doesn't support IN subqueries (at the time of this writing), but you can use a LEFT SEMI JOIN to do the same thing.

Consider this IN subquery, which finds all the items in the things table that are in the sales table:

```
SELECT *
FROM things
WHERE things.id IN (SELECT id from sales);
```

We can rewrite it as follows:

```
hive> SELECT *
    > FROM things LEFT SEMI JOIN sales ON (sales.id = things.id);
2    Tie
3    Hat
4    Coat
```

There is a restriction that we must observe for LEFT SEMI JOIN queries: the right table (sales) may appear only in the ON clause. It cannot be referenced in a SELECT expression, for example.

Map joins

If one table is small enough to fit in memory, Hive can load the smaller table into memory to perform the join in each of the mappers. The syntax for specifying a map join is a hint embedded in an SQL C-style comment:

```
hive> SELECT /*+ MAPJOIN(things) */ sales.*, things.*
    > FROM sales JOIN things ON (sales.id = things.id);
Joe     2   2   Tie
Hank    4   4   Coat
Eve     3   3   Hat
Hank    2   2   Tie
```

The job to execute this query has no reducers, so this query would not work for a RIGHT or FULL OUTER JOIN, since absence of matching can be detected only in an aggregating (reduce) step across all the inputs.

Map joins can take advantage of bucketed tables ("Buckets" on page 433), since a mapper working on a bucket of the left table needs to load only the corresponding buckets of the right table to perform the join. The syntax for the join is the same as for the in-memory case shown earlier; however, you also need to enable the optimization with the following:

```
SET hive.optimize.bucketmapjoin=true;
```

Subqueries

A subquery is a SELECT statement that is embedded in another SQL statement. Hive has limited support for subqueries, permitting a subquery only in the FROM clause of a SELECT statement.

> Other databases allow subqueries almost anywhere that an expression is valid, such as in the list of values to retrieve from a SELECT statement or in the WHERE clause. Many uses of subqueries can be rewritten as joins, so if you find yourself writing a subquery where Hive does not support it, see whether it can be expressed as a join. For example, an IN subquery can be written as a semi join or an inner join (see "Joins" on page 446).

The following query finds the mean maximum temperature for every year and weather station:

```
SELECT station, year, AVG(max_temperature)
FROM (
  SELECT station, year, MAX(temperature) AS max_temperature
  FROM records2
  WHERE temperature != 9999
    AND (quality = 0 OR quality = 1 OR quality = 4 OR quality = 5 OR quality = 9)
  GROUP BY station, year
) mt
GROUP BY station, year;
```

The subquery is used to find the maximum temperature for each station/date combination, and then the outer query uses the AVG aggregate function to find the average of the maximum temperature readings for each station/date combination.

The outer query accesses the results of the subquery like it does a table, which is why the subquery must be given an alias (mt). The columns of the subquery have to be given unique names so that the outer query can refer to them.

Views

A view is a sort of "virtual table" that is defined by a SELECT statement. Views can be used to present data to users in a way that differs from the way it is actually stored on disk. Often, the data from existing tables is simplified or aggregated in a particular way that makes it convenient for further processing. Views may also be used to restrict users' access to particular subsets of tables that they are authorized to see.

In Hive, a view is not materialized to disk when it is created; rather, the view's SELECT statement is executed when the statement that refers to the view is run. If a view performs extensive transformations on the base tables or is used frequently, you may choose to manually materialize it by creating a new table that stores the contents of the view (see "CREATE TABLE...AS SELECT" on page 442).

We can use views to rework the query from the previous section for finding the mean maximum temperature for every year and weather station. First, let's create a view for valid records, that is, records that have a particular quality value:

```
CREATE VIEW valid_records
AS
SELECT *
FROM records2
WHERE temperature != 9999
  AND (quality = 0 OR quality = 1 OR quality = 4 OR quality = 5 OR quality = 9);
```

When we create a view, the query is not run; it is simply stored in the metastore. Views are included in the output of the SHOW TABLES command, and you can see more details about a particular view, including the query used to define it, by issuing the DESCRIBE EXTENDED view_name command.

Next, let's create a second view of maximum temperatures for each station and year. It is based on the valid_records view:

```
CREATE VIEW max_temperatures (station, year, max_temperature)
AS
SELECT station, year, MAX(temperature)
FROM valid_records
GROUP BY station, year;
```

In this view definition, we list the column names explicitly. We do this because the maximum temperature column is an aggregate expression, and otherwise Hive would create a column alias for us (such as _c2). We could equally well have used an AS clause in the SELECT to name the column.

With the views in place, we can now use them by running a query:

```
SELECT station, year, AVG(max_temperature)
FROM max_temperatures
GROUP BY station, year;
```

The result of the query is the same as running the one that uses a subquery, and in particular, Hive creates the same number of MapReduce jobs for both: two in each case, one for each GROUP BY. This example shows that Hive can combine a query on a view into a sequence of jobs that is equivalent to writing the query without using a view. In other words, Hive won't needlessly materialize a view, even at execution time.

Views in Hive are read-only, so there is no way to load or insert data into an underlying base table via a view.

User-Defined Functions

Sometimes the query you want to write can't be expressed easily (or at all) using the built-in functions that Hive provides. By writing a *user-defined function* (UDF), Hive makes it easy to plug in your own processing code and invoke it from a Hive query.

UDFs have to be written in Java, the language that Hive itself is written in. For other languages, consider using a SELECT TRANSFORM query, which allows you to stream data through a user-defined script ("MapReduce Scripts" on page 445).

There are three types of UDF in Hive: (regular) UDFs, user-defined aggregate functions (UDAFs), and user-defined table-generating functions (UDTFs). They differ in the numbers of rows that they accept as input and produce as output:

- A UDF operates on a single row and produces a single row as its output. Most functions, such as mathematical functions and string functions, are of this type.
- A UDAF works on multiple input rows and creates a single output row. Aggregate functions include such functions as COUNT and MAX.
- A UDTF operates on a single row and produces multiple rows—a table—as output.

Table-generating functions are less well known than the other two types, so let's look at an example. Consider a table with a single column, x, which contains arrays of strings. It's instructive to take a slight detour to see how the table is defined and populated:

```
CREATE TABLE arrays (x ARRAY<STRING>)
ROW FORMAT DELIMITED
  FIELDS TERMINATED BY '\001'
  COLLECTION ITEMS TERMINATED BY '\002';
```

Notice that the ROW FORMAT clause specifies that the entries in the array are delimited by Control-B characters. The example file that we are going to load has the following contents, where ^B is a representation of the Control-B character to make it suitable for printing:

```
a^Bb
c^Bd^Be
```

After running a LOAD DATA command, the following query confirms that the data was loaded correctly:

```
hive> SELECT * FROM arrays;
["a","b"]
["c","d","e"]
```

Next, we can use the explode UDTF to transform this table. This function emits a row for each entry in the array, so in this case the type of the output column y is STRING. The result is that the table is flattened into five rows:

```
hive> SELECT explode(x) AS y FROM arrays;
a
b
c
d
e
```

SELECT statements using UDTFs have some restrictions (for example, they cannot retrieve additional column expressions), which make them less useful in practice. For this reason, Hive supports LATERAL VIEW queries, which are more powerful. LATERAL VIEW queries not covered here, but you may find out more about them at *https://cwiki .apache.org/confluence/display/Hive/LanguageManual+LateralView*.

Writing a UDF

To illustrate the process of writing and using a UDF, we'll write a simple UDF to trim characters from the ends of strings. Hive already has a built-in function called trim, so we'll call ours strip. The code for the Strip Java class is shown in Example 12-3.

Example 12-3. A UDF for stripping characters from the ends of strings

```
package com.hadoopbook.hive;

import org.apache.commons.lang.StringUtils;
import org.apache.hadoop.hive.ql.exec.UDF;
import org.apache.hadoop.io.Text;

public class Strip extends UDF {
  private Text result = new Text();

  public Text evaluate(Text str) {
    if (str == null) {
      return null;
    }
```

```
    result.set(StringUtils.strip(str.toString()));
    return result;
  }
  public Text evaluate(Text str, String stripChars) {
    if (str == null) {
      return null;
    }
    result.set(StringUtils.strip(str.toString(), stripChars));
    return result;
  }
}
```

A UDF must satisfy the following two properties:

- A UDF must be a subclass of `org.apache.hadoop.hive.ql.exec.UDF`.
- A UDF must implement at least one `evaluate()` method.

The `evaluate()` method is not defined by an interface, since it may take an arbitrary number of arguments, of arbitrary types, and it may return a value of arbitrary type. Hive introspects the UDF to find the `evaluate()` method that matches the Hive function that was invoked.

The `Strip` class has two `evaluate()` methods. The first strips leading and trailing white-space from the input, and the second can strip any of a set of supplied characters from the ends of the string. The actual string processing is delegated to the `StringUtils` class from the Apache Commons project, which makes the only noteworthy part of the code the use of `Text` from the Hadoop Writable library. Hive actually supports Java primitives in UDFs (and a few other types such as `java.util.List` and `java.util.Map`), so a signature like:

```
public String evaluate(String str)
```

would work equally well. However, by using `Text`, we can take advantage of object reuse, which can bring efficiency savings, and so is preferred in general.

To use the UDF in Hive, we need to package the compiled Java class in a JAR file (you can do this by typing `ant hive` with the book's example code) and register the file with Hive:

```
ADD JAR /path/to/hive-examples.jar;
```

We also need to create an alias for the Java classname:

```
CREATE TEMPORARY FUNCTION strip AS 'com.hadoopbook.hive.Strip';
```

The `TEMPORARY` keyword here highlights the fact that UDFs are defined only for the duration of the Hive session (they are not persisted in the metastore). In practice, this means you need to add the JAR file and either define the function at the beginning of each script, or create a *.hiverc* file in your home directory containing these commands, and the UDF will be running automatically at the beginning of each Hive session.

As an alternative to calling `ADD JAR` at launch time, you can specify a path where Hive looks for auxiliary JAR files to put on its classpath (including the MapReduce classpath). This technique is useful for automatically adding your own library of UDFs every time you run Hive.

There are two ways of specifying the path. Either pass the `--auxpath` option to the *hive* command:

```
% hive --auxpath /path/to/hive-examples.jar
```

or set the `HIVE_AUX_JARS_PATH` environment variable before invoking Hive. The auxiliary path may be a comma-separated list of JAR file paths or a directory containing JAR files.

The UDF is now ready to be used, just like a built-in function:

```
hive> SELECT strip(' bee ') FROM dummy;
bee
hive> SELECT strip('banana', 'ab') FROM dummy;
nan
```

Notice that the UDF's name is not case-sensitive:

```
hive> SELECT STRIP(' bee ') FROM dummy;
bee
```

Writing a UDAF

An aggregate function is more difficult to write than a regular UDF. Values are aggregated in chunks (potentially across many map or reduce tasks), so the implementation has to be capable of combining partial aggregations into a final result. The code to achieve this is best explained by example, so let's look at the implementation of a simple UDAF for calculating the maximum of a collection of integers (Example 12-4).

Example 12-4. A UDAF for calculating the maximum of a collection of integers

```
package com.hadoopbook.hive;

import org.apache.hadoop.hive.ql.exec.UDAF;
import org.apache.hadoop.hive.ql.exec.UDAFEvaluator;
import org.apache.hadoop.io.IntWritable;

public class Maximum extends UDAF {

  public static class MaximumIntUDAFEvaluator implements UDAFEvaluator {

    private IntWritable result;

    public void init() {
      result = null;
    }

    public boolean iterate(IntWritable value) {
```

```
    if (value == null) {
      return true;
    }
    if (result == null) {
      result = new IntWritable(value.get());
    } else {
      result.set(Math.max(result.get(), value.get()));
    }
    return true;
  }

  public IntWritable terminatePartial() {
    return result;
  }

  public boolean merge(IntWritable other) {
    return iterate(other);
  }

  public IntWritable terminate() {
    return result;
  }
 }
}
```

The class structure is slightly different from the one for UDFs. A UDAF must be a subclass of `org.apache.hadoop.hive.ql.exec.UDAF` (note the "A" in UDAF) and contain one or more nested static classes implementing `org.apache.hadoop.hive.ql.exec.UDA FEvaluator`. In this example, there is a single nested class, `MaximumIntUDAFEvaluator`, but we could add more evaluators such as `MaximumLongUDAFEvaluator`, `MaximumFloatU DAFEvaluator`, and so on, to provide overloaded forms of the UDAF for finding the maximum of a collection of longs, floats, and so on.

An evaluator must implement five methods, described in turn here (the flow is illustrated in Figure 12-4):

init()

The `init()` method initializes the evaluator and resets its internal state. In `MaximumIntUDAFEvaluator`, we set the `IntWritable` object holding the final result to null. We use null to indicate that no values have been aggregated yet, which has the desirable effect of making the maximum value of an empty set `NULL`.

iterate()

The `iterate()` method is called every time there is a new value to be aggregated. The evaluator should update its internal state with the result of performing the aggregation. The arguments that `iterate()` takes correspond to those in the Hive function from which it was called. In this example, there is only one argument. The value is first checked to see whether it is null, and if it is, it is ignored. Otherwise, the `result` instance variable is set to `value`'s integer value (if this is the first value that has been seen) or set to the larger of the current result and `value` (if one or more values have already been seen). We return `true` to indicate that the input value was valid.

`terminatePartial()`

The `terminatePartial()` method is called when Hive wants a result for the partial aggregation. The method must return an object that encapsulates the state of the aggregation. In this case, an `IntWritable` suffices because it encapsulates either the maximum value seen or `null` if no values have been processed.

`merge()`

The `merge()` method is called when Hive decides to combine one partial aggregation with another. The method takes a single object whose type must correspond to the return type of the `terminatePartial()` method. In this example, the `merge()` method can simply delegate to the `iterate()` method because the partial aggregation is represented in the same way as a value being aggregated. This is not generally the case (and we'll see a more general example later), and the method should implement the logic to combine the evaluator's state with the state of the partial aggregation.

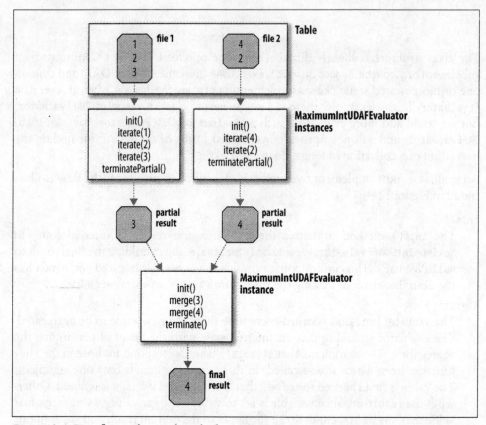

Figure 12-4. Data flow with partial results for a UDAF

terminate()

The terminate() method is called when the final result of the aggregation is needed. The evaluator should return its state as a value. In this case, we return the result instance variable.

Let's exercise our new function:

```
hive> CREATE TEMPORARY FUNCTION maximum AS 'com.hadoopbook.hive.Maximum';
hive> SELECT maximum(temperature) FROM records;
111
```

A more complex UDAF

The previous example is unusual in that a partial aggregation can be represented using the same type (IntWritable) as the final result. This is not generally the case for more complex aggregate functions, as can be seen by considering a UDAF for calculating the mean (average) of a collection of double values. It's not mathematically possible to combine partial means into a final mean value (see "Combiner Functions" on page 33). Instead, we can represent the partial aggregation as a pair of numbers: the cumulative sum of the double values processed so far, and the number of values.

This idea is implemented in the UDAF shown in Example 12-5. Notice that the partial aggregation is implemented as a "struct" nested static class, called PartialResult, which Hive is intelligent enough to serialize and deserialize, since we are using field types that Hive can handle (Java primitives in this case).

In this example, the merge() method is different from iterate() because it combines the partial sums and partial counts by pairwise addition. Also, the return type of terminatePartial() is PartialResult—which of course is never seen by the user calling the function—whereas the return type of terminate() is DoubleWritable, the final result seen by the user.

Example 12-5. A UDAF for calculating the mean of a collection of doubles

```
package com.hadoopbook.hive;

import org.apache.hadoop.hive.ql.exec.UDAF;
import org.apache.hadoop.hive.ql.exec.UDAFEvaluator;
import org.apache.hadoop.hive.serde2.io.DoubleWritable;

public class Mean extends UDAF {

  public static class MeanDoubleUDAFEvaluator implements UDAFEvaluator {
    public static class PartialResult {
      double sum;
      long count;
    }

    private PartialResult partial;
```

```
    public void init() {
      partial = null;
    }

    public boolean iterate(DoubleWritable value) {
      if (value == null) {
        return true;
      }
      if (partial == null) {
        partial = new PartialResult();
      }
      partial.sum += value.get();
      partial.count++;
      return true;
    }

    public PartialResult terminatePartial() {
      return partial;
    }

    public boolean merge(PartialResult other) {
      if (other == null) {
        return true;
      }
      if (partial == null) {
        partial = new PartialResult();
      }
      partial.sum += other.sum;
      partial.count += other.count;
      return true;
    }

    public DoubleWritable terminate() {
      if (partial == null) {
        return null;
      }
      return new DoubleWritable(partial.sum / partial.count);
    }
  }
}
```

HBase

Jonathan Gray and Michael Stack

HBasics

HBase is a distributed column-oriented database built on top of HDFS. HBase is the Hadoop application to use when you require real-time read/write random access to very large datasets.

Although there are countless strategies and implementations for database storage and retrieval, most solutions—especially those of the relational variety—are not built with very large scale and distribution in mind. Many vendors offer replication and partitioning solutions to grow the database beyond the confines of a single node, but these add-ons are generally an afterthought and are complicated to install and maintain. They also severely compromise the RDBMS feature set. Joins, complex queries, triggers, views, and foreign-key constraints become prohibitively expensive to run on a scaled RDBMS or do not work at all.

HBase comes at the scaling problem from the opposite direction. It is built from the ground up to scale linearly just by adding nodes. HBase is not relational and does not support SQL, but given the proper problem space, it is able to do what an RDBMS cannot: host very large, sparsely populated tables on clusters made from commodity hardware.

The canonical HBase use case is the *webtable*, a table of crawled web pages and their attributes (such as language and MIME type) keyed by the web page URL. The webtable is large, with row counts that run into the billions. Batch analytic and parsing MapReduce jobs are continuously run against the webtable, deriving statistics and adding new columns of verified MIME-type and parsed-text content for later indexing by a search engine. Concurrently, the table is randomly accessed by crawlers running at various rates and updating random rows while random web pages are served in real time as users click on a website's cached-page feature.

In this chapter we give an introduction to using HBase. For more in-depth information, consult *HBase: The Definitive Guide (http://shop.oreilly.com/product/0636920014348 .do)* by Lars George (O'Reilly, 2011).

Backdrop

The HBase project was started toward the end of 2006 by Chad Walters and Jim Kellerman at Powerset. It was modeled after Google's "Bigtable: A Distributed Storage System for Structured Data" by Chang et al. (*http://labs.google.com/papers/bigtable .html*), which had just been published. In February 2007, Mike Cafarella made a code drop of a mostly working system that Jim Kellerman then carried forward.

The first HBase release was bundled as part of Hadoop 0.15.0 in October 2007. In May 2010, HBase graduated from a Hadoop subproject to become an Apache Top Level Project. Production users of HBase include Adobe, StumbleUpon, Twitter, and groups at Yahoo!.

Concepts

In this section, we provide a quick overview of core HBase concepts. At a minimum, a passing familiarity will ease the digestion of all that follows.[1]

Whirlwind Tour of the Data Model

Applications store data into labeled tables. Tables are made of rows and columns. Table cells—the intersection of row and column coordinates—are versioned. By default, their version is a timestamp auto-assigned by HBase at the time of cell insertion. A cell's content is an uninterpreted array of bytes.

Table row keys are also byte arrays, so theoretically anything can serve as a row key, from strings to binary representations of long or even serialized data structures. Table rows are sorted by row key, the table's primary key. The sort is byte-ordered. All table accesses are via the table primary key.[2]

Row columns are grouped into *column families*. All column family members have a common prefix, so, for example, the columns *temperature:air* and *tempera-ture:dew_point* are both members of the *temperature* column family, whereas *station:identifier* belongs to the *station* family.[3] The column family prefix must be com-

---

1. For more detail than is provided here, see the HBase Architecture page (*http://wiki.apache.org/hadoop/ Hbase/HbaseArchitecture*) on the HBase wiki.

2. As of this writing, there are at least two projects up on github that add secondary indices to HBase.

3. In HBase, by convention, the colon character (:) delimits the column family from the column family *qualifier*. It is hardcoded.

posed of *printable* characters. The qualifying tail, the column family *qualifier*, can be made of any arbitrary bytes.

A table's column families must be specified up front as part of the table schema definition, but new column family members can be added on demand. For example, a new column *station:address* can be offered by a client as part of an update, and its value persisted, as long as the column family *station* is already in existence on the targeted table.

Physically, all column family members are stored together on the filesystem. So although earlier we described HBase as a column-oriented store, it would be more accurate if it were described as a column-*family*-oriented store. Because tunings and storage specifications are done at the column-family level, it is advised that all column family members have the same general access pattern and size characteristics.

In synopsis, HBase tables are like those in an RDBMS, only cells are versioned, rows are sorted, and columns can be added on the fly by the client as long as the column family they belong to preexists.

Regions

Tables are automatically partitioned horizontally by HBase into *regions*. Each region comprises a subset of a table's rows. A region is denoted by the table it belongs to, its first row, inclusive, and last row, exclusive. Initially, a table comprises a single region, but as the size of the region grows, after it crosses a configurable size threshold, it splits at a row boundary into two new regions of approximately equal size. Until this first split happens, all loading will be against the single server hosting the original region. As the table grows, the number of its regions grows. Regions are the units that get distributed over an HBase cluster. In this way, a table that is too big for any one server can be carried by a cluster of servers, with each node hosting a subset of the table's total regions. This is also the means by which the loading on a table gets distributed. The online set of sorted regions comprises the table's total content.

Locking

Row updates are atomic, no matter how many row columns constitute the row-level transaction. This keeps the locking model simple.

Implementation

Just as HDFS and MapReduce are built of clients, slaves, and a coordinating master—*namenode* and *datanodes* in HDFS and *jobtracker* and *tasktrackers* in MapReduce—so is HBase modeled with an HBase *master* node orchestrating a cluster of one or more *regionserver* slaves (see Figure 13-1). The HBase master is responsible for bootstrapping a virgin install, for assigning regions to registered regionservers, and for recovering regionserver failures. The master node is lightly loaded. The regionservers carry zero or more regions and field client read/write requests. They also manage region splits, informing the HBase master about the new daughter regions for it to manage the off-lining of parent region and assignment of the replacement daughters.

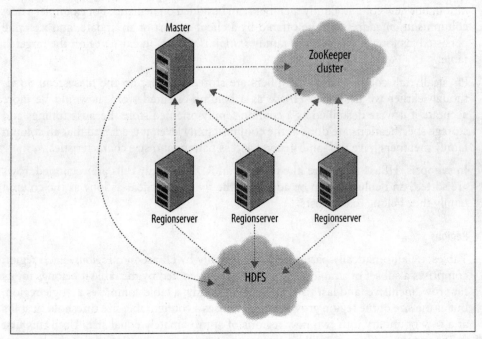

Figure 13-1. HBase cluster members

HBase depends on ZooKeeper (Chapter 14), and by default it manages a ZooKeeper instance as the authority on cluster state. HBase hosts vitals such as the location of the root catalog table and the address of the current cluster master. Assignment of regions is mediated via ZooKeeper in case participating servers crash mid-assignment. Hosting the assignment transaction state in ZooKeeper makes it so recovery can pick up on the assignment where the crashed server left off. At a minimum, when bootstrapping a client connection to an HBase cluster, the client must be passed the location of the ZooKeeper ensemble. Thereafter, the client navigates the ZooKeeper hierarchy to learn cluster attributes such as server locations.[4]

Regionserver slave nodes are listed in the HBase *conf/regionservers* file as you would list datanodes and tasktrackers in the Hadoop *conf/slaves* file. Start and stop scripts are like those in Hadoop and use the same SSH-based mechanism for running remote commands. A cluster's site-specific configuration is made in the HBase *conf/hbase-site.xml* and *conf/hbase-env.sh* files, which have the same format as that of their equivalents in the Hadoop parent project (see Chapter 9).

---

4. HBase can be configured to use an existing ZooKeeper cluster instead.

Where there is commonality to be found, HBase directly uses or sub-classes the parent Hadoop implementation, whether this is a service or type. When this is not possible, HBase will follow the Hadoop model where it can. For example, HBase uses the Hadoop Configuration system so configuration files have the same format. What this means for you, the user, is that you can leverage any Hadoop familiarity in your exploration of HBase. HBase deviates from this rule only when adding its specializations.

HBase persists data via the Hadoop filesystem API. Because there are multiple implementations of the filesystem interface—one for the local filesystem, and one for the KFS filesystem, Amazon's S3, and HDFS. Most people using HBase run it on HDFS for storage, though by default, and unless told otherwise, HBase writes to the local filesystem. The local filesystem is fine for experimenting with your initial HBase install, but thereafter, the first configuration made in an HBase cluster usually involves pointing HBase at the HDFS cluster it should use.

HBase in operation

Internally, HBase keeps special catalog tables named *-ROOT-* and *.META.*, within which it maintains the current list, state, and location of all regions afloat on the cluster. The -ROOT- table holds the list of .META. table regions. The .META. table holds the list of all user-space regions. Entries in these tables are keyed by region name, where a region name is made of the table name the region belongs to, the region's start row, its time of creation, and finally, an MD5 hash of all of the former (i.e., a hash of tablename, start row, and creation timestamp).[5] As noted previously, row keys are sorted, so finding the region that hosts a particular row is a matter of a lookup to find the first entry whose key is greater than or equal to that of the requested row key. As regions transition—are split, disabled/enabled, deleted, redeployed by the region load balancer, or redeployed due to a regionserver crash—the catalog tables are updated so the state of all regions on the cluster is kept current.

Fresh clients connect to the ZooKeeper cluster first to learn the location of -ROOT-. Clients consult -ROOT- to elicit the location of the .META. region whose scope covers that of the requested row. The client then does a lookup against the found .META. region to figure out the hosting user-space region and its location. Thereafter, the client interacts directly with the hosting regionserver.

To save on having to make three round-trips per row operation, clients cache all they learn while traversing -ROOT- and .META. caching locations as well as user-space region start and stop rows so they can figure hosting regions themselves without having to go

---

5. Here is an example region name from the table TestTable whose start row is xyz: TestTable,xyz, 1279729913622.1b6e176fb8d8aa88fd4ab6bc80247ece. A comma delimits the table name, start row, and timestamp. The name always ends in a period.

back to the .META. table. Clients continue to use the cached entry as they work until there is a fault. When this happens—i.e., when the region has moved—the client consults the .META. again to learn the new location. If the consulted .META. region has moved, then -ROOT- is reconsulted.

Writes arriving at a regionserver are first appended to a commit log and then are added to an in-memory *memstore*. When a memstore fills, its content is flushed to the filesystem.

The commit log is hosted on HDFS, so it remains available through a regionserver crash. When the master notices that a regionserver is no longer reachable, usually because the servers's znode has expired in ZooKeeper, it splits the dead regionserver's commit log by region. On reassignment and before they were open for business, regions that were on the dead regionserver will pick up their just-split file of not-yet-persisted edits and replay them to bring themselves up-to-date with the state they had just before the failure.

When reading, the region's memstore is consulted first. If sufficient versions are found reading memstore alone, the query completes there. Otherwise, flush files are consulted in order, from newest to oldest, either until versions sufficient to satisfy the query are found or until we run out of flush files.

A background process compacts flush files once their number has broached a threshold, rewriting many files as one, because the fewer files a read consults, the more performant it will be. On compaction, the process cleans out versions beyond the schema-configured maximum, deletes, and expired cells. A separate process running in the regionserver monitors flush file sizes, splitting the region when they grow in excess of the configured maximum.

Installation

Download a stable release from an Apache Download Mirror (*http://www.apache.org/ dyn/closer.cgi/hbase/*) and unpack it on your local filesystem. For example:

```
% tar xzf hbase-x.y.z.tar.gz
```

As with Hadoop, you first need to tell HBase where Java is located on your system. If you have the JAVA_HOME environment variable set to point to a suitable Java installation, then that will be used, and you don't have to configure anything further. Otherwise, you can set the Java installation that HBase uses by editing HBase's *conf/hbase-env.sh* and specifying the JAVA_HOME variable (see Appendix A for some examples) to point to version 1.6.0 of Java.

 HBase, just like Hadoop, requires Java 6.

For convenience, add the HBase binary directory to your command-line path. For example:

```
% export HBASE_HOME=/home/hbase/hbase-x.y.z
% export PATH=$PATH:$HBASE_HOME/bin
```

To get the list of HBase options, type:

```
% hbase
Usage: hbase <command>
where <command> is one of:
  shell           run the HBase shell
  master          run an HBase HMaster node
  regionserver    run an HBase HRegionServer node
  zookeeper       run a Zookeeper server
  rest            run an HBase REST server
  thrift          run an HBase Thrift server
  avro            run an HBase Avro server
  migrate         upgrade an hbase.rootdir
  hbck            run the hbase 'fsck' tool
 or
  CLASSNAME       run the class named CLASSNAME
Most commands print help when invoked w/o parameters.
```

Test Drive

To start a temporary instance of HBase that uses the */tmp* directory on the local file-system for persistence, type:

```
% start-hbase.sh
```

This will launch a standalone HBase instance that persists to the local filesystem; by default, HBase will write to */tmp/hbase-${USERID}*.[6]

To administer your HBase instance, launch the HBase shell by typing:

```
% hbase shell
HBase Shell; enter 'help<RETURN>' for list of supported commands.
Type "exit<RETURN>" to leave the HBase Shell
Version: 0.89.0-SNAPSHOT, ra4ea1a9a7b074a2e5b7b24f761302d4ea28ed1b2, Sun Jul 18
15:01:50 PDT 2010 hbase(main):001:0>
```

This will bring up a JRuby IRB interpreter that has had some HBase-specific commands added to it. Type help and then press RETURN to see the list of shell commands grouped into categories. Type help COMMAND_GROUP for help by category or help COMMAND for help on a specific command and example usage. Commands use Ruby formatting to specify lists and dictionaries. See the end of the main help screen for a quick tutorial.

Now let us create a simple table, add some data, and then clean up.

---

6. In standalone mode, the HBase master, regionserver, and a ZooKeeper instance are all run in the same JVM.

To create a table, you must name your table and define its schema. A table's schema comprises table attributes and the list of table column families. Column families themselves have attributes that you in turn set at schema definition time. Examples of column family attributes include whether the family content should be compressed on the filesystem and how many versions of a cell to keep. Schemas can be edited later by offlining the table using the shell `disable` command, making the necessary alterations using `alter`, then putting the table back online with `enable`.

To create a table named `test` with a single column family named `data` using defaults for table and column family attributes, enter:

```
hbase(main):007:0> create 'test', 'data'
0 row(s) in 1.3066 seconds
```

 If the previous command does not complete successfully, and the shell displays an error and a stack trace, your install was not successful. Check the master logs under the HBase *logs* directory—the default location for the logs directory is *${HBASE_HOME}/logs*—for a clue as to where things went awry.

See the `help` output for examples of adding table and column family attributes when specifying a schema.

To prove the new table was created successfully, run the `list` command. This will output all tables in user space:

```
hbase(main):019:0> list
test
1 row(s) in 0.1485 seconds
```

To insert data into three different rows and columns in the `data` column family, and then list the table content, do the following:

```
hbase(main):021:0> put 'test', 'row1', 'data:1', 'value1'
0 row(s) in 0.0454 seconds
hbase(main):022:0> put 'test', 'row2', 'data:2', 'value2'
0 row(s) in 0.0035 seconds
hbase(main):023:0> put 'test', 'row3', 'data:3', 'value3'
0 row(s) in 0.0090 seconds
hbase(main):024:0> scan 'test'
ROW                      COLUMN+CELL
 row1                    column=data:1, timestamp=1240148026198, value=value1
 row2                    column=data:2, timestamp=1240148040035, value=value2
 row3                    column=data:3, timestamp=1240148047497, value=value3
3 row(s) in 0.0825 seconds
```

Notice how we added three new columns without changing the schema.

To remove the table, you must first disable it before dropping it:

```
hbase(main):025:0> disable 'test'
09/04/19 06:40:13 INFO client.HBaseAdmin: Disabled test
```

```
0 row(s) in 6.0426 seconds
hbase(main):026:0> drop 'test'
09/04/19 06:40:17 INFO client.HBaseAdmin: Deleted test
0 row(s) in 0.0210 seconds
hbase(main):027:0> list
0 row(s) in 2.0645 seconds
```

Shut down your HBase instance by running:

```
% stop-hbase.sh
```

To learn how to set up a distributed HBase and point it at a running HDFS, see the Getting Started (*http://hadoop.apache.org/hbase/docs/current/api/overview-summary .html#overview_description*) section of the HBase documentation.

Clients

There are a number of client options for interacting with an HBase cluster.

Java

HBase, like Hadoop, is written in Java. Example 13-1 shows the Java version of how you would do the shell operations listed previously in "Test Drive" on page 465.

Example 13-1. Basic table administration and access

```java
public class ExampleClient {
  public static void main(String[] args) throws IOException {
    Configuration config = HBaseConfiguration.create();

    // Create table
    HBaseAdmin admin = new HBaseAdmin(config);
    HTableDescriptor htd = new HTableDescriptor("test");
    HColumnDescriptor hcd = new HColumnDescriptor("data");
    htd.addFamily(hcd);
    admin.createTable(htd);
    byte [] tablename = htd.getName();
    HTableDescriptor [] tables = admin.listTables();
    if (tables.length != 1 && Bytes.equals(tablename, tables[0].getName())) {
      throw new IOException("Failed create of table");
    }

    // Run some operations -- a put, a get, and a scan -- against the table.
    HTable table = new HTable(config, tablename);
    byte [] row1 = Bytes.toBytes("row1");
    Put p1 = new Put(row1);
    byte [] databytes = Bytes.toBytes("data");
    p1.add(databytes, Bytes.toBytes("1"), Bytes.toBytes("value1"));
    table.put(p1);
    Get g = new Get(row1);
    Result result = table.get(g);
    System.out.println("Get: " + result);
    Scan scan = new Scan();
```

```
    ResultScanner scanner = table.getScanner(scan);
    try {
      for (Result scannerResult: scanner) {
        System.out.println("Scan: " + scannerResult);
      }
    } finally {
      scanner.close();
    }

    // Drop the table
    admin.disableTable(tablename);
    admin.deleteTable(tablename);
  }
}
```

This class has a `main` method only. For the sake of brevity, we do not include the package name nor imports. In this class, we first create an instance of `org.apache.hadoop.conf.Configuration`. We ask the `org.apache.hadoop.hbase.HBase Configuration` class to create the instance. It will return a `Configuration` that has read the HBase configuration from the *hbase-site.xml* and *hbase-default.xml* files found on the program's classpath. This `Configuration` is subsequently used to create instances of `HBaseAdmin` and `HTable`, two classes found in the `org.apache.hadoop.hbase.client` Java package. `HBaseAdmin` is used for administering your HBase cluster, specifically for adding and dropping tables. `HTable` is used to access a specific table. The `Configura tion` instance points these classes at the cluster the code is to work against.

To create a table, we first need to create an instance of `HBaseAdmin` and then ask it to create the table named `test` with a single column family named `data`. In our example, our table schema is the default. Use methods on `org.apache.hadoop.hbase.HTableDe scriptor` and `org.apache.hadoop.hbase.HColumnDescriptor` to change the table schema. Next, the code asserts the table was actually created, and then it moves to run operations against the just-created table.

Operating on a table, we will need an instance of `org.apache.hadoop.hbase.cli ent.HTable`, passing it our `Configuration` instance and the name of the table we want to operate on. After creating an `HTable`, we then create an instance of `org.apache.hadoop.hbase.client.Put` puts a single cell value of `value1` into a row named `row1` on the column named `data:1`. (The column name is specified in two parts: the column family name as bytes—`databytes` in the preceding code—and then the column family qualifier, specified as `Bytes.toBytes("1")`.) Next, we create an `org. apache.hadoop.hbase.client.Get`, do a get of the just-added cell, and then use an `org. apache.hadoop.hbase.client.Scan` to scan over the table against the just-created table, printing out what we find.

Finally, we clean up by first disabling the table and then deleting it. A table must be disabled before it can be dropped.

MapReduce

HBase classes and utilities in the org.apache.hadoop.hbase.mapreduce package facilitate using HBase as a source and/or sink in MapReduce jobs. The TableInputFormat class makes splits on region boundaries so maps are handed a single region to work on. The TableOutputFormat will write the result of the reduce into HBase. The RowCounter class in Example 13-2, which can be found in the HBase mapreduce package, runs a map task to count rows using TableInputFormat.

Example 13-2. A MapReduce application to count the number of rows in an HBase table

```
public class RowCounter {
  /** Name of this 'program'. */
  static final String NAME = "rowcounter";

  static class RowCounterMapper
  extends TableMapper<ImmutableBytesWritable, Result> {
    /** Counter enumeration to count the actual rows. */
    public static enum Counters {ROWS}

    @Override
    public void map(ImmutableBytesWritable row, Result values,
      Context context)
    throws IOException {
      for (KeyValue value: values.list()) {
        if (value.getValue().length > 0) {
          context.getCounter(Counters.ROWS).increment(1);
          break;
        }
      }
    }
  }

  public static Job createSubmittableJob(Configuration conf, String[] args)
  throws IOException {
    String tableName = args[0];
    Job job = new Job(conf, NAME + "_" + tableName);
    job.setJarByClass(RowCounter.class);
    // Columns are space delimited
    StringBuilder sb = new StringBuilder();
    final int columnoffset = 1;
    for (int i = columnoffset; i < args.length; i++) {
      if (i > columnoffset) {
        sb.append(" ");
      }
      sb.append(args[i]);
    }
    Scan scan = new Scan();
    scan.setFilter(new FirstKeyOnlyFilter());
    if (sb.length() > 0) {
      for (String columnName :sb.toString().split(" ")) {
        String [] fields = columnName.split(":");
        if(fields.length == 1) {
          scan.addFamily(Bytes.toBytes(fields[0]));
```

```
      } else {
        scan.addColumn(Bytes.toBytes(fields[0]), Bytes.toBytes(fields[1]));
      }
    }
  }
  // Second argument is the table name.
  job.setOutputFormatClass(NullOutputFormat.class);
  TableMapReduceUtil.initTableMapperJob(tableName, scan,
    RowCounterMapper.class, ImmutableBytesWritable.class, Result.class, job);
  job.setNumReduceTasks(0);
  return job;
}

public static void main(String[] args) throws Exception {
  Configuration conf = HBaseConfiguration.create();
  String[] otherArgs = new GenericOptionsParser(conf, args).getRemainingArgs();
  if (otherArgs.length < 1) {
    System.err.println("ERROR: Wrong number of parameters: " + args.length);
    System.err.println("Usage: RowCounter <tablename> [<column1> <column2>...]");
    System.exit(-1);
  }
  Job job = createSubmittableJob(conf, otherArgs);
  System.exit(job.waitForCompletion(true) ? 0 : 1);
}
}
```

This class uses `GenericOptionsParser`, which is discussed in "GenericOptionsParser, Tool, and ToolRunner" on page 150, for parsing command-line arguments. The `Row CounterMapper` inner class implements the HBase `TableMapper` abstract, a specialization of `org.apache.hadoop.mapreduce.Mapper` that sets the map input types passed by `TableInputFormat`. The `createSubmittableJob()` method parses arguments added to the configuration that were passed on the command line and specify the table and columns we are to run `RowCounter` against. The column names are used to configure an instance of `org.apache.hadoop.hbase.client.Scan`, which is a scan object that will be passed through to `TableInputFormat` and used for constraining what our `Mapper` sees. Notice how we set a filter, an instance of `org.apache.hadoop.hbase.filter.FirstKeyOnlyFil ter`, on the scan. This filter instructs the server to short-circuit when running server-side, doing no more than verifying a row has an entry before returning. This speeds the row count. The `createSubmittableJob()` method also invokes the `TableMapReduceU til.initTableMapJob()` utility method, which among other things, such as setting the map class to use, sets the input format to `TableInputFormat`. The map is simple and just checks for empty values. If empty, it doesn't count the row. Otherwise, it increments `Counters.ROWS` by one.

Avro, REST, and Thrift

HBase ships with Avro, REST, and Thrift interfaces. These are useful when the interacting application is written in a language other than Java. In all cases, a Java server hosts an instance of the HBase client brokering Avro, REST, and Thrift application

---

requests in and out of the HBase cluster. This extra work to proxy requests and responses means these interfaces are slower than using the Java client directly.

REST

To put up a *stargate* instance (stargate is the name for the HBase REST service), start it using the following command:

```
% hbase-daemon.sh start rest
```

This will start a server instance (by default on port 8080), background it, and catch any emissions by the server in logfiles under the HBase *logs* directory.

Clients can ask for the response to be formatted as JSON, Google's protobufs, or as XML, depending on how the client *HTTP Accept* header is set. See the REST wiki page (*http://wiki.apache.org/hadoop/Hbase/Stargate*) for documentation and examples of making REST client requests.

To stop the REST server, type:

```
% hbase-daemon.sh stop rest
```

Thrift

Similarly, start a Thrift service by putting up a server to field Thrift clients by running the following:

```
% hbase-daemon.sh start thrift
```

This will start the server instance (by default on port 9090), background it, and catch any emissions by the server in logfiles under the HBase *logs* directory. The HBase Thrift documentation[7] notes that the Thrift version uses generating classes. The HBase Thrift IDL can be found at *src/main/resources/org/apache/hadoop/hbase/thrift/Hbase.thrift* in the HBase source code.

To stop the Thrift server, type:

```
% hbase-daemon.sh stop thrift
```

Avro

The Avro server is started and stopped in the same manner as you'd start and stop the Thrift or REST services. The Avro server uses port 9090 by default (the same as the Thrift server, although you wouldn't normally run both).

---

7. *http://hbase.apache.org/docs/current/api/org/apache/hadoop/hbase/thrift/package-summary.html*

Example

Although HDFS and MapReduce are powerful tools for processing batch operations over large datasets, they do not provide ways to read or write individual records efficiently. In this example, we'll explore using HBase as the tool to fill this gap.

The existing weather dataset described in previous chapters contains observations for tens of thousands of stations over 100 years, and this data is growing without bound. In this example, we will build a simple web interface that allows a user to navigate the different stations and page through their historical temperature observations in time order. For the sake of this example, let us allow that the dataset is massive, that the observations run to the billions, and that the rate at which temperature updates arrive is significant—say, hundreds to thousands of updates per second from around the world and across the whole range of weather stations. Also, let us allow that it is a requirement that the web application must display the most up-to-date observation within a second or so of receipt.

The first size requirement should preclude our use of a simple RDBMS instance and make HBase a candidate store. The second latency requirement rules out plain HDFS. A MapReduce job could build initial indices that allowed random access over all of the observation data, but keeping up this index as the updates arrived is not what HDFS and MapReduce are good at.

Schemas

In our example, there will be two tables:

stations
> This table holds station data. Let the row key be the `stationid`. Let this table have a column family `info` that acts as a key-value dictionary for station information. Let the dictionary keys be the column names `info:name`, `info:location`, and `info:description`. This table is static, and in this case, the *info* family closely mirrors a typical RDBMS table design.

observations
> This table holds temperature observations. Let the row key be a composite key of `stationid` plus a reverse-order timestamp. Give this table a column family `data` that will contain one column, `airtemp`, with the observed temperature as the column value.

Our choice of schema is derived from knowing the most efficient way we can read from HBase. Rows and columns are stored in increasing lexicographical order. Though there are facilities for secondary indexing and regular expression matching, they come at a performance penalty. It is vital that you understand the most efficient way to query your data in order to choose the most effective setup for storing and accessing.

For the `stations` table, the choice of `stationid` as the key is obvious because we will always access information for a particular station by its ID. The `observations` table, however, uses a composite key that adds the observation timestamp at the end. This will group all observations for a particular station together, and by using a reverse-order timestamp (`Long.MAX_VALUE - epoch`) and storing it as binary, observations for each station will be ordered with most recent observation first.

In the shell, you would define your tables as follows:

```
hbase(main):036:0> create 'stations', {NAME => 'info', VERSIONS => 1}
0 row(s) in 0.1304 seconds
hbase(main):037:0> create 'observations', {NAME => 'data', VERSIONS => 1}
0 row(s) in 0.1332 seconds
```

In both cases, we are interested only in the latest version of a table cell, so set `VERSIONS` to 1 (the default is 3).

Loading Data

There are a relatively small number of stations, so their static data is easily inserted using any of the available interfaces.

However, let's assume that there are billions of individual observations to be loaded. This kind of import is normally an extremely complex and long-running database operation, but MapReduce and HBase's distribution model allow us to make full use of the cluster. Copy the raw input data onto HDFS, and then run a MapReduce job that can read the input and write to HBase.

Example 13-3 shows an example MapReduce job that imports observations to HBase from the same input file used in the previous chapters' examples.

Example 13-3. A MapReduce application to import temperature data from HDFS into an HBase table

```
public class HBaseTemperatureImporter extends Configured implements Tool {

  // Inner-class for map
  static class HBaseTemperatureMapper<K, V> extends MapReduceBase implements
      Mapper<LongWritable, Text, K, V> {
    private NcdcRecordParser parser = new NcdcRecordParser();
    private HTable table;

    public void map(LongWritable key, Text value,
      OutputCollector<K, V> output, Reporter reporter)
    throws IOException {
      parser.parse(value.toString());
      if (parser.isValidTemperature()) {
        byte[] rowKey = RowKeyConverter.makeObservationRowKey(parser.getStationId(),
          parser.getObservationDate().getTime());
        Put p = new Put(rowKey);
        p.add(HBaseTemperatureCli.DATA_COLUMNFAMILY,
          HBaseTemperatureCli.AIRTEMP_QUALIFIER,
          Bytes.toBytes(parser.getAirTemperature()));
```

Example | 473

```
        table.put(p);
    }
}

public void configure(JobConf jc) {
    super.configure(jc);
    // Create the HBase table client once up-front and keep it around
    // rather than create on each map invocation.
    try {
        this.table = new HTable(new HBaseConfiguration(jc), "observations");
    } catch (IOException e) {
        throw new RuntimeException("Failed HTable construction", e);
    }
}

@Override
public void close() throws IOException {
    super.close();
    table.close();
}
}

public int run(String[] args) throws IOException {
    if (args.length != 1) {
        System.err.println("Usage: HBaseTemperatureImporter <input>");
        return -1;
    }
    JobConf jc = new JobConf(getConf(), getClass());
    FileInputFormat.addInputPath(jc, new Path(args[0]));
    jc.setMapperClass(HBaseTemperatureMapper.class);
    jc.setNumReduceTasks(0);
    jc.setOutputFormat(NullOutputFormat.class);
    JobClient.runJob(jc);
    return 0;
}

public static void main(String[] args) throws Exception {
    int exitCode = ToolRunner.run(new HBaseConfiguration(),
        new HBaseTemperatureImporter(), args);
    System.exit(exitCode);
}
}
```

HBaseTemperatureImporter has an inner class named HBaseTemperatureMapper that is like
the MaxTemperatureMapper class from Chapter 5. The outer class implements Tool and
does the setup to launch the HBaseTemperatureMapper inner class. HBaseTemperatureMap
per takes the same input as MaxTemperatureMapper and does the same parse—using the
NcdcRecordParser introduced in Chapter 5—to check for valid temperatures, but rather
than add valid temperatures to the output collector as MaxTemperatureMapper does,
instead it adds valid temperatures to the observations HBase table into the *data:air-
temp* column. (We are using static constants for data and airtemp, imported from the
HBaseTemperatureCli class described later.) In the configure() method, we create an
HTable instance once against the observations table and use it afterward in map

invocations talking to HBase. Finally, we call `close()` on our `HTable` instance to flush out any write buffers not yet cleared.

The row key used is created in the `makeObservationRowKey()` method on `RowKey Converter` from the station ID and observation time:

```java
public class RowKeyConverter {

    private static final int STATION_ID_LENGTH = 12;

    /**
     * @return A row key whose format is: <station_id> <reverse_order_epoch>
     */
    public static byte[] makeObservationRowKey(String stationId,
            long observationTime) {
        byte[] row = new byte[STATION_ID_LENGTH + Bytes.SIZEOF_LONG];
        Bytes.putBytes(row, 0, Bytes.toBytes(stationId), 0, STATION_ID_LENGTH);
        long reverseOrderEpoch = Long.MAX_VALUE - observationTime;
        Bytes.putLong(row, STATION_ID_LENGTH, reverseOrderEpoch);
        return row;
    }

}
```

The conversion takes advantage of the fact that the station ID is a fixed-length string. The `Bytes` class used in `makeObservationRowKey()` is from the HBase utility package. It includes methods for converting between byte arrays and common Java and Hadoop types. In `makeObservationRowKey()`, the `Bytes.putLong()` method is used to fill the key byte array. The `Bytes.SIZEOF_LONG` constant is used for sizing and positioning in the row key array.

We can run the program with the following:

```
% hbase HBaseTemperatureImporter input/ncdc/all
```

Optimization notes

- Watch for the phenomenon where an import walks in lockstep through the table, with all clients in concert pounding one of the table's regions (and thus, a single node), then moving on to the next, and so on, rather than evenly distributing the load over all regions. This is usually brought on by some interaction between sorted input and how the splitter works. Randomizing the ordering of your row keys prior to insertion may help. In our example, given the distribution of `stationid` values and how `TextInputFormat` makes splits, the upload should be sufficiently distributed.[8]

---

8. If a table is new, it will have only one region, and initially all updates will be to this single region until it splits. This will happen even if row keys are randomly distributed. This startup phenomenon means uploads run slowly at first until there are sufficient regions distributed so all cluster members are able to participate in the upload. Do not confuse this phenomenon with that noted in the main text.

Example | 475

- Obtain only one `HTable` instance per task. There is a cost to instantiating an `HTable`, so if you do this for each insert, you may have a negative impact on performance, hence our setup of `HTable` in the `configure()` step.

- By default, each `HTable.put(put)` actually performs the insert without any buffering. You can disable the `HTable` auto-flush feature using `HTable.setAuto Flush(false)` and then set the size of configurable write buffer. When the inserts committed fill the write buffer, it is then flushed. Remember, though, that you must call either a manual `HTable.flushCommits()` or `HTable.close()`, which will call through to `HTable.flushCommits()` at the end of each task to ensure that nothing is left unflushed in the buffer. You could do this in an override of the mapper's `close()` method.

- HBase includes `TableInputFormat` and `TableOutputFormat` to help with MapReduce jobs that source and sink HBase (see Example 13-2). One way to write the previous example would have been to use `MaxTemperatureMapper` from Chapter 5 as is, but add a reducer task that takes the output of the `MaxTemperatureMapper` and feeds it to HBase via `TableOutputFormat`.

Web Queries

To implement the web application, we will use the HBase Java API directly. Here it becomes clear how important your choice of schema and storage format is.

The simplest query will be to get the static station information. This type of query is simple in a traditional database, but HBase gives you additional control and flexibility. Using the `info` family as a key-value dictionary (column names as keys, column values as values), the code would look like this:

```
public Map<String, String> getStationInfo(HTable table, String stationId)
    throws IOException {
  Get get = new Get(Bytes.toBytes(stationId));
  get.addColumn(INFO_COLUMNFAMILY);
  Result res = table.get(get);
  if (res == null) {
    return null;
  }
  Map<String, String> resultMap = new HashMap<String, String>();
  resultMap.put("name", getValue(res, INFO_COLUMNFAMILY, NAME_QUALIFIER));
  resultMap.put("location", getValue(res, INFO_COLUMNFAMILY, LOCATION_QUALIFIER));
  resultMap.put("description", getValue(res, INFO_COLUMNFAMILY,
    DESCRIPTION_QUALIFIER));
  return resultMap;
}

private static String getValue(Result res, byte [] cf, byte [] qualifier) {
  byte [] value = res.getValue(cf, qualifier);
  return value == null? ": Bytes.toString(value);
}
```

In this example, getStationInfo() takes an HTable instance and a station ID. To get the station info, we use HTable.get(), passing a Get instance configured to get all the column values for the row identified by the station ID in the defined column family, INFO_COLUMNFAMILY.

The get() results are returned in Result. It contains the row, and you can fetch cell values by stipulating the column cell you want. The getStationInfo() method converts the Result Map into a more friendly Map of String keys and values.

We can already see how there is a need for utility functions when using HBase. There are an increasing number of abstractions being built atop HBase to deal with this low-level interaction, but it's important to understand how this works and how storage choices make a difference.

One of the strengths of HBase over a relational database is that you don't have to prespecify the columns. So, in the future, if each station now has at least these three attributes but there are hundreds of optional ones, we can just insert them without modifying the schema. Your application's reading and writing code would of course need to be changed. The example code might change in this case to looping through Result rather than grabbing each value explicitly.

We will make use of HBase scanners for retrieval of observations in our web application.

Here we are after a Map<ObservationTime, ObservedTemp> result. We will use a NavigableMap<Long, Integer> because it is sorted and has a descendingMap() method, so we can access observations in both ascending or descending order. The code is in Example 13-4.

Example 13-4. Methods for retrieving a range of rows of weather station observations from an HBase table

```java
public NavigableMap<Long, Integer> getStationObservations(HTable table,
    String stationId, long maxStamp, int maxCount) throws IOException {
  byte[] startRow = RowKeyConverter.makeObservationRowKey(stationId, maxStamp);
  NavigableMap<Long, Integer> resultMap = new TreeMap<Long, Integer>();
  Scan scan = new Scan(startRow);
  scan.addColumn(DATA_COLUMNFAMILY, AIRTEMP_QUALIFIER);
  ResultScanner scanner = table.getScanner(scan);
  Result res = null;
  int count = 0;
  try {
    while ((res = scanner.next()) != null && count++ < maxCount) {
      byte[] row = res.getRow();
      byte[] value = res.getValue(DATA_COLUMNFAMILY, AIRTEMP_QUALIFIER);
      Long stamp = Long.MAX_VALUE -
        Bytes.toLong(row, row.length - Bytes.SIZEOF_LONG, Bytes.SIZEOF_LONG);
      Integer temp = Bytes.toInt(value);
      resultMap.put(stamp, temp);
    }
  } finally {
    scanner.close();
```

Example | 477

```
    }
    return resultMap;
}
/**
 * Return the last ten observations.
 */
public NavigableMap<Long, Integer> getStationObservations(HTable table,
    String stationId) throws IOException {
    return getStationObservations(table, stationId, Long.MAX_VALUE, 10);
```

The getStationObservations() method takes a station ID and a range defined by max
Stamp and a maximum number of rows (maxCount). Note that the NavigableMap that is
returned is actually now in descending time order. If you want to read through it in
ascending order, you would make use of NavigableMap.descendingMap().

Scanners

HBase scanners are like cursors in a traditional database or Java iterators, except—
unlike the latter—they have to be closed after use. Scanners return rows in order. Users
obtain a scanner on an HBase table by calling HTable.getScanner(scan), where the
scan parameter is a configured instance of a Scan object. In the Scan instance, you can
pass the row at which to start and stop the scan, which columns in a row to return in
the row result, and optionally, a filter to run on the server side.[9] The ResultScanner
interface, which is returned when you call HTable.getScanner(), is as follows:

```
public interface ResultScanner extends Closeable, Iterable<Result> {
    public Result next() throws IOException;
    public Result [] next(int nbRows) throws IOException;
    public void close();
}
```

You can ask for the next row's results or a number of rows. Each invocation of
next() involves a trip back to the regionserver, so grabbing a bunch of rows at once can
make for significant performance savings.[10]

---

9. To learn more about the server-side filtering mechanism in HBase, see *http://hadoop.apache.org/hbase/
docs/current/api/org/apache/hadoop/hbase/filter/package-summary.html*.

10. The hbase.client.scanner.caching configuration option is set to 1 by default. You can also set how
much to cache/prefetch on the Scan instance itself. Scanners will, under the covers, fetch this many
results at a time, bringing them client-side, and returning to the server to fetch the next batch only
after the current batch has been exhausted. Higher caching values will enable faster scanning but will
eat up more memory in the client. Also, avoid setting the caching so high that the time spent processing
the batch client-side exceeds the scanner lease period. If a client fails to check back with the server
before the scanner lease expires, the server will go ahead and garbage-collect resources consumed by
the scanner server-side. The default scanner lease is 60 seconds, and can be changed by setting
hbase.regionserver.lease.period. Clients will see an UnknownScannerException if the scanner lease
has expired.

The advantage of storing things as `Long.MAX_VALUE - stamp` may not be clear in the previous example. It is more useful when you want to get the newest observations for a given offset and limit, which is often the case in web applications. If the observations were stored with the actual stamps, we would be able to get only the oldest observations for a given offset and limit efficiently. Getting the newest would mean getting all of them and then grabbing them off the end. One of the prime reasons for moving from RDBMS to HBase is to allow for these types of "early-out" scenarios.

HBase Versus RDBMS

HBase and other column-oriented databases are often compared to more traditional and popular relational databases or RDBMSs. Although they differ dramatically in their implementations and in what they set out to accomplish, the fact that they are potential solutions to the same problems means that despite their enormous differences, the comparison is a fair one to make.

As described previously, HBase is a distributed, column-oriented data storage system. It picks up where Hadoop left off by providing random reads and writes on top of HDFS. It has been designed from the ground up with a focus on scale in every direction: tall in numbers of rows (billions), wide in numbers of columns (millions), and to be horizontally partitioned and replicated across thousands of commodity nodes automatically. The table schemas mirror the physical storage, creating a system for efficient data structure serialization, storage, and retrieval. The burden is on the application developer to make use of this storage and retrieval in the right way.

Strictly speaking, an RDBMS is a database that follows Codd's 12 Rules (*http://en.wikipedia.org/wiki/Codd%27s_12_rules*). Typical RDBMSs are fixed-schema, row-oriented databases with ACID properties and a sophisticated SQL query engine. The emphasis is on strong consistency, referential integrity, abstraction from the physical layer, and complex queries through the SQL language. You can easily create secondary indexes, perform complex inner and outer joins, and count, sum, sort, group, and page your data across a number of tables, rows, and columns.

For a majority of small- to medium-volume applications, there is no substitute for the ease of use, flexibility, maturity, and powerful feature set of available open source RDBMS solutions such as MySQL and PostgreSQL. However, if you need to scale up in terms of dataset size, read/write concurrency, or both, you'll soon find that the conveniences of an RDBMS come at an enormous performance penalty and make distribution inherently difficult. The scaling of an RDBMS usually involves breaking Codd's rules, loosening ACID restrictions, forgetting conventional DBA wisdom, and on the way losing most of the desirable properties that made relational databases so convenient in the first place.

Successful Service

Here is a synopsis of how the typical RDBMS scaling story runs. The following list presumes a successful growing service:

Initial public launch
> Move from local workstation to shared, remotely hosted MySQL instance with a well-defined schema.

Service becomes more popular; too many reads hitting the database
> Add memcached to cache common queries. Reads are now no longer strictly ACID; cached data must expire.

Service continues to grow in popularity; too many writes hitting the database
> Scale MySQL vertically by buying a beefed-up server with 16 cores, 128 GB of RAM, and banks of 15 k RPM hard drives. Costly.

New features increases query complexity; now we have too many joins
> Denormalize your data to reduce joins. (That's not what they taught me in DBA school!)

Rising popularity swamps the server; things are too slow
> Stop doing any server-side computations.

Some queries are still too slow
> Periodically prematerialize the most complex queries, and try to stop joining in most cases.

Reads are OK, but writes are getting slower and slower
> Drop secondary indexes and triggers (no indexes?).

At this point, there are no clear solutions for how to solve your scaling problems. In any case, you'll need to begin to scale horizontally. You can attempt to build some type of partitioning on your largest tables, or look into some of the commercial solutions that provide multiple master capabilities.

Countless applications, businesses, and websites have successfully achieved scalable, fault-tolerant, and distributed data systems built on top of RDBMSs and are likely using many of the previous strategies. But what you end up with is something that is no longer a true RDBMS, sacrificing features and conveniences for compromises and complexities. Any form of slave replication or external caching introduces weak consistency into your now denormalized data. The inefficiency of joins and secondary indexes means almost all queries become primary key lookups. A multiwriter setup likely means no real joins at all, and distributed transactions are a nightmare. There's now an incredibly complex network topology to manage with an entirely separate cluster for caching. Even with this system and the compromises made, you will still worry about your primary master crashing and the daunting possibility of having 10 times the data and 10 times the load in a few months.

HBase

Enter HBase, which has the following characteristics:

No real indexes
> Rows are stored sequentially, as are the columns within each row. Therefore, no issues with index bloat, and insert performance is independent of table size.

Automatic partitioning
> As your tables grow, they will automatically be split into regions and distributed across all available nodes.

Scale linearly and automatically with new nodes
> Add a node, point it to the existing cluster, and run the regionserver. Regions will automatically rebalance, and load will spread evenly.

Commodity hardware
> Clusters are built on $1,000–$5,000 nodes rather than $50,000 nodes. RDBMSs are I/O hungry, requiring more costly hardware.

Fault tolerance
> Lots of nodes means each is relatively insignificant. No need to worry about individual node downtime.

Batch processing
> MapReduce integration allows fully parallel, distributed jobs against your data with locality awareness.

If you stay up at night worrying about your database (uptime, scale, or speed), you should seriously consider making a jump from the RDBMS world to HBase. Utilize a solution that was intended to scale rather than a solution based on stripping down and throwing money at what used to work. With HBase, the software is free, the hardware is cheap, and the distribution is intrinsic.

Use Case: HBase at Streamy.com

Streamy.com is a real-time news aggregator and social sharing platform. With a broad feature set, we started out with a complex implementation on top of PostgreSQL. It's a terrific product with a great community and a beautiful codebase. We tried every trick in the book to keep things fast as we scaled, going so far as to modify the PostgreSQL code directly to suit our needs. Originally taking advantage of all RDBMS goodies, we found that eventually, one by one, we had to let them all go. Along the way, our entire team became the DBA.

We did manage to solve many of the issues that we ran into, but there were two that eventually led to the decision to find another solution from outside the world of RDBMS.

Streamy crawls thousands of RSS feeds and aggregates hundreds of millions of items from them. In addition to having to store these items, one of our more complex queries reads a time-ordered list of all items from a set of sources. At the high end, this can run to several thousand sources and all of their items all in a single query.

Very large items tables

At first, this was a single items table, but the high number of secondary indexes made inserts and updates very slow. We started to divide items up into several one-to-one link tables to store other information, separating static fields from dynamic ones, grouping fields based on how they were queried, and denormalizing everything along the way. Even with these changes, single updates required rewriting the entire record, so tracking statistics on items was difficult to scale. The rewriting of records and having to update indexes along the way are intrinsic properties of the RDBMS we were using. They could not be decoupled. We partitioned our tables, which was not too difficult because of the natural partition of time, but the complexity got out of hand fast. We needed another solution!

Very large sort merges

Performing sorted merges of time-ordered lists is common in many Web 2.0 applications. An example SQL query might look like this:

```
SELECT id, stamp, type FROM streams
  WHERE type IN ('type1','type2','type3','type4',....,'typeN')
  ORDER BY stamp DESC LIMIT 10 OFFSET 0;
```

Assuming id is a primary key on streams, and that stamp and type have secondary indexes, an RDBMS query planner treats this query as follows:

```
MERGE (
  SELECT id, stamp, type FROM streams
    WHERE type = 'type1' ORDER BY stamp DESC,
  ...,
  SELECT id, stamp, type FROM streams
    WHERE type = 'typeN' ORDER BY stamp DESC
) ORDER BY stamp DESC LIMIT 10 OFFSET 0;
```

The problem here is that we are after only the top 10 IDs, but the query planner actually materializes an entire merge and then limits at the end. A simple heapsort across each of the types would allow you to "early out" once you have the top 10. In our case, each type could have tens of thousands of IDs in it, so materializing the entire list and sorting it was extremely slow and unnecessary. We actually went so far as to write a custom PL/Python script that performed a heapsort using a series of queries like the following:

```
SELECT id, stamp, type FROM streams
  WHERE type = 'typeN'
  ORDER BY stamp DESC LIMIT 1 OFFSET 0;
```

If we ended up taking from typeN (it was the next most recent in the heap), we would run another query:

```
SELECT id, stamp, type FROM streams
  WHERE type = 'typeN'
  ORDER BY stamp DESC LIMIT 1 OFFSET 1;
```

In nearly all cases, this outperformed the native SQL implementation and the query planner's strategy. In the worst cases for SQL, we were more than an order of magnitude faster using the Python procedure. We found ourselves continually trying to outsmart the query planner.

Again, at this point, we really needed another solution.

Life with HBase

Our RDBMS-based system was always capable of correctly implementing our requirements; the issue was scaling. When you start to focus on scale and performance rather than correctness, you end up shortcutting and optimizing for your domain-specific use cases everywhere possible. Once you start implementing your own solutions to your data problems, the overhead and complexity of an RDBMS gets in your way. The abstraction from the storage layer and ACID requirements are an enormous barrier and luxury that you cannot always afford when building for scale. HBase is a distributed, column-oriented, sorted map store and not much else. The only major part that is abstracted from the user is the distribution, and that's exactly what we don't want to deal with. Business logic, on the other hand, is very specialized and optimized. With HBase not trying to solve all of our problems, we've been able to solve them better ourselves and rely on HBase for scaling our storage, not our logic. It was an extremely liberating experience to be able to focus on our applications and logic rather than the scaling of the data itself.

We currently have tables with hundreds of millions of rows and tens of thousands of columns; the thought of storing billions of rows and millions of columns is exciting, not scary.

Praxis

In this section, we discuss some of the common issues users run into when running an HBase cluster under load.

Versions

Up until HBase 0.20, HBase aligned its versioning with that of Hadoop. A particular HBase version would run on any Hadoop that had a matching minor version, where minor version in this context is considered the number between the periods (e.g., 20 is the minor version of an HBase 0.20.5). HBase 0.20.5 would run on an Hadoop 0.20.2, but HBase 0.19.5 would not run on Hadoop 0.20.0.

With HBase 0.90,[11] the version relationship was broken. The Hadoop release cycle has slowed and no longer aligns with that of HBase developments. Also, the intent is that now a particular HBase version can run on multiple versions of Hadoop. For example, HBase 0.90.x will work with both Hadoop 0.20.x and 0.21.x.

This said, ensure you are running compatible versions of Hadoop and HBase. Check the requirements section of your download. Incompatible versions will throw an exception complaining about the version mismatch, if you are lucky. If they cannot talk to each sufficiently to pass versions, you may see your HBase cluster hang indefinitely, soon after startup. The mismatch exception or HBase hang can also happen on upgrade if older versions of either HBase or Hadoop can still be found on the classpath because of imperfect cleanup of the old software.

HDFS

HBase's use of HDFS is very different from how it's used by MapReduce. In MapReduce, generally, HDFS files are opened with their content streamed through a map task and then closed. In HBase, datafiles are opened on cluster startup and kept open so that we avoid paying the costs associated with opening files on each access. Because of this, HBase tends to see issues not normally encountered by MapReduce clients:

Running out of file descriptors
> Because we keep files open, and on a loaded cluster, it doesn't take long before we run into system- and Hadoop-imposed limits. For instance, say we have a cluster that has three nodes, each running an instance of a datanode and a regionserver, and we're running an upload into a table that is currently at 100 regions and 10 column families. Allow that each column family has on average two flush files. Doing the math, we can have $100 \times 10 \times 2$, or 2,000, files open at any one time. Add to this total other miscellaneous descriptors consumed by outstanding scanners and Java libraries. Each open file consumes at least one descriptor over on the remote datanode. The default limit on the number of file descriptors per process is 1,024. When we exceed the filesystem *ulimit*, we'll see the complaint about *Too many open files* in logs, but often you'll first see indeterminate behavior in HBase. The fix requires increasing the file descriptor *ulimit* count.[12] You can verify that the HBase process is running with sufficient file descriptors by looking at the first few lines of a regionserver's log. It emits vitals such as the JVM being used and environment settings, such as the file descriptor *ulimit*.

---

11. Why 0.90? We wanted there to be no confusion that a break had been made, so we put a large gap between our new versioning and that of Hadoop's.

12. See the HBase FAQ (*http://wiki.apache.org/hadoop/Hbase/FAQ*) for how to up the *ulimit* on your cluster.

Running out of datanode threads

Similarly, the Hadoop datanode has an upper bound of 256 on the number of threads it can run at any one time. Given the same table statistics quoted in the preceding description, it's easy to see how we can exceed this upper bound relatively early, given that as of this writing, in the datanode each open connection to a file block consumes a thread. If you look in the datanode log, you'll see a complaint like *xceiverCount 258 exceeds the limit of concurrent xcievers 256*, but again, you'll likely see HBase act erratically before you encounter this log entry. Increase the `dfs.datanode.max.xcievers` (note that the property name is misspelled) count in HDFS, and restart your cluster.[13]

Sync

You must run HBase on an HDFS that has a working sync. Otherwise, you will lose data. This means running HBase on Hadoop 0.20.205.0 or later.[14]

UI

HBase runs a web server on the master to present a view on the state of your running cluster. By default, it listens on port 60010. The master UI displays a list of basic attributes such as software versions, cluster load, request rates, lists of cluster tables, and participating regionservers. Click on a regionserver in the master UI, and you are taken to the web server running on the individual regionserver. It lists the regions this server is carrying and basic metrics such as resources consumed and request rates.

Metrics

Hadoop has a metrics system that can be used to emit vitals over a period to a *context* (this is covered in "Metrics" on page 352). Enabling Hadoop metrics, and in particular tying them to Ganglia or emitting them via JMX, will give you views on what is happening on your cluster, both currently and in the recent past. HBase also adds metrics of its own—request rates, counts of vitals, resources used—that can be caught by a Hadoop context. See the file *hadoop-metrics.properties* under the HBase *conf* directory.[15]

---

13. See the HBase troubleshooting guide (*http://wiki.apache.org/hadoop/Hbase/Troubleshooting*) for more detail on this issue.

14. On regionserver crash, when running on an older version of Hadoop, edits written to the commit log kept in HDFS were not recoverable, as files that had not been properly closed lost all edits, no matter how much had been written to them at the time of the crash.

15. Yes, this file is named for Hadoop, though it's for setting up HBase metrics.

Schema Design

HBase tables are like those in an RDBMS, except that cells are versioned, rows are sorted, and columns can be added on the fly by the client as long as the column family they belong to preexists. These factors should be considered when designing schemas for HBase, but far and away the most important concern when designing schemas is considering how the data will be accessed. All access is via primary key, so the key design should lend itself to how the data is going to be queried. The other property to keep in mind when designing schemas is that a defining attribute of column(-family)-oriented stores (*http://en.wikipedia.org/wiki/Column-oriented_DBMS*), such as HBase, is the ability to host wide and sparsely populated tables at no incurred cost.[16]

Joins

There is no native database join facility in HBase, but wide tables can make it so that there is no need for database joins to pull from secondary or tertiary tables. A wide row can sometimes be made to hold all data that pertains to a particular primary key.

Row keys

Take time designing your row key. In the weather data example in this chapter, the compound row key has a station prefix that served to group temperatures by station. The reversed timestamp suffix made it so temperatures could be scanned and ordered from most recent to oldest. A smart compound key can be used to cluster data in ways amenable to how it will be accessed.

Designing compound keys, you may have to zero-pad number components so row keys sort properly. Otherwise, you will run into the issue where 10 sorts before 2 when only the byte order is considered (02 sorts before 10).

If your keys are integers, use a binary representation rather than persist the string version of a number. The former consumes less space.

Counters

At StumbleUpon, the first production feature deployed on HBase was keeping counters for the stumbleupon.com frontend. Counters used to be kept in MySQL, but the rate of change was such that drops were frequent, and the load imposed by the counter writes was such that web designers self-imposed limits on what was counted. Using the incre mentColumnValue() method on org.apache.hadoop.hbase.HTable, counters can be incremented many thousands of times a second.

---

16. See "Column-Stores for Wide and Sparse Data" (*http://db.csail.mit.edu/projects/cstore/abadicidr07.pdf*) by Daniel J. Abadi.

Bulk Load

HBase has an efficient facility for bulk loading HBase by writing its internal data format directly into the filesystem from MapReduce. Going this route, it's possible to load an HBase instance at rates that are an order of magnitude or more beyond those attainable by writing via the HBase client API. The facility is described at *http://hbase.apache.org/docs/current/bulk-loads.html*. It's also possible to bulk load into a live table.

ZooKeeper

So far in this book, we have been studying large-scale data processing. This chapter is different: it is about building general distributed applications using Hadoop's distributed coordination service, called ZooKeeper.

Writing distributed applications is hard. It's hard primarily because of partial failure. When a message is sent across the network between two nodes and the network fails, the sender does not know whether the receiver got the message. It may have gotten through before the network failed, or it may not have. Or perhaps the receiver's process died. The only way that the sender can find out what happened is to reconnect to the receiver and ask it. This is partial failure: when we don't even know if an operation failed.

ZooKeeper can't make partial failures go away, since they are intrinsic to distributed systems. It certainly does not hide partial failures, either.[1] But what ZooKeeper does do is give you a set of tools to build distributed applications that can safely handle partial failures.

ZooKeeper also has the following characteristics:

ZooKeeper is simple
ZooKeeper is, at its core, a stripped-down filesystem that exposes a few simple operations, and some extra abstractions such as ordering and notifications.

ZooKeeper is expressive
The ZooKeeper primitives are a rich set of building blocks that can be used to build a large class of coordination data structures and protocols. Examples include: distributed queues, distributed locks, and leader election among a group of peers.

---

1. This is the message of J. Waldo et al., "A Note on Distributed Computing," (1994), *http://research.sun .com/techrep/1994/smli_tr-94-29.pdf*. That is, distributed programming is fundamentally different from local programming, and the differences cannot simply be papered over.

ZooKeeper is highly available

ZooKeeper runs on a collection of machines and is designed to be highly available, so applications can depend on it. ZooKeeper can help you avoid introducing single points of failure into your system, so you can build a reliable application.

ZooKeeper facilitates loosely coupled interactions

ZooKeeper interactions support participants that do not need to know about one another. For example, ZooKeeper can be used as a rendezvous mechanism so that processes that otherwise don't know of each other's existence (or network details) can discover and interact with each other. Coordinating parties may not even be contemporaneous, since one process may leave a message in ZooKeeper that is read by another after the first has shut down.

ZooKeeper is a library

ZooKeeper provides an open source, shared repository of implementations and recipes of common coordination patterns. Individual programmers are spared the burden of writing common protocols themselves (which are often difficult to get right). Over time, the community can add to and improve the libraries, which is to everyone's benefit.

ZooKeeper is highly performant, too. At Yahoo!, where it was created, the throughput for a ZooKeeper cluster has been benchmarked at over 10,000 operations per second for write-dominant workloads generated by hundreds of clients. For workloads where reads dominate, which is the norm, the throughput is several times higher.[2]

Installing and Running ZooKeeper

When trying out ZooKeeper for the first time, it's simplest to run it in standalone mode with a single ZooKeeper server. You can do this on a development machine, for example. ZooKeeper requires Java 6 to run, so make sure you have it installed first. You don't need Cygwin to run ZooKeeper on Windows, since there are Windows versions of the ZooKeeper scripts. (Windows is supported only as a development platform, not as a production platform.)

Download a stable release of ZooKeeper from the Apache ZooKeeper releases page at *http://zookeeper.apache.org/releases.html*, and unpack the tarball in a suitable location:

```
% tar xzf zookeeper-x.y.z.tar.gz
```

ZooKeeper provides a few binaries to run and interact with the service, and it's convenient to put the directory containing the binaries on your command-line path:

```
% export ZOOKEEPER_INSTALL=/home/tom/zookeeper-x.y.z
% export PATH=$PATH:$ZOOKEEPER_INSTALL/bin
```

---

2. Detailed benchmarks are available in the excellent paper "ZooKeeper: Wait-free coordination for Internet-scale systems," by Patrick Hunt, Mahadev Konar, Flavio P. Junqueira, and Benjamin Reed (USENIX Annual Technology Conference, 2010).

Before running the ZooKeeper service, we need to set up a configuration file. The configuration file is conventionally called *zoo.cfg* and placed in the *conf* subdirectory (although you can also place it in */etc/zookeeper*, or in the directory defined by the ZOOCFGDIR environment variable, if set). Here's an example:

```
tickTime=2000
dataDir=/Users/tom/zookeeper
clientPort=2181
```

This is a standard Java properties file, and the three properties defined in this example are the minimum required for running ZooKeeper in standalone mode. Briefly, tickTime is the basic time unit in ZooKeeper (specified in milliseconds), dataDir is the local filesystem location where ZooKeeper stores persistent data, and clientPort is the port the ZooKeeper listens on for client connections (2181 is a common choice). You should change dataDir to an appropriate setting for your system.

With a suitable configuration defined, we are now ready to start a local ZooKeeper server:

```
% zkServer.sh start
```

To check whether ZooKeeper is running, send the ruok command ("Are you OK?") to the client port using nc (telnet works, too):

```
% echo ruok | nc localhost 2181
imok
```

That's ZooKeeper saying, "I'm OK." There are other commands, known as the "four-letter words," for managing ZooKeeper and they are listed in Table 14-1.

Table 14-1. ZooKeeper commands: the four-letter words

Category	Command	Description
Server status	ruok	Prints imok if the server is running and not in an error state.
	conf	Prints the server configuration (from *zoo.cfg*).
	envi	Prints the server environment, including ZooKeeper version, Java version and other system properties.
	srvr	Prints server statistics, including latency statistics, the number of znodes, and the server mode (standalone, leader or follower).
	stat	Prints server statistics and connected clients.
	srst	Resets server statistics.
	isro	Shows whether the server is in read-only (ro) mode (due to a network partition) or read-write mode (rw).
Client connections	dump	Lists all the sessions and ephemeral znodes for the ensemble. You must connect to the leader (see srvr) for this command.
	cons	Lists connection statistics for all the server's clients.
	crst	Resets connection statistics.
Watches	wchs	Lists summary information for the server's watches.

Category	Command	Description
	wchc	Lists all the server's watches by connection. Caution: may impact server performance for large number of watches.
	wchp	Lists all the server's watches by znode path. Caution: may impact server performance for large number of watches.
Monitoring	mntr	Lists server statistics in Java Properties format, suitable as a source for monitoring systems such as Ganglia and Nagios.

In addition to the mntr command, ZooKeeper exposes statistics via JMX. For more details, see the ZooKeeper documentation at *http://zookeeper.apache.org/*. There are also monitoring tools and recipes in the *src/contrib* directory of the distribution.

An Example

Imagine a group of servers that provide some service to clients. We want clients to be able to locate one of the servers so they can use the service. One of the challenges is maintaining the list of servers in the group.

The membership list clearly cannot be stored on a single node in the network, as the failure of that node would mean the failure of the whole system (we would like the list to be highly available). Suppose for a moment that we had a robust way of storing the list. We would still have the problem of how to remove a server from the list if it failed. Some process needs to be responsible for removing failed servers, but note that it can't be the servers themselves because they are no longer running!

What we are describing is not a passive distributed data structure, but an active one, and one that can change the state of an entry when some external event occurs. Zoo-Keeper provides this service, so let's see how to build this group membership application (as it is known) with it.

Group Membership in ZooKeeper

One way of understanding ZooKeeper is to think of it as providing a high-availability filesystem. It doesn't have files and directories, but a unified concept of a node, called a *znode*, which acts both as a container of data (like a file) and a container of other znodes (like a directory). Znodes form a hierarchical namespace, and a natural way to build a membership list is to create a parent znode with the name of the group and child znodes with the name of the group members (servers). This is shown in Figure 14-1.

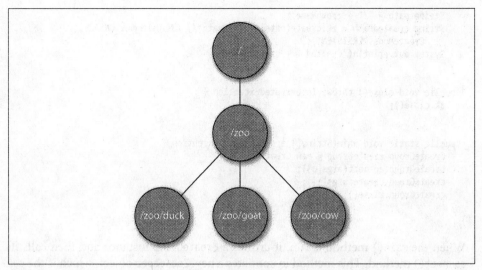

Figure 14-1. ZooKeeper znodes

In this example, we won't store data in any of the znodes, but in a real application, you could imagine storing data about the members, such as hostnames, in their znodes.

Creating the Group

Let's introduce ZooKeeper's Java API by writing a program to create a znode for the group, which is */zoo* in Example Example 14-1.

Example 14-1. A program to create a znode representing a group in ZooKeeper

```java
public class CreateGroup implements Watcher {

  private static final int SESSION_TIMEOUT = 5000;

  private ZooKeeper zk;
  private CountDownLatch connectedSignal = new CountDownLatch(1);

  public void connect(String hosts) throws IOException, InterruptedException {
    zk = new ZooKeeper(hosts, SESSION_TIMEOUT, this);
    connectedSignal.await();
  }

  @Override
  public void process(WatchedEvent event) { // Watcher interface
    if (event.getState() == KeeperState.SyncConnected) {
      connectedSignal.countDown();
    }
  }

  public void create(String groupName) throws KeeperException,
      InterruptedException {
```

```
    String path = "/" + groupName;
    String createdPath = zk.create(path, null/*data*/, Ids.OPEN_ACL_UNSAFE,
        CreateMode.PERSISTENT);
    System.out.println("Created " + createdPath);
  }

  public void close() throws InterruptedException {
    zk.close();
  }

  public static void main(String[] args) throws Exception {
    CreateGroup createGroup = new CreateGroup();
    createGroup.connect(args[0]);
    createGroup.create(args[1]);
    createGroup.close();
  }
}
```

When the main() method is run, it creates a CreateGroup instance and then calls its connect() method. This method instantiates a new ZooKeeper object, which is the central class of the client API and the one that maintains the connection between the client and the ZooKeeper service. The constructor takes three arguments: the first is the host address (and optional port, which defaults to 2181) of the ZooKeeper service;[3] the second is the session timeout in milliseconds (which we set to 5 seconds), explained in more detail later; and the third is an instance of a Watcher object. The Watcher object receives callbacks from ZooKeeper to inform it of various events. In this scenario, CreateGroup is a Watcher, so we pass this to the ZooKeeper constructor.

When a ZooKeeper instance is created, it starts a thread to connect to the ZooKeeper service. The call to the constructor returns immediately, so it is important to wait for the connection to be established before using the ZooKeeper object. We make use of Java's CountDownLatch class (in the java.util.concurrent package) to block until the ZooKeeper instance is ready. This is where the Watcher comes in. The Watcher interface has a single method:

```
    public void process(WatchedEvent event);
```

When the client has connected to ZooKeeper, the Watcher receives a call to its process() method with an event indicating that it has connected. On receiving a connection event (represented by the Watcher.Event.KeeperState enum, with value SyncConnected), we decrement the counter in the CountDownLatch, using its count Down() method. The latch was created with a count of one, representing the number of events that need to occur before it releases all waiting threads. After calling count Down() once, the counter reaches zero and the await() method returns.

The connect() method has now returned, and the next method to be invoked on the CreateGroup is the create() method. In this method, we create a new ZooKeeper znode

---

3. For a replicated ZooKeeper service, this parameter is the comma-separated list of servers (host and optional port) in the ensemble.

using the `create()` method on the ZooKeeper instance. The arguments it takes are the path (represented by a string), the contents of the znode (a byte array, null here), an access control list (or ACL for short, which here is a completely open ACL, allowing any client to read from or write to the znode), and the nature of the znode to be created.

Znodes may be ephemeral or persistent. An ephemeral znode will be deleted by the ZooKeeper service when the client that created it disconnects, either by explicitly disconnecting or if the client terminates for whatever reason. A persistent znode, on the other hand, is not deleted when the client disconnects. We want the znode representing a group to live longer than the lifetime of the program that creates it, so we create a persistent znode.

The return value of the `create()` method is the path that was created by ZooKeeper. We use it to print a message that the path was successfully created. We will see how the path returned by `create()` may differ from the one passed into the method when we look at sequential znodes.

To see the program in action, we need to have ZooKeeper running on the local machine, and then we can type:

```
% export CLASSPATH=ch14/target/classes/:$ZOOKEEPER_INSTALL/*:$ZOOKEEPER_INSTALL/lib/*:\
$ZOOKEEPER_INSTALL/conf
% java CreateGroup localhost zoo
Created /zoo
```

Joining a Group

The next part of the application is a program to register a member in a group. Each member will run as a program and join a group. When the program exits, it should be removed from the group, which we can do by creating an ephemeral znode that represents it in the ZooKeeper namespace.

The JoinGroup program implements this idea, and its listing is in Example 14-2. The logic for creating and connecting to a ZooKeeper instance has been refactored into a base class, ConnectionWatcher, and appears in Example 14-3.

Example 14-2. A program that joins a group

```java
public class JoinGroup extends ConnectionWatcher {

  public void join(String groupName, String memberName) throws KeeperException,
      InterruptedException {
    String path = "/" + groupName + "/" + memberName;
    String createdPath = zk.create(path, null/*data*/, Ids.OPEN_ACL_UNSAFE,
      CreateMode.EPHEMERAL);
    System.out.println("Created " + createdPath);
  }

  public static void main(String[] args) throws Exception {
    JoinGroup joinGroup = new JoinGroup();
    joinGroup.connect(args[0]);
```

```
    joinGroup.join(args[1], args[2]);

    // stay alive until process is killed or thread is interrupted
    Thread.sleep(Long.MAX_VALUE);
  }
}
```

Example 14-3. A helper class that waits for the connection to ZooKeeper to be established

```
public class ConnectionWatcher implements Watcher {

  private static final int SESSION_TIMEOUT = 5000;

  protected ZooKeeper zk;
  private CountDownLatch connectedSignal = new CountDownLatch(1);

  public void connect(String hosts) throws IOException, InterruptedException {
    zk = new ZooKeeper(hosts, SESSION_TIMEOUT, this);
    connectedSignal.await();
  }

  @Override
  public void process(WatchedEvent event) {
    if (event.getState() == KeeperState.SyncConnected) {
      connectedSignal.countDown();
    }
  }

  public void close() throws InterruptedException {
    zk.close();
  }
}
```

The code for JoinGroup is very similar to CreateGroup. It creates an ephemeral znode as
a child of the group znode in its join() method, then simulates doing work of some
kind by sleeping until the process is forcibly terminated. Later, you will see that upon
termination, the ephemeral znode is removed by ZooKeeper.

Listing Members in a Group

Now we need a program to find the members in a group (see Example 14-4).

Example 14-4. A program to list the members in a group

```
public class ListGroup extends ConnectionWatcher {

  public void list(String groupName) throws KeeperException,
      InterruptedException {
    String path = "/" + groupName;

    try {
      List<String> children = zk.getChildren(path, false);
      if (children.isEmpty()) {
        System.out.printf("No members in group %s\n", groupName);
```

```
      System.exit(1);
    }
    for (String child : children) {
      System.out.println(child);
    }
  } catch (KeeperException.NoNodeException e) {
    System.out.printf("Group %s does not exist\n", groupName);
    System.exit(1);
  }
}

public static void main(String[] args) throws Exception {
  ListGroup listGroup = new ListGroup();
  listGroup.connect(args[0]);
  listGroup.list(args[1]);
  listGroup.close();
}
}
```

In the list() method, we call getChildren() with a znode path and a watch flag to retrieve a list of child paths for the znode, which we print out. Placing a watch on a znode causes the registered Watcher to be triggered if the znode changes state. Although we're not using it here, watching a znode's children would permit a program to get notifications of members joining or leaving the group, or of the group being deleted.

We catch KeeperException.NoNodeException, which is thrown in the case when the group's znode does not exist.

Let's see ListGroup in action. As expected, the zoo group is empty, since we haven't added any members yet:

```
% java ListGroup localhost zoo
No members in group zoo
```

We can use JoinGroup to add some members. We launch them as background processes, since they don't terminate on their own (due to the sleep statement):

```
% java JoinGroup localhost zoo duck &
% java JoinGroup localhost zoo cow &
% java JoinGroup localhost zoo goat &
% goat_pid=$!
```

The last line saves the process ID of the Java process running the program that adds goat as a member. We need to remember the ID so that we can kill the process in a moment, after checking the members:

```
% java ListGroup localhost zoo
goat
duck
cow
```

To remove a member, we kill its process:

```
% kill $goat_pid
```

And a few seconds later, it has disappeared from the group because the process's Zoo-Keeper session has terminated (the timeout was set to 5 seconds) and its associated ephemeral node has been removed:

```
% java ListGroup localhost zoo
duck
cow
```

Let's stand back and see what we've built here. We have a way of building up a list of a group of nodes that are participating in a distributed system. The nodes may have no knowledge of each other. A client that wants to use the nodes in the list to perform some work, for example, can discover the nodes without them being aware of the client's existence.

Finally, note that group membership is not a substitution for handling network errors when communicating with a node. Even if a node is a group member, communications with it may fail, and such failures must be handled in the usual ways (retrying, trying a different member of the group, and so on).

ZooKeeper command-line tools

ZooKeeper comes with a command-line tool for interacting with the ZooKeeper name-space. We can use it to list the znodes under the /zoo znode as follows:

```
% zkCli.sh localhost ls /zoo
Processing ls
WatchedEvent: Server state change. New state: SyncConnected
[duck, cow]
```

You can run the command without arguments to display usage instructions.

Deleting a Group

To round off the example, let's see how to delete a group. The ZooKeeper class provides a delete() method that takes a path and a version number. ZooKeeper will delete a znode only if the version number specified is the same as the version number of the znode it is trying to delete, an optimistic locking mechanism that allows clients to detect conflicts over znode modification. You can bypass the version check, however, by using a version number of -1 to delete the znode regardless of its version number.

There is no recursive delete operation in ZooKeeper, so you have to delete child znodes before parents. This is what we do in the DeleteGroup class, which will remove a group and all its members (Example 14-5).

Example 14-5. A program to delete a group and its members

```
public class DeleteGroup extends ConnectionWatcher {

  public void delete(String groupName) throws KeeperException,
      InterruptedException {
    String path = "/" + groupName;
```

```
  try {
    List<String> children = zk.getChildren(path, false);
    for (String child : children) {
      zk.delete(path + "/" + child, -1);
    }
    zk.delete(path, -1);
  } catch (KeeperException.NoNodeException e) {
    System.out.printf("Group %s does not exist\n", groupName);
    System.exit(1);
  }
}

public static void main(String[] args) throws Exception {
  DeleteGroup deleteGroup = new DeleteGroup();
  deleteGroup.connect(args[0]);
  deleteGroup.delete(args[1]);
  deleteGroup.close();
}
}
```

Finally, we can delete the zoo group that we created earlier:

```
% java DeleteGroup localhost zoo
% java ListGroup localhost zoo
Group zoo does not exist
```

The ZooKeeper Service

ZooKeeper is a highly available, high-performance coordination service. In this section, we look at the nature of the service it provides: its model, operations, and implementation.

Data Model

ZooKeeper maintains a hierarchical tree of nodes called znodes. A znode stores data and has an associated ACL. ZooKeeper is designed for coordination (which typically uses small datafiles), not high-volume data storage, so there is a limit of 1 MB on the amount of data that may be stored in any znode.

Data access is atomic. A client reading the data stored at a znode will never receive only some of the data; either the data will be delivered in its entirety or the read will fail. Similarly, a write will replace all the data associated with a znode. ZooKeeper guarantees that the write will either succeed or fail; there is no such thing as a partial write, where only some of the data written by the client is stored. ZooKeeper does not support an append operation. These characteristics contrast with HDFS, which is designed for high-volume data storage with streaming data access and provides an append operation.

Znodes are referenced by paths, which in ZooKeeper are represented as slash-delimited Unicode character strings, like filesystem paths in Unix. Paths must be absolute, so they must begin with a slash character. Furthermore, they are canonical, which means that each path has a single representation, and so paths do not undergo resolution. For example, in Unix, a file with the path /a/b can equivalently be referred to by the path /a/./b because "." refers to the current directory at the point it is encountered in the path. In ZooKeeper, "." does not have this special meaning and is actually illegal as a path component (as is ".." for the parent of the current directory).

Path components are composed of Unicode characters, with a few restrictions (these are spelled out in the ZooKeeper reference documentation). The string "zookeeper" is a reserved word and may not be used as a path component. In particular, ZooKeeper uses the /zookeeper subtree to store management information, such as information on quotas.

Note that paths are not URIs, and they are represented in the Java API by a `java.lang.String`, rather than the Hadoop `Path` class (or by the `java.net.URI` class, for that matter).

Znodes have some properties that are very useful for building distributed applications, which we discuss in the following sections.

Ephemeral znodes

Znodes can be one of two types: ephemeral or persistent. A znode's type is set at creation time and may not be changed later. An ephemeral znode is deleted by ZooKeeper when the creating client's session ends. By contrast, a persistent znode is not tied to the client's session and is deleted only when explicitly deleted by a client (not necessarily the one that created it). An ephemeral znode may not have children, not even ephemeral ones.

Even though ephemeral nodes are tied to a client session, they are visible to all clients (subject to their ACL policy, of course).

Ephemeral znodes are ideal for building applications that need to know when certain distributed resources are available. The example earlier in this chapter uses ephemeral znodes to implement a group membership service, so any process can discover the members of the group at any particular time.

Sequence numbers

A *sequential* znode is given a sequence number by ZooKeeper as a part of its name. If a znode is created with the sequential flag set, then the value of a monotonically increasing counter (maintained by the parent znode) is appended to its name.

If a client asks to create a sequential znode with the name /a/b-, for example, the znode created may actually have the name /a/b-3.[4] If, later on, another sequential znode with the name /a/b- is created, it will be given a unique name with a larger value of the counter —for example, /a/b-5. In the Java API, the actual path given to sequential znodes is communicated back to the client as the return value of the create() call.

Sequence numbers can be used to impose a global ordering on events in a distributed system and may be used by the client to infer the ordering. In "A Lock Service" on page 519, you will learn how to use sequential znodes to build a shared lock.

Watches

Watches allow clients to get notifications when a znode changes in some way. Watches are set by operations on the ZooKeeper service and are triggered by other operations on the service. For example, a client might call the exists operation on a znode, placing a watch on it at the same time. If the znode doesn't exist, the exists operation will return false. If, some time later, the znode is created by a second client, the watch is triggered, notifying the first client of the znode's creation. You will see precisely which operations trigger others in the next section.

Watchers are triggered only once.[5] To receive multiple notifications, a client needs to reregister the watch. If the client in the previous example wishes to receive further notifications for the znode's existence (to be notified when it is deleted, for example), it needs to call the exists operation again to set a new watch.

There is an example in "A Configuration Service" on page 512 demonstrating how to use watches to update configuration across a cluster.

Operations

There are nine basic operations in ZooKeeper, listed in Table 14-2.

Table 14-2. Operations in the ZooKeeper service

Operation	Description
create	Creates a znode (the parent znode must already exist)
delete	Deletes a znode (the znode must not have any children)
exists	Tests whether a znode exists and retrieves its metadata
getACL, setACL	Gets/sets the ACL for a znode
getChildren	Gets a list of the children of a znode
getData, setData	Gets/sets the data associated with a znode

---

4. It is conventional (but not required) to have a trailing dash on pathnames for sequential nodes, to make their sequence numbers easy to read and parse (by the application).

5. Except for callbacks for connection events, which do not need reregistration.

Operation	Description
sync	Synchronizes a client's view of a znode with ZooKeeper

Update operations in ZooKeeper are conditional. A delete or setData operation has to specify the version number of the znode that is being updated (which is found from a previous exists call). If the version number does not match, the update will fail. Updates are a nonblocking operation, so a client that loses an update (because another process updated the znode in the meantime) can decide whether to try again or take some other action, and it can do so without blocking the progress of any other process.

Although ZooKeeper can be viewed as a filesystem, there are some filesystem primitives that it does away with in the name of simplicity. Because files are small and are written and read in their entirety, there is no need to provide open, close, or seek operations.

 The sync operation is not like fsync() in POSIX filesystems. As mentioned earlier, writes in ZooKeeper are atomic, and a successful write operation is guaranteed to have been written to persistent storage on a majority of ZooKeeper servers. However, it is permissible for reads to lag the latest state of the ZooKeeper service, and the sync operation exists to allow a client to bring itself up-to-date. This topic is covered in more detail in the section on "Consistency" on page 507.

Multiupdate

There is another ZooKeeper operation, called multi, which batches together multiple primitive operations into a single unit that either succeeds or fails in its entirety. The situation where some of the primitive operations succeed and some fail can never arise.

Multiupdate is very useful for building structures in ZooKeeper that maintain some global invariant. One example is an undirected graph. Each vertex in the graph is naturally represented as a znode in ZooKeeper, and to add or remove an edge we need to update the two znodes corresponding to its vertices because each has a reference to the other. If we used only primitive ZooKeeper operations, it would be possible for another client to observe the graph in an inconsistent state where one vertex is connected to another but the reverse connection is absent. Batching the updates on the two znodes into one multi operation ensures that the update is atomic, so a pair of vertices can never have a dangling connection.

APIs

There are two core language bindings for ZooKeeper clients, one for Java and one for C; there are also contrib bindings for Perl, Python, and REST clients. For each binding, there is a choice between performing operations synchronously or asynchronously. We've already seen the synchronous Java API. Here's the signature for the exists operation, which returns either a Stat object that encapsulates the znode's metadata or null if the znode doesn't exist:

```
public Stat exists(String path, Watcher watcher) throws KeeperException,
        InterruptedException
```

The asynchronous equivalent, which is also found in the ZooKeeper class, looks like this:

```
public void exists(String path, Watcher watcher, StatCallback cb, Object ctx)
```

In the Java API, all the asynchronous methods have void return types, since the result of the operation is conveyed via a callback. The caller passes a callback implementation whose method is invoked when a response is received from ZooKeeper. In this case, the callback is the StatCallback interface, which has the following method:

```
public void processResult(int rc, String path, Object ctx, Stat stat);
```

The rc argument is the return code, corresponding to the codes defined by KeeperEx ception. A nonzero code represents an exception, in which case the stat parameter will be null. The path and ctx arguments correspond to the equivalent arguments passed by the client to the exists() method, and can be used to identify the request for which this callback is a response. The ctx parameter can be an arbitrary object that may be used by the client when the path does not give enough context to disambiguate the request. If not needed, it may be set to null.

There are actually two C shared libraries. The single-threaded library, zookeeper_st, supports only the asynchronous API and is intended for platforms where the pthread library is not available or stable. Most developers will use the multithreaded library, zookeeper_mt, as it supports both the synchronous and asynchronous APIs. For details on how to build and use the C API, refer to the *README* file in the *src/c* directory of the ZooKeeper distribution.

Should I Use the Synchronous or Asynchronous API?

Both APIs offer the same functionality, so the one you use is largely a matter of style. The asynchronous API is appropriate if you have an event-driven programming model, for example.

The asynchronous API allows you to pipeline requests, which in some scenarios can offer better throughput. Imagine that you want to read a large batch of znodes and process them independently. Using the synchronous API, each read would block until it returned, whereas with the asynchronous API, you can fire off all the asynchronous reads very quickly and process the responses in a separate thread as they come back.

Watch triggers

The read operations exists, getChildren, and getData may have watches set on them, and the watches are triggered by write operations: create, delete, and setData. ACL operations do not participate in watches. When a watch is triggered, a watch event is generated, and the watch event's type depends both on the watch and the operation that triggered it:

- A watch set on an exists operation will be triggered when the znode being watched is created, deleted, or has its data updated.
- A watch set on a getData operation will be triggered when the znode being watched is deleted or has its data updated. No trigger can occur on creation because the znode must already exist for the getData operation to succeed.
- A watch set on a getChildren operation will be triggered when a child of the znode being watched is created or deleted, or when the znode itself is deleted. You can tell whether the znode or its child was deleted by looking at the watch event type: NodeDeleted shows the znode was deleted, and NodeChildrenChanged indicates that it was a child that was deleted.

The combinations are summarized in Table 14-3.

Table 14-3. Watch creation operations and their corresponding triggers

Watch creation	Watch trigger				setData
	create znode	create child	delete znode	delete child	
exists	NodeCreated		NodeDeleted		NodeData Changed
getData			NodeDeleted		NodeData Changed
getChildren		NodeChildren Changed	NodeDeleted	NodeChildren Changed	

A watch event includes the path of the znode that was involved in the event, so for NodeCreated and NodeDeleted events, you can tell which node was created or deleted simply by inspecting the path. To discover which children have changed after a Node ChildrenChanged event, you need to call getChildren again to retrieve the new list of children. Similarly, to discover the new data for a NodeDataChanged event, you need to call getData. In both of these cases, the state of the znodes may have changed between receiving the watch event and performing the read operation, so you should bear this in mind when writing applications.

ACLs

A znode is created with a list of ACLs, which determines who can perform certain operations on it.

ACLs depend on authentication, the process by which the client identifies itself to ZooKeeper. There are a few authentication schemes that ZooKeeper provides:

digest

The client is authenticated by a username and password.

sasl

The client is authenticated using Kerberos.

ip

The client is authenticated by its IP address.

Clients may authenticate themselves after establishing a ZooKeeper session. Authentication is optional, although a znode's ACL may require an authenticated client, in which case the client must authenticate itself to access the znode. Here is an example of using the digest scheme to authenticate with a username and password:

```
zk.addAuthInfo("digest", "tom:secret".getBytes());
```

An ACL is the combination of an authentication scheme, an identity for that scheme, and a set of permissions. For example, if we wanted to give a client with the IP address 10.0.0.1 read access to a znode, we would set an ACL on the znode with the ip scheme, an ID of 10.0.0.1, and READ permission. In Java, we would create the ACL object as follows:

```
new ACL(Perms.READ,
new Id("ip", "10.0.0.1"));
```

The full set of permissions are listed in Table 14-4. Note that the exists operation is not governed by an ACL permission, so any client may call exists to find the Stat for a znode or to discover that a znode does not in fact exist.

Table 14-4. ACL permissions

ACL permission	Permitted operations
CREATE	create (a child znode)
READ	getChildren
	getData
WRITE	setData
DELETE	delete (a child znode)
ADMIN	setACL

There are a number of predefined ACLs defined in the `ZooDefs.Ids` class, including `OPEN_ACL_UNSAFE`, which gives all permissions (except `ADMIN` permission) to everyone.

In addition, ZooKeeper has a pluggable authentication mechanism, which makes it possible to integrate third-party authentication systems if needed.

Implementation

The ZooKeeper service can run in two modes. In *standalone mode*, there is a single ZooKeeper server, which is useful for testing due to its simplicity (it can even be embedded in unit tests), but provides no guarantees of high-availability or resilience. In production, ZooKeeper runs in *replicated mode* on a cluster of machines called an *ensemble*. ZooKeeper achieves high-availability through replication, and can provide a service as long as a majority of the machines in the ensemble are up. For example, in a five-node ensemble, any two machines can fail and the service will still work because a majority of three remain. Note that a six-node ensemble can also tolerate only two machines failing, since with three failures the remaining three do not constitute a majority of the six. For this reason, it is usual to have an odd number of machines in an ensemble.

Conceptually, ZooKeeper is very simple: all it has to do is ensure that every modification to the tree of znodes is replicated to a majority of the ensemble. If a minority of the machines fail, then a minimum of one machine will survive with the latest state. The other remaining replicas will eventually catch up with this state.

The implementation of this simple idea, however, is nontrivial. ZooKeeper uses a protocol called Zab that runs in two phases, which may be repeated indefinitely:

Phase 1: Leader election
> The machines in an ensemble go through a process of electing a distinguished member, called the *leader*. The other machines are termed *followers*. This phase is finished once a majority (or *quorum*) of followers have synchronized their state with the leader.

Phase 2: Atomic broadcast
> All write requests are forwarded to the leader, which broadcasts the update to the followers. When a majority have persisted the change, the leader commits the update, and the client gets a response saying the update succeeded. The protocol for achieving consensus is designed to be atomic, so a change either succeeds or fails. It resembles a two-phase commit.

Does ZooKeeper Use Paxos?

No. ZooKeeper's Zab protocol is not the same as the well-known Paxos algorithm (Leslie Lamport, "Paxos Made Simple," *ACM SIGACT News [Distributed Computing Column]* 32, 4 [Whole Number 121, December 2001] 51–58.). Zab is similar, but it differs in several aspects of its operation, such as relying on TCP for its message ordering guarantees.

Zab is described in "A simple totally ordered broadcast protocol" by Benjamin Reed and Flavio Junqueira (*LADIS 2008, in: Proceedings of the 2nd Workshop on Large-Scale Distributed Systems and Middleware*, Article 2, New York, NY, USA, 2008. ACM).

Google's Chubby Lock Service (Mike Burrows, "The Chubby Lock Service for Loosely-Coupled Distributed Systems," November 2006, *http://labs.google.com/papers/chubby .html*), which shares similar goals with ZooKeeper, is based on Paxos.

If the leader fails, the remaining machines hold another leader election and continue as before with the new leader. If the old leader later recovers, it then starts as a follower. Leader election is very fast, around 200 ms according to one published result,[6] so performance does not noticeably degrade during an election.

All machines in the ensemble write updates to disk before updating their in-memory copy of the znode tree. Read requests may be serviced from any machine, and because they involve only a lookup from memory, they are very fast.

Consistency

Understanding the basis of ZooKeeper's implementation helps in understanding the consistency guarantees that the service makes. The terms "leader" and "follower" for the machines in an ensemble are apt because they make the point that a follower may lag the leader by a number of updates. This is a consequence of the fact that only a majority and not all of the ensemble needs to have persisted a change before it is committed. A good mental model for ZooKeeper is of clients connected to ZooKeeper servers that are following the leader. A client may actually be connected to the leader, but it has no control over this and cannot even know if this is the case.[7] See Figure 14-2.

Every update made to the znode tree is given a globally unique identifier, called a *zxid* (which stands for "ZooKeeper transaction ID"). Updates are ordered, so if *zxid* z_1 is less than z_2, then z_1 happened before z_2, according to ZooKeeper, which is the single authority on ordering in the distributed system.

---

6. Reported by Yahoo! at *http://zookeeper.apache.org/doc/current/zookeeperOver.html*.

7. It is possible to configure ZooKeeper so that the leader does not accept client connections. In this case, its only job is to coordinate updates. Do this by setting the `leaderServes` property to `no`. This is recommended for ensembles of more than three servers.

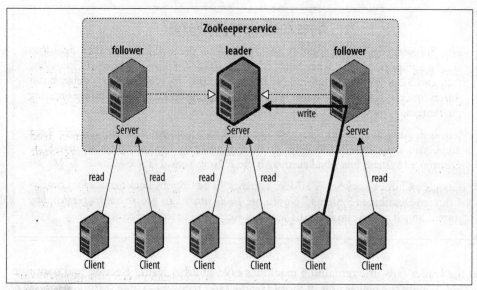

Figure 14-2. Reads are satisfied by followers, whereas writes are committed by the leader

The following guarantees for data consistency flow from ZooKeeper's design:

Sequential consistency

Updates from any particular client are applied in the order that they are sent. This means that if a client updates the znode z to the value a, and in a later operation, it updates z to the value b, then no client will ever see z with value a after it has seen it with value b (if no other updates are made to z).

Atomicity

Updates either succeed or fail. This means that if an update fails, no client will ever see it.

Single system image

A client will see the same view of the system, regardless of the server it connects to. This means that if a client connects to a new server during the same session, it will not see an older state of the system than the one it saw with the previous server. When a server fails and a client tries to connect to another in the ensemble, a server that is behind the one that failed will not accept connections from the client until it has caught up with the failed server.

Durability

Once an update has succeeded, it will persist and will not be undone. This means updates will survive server failures.

Timeliness

The lag in any client's view of the system is bounded, so it will not be out of date by more than some multiple of tens of seconds. This means that rather than allow a client to see data that is very stale, a server will shut down, forcing the client to switch to a more up-to-date server.

For performance reasons, reads are satisfied from a ZooKeeper server's memory and do not participate in the global ordering of writes. This property can lead to the appearance of inconsistent ZooKeeper states from clients that communicate through a mechanism outside ZooKeeper.

For example, client A updates znode z from a to a', A tells B to read z, and B reads the value of z as a, not a'. This is perfectly compatible with the guarantees that ZooKeeper makes (this condition that it does *not* promise is called "Simultaneously Consistent Cross-Client Views"). To prevent this condition from happening, B should call sync on z before reading z's value. The sync operation forces the ZooKeeper server to which B is connected to "catch up" with the leader, so that when B reads z's value, it will be the one that A set (or a later value).

 Slightly confusingly, the sync operation is available only as an *asynchronous* call. This is because you don't need to wait for it to return, since ZooKeeper guarantees that any subsequent operation will happen after the sync completes on the server, even if the operation is issued before the sync completes.

Sessions

A ZooKeeper client is configured with the list of servers in the ensemble. On startup, it tries to connect to one of the servers in the list. If the connection fails, it tries another server in the list, and so on, until it either successfully connects to one of them or fails if all ZooKeeper servers are unavailable.

Once a connection has been made with a ZooKeeper server, the server creates a new session for the client. A session has a timeout period that is decided on by the application that creates it. If the server hasn't received a request within the timeout period, it may expire the session. Once a session has expired, it may not be reopened, and any ephemeral nodes associated with the session will be lost. Although session expiry is a comparatively rare event, since sessions are long-lived, it is important for applications to handle it (we will see how in "The Resilient ZooKeeper Application" on page 515).

Sessions are kept alive by the client sending ping requests (also known as heartbeats) whenever the session is idle for longer than a certain period. (Pings are automatically sent by the ZooKeeper client library, so your code doesn't need to worry about maintaining the session.) The period is chosen to be low enough to detect server failure (manifested by a read timeout) and reconnect to another server within the session timeout period.

Failover to another ZooKeeper server is handled automatically by the ZooKeeper client, and, crucially, sessions (and associated ephemeral znodes) are still valid after another server takes over from the failed one.

During failover, the application will receive notifications of disconnections and connections to the service. Watch notifications will not be delivered while the client is disconnected, but they will be delivered when the client successfully reconnects. Also, if the application tries to perform an operation while the client is reconnecting to another server, the operation will fail. This underlines the importance of handling connection loss exceptions in real-world ZooKeeper applications (described in "The Resilient ZooKeeper Application" on page 515).

Time

There are several time parameters in ZooKeeper. The *tick time* is the fundamental period of time in ZooKeeper and is used by servers in the ensemble to define the schedule on which their interactions run. Other settings are defined in terms of tick time, or are at least constrained by it. The session timeout, for example, may not be less than 2 ticks or more than 20. If you attempt to set a session timeout outside this range, it will be modified to fall within the range.

A common tick time setting is 2 seconds (2,000 milliseconds). This translates to an allowable session timeout of between 4 and 40 seconds. There are a few considerations in selecting a session timeout.

A low session timeout leads to faster detection of machine failure. In the group membership example, the session timeout is the time it takes for a failed machine to be removed from the group. Beware of setting the session timeout too low, however, because a busy network can cause packets to be delayed and may cause inadvertent session expiry. In such an event, a machine would appear to "flap": leaving and then rejoining the group repeatedly in a short space of time.

Applications that create more complex ephemeral state should favor longer session timeouts, as the cost of reconstruction is higher. In some cases, it is possible to design the application so it can restart within the session timeout period and avoid session expiry. (This might be desirable to perform maintenance or upgrades.) Every session is given a unique identity and password by the server, and if these are passed to ZooKeeper while a connection is being made, it is possible to recover a session (as long as it hasn't expired). An application can therefore arrange a graceful shutdown, whereby it stores the session identity and password to stable storage before restarting the process, retrieving the stored session identity and password and recovering the session.

You should view this feature as an optimization that can help avoid expire sessions. It does not remove the need to handle session expiry, which can still occur if a machine fails unexpectedly, or even if an application is shut down gracefully but does not restart before its session expires—for whatever reason.

As a general rule, the larger the ZooKeeper ensemble, the larger the session timeout should be. Connection timeouts, read timeouts, and ping periods are all defined internally as a function of the number of servers in the ensemble, so as the ensemble grows, these periods decrease. Consider increasing the timeout if you experience frequent connection loss. You can monitor ZooKeeper metrics—such as request latency statistics—using JMX.

States

The `ZooKeeper` object transitions through different states in its lifecycle (see Figure 14-3). You can query its state at any time by using the `getState()` method:

```
public States getState()
```

`States` is an enum representing the different states that a `ZooKeeper` object may be in. (Despite the enum's name, an instance of `ZooKeeper` may be in only one state at a time.) A newly constructed `ZooKeeper` instance is in the `CONNECTING` state while it tries to establish a connection with the ZooKeeper service. Once a connection is established, it goes into the `CONNECTED` state.

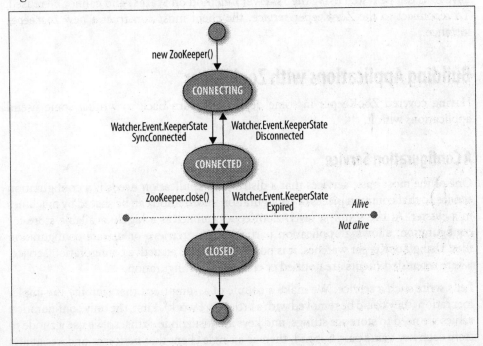

Figure 14-3. ZooKeeper state transitions

A client using the `ZooKeeper` object can receive notifications of the state transitions by registering a `Watcher` object. On entering the `CONNECTED` state, the watcher receives a `WatchedEvent` whose `KeeperState` value is `SyncConnected`.

A ZooKeeper Watcher object serves double duty: it can be used to be notified of changes in the ZooKeeper state (as described in this section), and it can be used to be notified of changes in znodes (described in "Watch triggers" on page 504). The (default) watcher passed into the ZooKeeper object constructor is used for state changes, but znode changes may either use a dedicated instance of Watcher (by passing one in to the appropriate read operation) or share the default one if using the form of the read operation that takes a Boolean flag to specify whether to use a watcher.

The ZooKeeper instance may disconnect and reconnect to the ZooKeeper service, moving between the CONNECTED and CONNECTING states. If it disconnects, the watcher receives a Disconnected event. Note that these state transitions are initiated by the ZooKeeper instance itself, and it will automatically try to reconnect if the connection is lost.

The ZooKeeper instance may transition to a third state, CLOSED, if either the close() method is called or the session times out as indicated by a KeeperState of type Expired. Once in the CLOSED state, the ZooKeeper object is no longer considered to be alive (this can be tested using the isAlive() method on States) and cannot be reused. To reconnect to the ZooKeeper service, the client must construct a new ZooKeeper instance.

Building Applications with ZooKeeper

Having covered ZooKeeper in some depth, let's turn back to writing some useful applications with it.

A Configuration Service

One of the most basic services that a distributed application needs is a configuration service so that common pieces of configuration information can be shared by machines in a cluster. At the simplest level, ZooKeeper can act as a highly available store for configuration, allowing application participants to retrieve or update configuration files. Using ZooKeeper watches, it is possible to create an active configuration service, where interested clients are notified of changes in configuration.

Let's write such a service. We make a couple of assumptions that simplify the implementation (they could be removed with a little more work). First, the only configuration values we need to store are strings, and keys are just znode paths, so we use a znode to store each key-value pair. Second, there is a single client that performs updates at any one time. Among other things, this model fits with the idea of a master (such as the namenode in HDFS) that wishes to update information that its workers need to follow.

We wrap the code up in a class called `ActiveKeyValueStore`:

```
public class ActiveKeyValueStore extends ConnectionWatcher {

  private static final Charset CHARSET = Charset.forName("UTF-8");

  public void write(String path, String value) throws InterruptedException,
      KeeperException {
    Stat stat = zk.exists(path, false);
    if (stat == null) {
      zk.create(path, value.getBytes(CHARSET), Ids.OPEN_ACL_UNSAFE,
          CreateMode.PERSISTENT);
    } else {
      zk.setData(path, value.getBytes(CHARSET), -1);
    }
  }
}
```

The contract of the `write()` method is that a key with the given value is written to ZooKeeper. It hides the difference between creating a new znode and updating an existing znode with a new value by testing first for the znode using the `exists` operation and then performing the appropriate operation. The other detail worth mentioning is the need to convert the string value to a byte array, for which we just use the `getBytes()` method with a UTF-8 encoding.

To illustrate the use of the `ActiveKeyValueStore`, consider a `ConfigUpdater` class that updates a configuration property with a value. The listing appears in Example 14-6.

Example 14-6. An application that updates a property in ZooKeeper at random times

```
public class ConfigUpdater {

  public static final String PATH = "/config";

  private ActiveKeyValueStore store;
  private Random random = new Random();

  public ConfigUpdater(String hosts) throws IOException, InterruptedException {
    store = new ActiveKeyValueStore();
    store.connect(hosts);
  }

  public void run() throws InterruptedException, KeeperException {
    while (true) {
      String value = random.nextInt(100) + ";
      store.write(PATH, value);
      System.out.printf("Set %s to %s\n", PATH, value);
      TimeUnit.SECONDS.sleep(random.nextInt(10));
    }
  }
}
```

```
  public static void main(String[] args) throws Exception {
    ConfigUpdater configUpdater = new ConfigUpdater(args[0]);
    configUpdater.run();
  }
}
```

The program is simple. A ConfigUpdater has an ActiveKeyValueStore that connects to
ZooKeeper in ConfigUpdater's constructor. The run() method loops forever, updating
the */config* znode at random times with random values.

Next, let's look at how to read the */config* configuration property. First, we add a read
method to ActiveKeyValueStore:

```
    public String read(String path, Watcher watcher) throws InterruptedException,
        KeeperException {
      byte[] data = zk.getData(path, watcher, null/*stat*/);
      return new String(data, CHARSET);
    }
```

The getData() method of ZooKeeper takes the path, a Watcher, and a Stat object. The
Stat object is filled in with values by getData() and is used to pass information back to
the caller. In this way, the caller can get both the data and the metadata for a znode,
although in this case, we pass a null Stat because we are not interested in the metadata.

As a consumer of the service, ConfigWatcher (see Example 14-7) creates an ActiveKey
ValueStore, and after starting, calls the store's read() method (in its displayConfig()
method) to pass a reference to itself as the watcher. It displays the initial value of the
configuration that it reads.

*Example 14-7. An application that watches for updates of a property in ZooKeeper and prints them
to the console*

```
public class ConfigWatcher implements Watcher {

  private ActiveKeyValueStore store;

  public ConfigWatcher(String hosts) throws IOException, InterruptedException {
    store = new ActiveKeyValueStore();
    store.connect(hosts);
  }

  public void displayConfig() throws InterruptedException, KeeperException {
    String value = store.read(ConfigUpdater.PATH, this);
    System.out.printf("Read %s as %s\n", ConfigUpdater.PATH, value);
  }

  @Override
  public void process(WatchedEvent event) {
    if (event.getType() == EventType.NodeDataChanged) {
      try {
        displayConfig();
      } catch (InterruptedException e) {
        System.err.println("Interrupted. Exiting.");
        Thread.currentThread().interrupt();
```

```
    } catch (KeeperException e) {
      System.err.printf("KeeperException: %s. Exiting.\n", e);
    }
  }
}

public static void main(String[] args) throws Exception {
  ConfigWatcher configWatcher = new ConfigWatcher(args[0]);
  configWatcher.displayConfig();

  // stay alive until process is killed or thread is interrupted
  Thread.sleep(Long.MAX_VALUE);
  }
}
```

When the ConfigUpdater updates the znode, ZooKeeper causes the watcher to fire with an event type of EventType.NodeDataChanged. ConfigWatcher acts on this event in its process() method by reading and displaying the latest version of the config.

Because watches are one-time signals, we tell ZooKeeper of the new watch each time we call read() on ActiveKeyValueStore, which ensures we see future updates. Furthermore, we are not guaranteed to receive every update, since between the receipt of the watch event and the next read, the znode may have been updated, possibly many times, and as the client has no watch registered during that period, it is not notified. For the configuration service, this is not a problem, because clients care only about the latest value of a property, as it takes precedence over previous values. However, in general you should be aware of this potential limitation.

Let's see the code in action. Launch the ConfigUpdater in one terminal window:

```
% java ConfigUpdater localhost
Set /config to 79
Set /config to 14
Set /config to 78
```

Then launch the ConfigWatcher in another window immediately afterward:

```
% java ConfigWatcher localhost
Read /config as 79
Read /config as 14
Read /config as 78
```

The Resilient ZooKeeper Application

The first of the Fallacies of Distributed Computing states that "the network is reliable."[8] As they stand, the programs so far have been assuming a reliable network, so when they run on a real network, they can fail in several ways. Let's examine possible failure modes and what we can do to correct them so that our programs are resilient in the face of failure.

8. See *http://en.wikipedia.org/wiki/Fallacies_of_Distributed_Computing*.

Every ZooKeeper operation in the Java API declares two types of exception in its throws clause: InterruptedException and KeeperException.

InterruptedException

An InterruptedException is thrown if the operation is interrupted. There is a standard Java mechanism for canceling blocking methods, which is to call interrupt() on the thread from which the blocking method was called. A successful cancellation will result in an InterruptedException. ZooKeeper adheres to this standard, so you can cancel a ZooKeeper operation in this way. Classes or libraries that use ZooKeeper usually should propagate the InterruptedException so that their clients can cancel their operations.[9]

An InterruptedException does not indicate a failure, but rather that the operation has been canceled, so in the configuration application example, it is appropriate to propagate the exception, causing the application to terminate.

KeeperException

A KeeperException is thrown if the ZooKeeper server signals an error or if there is a communication problem with the server. For different error cases, there are various subclasses of KeeperException. For example, KeeperException.NoNodeException is a subclass of KeeperException that is thrown if you try to perform an operation on a znode that doesn't exist.

Every subclass of KeeperException has a corresponding code with information about the type of error. For example, for KeeperException.NoNodeException the code is KeeperException.Code.NONODE (an enum value).

There are two ways then to handle KeeperException: either catch KeeperException and test its code to determine what remedying action to take, or catch the equivalent KeeperException subclasses and perform the appropriate action in each catch block.

KeeperExceptions fall into three broad categories.

State exceptions. A state exception occurs when the operation fails because it cannot be applied to the znode tree. State exceptions usually happen because another process is mutating a znode at the same time. For example, a setData operation with a version number will fail with a KeeperException.BadVersionException if the znode is updated by another process first because the version number does not match. The programmer is usually aware that this kind of conflict is possible and will code to deal with it.

Some state exceptions indicate an error in the program, such as KeeperException.NoChildrenForEphemeralsException, which is thrown when trying to create a child znode of an ephemeral znode.

---

9. For more detail, see the excellent article "Dealing with InterruptedException" (*http://www.ibm.com/developerworks/java/library/j-jtp05236.html*) by Brian Goetz.

Recoverable exceptions. Recoverable exceptions are those from which the application can recover within the same ZooKeeper session. A recoverable exception is manifested by `KeeperException.ConnectionLossException`, which means that the connection to ZooKeeper has been lost. ZooKeeper will try to reconnect, and in most cases the reconnection will succeed and ensure that the session is intact.

However, ZooKeeper cannot tell whether the operation that failed with `KeeperException.ConnectionLossException` was applied. This is an example of partial failure (which we introduced at the beginning of the chapter). The onus is therefore on the programmer to deal with the uncertainty, and the action that should be taken depends on the application.

At this point, it is useful to make a distinction between *idempotent* and *nonidempotent* operations. An idempotent operation is one that may be applied one or more times with the same result, such as a read request or an unconditional `setData`. These can simply be retried.

A nonidempotent operation cannot be retried indiscriminately, as the effect of applying it multiple times is not the same as applying it once. The program needs a way of detecting whether its update was applied by encoding information in the znode's pathname or its data. We discuss how to deal with failed nonidempotent operations in "Recoverable exceptions" on page 520, when we look at the implementation of a lock service.

Unrecoverable exceptions. In some cases, the ZooKeeper session becomes invalid—perhaps because of a timeout or because the session was closed (both get a `KeeperException.SessionExpiredException`), or perhaps because authentication failed (`KeeperException.AuthFailedException`). In any case, all ephemeral nodes associated with the session will be lost, so the application needs to rebuild its state before reconnecting to ZooKeeper.

A reliable configuration service

Going back to the `write()` method in `ActiveKeyValueStore`, recall that it is composed of an `exists` operation followed by either a `create` or a `setData`:

```
public void write(String path, String value) throws InterruptedException,
    KeeperException {
  Stat stat = zk.exists(path, false);
  if (stat == null) {
    zk.create(path, value.getBytes(CHARSET), Ids.OPEN_ACL_UNSAFE,
        CreateMode.PERSISTENT);
  } else {
    zk.setData(path, value.getBytes(CHARSET), -1);
  }
}
```

Taken as a whole, the `write()` method is idempotent, so we can afford to unconditionally retry it. Here's a modified version of the `write()` method that retries in a loop.

It is set to try a maximum number of retries (MAX_RETRIES) and sleeps for RETRY_PERIOD_SECONDS between each attempt:

```java
public void write(String path, String value) throws InterruptedException,
    KeeperException {
  int retries = 0;
  while (true) {
    try {
      Stat stat = zk.exists(path, false);
      if (stat == null) {
        zk.create(path, value.getBytes(CHARSET), Ids.OPEN_ACL_UNSAFE,
            CreateMode.PERSISTENT);
      } else {
        zk.setData(path, value.getBytes(CHARSET), stat.getVersion());
      }
      return;
    } catch (KeeperException.SessionExpiredException e) {
      throw e;
    } catch (KeeperException e) {
      if (retries++ == MAX_RETRIES) {
        throw e;
      }
      // sleep then retry
      TimeUnit.SECONDS.sleep(RETRY_PERIOD_SECONDS);
    }
  }
}
```

The code is careful not to retry KeeperException.SessionExpiredException, because when a session expires, the ZooKeeper object enters the CLOSED state, from which it can never reconnect (refer to Figure 14-3). We simply rethrow the exception[10] and let the caller create a new ZooKeeper instance, so that the whole write() method can be retried. A simple way to create a new instance is to create a new ConfigUpdater (which we've actually renamed ResilientConfigUpdater) to recover from an expired session:

```java
public static void main(String[] args) throws Exception {
  while (true) {
    try {
      ResilientConfigUpdater configUpdater =
        new ResilientConfigUpdater(args[0]);
      configUpdater.run();
    } catch (KeeperException.SessionExpiredException e) {
      // start a new session
    } catch (KeeperException e) {
      // already retried, so exit
      e.printStackTrace();
      break;
    }
  }
}
```

10. Another way of writing the code would be to have a single catch block, just for KeeperException, and a test to see whether its code has the value KeeperException.Code.SESSIONEXPIRED. Which method you use is a matter of style, since they both behave in the same way.

An alternative way of dealing with session expiry would be to look for a `KeeperState` of type `Expired` in the watcher (that would be the `ConnectionWatcher` in the example here), and create a new connection when this is detected. This way, we would just keep retrying in the `write()` method, even if we got a `KeeperException.SessionExpiredExcep tion`, since the connection should eventually be reestablished. Regardless of the precise mechanics of how we recover from an expired session, the important point is that it is a different kind of failure from connection loss and needs to be handled differently.

There's actually another failure mode that we've ignored here. When the `ZooKeeper` object is created, it tries to connect to a ZooKeeper server. If the connection fails or times out, then it tries another server in the ensemble. If, after trying all of the servers in the ensemble, it can't connect, then it throws an `IOException`. The likelihood of all ZooKeeper servers being unavailable is low; nevertheless, some applications may choose to retry the operation in a loop until ZooKeeper is available.

This is just one strategy for retry handling. There are many others, such as using exponential backoff where the period between retries is multiplied by a constant each time. The `org.apache.hadoop.io.retry` package in Hadoop Core is a set of utilities for adding retry logic into your code in a reusable way, and it may be helpful for building ZooKeeper applications.

A Lock Service

A distributed lock is a mechanism for providing mutual exclusion between a collection of processes. At any one time, only a single process may hold the lock. Distributed locks can be used for leader election in a large distributed system, where the leader is the process that holds the lock at any point in time.

Do not confuse ZooKeeper's own leader election with a general leader election service, which can be built using ZooKeeper primitives (and in fact, one implementation is included with ZooKeeper). ZooKeeper's own leader election is not exposed publicly, unlike the type of general leader election service we are describing here, which is designed to be used by distributed systems that need to agree upon a master process.

To implement a distributed lock using ZooKeeper, we use sequential znodes to impose an order on the processes vying for the lock. The idea is simple: first, designate a lock znode, typically describing the entity being locked on, say, */leader*; then, clients that want to acquire the lock create sequential ephemeral znodes as children of the lock znode. At any point in time, the client with the lowest sequence number holds the lock. For example, if two clients create the znodes at */leader/lock-1* and */leader/lock-2* around the same time, then the client that created */leader/lock-1* holds the lock, since its znode has the lowest sequence number. The ZooKeeper service is the arbiter of order because it assigns the sequence numbers.

The lock may be released simply by deleting the znode */leader/lock-1*; alternatively, if the client process dies, it will be deleted by virtue of being an ephemeral znode. The client that created */leader/lock-2* will then hold the lock because it has the next lowest sequence number. It will be notified that it has the lock by creating a watch that fires when znodes go away.

The pseudocode for lock acquisition is as follows:

1. Create an ephemeral sequential znode named *lock-* under the lock znode, and remember its actual pathname (the return value of the create operation).

2. Get the children of the lock znode and set a watch.

3. If the path name of the znode created in 1 has the lowest number of the children returned in 2, then the lock has been acquired. Exit.

4. Wait for the notification from the watch set in 2, and go to step 2.

The herd effect

Although this algorithm is correct, there are some problems with it. The first problem is that this implementation suffers from the *herd effect*. Consider hundreds or thousands of clients, all trying to acquire the lock. Each client places a watch on the lock znode for changes in its set of children. Every time the lock is released or another process starts the lock acquisition process, the watch fires, and every client receives a notification. The "herd effect" refers to a large number of clients being notified of the same event when only a small number of them can actually proceed. In this case, only one client will successfully acquire the lock, and the process of maintaining and sending watch events to all clients causes traffic spikes, which put pressure on the ZooKeeper servers.

To avoid the herd effect, the condition for notification needs to be refined. The key observation for implementing locks is that a client needs to be notified only when the child znode with the *previous* sequence number goes away, not when any child znode is deleted (or created). In our example, if clients have created the znodes */leader/ lock-1*, */leader/lock-2*, and */leader/lock-3*, then the client holding */leader/lock-3* needs to be notified only when */leader/lock-2* disappears. It does not need to be notified when */leader/lock-1* disappears or when a new znode */leader/lock-4* is added.

Recoverable exceptions

Another problem with the lock algorithm as it stands is that it doesn't handle the case when the create operation fails due to connection loss. Recall that in this case we do not know whether the operation succeeded or failed. Creating a sequential znode is a nonidempotent operation, so we can't simply retry, because if the first create had succeeded, we would have an orphaned znode that would never be deleted (until the client session ended, at least). Deadlock would be the unfortunate result.

The problem is that after reconnecting, the client can't tell whether it created any of the child znodes. By embedding an identifier in the znode name, if it suffers a connection loss, it can check to see whether any of the children of the lock node have its identifier in their name. If a child contains its identifier, it knows that the create operation succeeded, and it shouldn't create another child znode. If no child has the identifier in its name, the client can safely create a new sequential child znode.

The client's session identifier is a long integer that is unique for the ZooKeeper service and therefore ideal for the purpose of identifying a client across connection loss events. The session identifier can be obtained by calling the getSessionId() method on the ZooKeeper Java class.

The ephemeral sequential znode should be created with a name of the form *lock-<sessionId>-*, so that when the sequence number is appended by ZooKeeper, the name becomes *lock-<sessionId>-<sequenceNumber>*. The sequence numbers are unique to the parent, not to the name of the child, so this technique allows the child znodes to identify their creators as well as impose an order of creation.

Unrecoverable exceptions

If a client's ZooKeeper session expires, the ephemeral znode created by the client will be deleted, effectively relinquishing the lock or at least forfeiting the client's turn to acquire the lock. The application using the lock should realize that it no longer holds the lock, clean up its state, and then start again by creating a new lock object and trying to acquire it. Notice that it is the application that controls this process, not the lock implementation, since it cannot second-guess how the application needs to clean up its state.

Implementation

Implementing a distributed lock correctly is a delicate matter, since accounting for all of the failure modes is nontrivial. ZooKeeper comes with a production-quality lock implementation in Java called WriteLock that is very easy for clients to use.

More Distributed Data Structures and Protocols

There are many distributed data structures and protocols that can be built with Zoo-Keeper, such as barriers, queues, and two-phase commit. One interesting thing to note is that these are synchronous protocols, even though we use asynchronous ZooKeeper primitives (such as notifications) to build them.

The ZooKeeper website (*http://zookeeper.apache.org/*) describes several such data structures and protocols in pseudocode. ZooKeeper comes with implementations of some of these standard recipes (including locks, leader election, and queues); they can be found in the *recipes* directory of the distribution.

The Curator project (*https://github.com/Netflix/curator*) also provides an extensive set of ZooKeeper recipes.

BookKeeper and Hedwig

BookKeeper is a highly available and reliable logging service. It can be used to provide write-ahead logging, which is a common technique for ensuring data integrity in storage systems. In a system using write-ahead logging, every write operation is written to the transaction log before it is applied. Using this procedure, we don't have to write the data to permanent storage after every write operation, because in the event of a system failure, the latest state may be recovered by replaying the transaction log for any writes that were not applied.

BookKeeper clients create logs called *ledgers*, and each record appended to a ledger is called a *ledger entry*, which is simply a byte array. Ledgers are managed by *bookies*, which are servers that replicate the ledger data. Note that ledger data is not stored in ZooKeeper, only metadata is.

Traditionally, the challenge has been to make systems that use write-ahead logging robust in the face of failure of the node writing the transaction log. This is usually done by replicating the transaction log in some manner. Hadoop's HDFS namenode, for instance, writes its edit log to multiple disks, one of which is typically an NFS-mounted disk. However, in the event of failure of the primary, failover is still manual. By providing logging as a highly available service, BookKeeper promises to make failover transparent, since it can tolerate the loss of bookie servers. (In the case of HDFS High-Availability, described on page 48, a BookKeeper-based edit log will remove the requirement for using NFS for shared storage.)

Hedwig is a topic-based publish-subscribe system built on BookKeeper. Thanks to its ZooKeeper underpinnings, Hedwig is a highly available service and guarantees message delivery even if subscribers are offline for extended periods of time.

BookKeeper is a ZooKeeper subproject, and you can find more information on how to use it, as well as Hedwig, at *http://zookeeper.apache.org/bookkeeper/*.

ZooKeeper in Production

In production, you should run ZooKeeper in replicated mode. Here, we will cover some of the considerations for running an ensemble of ZooKeeper servers. However, this section is not exhaustive, so you should consult the ZooKeeper Administrator's Guide (*http://zookeeper.apache.org/doc/current/zookeeperAdmin.html*) for detailed, up-to-date instructions, including supported platforms, recommended hardware, maintenance procedures, and configuration properties.

Resilience and Performance

ZooKeeper machines should be located to minimize the impact of machine and network failure. In practice, this means that servers should be spread across racks, power supplies, and switches, so that the failure of any one of these does not cause the ensemble to lose a majority of its servers.

For applications that require low-latency service (on the order of a few milliseconds), it is important to run all the servers in an ensemble in a single data center. Some use cases don't require low-latency responses, however, which makes it feasible to spread servers across data centers (at least two per data center) for extra resilience. Example applications in this category are leader election and distributed coarse-grained locking, both of which have relatively infrequent state changes, so the overhead of a few tens of milliseconds incurred by inter-data-center messages is not significant relative to the overall functioning of the service.

ZooKeeper has the concept of an *observer node*, which is like a non-voting follower. Because they do not participate in the vote for consensus during write requests, observers allow a ZooKeeper cluster to improve read performance without hurting write performance.[11] Observers can be used to good advantage to allow a ZooKeeper cluster to span data centers without impacting latency as much as regular voting followers. This is achieved by placing the voting members in one data center and observers in the other.

ZooKeeper is a highly available system, and it is critical that it can perform its functions in a timely manner. Therefore, ZooKeeper should run on machines that are dedicated to ZooKeeper alone. Having other applications contend for resources can cause ZooKeeper's performance to degrade significantly.

Configure ZooKeeper to keep its transaction log on a different disk drive from its snapshots. By default, both go in the directory specified by the `dataDir` property, but by specifying a location for `dataLogDir`, the transaction log will be written there. By having its own dedicated device (not just a partition), a ZooKeeper server can maximize the rate at which it writes log entries to disk, which it does sequentially without seeking. Because all writes go through the leader, write throughput does not scale by adding servers, so it is crucial that writes are as fast as possible.

If the process swaps to disk, performance will be adversely affected. This can be avoided by setting the Java heap size to less than the amount of unused physical memory on the machine. From its configuration directory, the ZooKeeper scripts will source a file

---

11. This is discussed in more detail in "Observers: Making ZooKeeper Scale Even Further" (*http: //www.cloudera.com/blog/2009/12/observers-making-zookeeper-scale-even-further/*) by Henry Robinson.

called *java.env*, which can be used to set the JVMFLAGS environment variable to specify the heap size (and any other desired JVM arguments).

Configuration

Each server in the ensemble of ZooKeeper servers has a numeric identifier that is unique within the ensemble and must fall between 1 and 255. The server number is specified in plain text in a file named *myid* in the directory specified by the dataDir property.

Setting each server number is only half of the job. We also need to give every server all the identities and network locations of the others in the ensemble. The ZooKeeper configuration file must include a line for each server, of the form:

```
server.n=hostname:port:port
```

The value of *n* is replaced by the server number. There are two port settings: the first is the port that followers use to connect to the leader, and the second is used for leader election. Here is a sample configuration for a three-machine replicated ZooKeeper ensemble:

```
tickTime=2000
dataDir=/disk1/zookeeper
dataLogDir=/disk2/zookeeper
clientPort=2181
initLimit=5
syncLimit=2
server.1=zookeeper1:2888:3888
server.2=zookeeper2:2888:3888
server.3=zookeeper3:2888:3888
```

Servers listen on three ports: 2181 for client connections; 2888 for follower connections, if they are the leader; and 3888 for other server connections during the leader election phase. When a ZooKeeper server starts up, it reads the *myid* file to determine which server it is, and then reads the configuration file to determine the ports it should listen on and to discover the network addresses of the other servers in the ensemble.

Clients connecting to this ZooKeeper ensemble should use zookeeper1:2181,zoo keeper2:2181,zookeeper3:2181 as the host string in the constructor for the ZooKeeper object.

In replicated mode, there are two extra mandatory properties: initLimit and syncLimit, both measured in multiples of tickTime.

initLimit is the amount of time to allow for followers to connect to and sync with the leader. If a majority of followers fail to sync within this period, the leader renounces its leadership status and another leader election takes place. If this happens often (and you can discover if this is the case because it is logged), it is a sign that the setting is too low.

syncLimit is the amount of time to allow a follower to sync with the leader. If a follower fails to sync within this period, it will restart itself. Clients that were attached to this follower will connect to another one.

These are the minimum settings needed to get up and running with a cluster of Zoo-Keeper servers. There are, however, more configuration options, particularly for tuning performance, which are documented in the ZooKeeper Administrator's Guide.

Sqoop

Aaron Kimball

A great strength of the Hadoop platform is its ability to work with data in several different forms. HDFS can reliably store logs and other data from a plethora of sources, and MapReduce programs can parse diverse ad hoc data formats, extracting relevant information and combining multiple datasets into powerful results.

But to interact with data in storage repositories outside of HDFS, MapReduce programs need to use external APIs to get to this data. Often, valuable data in an organization is stored in structured data stores such as relational database systems (RDBMS). *Apache Sqoop* is an open source tool that allows users to extract data from a structured data store into Hadoop for further processing. This processing can be done with MapReduce programs or other higher-level tools such as Hive. (It's even possible to use Sqoop to move data from a database into HBase.) When the final results of an analytic pipeline are available, Sqoop can export these results back to the data store for consumption by other clients.

In this chapter, we'll take a look at how Sqoop works and how you can use it in your data processing pipeline.

Getting Sqoop

Sqoop is available in a few places. The primary home of the project is *http://sqoop .apache.org/*. This repository contains all the Sqoop source code and documentation. Official releases are available at this site, as well as the source code for the version currently under development. The repository itself contains instructions for compiling the project. Alternatively, Cloudera's Distribution Including Apache Hadoop (CDH) contains an installation package for Sqoop alongside compatible editions of Hadoop and other tools such as Hive.

If you download a release from Apache, it will be placed in a directory such as */home/ yourname/sqoop-x.y.z/*. We'll call this directory $SQOOP_HOME. You can run Sqoop by running the executable script $SQOOP_HOME/bin/sqoop.

If you've installed a release from Cloudera, the package will have placed Sqoop's scripts in a standard locations such as */usr/bin/sqoop*. You can run Sqoop by simply typing sqoop at the command line. (Regardless of how you install Sqoop, we'll refer to this script as just sqoop from here on.)

Running Sqoop with no arguments does not do much of interest:

```
% sqoop
Try sqoop help for usage.
```

Sqoop is organized as a set of tools or commands. Without selecting a tool, Sqoop does not know what to do. help is the name of one such tool; it can print out the list of available tools, like this:

```
% sqoop help
usage: sqoop COMMAND [ARGS]

Available commands:
  codegen            Generate code to interact with database records
  create-hive-table  Import a table definition into Hive
  eval               Evaluate a SQL statement and display the results
  export             Export an HDFS directory to a database table
  help               List available commands
  import             Import a table from a database to HDFS
  import-all-tables  Import tables from a database to HDFS
  job                Work with saved jobs
  list-databases     List available databases on a server
  list-tables        List available tables in a database
  merge              Merge results of incremental imports
  metastore          Run a standalone Sqoop metastore
  version            Display version information

See 'sqoop help COMMAND' for information on a specific command.
```

As it explains, the help tool can also provide specific usage instructions on a particular tool when you provide that tool's name as an argument:

```
% sqoop help import
usage: sqoop import [GENERIC-ARGS] [TOOL-ARGS]

Common arguments:
   --connect <jdbc-uri>     Specify JDBC connect string
   --driver <class-name>    Manually specify JDBC driver class to use
   --hadoop-home <dir>      Override $HADOOP_HOME
   --help                   Print usage instructions
-P                          Read password from console
   --password <password>    Set authentication password
   --username <username>    Set authentication username
   --verbose                Print more information while working
...
```

An alternate way of running a Sqoop tool is to use a tool-specific script. This script will be named sqoop-*toolname*—for example, sqoop-help, sqoop-import, etc. These commands are identical to running sqoop help or sqoop import.

Sqoop Connectors

Sqoop has an extension framework that makes it possible to import data from—and export data to—any external storage system that has bulk data transfer capabilities. A Sqoop *connector* is a modular component that uses this framework to enable Sqoop imports and exports. Sqoop ships with connectors for working with a range of popular relational databases, including MySQL, PostgreSQL, Oracle, SQL Server, and DB2. There is also a generic JDBC connector for connecting to any database that supports Java's JDBC protocol. Sqoop provides optimized MySQL and PostgreSQL connectors that use database-specific APIs to perform bulk transfers efficiently (this is discussed more in "Direct-mode Imports" on page 536).

As well as the built-in Sqoop connectors, various third-party connectors are available for data stores, ranging from enterprise data warehouses (including Netezza, Teradata, and Oracle) to NoSQL stores (such as Couchbase). These connectors must be downloaded separately and can be added to an existing Sqoop installation by following the instructions that come with the connector.

A Sample Import

After you install Sqoop, you can use it to import data to Hadoop. For the examples in this chapter we'll use MySQL, which is easy to use and available for a large number of platforms.

To install and configure MySQL, follow the documentation at *http://dev.mysql.com/doc/refman/5.1/en/*. Chapter 2 ("Installing and Upgrading MySQL") in particular should help. Users of Debian-based Linux systems (e.g., Ubuntu) can type sudo apt-get install mysql-client mysql-server. RedHat users can type sudo yum install mysql mysql-server.

Now that MySQL is installed, let's log in and create a database (Example 15-1).

Example 15-1. Creating a new MySQL database schema

```
% mysql -u root -p
Enter password:
Welcome to the MySQL monitor.  Commands end with ; or \g.
Your MySQL connection id is 349
Server version: 5.1.37-1ubuntu5.4 (Ubuntu)

Type 'help;' or '\h' for help. Type '\c' to clear the current input
statement.
```

```
mysql> CREATE DATABASE hadoopguide;
Query OK, 1 row affected (0.02 sec)

mysql> GRANT ALL PRIVILEGES ON hadoopguide.* TO '%'@'localhost';
Query OK, 0 rows affected (0.00 sec)

mysql> GRANT ALL PRIVILEGES ON hadoopguide.* TO ''@'localhost';
Query OK, 0 rows affected (0.00 sec)

mysql> quit;
Bye
```

The password prompt shown in this example asks for your root user password. This is likely the same as the password for the root shell login. If you are running Ubuntu or another variant of Linux where root cannot log in directly, enter the password you picked at MySQL installation time.

In this session, we created a new database schema called hadoopguide, which we'll use throughout this chapter. We then allowed any local user to view and modify the contents of the hadoopguide schema, and closed our session.[1]

Now let's log back into the database (not as root, but as yourself this time) and create a table to import into HDFS (Example 15-2).

Example 15-2. Populating the database

```
% mysql hadoopguide
Welcome to the MySQL monitor.  Commands end with ; or \g.
Your MySQL connection id is 352
Server version: 5.1.37-1ubuntu5.4 (Ubuntu)

Type 'help;' or '\h' for help. Type '\c' to clear the current input statement.

mysql> CREATE TABLE widgets(id INT NOT NULL PRIMARY KEY AUTO_INCREMENT,
    -> widget_name VARCHAR(64) NOT NULL,
    -> price DECIMAL(10,2),
    -> design_date DATE,
    -> version INT,
    -> design_comment VARCHAR(100));
Query OK, 0 rows affected (0.00 sec)

mysql> INSERT INTO widgets VALUES (NULL, 'sprocket', 0.25, '2010-02-10',
    -> 1, 'Connects two gizmos');
Query OK, 1 row affected (0.00 sec)

mysql> INSERT INTO widgets VALUES (NULL, 'gizmo', 4.00, '2009-11-30', 4,
    -> NULL);
```

---

1. Of course, in a production deployment, we'd need to be much more careful about access control, but this serves for demonstration purposes. The grant privilege shown in the example also assumes you're running a pseudo-distributed Hadoop instance. If you're working with a distributed Hadoop cluster, you'd need to enable remote access by at least one user, whose account would be used to perform imports and exports via Sqoop.

```
Query OK, 1 row affected (0.00 sec)

mysql> INSERT INTO widgets VALUES (NULL, 'gadget', 99.99, '1983-08-13',
    -> 13, 'Our flagship product');
Query OK, 1 row affected (0.00 sec)

mysql> quit;
```

In this listing, we created a new table called widgets. We'll be using this fictional product database in further examples in this chapter. The widgets table contains several fields representing a variety of data types.

Now let's use Sqoop to import this table into HDFS:

```
% sqoop import --connect jdbc:mysql://localhost/hadoopguide \
> --table widgets -m 1
10/06/23 14:44:18 INFO tool.CodeGenTool: Beginning code generation
...
10/06/23 14:44:20 INFO mapred.JobClient: Running job: job_201006231439_0002
10/06/23 14:44:21 INFO mapred.JobClient:  map 0% reduce 0%
10/06/23 14:44:32 INFO mapred.JobClient:  map 100% reduce 0%
10/06/23 14:44:34 INFO mapred.JobClient: Job complete:
job_201006231439_0002
...
10/06/23 14:44:34 INFO mapreduce.ImportJobBase: Retrieved 3 records.
```

Sqoop's import tool will run a MapReduce job that connects to the MySQL database and reads the table. By default, this will use four map tasks in parallel to speed up the import process. Each task will write its imported results to a different file, but all in a common directory. Because we knew that we had only three rows to import in this example, we specified that Sqoop should use a single map task (-m 1) so we get a single file in HDFS.

We can inspect this file's contents like so:

```
% hadoop fs -cat widgets/part-m-00000
1,sprocket,0.25,2010-02-10,1,Connects two gizmos
2,gizmo,4.00,2009-11-30,4,null
3,gadget,99.99,1983-08-13,13,Our flagship product
```

 The connect string (*jdbc:mysql://localhost/hadoopguide*) shown in the example will read from a database on the local machine. If a distributed Hadoop cluster is being used, localhost should not be specified in the connect string, because map tasks not running on the same machine as the database will fail to connect. Even if Sqoop is run from the same host as the database sever, the full hostname should be specified.

By default, Sqoop will generate comma-delimited text files for our imported data. Delimiters can be specified explicitly, as well as field enclosing and escape characters, to allow the presence of delimiters in the field contents. The command-line arguments that specify delimiter characters, file formats, compression, and more fine-grained control of the import process are described in the *Sqoop User Guide* distributed with Sqoop,[2] as well as in the online help (`sqoop help import`, or `man sqoop-import` in CDH).

Text and Binary File Formats

Sqoop is capable of importing into a few different file formats. Text files (the default) offer a human-readable representation of data, platform independence, and the simplest structure. However, they cannot hold binary fields (such as database columns of type `VARBINARY`) and distinguishing between `null` values and String-based fields containing the value "null" can be problematic (although using the `--null-string` import option allows you to control the representation of null values).

To handle these conditions, you can either use Sqoop's SequenceFile-based format or its Avro-based format. Both Avro datafiles and SequenceFiles provide the most precise representation possible of the imported data. They also allow data to be compressed while retaining MapReduce's ability to process different sections of the same file in parallel. However, current versions of Sqoop cannot load either Avro or SequenceFiles into Hive (although you can load Avro datafiles into Hive manually). A final disadvantage of SequenceFiles is that they are Java-specific, whereas Avro datafiles can be processed by a wide range of languages.

Generated Code

In addition to writing the contents of the database table to HDFS, Sqoop has also provided you with a generated Java source file (*widgets.java*) written to the current local directory. (After running the `sqoop import` command shown earlier, you can see this file by running `ls widgets.java`.)

As you'll learn in "Imports: A Deeper Look" on page 533, Sqoop can use generated code to handle the deserialization of table-specific data from the database source before writing it to HDFS.

The generated class (`widgets`) is capable of holding a single record retrieved from the imported table. It can manipulate such a record in MapReduce or store it in a SequenceFile in HDFS. (SequenceFiles written by Sqoop during the import process will store each imported row in the "value" element of the SequenceFile's key-value pair format, using the generated class.)

It is likely that you don't want to name your generated class `widgets` since each instance of the class refers to only a single record. We can use a different Sqoop tool to generate source code without performing an import; this generated code will still examine the database table to determine the appropriate data types for each field:

---

2. Available from the website at *http://sqoop.apache.org/*.

```
% sqoop codegen --connect jdbc:mysql://localhost/hadoopguide \
> --table widgets --class-name Widget
```

The codegen tool simply generates code; it does not perform the full import. We specified that we'd like it to generate a class named Widget; this will be written to *Widget.java*. We also could have specified --class-name and other code-generation arguments during the import process we performed earlier. This tool can be used to regenerate code if you accidentally remove the source file, or generate code with different settings than were used during the import.

If you're working with records imported to SequenceFiles, it is inevitable that you'll need to use the generated classes (to deserialize data from the SequenceFile storage). You can work with text-file-based records without using generated code, but as we'll see in "Working with Imported Data" on page 536, Sqoop's generated code can handle some tedious aspects of data processing for you.

Additional Serialization Systems

Recent versions of Sqoop support Avro-based serialization and schema generation as well (see "Avro" on page 110), allowing you to use Sqoop in your project without integrating with generated code.

Imports: A Deeper Look

As mentioned earlier, Sqoop imports a table from a database by running a MapReduce job that extracts rows from the table, and writes the records to HDFS. How does MapReduce read the rows? This section explains how Sqoop works under the hood.

At a high level, Figure 15-1 demonstrates how Sqoop interacts with both the database source and Hadoop. Like Hadoop itself, Sqoop is written in Java. Java provides an API called Java Database Connectivity, or JDBC, that allows applications to access data stored in an RDBMS as well as inspect the nature of this data. Most database vendors provide a JDBC *driver* that implements the JDBC API and contains the necessary code to connect to their database server.

 Based on the URL in the connect string used to access the database, Sqoop attempts to predict which driver it should load. You may still need to download the JDBC driver itself and install it on your Sqoop client. For cases where Sqoop does not know which JDBC driver is appropriate, users can specify exactly how to load the JDBC driver into Sqoop. This capability allows Sqoop to work with a wide variety of database platforms.

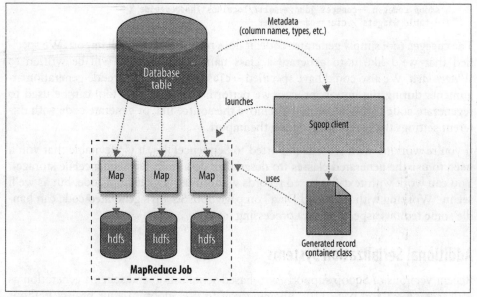

Figure 15-1. Sqoop's import process

Before the import can start, Sqoop uses JDBC to examine the table it is to import. It retrieves a list of all the columns and their SQL data types. These SQL types (VARCHAR, INTEGER, and so on) can then be mapped to Java data types (String, Integer, etc.), which will hold the field values in MapReduce applications. Sqoop's code generator will use this information to create a table-specific class to hold a record extracted from the table.

The Widget class from earlier, for example, contains the following methods that retrieve each column from an extracted record:

```
public Integer get_id();
public String get_widget_name();
public java.math.BigDecimal get_price();
public java.sql.Date get_design_date();
public Integer get_version();
public String get_design_comment();
```

More critical to the import system's operation, though, are the serialization methods that form the DBWritable interface, which allow the Widget class to interact with JDBC:

```
public void readFields(ResultSet __dbResults) throws SQLException;
public void write(PreparedStatement __dbStmt) throws SQLException;
```

JDBC's ResultSet interface provides a cursor that retrieves records from a query; the readFields() method here will populate the fields of the Widget object with the columns from one row of the ResultSet's data. The write() method shown here allows Sqoop to insert new Widget rows into a table, a process called *exporting*. Exports are discussed in "Performing an Export" on page 542.

The MapReduce job launched by Sqoop uses an InputFormat that can read sections of a table from a database via JDBC. The DataDrivenDBInputFormat provided with Hadoop partitions a query's results over several map tasks.

Reading a table is typically done with a simple query such as:

```
SELECT col1,col2,col3,... FROM tableName
```

But often, better import performance can be gained by dividing this query across multiple nodes. This is done using a *splitting column*. Using metadata about the table, Sqoop will guess a good column to use for splitting the table (typically the primary key for the table, if one exists). The minimum and maximum values for the primary key column are retrieved, and then these are used in conjunction with a target number of tasks to determine the queries that each map task should issue.

For example, suppose the widgets table had 100,000 entries, with the id column containing values 0 through 99,999. When importing this table, Sqoop would determine that id is the primary key column for the table. When starting the MapReduce job, the DataDrivenDBInputFormat used to perform the import would then issue a statement such as SELECT MIN(id), MAX(id) FROM widgets. These values would then be used to interpolate over the entire range of data. Assuming we specified that five map tasks should run in parallel (with -m 5), this would result in each map task executing queries such as SELECT id, widget_name, ... FROM widgets WHERE id >= 0 AND id < 20000, SELECT id, widget_name, ... FROM widgets WHERE id >= 20000 AND id < 40000, and so on.

The choice of splitting column is essential to parallelizing work efficiently. If the id column were not uniformly distributed (perhaps there are no widgets with IDs between 50,000 and 75,000), then some map tasks may have little or no work to perform, whereas others would have a great deal. Users can specify a particular splitting column when running an import job, to tune the job to the data's actual distribution. If an import job is run as a single (sequential) task with -m 1, this split process is not performed.

After generating the deserialization code and configuring the InputFormat, Sqoop sends the job to the MapReduce cluster. Map tasks execute the queries and deserialize rows from the ResultSet into instances of the generated class, which are either stored directly in SequenceFiles or transformed into delimited text before being written to HDFS.

Controlling the Import

Sqoop does not need to import an entire table at a time. For example, a subset of the table's columns can be specified for import. Users can also specify a WHERE clause to include in queries, which bound the rows of the table to import. For example, if widgets 0 through 99,999 were imported last month, but this month our vendor catalog included 1,000 new types of widget, an import could be configured with the clause WHERE id >= 100000; this will start an import job to retrieve all the new rows added to the source database since the previous import run. User-supplied WHERE clauses are applied before task splitting is performed, and are pushed down into the queries executed by each task.

Imports and Consistency

When importing data to HDFS, it is important that you ensure access to a consistent snapshot of the source data. Map tasks reading from a database in parallel are running in separate processes. Thus, they cannot share a single database transaction. The best way to do this is to ensure that any processes that update existing rows of a table are disabled during the import.

Direct-mode Imports

Sqoop's architecture allows it to choose from multiple available strategies for performing an import. Most databases will use the DataDrivenDBInputFormat-based approach described earlier. Some databases offer specific tools designed to extract data quickly. For example, MySQL's mysqldump application can read from a table with greater throughput than a JDBC channel. The use of these external tools is referred to as *direct mode* in Sqoop's documentation. Direct mode must be specifically enabled by the user (via the --direct argument), as it is not as general-purpose as the JDBC approach. (For example, MySQL's direct mode cannot handle large objects, such as CLOB or BLOB columns, because Sqoop needs to use a JDBC-specific API to load these columns into HDFS.)

For databases that provide such tools, Sqoop can use these to great effect. A direct-mode import from MySQL is usually much more efficient (in terms of map tasks and time required) than a comparable JDBC-based import. Sqoop will still launch multiple map tasks in parallel. These tasks will then spawn instances of the mysqldump program and read its output. The effect is similar to a distributed implementation of mk-parallel-dump from the Maatkit (*http://www.maatkit.org*) tool set. Sqoop can also perform direct-mode imports from PostgreSQL.

Even when direct mode is used to access the contents of a database, the metadata is still queried through JDBC.

Working with Imported Data

Once data has been imported to HDFS, it is now ready for processing by custom Map-Reduce programs. Text-based imports can be easily used in scripts run with Hadoop Streaming or in MapReduce jobs run with the default TextInputFormat.

To use individual fields of an imported record, though, the field delimiters (and any escape/enclosing characters) must be parsed and the field values extracted and converted to the appropriate data types. For example, the ID of the "sprocket" widget is represented as the string "1" in the text file, but should be parsed into an Integer or

---

int variable in Java. The generated table class provided by Sqoop can automate this process, allowing you to focus on the actual MapReduce job to run. Each auto-generated class has several overloaded methods named `parse()` that operate on the data represented as `Text`, `CharSequence`, `char[]`, or other common types.

The MapReduce application called `MaxWidgetId` (available in the example code) will find the widget with the highest ID.

The class can be compiled into a JAR file along with *Widget.java*. Both Hadoop (*hadoop-core-version.jar*) and Sqoop (*sqoop-version.jar*) will need to be on the classpath for compilation. The class files can then be combined into a JAR file and executed like so:

```
% jar cvvf widgets.jar *.class
% HADOOP_CLASSPATH=/usr/lib/sqoop/sqoop-version.jar hadoop jar \
> widgets.jar MaxWidgetId -libjars /usr/lib/sqoop/sqoop-version.jar
```

This command line ensures that Sqoop is on the classpath locally (via `$HADOOP_CLASS PATH`) when running the `MaxWidgetId.run()` method, as well as when map tasks are running on the cluster (via the `-libjars` argument).

When run, the *maxwidgets* path in HDFS will contain a file named *part-r-00000* with the following expected result:

```
3,gadget,99.99,1983-08-13,13,Our flagship product
```

It is worth noting that in this example MapReduce program, a `Widget` object was emitted from the mapper to the reducer; the autogenerated `Widget` class implements the `Writable` interface provided by Hadoop, which allows the object to be sent via Hadoop's serialization mechanism, as well as written to and read from SequenceFiles.

The `MaxWidgetId` example is built on the new MapReduce API. MapReduce applications that rely on Sqoop-generated code can be built on the new or old APIs, though some advanced features (such as working with large objects) are more convenient to use in the new API.

Avro-based imports can be processed using the APIs described in "Avro MapReduce" on page 124. With the generic Avro mapping, the MapReduce program does not need to use schema-specific generated code (although this is an option too, by using Avro's specific compiler; Sqoop does not do the code generation in this case). The example code includes a program called `MaxWidgetIdGenericAvro`, which finds the widget with the highest ID and writes out the result in an Avro datafile.

Imported Data and Hive

As noted in Chapter 12, for many types of analysis, using a system such as Hive to handle relational operations can dramatically ease the development of the analytic pipeline. Especially for data originally from a relational data source, using Hive makes a lot of sense. Hive and Sqoop together form a powerful toolchain for performing analysis.

Suppose we had another log of data in our system, coming from a web-based widget purchasing system. This may return logfiles containing a widget ID, a quantity, a shipping address, and an order date.

Here is a snippet from an example log of this type:

```
1,15,120 Any St.,Los Angeles,CA,90210,2010-08-01
3,4,120 Any St.,Los Angeles,CA,90210,2010-08-01
2,5,400 Some Pl.,Cupertino,CA,95014,2010-07-30
2,7,88 Mile Rd.,Manhattan,NY,10005,2010-07-18
```

By using Hadoop to analyze this purchase log, we can gain insight into our sales operation. By combining this data with the data extracted from our relational data source (the widgets table), we can do better. In this example session, we will compute which zip code is responsible for the most sales dollars, so we can better focus our sales team's operations. Doing this requires data from both the sales log and the widgets table.

The table shown in the previous code snippet should be in a local file named *sales.log* for this to work.

First, let's load the sales data into Hive:

```
hive> CREATE TABLE sales(widget_id INT, qty INT,
    > street STRING, city STRING, state STRING,
    > zip INT, sale_date STRING)
    > ROW FORMAT DELIMITED FIELDS TERMINATED BY ',';
OK
Time taken: 5.248 seconds
hive> LOAD DATA LOCAL INPATH "sales.log" INTO TABLE sales;
Copying data from file:/home/sales.log
Loading data to table sales
OK
Time taken: 0.188 seconds
```

Sqoop can generate a Hive table based on a table from an existing relational data source. Since we've already imported the widgets data to HDFS, we can generate the Hive table definition and then load in the HDFS-resident data:

```
% sqoop create-hive-table --connect jdbc:mysql://localhost/hadoopguide \
> --table widgets --fields-terminated-by ','
...
10/06/23 18:05:34 INFO hive.HiveImport: OK
10/06/23 18:05:34 INFO hive.HiveImport: Time taken: 3.22 seconds
10/06/23 18:05:35 INFO hive.HiveImport: Hive import complete.
% hive
hive> LOAD DATA INPATH "widgets" INTO TABLE widgets;
Loading data to table widgets
OK
Time taken: 3.265 seconds
```

When creating a Hive table definition with a specific already-imported dataset in mind, we need to specify the delimiters used in that dataset. Otherwise, Sqoop will allow Hive to use its default delimiters (which are different from Sqoop's default delimiters).

> Hive's type system is less rich than that of most SQL systems. Many SQL types do not have direct analogues in Hive. When Sqoop generates a Hive table definition for an import, it uses the best Hive type available to hold a column's values. This may result in a decrease in precision. When this occurs, Sqoop will provide you with a warning message such as this one:
>
> ```
> 10/06/23 18:09:36 WARN hive.TableDefWriter:
> Column design_date had to be
> cast to a less precise type in Hive
> ```

This three-step process of importing data to HDFS, creating the Hive table, and then loading the HDFS-resident data into Hive can be shortened to one step if you know that you want to import straight from a database directly into Hive. During an import, Sqoop can generate the Hive table definition and then load in the data. Had we not already performed the import, we could have executed this command, which re-creates the widgets table in Hive, based on the copy in MySQL:

```
% sqoop import --connect jdbc:mysql://localhost/hadoopguide \
> --table widgets -m 1 --hive-import
```

> The sqoop import tool run with the --hive-import argument will load the data directly from the source database into Hive; it infers a Hive schema automatically based on the schema for the table in the source database. Using this, you can get started working with your data in Hive with only one command.

Regardless of which data import route we chose, we can now use the widgets dataset and the sales data set together to calculate the most profitable zip code. Let's do so, and also save the result of this query in another table for later:

```
hive> CREATE TABLE zip_profits (sales_vol DOUBLE, zip INT);
OK

hive> INSERT OVERWRITE TABLE zip_profits
    > SELECT SUM(w.price * s.qty) AS sales_vol, s.zip  FROM SALES s
    > JOIN widgets w ON (s.widget_id = w.id) GROUP BY s.zip;
...
3 Rows loaded to zip_profits
OK

hive> SELECT * FROM zip_profits ORDER BY sales_vol DESC;
...
OK
403.71  90210
```

```
28.0    10005
20.0    95014
```

Importing Large Objects

Most databases provide the capability to store large amounts of data in a single field. Depending on whether this data is textual or binary in nature, it is usually represented as a `CLOB` or `BLOB` column in the table. These "large objects" are often handled specially by the database itself. In particular, most tables are physically laid out on disk as in Figure 15-2. When scanning through rows to determine which rows match the criteria for a particular query, this typically involves reading all columns of each row from disk. If large objects were stored "inline" in this fashion, they would adversely affect the performance of such scans. Therefore, large objects are often stored externally from their rows, as in Figure 15-3. Accessing a large object often requires "opening" it through the reference contained in the row.

Figure 15-2. Database tables are typically physically represented as an array of rows, with all the columns in a row stored adjacent to one another

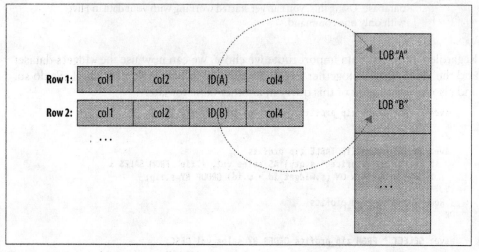

Figure 15-3. Large objects are usually held in a separate area of storage; the main row storage contains indirect references to the large objects

---

The difficulty of working with large objects in a database suggests that a system such as Hadoop, which is much better suited to storing and processing large, complex data objects, is an ideal repository for such information. Sqoop can extract large objects from tables and store them in HDFS for further processing.

As in a database, MapReduce typically *materializes* every record before passing it along to the mapper. If individual records are truly large, this can be very inefficient.

As shown earlier, records imported by Sqoop are laid out on disk in a fashion very similar to a database's internal structure: an array of records with all fields of a record concatenated together. When running a MapReduce program over imported records, each map task must fully materialize all fields of each record in its input split. If the contents of a large object field are relevant only for a small subset of the total number of records used as input to a MapReduce program, it would be inefficient to fully materialize all these records. Furthermore, depending on the size of the large object, full materialization in memory may be impossible.

To overcome these difficulties, Sqoop will store imported large objects in a separate file called a LobFile. The LobFile format can store individual records of very large size (a 64-bit address space is used). Each record in a LobFile holds a single large object. The LobFile format allows clients to hold a reference to a record without accessing the record contents. When records are accessed, this is done through a `java.io.Input Stream` (for binary objects) or `java.io.Reader` (for character-based objects).

When a record is imported, the "normal" fields will be materialized together in a text file, along with a reference to the LobFile where a CLOB or BLOB column is stored. For example, suppose our `widgets` table contained a BLOB field named `schematic` holding the actual schematic diagram for each widget.

An imported record might then look like:

```
2,gizmo,4.00,2009-11-30,4,null,externalLob(lf,lobfile0,100,5011714)
```

The `externalLob(...)` text is a reference to an externally stored large object, stored in LobFile format (`lf`) in a file named *lobfile0*, with the specified byte offset and length inside that file.

When working with this record, the `Widget.get_schematic()` method would return an object of type `BlobRef` referencing the `schematic` column, but not actually containing its contents. The `BlobRef.getDataStream()` method actually opens the LobFile and returns an `InputStream`, allowing you to access the `schematic` field's contents.

When running a MapReduce job processing many `Widget` records, you might need to access the `schematic` field of only a handful of records. This system allows you to incur the I/O costs of accessing only the required large object entries, as individual schematics may be several megabytes or more of data.

The `BlobRef` and `ClobRef` classes cache references to underlying LobFiles within a map task. If you do access the `schematic` field of several sequentially ordered records, they will take advantage of the existing file pointer's alignment on the next record body.

Performing an Export

In Sqoop, an *import* refers to the movement of data from a database system into HDFS. By contrast, an *export* uses HDFS as the source of data and a remote database as the destination. In the previous sections, we imported some data and then performed some analysis using Hive. We can export the results of this analysis to a database for consumption by other tools.

Before exporting a table from HDFS to a database, we must prepare the database to receive the data by creating the target table. Although Sqoop can infer which Java types are appropriate to hold SQL data types, this translation does not work in both directions (for example, there are several possible SQL column definitions that can hold data in a Java `String`; this could be `CHAR(64)`, `VARCHAR(200)`, or something else entirely). Consequently, you must determine which types are most appropriate.

We are going to export the `zip_profits` table from Hive. We need to create a table in MySQL that has target columns in the same order, with the appropriate SQL types:

```
% mysql hadoopguide
mysql> CREATE TABLE sales_by_zip (volume DECIMAL(8,2), zip INTEGER);
Query OK, 0 rows affected (0.01 sec)
```

Then we run the export command:

```
% sqoop export --connect jdbc:mysql://localhost/hadoopguide -m 1 \
> --table sales_by_zip --export-dir /user/hive/warehouse/zip_profits \
> --input-fields-terminated-by '\0001'
...
10/07/02 16:16:50 INFO mapreduce.ExportJobBase: Transferred 41 bytes in 10.8947
seconds (3.7633 bytes/sec)
10/07/02 16:16:50 INFO mapreduce.ExportJobBase: Exported 3 records.
```

Finally, we can verify that the export worked by checking MySQL:

```
% mysql hadoopguide -e 'SELECT * FROM sales_by_zip'
+--------+-------+
| volume | zip   |
+--------+-------+
|  28.00 | 10005 |
| 403.71 | 90210 |
|  20.00 | 95014 |
+--------+-------+
```

When we created the `zip_profits` table in Hive, we did not specify any delimiters. So Hive used its default delimiters: a Ctrl-A character (Unicode 0x0001) between fields and a newline at the end of each record. When we used Hive to access the contents of this table (in a `SELECT` statement), Hive converted this to a tab-delimited representation for display on the console. But when reading the tables directly from files, we need to tell Sqoop which delimiters to use. Sqoop assumes records are newline-delimited by default, but needs to be told about the Ctrl-A field delimiters. The `--input-fields-ter minated-by` argument to `sqoop export` specified this information. Sqoop supports several escape sequences, which start with a backslash (\) character, when specifying delimiters.

In the example syntax, the escape sequence is enclosed in single quotes to ensure that the shell processes it literally. Without the quotes, the leading backslash itself may need to be escaped (for example, `--input-fields-terminated-by \\0001`). The escape sequences supported by Sqoop are listed in Table 15-1.

Table 15-1. *Escape sequences can be used to specify nonprintable characters as field and record delimiters in Sqoop*

Escape	Description
\b	Backspace
\n	Newline
\r	Carriage return
\t	Tab
\'	Single quote
\"	Double quote
\\	Backslash
\0	NUL. This will insert NUL characters between fields or lines, or will disable enclosing/escaping if used for one of the `--enclosed-by`, `--optionally-enclosed-by`, or `--escaped-by` arguments.
\0ooo	The octal representation of a Unicode character's code point. The actual character is specified by the octal value ooo.
\0xhhh	The hexadecimal representation of a Unicode character's code point. This should be of the form \0x*hhh*, where *hhh* is the hex value. For example, `--fields-terminated-by '\0x10'` specifies the carriage return character.

Exports: A Deeper Look

The architecture of Sqoop's export capability is very similar in nature to how Sqoop performs imports. (See Figure 15-4.) Before performing the export, Sqoop picks a strategy based on the database connect string. For most systems, Sqoop uses JDBC. Sqoop then generates a Java class based on the target table definition. This generated class has the ability to parse records from text files and insert values of the appropriate types into a table (in addition to the ability to read the columns from a ResultSet). A MapReduce job is then launched that reads the source datafiles from HDFS, parses the records using the generated class, and executes the chosen export strategy.

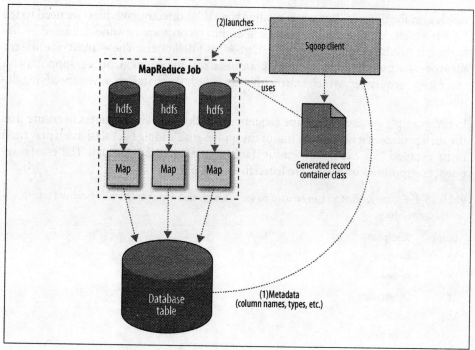

Figure 15-4. Exports are performed in parallel using MapReduce

The JDBC-based export strategy builds up batch INSERT statements that will each add multiple records to the target table. Inserting many records per statement performs much better than executing many single-row INSERT statements on most database systems. Separate threads are used to read from HDFS and communicate with the database, to ensure that I/O operations involving different systems are overlapped as much as possible.

For MySQL, Sqoop can employ a direct-mode strategy using mysqlimport. Each map task spawns a mysqlimport process that it communicates with via a named FIFO on the local filesystem. Data is then streamed into mysqlimport via the FIFO channel, and from there into the database.

Whereas most MapReduce jobs reading from HDFS pick the degree of parallelism (number of map tasks) based on the number and size of the files to process, Sqoop's export system allows users explicit control over the number of tasks. The performance of the export can be affected by the number of parallel writers to the database, so Sqoop uses the CombineFileInputFormat class to group the input files into a smaller number of map tasks.

Exports and Transactionality

Due to the parallel nature of the process, often an export is not an atomic operation. Sqoop will spawn multiple tasks to export slices of the data in parallel. These tasks can complete at different times, meaning that even though transactions are used inside tasks, results from one task may be visible before the results of another task. Moreover, databases often use fixed-size buffers to store transactions. As a result, one transaction cannot necessarily contain the entire set of operations performed by a task. Sqoop commits results every few thousand rows, to ensure that it does not run out of memory. These intermediate results are visible while the export continues. Applications that will use the results of an export should not be started until the export process is complete, or they may see partial results.

To solve this problem, Sqoop can export to a temporary staging table, and then at the end of the job—if the export has succeeded—move the staged data into the destination table in a single transaction. You can specify a staging table with the `--staging-table` option. The staging table must already exist and have the same schema as the destination. It must also be empty, unless the `--clear-staging-table` option is also supplied.

Exports and SequenceFiles

The example export reads source data from a Hive table, which is stored in HDFS as a delimited text file. Sqoop can also export delimited text files that were not Hive tables. For example, it can export text files that are the output of a MapReduce job.

Sqoop can also export records stored in SequenceFiles to an output table, although some restrictions apply. A SequenceFile can contain arbitrary record types. Sqoop's export tool will read objects from SequenceFiles and send them directly to the `Output Collector`, which passes the objects to the database export `OutputFormat`. To work with Sqoop, the record must be stored in the "value" portion of the SequenceFile's key-value pair format and must subclass the `org.apache.sqoop.lib.SqoopRecord` abstract class (as is done by all classes generated by Sqoop).

If you use the codegen tool (`sqoop-codegen`) to generate a `SqoopRecord` implementation for a record based on your export target table, you can then write a MapReduce program, which populates instances of this class and writes them to SequenceFiles. `sqoop-export` can then export these SequenceFiles to the table. Another means by which data may be in `SqoopRecord` instances in SequenceFiles is if data is imported from a database table to HDFS and modified in some fashion, and then the results are stored in SequenceFiles holding records of the same data type.

In this case, Sqoop should reuse the existing class definition to read data from SequenceFiles, rather than generate a new (temporary) record container class to perform the export, as is done when converting text-based records to database rows. You can suppress code generation and instead use an existing record class and JAR by providing the `--class-name` and `--jar-file` arguments to Sqoop. Sqoop will use the specified class, loaded from the specified JAR, when exporting records.

In the following example, we reimport the `widgets` table as SequenceFiles, and then export it back to the database in a different table:

```
% sqoop import --connect jdbc:mysql://localhost/hadoopguide \
> --table widgets -m 1 --class-name WidgetHolder --as-sequencefile \
> --target-dir widget_sequence_files --bindir .
...
10/07/05 17:09:13 INFO mapreduce.ImportJobBase: Retrieved 3 records.

% mysql hadoopguide
mysql> CREATE TABLE widgets2(id INT, widget_name VARCHAR(100),
    -> price DOUBLE, designed DATE, version INT, notes VARCHAR(200));
Query OK, 0 rows affected (0.03 sec)

mysql> exit;

% sqoop export --connect jdbc:mysql://localhost/hadoopguide \
> --table widgets2 -m 1 --class-name WidgetHolder \
> --jar-file widgets.jar --export-dir widget_sequence_files
...
10/07/05 17:26:44 INFO mapreduce.ExportJobBase: Exported 3 records.
```

During the import, we specified the SequenceFile format and indicated that we wanted the JAR file to be placed in the current directory (with `--bindir`) so we can reuse it. Otherwise, it would be placed in a temporary directory. We then created a destination table for the export, which had a slightly different schema, albeit one that is compatible with the original data. We then ran an export that used the existing generated code to read the records from the SequenceFile and write them to the database.

Case Studies

Hadoop Usage at Last.fm

Last.fm: The Social Music Revolution

Founded in 2002, Last.fm is an Internet radio and music community website that offers many services to its users, such as free music streams and downloads, music and event recommendations, personalized charts, and much more. There are about 25 million people who use Last.fm every month, generating huge amounts of data that need to be processed. One example of this is users transmitting information indicating which songs they are listening to (this is known as "scrobbling"). This data is processed and stored by Last.fm, so the user can access it directly (in the form of charts), and it is also used to make decisions about users' musical tastes and compatibility, and artist and track similarity.

Hadoop at Last.fm

As Last.fm's service developed and the number of users grew from thousands to millions, storing, processing, and managing all the incoming data became increasingly challenging. Fortunately, Hadoop was quickly becoming stable enough and was enthusiastically adopted as it became clear how many problems it solved. It was first used at Last.fm in early 2006 and was put into production a few months later. There were several reasons for adopting Hadoop at Last.fm:

- The distributed filesystem provided redundant backups for the data stored on it (e.g., web logs, user listening data) at no extra cost.
- Scalability was simplified through the ability to add cheap commodity hardware when required.
- The cost was right (free) at a time when Last.fm had limited financial resources.

- The open source code and active community meant that Last.fm could freely modify Hadoop to add custom features and patches.

- Hadoop provided a flexible framework for running distributed computing algorithms with a relatively easy learning curve.

Hadoop has now become a crucial part of Last.fm's infrastructure, currently consisting of two Hadoop clusters spanning over 50 machines, 300 cores, and 100 TB of disk space. Hundreds of daily jobs are run on the clusters performing operations, such as logfile analysis, evaluation of A/B tests, ad hoc processing, and charts generation. This case study will focus on the process of generating charts, as this was the first usage of Hadoop at Last.fm and illustrates the power and flexibility that Hadoop provides over other approaches when working with very large datasets.

Generating Charts with Hadoop

Last.fm uses user-generated track listening data to produce many different types of charts, such as weekly charts for tracks, per country and per user. A number of Hadoop programs are used to process the listening data and generate these charts, and these run on a daily, weekly, or monthly basis. Figure 16-1 shows an example of how this data is displayed on the site, in this case, the weekly top tracks.

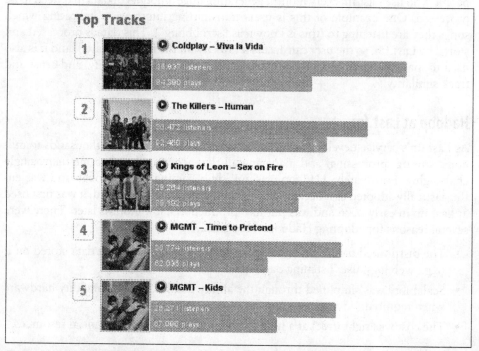

Figure 16-1. Last.fm top tracks chart

Listening data typically arrives at Last.fm from one of two sources:

- A user plays a track of his own (e.g., listening to an MP3 file on a PC or other device), and this information is sent to Last.fm using either the official Last.fm client application or one of many hundreds of third-party applications.
- A user tunes into one of Last.fm's Internet radio stations and streams a song to his computer. The Last.fm player or website can be used to access these streams and extra functionality is made available to the user, allowing him to love, skip, or ban each track that he listens to.

When processing the received data, we distinguish between a track listen submitted by a user (the first source in the previous list, referred to as a *scrobble* from here on) and a track listened to on the Last.fm radio (the second source, mentioned earlier, referred to as a *radio listen* from here on). This distinction is very important in order to prevent a feedback loop in the Last.fm recommendation system, which is based only on scrobbles. One of the most fundamental Hadoop jobs at Last.fm takes the incoming listening data and summarizes it into a format that can be used for display purposes on the Last.fm website as well as for input to other Hadoop programs. This is achieved by the Track Statistics program, which is the example described in the following sections.

The Track Statistics Program

When track listening data is submitted to Last.fm, it undergoes a validation and conversion phase, the end result of which is a number of space-delimited text files containing the user ID, the track ID, the number of times the track was scrobbled, the number of times the track was listened to on the radio, and the number of times it was skipped. Table 16-1 contains sample listening data, which is used in the following examples as input to the Track Statistics program (the real data is gigabytes in size and includes many more fields that have been omitted here for simplicity's sake).

Table 16-1. Listening data

UserId	TrackId	Scrobble	Radio	Skip
111115	222	0	1	0
111113	225	1	0	0
111117	223	0	1	1
111115	225	1	0	0

These text files are the initial input provided to the Track Statistics program, which consists of two jobs that calculate various values from this data and a third job that merges the results (see Figure 16-2).

The Unique Listeners job calculates the total number of unique listeners for a track by counting the first listen by a user and ignoring all other listens by the same user. The Sum job accumulates the total listens, scrobbles, radio listens, and skips for each track

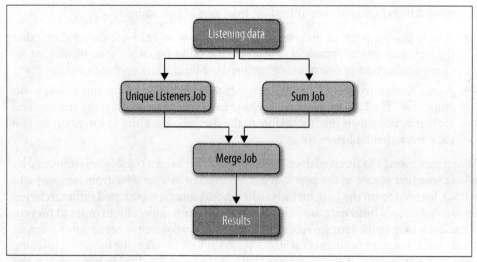

Figure 16-2. TrackStats jobs

by counting these values for all listens by all users. Although the input format of these two jobs is identical, two separate jobs are needed, as the Unique Listeners job is responsible for emitting values per track per user, and the Sum job emits values per track. The final Merge job is responsible for merging the intermediate output of the two other jobs into the final result. The end results of running the program are the following values per track:

- Number of unique listeners
- Number of times the track was scrobbled
- Number of times the track was listened to on the radio
- Number of times the track was listened to in total
- Number of times the track was skipped on the radio

Each job and its MapReduce phases are described in more detail next. Please note that the provided code snippets have been simplified due to space constraints; for download details for the full code listings, refer to the Preface.

Calculating the number of unique listeners

The Unique Listeners job calculates, per track, the number of unique listeners.

UniqueListenersMapper. The `UniqueListenersMapper` processes the space-delimited raw listening data and emits the user ID associated with each track ID:

```
public void map(LongWritable position, Text rawLine, OutputCollector<IntWritable,
    IntWritable> output, Reporter reporter) throws IOException {

    String[] parts = (rawLine.toString()).split(" ");
```

```
int scrobbles = Integer.parseInt(parts[TrackStatisticsProgram.COL_SCROBBLES]);
int radioListens = Integer.parseInt(parts[TrackStatisticsProgram.COL_RADIO]);
// if track somehow is marked with zero plays - ignore
if (scrobbles <= 0 && radioListens <= 0) {
  return;
}
// if we get to here then user has listened to track,
// so output user id against track id
IntWritable trackId = new IntWritable(
  Integer.parseInt(parts[TrackStatisticsProgram.COL_TRACKID]));
IntWritable userId = new IntWritable(
  Integer.parseInt(parts[TrackStatisticsProgram.COL_USERID]));
output.collect(trackId, userId);
}
```

UniqueListenersReducer. The UniqueListenersReducers receives a list of user IDs per track
ID and puts these IDs into a Set to remove any duplicates. The size of this set is then
emitted (i.e., the number of unique listeners) for each track ID. Storing all the reduce
values in a Set runs the risk of running out of memory if there are many values for a
certain key. This hasn't happened in practice, but to overcome this, an extra
MapReduce step could be introduced to remove all the duplicate values, or a secondary
sort could be used (for more details, see "Secondary Sort" on page 277):

```
public void reduce(IntWritable trackId, Iterator<IntWritable> values,
    OutputCollector<IntWritable, IntWritable> output, Reporter reporter)
    throws IOException {

  Set<Integer> userIds = new HashSet<Integer>();
  // add all userIds to the set, duplicates automatically removed (set contract)
  while (values.hasNext()) {
    IntWritable userId = values.next();
    userIds.add(Integer.valueOf(userId.get()));
  }
  // output trackId -> number of unique listeners per track
  output.collect(trackId, new IntWritable(userIds.size()));
}
```

Table 16-2 shows the sample input data for the job. The map output appears in Table 16-3 and the reduce output in Table 16-4.

Table 16-2. Job input

Line of file	UserId	TrackId	Scrobbled	Radio play	Skip
LongWritable	IntWritable	IntWritable	Boolean	Boolean	Boolean
0	11115	222	0	1	0
1	11113	225	1	0	0
2	11117	223	0	1	1
3	11115	225	1	0	0

Table 16-3. Mapper output

TrackId	UserId
IntWritable	IntWritable
222	11115
225	11113
223	11117
225	11115

Table 16-4. Reducer output

TrackId	#listeners
IntWritable	IntWritable
222	1
225	2
223	1

Summing the track totals

The Sum job is relatively simple; it just adds up the values we are interested in for each track.

SumMapper. The input data is again the raw text files, but in this case, it is handled quite differently. The desired end result is a number of totals (unique listener count, play count, scrobble count, radio listen count, skip count) associated with each track. To simplify things, we use an intermediate TrackStats object generated using Hadoop Record I/O, which implements WritableComparable (so it can be used as output) to hold these values. The Mapper creates a TrackStats object and sets the values on it for each line in the file, except for the unique listener count, which is left empty (it will be filled in by the final merge job):

```
public void map(LongWritable position, Text rawLine,
    OutputCollector<IntWritable, TrackStats> output, Reporter reporter)
    throws IOException {

    String[] parts = (rawLine.toString()).split(" ");
    int trackId = Integer.parseInt(parts[TrackStatisticsProgram.COL_TRACKID]);
    int scrobbles = Integer.parseInt(parts[TrackStatisticsProgram.COL_SCROBBLES]);
    int radio = Integer.parseInt(parts[TrackStatisticsProgram.COL_RADIO]);
    int skip = Integer.parseInt(parts[TrackStatisticsProgram.COL_SKIP]);
    // set number of listeners to 0 (this is calculated later)
    // and other values as provided in text file
    TrackStats trackstat = new TrackStats(0, scrobbles + radio, scrobbles, radio, skip);
    output.collect(new IntWritable(trackId), trackstat);
}
```

SumReducer. In this case, the reducer performs a very similar function to the Mapper, summing the statistics per track and returning an overall total:

```
public void reduce(IntWritable trackId, Iterator<TrackStats> values,
    OutputCollector<IntWritable, TrackStats> output, Reporter reporter)
    throws IOException {

  TrackStats sum = new TrackStats(); // holds the totals for this track
  while (values.hasNext()) {
    TrackStats trackStats = (TrackStats) values.next();
    sum.setListeners(sum.getListeners() + trackStats.getListeners());
    sum.setPlays(sum.getPlays() + trackStats.getPlays());
    sum.setSkips(sum.getSkips() + trackStats.getSkips());
    sum.setScrobbles(sum.getScrobbles() + trackStats.getScrobbles());
    sum.setRadioPlays(sum.getRadioPlays() + trackStats.getRadioPlays());
  }
  output.collect(trackId, sum);
}
```

Table 16-5 shows the input data for the job (the same as for the Unique Listeners job). The map output appears in Table 16-6 and the reduce output in Table 16-7.

Table 16-5. Job input

Line	UserId	TrackId	Scrobbled	Radio play	Skip
LongWritable	IntWritable	IntWritable	Boolean	Boolean	Boolean
0	11115	222	0	1	0
1	11113	225	1	0	0
2	11117	223	0	1	1
3	11115	225	1	0	0

Table 16-6. Map output

TrackId	#listeners	#plays	#scrobbles	#radio plays	#skips
IntWritable	IntWritable	IntWritable	IntWritable	IntWritable	IntWritable
222	0	1	0	1	0
225	0	1	1	0	0
223	0	1	0	1	1
225	0	1	1	0	0

Table 16-7. Reduce output

TrackId	#listeners	#plays	#scrobbles	#radio plays	#skips
IntWritable	IntWritable	IntWritable	IntWritable	IntWritable	IntWritable
222	0	1	0	1	0
225	0	2	2	0	0
223	0	1	0	1	1

Merging the results

The final job needs to merge the output from the two previous jobs: the number of unique listeners per track and the statistics per track. In order to merge these different inputs, two different mappers (one for each type of input) are used. The two intermediate jobs are configured to write their results to different paths, and the MultipleInputs class is used to specify which Mapper will process which files. The following code shows how the JobConf for the job is set up to do this:

```
MultipleInputs.addInputPath(conf, sumInputDir,
    SequenceFileInputFormat.class, IdentityMapper.class);

MultipleInputs.addInputPath(conf, listenersInputDir,
    SequenceFileInputFormat.class, MergeListenersMapper.class);
```

It is possible to use a single Mapper to handle different inputs, but the example solution is more convenient and elegant.

MergeListenersMapper. This Mapper is used to process the UniqueListenerJob's output of unique listeners per track. It creates a TrackStats object in a similar manner to the SumMapper, but this time, it fills in only the unique listener count per track and leaves the other values empty:

```
public void map(IntWritable trackId, IntWritable uniqueListenerCount,
    OutputCollector<IntWritable, TrackStats> output, Reporter reporter)
    throws IOException {
  TrackStats trackStats = new TrackStats();
  trackStats.setListeners(uniqueListenerCount.get());
  output.collect(trackId, trackStats);
}
```

Table 16-8 shows some input for the Mapper; the corresponding output is shown in Table 16-9.

Table 16-8. MergeListenersMapper input

TrackId	#listeners
IntWritable	IntWritable
222	1
225	2
223	1

Table 16-9. MergeListenersMapper output

TrackId	#listeners	#plays	#scrobbles	#radio	#skips
222	1	0	0	0	0
225	2	0	0	0	0
223	1	0	0	0	0

IdentityMapper. The IdentityMapper is configured to process the SumJob's output of TrackStats objects and, as no additional processing is required, directly emits the input data (see Table 16-10).

Table 16-10. IdentityMapper input and output

TrackId	#listeners	#plays	#scrobbles	#radio	#skips
IntWritable	IntWritable	IntWritable	IntWritable	IntWritable	IntWritable
222	0	1	0	1	0
225	0	2	2	0	0
223	0	1	0	1	1

SumReducer. The two Mappers emit values of the same type: a TrackStats object per track, with different values filled in. The final reduce phase can reuse the SumReducer described earlier to create a TrackStats object per track, sum up all the values, and emit it (see Table 16-11).

Table 16-11. Final SumReducer output

TrackId	#listeners	#plays	#scrobbles	#radio	#skips
IntWritable	IntWritable	IntWritable	IntWritable	IntWritable	IntWritable
222	1	1	0	1	0
225	2	2	2	0	0
223	1	1	0	1	1

The final output files are then accumulated and copied to a server, where a web service makes the data available to the Last.fm website for display. An example of this is shown in Figure 16-3, where the total number of listeners and plays are displayed for a track.

Figure 16-3. TrackStats result

Summary

Hadoop has become an essential part of Last.fm's infrastructure and is used to generate and process a wide variety of datasets ranging from web logs to user listening data. The example covered here has been simplified considerably in order to get the key concepts across; in real-world usage, the input data has a more complicated structure and the code that processes it is more complex. Hadoop itself, although mature enough for production use, is still in active development, and new features and improvements are added by the Hadoop community every week. We at Last.fm are happy to be part of this community as a contributor of code and ideas, and as end users of a great piece of open source technology.

—Adrian Woodhead and Marc de Palol

Hadoop and Hive at Facebook

Hadoop can be used to form core backend batch and near real-time computing infrastructures. It can also be used to store and archive massive datasets. In this case study, we will explore backend data architectures and the role Hadoop can play in them. We will describe hypothetical Hadoop configurations, potential uses of Hive—an open source data warehousing and SQL infrastructure built on top of Hadoop—and the different kinds of business and product applications that have been built using this infrastructure.

Hadoop at Facebook

History

The amount of log and dimension data in Facebook that needs to be processed and stored has exploded as the usage of the site has increased. A key requirement for any data processing platform for this environment is the ability to scale rapidly. Further, with limited engineering resources, the system should be very reliable and easy to use and maintain.

Initially, data warehousing at Facebook was performed entirely on an Oracle instance. After we started hitting scalability and performance problems, we investigated whether there were open source technologies that could be used in our environment. As part of this investigation, we deployed a relatively small Hadoop instance and started publishing some of our core datasets into this instance. Hadoop was attractive because Yahoo! was using it internally for its batch processing needs and because we were familiar with the simplicity and scalability of the MapReduce model as popularized by Google.

Our initial prototype was very successful: the engineers loved the ability to process massive amounts of data in reasonable timeframes, an ability that we just did not have before. They also loved being able to use their favorite programming language for processing (using Hadoop streaming). Having our core datasets published in one centralized data store was also very convenient. At around the same time, we started developing Hive. This made it even easier for users to process data in the Hadoop cluster by being able to express common computations in the form of SQL, a language with which most engineers and analysts are familiar.

As a result, the cluster size and usage grew by leaps and bounds, and today Facebook is running the second-largest Hadoop cluster in the world. As of this writing, we hold more than 2 PB of data in Hadoop and load more than 10 TB of data into it every day. Our Hadoop instance has 2,400 cores and about 9 TB of memory, and runs at 100% utilization at many points during the day. We are able to scale out this cluster rapidly in response to our growth, and we have been able to take advantage of open source by modifying Hadoop where required to suit our needs. We have contributed back to open source, both in the form of contributions to some core components of Hadoop as well as by open-sourcing Hive, which is now a Hadoop top-level project.

Use cases

There are at least four interrelated but distinct classes of uses for Hadoop at Facebook:

- Producing daily and hourly summaries over large amounts of data. These summaries are used for a number of different purposes within the company:
  - Reports based on these summaries are used by engineering and nonengineering functional teams to drive product decisions. These summaries include reports on growth of the users, page views, and average time spent on the site by the users.
  - Providing performance numbers about advertisement campaigns that are run on Facebook.
  - Backend processing for site features such as people you may like and applications you may like.
- Running ad hoc jobs over historical data. These analyses help answer questions from our product groups and executive team.
- As a de facto long-term archival store for our log datasets.
- To look up log events by specific attributes (where logs are indexed by such attributes), which is used to maintain the integrity of the site and protect users against spambots.

Data architecture

Figure 16-4 shows the basic components of our architecture and the data flow within these components.

Web servers Scribe servers

Filers

Hive on Hadoop cluster

Oracle RAC Federated MySQL

Figure 16-4. Data warehousing architecture at Facebook

As shown in Figure 16-4, the following components are used in processing data:

Scribe

Log data is generated by web servers as well as internal services such as the Search backend. We use Scribe, an open source log collection service developed in Facebook that deposits hundreds of log datasets with a daily volume in the tens of terabytes into a handful of NFS servers.

HDFS

A large fraction of this log data is copied into one central HDFS instance. Dimension data is also scraped from our internal MySQL databases and copied over into HDFS daily.

Hive/Hadoop

We use Hive, a Hadoop subproject developed in Facebook, to build a data warehouse over all the data collected in HDFS. Files in HDFS, including log data from Scribe and dimension data from the MySQL tier, are made available as tables with logical partitions. A SQL-like query language provided by Hive is used in conjunction with MapReduce to create/publish a variety of summaries and reports, as well as to perform historical analysis over these tables.

Tools

Browser-based interfaces built on top of Hive allow users to compose and launch Hive queries (which in turn launch MapReduce jobs) using just a few mouse clicks.

Traditional RDBMS

We use Oracle and MySQL databases to publish these summaries. The volume of data here is relatively small, but the query rate is high and needs real-time response.

DataBee

An in-house Extract, Transform, Load (ETL) workflow software that is used to provide a common framework for reliable batch processing across all data processing jobs.

Data from the NFS tier storing Scribe data is continuously replicated to the HDFS cluster by copier jobs. The NFS devices are mounted on the Hadoop tier, and the copier processes run as Map-only jobs on the Hadoop cluster. This makes it easy to scale the copier processes and makes them fault-resilient. Currently, we copy over 6 TB per day from Scribe to HDFS in this manner. We also download up to 4 TB of dimension data from our MySQL tier to HDFS every day. These are also conveniently arranged on the Hadoop cluster as Map-only jobs that copy data out of MySQL boxes.

Hadoop configuration

The central philosophy behind our Hadoop deployment is consolidation. We use a single HDFS instance, and a vast majority of processing is done in a single MapReduce cluster (running a single jobtracker). The reasons for this are fairly straightforward:

- We can minimize the administrative overheads by operating a single cluster.
- Data does not need to be duplicated. All data is available in a single place for all the use cases described previously.
- By using the same compute cluster across all departments, we get tremendous efficiencies.
- Our users work in a collaborative environment, so requirements in terms of quality of service are not onerous (yet).

We also have a single shared Hive metastore (using a MySQL database) that holds metadata about all the Hive tables stored in HDFS.

Hypothetical Use Case Studies

In this section, we will describe some typical problems that are common for large websites, which are difficult to solve through traditional warehousing technologies, simply because the costs and scales involved are prohibitively high. Hadoop and Hive can provide a more scalable and more cost-effective solution in such situations.

Advertiser insights and performance

One of the most common uses of Hadoop is to produce summaries from large volumes of data. It is very typical of large ad networks, such as the Facebook ad network, Google AdSense, and many others, to provide advertisers with standard aggregated statistics about their ads that help the advertisers tune their campaigns effectively. Computing advertisement performance numbers on large datasets is a very data-intensive operation, and the scalability and cost advantages of Hadoop and Hive can really help in computing these numbers in a reasonable time frame and at a reasonable cost.

Many ad networks provide standardized CPC- and CPM-based ad units to the advertisers. The CPC ads are cost-per-click ads: the advertiser pays the ad network amounts that are dependent on the number of clicks that the particular ad gets from the users visiting the site. The CPM ads (short for *cost per mille*, that is, the cost per thousand impressions), on the other hand, bill the advertisers amounts that are proportional to the number of users who see the ad on the site. Apart from these standardized ad units, in the last few years ads with more dynamic content that is tailored to each individual user have also become common in the online advertisement industry. Yahoo! does this through SmartAds, whereas Facebook provides its advertisers with Social Ads. The latter allows the advertisers to embed information from a user's network of friends; for example, a Nike ad may refer to a friend of the user who recently fanned Nike and shared that information with her friends on Facebook. In addition, Facebook also provides Engagement Ad units to the advertisers, wherein the users can more effectively interact with the ad, be it by commenting on it or by playing embedded videos. In general, a wide variety of ads are provided to the advertisers by the online ad networks, and this variety adds yet another dimension to the various kinds of performance numbers that the advertisers are interested in getting about their campaigns.

At the most basic level, advertisers are interested in knowing the total number of users, as well as the number of unique users, who have seen the ad or have clicked on it. For more dynamic ads, they may even be interested in getting the breakdown of these aggregated numbers by the kind of dynamic information shown in the ad unit or the kind of engagement action undertaken by the users on the ad. For example, a particular advertisement may have been shown 100,000 times to 30,000 unique users. Similarly, a video embedded inside an Engagement Ad may have been watched by 100,000 unique users. In addition, these performance numbers are typically reported for each ad, campaign, and account. An account may have multiple campaigns, with each campaign running multiple ads on the network. Finally, these numbers are typically reported for different time durations by the ad networks. Typical durations are daily, rolling week, month to date, rolling month, and sometimes even for the entire lifetime of the campaign. Moreover, advertisers also look at the geographic breakdown of these numbers, among other ways of slicing and dicing this data, such as what percentage of the total viewers or clickers of a particular ad are in the Asia Pacific region.

As is evident, there are four predominant dimension hierarchies: the account, campaign, and ad dimension; the time period; the type of interaction; and the user dimension. The last of these is used to report unique numbers, whereas the other three are the reporting dimensions. The user dimension is also used to create aggregated geographic profiles for the viewers and clickers of ads. All this information in totality allows the advertisers to tune their campaigns to improve their effectiveness on any given ad network. Aside from the multidimensional nature of this set of pipelines, the volumes of data processed and the rate at which this data is growing on a daily basis make this difficult to scale without a technology such as Hadoop for large ad networks. As of this writing, for example, the ad log volume that is processed for ad performance numbers at Facebook is approximately 1 TB per day of (uncompressed) logs. This volume has seen a 30-fold increase since January 2008, when the volumes were in the range of 30 GB per day. Hadoop's ability to scale with hardware has been a major factor behind the ability of these pipelines to keep up with this data growth with only minor tweaking of job configurations. Typically, these configuration changes involve increasing the number of reducers for the Hadoop jobs that are processing the intensive portions of these pipelines. The largest of these stages currently runs with 400 reducers (an increase of eight times from the 50 reducers that were being used in January 2008).

Ad hoc analysis and product feedback

Apart from regular reports, another primary use case for a data warehousing solution is to support ad hoc analysis and product feedback solutions. Any typical website, for example, makes product changes, and product managers or engineers often need to understand the impact of a new feature, based on user engagement as well as on the click-through rate on that feature. The product team may even wish to perform a deeper analysis on the impact of the change based on various regions and countries, such as whether this change increases the click-through rate of the users in the US or whether it reduces the engagement of users in India. A lot of this type of analysis could be done with Hadoop by using Hive and regular SQL. The measurement of click-through rate can be easily expressed as a join of the impressions and clicks for the particular link related to the feature. This information can be joined with geographic information to compute the effect of product changes on different regions. Subsequently, one can compute average click-through rate for different geographic regions by performing aggregations over them. All of these are easily expressible in Hive using a couple of SQL queries (that would, in turn, generate multiple Hadoop jobs). If only an estimate were required, the same queries can be run for a sample set of the users using the sampling functionality natively supported by Hive. Some of this analysis needs the use of custom map and reduce scripts in conjunction with the Hive SQL, and that is also easy to plug into a Hive query.

A good example of a more complex analysis is estimating the peak number of users logging into the site per minute for the entire past year. This would involve sampling page view logs (because the total page view data for a popular website is huge), grouping it by time, and then finding the number of new users at different time points via a custom reduce script. This is a good example where both SQL and MapReduce are required for solving the end user problem, and something that is possible to achieve easily with Hive.

Data analysis

Hive and Hadoop are easy to use for training and scoring for data analysis applications. These data analysis applications can span multiple domains, such as popular websites, bioinformatics companies, and oil exploration companies. A typical example of such an application in the online ad network industry would be the prediction of what features of an ad make it more likely to be noticed by the user. The training phase typically would involve identifying the response metric and the predictive features. In this case, a good metric to measure the effectiveness of an ad could be its click-through rate. Some interesting features of the ad could be the industry vertical that it belongs to, the content of the ad, the placement of the ad on the page, and so on. Hive is useful for assembling training data and then feeding the same into a data analysis engine (typically R or user programs written in MapReduce). In this particular case, different ad performance numbers and features can be structured as tables in Hive. One can easily sample this data (sampling is required, as R can handle only limited data volume) and perform the appropriate aggregations and joins using Hive queries to assemble a response table containing the most important ad features that determine the effectiveness of an advertisement. However, because sampling loses information, some of the more important data analysis applications use parallel implementations of popular data analysis kernels using the MapReduce framework.

Once the model has been trained, it may be deployed for scoring on a daily basis. The bulk of the data analysis tasks do not perform daily scoring, though. Many of them are ad hoc in nature and require one-time analysis that can be used as input into the product design process.

Hive

When we started using Hadoop, we very quickly became impressed by its scalability and availability. However, we were worried about widespread adoption, primarily because of the complexity involved in writing MapReduce programs in Java (as well as the cost of training users to write them). We were aware that a lot of engineers and analysts in the company understood SQL as a tool to query and analyze data, and that many of them were proficient in a number of scripting languages, such as PHP and Python. As a result, it was imperative for us to develop software that could bridge this gap between the languages that the users were proficient in and the languages required to program Hadoop.

It was also evident that a lot of our datasets were structured and could be easily partitioned. The natural consequence of these requirements was a system that could model data as tables and partitions and that could also provide a SQL-like language for query and analysis. Also essential was the ability to plug in customized MapReduce programs written in the programming language of the user's choice into the query. This system was called Hive. Hive is a data warehouse infrastructure built on top of Hadoop and serves as the predominant tool that is used to query the data stored in Hadoop at Facebook. In the following sections, we describe this system in more detail.

Data organization

Data is organized consistently across all datasets and is compressed, partitioned, and sorted:

Compression
Almost all datasets are stored as sequence files using the gzip codec. Older datasets are recompressed to use the bzip codec, which affords substantially more compression than gzip. Bzip is slower than gzip, but older data is accessed much less frequently, and this performance hit is well worth the savings in terms of disk space.

Partitioning
Most datasets are partitioned by date. Individual partitions are loaded into Hive, which loads each partition into a separate HDFS directory. In most cases, this partitioning is based simply on datestamps associated with Scribe logfiles. However, in some cases, we scan data and collate them based on the timestamp available inside a log entry. Going forward, we are also going to be partitioning data on multiple attributes (for example, country and date).

Sorting
Each partition within a table is often sorted (and hash-partitioned) by unique ID (if one is present). This has a few key advantages:
- It is easy to run sampled queries on such datasets.
- We can build indexes on sorted data.
- Aggregates and joins involving unique IDs can be done very efficiently on such datasets.

Loading data into this long-term format is done by daily MapReduce jobs (and is distinct from the near real-time data import processes).

Query language

The Hive Query language is very SQL-like. It has traditional SQL constructs such as joins, group bys, where, select, from clauses, and from clause subqueries. It tries to convert SQL commands into a set of MapReduce jobs. Apart from the normal SQL clauses, it has a bunch of other extensions, such as the ability to specify custom Mapper and reducer scripts in the query itself; the ability to insert into multiple tables, partitions, HDFS, or local files while doing a single scan of the data; and the ability to run the query on data samples rather than the full dataset (this ability is fairly useful when testing queries). The Hive metastore stores the metadata for a table and provides this metadata to the Hive compiler for converting SQL commands to MapReduce jobs. Through partition pruning, map-side aggregations, and other features, the compiler tries to create plans that can optimize the runtime for the query.

Data pipelines using Hive

Additionally, the ability provided by Hive in terms of expressing data pipelines in SQL can and has provided the much-needed flexibility in putting these pipelines together in an easy and expedient manner. This is especially useful for organizations and products that are still evolving and growing. Many of the operations needed in processing data pipelines are the well-understood SQL operations such as join, group by, and distinct aggregations. With Hive's ability to convert SQL into a series of Hadoop Map-Reduce jobs, it becomes fairly easy to create and maintain these pipelines. We illustrate these facets of Hive in this section by using an example of a hypothetical ad network and showing how some typical aggregated reports needed by the advertisers can be computed using Hive. As an example, assuming that an online ad network stores information on ads in a table named dim_ads and stores all the impressions served to that ad in a table named impression_logs in Hive, with the latter table being partitioned by date, the daily impression numbers (both unique and total by campaign, which are numbers that ad networks routinely give to the advertisers) for 2008-12-01 are expressible as the following SQL in Hive:

```
SELECT a.campaign_id, count(1), count(DISTINCT b.user_id)
FROM dim_ads a JOIN impression_logs b ON(b.ad_id = a.ad_id)
WHERE b.dateid = '2008-12-01'
GROUP BY a.campaign_id;
```

This would also be the typical SQL statement that one could use in other RDBMSs, such as Oracle, DB2, and so on.

In order to compute the daily impression numbers by ad and account from the same joined data as earlier, Hive provides the ability to do multiple group bys simultaneously, as shown in the following query (which is SQL-like, but not strictly SQL):

```
FROM(
  SELECT a.ad_id, a.campaign_id, a.account_id, b.user_id
  FROM dim_ads a JOIN impression_logs b ON (b.ad_id = a.ad_id)
  WHERE b.dateid = '2008-12-01') x
INSERT OVERWRITE DIRECTORY 'results_gby_adid'
  SELECT x.ad_id, count(1), count(DISTINCT x.user_id) GROUP BY x.ad_id
INSERT OVERWRITE DIRECTORY 'results_gby_campaignid'
  SELECT x.campaign_id, count(1), count(DISTINCT x.user_id) GROUP BY x.campaign_id
INSERT OVERWRITE DIRECTORY 'results_gby_accountid'
  SELECT x.account_id, count(1), count(DISTINCT x.user_id) GROUP BY x.account_id;
```

In one of the optimizations that is being added to Hive, the query can be converted into a sequence of Hadoop MapReduce jobs that are able to scale with data skew. Essentially, the join is converted into one MapReduce job ,and the three group bys are converted into four MapReduce jobs, with the first one generating a partial aggregate on unique_id. This is especially useful because the distribution of impression_logs over unique_id is much more uniform compared to ad_id (in an ad network, it is typical for a few ads to dominate in that they are shown more uniformly to the users). As a result, computing the partial aggregation by unique_id allows the pipeline to distribute the work more uniformly to the reducers. The same template can be used to compute performance numbers for different time periods by simply changing the date predicate in the query.

Computing the lifetime numbers can be more tricky, though, because using the strategy described previously, one would have to scan all the partitions of the `impres sion_logs` table. Therefore, in order to compute the lifetime numbers, a more viable strategy is to store the lifetime counts on a per `ad_id`, `unique_id` grouping every day in a partition of an intermediate table. The data in this table combined with the next day's `impression_logs` can be used to incrementally generate the lifetime ad performance numbers. As an example, in order to get the impression numbers for 2008-12-01, the intermediate table partition for 2008-11-30 is used. The Hive queries that can be used to achieve this are as follows:

```
INSERT OVERWRITE lifetime_partial_imps PARTITION(dateid='2008-12-01')
SELECT x.ad_id, x.user_id, sum(x.cnt)
FROM (
  SELECT a.ad_id, a.user_id, a.cnt
  FROM lifetime_partial_imps a
  WHERE a.dateid = '2008-11-30'
  UNION ALL
  SELECT b.ad_id, b.user_id, 1 as cnt
  FROM impression_log b
  WHERE b.dateid = '2008-12-01'
) x
GROUP BY x.ad_id, x.user_id;
```

This query computes the partial sums for 2008-12-01, which can be used for computing the 2008-12-01 numbers as well as the 2008-12-02 numbers (not shown here). The SQL is converted to a single Hadoop MapReduce job that essentially computes the group by statement on the combined stream of inputs. This SQL can be followed by the next Hive query, which computes the actual numbers for different groupings (similar to the one in the daily pipelines):

```
FROM(
  SELECT a.ad_id, a.campaign_id, a.account_id, b.user_id, b.cnt
    FROM dim_ads a JOIN lifetime_partial_imps b ON (b.ad_id = a.ad_id)
    WHERE b.dateid = '2008-12-01') x
INSERT OVERWRITE DIRECTORY 'results_gby_adid'
  SELECT x.ad_id, sum(x.cnt), count(DISTINCT x.user_id) GROUP BY x.ad_id
INSERT OVERWRITE DIRECTORY 'results_gby_campaignid'
  SELECT x.campaign_id, sum(x.cnt), count(DISTINCT x.user_id) GROUP BY x.campaign_id
INSERT OVERWRITE DIRECTORY 'results_gby_accountid'
  SELECT x.account_id, sum(x.cnt), count(DISTINCT x.user_id) GROUP BY x.account_id;
```

Hive and Hadoop are batch processing systems that cannot serve the computed data with the same latency as a standard RDBMS, such as Oracle or MySQL. Therefore, on many occasions, it is still useful to load the summaries generated through Hive and Hadoop to a more traditional RDBMS for serving this data to users through different business intelligence (BI) tools, or even though a web portal.

Problems and Future Work

Fair sharing

Hadoop clusters typically run a mix of daily production jobs that need to finish computation within a reasonable time frame as well as ad hoc jobs that may be of different priorities and sizes. In typical installations, these production jobs tend to run overnight, when interference from ad hoc jobs run by users is minimal. However, overlap between large ad hoc and production jobs is often unavoidable and, without adequate safeguards, can impact the latency of production jobs. ETL processing also contains several near real-time jobs that must be performed at hourly intervals (these include processes to copy Scribe data from NFS servers, as well as hourly summaries computed over some datasets). It also means that a single rogue job can bring down the entire cluster and put production processes at risk.

The fair-sharing Hadoop job scheduler, developed at Facebook and contributed back to Hadoop, provides a solution to many of these issues. It reserves guaranteed compute resources for specific pools of jobs while at the same time letting idle resources be used by everyone. It also prevents large jobs from hogging cluster resources by allocating compute resources in a fair manner across these pools. Memory can become one of the most contended resources in the cluster. We have made some changes to Hadoop so that if the job tracker is low on memory, Hadoop job submissions are throttled. This can allow the user processes to run with reasonable per-process memory limits, and it is possible to put in place some monitoring scripts in order to prevent MapReduce jobs from impacting HDFS daemons (due primarily to high memory consumption) running on the same node. Log directories are stored in separate disk partitions and cleaned regularly, and we think it can also be useful to put MapReduce intermediate storage in separate disk partitions as well.

Space management

Capacity management continues to be a big challenge. Utilization is increasing at a fast rate with the growth of data, and many growing companies with expanding datasets have the same pain. In many situations, much of this data is temporary in nature. In such cases, one can use retention settings in Hive and also recompress older data in bzip format to save on space. Although configurations are largely symmetrical from a disk storage point of view, adding a separate tier of high-storage-density machines to hold older data may prove beneficial. This will make it cheaper to store archival data in Hadoop. However, access to such data should be transparent. We are currently working on a data archival layer to make this possible and to unify all the aspects of dealing with older data.

Scribe-HDFS integration

Currently, Scribe writes to a handful of NFS filers from where data is picked up and delivered to HDFS by custom copier jobs, as described earlier. We are working on making Scribe write directly to another HDFS instance. This will make it very easy to scale and administer Scribe. Due to the high uptime requirements for Scribe, its target HDFS instance is likely to be different from the production HDFS instance (so that it is isolated from any load/downtime issues due to user jobs).

Improvements to Hive

Hive is still under active development. We are working on a number of key features, such as support for order by and having clause supports, more aggregate functions, more built-in functions, a datetime data type, and so on. At the same time, a number of performance optimizations are being worked on, such as predicate pushdown and common subexpression elimination. On the integration side, JDBC and ODBC drivers are being developed in order to integrate with OLAP and BI tools. With all these optimizations, we hope that we can unlock the power of MapReduce and Hadoop, and bring it closer to nonengineering communities as well as within Facebook. For more information on this project, please visit *http://hadoop.apache.org/hive/*.

—Joydeep Sen Sarma and Ashish Thusoo

Nutch Search Engine

Nutch is a framework for building scalable Internet crawlers and search engines. It's an Apache Software Foundation project and a subproject of Lucene, and it's available under the Apache 2.0 license.

We won't go deeply into the anatomy of a web crawler as such; instead, the purpose of this case study is to show how Hadoop can be used to implement various complex processing tasks typical for a search engine. Interested readers can find plenty of Nutch-specific information on the official site of the project (*http://lucene.apache.org/nutch*). Suffice it to say that in order to create and maintain a search engine, one needs the following subsystems:

Database of pages
> This database keeps track of all pages known to the crawler and their status, such as the last time it visited the page, its fetching status, refresh interval, content checksum, etc. In Nutch terminology, this database is called *CrawlDb*.

List of pages to fetch
> As crawlers periodically refresh their view of the Web, they download new pages (previously unseen) or refresh pages that they think have already expired. Nutch calls such a list of candidate pages prepared for fetching a *fetchlist*.

Raw page data

Page content is downloaded from remote sites and stored locally in the original uninterpreted format, as a byte array. This data is called the *page content* in Nutch.

Parsed page data

Page content is then parsed using a suitable parser. Nutch provides parsers for documents in many popular formats, such as HTML, PDF, Open Office and Microsoft Office, RSS, and others.

Link graph database

This database is necessary to compute link-based page ranking scores, such as PageRank. For each URL known to Nutch, it contains a list of other URLs pointing to it and their associated anchor text (from HTML `<a href="..">`anchor text`</a>` elements). This database is called *LinkDb*.

Full-text search index

This is a classical inverted index, built from the collected page metadata and from the extracted plain-text content. It is implemented using the excellent Lucene library (*http://lucene.apache.org/java*).

We briefly mentioned before that Hadoop began its life as a component in Nutch, intended to improve its scalability and to address clear performance bottlenecks caused by a centralized data processing model. Nutch was also the first public proof-of-concept application ported to the framework that would later become Hadoop, and the effort required to port Nutch algorithms and data structures to Hadoop proved to be surprisingly small. This probably encouraged the following development of Hadoop as a separate subproject with the aim of providing a reusable framework for applications other than Nutch.

Currently, nearly all Nutch tools process data by running one or more MapReduce jobs.

Data Structures

There are several major data structures maintained in Nutch, and they all make use of Hadoop I/O classes and formats. Depending on the purpose of the data and the way it's accessed once it's created, the data is kept using either Hadoop map files or sequence files.

Since the data is produced and processed by MapReduce jobs, which in turn run several map and reduce tasks, its on-disk layout corresponds to the common Hadoop output formats, that is, `MapFileOutputFormat` and `SequenceFileOutputFormat`. So to be precise, we should say that data is kept in several partial map files or sequence files, with as many parts as there were reduce tasks in the job that created the data. For simplicity, we omit this distinction in the following sections.

CrawlDb

CrawlDb stores the current status of each URL as a map file of `<url, CrawlDatum>`, where keys use `Text` and values use a Nutch-specific `CrawlDatum` class (which implements the `Writable` interface).

In order to provide quick random access to the records (sometimes useful for diagnostic reasons, when users want to examine individual records in CrawlDb), this data is stored in map files and not in sequence files.

CrawlDb is initially created using the Injector tool, which simply converts a plain-text representation of the initial list of URLs (called the seed list) to a map file in the format described earlier. Subsequently, it is updated with the information from the fetched and parsed pages—more on that shortly.

LinkDb

This database stores the incoming link information for every URL known to Nutch. It is a map file of `<url, Inlinks>`, where `Inlinks` is a list of URL and anchor text data. It's worth noting that this information is not immediately available during page collection, but the reverse information is available, namely that of outgoing links from a page. The process of inverting this relationship is implemented as a MapReduce job, described shortly.

Segments

Segments in Nutch parlance correspond to fetching and parsing a batch of URLs. Figure 16-5 presents how segments are created and processed.

A segment (which is really a directory in a filesystem) contains the following parts (which are simply subdirectories containing `MapFileOutputFormat` or `SequenceFileOutputFormat` data):

content
> Contains the raw data of downloaded pages as a map file of `<url, Content>`. Nutch uses a map file here because it needs fast random access in order to present a cached view of a page.

crawl_generate
> Contains the list of URLs to be fetched, together with their current status retrieved from CrawlDb, as a sequence file of `<url, CrawlDatum>`. This data uses the sequence file format, first because it's processed sequentially, and second because we couldn't satisfy the map file invariants of sorted keys. We need to spread URLs that belong to the same host as far apart as possible to minimize the load per target host, and this means that records are sorted more or less randomly.

crawl_fetch
> Contains status reports from the fetching, that is, whether it was successful, what was the response code, etc. This is stored in a map file of `<url, CrawlDatum>`.

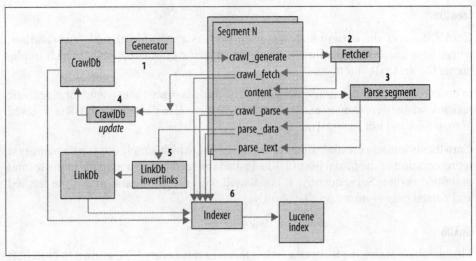

Figure 16-5. Segments

crawl_parse

> The list of outlinks for each successfully fetched and parsed page is stored here so that Nutch can expand its crawling frontier by learning new URLs.

parse_data

> Metadata collected during parsing; this includes, among others, the list of outgoing links (outlinks) for a page. This information is crucial later on to build an inverted graph (of incoming links, or inlinks).

parse_text

> Plain-text version of the page, suitable for indexing in Lucene. These are stored as a map file of <url, ParseText> so that Nutch can access them quickly when building summaries (snippets) to display the list of search results.

New segments are created from CrawlDb when the Generator tool is run (labeled as 1 in Figure 16-5), and initially contain just a list of URLs to fetch (the *crawl_generate* subdirectory). As this list is processed in several steps, the segment collects output data from the processing tools in a set of subdirectories.

For example, the *content* part is populated by a tool called Fetcher, which downloads raw data from URLs on the fetchlist (2). This tool also saves the status information in *crawl_fetch* so that this data can be used later on for updating the status of the page in CrawlDb.

The remaining parts of the segment are populated by the Parse segment tool (3), which reads the content section, selects appropriate content parser based on the declared (or detected) MIME type, and saves the results of parsing in three parts: *crawl_parse*, *parse_data*, and *parse_text*. This data is then used to update the CrawlDb with new information (4) and to create the LinkDb (5).

Segments are kept around until all pages present in them are expired. Nutch applies a configurable maximum time limit, after which a page is forcibly selected for refetching; this helps the operator phase out all segments older than this limit (because she can be sure that by that time, all pages in this segment would have been refetched).

Segment data is used to create Lucene indexes (primarily the *parse_text* and *parse_data* parts; 6 in the figure), but it also provides a data storage mechanism for quick retrieval of plain-text and raw content data. The former is needed so that Nutch can generate snippets (fragments of document text best matching a query); the latter provides the ability to present a "cached view" of the page. In both cases, this data is accessed directly from map files in response to requests for snippet generation or for cached content. In practice, even for large collections the performance of accessing data directly from map files is quite sufficient.

Selected Examples of Hadoop Data Processing in Nutch

The following sections present relevant details of some Nutch tools to illustrate how the MapReduce paradigm is applied to a concrete data processing task in Nutch.

Link inversion

HTML pages collected during crawling contain HTML links, which may point either to the same page (internal links) or to other pages. HTML links are directed from source page to target page. See Figure 16-6.

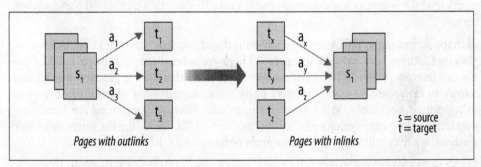

Figure 16-6. Link inversion

However, most algorithms for calculating a page's importance (or quality) need the opposite information, that is, what pages contain outlinks that point to the current page. This information is not readily available when crawling. Also, the indexing process benefits from taking into account the anchor text on inlinks so that this text may semantically enrich the text of the current page.

As mentioned earlier, Nutch collects the outlink information and then uses this data to build a LinkDb, which contains this reversed link data in the form of inlinks and anchor text.

This section presents a rough outline of the implementation of the LinkDb tool. Many details have been omitted (such as URL normalization and filtering) in order to present a clear picture of the process. What's left gives a classical example of why the MapReduce paradigm fits so well with the key data transformation processes required to run a search engine. Large search engines need to deal with massive web graph data (many pages with a lot of outlinks/inlinks), and the parallelism and fault tolerance offered by Hadoop make this possible. Additionally, it's easy to express the link inversion using the Map-sort-Reduce primitives, as illustrated next.

The snippet here presents the job initialization of the LinkDb tool:

```
JobConf job = new JobConf(configuration);
FileInputFormat.addInputPath(job, new Path(segmentPath, "parse_data"));
job.setInputFormat(SequenceFileInputFormat.class);
job.setMapperClass(LinkDb.class);
job.setReducerClass(LinkDb.class);
job.setOutputKeyClass(Text.class);
job.setOutputValueClass(Inlinks.class);
job.setOutputFormat(MapFileOutputFormat.class);
FileOutputFormat.setOutputPath(job, newLinkDbPath);
```

As we can see, the source data for this job is the list of fetched URLs (keys) and the corresponding ParseData records that contain, among others, the outlink information for each page as an array of outlinks. An outlink contains both the target URL and the anchor text.

The output from the job is again a list of URLs (keys), but the values are instances of inlinks, which is simply a specialized set of inlinks that contain target URLs and anchor text.

Perhaps surprisingly, URLs are typically stored and processed as plain text and not as java.net.URL or java.net.URI instances. There are several reasons for this: URLs extracted from downloaded content usually need normalization (e.g., converting hostnames to lowercase, resolving relative paths), are often broken or invalid, or refer to unsupported protocols. Many normalization and filtering operations are better expressed as text patterns that span several parts of a URL. Also, for the purpose of link analysis, we may still want to process and count invalid URLs.

Let's take a closer look now at the map() and reduce() implementations. In this case, they are simple enough to be implemented in the body of the same class:

```
public void map(Text fromUrl, ParseData parseData,
    OutputCollector<Text, Inlinks> output, Reporter reporter) {
  ...
  Outlink[] outlinks = parseData.getOutlinks();
  Inlinks inlinks = new Inlinks();
  for (Outlink out : outlinks) {
    inlinks.clear(); // instance reuse to avoid excessive GC
    String toUrl = out.getToUrl();
    String anchor = out.getAnchor();
    inlinks.add(new Inlink(fromUrl, anchor));
    output.collect(new Text(toUrl), inlinks);
```

```
        }
    }
```

You can see from this listing that for each `Outlink`, our `map()` implementation produces a pair of `<toUrl, Inlinks>`, where `Inlinks` contains just a single `Inlink` containing `fromUrl` and the anchor text. The direction of the link has been inverted.

Subsequently, these one-element-long `Inlinks` are aggregated in the `reduce()` method:

```
    public void reduce(Text toUrl, Iterator<Inlinks> values,
        OutputCollector<Text, Inlinks> output, Reporter reporter) {
      Inlinks result = new Inlinks();
      while (values.hasNext()) {
        result.add(values.next());
      }
      output.collect(toUrl, result);
    }
```

From this code, it's obvious that we got exactly what we wanted—that is, a list of all `fromUrls` that point to our `toUrl`, together with their anchor text. The inversion process has been accomplished.

This data is then saved using the `MapFileOutputFormat` and becomes the new version of LinkDb.

Generation of fetchlists

Let's take a look now at a more complicated use case. Fetchlists are produced from the CrawlDb (which is a map file of `<url, crawlDatum>`, with the `crawlDatum` containing a status of this URL), and they contain URLs ready to be fetched, which are then processed by the Nutch Fetcher tool. Fetcher is itself a MapReduce application (described shortly). This means that the input data (partitioned in N parts) will be processed by N map tasks; the Fetcher tool enforces that `SequenceFileInputFormat` should not further split the data into more parts than there are already input partitions. Earlier, we mentioned briefly that fetchlists need to be generated in a special way so that the data in each part of the fetchlist (and consequently processed in each map task) meets certain requirements:

1. All URLs from the same host need to end up in the same partition. This is required so that Nutch can easily implement in-JVM host-level blocking to avoid overwhelming target hosts.

2. URLs from the same host should be as far apart as possible (i.e., well mixed with URLs from other hosts) in order to minimize the host-level blocking.

3. There should be no more than x URLs from any single host so that large sites with many URLs don't dominate smaller sites (and URLs from smaller sites still have a chance to be scheduled for fetching).

4. URLs with high scores should be preferred over URLs with low scores.

5. There should be, at most, *y* URLs in total in the fetchlist.

6. The number of output partitions should match the optimum number of fetching map tasks.

In this case, two MapReduce jobs are needed to satisfy all these requirements, as illustrated in Figure 16-7. Again, in the following listings, we are going to skip some details of these steps for the sake of brevity.

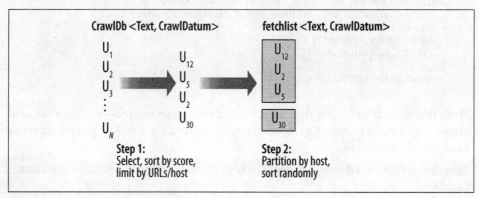

Figure 16-7. Generation of fetchlists

Step 1: Select, sort by score, limit by URL count per host. In this step, Nutch runs a MapReduce job to select URLs that are considered eligible for fetching and to sort them by their score (a floating-point value assigned to each URL, e.g., a PageRank score). The input data comes from CrawlDb, which is a map file of `<url, datum>`. The output from this job is a sequence file with `<score, <url, datum>>`, sorted in descending order by score.

First, let's look at the job setup:

```
FileInputFormat.addInputPath(job, crawlDbPath);
job.setInputFormat(SequenceFileInputFormat.class);
job.setMapperClass(Selector.class);
job.setPartitionerClass(Selector.class);
job.setReducerClass(Selector.class);
FileOutputFormat.setOutputPath(job, tempDir);
job.setOutputFormat(SequenceFileOutputFormat.class);
job.setOutputKeyClass(FloatWritable.class);
job.setOutputKeyComparatorClass(DecreasingFloatComparator.class);
job.setOutputValueClass(SelectorEntry.class);
```

The `Selector` class implements three functions: mapper, reducer, and partitioner. The last function is especially interesting: `Selector` uses a custom `Partitioner` to assign URLs from the same host to the same reduce task so that we can satisfy criteria 3–5 from the previous list. If we didn't override the default partitioner, URLs from the same host would end up in different partitions of the output, and we wouldn't be able to track and limit the total counts, because MapReduce tasks don't communicate between themselves. As it is now, all URLs that belong to the same host will end up being processed by the same reduce task, which means we can control how many URLs per host are selected.

It's easy to implement a custom partitioner so that data that needs to be processed in the same task ends up in the same partition. Let's take a look first at how the `Selector` class implements the `Partitioner` interface (which consists of a single method):

```
/** Partition by host. */
public int getPartition(FloatWritable key, Writable value, int numReduceTasks) {
  return hostPartitioner.getPartition((((SelectorEntry)value).url, key,
    numReduceTasks);
}
```

The method returns an integer number from 0 to numReduceTasks - 1. It simply replaces the key with the original URL from `SelectorEntry` to pass the URL (instead of the score) to an instance of `PartitionUrlByHost`, where the partition number is calculated:

```
/** Hash by hostname. */
public int getPartition(Text key, Writable value, int numReduceTasks) {
  String urlString = key.toString();
  URL url = null;
  try {
    url = new URL(urlString);
  } catch (MalformedURLException e) {
    LOG.warn("Malformed URL: '" + urlString + "'");
  }
  int hashCode = (url == null ? urlString : url.getHost()).hashCode();
  // make hosts wind up in different partitions on different runs
  hashCode ^= seed;

  return (hashCode & Integer.MAX_VALUE) % numReduceTasks;
}
```

As you can see from the code snippet, the partition number is a function of only the host part of the URL, which means that all URLs that belong to the same host will end up in the same partition.

The output from this job is sorted in decreasing order by score. Since there are many records in CrawlDb with the same score, we couldn't use `MapFileOutputFormat` because we would violate the map file's invariant of strict key ordering.

Observant readers will notice that we had to use something other than the original keys, but we still want to preserve the original key-value pairs. We use here a `SelectorEntry` class to pass the original key-value pairs to the next step of processing.

`Selector.reduce()` keeps track of the total number of URLs and the maximum number of URLs per host, and simply discards excessive records. Please note that the enforcement of the total count limit is necessarily approximate. We calculate the limit for the current task as the total limit divided by the number of reduce tasks. But we don't know for sure from within the task that it is going to get an equal share of URLs;

indeed, in most cases it doesn't, because of the uneven distribution of URLs among hosts. However, for Nutch this approximation is sufficient.

Step 2: Invert, partition by host, sort randomly. In the previous step, we ended up with a sequence file of `<score, selectorEntry>`. Now we have to produce a sequence file of `<url, datum>` and satisfy criteria 1, 2, and 6 just described. The input data for this step is the output data produced in step 1.

The following is a snippet showing the setup of this job:

```
FileInputFormat.addInputPath(job, tempDir);
job.setInputFormat(SequenceFileInputFormat.class);
job.setMapperClass(SelectorInverseMapper.class);
job.setMapOutputKeyClass(Text.class);
job.setMapOutputValueClass(SelectorEntry.class);
job.setPartitionerClass(PartitionUrlByHost.class);
job.setReducerClass(PartitionReducer.class);
job.setNumReduceTasks(numParts);
FileOutputFormat.setOutputPath(job, output);
job.setOutputFormat(SequenceFileOutputFormat.class);
job.setOutputKeyClass(Text.class);
job.setOutputValueClass(CrawlDatum.class);
job.setOutputKeyComparatorClass(HashComparator.class);
```

The `SelectorInverseMapper` class simply discards the current key (the score value), extracts the original URL and uses it as a key, and uses the `SelectorEntry` as the value. Careful readers may wonder why we don't go one step further, extracting also the original `CrawlDatum` and using it as the value—more on this shortly.

The final output from this job is a sequence file of `<Text, CrawlDatum>`, but our output from the map phase uses `<Text, SelectorEntry>`. We have to specify that we use different key-value classes for the map output, using the `setMapOutputKeyClass()` and `setMapOutputValueClass()` setters. Otherwise, Hadoop assumes that we use the same classes as declared for the reduce output (this conflict usually would cause a job to fail).

The output from the map phase is partitioned using the `PartitionUrlByHost` class so that it again assigns URLs from the same host to the same partition. This satisfies requirement 1.

Once the data is shuffled from map to reduce tasks, it's sorted by Hadoop according to the output key comparator, in this case the `HashComparator`. This class uses a simple hashing scheme to mix URLs in a way that is least likely to put URLs from the same host close to each other.

In order to meet requirement 6, we set the number of reduce tasks to the desired number of `Fetcher` map tasks (the `numParts` mentioned earlier), keeping in mind that each reduce partition will be used later on to create a single `Fetcher` map task.

The `PartitionReducer` class is responsible for the final step, that is, to convert `<url, selectorEntry>` to `<url, crawlDatum>`. A surprising side effect of using `HashComparator` is that several URLs may be hashed to the same hash value, and Hadoop will call the reduce() method, passing only the first such key; all other keys considered equal will be discarded. Now it becomes clear why we had to preserve all URLs in SelectorEntry records, because now we can extract them from the iterated values. Here is the implementation of this method:

```
public void reduce(Text key, Iterator<SelectorEntry> values,
    OutputCollector<Text, CrawlDatum> output, Reporter reporter) throws IOException {
  // when using HashComparator, we get only one input key in case of hash collisions
  // so use only URLs extracted from values
  while (values.hasNext()) {
    SelectorEntry entry = values.next();
    output.collect(entry.url, entry.datum);
  }
}
```

Finally, the output from reduce tasks is stored as a SequenceFileOutputFormat in a *crawl_generate* subdirectory of a Nutch segment directory. This output satisfies all criteria from 1 to 6.

Fetcher: A multithreaded MapRunner in action

The Fetcher application in Nutch is responsible for downloading the page content from remote sites. As such, it is important that the process uses every opportunity for parallelism, in order to minimize the time it takes to crawl a fetchlist.

There is already one level of parallelism present in Fetcher; multiple parts of the input fetchlists are assigned to multiple map tasks. However, in practice this is not sufficient: sequential download of URLs, from different hosts (see the earlier section on HashComparator), would be a tremendous waste of time. For this reason, the Fetcher map tasks process this data using multiple worker threads.

Hadoop uses the MapRunner class to implement the sequential processing of input data records. The Fetcher class implements its own MapRunner that uses multiple threads to process input records in parallel.

Let's begin with the setup of the job:

```
job.setSpeculativeExecution(false);
FileInputFormat.addInputPath(job, "segment/crawl_generate");
job.setInputFormat(InputFormat.class);
job.setMapRunnerClass(Fetcher.class);
FileOutputFormat.setOutputPath(job, segment);
job.setOutputFormat(FetcherOutputFormat.class);
job.setOutputKeyClass(Text.class);
job.setOutputValueClass(NutchWritable.class);
```

First, we turn off speculative execution. We can't run several map tasks to download content from the same hosts, because it would violate the host-level load limits (such as the number of concurrent requests and the number of requests per second).

Next, we use a custom InputFormat implementation that prevents Hadoop from splitting partitions of input data into smaller chunks (splits), thus creating more map tasks than there are input partitions. This again ensures that we control host-level access limits.

Output data is stored using a custom `OutputFormat` implementation, which uses data contained in `NutchWritable` values to create several output map files and sequence files. The `NutchWritable` class is a subclass of `GenericWritable`, able to pass instances of several different `Writable` classes declared in advance.

The Fetcher class implements the `MapRunner` interface, and we set this class as the job's `MapRunner` implementation. The relevant parts of the code are listed here:

```
public void run(RecordReader<Text, CrawlDatum> input,
    OutputCollector<Text, NutchWritable> output,
                Reporter reporter) throws IOException {
  int threadCount = getConf().getInt("fetcher.threads.fetch", 10);
  feeder = new QueueFeeder(input, fetchQueues, threadCount * 50);
  feeder.start();

  for (int i = 0; i < threadCount; i++) {          // spawn threads
    new FetcherThread(getConf()).start();
  }
  do {                                             // wait for threads to exit
    try {
      Thread.sleep(1000);
    } catch (InterruptedException e) {}
    reportStatus(reporter);
  } while (activeThreads.get() > 0);
}
```

Fetcher reads many input records in advance, using the `QueueFeeder` thread that puts input records into a set of per-host queues. Then several `FetcherThread` instances are started, which consume items from per-host queues, while `QueueFeeder` keeps reading input data to keep the queues filled. Each `FetcherThread` consumes items from any nonempty queue.

In the meantime, the main thread of the map task spins around, waiting for all threads to finish their job. Periodically, it reports the status to the framework to ensure that Hadoop doesn't consider this task to be dead and kill it. Once all items are processed, the loop is finished and the control is returned to Hadoop, which considers this map task to be completed.

Indexer: Using custom OutputFormat

This is an example of a MapReduce application that doesn't produce sequence file or map file output; instead, the output from this application is a Lucene index. Again, as MapReduce applications may consist of several reduce tasks, the output from this application may consist of several partial Lucene indexes.

The Nutch Indexer tool uses information from CrawlDb, LinkDb, and Nutch segments (fetch status, parsing status, page metadata, and plain-text data), so the job setup section involves adding several input paths:

```
FileInputFormat.addInputPath(job, crawlDbPath);
FileInputFormat.addInputPath(job, linkDbPath);
// add segment data
FileInputFormat.addInputPath(job, "segment/crawl_fetch");
FileInputFormat.addInputPath(job, "segment/crawl_parse");
FileInputFormat.addInputPath(job, "segment/parse_data");
FileInputFormat.addInputPath(job, "segment/parse_text");
job.setInputFormat(SequenceFileInputFormat.class);
job.setMapperClass(Indexer.class);
job.setReducerClass(Indexer.class);
FileOutputFormat.setOutputPath(job, indexDir);
job.setOutputFormat(OutputFormat.class);
job.setOutputKeyClass(Text.class);
job.setOutputValueClass(LuceneDocumentWrapper.class);
```

All corresponding records for a URL dispersed among these input locations need to be combined to create Lucene documents for addition to the index.

The Mapper implementation in Indexer simply wraps input data, whatever its source and implementation class, in a NutchWritable so that the reduce phase may receive data from different sources, using different classes, and still be able to consistently declare a single output value class (as NutchWritable) from both map and reduce steps.

The Reducer implementation iterates over all values that fall under the same key (URL), unwraps the data (fetch CrawlDatum, CrawlDb CrawlDatum, LinkDb Inlinks, Parse Data, and ParseText) and, using this information, builds a Lucene document, which is then wrapped in a Writable LuceneDocumentWrapper and collected. In addition to all textual content (coming either from the plain-text data or from metadata), this document also contains PageRank-like score information (obtained from CrawlDb data). Nutch uses this score to set the boost value of the Lucene document.

The OutputFormat implementation is the most interesting part of this tool:

```
public static class OutputFormat extends
    FileOutputFormat<WritableComparable, LuceneDocumentWrapper> {

  public RecordWriter<WritableComparable, LuceneDocumentWrapper>
    getRecordWriter(final FileSystem fs, JobConf job,
                    String name, final Progressable progress) throws IOException {
    final Path out = new Path(FileOutputFormat.getOutputPath(job), name);
    final IndexWriter writer = new IndexWriter(out.toString(),
                    new NutchDocumentAnalyzer(job), true);

    return new RecordWriter<WritableComparable, LuceneDocumentWrapper>() {
      boolean closed;
      public void write(WritableComparable key, LuceneDocumentWrapper value)
        throws IOException {                        // unwrap & index doc
        Document doc = value.get();
        writer.addDocument(doc);
        progress.progress();
      }

      public void close(final Reporter reporter) throws IOException {
        // spawn a thread to give progress heartbeats
```

```
        Thread prog = new Thread() {
            public void run() {
                while (!closed) {
                    try {
                        reporter.setStatus("closing");
                        Thread.sleep(1000);
                    } catch (InterruptedException e) { continue; }
                    catch (Throwable e) { return; }
                }
            }
        };

        try {
            prog.start();
            // optimize & close index
            writer.optimize();
            writer.close();
        } finally {
            closed = true;
        }
    }
};
```

When an instance of RecordWriter is requested, the OutputFormat creates a new Lucene index by opening an IndexWriter. Then, for each new output record collected in the reduce method, it unwraps the Lucene document from the LuceneDocumentWrapper value and adds it to the index.

When a reduce task is finished, Hadoop will try to close the RecordWriter. In this case, the process of closing may take a long time because we would like to optimize the index before closing. During this time, Hadoop may conclude that the task is hung, since there are no progress updates, and it may attempt to kill it. For this reason, we first start a background thread to give reassuring progress updates, and then proceed to perform the index optimization. Once the optimization is completed, we stop the progress updater thread. The output index is now created, optimized, and closed, after which it is ready for use in a searcher application.

Summary

This short overview of Nutch necessarily omits many details, such as error handling, logging, URL filtering and normalization, dealing with redirects or other forms of "aliased" pages (such as mirrors), removing duplicate content, calculating PageRank scoring, etc. You can find this and much more information on the official page of the project and on the wiki (*http://wiki.apache.org/nutch*).

Today, Nutch is used by many organizations and individual users. Still, operating a search engine requires nontrivial investments in hardware, integration, customization, and the maintenance of the index, so in most cases, Nutch is used to build commercial vertical- or field-specific search engines.

Nutch is under active development, and the project closely follows new releases of Hadoop. As such, it will continue to be a practical example of a real-life application that uses Hadoop at its core, with excellent results.

—Andrzej Białecki

Log Processing at Rackspace

Rackspace Hosting has always provided managed systems for enterprises, and in that vein, Mailtrust became Rackspace's mail division in Fall 2007. Rackspace currently hosts email for over 1 million users and thousands of companies on hundreds of servers.

Requirements/The Problem

Transferring the mail generated by Rackspace customers through the system generates a considerable "paper" trail, in the form of around 150 GB per day of logs in various formats. It is extremely helpful to aggregate that data for growth planning purposes and to understand how customers use our applications, and the records are also a boon for troubleshooting problems in the system.

If an email fails to be delivered, or a customer is unable to log in, it is vital that our customer support team is able to find enough information about the problem to begin the debugging process. To make it possible to find that information quickly, we cannot leave the logs on the machines that generated them or in their original format. Instead, we use Hadoop to do a considerable amount of processing, with the end result being Lucene indexes that customer support can query.

Logs

Two of our highest-volume log formats are produced by the Postfix mail transfer agent and Microsoft Exchange Server. All mail that travels through our systems touches Postfix at some point, and the majority of messages travel through multiple Postfix servers. The Exchange environment is independent by necessity, but one class of Postfix machines acts as an added layer of protection and uses SMTP to transfer messages between mailboxes hosted in each environment.

The messages travel through many machines, but each server knows only enough about the destination of the mail to transfer it to the next responsible server. Thus, in order to build the complete history of a message, our log processing system needs to have a global view of the system. This is where Hadoop helps us immensely: as our system grows, so does the volume of logs. For our log processing logic to stay viable, we had to ensure that it would scale, and MapReduce was the perfect framework for that growth.

Brief History

Earlier versions of our log processing system were based on MySQL, but as we gained more and more logging machines, we reached the limits of what a single MySQL server could process. The database schema was already reasonably denormalized, which would have made it less difficult to shard, but MySQL's partitioning support was still very weak at that point in time. Rather than implementing our own sharding and processing solution around MySQL, we chose to use Hadoop.

Choosing Hadoop

As soon as you shard the data in a RDBMS system, you lose a lot of the advantages of SQL for performing analysis of your dataset. Hadoop gives us the ability to easily process all of our data in parallel using the same algorithms we would for smaller datasets.

Collection and Storage

Log collection

The servers generating the logs we process are distributed across multiple data centers, but we currently have a single Hadoop cluster, located in one of those data centers (see Figure 16-8). In order to aggregate the logs and place them into the cluster, we use the Unix syslog replacement syslog-ng and some simple scripts to control the creation of files in Hadoop.

Figure 16-8. Hadoop data flow at Rackspace

Within a data center, syslog-ng is used to transfer logs from a *source* machine to a load-balanced set of *collector* machines. On the collectors, each type of log is aggregated into a single stream and lightly compressed with gzip (step A in Figure 16-8). From remote collectors, logs can be transferred through an SSH tunnel cross-data center to collectors that are local to the Hadoop cluster (step B).

Once the compressed log stream reaches a local collector, it can be written to Hadoop (step C). We currently use a simple Python script that buffers input data to disk and periodically pushes the data into the Hadoop cluster using the Hadoop command-line interface. The script copies the log buffers to input folders in Hadoop when they reach a multiple of the Hadoop block size or when enough time has passed.

This method of securely aggregating logs from different data centers was developed before SOCKet Secure (SOCKS) support was added to Hadoop via the hadoop.rpc.socket.factory.class.default parameter and SocksSocketFactory class. By using SOCKS support and the HDFS API directly from remote collectors, we could eliminate one disk write and a lot of complexity from the system. We plan to implement a replacement using these features in future development sprints.

Once the raw logs have been placed in Hadoop, they are ready for processing by our MapReduce jobs.

Log storage

Our Hadoop cluster currently contains 15 datanodes with commodity CPUs and three 500 GB disks each. We use a default replication factor of three for files that need to survive for our archive period of six months and a factor of two for anything else.

The Hadoop namenode uses hardware identical to the datanodes. To provide reasonably high availability, we use two secondary namenodes and a virtual IP that can easily be pointed at any of the three machines with snapshots of the HDFS. This means that in a failover situation, there is potential for us to lose up to 30 minutes of data, depending on the ages of the snapshots on the secondary namenodes. This is acceptable for our log processing application, but other Hadoop applications may require lossless failover by using shared storage for the namenode's image.

MapReduce for Logs

Processing

In distributed systems, the sad truth of unique identifiers is that they are rarely truly unique. All email messages have a (supposedly) unique identifier called a *message-id* that is generated by the host where they originated, but a bad client could easily send out duplicates. In addition, since the designers of Postfix could not trust the message-id to uniquely identify the message, they were forced to come up with a separate ID called a *queue-id*, which is guaranteed to be unique only for the lifetime of the message on a local machine.

Although the message-id tends to be the definitive identifier for a message, in Postfix logs, it is necessary to use queue-ids to find the message-id. Looking at the second line in Example 16-1 (which is formatted to better fit the page), you will see the hex string 1DBD21B48AE, which is the queue-id of the message that the log line refers to. Because information about a message (including its message-id) is output as separate lines when it is collected (potentially hours apart), it is necessary for our parsing code to keep state about messages.

Example 16-1. Postfix log lines

```
Nov 12 17:36:54 gate8.gate.sat.mlsrvr.com postfix/smtpd[2552]: connect from hostname
Nov 12 17:36:54 relay2.relay.sat.mlsrvr.com postfix/qmgr[9489]: 1DBD21B48AE:
from=<mapreduce@rackspace.com>, size=5950, nrcpt=1 (queue active)
Nov 12 17:36:54 relay2.relay.sat.mlsrvr.com postfix/smtpd[28085]: disconnect from
hostname
Nov 12 17:36:54 gate5.gate.sat.mlsrvr.com postfix/smtpd[22593]: too many errors
after DATA from hostname
Nov 12 17:36:54 gate5.gate.sat.mlsrvr.com postfix/smtpd[22593]: disconnect from
hostname
Nov 12 17:36:54 gate10.gate.sat.mlsrvr.com postfix/smtpd[10311]: connect from
hostname
Nov 12 17:36:54 relay2.relay.sat.mlsrvr.com postfix/smtp[28107]: D42001B48B5:
to=<mapreduce@rackspace.com>, relay=hostname[ip], delay=0.32, delays=0.28/0/0/0.04,
dsn=2.0.0, status=sent (250 2.0.0 Ok: queued as 1DBD21B48AE)
Nov 12 17:36:54 gate20.gate.sat.mlsrvr.com postfix/smtpd[27168]: disconnect from
hostname
Nov 12 17:36:54 gate5.gate.sat.mlsrvr.com postfix/qmgr[1209]: 645965A0224: removed
Nov 12 17:36:54 gate2.gate.sat.mlsrvr.com postfix/smtp[15928]: 732196384ED: to=<m
apreduce@rackspace.com>, relay=hostname[ip], conn_use=2, delay=0.69, delays=0.04/
0.44/0.04/0.17, dsn=2.0.0, status=sent (250 2.0.0 Ok: queued as 02E1544C005)
Nov 12 17:36:54 gate2.gate.sat.mlsrvr.com postfix/qmgr[13764]: 732196384ED: removed
Nov 12 17:36:54 gate1.gate.sat.mlsrvr.com postfix/smtpd[26394]: NOQUEUE: reject: RCP
T from hostname 554 5.7.1 <mapreduce@rackspace.com>: Client host rejected: The
sender's mail server is blocked; from=<mapreduce@rackspace.com> to=<mapred
uce@rackspace.com> proto=ESMTP helo=<mapreduce@rackspace.com>
```

From a MapReduce perspective, each line of the log is a single key-value pair. In phase 1, we need to map all lines with a single queue-id key together, and then reduce them to determine whether the log message values indicate that the queue-id is complete.

Similarly, once we have a completed the queue-id phase for a message, we need to group by the message-id in phase 2. We map each completed queue-id with its message-id as key and a list of its log lines as the value. In the reduce, we determine whether all of the queue-ids for the message-id indicate that the message left our system.

Together, the two phases of the mail log MapReduce job and their InputFormat and OutputFormat form a type of *staged event-driven architecture* (SEDA). In SEDA, an application is broken up into multiple "stages," which are separated by queues. In a Hadoop context, a queue could be either an input folder in HDFS that a MapReduce job consumes from or the implicit queue that MapReduce forms between the map and reduce steps.

In Figure 16-9, the arrows between stages represent the queues, with a dashed arrow being the implicit MapReduce queue. Each stage can send a key-value pair (SEDA calls them events or messages) to another stage via these queues.

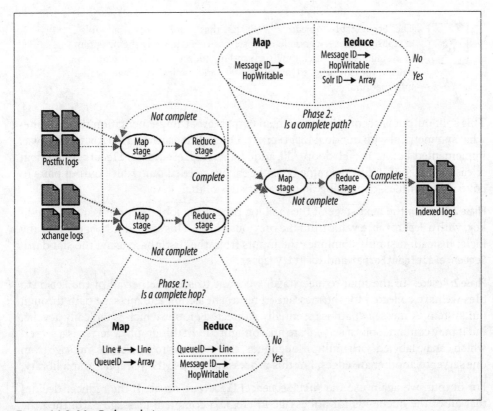

Figure 16-9. MapReduce chain

Phase 1: Map. During the first phase of our Mail log processing job, the inputs to the map stage are either a line number key and log message value or a queue-id key to an array of log-message values. The first type of input is generated when we process a raw logfile from the queue of input files, and the second type is an intermediate format that represents the state of a queue-id we have already attempted to process but that was requeued because it was incomplete.

In order to accomplish this dual input, we implemented a Hadoop `InputFormat` that delegates the work to an underlying `SequenceFileRecordReader` or `LineRecordReader`, depending on the file extension of the input `FileSplit`. The two input formats come from different input folders (queues) in HDFS.

Phase 1: Reduce. During this phase, the reduce stage determines whether the queue-id has enough lines to be considered completed. If the queue-id is completed, we output the message-id as key and a `HopWritable` object as value. Otherwise, the queue-id is set as the key, and the array of log lines is requeued to be Mapped with the next set of raw logs. This will continue until we complete the queue-id or until it times out.

The `HopWritable` object is a POJO that implements Hadoop's `Writable` interface. It completely describes a message from the viewpoint of a single server, including the sending address and IP, attempts to deliver the message to other servers, and typical message header information.

This split output is accomplished with an `OutputFormat` implementation that is somewhat symmetrical with our dual `InputFormat`. Our `MultiSequenceFileOutputFormat` was implemented before the Hadoop API added a `MultipleSequenceFileOutputFormat` in release0.17.0, but fulfills the same type of goal: we needed our reduce output pairs to go to different files, depending on characteristics of their keys.

Phase 2: Map. In the next stage of the mail log processing job, the input is a message-id key, with a `HopWritable` value from the previous phase. This stage does not contain any logic; instead, it simply combines the inputs from the first phase using the standard `SequenceFileInputFormat` and `IdentityMapper`.

Phase 2: Reduce. In the final reduce stage, we want to see whether all of the `HopWrita bles` we have collected for the message-id represent a complete message path through our system. A message path is essentially a directed graph (which is typically acyclic, but it may contain loops if servers are misconfigured). In this graph, a vertex is a server, which can be labeled with multiple queue-ids, and attempts to deliver the message from one server to another are edges. For this processing, we use the JGraphT graph library.

For output, we again use the `MultiSequenceFileOutputFormat`. If the reducer decides that all of the queue-ids for a message-id create a complete message path, then the message is serialized and queued for the `SolrOutputFormat`. Otherwise, the `HopWritables` for the message are queued for the phase 2: map stage to be reprocessed with the next batch of queue-ids.

The `SolrOutputFormat` contains an embedded Apache Solr instance—in the fashion that was originally recommended by the Solr wiki (*http://wiki.apache.org/solr/Embedded Solr*)—to generate an index on local disk. Closing the `OutputFormat` then involves compressing the disk index to the final destination for the output file. This approach has a few advantages over using Solr's HTTP interface or using Lucene directly:

- We can enforce a Solr schema (*http://wiki.apache.org/solr/SchemaXml*).
- Map and reduce remain idempotent.
- Indexing load is removed from the search nodes.

We currently use the default `HashPartitioner` class to decide which reduce task will receive particular keys, which means that the keys are semirandomly distributed. In a future iteration of the system, we'd like to implement a new `Partitioner` to split by the sending address instead (our most common search term). Once the indexes are split by sender, we can use the hash of the address to determine where to merge or query for an index, and our search API will need to communicate only with the relevant nodes.

Merging for near-term search

After a set of MapReduce phases have completed, a different set of machines are notified of the new indexes and can pull them for merging. These search nodes are running Apache Tomcat and Solr instances to host completed indexes, along with a service to pull and merge the indexes to local disk (step D in Figure 16-8).

Each compressed file from `SolrOutputFormat` is a complete Lucene index, and Lucene provides the `IndexWriter.addIndexes()` methods for quickly merging multiple indexes. Our `MergeAgent` service decompresses each new index into a Lucene `RAMDirectory` or `FSDirectory` (depending on size), merges them to local disk, and sends a `<commit/>` request to the Solr instance hosting the index to make the changed index visible to queries.

Sharding. The Query/Management API is a thin layer of PHP code that handles sharding the output indexes across all of the search nodes. We use a simple implementation of consistent hashing to decide which search nodes are responsible for each index file. Currently, indexes are sharded by their creation time and then by their hashed filename, but we plan to replace the filename hash with a sending address hash at some point in the future (see "Phase 2: reduce").

Because HDFS already handles replication of the Lucene indexes, there is no need to keep multiple copies available in Solr. Instead, in a failover situation, the search node is completely removed, and other nodes become responsible for merging the indexes.

Search results. With this system, we've achieved a 15-minute turnaround time from log generation to availability of a search result for our Customer Support team.

Our search API supports the full Lucene query syntax, so we commonly see complex queries like:

```
sender:"mapreduce@rackspace.com" -recipient:"hadoop@rackspace.com"
  recipient:"@rackspace.com" short-status:deferred timestamp:[1228140900 TO 2145916799]
```

Each result returned by a query is a complete serialized message path that indicates whether individual servers and recipients received the message. We currently display the path as a 2D graph (Figure 16-10) that the user can interact with to expand points of interest, but there is a lot of room for improvement in the visualization of this data.

Archiving for analysis

In addition to providing short-term search for Customer Support, we are also interested in performing analyses of our log data.

Every night, we run a series of MapReduce jobs with the day's indexes as input. We implemented a `SolrInputFormat` that can pull and decompress an index, and emit each document as a key-value pair. With this `InputFormat`, we can iterate over all message paths for a day and answer almost any question about our mail system, including:

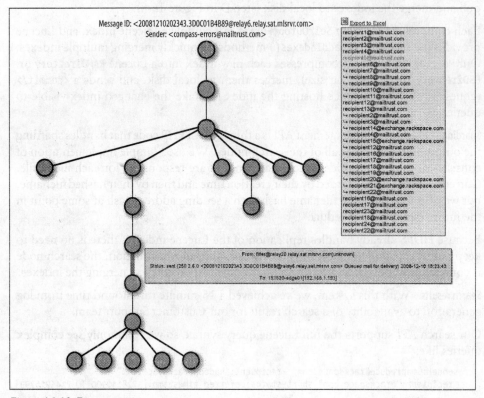

Figure 16-10. Data tree

- Per-domain data (viruses, spam, connections, recipients)
- Most effective spam rules
- Load generated by specific users
- Reasons for message bounces
- Geographical sources of connections
- Average latency between specific machines

Because we have months of compressed indexes archived in Hadoop, we are also able to retrospectively answer questions that our nightly log summaries leave out. For instance, we recently wanted to determine the top sending IP addresses per month, which we accomplished with a simple one-off MapReduce job.

—Stu Hood

Cascading

Cascading is an open source Java library and API that provides an abstraction layer for MapReduce. It allows developers to build complex, mission-critical data processing applications that run on Hadoop clusters.

The Cascading project began in the summer of 2007. Its first public release, version 0.1, launched in January 2008. Version 1.0 was released in January 2009. Binaries, source code, and add-on modules can be downloaded from the project website, *http://www.cascading.org/*.

Map and reduce operations offer powerful primitives. However, they tend to be at the wrong level of granularity for creating sophisticated, highly composable code that can be shared among different developers. Moreover, many developers find it difficult to "think" in terms of MapReduce when faced with real-world problems.

To address the first issue, Cascading substitutes the keys and values used in MapReduce with simple field names and a data tuple model, where a tuple is simply a list of values. For the second issue, Cascading departs from map and reduce operations directly by introducing higher-level abstractions as alternatives: Functions, Filters, Aggregators, and Buffers.

Other alternatives began to emerge at about the same time as the project's initial public release, but Cascading was designed to complement them. Consider that most of these alternative frameworks impose pre- and post-conditions, or other expectations.

For example, in several other MapReduce tools, you must preformat, filter, or import your data into HDFS prior to running the application. That step of preparing the data must be performed outside of the programming abstraction. In contrast, Cascading provides the means to prepare and manage your data as integral parts of the programming abstraction.

This case study begins with an introduction to the main concepts of Cascading, then finishes with an overview of how ShareThis (*http://www.sharethis.com/*) uses Cascading in its infrastructure.

See the Cascading User Guide on the project website for a more in-depth presentation of the Cascading processing model.

Fields, Tuples, and Pipes

The MapReduce model uses keys and values to link input data to the map function, the map function to the reduce function, and the reduce function to the output data.

But as we know, real-world Hadoop applications usually consist of more than one MapReduce job chained together. Consider the canonical word count example implemented in MapReduce. If you needed to sort the numeric counts in descending order, which is not an unlikely requirement, it would need to be done in a second MapReduce job.

So, in the abstract, keys and values not only bind map to reduce, but reduce to the next map, and then to the next reduce, and so on (Figure 16-11). That is, key-value pairs are sourced from input files and stream through chains of map and reduce operations, and finally rest in an output file. When you implement enough of these chained Map-Reduce applications, you start to see a well-defined set of key-value manipulations used over and over again to modify the key-value data stream.

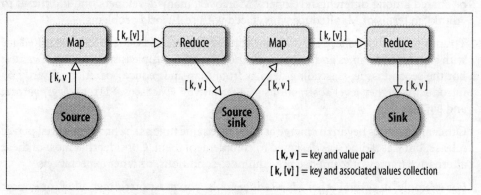

Figure 16-11. Counting and sorting in MapReduce

Cascading simplifies this by abstracting away keys and values and replacing them with tuples that have corresponding field names, similar in concept to tables and column names in a relational database. And during processing, streams of these fields and tuples are then manipulated as they pass through user-defined operations linked together by pipes (Figure 16-12).

Figure 16-12. Pipes linked by fields and tuples

So, MapReduce keys and values are reduced to:

Fields

Fields are a collection of either `String` names (such as "first_name"), numeric positions (such as 2, or −1, for the third and last position, respectively), or a combination of both, very much like column names. So fields are used to declare the names of values in a tuple and to select values by name from a tuple. The latter is like a SQL `select` call.

Tuple

A tuple is simply an array of `java.lang.Comparable` objects. A tuple is very much like a database row or record.

And the map and reduce operations are abstracted behind one or more pipe instances (Figure 16-13):

`Each`

The `Each` pipe processes a single input tuple at a time. It may apply either a `Function` or a `Filter` operation (described shortly) to the input tuple.

`GroupBy`

The `GroupBy` pipe groups tuples on grouping fields. It behaves just like the SQL `group by` statement. It can also merge multiple input tuple streams into a single stream if they all share the same field names.

`CoGroup`

The `CoGroup` pipe joins multiple tuple streams together by common field names, and it also groups the tuples by the common grouping fields. All standard join types (inner, outer, etc.) and custom joins can be used across two or more tuple streams.

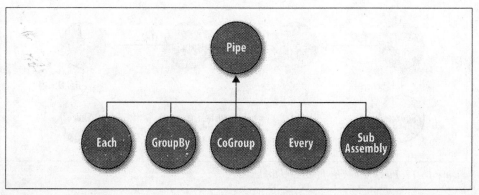

Figure 16-13. Pipe types

Every

The Every pipe processes a single grouping of tuples at a time, where the group was grouped by a GroupBy or CoGroup pipe. The Every pipe may apply either an Aggregator or a Buffer operation to the grouping.

SubAssembly

The SubAssembly pipe allows for nesting of assemblies inside a single pipe, which can, in turn, be nested in more complex assemblies.

All these pipes are chained together by the developer into "pipe assemblies" in which each assembly can have many input tuple streams (sources) and many output tuple streams (sinks). See Figure 16-14.

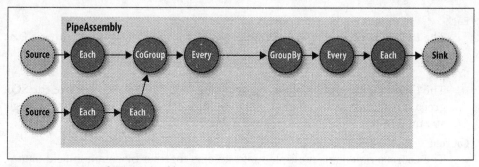

Figure 16-14. A simple PipeAssembly

On the surface, this might seem more complex than the traditional MapReduce model. And admittedly there are more concepts here than Map, Reduce, Key, and Value. But in practice, there are many more concepts that must all work in tandem to provide different behaviors.

For example, if a developer wanted to provide a "secondary sorting" of reducer values, he would need to implement a map, a reduce, a "composite" Key (two Keys nested in a parent Key), a Value, a Partitioner, an "output value grouping" Comparator, and an "output key" Comparator, all of which would be coupled to one another in varying ways and, very likely, would not be reusable in subsequent applications.

In Cascading, this would be one line of code: `new GroupBy(<previous>, <grouping fields>, <secondary sorting fields>)`, where `previous` is the pipe that came before.

Operations

As mentioned earlier, Cascading departs from MapReduce by introducing alternative operations that are applied either to individual tuples or groups of tuples (Figure 16-15):

Function
> A `Function` operates on individual input tuples and may return zero or more output tuples for every one input. Functions are applied by the `Each` pipe.

Filter
> A `Filter` is a special kind of function that returns a Boolean value indicating whether the current input tuple should be removed from the tuple stream. A `function` could serve this purpose, but the `Filter` is optimized for this case, and many filters can be grouped by "logical" filters such as `And`, `Or`, `Xor`, and `Not`, rapidly creating more complex filtering operations.

Aggregator
> An `Aggregator` performs some operation against a group of tuples, where the grouped tuples are grouped by a common set of field values. For example, all tuples having the same "last-name" value. Common `Aggregator` implementations would be `Sum`, `Count`, `Average`, `Max`, and `Min`.

Buffer
> A `Buffer` is similar to the `Aggregator`, except it is optimized to act as a "sliding window" across all the tuples in a unique grouping. This is useful when the developer needs to efficiently insert missing values in an ordered set of tuples (such as a missing date or duration) or create a running average. Usually `Aggregator` is the operation of choice when working with groups of tuples, since many `Aggregators` can be chained together very efficiently, but sometimes a `Buffer` is the best tool for the job.

Operations are bound to pipes when the pipe assembly is created (Figure 16-16).

The `Each` and `Every` pipes provide a simple mechanism for selecting some or all values out of an input tuple before being passed to its child operation. And there is a simple mechanism for merging the operation results with the original input tuple to create the output tuple. Without going into great detail, this allows for each operation only to care about argument tuple values and fields, not the whole set of fields in the current input tuple. Subsequently, operations can be reusable across applications in the same way that Java methods can be reusable.

Figure 16-15. Operation types

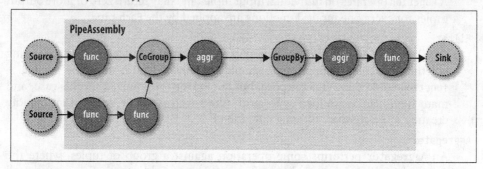

Figure 16-16. An assembly of operations

For example, in Java, a method declared as concatenate(String first, String second) is more abstract than concatenate(Person person). In the second case, the concatenate() function must "know" about the Person object; in the first case, it is agnostic to where the data came from. Cascading operations exhibit this same quality.

Taps, Schemes, and Flows

In many of the previous diagrams, there are references to "sources" and "sinks." In Cascading, all data is read from or written to Tap instances, but is converted to and from tuple instances via Scheme objects:

Tap

A Tap is responsible for the "how" and "where" parts of accessing data. For example, is the data on HDFS or the local filesystem? In Amazon S3 or over HTTP?

Scheme

A Scheme is responsible for reading raw data and converting it to a tuple and/or writing a tuple out into raw data, where this "raw" data can be lines of text, Hadoop binary sequence files, or some proprietary format.

Note that Taps are not part of a pipe assembly, and so they are not a type of Pipe.

But they are connected with pipe assemblies when they are made cluster-executable. When a pipe assembly is connected with the necessary number of source and sink Tap instances, we get a Flow. A Flow is created when a pipe assembly is connected with its required number of source and sink Taps, and the Taps either emit or capture the field names the pipe assembly expects. That is, if a Tap emits a tuple with the field name "line" (by reading data from a file on HDFS), the head of the pipe assembly must be expecting a "line" value as well. Otherwise, the process that connects the pipe assembly with the Taps will immediately fail with an error.

So pipe assemblies are really data process definitions, and are not "executable" on their own. They must be connected to source and sink Tap instances before they can run on a cluster. This separation between Taps and pipe assemblies is part of what makes Cascading so powerful.

If you think of pipe assemblies like a Java class, then a Flow is like a Java Object instance (Figure 16-17). That is, the same pipe assembly can be "instantiated" many times into new Flow, in the same application, without fear of any interference between them. This allows pipe assemblies to be created and shared like standard Java libraries.

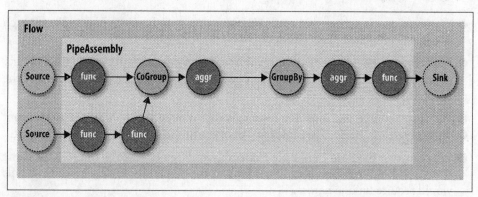

Figure 16-17. A Flow

Cascading in Practice

Now that we know what Cascading is and have a good idea of how it works, what does an application written in Cascading look like? See Example 16-2.

Example 16-2. Word count and sort

```
Scheme sourceScheme =
  new TextLine(new Fields("line")); ❶
Tap source =
  new Hfs(sourceScheme, inputPath); ❷

Scheme sinkScheme = new TextLine(); ❸
Tap sink =
  new Hfs(sinkScheme, outputPath, SinkMode.REPLACE); ❹
```

```
Pipe assembly = new Pipe("wordcount"); ❺

String regexString = "(?<!\\pL)(?=\\pL)[^ ]*(?<=\\pL)(?!\\pL)";
Function regex = new RegexGenerator(new Fields("word"), regexString);
assembly =
  new Each(assembly, new Fields("line"), regex); ❻

assembly =
  new GroupBy(assembly, new Fields("word")); ❼

Aggregator count = new Count(new Fields("count"));
assembly = new Every(assembly, count); ❽

assembly =
  new GroupBy(assembly, new Fields("count"), new Fields("word")); ❾

FlowConnector flowConnector = new FlowConnector();
Flow flow =
  flowConnector.connect("word-count", source, sink, assembly); ❿

flow.complete();⓫
```

❶ We create a new Scheme that reads simple text files and emits a new Tuple for each line in a field named "line," as declared by the Fields instance.

❸ We create a new Scheme that writes simple text files and expects a Tuple with any number of fields/values. If more than one value, they will be tab-delimited in the output file.

❷ We create source and sink Tap instances that reference the input file and output
❹ directory, respectively. The sink Tap will overwrite any file that may already exist.

❺ We construct the head of our pipe assembly and name it "wordcount." This name is used to bind the source and sink Taps to the assembly. Multiple heads or tails would require unique names.

❻ We construct an Each pipe with a function that will parse the "line" field into a new Tuple for each word encountered.

❼ We construct a GroupBy pipe that will create a new Tuple grouping for each unique value in the field "word."

❽ We construct an Every pipe with an Aggregator that will count the number of Tuples in every unique word group. The result is stored in a field named "count."

❾ We construct a GroupBy pipe that will create a new Tuple grouping for each unique value in the field "count" and secondary sort each value in the field "word." The result will be a list of "count" and "word" values with "count" sorted in increasing order.

❿ We connect the pipe assembly to its sources and sinks into a Flow, and then execute
⓫ the Flow on the cluster.

In the example, we count the words encountered in the input document, and we sort the counts in their natural order (ascending). And if some words have the same "count" value, these words are sorted in their natural order (alphabetical).

One obvious problem with this example is that some words might have uppercase letters—for example, "the" and "The" when the word comes at the beginning of a sentence. So we might decide to insert a new operation to force all the words to lowercase, but we realize that all future applications that need to parse words from documents should have the same behavior, so we decide to create a reusable pipe called SubAssembly, just like we would by creating a subroutine in a traditional application (see Example 16-3).

Example 16-3. Creating a SubAssembly

```
public class ParseWordsAssembly extends SubAssembly ❶
  {
  public ParseWordsAssembly(Pipe previous)
    {
    String regexString = "(?<!\\pL)(?=\\pL)[^ ]*(?<=\\pL)(?!\\pL)";
    Function regex = new RegexGenerator(new Fields("word"), regexString);
    previous = new Each(previous, new Fields("line"), regex);

    String exprString = "word.toLowerCase()";
    Function expression =
      new ExpressionFunction(new Fields("word"), exprString, String.class); ❷
    previous = new Each(previous, new Fields("word"), expression);

    setTails(previous); ❸
    }
  }
```

❶ We subclass the SubAssembly class, which is itself a kind of Pipe.

❷ We create a Java expression function that will call toLowerCase() on the String value in the field named "word." We must also pass in the Java type the expression expects "word" to be, in this case, String. (*http://www.janino.net/* is used under the covers.)

❸ We must tell the SubAssembly superclass where the tail ends of our pipe subassembly are.

First, we create a SubAssembly pipe to hold our "parse words" pipe assembly. Because this is a Java class, it can be reused in any other application, as long as there is an incoming field named "word" (Example 16-4). Note that there are ways to make this function even more generic, but they are covered in the Cascading User Guide.

Example 16-4. Extending word count and sort with a SubAssembly

```
Scheme sourceScheme = new TextLine(new Fields("line"));
Tap source = new Hfs(sourceScheme, inputPath);

Scheme sinkScheme = new TextLine(new Fields("word", "count"));
Tap sink = new Hfs(sinkScheme, outputPath, SinkMode.REPLACE);
```

```
Pipe assembly = new Pipe("wordcount");

assembly =
  new ParseWordsAssembly(assembly); ❶

assembly = new GroupBy(assembly, new Fields("word"));

Aggregator count = new Count(new Fields("count"));
assembly = new Every(assembly, count);

assembly = new GroupBy(assembly, new Fields("count"), new Fields("word"));

FlowConnector flowConnector = new FlowConnector();
Flow flow = flowConnector.connect("word-count", source, sink, assembly);

flow.complete();
```

❶ We replace the Each from the previous example with our ParseWordsAssembly pipe.

Finally, we just substitute in our new SubAssembly right where the previous Every and word parser function was used in the previous example. This nesting can continue as deep as necessary.

Flexibility

Take a step back and see what this new model has given us or, better yet, what it has taken away.

You see, we no longer think in terms of MapReduce jobs, or Mapper and Reducer interface implementations and how to bind or link subsequent MapReduce jobs to the ones that precede them. During runtime, the Cascading "planner" figures out the optimal way to partition the pipe assembly into MapReduce jobs and manages the linkages between them (Figure 16-18).

Figure 16-18. How a Flow translates to chained MapReduce jobs

Because of this, developers can build applications of arbitrary granularity. They can start with a small application that just filters a logfile, but then can iteratively build up more features into the application as needed.

Since Cascading is an API and not a syntax like strings of SQL, it is more flexible. First off, developers can create domain-specific languages (DSLs) using their favorite language, such as Groovy, JRuby, Jython, Scala, and others (see the project site for examples). Second, developers can extend various parts of Cascading, such as allowing custom Thrift or JSON objects to be read and written to and allowing them to be passed through the tuple stream.

Hadoop and Cascading at ShareThis

ShareThis is a sharing network that makes it simple to share any online content. With the click of a button on a web page or browser plug-in, ShareThis allows users to seamlessly access their contacts and networks from anywhere online and share the content through email, IM, Facebook, Digg, mobile SMS, etc., without ever leaving the current page. Publishers can deploy the ShareThis button to tap the service's universal sharing capabilities to drive traffic, stimulate viral activity, and track the sharing of online content. ShareThis also simplifies social media services by reducing clutter on web pages and providing instant distribution of content across social networks, affiliate groups, and communities.

As ShareThis users share pages and information through the online widgets, a continuous stream of events enter the ShareThis network. These events are first filtered and processed, and then handed to various backend systems, including AsterData, Hypertable, and Katta.

The volume of these events can be huge, too large to process with traditional systems. This data can also be very "dirty" thanks to "injection attacks" from rogue systems, browser bugs, or faulty widgets. For this reason, ShareThis chose to deploy Hadoop as the preprocessing and orchestration frontend to their backend systems. They also chose to use Amazon Web Services to host their servers, on the Elastic Computing Cloud (EC2), and provide long-term storage, on the Simple Storage Service (S3), with an eye toward leveraging Elastic MapReduce (EMR).

In this overview, we will focus on the "log processing pipeline" (Figure 16-19). This pipeline simply takes data stored in an S3 bucket, processes it (described shortly), and stores the results back into another bucket. Simple Queue Service (SQS) is used to coordinate the events that mark the start and completion of data processing runs. Downstream, other processes pull data that load AsterData, pull URL lists from Hypertable to source a web crawl, or pull crawled page data to create Lucene indexes for use by Katta. Note that Hadoop is central to the ShareThis architecture. It is used to coordinate the processing and movement of data between architectural components.

Figure 16-19. The ShareThis log processing pipeline

With Hadoop as the frontend, all the event logs can be parsed, filtered, cleaned, and organized by a set of rules before ever being loaded into the AsterData cluster or used by any other component. AsterData is a clustered data warehouse that can support large datasets and allow for complex ad hoc queries using a standard SQL syntax. ShareThis chose to clean and prepare the incoming datasets on the Hadoop cluster and then to load that data into the AsterData cluster for ad hoc analysis and reporting. Though possible with AsterData, it made a lot of sense to use Hadoop as the first stage in the processing pipeline to offset load on the main data warehouse.

Cascading was chosen as the primary data processing API to simplify the development process, codify how data is coordinated between architectural components, and provide the developer-facing interface to those components. This represents a departure from more "traditional" Hadoop use cases, which essentially just query stored data. Instead, Cascading and Hadoop together provide a better and simpler structure to the complete solution, end-to-end, and thus provide more value to the users.

For developers, Cascading made it easy to start with a simple unit test (by subclassing `cascading.ClusterTestCase`) that did simple text parsing and then to layer in more processing rules while keeping the application logically organized for maintenance. Cascading aided this organization in a couple of ways. First, standalone operations (`Functions`, `Filters`, etc.) could be written and tested independently. Second, the application was segmented into stages: one for parsing, one for rules, and a final stage for binning/collating the data, all via the `SubAssembly` base class described earlier.

The data coming from the ShareThis loggers looks a lot like Apache logs, with date/timestamps, share URLs, referrer URLs, and a bit of metadata. To use the data for analysis downstream, the URLs needed to be unpacked (parsing query-string data, domain names, etc.). So a top-level SubAssembly was created to encapsulate the parsing, and child subassemblies were nested inside to handle specific fields if they were sufficiently complex to parse.

The same was done for applying rules. As every Tuple passed through the rules SubAssembly, it was marked as "bad" if any of the rules were triggered. Along with the "bad" tag, a description of why the record was bad was added to the Tuple for later review.

Finally, a splitter SubAssembly was created to do two things. First, it allows for the tuple stream to split into two: one stream for "good" data and one for "bad" data. Second, the splitter binned the data into intervals, such as every hour. To do this, only two operations were necessary: the first to create the interval from the *timestamp* value already present in the stream, and the second to use the *interval* and *good/bad* metadata to create a directory path (for example, *05/good/*, where "05" is 5 a.m. and "good" means the tuple passed all the rules). This path would then be used by the Cascading TemplateTap, a special Tap that can dynamically output tuple streams to different locations based on values in the Tuple. In this case, the TemplateTap used the "path" value to create the final output path.

The developers also created a fourth SubAssembly—this one to apply Cascading Assertions during unit testing. These assertions double-checked that rules and parsing subassemblies did their job.

In the unit test in Example 16-5, we see the splitter isn't being tested, but it is added in another integration test not shown.

Example 16-5. Unit testing a Flow

```
public void testLogParsing() throws IOException
  {
  Hfs source = new Hfs(new TextLine(new Fields("line")), sampleData);
  Hfs sink =
    new Hfs(new TextLine(), outputPath + "/parser", SinkMode.REPLACE);

  Pipe pipe = new Pipe("parser");

  // split "line" on tabs
  pipe = new Each(pipe, new Fields("line"), new RegexSplitter("\t"));

  pipe = new LogParser(pipe);

  pipe = new LogRules(pipe);
```

```
// testing only assertions
pipe = new ParserAssertions(pipe);

Flow flow = new FlowConnector().connect(source, sink, pipe);

flow.complete(); // run the test flow

// verify there are 98 tuples, 2 fields, and matches the regex pattern
// for TextLine schemes the tuples are { "offset", "line }
validateLength(flow, 98, 2, Pattern.compile("^[0-9]+(\\t[^\\t]*){19}$"));
}
```

For integration and deployment, many of the features built into Cascading allowed for easier integration with external systems and for greater process tolerance.

In production, all the subassemblies are joined and planned into a Flow, but instead of just source and sink Taps, trap Taps were planned in (Figure 16-20). Normally, when an operation throws an exception from a remote mapper or reducer task, the Flow will fail and kill all its managed MapReduce jobs. When a Flow has traps, any exceptions are caught and the data causing the exception is saved to the Tap associated with the current trap. Then the next Tuple is processed without stopping the Flow. Sometimes you want your Flows to fail on errors, but in this case, the ShareThis developers knew they could go back and look at the "failed" data and update their unit tests while the production system kept running. Losing a few hours of processing time was worse than losing a couple of bad records.

Using Cascading's event listeners, Amazon SQS could be integrated. When a Flow finishes, a message is sent to notify other systems that there is data ready to be picked up from Amazon S3. On failure, a different message is sent, alerting other processes.

The remaining downstream processes pick up where the log processing pipeline leaves off on different independent clusters. The log processing pipeline today runs once a day, so there is no need to keep a 100-node cluster sitting around for the 23 hours it has nothing to do. So it is decommissioned and recommissioned 24 hours later.

In the future, it would be trivial to increase this interval on smaller clusters to every 6 hours, or 1 hour, as the business demands. Independently, other clusters are booting and shutting down at different intervals based on the needs of the business unit responsible for that component. For example, the web crawler component (using Bixo, a Cascading-based web-crawler toolkit developed by EMI and ShareThis) may run continuously on a small cluster with a companion Hypertable cluster. This on-demand model works very well with Hadoop, where each cluster can be tuned for the kind of workload it is expected to handle.

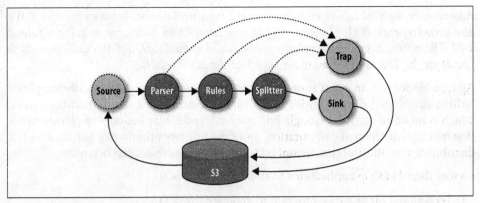

Figure 16-20. The ShareThis log processing Flow

Summary

Hadoop is a very powerful platform for processing and coordinating the movement of data across various architectural components. Its only drawback is that the primary computing model is MapReduce.

Cascading aims to help developers build powerful applications quickly and simply, through a well-reasoned API, without needing to think in MapReduce, and while leaving the heavy lifting of data distribution, replication, distributed process management, and liveness to Hadoop.

Read more about Cascading, join the online community, and download sample applications by visiting the project website (*http://www.cascading.org/*).

—Chris K. Wensel

TeraByte Sort on Apache Hadoop

This article is reproduced from http://sortbenchmark.org/YahooHadoop.pdf, which was written in May 2008. Jim Gray and his successors define a family of benchmarks to find the fastest sort programs every year. TeraByte Sort and other sort benchmarks are listed with winners over the years at http://sortbenchmark.org/. In April 2009, Arun Murthy and I won the minute sort (where the aim is to sort as much data as possible in under one minute) by sorting 500 GB in 59 seconds on 1,406 Hadoop nodes. We also sorted a terabyte in 62 seconds on the same cluster. The cluster we used in 2009 was similar to the hardware listed in the following article, except that the network was much better, with only 2-to-1 oversubscription between racks instead of 5-to-1 in the previous year.

Additionally, we used LZO compression on the intermediate data between the nodes. We also sorted a petabyte (10^{15} bytes) in 975 minutes on 3,658 nodes, for an average rate of 1.03 TB/minute. See http://developer.yahoo.net/blogs/hadoop/2009/05/hadoop_sorts_a _petabyte_in_162.html for more details about the 2009 results.

Apache Hadoop is an open source software framework that dramatically simplifies writing distributed data-intensive applications. It provides a distributed filesystem, which is modeled after the Google File System,[1] and a MapReduce[2] implementation that manages distributed computation. Since the primary primitive of MapReduce is a distributed sort, most of the custom code is glue to get the desired behavior.

I wrote three Hadoop applications to run the terabyte sort:

1. TeraGen is a MapReduce program to generate the data.
2. TeraSort samples the input data and uses MapReduce to sort the data into a total order.
3. TeraValidate is a MapReduce program that validates the output is sorted.

The total is around 1,000 lines of Java code, which will be checked in (*http://issues .apache.org/jira/browse/HADOOP-3402*) to the Hadoop example directory.

TeraGen generates output data that is byte-for-byte equivalent to the C version, including the newlines and specific keys. It divides the desired number of rows by the desired number of tasks and assigns ranges of rows to each map. The map jumps the random number generator to the correct value for the first row and generates the following rows. For the final run, I configured TeraGen to use 1,800 tasks to generate a total of 10 billion rows in HDFS, with a block size of 512 MB.

TeraSort is a standard MapReduce sort, except for a custom partitioner that uses a sorted list of *N*–1 sampled keys that define the key range for each reduce. In particular, all keys such that *sample*[*i*–1] <= *key* < *sample*[*i*] are sent to reduce *i*. This guarantees that the output of reduce *i* are all less than the output of reduce *i*+1. To speed up the partitioning, the partitioner builds a two-level trie that quickly indexes into the list of sample keys based on the first two bytes of the key. TeraSort generates the sample keys by sampling the input before the job is submitted and writing the list of keys into HDFS.

I wrote an input and output format, which are used by all three applications, that read and write the text files in the right format. The output of the reduce has replication set to 1, instead of the default 3, because the contest does not require the output data be replicated on to multiple nodes. I configured the job with 1,800 maps and 1,800 reduces and io.sort.mb, io.sort.factor, fs.inmemory.size.mb, and a task heap size sufficient that transient data was never spilled to disk other at the end of the map. The sampler

---

1. S. Ghemawat, H. Gobioff, and S.-T. Leung. "The Google File System." In *19th Symposium on Operating Systems Principles* (October 2003), Lake George, NY: ACM.

2. J. Dean and S. Ghemawat. "MapReduce: Simplified Data Processing on Large Clusters." In *Sixth Symposium on Operating System Design and Implementation* (December 2004), San Francisco, CA.

used 100,000 keys to determine the reduce boundaries, although as can be seen in Figure 16-21, the distribution between reduces was hardly perfect and would benefit from more samples. You can see the distribution of running tasks over the job run in Figure 16-22.

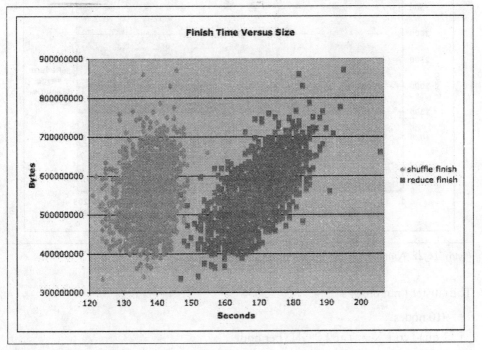

Figure 16-21. Plot of reduce output size versus finish time

TeraValidate ensures that the output is globally sorted. It creates one map per file in the output directory, and each map ensures that each key is less than or equal to the previous one. The map also generates records with the first and last keys of the file, and the reduce ensures that the first key of file *i* is greater than the last key of file *i*–1. Any problems are reported as output of the reduce with the keys that are out of order.

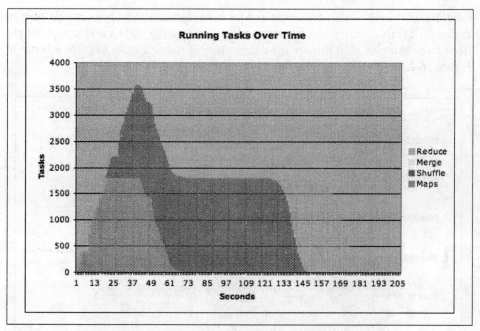

Figure 16-22. Number of tasks in each phase across time

The cluster I ran on was:

- 910 nodes
- 2 quad core Xeons at 2.0 GHz per node
- 4 SATA disks per node
- 8 G RAM per node
- 1 gigabit Ethernet on each node
- 40 nodes per rack
- 8 gigabit Ethernet uplinks from each rack to the core
- Red Hat Enterprise Linux Server release 5.1 (kernel 2.6.18)
- Sun Java JDK 1.6.0_05-b13

The sort completed in *209 seconds (3.48 minutes)*. I ran Hadoop trunk (pre-0.18.0) with patches for HADOOP-3443 (*http://issues.apache.org/jira/browse/HADOOP-3443*) and HADOOP-3446 (*http://issues.apache.org/jira/browse/HADOOP-3446*), which were required to remove intermediate writes to disk. Although I had the 910 nodes mostly to myself, the network core was shared with another active 2,000-node cluster, so the times varied a lot depending on the other activity.

—Owen O'Malley, Yahoo!

Using Pig and Wukong to Explore Billion-edge Network Graphs

Networks at massive scale are fascinating. The number of things they model are extremely general: if you have a collection of things (that we'll call nodes), they are related (edges), and if the nodes and edges tell a story (node/edge metadata), you have a network graph.

I started the Infochimps project, a site to find, share, or sell any dataset in the world. At Infochimps, we have a whole bag of tricks ready to apply to any interesting network graph that comes into the collection. We chiefly use Pig (described in Chapter 11) and Wukong (*http://github.com/mrflip/wukong*), a toolkit we've developed for Hadoop streaming in the Ruby programming language. They let us write simple scripts like the ones that follow—almost all of which fit on a single printed page—to process terabyte-scale graphs. Here are a few datasets that come up in a search for "network" on infochimps.org[3]:

- A social network, such as Twitter or Facebook. We somewhat impersonally model people as nodes, and relationships (@mrflip is friends with @tom_e_white) or actions (@infochimps mentioned @hadoop) as edges. The number of messages a user has sent and the bag of words from all those messages are each important pieces of node metadata.

- A linked document collection such as Wikipedia or the entire Web.[4] Each page is a node (carrying its title, view count, and categories as node metadata). Each hyperlink is an edge, and the frequency at which people click from one page to the next is edge metadata.

- The connections of neurons (nodes) and synapses (edges) in the *C. elegans* roundworm.[5]

---

3. See *http://infochimps.org/search?query=network*

4. *http://www.datawrangling.com/wikipedia-page-traffic-statistics-dataset*

5. *http://www.wormatlas.org/neuronalwiring.html*

- A highway map, with exits as nodes and highway segments as edges. The Open Street Map project's dataset has global coverage of place names (node metadata), street number ranges (edge metadata), and more.[6]
- Or the many esoteric graphs that fall out when you take an interesting system and shake it just right. Stream through a few million Twitter messages, and emit an edge for every pair of nonkeyboard characters occurring within the same message. Simply by observing "often, when humans use 最, they also use 近," you can re-create a map of human languages (see Figure 16-23).

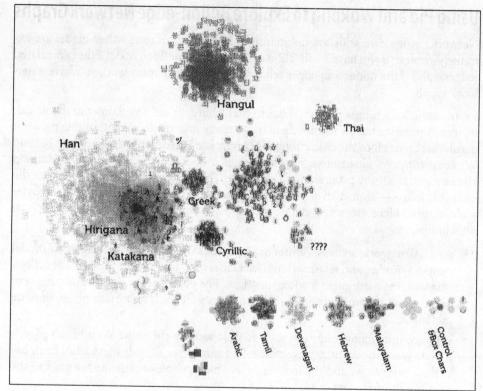

Figure 16-23. Twitter language map

6. *http://www.openstreetmap.org/*

What's amazing about these organic network graphs is that given enough data, a collection of powerful tools are able to *generically* use this network structure to expose insight. For example, we've used variants of the same algorithm[7] to do each of:

- Rank the most important pages in the Wikipedia linked-document collection. Google uses a vastly more refined version of this approach to identify top search hits.

- Identify celebrities and experts in the Twitter social graph. Users who have many more followers than their "trstrank" would imply are often spammers.

- Predict a school's impact on student education, using millions of anonymized exam scores gathered over five years.

Measuring Community

The most interesting network in the Infochimps collection is a massive crawl of the Twitter social graph. With more than 90 million nodes and 2 billion edges, it is a marvelous instrument for understanding what people talk about and how they relate to each other. Here is an exploration, using the subgraph of "People who talk about Infochimps or Hadoop,"[8] of three ways to characterize a user's community:

- Who are the people they converse with (the @reply graph)?
- Do the people they engage with reciprocate that attention (symmetric links)?
- Among the user's community, how many engage with each other (clustering coefficient)?

Everybody's Talkin' at Me: The Twitter Reply Graph

Twitter lets you reply to another user's message and thus engage in conversation. Since it's an expressly public activity, a reply is a strong *social token*: it shows interest in what the other is saying and demonstrates that interest is worth rebroadcasting.

The first step in our processing is done in Wukong, a Ruby language library for Hadoop. It lets us write small, agile programs capable of handling multiterabyte data streams. Here is a snippet from the class that represents a twitter message (or *tweet*):[9]

---

7. All are steady-state network flow problems. A flowing crowd of websurfers wandering the linked-document collection will visit the most interesting pages the most often. The transfer of social capital implied by social network interactions highlights the most central actors within each community. The year-to-year progress of students to higher or lower test scores implies what each school's effect on a generic class would be.

8. Chosen without apology, in keeping with the ego-centered ethos of social networks.

9. You can find full working source code on this book's website (*http://oreilly.com/catalog/0636920010388/*).

```
class Tweet < Struct.new(:tweet_id, :screen_name, :created_at,
                         :reply_tweet_id, :reply_screen_name, :text)
  def initialize(raw_tweet)
    # ... gory details of parsing raw tweet omitted
  end

  # Tweet is a reply if there's something in the reply_tweet_id slot
  def is_reply?
    not reply_tweet_id.blank?
    true
  end
end
```

Twitter's Stream API lets anyone easily pull gigabytes of messages.[10] They arrive in a raw JSON format:

```
{"text":"Just finished the final draft for Hadoop: the Definitive Guide!",
 "screen_name":"tom_e_white","reply_screen_name":null,"id":3239897342,
 "reply_tweet_id":null,...}
{"text":"@tom_e_white Can't wait to get a copy!",
 "screen_name":"mrflip","reply_screen_name":"tom_e_white","id":3239873453,
 "reply_tweet_id":3239897342,...}
{"text":"@josephkelly great job on the #InfoChimps API.
 Remind me to tell you about the time a baboon broke into our house.",
 "screen_name":"wattsteve","reply_screen_name":"josephkelly","id":16434069252,...}
{"text":"@mza Re: http://j.mp/atbroxmr Check out @James_Rubino's
 http://bit.ly/clusterfork ? Lots of good hadoop refs there too",
 "screen_name":"mrflip","reply_screen_name":"@mza","id":7809927173,...}
{"text":"@tlipcon divide lots of data into little parts. Magic software gnomes
 fix up the parts, elves then assemble those into whole things #hadoop",
 "screen_name":"nealrichter","reply_screen_name":"tlipcon","id":4491069515,...}
```

The reply_screen_name and reply_tweet_id let you follow the conversation (as you can see, they're otherwise null). Let's find each reply and emit the respective user IDs as an edge:[11]

```
class ReplyGraphMapper < LineStreamer
  def process(raw_tweet)
    tweet = Tweet.new(raw_tweet)
    if tweet.is_reply?
      emit [tweet.screen_name, tweet.reply_screen_name]
    end
  end
end
```

The Mapper derives from LineStreamer, a class that feeds each line as a single record to its process method. We only have to define that process method; Wukong and Hadoop take care of the rest. In this case, we use the raw JSON record to create a tweet

---

10. Refer to the Twitter developer site (*http://dev.twitter.com*), or use a tool like Hayes Davis' Flamingo (*http://github.com/hayesdavis/flamingo*).

11. In practice, we of course use numeric IDs and not screen names, but it's easier to follow along with screen names. In order to keep the graph-theory discussion general, I'm going to play loose with some details and leave out various janitorial details of loading and running.

object. Where user A replies to user B, emit the edge as A and B separated by a tab. The raw output will look like this:

```
% reply_graph_mapper --run raw_tweets.json a_replies_b.tsv
mrflip          tom_e_white
wattsteve       josephkelly
mrflip          mza
nealrichter     tlipcon
```

You should read this as "a replies b" and interpret it as a directed "out" edge: @watt steve conveys social capital to @josephkelly.

Edge pairs versus adjacency list

That is the *edge pairs* representation of a network. It's simple, and it gives an equal jumping-off point for in- or out-edges, but there's some duplication of data. You can tell the same story from the node's point of view (and save some disk space) by rolling up on the source node. We call this the *adjacency list*, and it can be generated in Pig by a simple GROUP BY. Load the file:

```
a_replies_b = LOAD 'a_replies_b.tsv' AS (src:chararray, dest:chararray);
```

Then find all edges out from each node by grouping on source:

```
replies_out = GROUP a_replies_b BY src;
DUMP replies_out

(cutting,{(tom_e_white)})
(josephkelly,{(wattsteve)})
(mikeolson,{(LusciousPear),(kevinweil),(LusciousPear),(tlipcon)})
(mndoci,{(mrflip),(peteskomoroch),(LusciousPear),(mrflip)})
(mrflip,{(LusciousPear),(mndoci),(mndoci),(esammer),(ogrisel),(esammer),(wattsteve)})
(peteskomoroch,{(CMastication),(esammer),(DataJunkie),(mndoci),(nealrichter),...
(tlipcon,{(LusciousPear),(LusciousPear),(nealrichter),(mrflip),(kevinweil)})
(tom_e_white,{(mrflip),(lenbust)})
```

Degree

A simple, useful measure of influence is the number of replies a user receives. In graph terms, this is the *degree* (specifically the *in-degree*, since this is a directed graph).

Pig's nested FOREACH syntax lets us count the distinct incoming repliers (neighbor nodes) and the total incoming replies in one pass:[12]

```
a_replies_b = LOAD 'a_replies_b.tsv' AS (src:chararray, dest:chararray);
replies_in  = GROUP a_replies_b BY dest; -- group on dest to get in-links
replies_in_degree = FOREACH replies_in {
  nbrs = DISTINCT a_replies_b.src;
  GENERATE group, COUNT(nbrs), COUNT(a_replies_b);
```

12. Due to the small size of the edge pair records and a pesky Hadoop implementation detail, the Mapper may spill data to disk early. If the jobtracker dashboard shows "spilled records" greatly exceeding "map output records," try bumping up the io.sort.record.percent:

```
PIG_OPTS="-Dio.sort.record.percent=0.25 -Dio.sort.mb=350" pig my_file.pig
```

```
};
DUMP replies_in_degree

(cutting,1L,1L)
(josephkelly,1L,1L)
(mikeolson,3L,4L)
(mndoci,3L,4L)
(mrflip,5L,9L)
(peteskomoroch,9L,18L)
(tlipcon,4L,8L)
(tom_e_white,2L,2L)
```

In this sample, @peteskomoroch has nine neighbors and 18 incoming replies, far more than most. This large variation in degree is typical for social networks. Most users see a small number of replies, but a few celebrities—such as @THE_REAL_SHAQ (basketball star Shaquille O'Neill) or @sockington (a fictional cat)—receive millions. By contrast, almost every intersection on a road map is four-way.[13] The skewed dataflow produced by this wild variation in degree has important ramifications for how you process such graphs—more later.

Symmetric Links

Although millions of people have given @THE_REAL_SHAQ a shout-out on twitter, he has understandably not reciprocated with millions of replies. As the graph shows, I frequently converse with @mndoci,[14] making ours a *symmetric link*. This accurately reflects the fact that I have more in common with @mndoci than with @THE_REAL_SHAQ.

One way to find symmetric links is to take the edges in A Replied To B that are also in A Replied By B. We can do that set intersection with an inner self-join:[15]

```
a_repl_to_b = LOAD 'a_replies_b.tsv' AS (user_a:chararray, user_b:chararray);
a_repl_by_b = LOAD 'a_replies_b.tsv' AS (user_b:chararray, user_a:chararray);
-- symmetric edges appear in both sets
a_symm_b_j  = JOIN a_repl_to_b BY (user_a, user_b),
                   a_repl_by_b BY (user_a, user_b);
...
```

However, this sends two full copies of the edge-pairs list to the reduce phase, doubling the memory required. We can do better by noticing that from a node's point of view, a symmetric link is equivalent to a paired edge: one out and one in. Make the graph undirected by putting the node with lowest sort order in the first slot—but preserve the direction as a piece of edge metadata:

---

13. The largest outlier that comes to mind is the famous "Magic Roundabout" in Swindon, England, with degree 10. See *http://en.wikipedia.org/wiki/Magic_Roundabout_%28Swindon%29*.

14. Deepak Singh, open data advocate and bizdev manager of the Amazon AWS cloud.

15. Current versions of Pig get confused on self-joins, so just load the table with differently named relations as shown here.

```
a_replies_b = LOAD 'a_replies_b.tsv' AS (src:chararray, dest:chararray);
a_b_rels = FOREACH a_replies_b GENERATE
  ((src <= dest) ? src  : dest) AS user_a,
  ((src <= dest) ? dest : src)  AS user_b,
  ((src <= dest) ? 1 : 0)       AS a_re_b:int,
  ((src <= dest) ? 0 : 1)       AS b_re_a:int;
DUMP a_b_rels

(mrflip,tom_e_white,1,0)
(josephkelly,wattsteve,0,1)
(mrflip,mza,1,0)
(nealrichter,tlipcon,0,1)
```

Now gather all edges for each node pair. A symmetric edge has at least one reply in each direction:

```
a_b_rels_g   = GROUP a_b_rels BY (user_a, user_b);
a_symm_b_all = FOREACH a_b_rels_g GENERATE
  group.user_a AS user_a,
  group.user_b AS user_b,
  (( ( SUM(a_b_rels.a_re_b) > 0) AND
      (SUM(a_b_rels.b_re_a) > 0)    ) ? 1 : 0) AS is_symmetric:int;
DUMP a_symm_b_all

(mrflip,tom_e_white,1)
(mrflip,mza,0)
(josephkelly,wattsteve,0)
(nealrichter,tlipcon,1)
...

a_symm_b = FILTER a_symm_b_all BY (is_symmetric == 1);
STORE a_symm_b INTO 'a_symm_b.tsv';
```

Here's a portion of the output, showing that @mrflip and @tom_e_white have a symmetric link:

```
(mrflip,tom_e_white,1)
(nealrichter,tlipcon,1)
...
```

Community Extraction

So far, we've generated a node measure (in-degree) and an edge measure (symmetric link identification). Let's move out one step and look at a neighborhood measure: how many of a given person's friends are friends with each other? Along the way, we'll produce the edge set for a visualization like the one discussed earlier.

Get neighbors

Choose a seed node (here, @hadoop). First, round up the seed's neighbors:

```
a_replies_b = LOAD 'a_replies_b.tsv' AS (src:chararray, dest:chararray);
-- Extract edges that originate or terminate on the seed
n0_edges    = FILTER a_replies_b BY (src == 'hadoop') OR (dest == 'hadoop');
-- Choose the node in each pair that *isn't* our seed:
```

```
n1_nodes_all = FOREACH n0_edges GENERATE
  ((src == 'hadoop') ? dest : src) AS screen_name;
n1_nodes     = DISTINCT n1_nodes_all;
DUMP n1_nodes
```

Now intersect the set of neighbors with the set of starting nodes to find all edges originating in n1_nodes:

```
n1_edges_out_j = JOIN a_replies_b BY src,
                      n1_nodes     BY screen_name USING 'replicated';
n1_edges_out   = FOREACH n1_edges_out_j GENERATE src, dest;
```

Our copy of the graph (with more than 1 billion edges) is far too large to fit in memory. On the other hand, the neighbor count for a single user rarely exceeds a couple of million, which fits easily in memory. Including USING 'replicated' in the JOIN command instructs Pig to do a map-side join (also called a *fragment replicate join*). Pig holds the n1_nodes relation in memory as a lookup table and streams the full edge list past. Whenever the join condition is met—src is in the n1_nodes lookup table—it produces output. No reduce step means an enormous speedup!

To leave only edges where both source and destination are neighbors of the seed node, repeat the join:

```
n1_edges_j = JOIN n1_edges_out BY dest,
                  n1_nodes      BY screen_name USING 'replicated';
n1_edges   = FOREACH n1_edges_j GENERATE src, dest;
DUMP n1_edges

(mrflip,tom_e_white)
(mrflip,mza)
(wattsteve,josephkelly)
(nealrichter,tlipcon)
(bradfordcross,lusciouspear)
(mrflip,jeromatron)
(mndoci,mrflip)
(nealrichter,datajunkie)
```

Community metrics and the 1 million × 1 million problem

With @hadoop, @cloudera, and @infochimps as seeds, I applied similar scripts to 2 billion messages to create Figure 16-24 (this image is also hosted on this book's website (*http://hadoopbook.com*)).

As you can see, the big data community is very interconnected. The link neighborhood of a celebrity such as @THE_REAL_SHAQ is far more sparse. We can characterize this using the *clustering coefficient*: the ratio of actual n1_edges to the maximum number of possible n1_edges. It ranges from zero (no neighbor links to any other neighbor) to one (every neighbor links to every other neighbor). A moderately high clustering coefficient indicates a cohesive community. A low clustering coefficient could indicate widely dispersed interest (as it does with @THE_REAL_SHAQ), or it could indicate the kind of inorganic community that a spam account would engender.

Local properties at global scale

We've calculated community metrics at the scale of a node, an edge, and a neighborhood. How about the whole globe? There's not enough space here to cover it, but you can simultaneously determine the clustering coefficient for every node by generating every "triangle" in the graph. For each user, comparing the number of triangles they belong to with their degree leads to the clustering coefficient.

Be careful, though! Remember the wide variation in node degree discussed earlier? Recklessly extending the previous method will lead to an explosion of data—pop star @britneyspears (5.2 million followers, 420,000 following as of July 2010) or @Whole Foods (1.7 million followers, 600,000 following) will each generate trillions of entries. What's worse, because large communities have a sparse clustering coefficient, almost all of these will be thrown away! There is a very elegant way to do this on the full graph,[16] but always keep in mind what the real world says about the problem. If you're willing to assert that @britneyspears isn't *really* friends with 420,000 people, you can keep only the strong links. Weight each edge (by number of replies, whether it's symmetric, and so on), and set limits on the number of links from any node. This sharply reduces the intermediate data size, yet still does a reasonable job of estimating cohesiveness.

—Philip (flip) Kromer, Infochimps

---

16. See *http://www.slideshare.net/ydn/3-xxl-graphalgohadoopsummit2010*. Sergei Vassilvitskii (@vsergei) and Jake Hofman (@jakehofman) of Yahoo! Research solve several graph problems by very intelligently throwing away most of the graph.

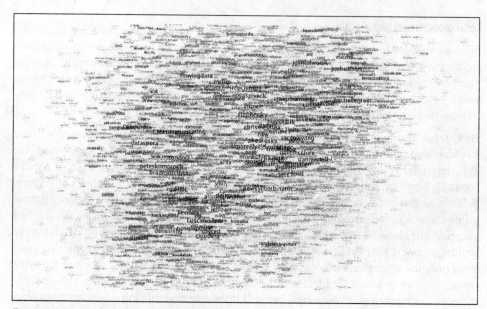

Figure 16-24. Big data community on Twitter

Installing Apache Hadoop

It's easy to install Hadoop on a single machine to try it out. (For installation on a cluster, please refer to Chapter 9.) The quickest way is to download and run a binary release from an Apache Software Foundation Mirror.

In this appendix, we cover how to install Hadoop Common, HDFS, and MapReduce. Instructions for installing the other projects covered in this book are included at the start of the relevant chapters.

Prerequisites

Hadoop is written in Java, so you will need to have Java installed on your machine, version 6 or later. Sun's JDK is the one most widely used with Hadoop, although others have been reported to work.

Hadoop runs on Unix and on Windows. Linux is the only supported production platform, but other flavors of Unix (including Mac OS X) can be used to run Hadoop for development. Windows is supported only as a development platform, and additionally requires Cygwin to run. During the Cygwin installation process, you should include the *openssh* package if you plan to run Hadoop in pseudodistributed mode (see the following explanation).

Installation

Start by deciding which user you'd like to run Hadoop as. For trying out Hadoop or developing Hadoop programs, it is simplest to run Hadoop on a single machine using your own user account.

Download a stable release, which is packaged as a gzipped tar file, from the Apache Hadoop releases page (*http://hadoop.apache.org/common/releases.html*), and unpack it somewhere on your filesystem:

```
% tar xzf hadoop-x.y.z.tar.gz
```

Before you can run Hadoop, you need to tell it where Java is located on your system. If you have the `JAVA_HOME` environment variable set to point to a suitable Java installation, that will be used, and you don't have to configure anything further. (It is often set in a shell startup file, such as *~/.bash_profile* or *~/.bashrc*.) Otherwise, you can set the Java installation that Hadoop uses by editing *conf/hadoop-env.sh* and specifying the `JAVA_HOME` variable. For example, on my Mac, I changed the line to read:

```
export JAVA_HOME=/System/Library/Frameworks/JavaVM.framework/Versions/1.6/Home/
```

to point to the latest 1.6 version of Java. On Ubuntu, the equivalent line is:

```
export JAVA_HOME=/usr/lib/jvm/java-6-sun
```

It's very convenient to create an environment variable that points to the Hadoop installation directory (`HADOOP_INSTALL`, say) and to put the Hadoop binary directory on your command-line path. (In Hadoop 2.0, you may need to put the *sbin* directory on the path too.) For example:

```
% export HADOOP_INSTALL=/home/tom/hadoop-x.y.z
% export PATH=$PATH:$HADOOP_INSTALL/bin:$HADOOP_INSTALL/sbin
```

Check that Hadoop runs by typing:

```
% hadoop version
Hadoop 1.0.0
Subversion https://svn.apache.org/repos/asf/hadoop/common/branches/branch-1.0
 -r 1214675
Compiled by hortonfo on Thu Dec 15 16:36:35 UTC 2011
```

Configuration

Each component in Hadoop is configured using an XML file. Common properties go in *core-site.xml*, HDFS properties go in *hdfs-site.xml*, and MapReduce properties go in *mapred-site.xml*. These files are all located in the *conf* subdirectory.

> In earlier versions of Hadoop, there was a single site configuration file for the Common, HDFS, and MapReduce components, called *hadoop-site.xml*. From release 0.20.0 onward, this file has been split into three: one for each component. The property names have not changed, just the configuration file they have to go in. You can see the default settings for all the properties that are governed by these configuration files by looking in the *docs* directory of your Hadoop installation for HTML files called *core-default.html*, *hdfs-default.html*, and *mapred-default.html*.

In Hadoop 2.0 and later, MapReduce runs on YARN and there is an additional configuration file called *yarn-site.xml*. All the configuration files should go in the *etc/hadoop* subdirectory.

Hadoop can be run in one of three modes:

Standalone (or local) mode

There are no daemons running and everything runs in a single JVM. Standalone mode is suitable for running MapReduce programs during development, since it is easy to test and debug them.

Pseudodistributed mode

The Hadoop daemons run on the local machine, thus simulating a cluster on a small scale.

Fully distributed mode

The Hadoop daemons run on a cluster of machines. This setup is described in Chapter 9.

To run Hadoop in a particular mode, you need to do two things: set the appropriate properties, and start the Hadoop daemons. Table A-1 shows the minimal set of properties to configure each mode. In standalone mode, the local filesystem and the local MapReduce job runner are used, whereas in the distributed modes the HDFS and MapReduce (or YARN) daemons are started.

Table A-1. Key configuration properties for different modes

Component	Property	Standalone	Pseudodistributed	Fully distributed
Common	`fs.default.name`	`file:///` (default)	`hdfs://local host/`	`hdfs://name node/`
HDFS	`dfs.replication`	N/A	1	3 (default)
MapReduce 1	`mapred.job.tracker`	`local` (default)	`localhost:8021`	`jobtracker:8021`
YARN (MapReduce 2)	`yarn.resource manager.address`	N/A	`localhost:8032`	`resourceman ager:8032`

You can read more about configuration in "Hadoop Configuration" on page 304 and "YARN Configuration" on page 320.

Standalone Mode

In standalone mode, there is no further action to take, since the default properties are set for standalone mode and there are no daemons to run.

Pseudodistributed Mode

The configuration files should be created with the following contents and placed in the *conf* directory (although you can place configuration files in any directory as long as you start the daemons with the `--config` option):

```
<?xml version="1.0"?>
<!-- core-site.xml -->
<configuration>
  <property>
```

```
        <name>fs.default.name</name>
        <value>hdfs://localhost/</value>
    </property>
</configuration>

<?xml version="1.0"?>
<!-- hdfs-site.xml -->
<configuration>
    <property>
        <name>dfs.replication</name>
        <value>1</value>
    </property>
</configuration>

<?xml version="1.0"?>
<!-- mapred-site.xml -->
<configuration>
    <property>
        <name>mapred.job.tracker</name>
        <value>localhost:8021</value>
    </property>
</configuration>
```

If you are running YARN, use the *yarn-site.xml* file:

```
<?xml version="1.0"?>
<!-- yarn-site.xml -->
<configuration>
    <property>
        <name>yarn.resourcemanager.address</name>
        <value>localhost:8032</value>
    </property>
    <property>
        <name>yarn.nodemanager.aux-services</name>
        <value>mapreduce.shuffle</value>
    </property>
</configuration>
```

Configuring SSH

In pseudodistributed mode, we have to start daemons, and to do that, we need to have
SSH installed. Hadoop doesn't actually distinguish between pseudodistributed and
fully distributed modes; it merely starts daemons on the set of hosts in the cluster
(defined by the *slaves* file) by SSH-ing to each host and starting a daemon process.
Pseudodistributed mode is just a special case of fully distributed mode in which the
(single) host is localhost, so we need to make sure that we can SSH to localhost and log
in without having to enter a password.

First, make sure that SSH is installed and a server is running. On Ubuntu, for example,
this is achieved with:

```
% sudo apt-get install ssh
```

On Windows with Cygwin, you can set up an SSH server (after having installed the openssh package) by running ssh-host-config -y.

On Mac OS X, make sure Remote Login (under System Preferences→Sharing) is enabled for the current user (or all users).

Then, to enable password-less login, generate a new SSH key with an empty passphrase:

```
% ssh-keygen -t rsa -P '' -f ~/.ssh/id_rsa
% cat ~/.ssh/id_rsa.pub >> ~/.ssh/authorized_keys
```

Test this with:

```
% ssh localhost
```

If successful, you should not have to type in a password.

Formatting the HDFS filesystem

Before it can be used, a brand-new HDFS installation needs to be formatted. The formatting process creates an empty filesystem by creating the storage directories and the initial versions of the namenode's persistent data structures. Datanodes are not involved in the initial formatting process, since the namenode manages all of the filesystem's metadata, and datanodes can join or leave the cluster dynamically. For the same reason, you don't need to say how large a filesystem to create, since this is determined by the number of datanodes in the cluster, which can be increased as needed, long after the filesystem is formatted.

Formatting HDFS is a fast operation. Just type the following:

```
% hadoop namenode -format
```

Starting and stopping the daemons (MapReduce 1)

To start the HDFS and MapReduce daemons, type:

```
% start-dfs.sh
% start-mapred.sh
```

If you have placed configuration files outside the default *conf* directory, start the daemons with the --config option, which takes an absolute path to the configuration directory:

```
% start-dfs.sh --config path-to-config-directory
% start-mapred.sh --config path-to-config-directory
```

The following daemons will be started on your local machine: a namenode, a secondary namenode, a datanode, a jobtracker, and a tasktracker. You can check whether the daemons started successfully by looking at the logfiles in the *logs* directory (in the Hadoop installation directory) or by looking at the web UIs, at *http://localhost:*

50030/ for the jobtracker and at *http://localhost:50070/* for the namenode. You can also use Java's jps command to see whether they are running.

Stopping the daemons is done in the obvious way:

```
% stop-dfs.sh
% stop-mapred.sh
```

Starting and stopping the daemons (MapReduce 2)

To start the HDFS and YARN daemons, type:

```
% start-dfs.sh
% start-yarn.sh
```

These commands will start the HDFS daemons, and for YARN, a resource manager and a node manager. The resource manager web UI is at *http://localhost:8088/*.

You can stop the daemons with:

```
% stop-dfs.sh
% stop-yarn.sh
```

Fully Distributed Mode

Setting up a cluster of machines brings many additional considerations, so this mode is covered in Chapter 9.

Cloudera's Distribution Including Apache Hadoop

Cloudera's Distribution Including Apache Hadoop (hereafter *CDH*) is an integrated Apache Hadoop-based stack containing all the components needed for production use, tested and packaged to work together. Cloudera makes the distribution available in a number of different formats: Linux packages, virtual machine images, tarballs, and scripts for running CDH in the cloud. CDH is free, released under the Apache 2.0 license and available at *http://www.cloudera.com/hadoop/*.

As of CDH3, the following components are included, many of which are covered elsewhere in this book:

- HDFS: Self-healing distributed filesystem
- MapReduce: Powerful, parallel data processing framework
- Hadoop Common: A set of utilities that support the Hadoop subprojects
- HBase: Hadoop database for random read/write access
- Hive: SQL-like queries and tables on large datasets
- Pig: Dataflow language and compiler
- Oozie: Workflow for interdependent Hadoop jobs
- Sqoop: Integrate databases and data warehouses with Hadoop
- Flume: Highly reliable, configurable streaming data collection
- ZooKeeper: Coordination service for distributed applications
- Hue: User interface framework and SDK for visual Hadoop applications
- Whirr: Libraries and scripts for running Hadoop and related services in the cloud
- Mahout: Scalable machine-learning and data-mining algorithms

Cloudera also provides *Cloudera Manager* for deploying and operating Hadoop clusters running CDH.

To download CDH and Cloudera Manager, visit *http://www.cloudera.com/downloads/*.

Preparing the NCDC Weather Data

This appendix gives a runthrough of the steps taken to prepare the raw weather datafiles so they are in a form that is amenable for analysis using Hadoop. If you want to get a copy of the data to process using Hadoop, you can do so by following the instructions given at the website that accompanies this book at *http://www.hadoopbook.com/*. The rest of this appendix explains how the raw weather datafiles were processed.

The raw data is provided as a collection of *tar* files, compressed with *bzip2*. Each year of readings comes in a separate file. Here's a partial directory listing of the files:

```
1901.tar.bz2
1902.tar.bz2
1903.tar.bz2
...
2000.tar.bz2
```

Each *tar* file contains a file for each weather station's readings for the year, compressed with *gzip*. (The fact that the files in the archive are compressed makes the *bzip2* compression on the archive itself redundant.) For example:

```
% tar jxf 1901.tar.bz2
% ls -l 1901 | head
011990-99999-1950.gz
011990-99999-1950.gz
...
011990-99999-1950.gz
```

Because there are tens of thousands of weather stations, the whole dataset is made up of a large number of relatively small files. It's generally easier and more efficient to process a smaller number of relatively large files in Hadoop (see "Small files and CombineFileInputFormat" on page 239), so in this case, I concatenated the decompressed files for a whole year into a single file, named by the year. I did this using a MapReduce program, to take advantage of its parallel processing capabilities. Let's take a closer look at the program.

The program has only a map function. No reduce function is needed because the map does all the file processing in parallel with no combine stage. The processing can be done with a Unix script, so the Streaming interface to MapReduce is appropriate in this case; see Example C-1.

Example C-1. Bash script to process raw NCDC datafiles and store in HDFS

```bash
#!/usr/bin/env bash

# NLineInputFormat gives a single line: key is offset, value is S3 URI
read offset s3file

# Retrieve file from S3 to local disk
echo "reporter:status:Retrieving $s3file" >&2
$HADOOP_INSTALL/bin/hadoop fs -get $s3file .

# Un-bzip and un-tar the local file
target=`basename $s3file .tar.bz2`
mkdir -p $target
echo "reporter:status:Un-tarring $s3file to $target" >&2
tar jxf `basename $s3file` -C $target

# Un-gzip each station file and concat into one file
echo "reporter:status:Un-gzipping $target" >&2
for file in $target/*/*
do
  gunzip -c $file >> $target.all
  echo "reporter:status:Processed $file" >&2
done

# Put gzipped version into HDFS
echo "reporter:status:Gzipping $target and putting in HDFS" >&2
gzip -c $target.all | $HADOOP_INSTALL/bin/hadoop fs -put - gz/$target.gz
```

The input is a small text file (*ncdc_files.txt*) listing all the files to be processed (the files start out on S3, so the files are referenced using S3 URIs that Hadoop understands). Here is a sample:

```
s3n://hadoopbook/ncdc/raw/isd-1901.tar.bz2
s3n://hadoopbook/ncdc/raw/isd-1902.tar.bz2
...
s3n://hadoopbook/ncdc/raw/isd-2000.tar.bz2
```

By specifying the input format to be `NLineInputFormat`, each mapper receives one line of input, which contains the file it has to process. The processing is explained in the script, but briefly, it unpacks the *bzip2* file and then concatenates each station file into a single file for the whole year. Finally, the file is gzipped and copied into HDFS. Note the use of `hadoop fs -put -` to consume from standard input.

Status messages are echoed to standard error with a `reporter:status` prefix so that they get interpreted as a MapReduce status update. This tells Hadoop that the script is making progress and is not hanging.

The script to run the Streaming job is as follows:

```
% hadoop jar $HADOOP_INSTALL/contrib/streaming/hadoop-*-streaming.jar \
  -D mapred.reduce.tasks=0 \
  -D mapred.map.tasks.speculative.execution=false \
  -D mapred.task.timeout=12000000 \
  -input ncdc_files.txt \
  -inputformat org.apache.hadoop.mapred.lib.NLineInputFormat \
  -output output \
  -mapper load_ncdc_map.sh \
  -file load_ncdc_map.sh
```

I set the number of reduce tasks to zero, since this is a map-only job. I also turned off speculative execution so duplicate tasks wouldn't write the same files (although the approach discussed in "Task side-effect files" on page 218 would have worked, too). The task timeout was set to a high value so that Hadoop doesn't kill tasks that are taking a long time (for example, when unarchiving files or copying to HDFS, when no progress is reported).

Finally, the files were archived on S3 by copying them from HDFS using *distcp*.

Index

Symbols

--class-name argument, 533, 546
--clear-staging-table option, 545
--config option, 187, 303, 305, 335, 417, 619, 621
--direct argument, 536
--enclosed-by argument, 543
--escaped-by argument, 543
--jar-file argument, 546
--private-key-file, 335
-clean argument, 332
-cmdenv option, 215
-combiner option, 38, 232
-conf command, 150, 153, 163
-copyFromLocal command, 50
-copyToLocal command, 82
-counter option, 174
-debug option, 380
-delete option, 349
-dryrun option, 390, 411
-exectype option, 369
-getmerge option, 170
-hiveconf option, 418
-ignoreCrc option, 82
-importCheckpoint option, 343
-input option, 238
-lazyOutput option, 258
-libjars, 163, 289, 292, 537
-no_multiquery, 378
-param_file, 410
.class.default parameter, 583

A

abortJob( ) method, 218
abortTask( ) method, 218
ACL object, 505
ACLs, for ZooKeeper, 505–506
ActiveKeyValueStore, 513, 514, 515, 517
add( ) method, 293
addFileToClassPath( ) method, 163, 293
addInputPath( ) method, 24, 236, 251
addInputPaths( ) method, 236
addresses, daemon properties
    for clusters, 316–317
    for MapReduce 2, 324
addXXXXToClassPath( ) method, 293
administration
    HDFS, 339–351
        audit logging, 346
        balancer program, 350–351
        datanode block scanner, 349–350
        datanode directory structure, 343–344
        dfsadmin, 347
        edit log, 340–342
        fsck, 347–349
        fsimage file, 340–342
        namenode directory structure, 339–340
        safe mode, 344–346
        secondary namenode directory
            structure, 342–343
    maintenance, 358–365
        commissioning new nodes, 359–360
        data backups, 358–359
        decommissioning old nodes, 361–362
        filesystem balancer, 359
        filesystem check, 359
        metadata backups, 358
    monitoring, 351–357
        logging, 352

We'd like to hear your suggestions for improving our indexes. Send email to *index@oreilly.com*.

metrics, 352–355
  using JMX, 355–357
upgrades, 362–365
  checking process of, 364
  finalizing, 365
  rolling back, 364–365
  starting, 364
  testing, 364
Aggregators, 589, 593, 596
Algebraic class, 395
aliases, 123, 372
analyzing data
  with Hadoop, 20–29
  with Unix tools, 19–20
Apache Oozie, 183–187
  defining workflow, 184–186
  packaging workflow, 186–187
  running workflow job, 187
Apache Whirr project, 334–338
  configuring, 335–336
  installing, 334–335
  launching cluster, 335
  running MapReduce job, 337
  running proxy, 336
  shutting down cluster, 338
APIs
  for distributed cache, 292–294
  for MapReduce model
    and releases for Hadoop, 15
    differences between, 27–29
  for ZooKeeper, 502–503
append( ) method, 60, 117, 131, 138
appendRaw( ) method, 250
application master failure, in MapReduce 2,
    205
arity property, 355
array( ) method, 427
ArrayFile, 141
ArrayPrimitiveWritable, 102, 103
ArrayWritable, 102, 103
audit logging, for HDFS, 346
authentication, 325, 326
authorization, 325
Avro, 110–130
  clients, for HBase, 471
  data types, 111–113
  datafiles for, 117–118, 438–439
  in-memory serialization and deserialization,
    114, 115–117

interoperability, 118–121
  C API for, 120–121
  Python API for, 118–119
processing in other languages, 130
schema resolution in, 121–123
sort order for objects, 123, 128–129
using MapReduce on, 124, 128–129
avro.java.string property, 113
AvroAsTextInputFormat, 130
AvroJob, 127
AvroMapper class, 124, 128
AvroOutputFormat, 127
AvroReducer class, 124, 128
AvroSpecificMaxTemperature class, 127
AvroTextOutputFormat, 130
avro_datum_t object, 121
avro_file_reader_read function, 121
await( ) method, 494

B

backups
  data, 358–359
  metadata, 358
balancer program, 76–77, 350, 359
benchmarking, 331–334
  example benchmarks, 333
  MapReduce with sort, 332–333
  user jobs, 333–334
  with TestDFSIO, 331–332
big data
  and disk storage, 3–4
  sizes of, 1–3
BINARY data type, 427
binaryDecoder( ) method, 115
BinarySortableSerDe class, 437
bitmaps, 424
BlobRef class, 541, 542
BlobRef.getDataStream( ) method, 541
blocks
  finding for file using fsck, 349
  in HDFS, 45–46, 317
blockSize, 239
BloomMapFile, 141
bookies, 522
BookKeeper logging service, 522
bucketed_users table, 434
buckets, in Hive, 433–435
buffer size, for clusters, 317
built-in counters, 259–263

job counters, 263
task counters, 260
bulk loading, in HBase, 487
bytearray type, 383, 384, 387, 393, 398
Bytes class, 475
bytesToCodePoint( ) method, 100
BytesWritable class, 101, 242, 244, 250

C

C API
  for Avro, 120–121
  for Hadoop Filesystems, 55
C++ (see Hadoop Pipes)
Capacity Scheduler, 207–208
Cascading case study, 589–603
  example using, 595–598
  fields, 590–593
  flexibility of, 598–599
  flows, 594–595
  operations, 593–594
  pipes, 590–593
  schemes, 594–595
  ShareThis example, 599–602
  taps, 594–595
  tuples, 590–593
case studies
  Cascading, 589–603
    example using, 595–598
    fields, 590–593
    flexibility of, 598–599
    flows, 594–595
    operations, 593–594
    pipes, 590–593
    schemes, 594–595
    ShareThis example, 599–602
    taps, 594–595
    tuples, 590–593
  Facebook, 556–567
    data architecture, 557–559
    fair sharing scheduler, 566
    Hadoop configuration at, 559
    history of Hadoop at, 556–557
    Scribe-HDFS integration, 567
    space management, 566
    uses for Hadoop, 557
    using Hive, 562–565
  hypothetical, for large ad networks, 559–
    562
  Infochimps, 607–615

community extraction, 613–615
measuring communities, 609
symmetric links, 612–613
Twitter reply graph, 609–612
Last.fm, 547–556
  generating charts, 548–549
  Track Statistics program, 549–555
Nutch, 567–581
  data structures, 568–571
  Fetcher application in, 577–578
  generating fetchlists, 573–577
  Indexer tool in, 578–580
  link inversion, 571–573
Rackspace, 581–589
  log collection, 582–583
  log storage, 583
  mail log processing, 583–589
  need for Hadoop, 581–582
Streamy.com, 481–483
  benefits of using HBase, 483
  very large items tables, 482
  very large sort merges, 482–483
TeraByte Sort, 603–607
cat command, 56, 377
ChainMapper, 183, 295
ChainReducer, 183
char, 96, 98, 99, 100, 383
chararray, 371, 382, 383, 384, 394, 395, 400
charAt( ) method, 98, 100
CharSequence, 537
charts, Last.fm case study, 548–549
checkOutput( ) method, 161
checksum, 81
ChecksumException, 82, 83
ChecksumFileSystem class, 83
cleanup( ) method, 235
client classpath, for jobs, 162
clientPort, 491
ClientProtocol class, 199
clients
  for HBase, 467–471
    Avro, 471
    Java, 467–470
    REST, 471
    Thrift, 471
  for Hive, 420–421
CLOB, 536, 540
ClobRef, 542

close( ) method, 37, 68, 71, 131, 244, 475, 476, 512
cloud, clusters in, 1, 334–338
  (see also Apache Whirr project)
Cloudera Distribution, with Hadoop, 623–624
Cluster object, 268
ClusterMapReduceTestCase, 161
clusters
  benchmarking, 331–334
    example benchmarks, 333
    MapReduce with sort, 332–333
    user jobs, 333–334
    with TestDFSIO, 331–332
  Hadoop configuration, 304–320
    buffer size, 317
    cluster membership, 317
    control scripts, 305–306
    creating user accounts, 320
    daemon addresses and ports, 316–317
    daemon properties, 311–315
    environment variables for, 307–311
    HDFS block size, 317
    job scheduler, 318
    master node scenarios, 306–307
    reserved storage space, 317
    slow start, 318
    task memory limits, 318–319
    trash, 318
  in cloud, 1, 334–338
    (see also Apache Whirr project)
  MapReduce applications on, 161–178
    debugging, 170–174
    launching job, 163–165
    logs for, 175–177
    MapReduce Web UI, 165–168
    packaging job, 162–163
    retrieving results, 168–170
  security, 325–330
    and delegation tokens, 328–329
    enhancements to, 329–330
    using Kerberos, 326–328
  setting up, 301–303
    creating Hadoop user, 302
    installing Hadoop, 302–303
    installing Java, 302
    testing installation, 303
  specifications for, 297–301
    network topology, 299–301

    rack awareness in Hadoop, 300–301
    SSH configuration of, 303–304
    YARN Configuration, 320–324
      daemon addresses and ports, 324
      daemon properties, 321–324
codec, 85
CodecPool, 88
CodecPool class, 88–89
codecs for compression, 85
codegen, 533
codePointAt( ) method, 100
CoGroup, 591, 592
COGROUP statement, 403–405, 404
coherency model, of HDFS, 72–74
collect( ) method, 261
collector class, 582
ColumnarSerDe class, 437
CombineFileInputFormat class, 239–240, 245, 544
combiner functions, for scaling, 33–35
command-line interface
  for HDFS, 49–52
  for ZooKeeper, 498
commissioning new nodes, 359–360
commitJob( ) method, 218
commitTask( ) method, 218
COMMITTED_HEAP_BYTES, 260, 324
compare( ) method, 95, 107
compareTo( ) method, 106, 271
compatibility of releases for Hadoop, 15–16
compiling Hadoop Pipes, 41–42
complex types, for Hive, 428
CompositeContext class, 355
CompositeInputFormat, 285
compression, 83–92
  and splits, 89–90
  codecs for, 85
  CompressionCodec class, 85–86
  in MapReduce, 90–92
  native libraries for, 87–89
  using CompressionCodecFactory class, 86–87
CompressionCodec class, 85–86, 85, 86, 89, 330
CompressionCodecFactory class, 86–87, 86, 87
CompressionInputStream, 85
CompressionOutputStream, 85, 86
computeSplitSize( ) method, 239

concat function, 428

concatenate( ) function, 594

conciseness, 373

ConfigUpdater, 513, 514, 515, 518

Configuration API, for MapReduce, 144–146
  adding resources to, 145
  properties in, 146

Configuration class, 28, 57, 144, 145, 151, 160, 288, 468

configuration names and releases for Hadoop, 15

Configuration object, 28, 131, 150, 151, 153

Configuration parameters, 335

Configuration property, 15

Configuration Service example, 512–515

ConfigurationPrinter, 151, 152

configure( ) method, 215, 241, 288, 474, 476

configuring
  Apache Whirr, 335–336
  clusters, 304–320
    buffer size, 317
    cluster membership, 317
    control scripts, 305–306
    creating user accounts, 320
    daemon addresses and ports, 316–317
    daemon properties, 311–315
    environment variables for, 307–311
    HDFS block size, 317
    job scheduler, 318
    master node scenarios, 306–307
    reserved storage space, 317
    slow start, 318
    task memory limits, 318–319
    trash, 318
  Facebook case study, 559
  Hive, 417–419
  ZooKeeper, 524–525

ConfigWatcher, 514, 515

connect( ) method, 494

ConnectionWatcher, 495

connectors, for Sqoop, 529

ConnectTimeout, 310, 519

consistency
  and Sqoop, 536
  of ZooKeeper, 507–509

content class, 570

Context object, 28, 155, 172, 235, 241

control scripts, for clusters, 305–306

conversions, in Hive, 429

copyBytes( ) method, 56, 86

copying in parallel, for HDFS, 75–77

countDown( ) method, 494

CountDownLatch class, 494

CounterGroupName, 266

counters, 259–268
  built-in, 259–263
    job counters, 263
    task counters, 260
  in HBase, 486
  user-defined Java, 264–268
    dynamic counters, 265–266
    readable names for, 266
    retrieving values for, 266–268
  user-defined Streaming, 268

Counters class, 267

Counters object, 267

CrawlDatum class, 569, 576, 579

CrawlDb, Nutch case study, 569

crawl_fetch class, 570

crawl_generate class, 570

crawl_parse class, 570

CREATE TABLE...AS SELECT statement, in Hive, 442

create( ) method, 60, 61, 62, 70, 117, 494, 495, 501

CreateGroup, 494, 496

createOutputStream( ) method, 89

createRecordReader( ) method, 235, 242

createSubmittableJob( ) method, 470

createSymlink( ) method, 294

createWriter( ) method, 131

CROSS statement, in Pig, 405–406

CTAS, 441

cTime property, 340, 344

ctx parameter, 503

cut command, 295, 396, 401

CutLoadFunc, 396, 397, 398, 399

D

daemon properties
  for clusters, 311–315
    addresses and ports, 316–317
    for HDFS, 312–314
    for MapReduce, 314–315
    for MapReduce 2, 321–324
    addresses and ports, 324
    memory, 323–324

daemons, in pseudodistributed mode, 621, 622
data architecture, Facebook case study, 557–559
data backups, 358–359
data flow, for HDFS, 67–74
    coherency model of, 72–74
    reading files, 67–69
    writing files, 70–72
data format, for weather dataset, 17–19
data integrity, 81–83
    ChecksumFileSystem class, 83
    in HDFS, 81–82
    LocalFileSystem class, 82–83
data locality, and MapReduce model, 7
data model
    for HBase, 460–461
        locking, 461
        regions, 461
    for ZooKeeper, 499–501
        ephemeral znodes, 500
        sequential znodes, 500–501
        watches, 501
data structures, Nutch case study, 568–571
    CrawlDb, 569
    LinkDb, 569
    segments, 569–571
data types
    for Hive, 426–428
        complex types, 428
        primitive types, 427–428
    in Avro, 111–113
data:airtemp column class, 474
databases
    as input format for MapReduce, 251
    as output format for MapReduce, 251
    vs. Hive, 423–425
        indexes, 424–425
        schema on read vs. schema on write, 423–424
        transactions, 424–425
        updates, 424–425
    vs. Pig, 374–375
DataBlockScanner, 82, 349
DataByteArray type, 393, 398
dataDir property, 491, 523, 524
DataDrivenDBInputFormat, 535, 536
DataFileReader, 117, 118
datafiles, for Avro, 117–118

DataFileStream, 118
DataFileWriter, 117, 118, 119
DataInput, 94, 105
dataLogDir, 523
DataNodeProtocol class, 330
datanodes, in HDFS, 46–47
    block scanner, 349–350
    directory structure, 343–344
DataOutput, 94, 105
DataStreamer, 70, 72
DataType class, 393
data_join, 285
DatumWriter, 115, 117, 118
DBInputFormat, 234, 251
DBOutputFormat, 251
DBWritable, 534
DEBUG, 176, 177, 352
debugging, 170–174
    handling malformed data, 174
    remotely, 177–178
    task details page, 172–174
    tasks page, 172
decodeVIntSize( ) method, 107
decommissioning old nodes, 361–362
DefaultStringifier, 288
default_parallel, 409
delegation tokens, security and, 328–329
delete( ) method, 67, 498
DeleteGroup class, 498
deleting
    data, 67
    groups in ZooKeeper, 498–499
    HAR files, 78
DELIMITED keyword, 440
delimited text, storage formats in Hive, 435–437
dependencies, for jobs, 163
descendingMap( ) method, 477
deserialization, 93
deserialize( ) method, 95
design, of HDFS, 43–44
destroy-cluster, 338
dfs command, 416
dfs.balance.bandwidthPerSec property, 351
dfs.block.access.token.enable, 329
dfs.block.size property, 317
dfs.data.dir property, 313, 315, 344
dfs.datanode.address property, 316
dfs.datanode.dns.interface, 317

dfs.datanode.du.reserved, 317
dfs.datanode.kerberos.principal, 330
dfs.datanode.keytab.file property, 330
dfs.datanode.numblocks, 344
dfs.datanode.scan.period.hours property, 349
dfs.hosts property, 317, 360
dfs.hosts.exclude property, 317, 361
dfs.http.address property, 76
dfs.name.dir property, 15, 313, 339, 343
dfs.permissions, 51
dfs.replication, 50, 71
dfs.replication.min, 71, 345
dfs.safemode.threshold.pct, 345, 346
dfs.web.ugi property, 150, 173
dfs.webhdfs.enabled, 54
dfsadmin, for HDFS, 347
DFSInputStream, 68
DFSOutputStream, 70, 71
dict object, 119
direct-mode imports, with Sqoop, 536
directories, creating, 62
disable command, 466
disk storage, and big data, 3–4
displayConfig( ) method, 514
displaying SequenceFile, 135
distcp, copying in parallel with, 75–77
distributed cache, side data distribution
        through, 289
    API for, 292–294
    overview, 292
DistributedCache, 163, 294
DistributedFileSystem, 53, 55, 67, 68, 70
DNSToSwitchMapping interface, 300, 301
double type, 112
DoubleWritable, 457
downloading, Sqoop, 527–529
Dreadnaught, 11
drivers, running MapReduce applications
        locally, 160–161
DROP, 430, 431
dropping tables, in Hive, 443–444
DUMP statement, 377
dynamic counters, 265–266
dynamic invokers, and Pig UDFs, 395–396
dynamic parameters, in Pig, 410–411

E

ecosystem, of Hadoop, 12–13
edit log, for HDFS, 340–342

EMR (Elastic MapReduce), 599
Encoder class, 115, 117
end control, 185
Entry class, 577
EnumSetWritable, 102, 103
environment variables
    for clusters, 307–311
        Java, 309
        memory, 307–309
        SSH settings, 310–311
        system logfiles, 309–310
    for tasks, 215
EOFException, 60
ephemeral znodes, for ZooKeeper, 500
equals( ) method, 105
eval UDF, for Pig, 394–396
EvalFunc, 391, 393, 395
evaluate( ) method, 453
EventType.NodeDataChanged, 515
Every class, 592, 593, 596, 598
exec( ) method, 391, 393, 394, 395
execution types, for Pig, 368–370
    local mode, 369
    MapReduce mode, 369–370
exists( ) method, 60, 63, 503
EXPLAIN command, 378, 447
exporting data, with Sqoop, 542–546
    and SequenceFiles, 545–546
    and transactionality, 545
expressions, in Pig Latin, 381
expunge( ) method, 318
external tables, in Hive, 429–431

F

Facebook case study, 556–567
    data architecture, 557–559
    fair sharing scheduler, 566
    Hadoop configuration at, 559
    history of Hadoop at, 556–557
    Scribe-HDFS integration, 567
    space management, 566
    uses for Hadoop, 557
    using Hive, 562–565
        data organization, 563
        data pipelines, 564–565
        improvements to, 567
        query language, 563
failover, for high-availability of HDFS, 49
failures

with MapReduce 1, 202–204
  of jobtracker, 204
  of tasks, 202–204
  of tasktracker, 204
with MapReduce 2, 204–206
  application master failure, 205
  node manager failure, 205–206
  of tasks, 205
  resource manager failure, 206
Fair Scheduler
  Facebook case study, 566
  scheduling jobs using, 207
federation, in HDFS, 47
Fetcher application, in Nutch case study, 577–578
Fetcher class, 576, 577, 578
FetcherThread class, 578
Fields class, 596
FieldSchema, 393
FieldSelectionMapper, 295
FieldSelectionMapReduce, 295
FieldSelectionReducer, 295
file-based data structures, 130–142
  MapFile, 137–142
    converting SequenceFile to, 141–142
    reading, 140–141
    variants of, 141
    writing, 138–140
  SequenceFile, 130–137
    displaying, 135
    format for, 136–137
    merging, 136
    reading, 132–135
    sorting, 136
    writing, 131–132
FileContext class, 55, 353–354, 353, 354, 355
FileInputFormat class, 236–242
  and splits, 238–239
  file information in mapper, 241–242
  input paths for, 236–238
fileName property, 353, 354
FileNotFoundException, 63
FileOutputCommitter, 192, 217, 218
FileOutputFormat, 24, 90, 186, 219, 253, 257
FileSplit, 241, 242, 243, 245, 585
FileStatus class, 62–66, 62, 65
  listStatus( ) method, 64
  using patterns with, 65–66
FileStatus object, 62, 64

FileSystem API
  reading data using, 57–60
    FSDataInputStream class, 58–60
Filesystem in Userspace (FUSE) interface, for
    Hadoop Filesystems, 55
FileSystemCounters, 260
filesystems, 1
  (see also Hadoop Filesystems)
  balancing, 359
  checking, 359
FileUtil, 64
FILTER statement, 374
filter UDF, for Pig, 391–394
filtered_records, 373, 390
FilterFunc, 391
find( ) method, 98, 100
finish( ) method, 86
FirstComparator, 107, 287
FirstPartitioner, 281
fix( ) method, 141, 142
Flow class, 595, 596, 602
Flume, with HDFS, 74–75
FOREACH...GENERATE statement, in Pig,
    400–401
formats
  for SequenceFile, 136–137
  for Sqoop, 532
frameworks, for serialization, 1, 108–110
  (see also Avro)
fromUrl class, 573
from_utc_timestamp function, 428
fs command, 380
fs.checkpoint.dir property, 313, 314, 343, 358
fs.default.name property, 50, 161, 312, 313,
    315, 369, 380, 416, 418
fsck utility, for HDFS, 347–349
FSDataInputStream class, 58–60
FSDataOutputStream class, 61–62, 131
FSDirectory, 587
fsimage file, 340–342
FsUrlStreamHandlerFactory, 56
fsync( ) method, 74, 502
fully distributed mode, 622
FuncSpec object, 393
functions
  in Hive, 428–429
  in Pig Latin, 388–390
FUSE (Filesystem in Userspace) interface, for
    Hadoop Filesystems, 55

G

GangliaContext class, 354
GarbageCollectorMXBean.getCollectionTime( ) method, 262
GENERATE statement, 401
Generated class, 114
GenericDatumReader class, 122
GenericDatumWriter class, 115
GenericOptionsParser, setting up IDE, 150–153
GenericRecord class, 115, 116, 127
GenericWritable class, 102, 103, 578
Get class, 477
get( ) method, 95, 96, 103, 140, 141, 145, 273, 391, 477
getArchiveClassPaths( ) method, 294
getArgToFuncMapping( ) method, 393, 395
getBytes( ) method, 101, 513
getChecksumFile( ) method, 83
getChildren( ) method, 497, 504
getClosest( ) method, 140
getCodec( ) method, 86
getConf( ) method, 151
getConfiguration( ) method, 288
getCounter( ) method, 267
getCounters( ) method, 267, 268
getCurrentKey( ) method, 236
getCurrentValue( ) method, 133, 236
getData( ) method, 501, 504, 514
getEntry( ) method, 273
getFileClassPaths( ) method, 294
getFileStatus( ) method, 62
getInputFormat( ) method, 398
getInputSplit( ) method, 241
getJob( ) method, 267
getKeyClass( ) method, 133
getLength( ) method, 101, 132
getLoadCaster( ) method, 398, 399
getLocal( ) method, 294
getLocalCacheArchives( ) method, 294
getLocalCacheFiles( ), 294
getNewJobId( ) method, 190
getNext( ) method, 398
getOutputCommitter( ) method, 217
getRawFileSystem( ) method, 83
getReaders( ) method, 273
getRecordReader( ) method, 240
getSchema( ) method, 117
getSessionId( ) method, 521

getSplits( ) method, 235
getState( ) method, 511
getStationInfo( ) method, 477
getStationObservations( ) method, 478
getStatus( ) method, 195
getValueClass( ) method, 133
getWorkOutputPath( ) method, 219
globbing, 65
globStatus( ) method, 65, 66
GrantingTicket (TGT), 326
Grid Computing, vs. Hadoop, 6–8
Gridmix, 333
GROUP statement, in Pig, 406–407
GroupBy class, 591, 592, 596
groups, in ZooKeeper
    creating, 493–495
    deleting, 498–499
    joining, 495–496
    listing members in, 496–498
    membership for, 492–493
Grunt shell, for Pig, 370–371
GzipCodec, 85, 86

H

Hadoop
    and Hadoop ecosystem, 12–13
    creating user for, 302
    history of, 9–12
    installing, 302–303
    releases for, 13–16
        and configuration names, 15
        and MapReduce APIs, 15
        compatibility of, 15–16
    vs. Grid Computing, 6–8
    vs. RDBMS, 4–6
    vs. Volunteer Computing, 8
    Yahoo! using, 11–12
Hadoop 2.0, xix
Hadoop Archives (see HAR files)
hadoop command, 26, 38
Hadoop Distributed Filesystem (see HDFS)
Hadoop Filesystems, interfaces for, 53–55
    C library, 55
    FUSE, 55
    HTTP, 53–54
Hadoop Pipes, 40–42
Hadoop Streaming, 36–40
    in Python, 39–40
    in Ruby, 36–39

hadoop-core, 148
hadoop-datanode, 336
hadoop-jobtracker, 336
hadoop-namenode, 336
hadoop-tasktracker, 336
hadoop-test, 148
hadoop.job.ugi property, 150
hadoop.native.lib, 88
hadoop.pipes.java.recordreader, 42
hadoop.pipes.java.recordwriter, 42
hadoop.security.authentication property, 327
hadoop.security.authorization, 328
hadoop.tmp.dir property, 314
hadoopguide, 530
HadoopPipes, 41
HADOOP_CLASSPATH environment
        variable, 26, 162, 163, 164
HADOOP_CONF_DIR environment variable,
        337, 369
HADOOP_HEAPSIZE environment variable,
        307
HADOOP_HOME environment variable, 369,
        414
HADOOP_IDENT_STRING environment
        variable, 310
HADOOP_INSTALL environment variable,
        42, 310, 618
HADOOP_LOG_DIR environment variable,
        175, 176, 309
HADOOP_MASTER environment variable,
        310
HADOOP_NAMENODE_OPTS environment
        variable, 308, 309
HADOOP_SECONDARYNAMENODE_OPT
        S environment variable, 309
HADOOP_SLAVES environment variable,
        305
HADOOP_SLAVE_SLEEP environment
        variable, 310
HADOOP_SSH_OPTS environment variable,
        310
HADOOP_USER_CLASSPATH_FIRST
        environment variable, 163
Haivvreo, 438
hamcrest-all, 148
HAR files (Hadoop Archives), in HDFS, 77–
        79
    creating, 77–78
    deleting, 78

limitations of, 79
hashCode( ) method, 105, 124
HashComparator class, 576
HashPartitioner class, 105, 230, 255, 586
hasNext( ) method, 118
HBase, 459–460
    and HDFS, 484–485
    bulk loading, 487
    clients for, 467–471
        Avro, 471
        Java, 467–470
        REST, 471
        Thrift, 471
    counters in, 486
    data model for, 460–461
        locking, 461
        regions, 461
    history of, 460
    installing, 464–467
    loading data, 473–476
    metrics for, 485
    overview, 461–464
    querying data, 476–479
    schemas for, 472, 486
        joins, 486
        row keys, 486
    Streamy.com case study, 481–483
    UI for, 485
    versions for, 483–484
    vs. RDBMS, 479–483
HBase-specific commands, 465
hbase.client class, 468
hbase.client.scanner.caching, 478
hbase.regionserver.lease.period, 478
HBaseAdmin class, 468
HBaseSerDe class, 437
HBaseTemperatureCli class, 474
HBaseTemperatureImporter class, 474
HBaseTemperatureMapper class, 474
HDFS (Hadoop Distributed Filesystem), 3
    administration of, 339–351
        audit logging, 346
        balancer program, 350–351
        datanode block scanner, 349–350
        datanode directory structure, 343–344
        dfsadmin, 347
        edit log, 340–342
        fsck, 347–349
        fsimage file, 340–342

namenode directory structure, 339–340
  safe mode, 344–346
  secondary namenode directory
      structure, 342–343
and Hadoop Filesystems, 52–55
and HBase, 484–485
and high-availability, 48–49
balancer tool for, 76–77
blocks in, 45–46
command-line interface for, 49–52
copying in parallel with distcp, 75–77
daemon properties for, 312–314
data flow for, 67–74
  coherency model of, 72–74
  reading files, 67–69
  writing files, 70–72
data integrity in, 81–82
datanodes in, 46–47
design of, 43–44
federation in, 47
for clusters, block size, 317
formatting, for pseudodistributed mode,
    621
HAR files in, 77–79
  creating, 77–78
  deleting, 78
  limitations of, 79
Java interface for, 55–67
  creating directories, 62
  deleting data, 67
  FileStatus class, 62–66
  PathFilter class, 66–67
  reading data from URL, 55–57
  reading data using FileSystem API, 57–
    60
  writing data, 60–62
namenodes in, 46–47
using Flume with, 74–75
using Sqoop with, 75
Hedwig publish-subscribe system, 522
help command, 371
herd effect, and ZooKeeper, 520
hexdump, 436
hflush( ) method, 73
high-availability of HDFS, 48–49
history
  of Hadoop, 9–12
  of HBase, 460
Hive

and Sqoop, 537–539
configuring, 417–419
example using, 416–417
Facebook case study, 562–565
  data organization, 563
  data pipelines, 564–565
  improvements to, 567
  query language, 563
HiveQL, 425–429
  conversions in, 429
  data types, 426–428
  functions, 428–429
  operators, 428–429
installing, 414–416
metastore, 421–423
querying data, 444–451
  in MapReduce scripts, 445
  joins, 446–449
  sorting, 444
  subqueries, 449–450
  views, 450–451
services for, 419–421
shell for, 415–416
tables in, 429–444
  altering, 443
  buckets, 433–435
  CREATE TABLE...AS SELECT
    statement, 442
  dropping, 443–444
  INSERT statement, 441
  managed tables vs. external tables, 429–
    431
  multitable insert, 442
  partitions, 431–433
  storage formats, 435–440
UDFs, 451–457
  example of, 452–454
  UDAFs, 454–457
vs. databases, 423–425
  indexes, 424–425
  schema on read vs. schema on write,
    423–424
  transactions, 424–425
  updates, 424–425
hive command, 414, 415, 417, 418, 419
hive.enforce.bucketing property, 434
HiveQL, 415
HIVE_AUX_JARS_PATH environment
    variable, 454

HIVE_CONF_DIR environment variable, 417
HIVE_PORT environment variable, 419
HopWritable object, 585, 586
HPROF profiler, 179–181
hsync( ) method, 73
HTable class, 468, 474, 475, 476, 477
HTable.flushCommits( ) method, 476
HTable.getScanner( ) method, 478
HTable.put(put) method, 476
HTable.setAutoFlush(false) class, 476
HTTP interface, for Hadoop Filesystems, 53–54
hypothetical case study, for large ad networks, 559–562

I

IDE (integrated development environment), setting up, 146
    managing configurations, 148–150
    using GenericOptionsParser, 150
    using Tool, 150
    using ToolRunner, 150
idempotent operation, 517
IdentityMapper, 555, 586
IDL (interface description language), 109–110
If object, 118
imok, 491
importing data, with Sqoop
    and consistency, 536
    controlling, 535–536
    direct-mode imports, 536
    formats for, 532
    large objects, 540–542
impression_logs, 564, 565
incrCounter( ) method, 195
incrementColumnValue( ) method, 486
Indexer class, 11, 579
Indexer tool, in Nutch case study, 578–580
indexing
    and Hive, 424–425
    of Text class, 98
indexOf( ) method, 100
IndexWriter class, 580
IndexWriter.addIndexes( ) methods, 587
Infochimps case study, 607–615
    community extraction, 613–615
    measuring communities, 609
    symmetric links, 612–613
    Twitter reply graph, 609–612

init( ) method, 455
initializing jobs
    in MapReduce 1, 191–192
    in MapReduce 2, 199
initLimit, 524
Inlink class, 573
Inlinks class, 569, 573, 579
inner joins, in Hive, 446–447
input formats, for MapReduce, 234–251
    CombineFileInputFormat class, 239–240
    database, 251
    FileInputFormat class, 236–242
    KeyValueTextInputFormat class, 247
    multiple inputs, 250–251
    NLineInputFormat class, 247–248
    preventing splitting, 241
    processing whole file as record, 242–245
    SequenceFileAsBinaryInputFormat class, 250
    SequenceFileAsTextInputFormat class, 250
    SequenceFileInputFormat class, 249–250
    TextInputFormat class, 246
    XML, 248–249
input.regex property, 440
InputFormat class, 79, 235, 236, 237, 246, 247, 250, 275, 397, 535, 577, 584, 585, 586, 588
InputSampler class, 275, 276, 277
InputSplit, 234, 235, 241, 245
InputStream class, 118, 541
INSERT statement, in Hive, 441
installing
    Apache Whirr, 334–335
    fully distributed mode, 622
    Hadoop, 302–303
    HBase, 464–467
    Hive, 414–416
    Java, 302
    location for, 617–618
    Pig, 368
    prerequisites for, 617
    pseudodistributed mode, 619–622
        configuring SSH, 620–621
        formatting HDFS filesystem, 621
        starting and stopping daemons, 621, 622
    standalone mode, 619
    ZooKeeper, 490–492
Integer class, 108, 393, 534, 536

INTEGER constant, 393
integrated development environment (see IDE)
interface description language (IDL), 109–110
interfaces for Hadoop Filesystems, 53–55
    C library, 55
    FUSE, 55
    HTTP, 53–54
    Java, 55–67
InterfaceStability.Evolving, 16
InterfaceStability.Stable, 16
InterfaceStability.Unstable, 16
interrupt( ) method, 516
InterruptedException, 516
IntervalSampler, 277
IntPair, 281
IntSumReducer, 295
IntWritable class, 23, 94, 95, 96, 97, 132, 154,
        156, 181, 249, 269, 270, 455, 456
InvokeForDouble, 396
InvokeForFloat, 396
InvokeForInt, 396
InvokeForLong, 396
InvokeForString, 396
io.bytes.per.checksum property, 81, 82
io.map.index.skip property, 140
io.mapfile.bloom.error.rate parameter, 141
io.mapfile.bloom.size parameter, 141
io.seqfile.compress.blocksize property, 137
io.serializations property, 108, 133
io.sort.factor property, 209, 210
io.sort.mb property, 209, 212, 213
IOException, 58, 67, 70, 82, 89, 138, 183, 519
IOUtils class, 56, 86, 244
isAlive( ) method, 512
IsEmpty, 388
IsGoodQuality, 391, 395
IsolationRunner, 177
isSplitable( ) method, 241, 242
isValidTemperature( ) method, 160
iterate( ) method, 455, 456, 457
iteration, of Text class, 100

J

Java
    clients for HBase, 467–470
    environment variables for clusters, 309
    installing, 302
    interface for HDFS, 55–67
        creating directories, 62

deleting data, 67
FileStatus class, 62–66
PathFilter class, 66–67
reading data from URL, 55–57
reading data using FileSystem API, 57–
    60
writing data, 60–62
    secondary sort in, 279–281
java command, 153
Java Data Objects (JDO), 422
Java Management Extensions (JMX), 355–357,
    355
Java Virtual Machine (JVM), 26, 219–220
java.io class, 58
java.io.ByteArrayOutputStream, 94
java.io.DataInputStream, 58
java.io.DataOutput, 94, 137
java.io.DataOutputStream, 94
java.io.Externalizable, 109
java.io.File, 117, 144, 294
java.io.FileFilter, 66
java.io.InputStream, 58, 541
java.io.OutputStream, 117
java.io.Reader, 541
java.io.Serializable, 109
java.lang.CharSequence interface, 113
java.lang.Comparable, 95, 591
java.lang.InterruptedException, 28
java.lang.Iterable, 28
java.lang.Iterator, 28
java.lang.Object, 105
java.lang.String, 98, 101, 383, 394, 500
java.lang.System class, 153
java.library.path, 88
java.net.URI class, 500, 572
java.net.URL class, 572
java.net.URL object, 55
java.util.zip.DeflaterInputStream, 85
java.util.zip.DeflaterOutputStream, 85
JavaSerialization, 108
JAVA_HOME environment variable, 309, 368,
    618
JDO (Java Data Objects), 422
JMX (Java Management Extensions), 355–357,
    355
Job class, 24, 25, 28, 35, 163, 164, 165, 166,
        187, 190, 192, 195, 202, 225, 236,
        268, 271, 292, 294
Job control, 28

job counters, 263
Job object, 24, 157, 189
job page, in MapReduce Web UI, 168
job scheduler, for clusters, 318
job-tracker, 186
job.end.notification.url property, 196
job.setMapperClass( ) method, 251
JobBuilder class, 229
JobClient, 28, 207, 267
JobConf class, 28, 41, 162, 179, 217, 219, 225,
     258, 271, 288, 554
JobConf object, 28, 92, 241
JobContext, 294
JobContext.NUM_MAP_PROFILES, 180
JobContext.NUM_REDUCE_PROFILES, 180
JobContext.TASK_PROFILE, 180
JobContext.TASK_PROFILE_PARAMS, 180
JobControl class, 183, 184
jobs
    benchmarking, 333–334
    converting problem into, 181–183
    in MapReduce model, 30
    launching, 163–165
    packaging, 162–163
        classpath precedence, 163
        client classpath for, 162
        dependencies for, 163
        task classpath for, 162–163
    running in MapReduce 1, 190–196
        job completion, 195–196
        job initialization, 191–192
        job submission, 190–191
        status updates, 193–195
        task assignment, 192
        task execution, 193
    running in MapReduce 2, 196–202
        job completion, 202
        job initialization, 199
        job submission, 199
        status updates, 201–202
        task assignment, 200
        task execution, 200–201
    running using Apache Whirr, 337
    scheduling, 206–208
        using Capacity Scheduler, 207–208
        using Fair Scheduler, 207
    side data distribution in configuration, 288–
        289
JobStatus, 195

JobSummitter, 190
JobTracker class, 9, 190, 191, 352
jobtrackers
    failure of, with MapReduce 1, 204
    in MapReduce model, 30
    page for, in MapReduce Web UI, 165–168
JOIN statement, in Pig, 402–403
join( ) method, 496
JoinGroup, 495, 496, 497
joins, 283–288
    for groups in ZooKeeper, 495–496
    for HBase, 486
    in Hive, 446–449
        inner joins, 446–447
        map joins, 449
        outer joins, 447–448
        semi joins, 448
    map-side joins, 284–285
    reduce-side joins, 285–288
jps command, 622
JSON objects, 599
JsonLoader, 389
JVM (Java Virtual Machine), 26, 219–220
JVMFLAGS, 524

K

kdestroy command, 328
KeeperException, in ZooKeeper, 516–517
    recoverable exceptions, 517
    state exceptions, 516
    unrecoverable exceptions, 517
KeeperException.BadVersionException, 516
KeeperException.Code.NONODE, 516
KeeperException.Code.SESSIONEXPIRED,
    518
KeeperException.ConnectionLossException,
    517
KeeperException.NoNodeException, 497, 516
KeeperException.SessionExpiredException,
    518, 519
KeeperState, 511, 512, 519
Kerberos, 326–328, 327
KeyFieldBasedComparator, 282, 283
KeyFieldBasedPartitioner, 282, 283
KEYIN, 224
KeyValueTextInputFormat class, 247, 252
kill control, 185
kinit command, 327, 328, 329
klist command, 328

ktutil command, 327, 330

L

large ad networks, hypothetical case study for, 559–562
large objects, and Sqoop, 540–542
Last.fm case study, 547–556
    generating charts, 548–549
    Track Statistics program, 549–555
        calculating unique listeners, 550–551
        merging results, 554–555
        summing track totals, 552–553
LazyBinarySerDe, 437
LazyOutputFormat class, 257–258, 257, 258
LazySimpleSerDe, 436, 437
leaderServes property, 507
ledgers, 522
LIKE statement, 444
LIMIT statement, 408, 426
LineRecordReader, 585
LineStreamer, 610
link inversion, Nutch case study, 571–573
LinkDb, 568, 569
LinuxTaskController, 330
list command, 466
list( ) method, 497
listblocks, 350
ListGroup, 497
listStatus( ) method, 64, 66
ListWritable, 103
LOAD statement, 372, 377, 384, 430
LoadCaster interface, 398
LoadFunc, 397, 398, 399
loading
    data, in HBase, 473–476
    UDF, for Pig, 396–399
LoadMetadata class, 399
LoadPushDown class, 399
local job runner, for MapReduce applications, 157–160
local method, 294
local mode, for Pig, 369
LocalFileSystem class, 82–83, 82, 83
localhost, 50, 531
location, for installing, 617–618
Lock Service example, 519–521
    herd effect, 520
    recoverable exceptions, 520–521
    unrecoverable exceptions, 521

locking, in HBase, 461
logging, 352
    for Hive, 419
    for MapReduce applications, 175–177
    getting stack traces, 352
    log levels, 352
long type, 239
Long.MAX_VALUE, 238, 239, 241
LongWritable, 23, 130, 158, 224, 225, 230, 231, 232, 246
ls command, 55, 376
LuceneDocumentWrapper, 579, 580
LzoCodec, 85
LzopCodec, 85

M

macros, in Pig Latin, 390–391
MAGIC_PARAMETER, 215
main( ) method, 41, 151, 468, 494
maintenance, 358–365
    commissioning new nodes, 359–360
    data backups, 358–359
    decommissioning old nodes, 361–362
    filesystem balancer, 359
    filesystem check, 359
    metadata backups, 358
makeObservationRowKey( ) method, 475
malformed data, handling, 174
managed tables, in Hive, 429–431
Map class, 477
map joins, in Hive, 449
map( ) method, 23, 29, 41, 235, 236, 261, 288, 427, 572, 573
map-side joins, 284–285
MapContext, 41
MapDriver, 154, 155
MapFile
    converting SequenceFile to, 141–142
    reading, 140–141
    variants of, 141
    writing, 138–140
MapFile.Reader, 140, 273
MapFile.Writer, 138, 139
MapFileInputFormat class, 250
MapFileOutputFormat class, 253, 271, 272, 568, 569, 573, 575
Mapper class, 22, 27, 29, 37, 41, 125, 155, 215, 224, 230, 241, 250, 288, 470, 579, 598

mapred.child.java.opts property, 177, 211, 307, 315, 319, 321, 323
mapred.hosts property, 317, 360
mapred.hosts.exclude property, 361
mapred.job.id property, 215
mapred.job.priority property, 207
mapred.job.tracker property, 158, 161, 189, 314, 369, 418
mapred.local.dir property, 178, 209, 314, 322
mapred.map.max.attempts property, 203, 221
mapred.max.split.size property, 238, 240
mapred.output.compress property, 90
mapred.output.compression.codec property, 90
mapred.reduce.parallel.copies property, 210
mapred.reduce.tasks property, 192
mapred.submit.replication property, 191
mapred.system.dir property, 315
mapred.task.profile.params property, 180
mapred.task.timeout property, 203
mapred.tasktracker.expiry.interval property, 204
mapred.text.key.comparator.options property, 282
mapred.userlog.limit.kb property, 177
mapred.userlog.retain.hours, 177
mapred.work.output.dir, 219
MapReduce
    benchmarking, 332–333
    compression in, 90–92
    daemon properties for, 314–315
    in HBase, 469–470
    in Hive, 445
    job scheduling in, 206–208
        using Capacity Scheduler, 207–208
        using Fair Scheduler, 207
    mode for Pig, 369–370
    shuffle process, 208–213
        map side of, 208–209
        performance tuning of, 211–213
        reduce side of, 210–211
    task execution, 214–221
        environment for, 215
        output committers for, 217–219
        reusing JVM for, 219–220
        skipping bad records, 220–221
        speculative execution of, 215–217
    using in Avro, 124, 128–129
MapReduce 1

failures with, 202–204
    of jobtracker, 204
    of tasks, 202–204
    of tasktracker, 204
running job with, 190–196
    job completion, 195–196
    job initialization, 191–192
    job submission, 190–191
    status updates, 193–195
    task assignment, 192
    task execution, 193
MapReduce 2 (YARN), 320–324
    daemon properties, 321–324
        addresses and ports, 324
        memory, 323–324
    failures with, 204–206
        application master failure, 205
        node manager failure, 205–206
        of tasks, 205
        resource manager failure, 206
    running job with, 196–202
        job completion, 202
        job initialization, 199
        job submission, 199
        status updates, 201–202
        task assignment, 200
        task execution, 200–201
MapReduce applications
    Configuration API, 144–146
        adding resources to, 145
        properties in, 146
    performance tuning, 178–181
        profiling tasks, 179–181
    running locally on test data, 157–161
        in local job runner, 157–160
        testing driver, 160–161
    running on cluster, 161–178
        debugging, 170–174
        launching job, 163–165
        logs for, 175–177
        MapReduce Web UI, 165–168
        packaging job, 162–163
        retrieving results, 168–170
    setting up IDE, 146–153
        managing configurations, 148–150
        using GenericOptionsParser, 150–153
        using Tool, 150–153
        using ToolRunner, 150–153

unit testing with MRUnit testing library, 154–156
    mapper, 154–156
    reducer, 156
workflows for, 181–187
    converting problem into MapReduce jobs, 181–183
    JobControl class, 183
    using Apache Oozie, 183–187
MapReduce formats
  input, 234–251
    CombineFileInputFormat class, 239–240
    database, 251
    FileInputFormat class, 236–242
    KeyValueTextInputFormat class, 247
    multiple inputs, 250–251
    NLineInputFormat class, 247–248
    preventing splitting, 241
    processing whole file as record, 242–245
    SequenceFileAsBinaryInputFormat class, 250
    SequenceFileAsTextInputFormat class, 250
    SequenceFileInputFormat class, 249–250
    TextInputFormat class, 246
    XML, 248–249
  output, 251–258
    database, 251
    LazyOutputFormat class, 257–258
    MapFileOutputFormat class, 253
    MultipleOutputs class, 253–257
    SequenceFileAsBinaryOutputFormat class, 253
    SequenceFileOutputFormat class, 253
    text, 252
MapReduce library classes, 295
MapReduce model
  and data locality, 7
  and normalization, 6
  and RDBMS, 5
  APIs for
    and releases for Hadoop, 15
    differences between, 27–29
  Hadoop Pipes, 40–42
  Hadoop Streaming, 36–40
    in Python, 39–40

    in Ruby, 36–39
  jobs, 30
  jobtrackers, 30
  partitions, 33
  scaling, 30–36
    combiner functions for, 33–35
    data flow for, 30–33
  splits, 30
  tasktrackers, 30
  vs. SETI@home, 8
  weather dataset, 17–19
    analyzing with Hadoop, 20–29
    analyzing with Unix tools, 19–20
    data format for, 17–19
    Java class for, 22–29
MapReduce types
  in default job, 223–232
  in default Streaming job, 232–233
MapReduce Web UI, 165–168
  job page, 168
  jobtracker page, 165–168
mapreduce.framework.name property, 158, 189, 199, 322
mapreduce.input.keyvaluelinerecordreader.key.value.separator property, 247
mapreduce.input.lineinputformat.linespermap, 247
mapreduce.job.acl-modify-job, 330
mapreduce.job.acl-view-job, 330
mapreduce.job.hdfs-servers, 329
mapreduce.job.maxtaskfailures.per.tracker, 206
mapreduce.job.name, 15
mapreduce.job.reduces property, 199
mapreduce.job.ubertask.enable, 199
mapreduce.job.ubertask.maxbytes, 199
mapreduce.job.ubertask.maxmaps, 199
mapreduce.job.ubertask.maxreduces, 199
mapreduce.map.failures.maxpercent, 205
mapreduce.map.java.opts, 321
mapreduce.map.maxattempts, 205
mapreduce.map.memory.mb, 200, 323
mapreduce.output.textoutputformat.separator, 252
mapreduce.reduce.failures.maxpercent, 205
mapreduce.reduce.java.opts, 321
mapreduce.reduce.maxattempts, 205
mapreduce.reduce.memory.mb, 200
mapreduce.shuffle, 322

mapreduce.task.classpath.first, 163
MapRunnable, 28
MapRunner class, 577, 578
MapWritable, 102, 103
MAP_INPUT_RECORDS, 260
master node scenarios, for clusters, 306–307
MAX function, 373, 387, 388, 393, 417, 451, 593
MaximumFloatUDAFEvaluator, 455
MaximumIntUDAFEvaluator, 455
MaximumLongUDAFEvaluator, 455
MaxTemperature, 28
MaxTemperatureByStationNameUsingDistrib utedCacheFile, 290
MaxTemperatureDriver class, 157, 158, 161, 164, 179
MaxTemperatureDriverMiniTest class, 161
MaxTemperatureMapper class, 41, 127, 155, 251, 474, 476
MaxTemperatureReducer, 35, 127, 156, 291
MaxWidgetId class, 537
MaxWidgetId.run( ) method, 537
MaxWidgetIdGenericAvro, 537
max_by_group macro, 390
max_field parameter, 390
membership
    for clusters, 317
    for groups in ZooKeeper, 492–493
memory
    environment variables for clusters, 307–309
    for MapReduce 2, daemon properties, 323–324
merge( ) method, 136, 456, 457
MergeAgent, 587
merging
    schemas, for Pig Latin, 387–388
    SequenceFile, 136
message-id class, 583
metadata backups, 358
metastore, 414, 421–423, 421
metastore.uris, 423
METASTORE_PORT, 419, 423
MetOfficeMaxTemperatureMapper, 251
metrics, 352–355
    CompositeContext class, 355
    FileContext class, 353–354
    for HBase, 485
    GangliaContext class, 354

NullContextWithUpdateThread class, 354–355
MetricsContext, 353, 355, 356
MIME type, 570
min.num.spills.for.combine property, 209
MiniDFSCluster, 161
MinimalMapReduce, 228
MinimalMapReduceWithDefaults, 230
MiniMRCluster, 161
MiniYARNCluster, 161
mkdirs( ) method, 62
mntr command, 492
monitoring, 351–357
    logging, 352
        getting stack traces, 352
        log levels, 352
    metrics, 352–355
        CompositeContext class, 355
        FileContext class, 353–354
        GangliaContext class, 354
        NullContextWithUpdateThread class, 354–355
    using JMX, 355–357
moveToTrash( ) method, 318
MRAppMaster, 199
MRBench, 333
MRUnit testing library, unit testing with, 154–156
    mapper, 154–156
    reducer, 156
MultipleInputs class, 250, 251, 285, 554
MultipleOutputFormat, 253
MultipleOutputs class, 253, 254–257, 255, 257
MultipleSequenceFileOutputFormat, 586
MultiSequenceFileOutputFormat, 586
multitable insert, in Hive, 442
MultithreadedMapper, 236, 295
MultithreadedMapRunner, 295
multiupdate, for ZooKeeper, 502
mutability, of Text class, 101
mysqldump, 536
mysqlimport, 544

N

namenode, 46, 461
namenode-host, 357
namenodes, in HDFS, 46–47, 339–340
names parameter, 301

namespace, 113
namespaceID, 340, 344
native libraries, for compression, 87–89
NavigableMap, 478
NCDC weather data, preparing, 625–627
NcdcRecordParser, 474
NDFS (Nutch DistributedFilesystem), 9
needsTaskCommit( ) method, 218
network topology
    for clusters, 299–301
    rack awareness in Hadoop, 300–301
New York Times example, using Hadoop, 10
newTuple( ) method, 398
NEW_HADOOP_INSTALL, 364
next( ) method, 118, 132, 133, 134, 140, 244,
    273, 478
nextKeyValue( ) method, 235, 236, 243
NLineInputFormat class, 219, 247–248, 247,
    626
NNBench, 333
NoChildrenForEphemeralsException, 516
node manager, in MapReduce 2, 205–206
NodeChildrenChanged, 504
NodeCreated, 504
NodeDataChanged, 504
NodeDeleted, 504
nodes
    commissioning, 359–360
    decommissioning, 361–362
normalization, and MapReduce model, 6
NullContext, 353, 354, 355, 356
NullContextWithUpdateThread class, 354–
    355, 354, 355, 356
NullOutputFormat, 252
nulls, in Pig Latin, 385–387
NullWritable class, 101, 102, 103, 240, 242,
    252, 281
NullWritable.get( ) method, 102
NumberFormatException, 155
numParts class, 576
Nutch case study, 567–581
    data structures, 568–571
        CrawlDb, 569
        LinkDb, 569
        segments, 569–571
    Fetcher application in, 577–578
    generating fetchlists, 573–577
    Indexer tool in, 578–580
    link inversion, 571–573

Nutch DistributedFilesystem (NDFS), 9
NutchWritable class, 578, 579

O

Object object, 392
ObjectWritable class, 102
OLD_HADOOP_INSTALL, 364
Oozie (see Apache Oozie)
oozie command, 187
oozie.wf.application.path, 187
OOZIE_URL, 187
open( ) method, 57, 58, 67, 82
OPEN_ACL_UNSAFE, 506
operators
    for Pig, 399–409
        COGROUP statement, 403–405
        CROSS statement, 405–406
        FOREACH…GENERATE statement,
            400–401
        GROUP statement, 406–407
        JOIN statement, 402–403
        ORDER statement, 407–408
        SPLIT statement, 408–409
        storing data, 399
        STREAM statement, 401–402
        UNION statement, 408–409
    in Hive, 428–429
ORDER statement, 407–408
org.apache.avro.mapred, 124, 130
org.apache.avro.mapred.AvroMapper, 127
org.apache.avro.mapred.AvroReducer, 127
org.apache.avro.mapred.Pair object, 127, 129
org.apache.avro.mapred.tether, 130
org.apache.avro.specific.SchemaTask, 116
org.apache.hadoop.classification, 16
org.apache.hadoop.conf, 144
org.apache.hadoop.conf.Configuration class,
    468
org.apache.hadoop.examples.Join, 285
org.apache.hadoop.filecache.DistributedCach
    e, 292
org.apache.hadoop.fs.FileSystem, 52
org.apache.hadoop.fs.RawLocalFileSystem,
    83
org.apache.hadoop.hbase.client.Get class, 468
org.apache.hadoop.hbase.client.Scan class,
    468, 470
org.apache.hadoop.hbase.filter.FirstKeyOnlyF
    ilter class, 470

org.apache.hadoop.hbase.HBaseConfiguratio n class, 468

org.apache.hadoop.hbase.HColumnDescripto r class, 468

org.apache.hadoop.hbase.HTable class, 486

org.apache.hadoop.hbase.mapreduce class, 469

org.apache.hadoop.hive.jdbc.HiveDriver class, 421

org.apache.hadoop.hive.ql.exec.UDAF class, 455

org.apache.hadoop.hive.ql.exec.UDAFEvaluat or class, 455

org.apache.hadoop.hive.ql.exec.UDF class, 453

org.apache.hadoop.io, 23, 96, 102, 103, 107

org.apache.hadoop.io.retry, 519

org.apache.hadoop.io.serializer, 108

org.apache.hadoop.io.serializer.WritableSerial ization, 108

org.apache.hadoop.mapred, 28, 234

org.apache.hadoop.mapred.FileInputFormat $Counter, 260

org.apache.hadoop.mapred.FileOutputForma t$Counter, 260

org.apache.hadoop.mapred.jobcontrol, 183

org.apache.hadoop.mapred.JobInProgress $Counter, 260

org.apache.hadoop.mapred.JobTracker, 352

org.apache.hadoop.mapred.LinuxTaskContro ller, 203, 330

org.apache.hadoop.mapred.Task$Counter, 260

org.apache.hadoop.mapred.Task.Counter, 268

org.apache.hadoop.mapreduce, 28, 234, 398

org.apache.hadoop.mapreduce.FileSystemCo unter, 260

org.apache.hadoop.mapreduce.jobcontrol, 183

org.apache.hadoop.mapreduce.JobCounter, 260

org.apache.hadoop.mapreduce.join, 285

org.apache.hadoop.mapreduce.lib.input.FileI nputFormatCounter, 260

org.apache.hadoop.mapreduce.lib.output.File OutputFormatCounter, 260

org.apache.hadoop.mapreduce.Mapper, 470

org.apache.hadoop.mapreduce.TaskCounter, 260, 268

org.apache.hadoop.record, 109

org.apache.hadoop.streaming, 249

org.apache.hadoop.streaming.StreamXmlReco rdReader, 249

org.apache.hadoop.yarn.server.resourcemana ger.recovery.MemStore, 206

org.apache.pig, 401

org.apache.pig.builtin, 393

org.apache.pig.builtin.MAX, 393

org.apache.sqoop.lib.SqoopRecord, 545

Other databases, 449

outer joins, in Hive, 447–448

Outlink class, 573

output committers, for tasks, 217–219

output formats, for MapReduce, 251–258
  database, 251
  LazyOutputFormat class, 257–258
  MapFileOutputFormat class, 253
  MultipleOutputs class, 253–257
  SequenceFileAsBinaryOutputFormat class, 253
  SequenceFileOutputFormat class, 253
  text, 252

output.field.separator, 233

OutputCollector class, 28, 218, 261, 545

OutputCommitter, 192, 193, 217, 219

OutputFormat class, 217, 247, 251, 252, 257, 397, 545, 578, 579, 580, 584, 586

outputSchema( ) method, 395

OutputStream class, 117

OVERWRITE keyword, 417, 441

P

packaging jobs
  classpath precedence, 163
  client classpath for, 162
  dependencies for, 163
  task classpath for, 162–163

parallel-dump, 536

parallelism, with Pig, 409

parameter substitution, in Pig, 410–411
  dynamic parameters, 410–411
  processing of, 411

parse( ) method, 159, 537

ParseData class, 572, 579

parseInt( ) method, 155

ParseWordsAssembly class, 598

parse_data class, 570, 571
parse_text class, 570, 571
partial sort, 270–274
PartialResult class, 457
PARTITION clause, 441
Partitioner class, 287, 574, 575, 586
PartitionReducer class, 576
partitions, 431
    in Hive, 431–433
    in MapReduce model, 33
PartitionUrlByHost class, 575, 576
Path class, 118, 500
Path object, 57, 60, 86, 219
PathFilter class, 64, 65, 66–67, 66, 67, 238
paths, for FileInputFormat class, 236–238
patterns, in FileStatus class, 65–66
performance tuning, 178–181
    of shuffle process, 211–213
    of ZooKeeper, 523–524
    profiling tasks, 179–181
Person object, 594
PHYSICAL_MEMORY_BYTES, 260, 324
Pig
    data processing operators, 399–409
        COGROUP statement, 403–405
        CROSS statement, 405–406
        FOREACH...GENERATE statement,
            400–401
        GROUP statement, 406–407
        JOIN statement, 402–403
        ORDER statement, 407–408
        SPLIT statement, 408–409
        storing data, 399
        STREAM statement, 401–402
        UNION statement, 408–409
    example of, 371–374
    execution types, 368–370
        local mode, 369
        MapReduce mode, 369–370
    Grunt shell for, 370–371
    installing, 368
    parallelism with, 409
    parameter substitution in, 410–411
        dynamic parameters, 410–411
        processing of, 411
    Pig Latin, 375–391
        expressions in, 381
        functions in, 388–390
        macros in, 390–391

        schemas for, 384–388
        statements in, 377–381
        structure of, 376–377
        types in, 382–384
    Pig Latin editors, 371
    running Pig programs, 370
    UDFs, 391–399
        and dynamic invokers, 395–396
        eval UDF, 394–396
        filter UDF, 391–394
        load UDF, 396–399
        vs. databases, 374–375
pig.exec.reducers.bytes.per.reducer, 409
pig.exec.reducers.max, 409
PigMix, 333
PigRunner, 370
PigServer class, 370
PigStorage, 383, 388
PigToStream, 401
Pipe class, 597
pipes command, 42
Pipes, in task execution, 193
PLATFORM environment variable, 42
ports, daemon properties
    for clusters, 316–317
    for MapReduce 2, 324
PositionedReadable, 59
prepareToRead( ) method, 398
prerequisites, for installion, 617
primitive types, for Hive, 427–428
process( ) method, 494, 515, 610
profiling tasks, 179–181
progress( ) method, 61, 195
pseudodistributed mode, 619–622
    configuring SSH, 620–621
    formatting HDFS filesystem, 621
    starting and stopping daemons, 621, 622
Python
    API for Avro, 118–119
    Hadoop Streaming in, 39–40

Q

querying data
    in HBase, 476–479
    in Hive, 444–451
        in MapReduce scripts, 445
        joins, 446–449
        sorting, 444
        subqueries, 449–450

views, 450–451
QueueFeeder, 578

R

rack awareness, in Hadoop, 300–301
Rackspace case study, 581–589
    log collection, 582–583
    log storage, 583
    mail log processing, 583–589
        archiving, 587–589
        Map stage, 585, 586
        merging, 587
        Reduce stage, 585, 586
    need for Hadoop, 581–582
RAID (Redundant Array of Independent
        Disks), 298
RaidNode, 53
RAMDirectory, 587
rand( ) function, 435
RandomSampler, 276, 277
RandomWriter, 332, 333
Range class, 398
RawComparator class, 95, 96, 106–107, 106,
        107, 179, 271
RawLocalFileSystem, 52, 83
RCFiles, storage formats in Hive, 438–439
RDBMS (relational database management
        systems)
    and MapReduce model, 5
    vs. Hadoop, 4–6
    vs. HBase, 479–483
read( ) method, 59, 68, 115, 514, 515
readable names, for counters, 266
readFields( ) method, 105, 534
reading data
    data flow for, 67–69
    from URL, 55–57
    MapFile, 140–141
    SequenceFile, 132–135
    using FileSystem API, 57–60
RecordReader class, 235, 236, 242, 261, 398
records, processing whole file as, 242–245
RecordWriter class, 580
recoverable exceptions, in ZooKeeper, 517,
        520–521
REDUCE clause, 425, 445
reduce( ) method, 28, 29, 257, 261, 287, 288,
        572, 573, 577
reduce-side joins, 285–288

Reducer class, 23, 29, 35, 41, 125, 215, 224,
        231, 288, 579, 598
Redundant Array of Independent Disks
        (RAID), 298
ReflectionUtils, 86, 133
RegexSerDe, 437, 440
regions, in HBase, 461
relational database management systems (see
        RDBMS)
releases for Hadoop, 13–16
    and configuration names, 15
    and MapReduce APIs, 15
    compatibility of, 15–16
removeSuffix( ) method, 87
reportChecksumFailure( ) method, 83
Reporter object, 28, 266
reserved storage space, for clusters, 317
Resilient Applications example, 515–519
    InterruptedException, 516
    KeeperException, 516–517
        recoverable exceptions, 517
        state exceptions, 516
        unrecoverable exceptions, 517
resource manager, in MapReduce 2, 206
resources, in MapReduce Configuration API,
        145
REST clients, for HBase, 471
Result class, 477
result.getLeft( ) method, 117
ResultScanner class, 478
ResultSet class, 534, 535
RETRY_PERIOD_SECONDS, 518
rolling back, upgrades, 364–365
row keys, for HBase, 486
RowCounter class, 469, 470
RowCounterMapper class, 470
RowKeyConverter class, 475
Ruby, Hadoop Streaming in, 36–39
run( ) method, 28, 151, 157, 229, 235, 236,
        514
runJob( ) method, 183
RunningJob object, 267
runTask( ) method, 41
runTest( ) method, 154
ruok command, 491

S

Safari® Books Online, xxi
safe mode, for HDFS, 344–346

Sampler interface, 275, 277
sampling, 275
scaling, MapReduce model, 30–36
    combiner functions for, 33–35
    data flow for, 30–33
Scan class, 478
scheduling jobs, 206–208
    using Capacity Scheduler, 207–208
    using Fair Scheduler, 207
schema on read, 423–424
schema on write, 423–424
schema resolution, in Avro, 121–123
schemas
    for HBase, 472, 486
        joins, 486
        row keys, 486
    for Pig Latin, 384–388
        merging of, 387–388
        validation and nulls, 385–387
Scheme class, 594, 596
Scribe-HDFS integration, Facebook case study,
        567
script.pig, 370
ScriptBasedMapping, 301
scrobble, 549
secondary namenode directory structure, for
        HDFS, 342–343
secondary sort, 277–283
    in Java, 279–281
    in Streaming, 281–283
security, 325–330
    and delegation tokens, 328–329
    enhancements to, 329–330
    using Kerberos, 326–328
security.datanode.protocol.acl, 330
seek( ) method, 58, 60, 118, 134
segments, Nutch case study, 569–571
SELECT statement, 415, 417, 430, 441, 442,
        443, 444, 447, 448, 449, 450, 451,
        542
Selector class, 574, 575
Selector.reduce( ) method, 575
SelectorEntry class, 575, 576
SelectorInverseMapper class, 576
semi joins, in Hive, 448
SequenceFile, 130–137
    and Sqoop, 545–546
    converting to MapFile, 141–142
    displaying, 135

format for, 136–137
merging, 136
reading, 132–135
sorting, 136
storage formats in Hive, 438–439
writing, 131–132
SequenceFile.Reader, 132, 133, 135
SequenceFile.Sorter class, 136
SequenceFile.Writer, 131, 132, 134, 135
SequenceFileAsBinaryInputFormat class, 250,
        253
SequenceFileAsBinaryOutputFormat class,
        250, 253
SequenceFileAsTextInputFormat class, 250
SequenceFileInputFormat class, 249–250, 249,
        250, 573, 586
SequenceFileOutputFormat class, 91, 253, 568,
        569, 577
SequenceFileRecordReader, 585
SequenceFiles, 131, 139
sequential znodes, for ZooKeeper, 500–501
SERDE keyword, 440
serialization, 93–110
    BytesWritable class, 101
    custom Writable classes, 103–107
        custom comparators, 107
        RawComparator class, 106–107
    frameworks for, 1, 108–110
        (see also Avro)
    GenericWritable class, 102
    in-memory with Avro, 114–117
    NullWritable class, 102
    ObjectWritable class, 102
    systems for Sqoop, 533
    Text class, 98–101
        converting to String object, 101
        indexing of, 98
        iteration of, 100
        mutability of, 101
        Unicode characters, 99–100
    Writable collection objects, 102–103
    Writable interface, 94–96
    Writable wrappers for Java primitives, 96–
        98
    WritableComparable interface, 95–96
SET command, 418
set( ) method, 94, 96, 101, 103, 293
set( ) methods, 103
setCacheXXXXs( ) method, 293

setData, 502, 504, 516, 517
SetFile, 141
setGroupingComparatorClass( ) method, 281
SETI@home, vs. MapReduce model, 8
setIndexInterval( ) method, 139
setInputPathFilter( ) method, 237, 238
setInputPaths( ) method, 236
setJar( ) method, 162
setJarByClass( ) method, 24, 162
setJobName( ) method, 166
setJobPriority( ) method, 207
setLocation( ) method, 398
setMapOutputKeyClass( ) method, 25, 225,
        576
setMapOutputValueClass( ) method, 25, 576
setMapperClass( ) method, 25, 251
setNumMapTasks( ) method, 238
setNumReduceTasks( ) method, 192, 248
setNumTasksToExecutePerJvm( ) method,
        219
setOutputCommitter( ) method, 217
setOutputCompressionType( ) method, 91
setOutputFormatClass( ) method, 258
setOutputKeyClass( ) method, 25, 225
setOutputKeyComparatorClass( ) method,
        271
setOutputPath( ) method, 24
setOutputValueClass( ) method, 25, 225
setReducerClass( ) method, 25
setsid command, 203
setSortComparatorClass( ) method, 271, 281
setStatus( ) method, 172, 195
setup( ) method, 161, 235, 257, 291, 294
setupJob( ) method, 218
setupTask( ) method, 218
setURLStreamHandlerFactory method, 56
setVerifyChecksum( ) method, 82
ShareThis case study, 599–602
shell, for Hive, 415–416
shuffle process, 208–213
    map side of, 208–209
    performance tuning of, 211–213
    reduce side of, 210–211
side data distribution, 288–294
    through distributed cache, 289–294
        API for, 292–294
        overview, 292
    using job configuration, 288–289
side-effect files, 218–219

single point of failure (SPOF), 48, 204, 490
SIZE function, 387
sizes, of big data, 1–3
skip( ) method, 58
SkipBadRecords class, 221
skipping bad records, in tasks, 220–221
slow start, for clusters, 318
SMALLINT, 427, 429
SocksSocketFactory class, 583
SolrInputFormat, 588
SolrOutputFormat, 586, 587
sort( ) method, 136
SortedMapWritable, 102, 103
sorting, 268–283
    benchmarking, 332–333
    in Avro, 123, 128–129
    in Hive, 444
    partial sort, 270–274
    preparing format for, 269
    secondary sort, 277–283
        in Java, 279–281
        in Streaming, 281–283
    SequenceFile, 136
    total sort, 274–277
SortValidator, 333
SortValidator.RecordStatsChecker, 241
space management, Facebook case study, 566
SpecificDatumWriter, 116
speculative execution of tasks, 215–217
Speculator, 216, 217
SPLIT statement, in Pig, 408–409
splits, 30
    and compression, 89–90
    and FileInputFormat class, 238–239
    in MapReduce model, 30
    preventing, 241
SplitSampler, 277
SPOF (single point of failure), 48, 204, 490
Sqoop
    code generated by, 532–533
    connectors for, 529
    downloading, 527–529
    exporting data with, 542–546
        and SequenceFiles, 545–546
        and transactionality, 545
    importing data with
        and consistency, 536
        controlling, 535–536
        direct-mode imports, 536

formats for, 532
    large objects, 540–542
  processing data, 536–539
  with HDFS, 75
sqoop-export, 545
sqoop-help, 529
sqoop-import, 529
SqoopRecord, 545
SSH configuration
  environment variables for clusters, 310–311
  for pseudodistributed mode, 620–621
  of clusters, 303–304
ssh_config, 310
stack traces, logging of, 352
standalone mode, 619
Standard Template Library (STL), 41
stargate, 471
Stat object, 502, 505, 514
stat parameter, 503
StatCallback interface, 503
state exceptions, in ZooKeeper, 516
statements, in Pig Latin, 377–381
states, of ZooKeeper, 511–512
stationName, 287
status updates
  in MapReduce 2, 201–202
  of jobs, in MapReduce 1, 193–195
STDIN constant, 37
STL (Standard Template Library), 41
STONITH technique, 49
storage formats, in Hive, 435–440
  Avro datafiles, 438–439
  delimited text, 435–437
  example using, 440
  RCFiles, 438–439
  sequence files, 438–439
storageID, 344
storageType, 340, 344
STORE statement, 377, 378, 379
STREAM statement, 401–402
stream.map.input.ignoreKey, 232
stream.non.zero.exit.is.failure, 202
stream.num.map.output.key.fields, 233, 282
stream.recordreader.class property, 249
stream.reduce.output.field.separator, 233
StreamCompressor, 86
Streaming
  environment variables for, 215
  in task execution, 193
  MapReduce types in, 232–233
  secondary sort in, 281–283
Streaming counters, 268
StreamInputFormat, 249
StreamToPig class, 401
StreamXmlRecordReader, 249
Streamy.com case study, 481–483
  benefits of using HBase, 483
  very large items tables, 482
  very large sort merges, 482–483
StrictHostKeyChecking, 310
STRING, 427, 429, 452
String class, converting Text object to, 101
Stringifier class, 288
StringPair class, 115, 116, 118, 123, 124
stringType, 113
StringUtils class, 396, 453
Strip class, 453
STRUCT, 428, 436
struct( ) method, 427
SubAssembly class, 592, 597, 598, 600, 601
submit( ) method, 189, 190
submitApplication( ) method, 199
submitJob( ) method, 191
submitJobInternal( ) method, 190
subqueries, in Hive, 449–450
substring( ) method, 23
SumMapper, 554
SumReducer, 555
sync( ) method, 73, 74, 118, 135
Syncable interface, 135
SyncConnected, 511
syncLimit, 524
System class, 153
system logfiles, 1, 309–310
  (see also Rackspace case study)
System.out, 56, 86

T

TableInputFormat class, 251, 469, 470, 476
TableMapper, 470
TableMapReduceUtil.initTableMapJob( ) method, 470
TableOutputFormat, 251, 469, 476
tables, in Hive, 429–444
  altering, 443
  buckets, 433–435

CREATE TABLE...AS SELECT statement, 442

dropping, 443–444

INSERT statement, 441

managed tables vs. external tables, 429–431

multitable insert, 442

partitions, 431–433

storage formats, 435–440

Avro datafiles, 438–439

delimited text, 435–437

example using, 440

RCFiles, 438–439

sequence files, 438–439

TABLESAMPLE, 434, 435

Tap class, 594, 595, 596, 601, 602

task classpath, for jobs, 162–163

task counters, 260

task details page, debugging, 172–174

task memory limits, for clusters, 318–319

TaskRunner, 193

TaskRuntimeEstimator, 217

tasks, 214–221

environment for, 215

in MapReduce 1

assignment of, 192

execution of, 193

failure of, 202–204

in MapReduce 2

assignment of, 200

execution of, 200–201

failure of, 205

output committers for, 217–219

page for, debugging, 172

reusing JVM for, 219–220

skipping bad records, 220–221

speculative execution of, 215–217

TaskTracker, 190

tasktracker.http.threads property, 209

tasktrackers, 30, 461

failure of, with MapReduce 1, 204

in MapReduce model, 30

tearDown( ) method, 161

TemplateTap, 601

TEMPORARY statement, 453

TeraByte Sort case study, 603–607

TeraGen, 604

TeraSort, 604

TeraValidate, 604, 605

terminate( ) method, 457

terminatePartial( ) method, 456, 457

test.randomwriter.maps_per_host, 332

TestDFSIO, 331–332, 331

testing upgrades, 364

TestTable, 463

Text class, 98–101, 98, 537, 569

and Unicode characters, 99–100

converting to String object, 101

indexing of, 98

iteration of, 100

mutability of, 101

Text object, 23, 100, 105, 106, 154, 236, 245, 246, 287

text, as output format for MapReduce, 252

TextArrayWritable, 106

TEXTFILE, 437

TextInputFormat class, 25, 158, 220, 225, 230, 232, 240, 246, 247, 248, 249, 251, 252, 398, 475, 536

TextOutputFormat class, 105, 232, 233, 247, 252, 257

TextPair class, 104, 105, 106, 107, 281, 286, 287

TGT (GrantingTicket), 326

Thrift clients, for HBase, 471

ThriftByteStreamTypedSerDe, 437

tickTime, 491, 524

time parameters, for ZooKeeper sessions, 510–511

TIMESTAMP data type, 427, 429

TINYINT type, 427, 429

toArray( ) method, 103

TOBAG statement, 383

tojson command, 120

toLowerCase( ) method, 597

TOMAP statement, 383

Tool class, 150–153, 151, 157, 160, 474

ToolRunner, 150–153, 150, 151, 152

topology.node.switch.mapping.impl, 301

topology.script.file.name, 301

toString( ) method, 101, 105, 113, 115, 135, 250, 252, 281

total sort, 274–277

TotalOrderPartitioner, 275, 277

TOTAL_LAUNCHED_MAPS, 263

TOTUPLE, 383

to_utc_timestamp function, 428

Track Statistics program, Last.fm case study, 549–555
    calculating unique listeners, 550–551
    merging results, 554–555
    summing track totals, 552–553
TrackStats object, 552, 554, 555
transactions
    and Hive, 424–425
    and Sqoop, 545
Trash class, 318
trash, for clusters, 318
Trim class, 395
Trim function, 395
trim( ) method, 394
TRUNCATE, 443
Tuple class, 391, 398, 596, 601, 602
TupleFactory, 398
Twitter reply graph, Infochimps case study, 609–612
TwoDArrayWritable, 102, 103
types, in Pig Latin, 382–384

U

UDAFs (user-defined aggregate functions), in Hive, 454
UDFs (user-defined functions)
    for Pig, 391–399
        and dynamic invokers, 395–396
        eval UDF, 394–396
        filter UDF, 391–394
        load UDF, 396–399
    in Hive, 451–457
        example of, 452–454
        UDAFs, 454–457
UI (user interface), for HBase, 485
umbilical interface, 193
UnderReplicatedBlocks, 357
Unicode characters, and Text class, 99–100
UNION statement, 408–409, 408
UniqueListenersMapper, 550
UniqueListenersReducers, 551
unit testing, with MRUnit testing library, 154–156
    mapper, 154–156
    reducer, 156
Unix tools, analyzing data with, 19–20
UnknownScannerException, 478
unrecoverable exceptions, in ZooKeeper, 517, 521

UPDATE statement, 425
upgrades, 362–365
    and Hive, 424–425
    checking process of, 364
    finalizing, 365
    rolling back, 364–365
    starting, 364
    testing, 364
URL, reading data from, 55–57
URLStreamHandlerFactory, 56, 57
user accounts, for clusters, 320
user interface (UI), for HBase, 485
user-defined aggregate functions (see UDAFs)
user-defined counters, 264–268
    dynamic counters, 265–266
    readable names for, 266
    retrieving values for, 266–268
    Streaming, 268
user-defined functions (see UDFs)

V

validation, in Pig Latin, 385–387
values, for counters, 266–268
VARCHAR, 427, 534
ViewFileSystem, 47
views, in Hive, 450–451
VIntWritable, 97, 98
VIRTUAL_MEMORY_BYTES, 260, 324
VLongWritable, 98
Volunteer Computing, vs. Hadoop, 8

W

waitForCompletion( ) method, 25, 164, 183, 189, 190, 195, 202
WatchedEvent, 511
Watcher object, 494, 511
Watcher.Event.KeeperState, 494
watches, for ZooKeeper, 501
weather dataset, 17–19
    analyzing
        with Hadoop, 20–29
        with Unix tools, 19–20
    data format for, 17–19
    Java class for, 22–29
        differences between APIs, 27–29
        testing, 25–27
webinterface.private.actions, 172, 173
WebMap, 11

weight property, 145
WHERE, 426, 447, 449, 535
Whirr project (see Apache Whirr project)
whirr.cluster-name, 335
whirr.credential, 336
whirr.identity, 336
whirr.instance-templates, 335, 336
whirr.provider, 336
whoami, 150
WholeFileInputFormat, 242, 244, 245
WholeFileRecordReader, 243
Widget class, 533, 534, 537, 541
Widget.get_schematic( ) method, 541
withOutput( ) method, 155
workflows, for MapReduce applications, 181–
    187
    converting problem into MapReduce jobs,
        181–183
    JobControl class, 183
    using Apache Oozie, 183–187
        defining Oozie workflow, 184–186
        packaging workflow, 186–187
        running workflow job, 187
Writable class, 97, 569, 578, 579
Writable collection objects, 102–103
Writable interface, 94, 103–107, 586
Writable object, 95, 105
Writable types, 103, 108, 132
Writable wrappers for Java primitives, 96–98
WritableComparable, 95–96, 95, 106, 138,
    271, 552
WritableComparator, 95, 107
Writables, 103
WritableSerialization, 108
WritableUtils, 107
write( ) method, 105, 115, 224, 257, 513, 517,
    518, 519, 534
writeInt( ) method, 137
WriteLock, 521
writePartitionFile( ) method, 275
writing data, 60–62
    data flow for, 70–72
    FSDataOutputStream class, 61–62
    MapFile, 138–140
    SequenceFile, 131–132

X

XML, as input format for MapReduce, 248–
    249

XmlInputFormat, 249
xpath, 428

Y

Yahoo!, using Hadoop, 11–12
YARN (Yet Another Resource Negotiator) (see
    MapReduce 2 [YARN])
yarn.app.mapreduce.am.compute-splits-in-
    cluster, 199
yarn.app.mapreduce.am.job.recovery.enable,
    205
yarn.nodemanager.aux-services property, 322
yarn.nodemanager.local-dirs, 322
yarn.nodemanager.resource.memory-mb, 323
yarn.nodemanager.vmem-pmem-ratio, 324
yarn.resourcemanager.address, 322
yarn.resourcemanager.am.max-retries, 205
yarn.resourcemanager.nm.liveness-
    monitor.expiry-interval-ms, 205
yarn.resourcemanager.store.class, 206
YarnChild, 200, 201
Yet Another Resource Negotiator (see
    MapReduce 2 [YARN])

Z

ZOOCFGDIR, 491
ZooDefs.Ids class, 506
ZooKeeper
    BookKeeper logging service, 522
    command-line tools, 498
    Configuration Service example, 512–515
    consistency of, 507–509
    data model for, 499–501
        ephemeral znodes, 500
        sequential znodes, 500–501
        watches, 501
    groups
        creating, 493–495
        deleting, 498–499
        joining, 495–496
        listing members in, 496–498
        membership for, 492–493
    Hedwig publish-subscribe system, 522
    implementing, 506–507
    in production, 522–525
        configuring, 524–525
        performance of, 523–524
    installing, 490–492

Lock Service example, 519–521
    herd effect, 520
    recoverable exceptions, 520–521
    unrecoverable exceptions, 521
operations, 501–506
    ACLs, 505–506
    APIs for, 502–503
    multiupdate, 502
    watch triggers, 504
Resilient Applications example, 515–519
    InterruptedException, 516
    KeeperException, 516–517
sessions for, 509–511
    time parameters, 510–511

About the Author

Tom White is one of the foremost experts on Hadoop. He has been an Apache Hadoop committer since February 2007, and is a Member of the Apache Software Foundation. Tom is a software engineer at Cloudera, where he has worked since its foundation, on the core distributions from Apache and Cloudera. Previously he was an independent Hadoop consultant, working with companies to set up, use, and extend Hadoop. He has written numerous articles for O'Reilly, java.net and IBM's developerWorks, and has spoken at many conferences, including ApacheCon and OSCON. Tom has a B.A. in mathematics from the University of Cambridge and an M.A. in philosophy of science from the University of Leeds, UK. He currently lives in San Francisco with his family.

Colophon

The animal on the cover of *Hadoop: The Definitive Guide* is an African elephant. These members of the genus *Loxodonta* are the largest land animals on earth (slightly larger than their cousin, the Asian elephant) and can be identified by their ears, which have been said to look somewhat like the continent of Asia. Males stand 12 feet tall at the shoulder and weigh 12,000 pounds, but they can get as big as 15,000 pounds, whereas females stand 10 feet tall and weigh 8,000–11,000 pounds. Even young elephants are very large: at birth, they already weigh approximately 200 pounds and stand about 3 feet tall.

African elephants live throughout sub-Saharan Africa. Most of the continent's elephants live on savannas and in dry woodlands. In some regions, they can be found in desert areas; in others, they are found in mountains.

The species plays an important role in the forest and savanna ecosystems in which they live. Many plant species are dependent on passing through an elephant's digestive tract before they can germinate; it is estimated that at least a third of tree species in west African forests rely on elephants in this way. Elephants grazing on vegetation also affect the structure of habitats and influence bush fire patterns. For example, under natural conditions, elephants make gaps through the rainforest, enabling the sunlight to enter, which allows the growth of various plant species. This, in turn, facilitates more abundance and more diversity of smaller animals. As a result of the influence elephants have over many plants and animals, they are often referred to as a *keystone species* because they are vital to the long-term survival of the ecosystems in which they live.

The cover image is from the Dover Pictorial Archive. The cover font is Adobe ITC Garamond. The text font is Linotype Birka; the heading font is Adobe Myriad Condensed; and the code font is LucasFont's TheSansMonoCondensed.

ISBN	Title	Author	Year	Price
	Shroff / O'Reilly			
9789350236772	**#tweetsmart, 124 Pages**	**McDougall**	**2012**	**200.00**
9788173669200	.NET Compact Framework Pocket Guide, 122 Pages	Lee	2004	125.00
9788173666544	.NET Framework Essentials, 3rd Edition, 400 Pages	Thai	2003	475.00
9789350236437	**20 Recipes for Programming MVC 3, 138 Pages**	**Munro**	**2012**	**225.00**
9789350237274	**20 Recipes for Programming PhoneGap, 96 Pages**	**Munro**	**2012**	**150.00**
9789350234051	21 Recipes for Mining Twitter, 96 Pages	Russell	2011	150.00
9789350239957	21st Century C, 316 Pages	Klemens	2012	550.00
9789350233993	50 Tips and Tricks for MongoDB Developers, 88 Pages	Chodorow	2011	125.00
9788184041637	802.11 Wireless Networks: The Definitive Guide, 2nd Edition (Covers 802.11a, g, n & i), 668 Pages	Gast	2005	550.00
9789350237267	**802.11n: A Survival Guide, 164 Pages**	**Gast**	**2012**	**250.00**
9788184049510	97 Things Every Programmer Should Know, 272 Pages	Henney	2010	350.00
9788184048131	97 Things Every Project Manager Should Know, 268 Pages	Davis	2009	350.00
9788184046892	97 Things Every Software Architect Should Know, 236 Pages	Monson	2009	300.00
9789350230503	Access 2010: The Missing Manual, 852 Pages	MacDonald	2010	950.00
9788184043334	Access Data Analysis Cookbook, 384 Pages	Bluttman	2007	375.00
9788173664281	Access Database Design & Programming, 3/ed, 454 Pages	Roman	2002	375.00
9788173666377	Access Hacks: Tips & Tools for Wrangling Your Data, 362 Pages	Bluttman	2005	325.00
9789350238745	**Accessibility Handbook, 116 Pages**	**Cunningham**	**2012**	**175.00**
9788184042832	ActionScript 3.0 Cookbook, 600 Pages	Lott	2006	475.00
9788184043747	ActionScript 3.0 Design Patterns: Object Oriented Programming Techniques (Adobe Developer Library), 552 Pages	Sanders	2007	500.00
9788184046120	ActionScript 3.0 Quick Reference Guide, The, 508 Pages	Stiller	2008	425.00
9789350236246	**ActionScript Developer's Guide to PureMVC, 144 Pages**	**Hall**	**2012**	**450.00**
9789350234914	ActionScript Developer's Guide to Robotlegs, 160 Pages	Hooks	2011	250.00
9788173666551	ActionScript for Flash MX Pocket Reference, 152 Pages	Moock	2003	125.00
9788184047103	Active Directory Cookbook, 3/ed: Solutions for Administrators & Developers, 1104 Pages	Hunter	2009	750.00
9788184046496	Active Directory: Designing, Deploying, and Running Active Directory, 4/ed, 876 Pages	Desmond	2008	600.00
9788184043501	Adding Ajax, 418 Pages	Power	2007	400.00
9788184044980	ADO.NET 3.5 Cookbook, 2/ed (Updated for .NET 3.5, LINQ, and SQL Server 2008), 1,098 Pages	Hamilton	2008	750.00
9788184046441	Adobe AIR 1.5 Cookbook: Solutions and Examples for Rich Internet Application Developers, 460 Pages	Tucker	2008	425.00
9788184045390	Adobe AIR for JavaScript Developers Pocket Guide, 220 Pages	Chambers	2008	150.00
9789350238844	**Adobe Edge Animate Preview 7: The Missing Manual, 300 Pages**	**Grover**	**2012**	**475.00**
9789350231197	Adobe InDesign CS4 One-on-One, 580 Pages	McClelland	2010	875.00
9788184043563	Adobe Integrated Runtime(AIR) for JavaScript Developers Pocket Reference, 192 Pages	Dura	2007	150.00
9788173668302	Advanced Perl Programming, 2/ed, 308 Pages	Cozens	2005	325.00
9788184044409	Advanced Rails, 374 Pages	Ediger	2008	375.00
9788184041576	Ajax Design Patterns, 668 Pages	Mahemoff	2006	500.00

ISBN	Title	Author	Year	Price
9788184043082	Ajax on Java, 176 Pages	Olson	2007	350.00
9788184042610	Ajax on Rails, 364 Pages	Raymond	2007	350.00
9788184044898	Ajax: The Definitive Guide, 996 Pages	Holdener	2008	800.00
9788184046083	Algorithms in a Nutshell: A Desktop Quick Reference, 376 Pages	Heineman	2008	350.00
9788173667299	Amazon Hacks: 100 Industrial Strength Tips & Tricks, 312 Pages	Bausch	2003	250.00
9788173667794	Analyzing Business Data with Excel, 276 Pages	Knight	2006	425.00
9788184047332	Android Application Development, 354 Pages	Rogers	2009	500.00
9789350237328	**Android Cookbook, 704 Pages**	**Darwin**	**2012**	**650.00**
9789351101260	**AngularJS, 216 Pages**	**Green**	**2013**	**375.00**
9788184040807	ANT: The Definitive Guide, 2/ed (Cover ANT 1.6), 346 Pages	Holzner	2005	475.00
9788184046007	Apache 2 Pocket Reference, 230 Pages	Ford	2008	150.00
9788184044416	Apache Cookbook, 2/ed, 322 Pages	Bowen	2008	475.00
9788173662270	Apache Security, 428 Pages	Ristic	2005	400.00
9788173665134	Apache: The Definitive Guide, 3/ed, 594 Pages	Laurie	2002	750.00
9789350238530	**APIs: A Strategy Guide, 168 Pages**	**Jacobson**	**2012**	**275.00**
9788184043549	Apollo for Adobe Flex Developers Pocket Guide, 154 Pages	Dixon	2007	125.00
9789350233962	App Inventor, 352 Pages	Wolber	2011	625.00
9789351100775	**Appcelerator Titanium: Up and Running, 174 Pages**	**Anderson**	**2013**	**300.00**
9789350239513	**Application Security for the Android Platform, 132 Pages**	**Six**	**2012**	**225.00**
9788184040395	Applied Software Project Management, 304 Pages	Stellman	2005	550.00
9788184048452	Apprenticeship Patterns: Guidance for the Aspiring Sofware Craftsman, 184 pgs	Hoover	2009	275.00
9789350236123	**Arduino Cookbook, 2/ed, 752 Pages**	**Margolis**	**2012**	**950.00**
9789350239490	**Arista Warrior, 440 Pages**	**Donahue**	**2012**	**750.00**
9789350237588	**Art of Community, 2nd Edition, The, 592 Pages**	**Bacon**	**2012**	**600.00**
9788173664588	ASP.NET 2.0: Developer's Notebook, 358 Pages	Lee	2005	525.00
9788173669385	AspectJ Cookbook, 364 Pages	Miles	2004	350.00
9789350234518	Asterisk Cookbook, 88 Pages	Madsen	2011	150.00
9788184045468	Asterisk: The Future of Telephony, 2/ed, 618 Pages	Meggelen	2008	575.00
9788184042702	Astronomy Hacks, 420 Pages	Thompson	2005	450.00
9789351100300	**Async in C# 5.0, 124 Pages**	**Davies**	**2013**	**200.00**
9789350239711	**Atmospheric Monitoring with Arduino, 106 Pages**	**Gertz**	**2013**	**175.00**
9789350235607	Automating ActionScript Projects with Eclipse and Ant, 120 Pages	Koning	2011	200.00
9788184047318	Automating System Administration with Perl, 2/ed, 686 Pages	Edelman	2009	600.00
9788184042900	Backup & Recovery, 774 Pages	Preston	2007	600.00
9789350239872	**Bad Data Handbook, 282**	**McCallum**	**2013**	**475.00**
9789350239735	**Bandit Algorithms for Website Optimization, 106 Pages**	**White**	**2013**	**175.00**
9788184043471	Bash Cookbook, 640 Pages	Albing	2007	875.00
9789350230312	Bash Pocket Reference, 148 Pages	Robbins	2010	225.00
9789350234662	Basic Sensors in iOS, 128 Pages	Allan	2011	200.00
9788184046908	Beautiful Architecture, 442 Pages	Gousios	2009	650.00
9788184043556	Beautiful Code: Leading Programmers Explain How They Think, 634 Pages	Wilson	2007	825.00
9788184047967	Beautiful Data, 404 Pages	Segaran	2009	650.00
9788184047110	Beautiful Security, 316 Pages	Oram	2009	350.00
9788184047035	Beautiful Teams, 524 Pages	Stellman	2009	475.00
9788184048650	Beautiful Testing, 358 Pages	Goucher	2009	550.00
9789350230510	Beautiful Visualization, 404 Pages	Steele	2010	600.00
9788173663956	Beginning Perl for Bioinformatics, 390 Pages	Tisdall	2001	550.00
9789350230657	Being Geek: The Software Developer's Career Handbook, 356 Pages	Lopp	2010	525.00
9789350231142	Best iPhone Apps, 2/ed, 272 Pages	Biersdorfer	2010	375.00
9788173668982	Better, Faster, Lighter Java, 270 Pages	Tate	2004	400.00

ISBN	Title	Author	Year	Price
9788184040036	Beyond Java, 206 Pages	Tate	2005	200.00
9789350235140	Big Data Glossary, 80 Pages	Warden	2011	150.00
9789350239704	**Big Data Now: 2012 Edition, 148 Pages**	**OReilly Media Inc.**	**2013**	**250.00**
9788184048988	Bioinformatics Programming Using Python, 540 Pages	Model	2010	550.00
9789350238400	**Book: A Futurist's Manifesto, 336 Pages**	**McGuire**	**2012**	**550.00**
9788184044393	Building A Web 2.0 Portal with ASP.NET 3.5, 324 Pages	Zabir	2008	350.00
9789350239247	**Building a Windows IT Infrastructure in the Cloud, 204 Pages**	**Rensin**	**2012**	**350.00**
9789350234488	Building and Testing with Gradle, 136 Pages	Berglund	2011	225.00
9789350231173	Building Android Apps with HTML, CSS, & JavaScript, 204 Pgs	Stark	2010	300.00
9789350236406	**Building Android Apps with HTML, CSS, and JavaScript, 2nd Edition, 204 Pages**	**Stark**	**2012**	**300.00**
9788184047127	Building Embedded Linux Systems, 2/ed: Concepts, techniques, tricks, and traps, 478 Pages	Gerum	2009	475.00
9789350235911	Building Hypermedia APIs with HTML5 and Node, 264 Pages	Amundsen	2011	425.00
9788184049428	Building iPhone Apps with HTML, CSS, & JavaScript, 202 Pgs	Stark	2010	300.00
9789350237250	**Building Mobile Applications with Java, 104 Pages**	**Marinacci**	**2012**	**150.00**
9789350239742	**Building Node Applications with MongoDB and Backbone, 224 Pages**	**Wilson**	**2013**	**375.00**
9789350234525	Building on SugarCRM, 104 Pages	Mertic	2011	175.00
9788184041545	Building Scalable Web Sites, 362 Pages	Henderson	2006	500.00
9788184048322	Building Social Web Applications, 452 Pages	Bell	2009	675.00
9789350231906	Building the Perfect PC, 3/ed, 368 Pages	Thompson	2010	825.00
9789350230527	Building the Realtime User Experience, 344 Pages	Roden	2010	525.00
9789350237984	**Building Web Applications with Erlang, 172 Pages**	**Kessin**	**2012**	**275.00**
9789350234471	Building Web Apps for Google TV, 140 Pages	Shen	2011	225.00
9789350239865	**Building Web, Cloud, and Mobile Solutions with F#, 196 Pages**	**Mohl**	**2013**	**325.00**
9789350232897	Building Wireless Sensor Networks, 344 Pages	Faludi	2011	525.00
9788184040494	C in a Nutshell, 618 Pages	Prinz	2005	400.00
9788173666605	C Pocket Reference, 142 Pages	Prinz	2002	175.00
9788173664434	C# & VB .NET Conversion Pocket Reference, 156 Pages	Mojica	2002	125.00
9788184044423	C# 3.0 Cookbook, 3/ed, 902 Pages	Hilyard	2008	650.00
9788184044379	C# 3.0 Design Patterns, 338 Pages	Bishop	2008	425.00
9788184049459	C# 4.0 in a Nutshell, 1064 Pages	Albahari	2010	725.00
9789350230831	C# 4.0 Pocket Reference, 3/ed, 232 Pages	Albahari	2010	225.00
9789350237625	**C# 5.0 in a Nutshell, 5th Edition, 1,060 Pages**	**Albahari**	**2012**	**750.00**
9789350237632	**C# 5.0 Pocket Reference, 240 Pages**	**Albahari**	**2012**	**200.00**
9789350236611	**C# Database Basics, 134 Pages**	**Schmalz**	**2012**	**200.00**
9788173663192	C# Essentials, 2/ed, 224 Pages	Albahari	2002	275.00
9788184040364	C++ Cookbook, 604 Pages	Stephens	2005	400.00
9788173666629	C++ in a Nutshell, (Cover ISO/IEC 14882 STD) 816 Pages	Lischner	2003	500.00
9788173667107	C++ Pocket Reference, 148 Pages	Loudon	2003	125.00
9789350232392	Canvas Pocket Reference, 127 Pages	Flanagan	2011	125.00
9789350231937	Cassandra: The Definitive Guide, 352 Pages	Hewitt	2010	525.00
9788173660450	CGI Programming with Perl 2/ed, 476 Pages	Gundavaram	2000	425.00
9788184042849	Cisco IOS Cookbook, 2/ed, 1,250 Pages	Dooley	2006	900.00
9788173669842	Cisco IOS in a Nutshell, 2/ed: A Desktop Quick Reference for IOS on IP Network, 808 Pages	Boney	2005	500.00
9789350238837	**Civic Apps Competition Handbook, 94 Pages**	**Carlson**	**2012**	**150.00**
9788184047134	CJKV Information Processing, 2/ed, 916 Pages	Lunde	2009	700.00
9788173668463	Classic Shell Scripting, 568 Pages	Robbins	2005	700.00
9789350237151	**Clojure Programming, 648 Pages**	**Emerick**	**2012**	**950.00**
9789350239667	**ClojureScript: Up and Running, 136 Pages**	**Sierra**	**2013**	**225.00**

ISBN	Title	Author	Year	Price
9789350231111	Closure: The Definitive Guide, 616 Pages	Bolin	2010	925.00
9788184047141	Cloud Application Architectures: Building Applications and Infrastructure in the Cloud, 220 Pages	Reese	2009	300.00
9789350239155	**Cloud Architecture Patterns, 200 Pages**	**Wilder**	**2012**	**250.00**
9788184048155	Cloud Security and Privacy, 352 Pages	Mather	2009	450.00
9789350230152	Cocoa and Objective-C: Up and Running, 436 Pages	Stevenson	2010	650.00
9789350237243	**Code Simplicity, 108 Pages**	**Alexander**	**2012**	**175.00**
9789350234921	Codermetrics: Analytics for Improving Software Teams, 284 Pages	Alexander	2011	450.00
9789351100331	**Coding with Coda, 84 Pages**	**Gruber**	**2013**	**125.00**
9788184047455	Complete Web Monitoring, 682 Pages	Croll	2009	975.00
9789351101277	**Computer Science Programming Basics in Ruby, 208 Pages**	**Frieder**	**2013**	**350.00**
9788184041583	Computer Security Basics, 2/ed, 324 Pages	Lehtinen	2006	400.00
9789350234204	Concurrent Programming in Mac OS X and iOS, 80 Pages	Nahavandipoor	2011	125.00
9788184049473	CouchDB: The Definitive Guide, 288 Pages	Anderson	2010	425.00
9789350233955	Creating a Web Site: The Missing Manual, 3/ed: 604 Pages	MacDonald	2011	650.00
9789350234990	Creating HTML5 Animations with Flash and Wallaby, 84 Pages	McLean	2011	125.00
9788184048971	CSS Cookbook, 3/ed, 746 Pages	Schmitt	2009	850.00
9788184047165	CSS Pocket Reference: Visual Presentation for the Web, 3/ed: 184 Pgs	Meyer	2009	150.00
9788184042788	CSS: The Definitive Guide, 3/ed, 550 Pages	Meyer	2006	700.00
9788184048124	CSS: The Missing Manual, 2/ed, 580 Pages	McFarland	2009	700.00
9789351100256	**CSS3: The Missing Manual, 3rd Edition, 668 Pages**	**McFarland**	**2013**	**675.00**
9789350231777	Data Analysis with Open Source Tools, 556 Pages	Janert	2010	825.00
9789350238394	**Data Journalism Handbook, The, 260 Pages**	**Chambers**	**2012**	**400.00**
9789350237298	**Database Design and Relational Theory, 294 Pages**	**Date**	**2012**	**375.00**
9788173662362	Database Nation: The Death of Privacy in the 21st Century, 336 Pages	Garfinkel	2000	235.00
9788173662898	Database Programming with JDBC & Java 2/ed, 348 Pages	Reese	2000	575.00
9788184046632	Data-Driven Services with Silverlight 2, 372 Pages	Papa	2009	400.00
9789350230992	Delphi in a Nutshell: A Desktop Quick Reference, 596 Pages	Lischner	2010	825.00
9789350234945	Deploying OpenStack, 108 Pages	Pepple	2011	175.00
9789350236093	**Design and Prototyping Drupal for Designers, 184 Pages**	**Nordin**	**2012**	**300.00**
9789350236840	**Designing Data Visualizations, 128 Pages**	**Steele**	**2012**	**200.00**
9788184042597	Designing Embedded Hardware, 2/ed, 406 Pages	Catsoulis	2005	400.00
9789350234532	Designing for XOOPS, 148 Pages	Ruoyu	2011	225.00
9789351100768	**Designing Games, 436 Pages**	**Sylvester**	**2013**	**700.00**
9789350232408	Designing Interfaces, 2/ed, 600 Pages	Tidwell	2011	750.00
9789350235690	Designing Mobile Interfaces, 608 Pages	Hoober	2011	600.00
9789350234006	Developing Android Applications with Adobe AIR, 340 Pages	Brossier	2011	500.00
9789350234129	Developing Android Applications with Flex 4.5, 136 Pages	Tretola	2011	200.00
9788173662423	Developing Bio-informatics Computer Skills, 504 Pages	Gibas	2001	575.00
9789350234464	Developing BlackBerry Tablet Applications with Flex 4.5, 136 Pages	Tretola	2011	225.00
9789350236109	**Developing Enterprise iOS Applications, 140 Pages**	**Turner**	**2012**	**225.00**
9788173669477	Developing Feeds with RSS and Atom, 280 Pages	Hammersley	2005	300.00
9789350235003	Developing iOS Applications with Flex 4.5, 156 Pages	Tretola	2011	225.00
9788184049626	Developing Large Web Applications, 306 Pages	Loudon	2010	475.00
9789350237304	**Developing Web Applications with Haskell and Yesod: Safety-Driven Web Development, 316 Pages**	**Snoyman**	**2012**	**400.00**
9789351100515	**Developing with Couchbase Server, 106 Pages**	**Brown**	**2013**	**175.00**
9789350238813	**Developing with Google+, 124 Pages**	**Murphy**	**2012**	**200.00**
9788184040111	Digital Identity, 266 Pages	Windley	2005	275.00
9789351100782	**Distributed Network Data, 188 Pages**	**Allan**	**2013**	**325.00**

ISBN	Title	Author	Year	Price
9789350236628	**DIY Satellite Platforms, 110 Pages**	**Antunes**	**2012**	**175.00**
9788184041965	DNS & BIND (Covers BIND 9.3), 5/ed, 654 Pages	Albitz	2006	800.00
9788173665677	DNS & BIND Cookbook, 248 Pages	Liu	2002	250.00
9789350234112	DNS and BIND on IPv6, 76 Pages	Liu	2011	100.00
9789350233702	DNS on Windows Server 2003, 3rd Edition, 450 Pages	Liu	2011	650.00
9789350230374	DocBook 5: The Definitive Guide, 568 Pages	Walsh	2010	850.00
9788184045567	Dojo: The Definitive Guide, 502 Pages	Russell	2008	800.00
9789350230534	Dreamweaver CS5: The Missing Manual, 1116 Pages	McFarland	2010	1,225.00
9789350238448	**Dreamweaver CS6: The Missing Manual, 1052 Pages**	**McFarland**	**2012**	**1,350.00**
9788184041200	Dreawweaver 8 Design and Construction, 330 Pages	Campbell	2006	750.00
9789350232958	Droid 2: The Missing Manual, 414 Pages	Gralla	2011	625.00
9789350235225	Droid X2: The Missing Manual, 440 Pages	Gralla	2011	625.00
9789350237236	**Drupal Development Tricks for Designers, 108 Pages**	**Nordin**	**2012**	**175.00**
9789350238455	**Drupal for Designers, 344 Pages**	**Nordin**	**2012**	**550.00**
9788184042771	Dynamic HTML: The Definitive Reference, 3/ed, 1,336 Pages	Goodman	2006	800.00
9788173669019	Eclipse (Coverage of 3.0), 344 Pages	Holzner	2004	325.00
9788173669309	Eclipse Cookbook (Cover 3.0), 372 Pages	Holzner	2004	350.00
9788173669941	Eclipse IDE Pocket Guide, 140 Pages	Burnette	2005	125.00
9788173663017	Effective awk Programming, 3/ed, 454 Pages	Robbins	2001	325.00
9789350239858	**Effective Monitoring and Alerting, 184 Pages**	**Ligus**	**2013**	**325.00**
9789350234679	Elastic Beanstalk, 108 Pages	Paganelli	2011	175.00
9789350237229	**Enabling Programmable Self with HealthVault, 136 Pages**	**Bhandari**	**2012**	**225.00**
9788184049886	Enterprise Development with Flex, 700 Pages	Fain	2010	850.00
9789351100287	**Enterprise Games, 236 Pages**	**Hugos**	**2013**	**400.00**
9789350231135	Enterprise JavaBeans 3.1, 6/ed, 788 Pages	Rubinger	2010	575.00
9788184046137	Enterprise Rails, 366 Pages	Chak	2008	350.00
9789350239698	**Enterprise Search, 208 Pages**	**White**	**2013**	**350.00**
9788173666780	Enterprise Service Bus, 284 Pages	Chappell	2004	425.00
9788184041446	Enterprise SOA, 468 Pages	Woods	2006	600.00
9789350236444	**Environmental Monitoring with Arduino, 124 Pages**	**Gertz**	**2012**	**175.00**
9788184047493	Erlang Programming, 514 Pages	Cesarini	2009	850.00
9788184040241	Essentail PHP Security, 310 Pages	Shiflett	2005	200.00
9788184045437	Essentail SharePoint 2007, 2/ed, 462 Pages	Webb	2008	475.00
9788184042825	Essentail SNMP, 2/ed, 480 Pages	Mauro	2005	400.00
9788173669316	Essential ActionScript 2.0, 528 Pages	Moock	2004	475.00
9788184043662	Essential ActionScript 3.0, 962 Pages	Moock	2007	800.00
9788184048308	Essential Blogging, 280 Pages	Doctorow	2009	425.00
9788184040104	Essential Business Process Modeling, 362 Pages	Havey	2005	350.00
9788184042757	Essential CVS, 2/ed, 442 Pages	Vesperman	2006	425.00
9789350236260	**Essential iOS Build and Release, 144 Pages**	**Roche**	**2012**	**225.00**
9788184045277	Essential SQLAlchemy, 242 Pages	Copeland	2008	275.00
9788173666643	Essential System Administration Pocket Reference, 152 Pages	Frisch	2002	125.00
9788173665295	Essential System Administration, 3/ed, 1,178 Pages	Frisch	2002	650.00
9788173660252	Essential Windows NT System Administration, 488 Pages	Frisch	1998	225.00
9789351101246	**Ethernet Switches, 98 Pages**	**Spurgeon**	**2013**	**175.00**
9788173662492	Ethernet: The Definitive Guide, 528 Pages	Spurgeon	2000	300.00
9789350238806	**Ethics of Big Data, 100 Pages**	**Davis**	**2012**	**150.00**
9788184047462	Even Faster Web Sites, 274 Pages	Souders	2009	500.00
9788184044058	Excel 2007 Pocket Guide, 2/ed, 180 Pages	Frye	2007	125.00
9789350230541	Excel 2010: The Missing Manual, 916 Pages	MacDonald	2010	900.00

ISBN	Title	Author	Year	Price
9788184043518	Excel Hacks, 2/ed, Tips & Tools for Streamlining Your Spreadsheets, 428 Pages	David	2007	400.00
9789350238240	**Exploring Everyday Things with R and Ruby, 276 Pages**	**Sheong**	**2012**	**425.00**
9789350233764	Facebook: The Missing Manual, 3rd Edition, 304 Pages	Veer	2011	600.00
9789350238462	**FileMaker Pro 12: The Missing Manual, 976 Pages**	**Prosser**	**2012**	**1,500.00**
9788184041361	Flash 8 Cookbook, 548 Pages	Lott	2006	400.00
9788184041040	Flash 8 Project for Learning Animation and Interactivity (B/CD), 372 Pages	Shupe	2006	400.00
9789350230985	Flash 8: The Missing Manual, 484 Pages	Veer	2010	725.00
9789350230381	Flash CS5: The Missing Manual, 796 Pages	Grover	2010	725.00
9789350237649	**Flash CS6: The Missing Manual, 864 Pages**	**Grover**	**2012**	**1,075.00**
9788173667473	Flash Hacks: 100 Industrial Strength Tips & Tools, 504 Pages	Bhangal	2004	400.00
9788173668593	Flash Out of the Box: A User-Centric Beginner's Guide to Flash (B/CD), 264 Pages	Hoekman	2004	300.00
9788173667312	Flash Remoting MX: The Definitive Guide, 652 Pages	Muck	2003	550.00
9788184048162	flex & bison, 310 Pages	Levine	2009	475.00
9788184045246	Flex 3 Cookbook, 798 Pages	Noble	2008	800.00
9788184048940	Flex 3 with Java, 309 Pages	Kore	2009	525.00
9789350230428	Flex 4 Cookbook, 780 Pages	Noble	2010	900.00
9789350234686	Functional Programming for Java Developers, 112 Pages	Wampler	2011	175.00
9789350236079	**Galaxy S II: The Missing Manual, 456 Pages**	**Gralla**	**2012**	**650.00**
9789350235133	Galaxy Tab: The Missing Manual, 460 Pages	Gralla	2011	525.00
9789350230664	Gamestorming: A Playbook for Innovators, Rulebreakers, and Changemakers, 308 Pages	Gray	2010	450.00
9789350234549	Gamification by Design, 228 Pages	Cunningham	2011	350.00
9788173668685	GDB Pocket Reference, 78 Pages	Robbins	2005	75.00
9789350239445	**Geolocation in iOS, 132 Pages**	**Allan**	**2012**	**225.00**
9789350237618	**Getting Started with .NET Gadgeteer, 108 Pages**	**Monk**	**2012**	**150.00**
9789350235010	Getting Started with Arduino, 2nd Edition 152 Pages	Banzi	2011	200.00
9789350237991	**Getting Started with Couchbase Server, 108 Pages**	**Brown**	**2012**	**175.00**
9789350238028	**Getting Started with CouchDB, 108 Pages**	**Brown**	**2012**	**175.00**
9789350238264	**Getting Started with D3, 86 Pages**	**Dewar**	**2012**	**150.00**
9789350237700	**Getting Started with Dwarf Fortress, 256 Pages**	**Tyson**	**2012**	**400.00**
9788184045284	Getting Started with Flex 3: An Adobe Developer Library Pocket Guide, 162 Pages	Herrington	2008	175.00
9789350236697	**Getting Started with Fluidinfo, 156 Pages**	**Radcliffe**	**2012**	**250.00**
9789350234624	Getting Started with GEO, CouchDB, and Node.js, 84 Pages	Thompson	2011	150.00
9789350239766	Getting Started with MakerBot, 244 Pages	Pettis	2013	425.00
9789350238387	**Getting Started with Metro Style Apps, 128 Pages**	**Dewey**	**2012**	**200.00**
9789351100003	Getting Started with Mule Cloud Connect, 132 Pages	Carter	2013	225.00
9789350236765	**Getting Started with Netduino, 120 Pages**	**Walker**	**2012**	**200.00**
9789350236703	**Getting Started with OAuth 2.0, 100 Pages**	**Boyd**	**2012**	**150.00**
9789350230596	Getting Started with Processing, 232 Pages	Reas	2010	300.00
9789350239759	Getting Started with Raspberry Pi, 196 Pages	Richardson	2013	325.00
9789350237212	**Getting Started with RFID, 60 Pages**	**Igoe**	**2012**	**100.00**
9789350235027	Getting Started with Roo, 84 Pages	Long	2011	150.00
9789350238752	**Getting Started with Storm, 124 Pages**	**Leibiusky**	**2012**	**200.00**
9789350234136	Getting Started with the Internet of Things, 212 Pages	Pfister	2011	275.00
9788184049503	Google Advertising Tools, 2nd Edition, 452 Pages	Davis	2010	675.00
9789350235881	Google AdWords, 216 Pages	Holdren	2011	350.00
9789350230923	Google Analytics, 240 Pages	Cutroni	2010	375.00
9788184045079	Google Apps Hacks, 396 Pages	Lenssen	2008	525.00

ISBN	Title	Author	Year	Price
9788184044942	Google Hacks, 3/ed, Tips & Tools for Finding and Using the World's Information, 558 Pages	Dornfest	2008	400.00
9788184040876	Google Maps Hacks: Tips & Tools for Geographic Searching & Remixing, 366 Pages	Gibson	2006	350.00
9788173667138	Google Pocket Guide, 144 Pages	Calishain	2003	125.00
9789350234556	Google Power Search, 96 Pages	Spencer	2011	150.00
9789350236390	**Google Script: Enterprise Application Essentials, 240 Pages**	**Ferreira**	**2012**	**375.00**
9788184048285	Google SketchUp: The Missing Manual, 616 Pages	Grover	2009	925.00
9788184042856	Google: The Missing Manual, 2/ed, 478 Pages	Milstein	2006	425.00
9789350236062	**Google+: The Missing Manual, 252 Pages**	**Purdy**	**2012**	**375.00**
9789350234013	Graphics and Animation on iOS, 104 Pages	Nahavandipoor	2011	150.00
9788184046915	Grep Pocket Reference, 98 Pages	Bambenek	2009	125.00
9789350230398	Hackers & Painters: Big Ideas from the Computer Age, 292 Pages	Graham	2010	450.00
9789350230404	Hackers: Heroes of the Computer Revolution, 540 Pages	Levy	2010	675.00
9789350238066	**Hacking and Securing iOS Applications, 376 Pages**	**Zdziarski**	**2012**	**600.00**
9788184048148	Hacking: The Next Generation, 314 Pages	Dhanjani	2009	475.00
9789350239261	**Hadoop Operations, 316 Pages**	**Sammer**	**2012**	**375.00**
9789350237564	**Hadoop: The Definitive Guide, 3rd Edition, 704 Pages**	**White**	**2012**	**650.00**
9788173668258	Hardcore Java, 354 Pages	Simmons	2004	300.00
9788184045024	Harnessing Hibernate, 396 Pages	Elliott	2008	500.00
9789350235034	HBase: The Definitive Guide, 576 Pages	George	2011	700.00
9788184048735	Head First 2D Geometry, 372 Pages	Fallow	2009	400.00
9788184045819	Head First Ajax: A Brain-Friendly Guide, 544 Pages	Riordan	2008	525.00
9788184046595	Head First Algebra: A Brain-Friendly Guide, 576 Pages	Pilone	2009	550.00
9789350230350	Head First C#: A Brain-Friendly Guide, 2nd/ed 504 Pages	Stellman	2010	650.00
9769350236925	**Head First C, 652 Pages**	**Griffiths**	**2012**	**450.00**
9788184047998	Head First Data Analysis, 504 Pages	Milton	2009	500.00
9788173664663	Head First Design Patterns, 688 Pages	Sierra	2004	625.00
9788173665264	Head First EJB: Passing the Sun Certified Business Component Developer Exam, 744 Pages	Sierra	2003	650.00
9788184049893	Head First Excel: A Brain-Friendly Guide, 458 Pages	Milton	2010	450.00
9789350238790	**Head First HTML and CSS, 2nd Edition, 782 Pages**	**Freeman**	**2012**	**750.00**
9789350235324	Head First HTML5 Programming, 632 Pages	Freeman	2011	575.00
9789350235331	Head First iPhone and iPad Development, 2nd Edition	Pilone	2011	600.00
9788173666025	Head First Java: Your Brain on Java - A Learner's Guide, 2nd Edition (Cover Java 5.0), 730 Pages	Sierra	2005	625.00
9788184044362	Head First JavaScript: A Brain-Friendly Guide, 666 Pages	Morrison	2008	600.00
9789350235164	Head First jQuery, 560 Pages	Benedetti	2011	650.00
9789350236024	**Head First Mobile Web, 500 Pages**	**Gardner**	**2012**	**600.00**
9788184047301	Head First Networking: A Brain-Friendly Guide, 556 Pages	Anderson	2009	550.00
9788184042214	Head First Object - Oriented Analysis & Design, 648 Pages	McLaughlin	2006	650.00
9788184046588	Head First PHP & MySQL : A Brain-Friendly Guide, 828 Pages	Beighley	2009	650.00
9788184045994	Head First Physics: A Learner's Companion to Mechanics and Practical Physics, 956 Pages	Lang	2008	875.00
9788184048001	Head First PMP, 2nd Edition 852 Pages	Greene	2009	700.00
9788184048766	Head First Programming, 460 Pages	Griffiths	2009	550.00
9789350231883	Head First Python, 516 Pages	Barry	2010	500.00
9788184046571	Head First Rails: A learner's companion to Ruby on Rails, 478 Pgs	Griffiths	2009	500.00
9788184044973	Head First Servlets & JSP, 2/ed (COVER J2EE 1.5): Passing the Sun Certified Web Component Developer Exam, 948 Pages	Basham	2008	750.00

ISBN	Title	Author	Year	Price
9788184044508	Head First Software Development, 512 Pages	Pilone	2008	500.00
9788184043686	Head First SQL: Your Brain on SQL -- A Learner's Guide, 624 Pgs	Beighley	2007	575.00
9788184045826	Head First Statistics: A Brain-Friendly Guide, 732 Pages	Griffiths	2008	675.00
9788184046601	Head First Web Design: A Brain-Friendly Guide, 512 Pages	Watrall	2009	500.00
9789350230671	Head First WordPress: A Brain-Friendly Guide, 386 Pages	Siarto	2010	450.00
9788173669347	Hibernate: A Developer's Notebook, 190 Pages	Elliott	2004	275.00
9788184049909	High Performance JavaScript, 252 Pages	Zakas	2010	375.00
9788173669262	High Performance Linux Cluster with OSCAR, Rocks, OpenMosix, and MPI, 380 Pages	Sloan	2004	350.00
9788184047189	High Performance MySQL: Optimization, Backups, Replication 2/ed, 724 Pages	Schwartz	2009	875.00
9788184043808	High Performance Web Sites: Essential Knowledge for Front-End Engineers, 184 Pages	Souders	2007	275.00
9789350238479	**HLSL and Pixel Shaders for XAML Developers, 220 Pages**	**Ritscher**	**2012**	**350.00**
9788184049527	HTML & CSS: The Good Parts, 368 Pages	Henick	2010	550.00
9788184048995	HTML & XHTML Pockte Reference, 4/ed, 206 Pages	Robbins	2010	250.00
9788184042146	HTML & XHTML The Definitive Guide, 6/ed, 692 Pages	Musciano	2006	775.00
9789350239506	**HTML5 and JavaScript Web Apps, 192 Pages**	**Hales**	**2012**	**300.00**
9789351101284	**HTML5 Canvas, 2nd Edition, 768 Pages**	**Fulton**	**2013**	**1,100.00**
9789350234020	HTML5 Canvas, 676 Pages	Fulton	2011	825.00
9789350235898	HTML5 Cookbook, 304 Pages	Schmitt	2011	475.00
9789350234174	HTML5 Geolocation, 136 Pages	Holdener	2011	175.00
9789350239889	**HTML5 Hacks, 520 Pages**	**Cravens**	**2013**	**800.00**
9789350234938	HTML5 Media, 160 Pages	Powers	2011	250.00
9789350235041	HTML5: The Missing Manual, 472 Pages	MacDonald	2011	450.00
9789350230824	HTML5: Up and Running, 244 Pages	Pilgrim	2010	375.00
9788184049466	HTTP: The Definitive Guide, 676 Pages	Gourley	2010	800.00
9789350238721	**Illustrated Guide to Home Forensic Science Experiments, 468 Pages**	**Thompson**	**2012**	**725.00**
9789350233801	iMovie '11 & iDVD: The Missing Manual, 568 Pages	Pogue	2011	850.00
9788184042917	Information Architecture for The World Wide Web, 3/ed, 540 Pgs	Morville	2006	650.00
9789350236277	**Information Diet, The, 188 Pages**	**Johnson**	**2012**	**300.00**
9789350236116	**Inside Cyber Warfare, 2/ed, 332 Pages**	**Carr**	**2012**	**525.00**
9788184040388	Integrating Excel and Access, 232 Pages	Schmalz	2005	250.00
9789350235195	Integrating PHP Projects with Jenkins, 80 Pages	Bergmann	2011	125.00
9788184043617	Intel Threading Building Blocks Out fitting C++ for Multi-Core Processor Parallelism, 348 Pages	Reinders	2007	350.00
9788184045635	Intellectual Property and Open Source: A Practical Guide to Protecting Code, 406 Pages	Lindberg	2008	450.00
9789351100850	**Interactive Data Visualization for the Web, 292 Pages**	**Murray**	**2013**	**500.00**
9789350238431	**Intermediate Perl, 2nd Edition, 416 Pages**	**Schwartz**	**2012**	**400.00**
9789350236710	**Introducing HTML5 Game Development, 140 Pages**	**Freeman**	**2012**	**225.00**
9789350238486	**Introducing Regular Expressions, 172 Pages**	**Fitzgerald**	**2012**	**275.00**
9789350234037	Introduction to Search with Sphinx, 168 Pages	Aksyonoff	2011	250.00
9789350237205	**Introduction to Tornado, 156 Pages**	**Dory**	**2012**	**250.00**
9789350232934	iOS 4 Programming Cookbook, 664 Pages	Nahavandipoor	2011	800.00
9789350238073	**iOS 5 Programming Cookbook, 892 Pages**	**Nahavandipoor**	**2012**	**1,350.00**
9789351100270	**iOS 6 Programming Cookbook, 996 Pages**	**Nahavandipoor**	**2013**	**1,350.00**
9789350235157	iOS Sensor Apps with Arduino, 148 Pages	Allan	2011	225.00
9788173663376	IP Routing, 244 Pages	Malhotra	2002	250.00
9789350233979	iPad 2: The Missing Manual, 352 Pages	Biersdorfer	2011	500.00

ISBN	Title	Author	Year	Price
9789350236291	**iPad 2: The Missing Manual, 3rd Edition, 380 Pages**	**Biersdorfer**	**2012**	**600.00**
9789350239803	**iPad: The Missing Manual, 5th Edition, 420 Pages**	**Biersdorfer**	**2013**	**600.00**
9789350230336	iPhone 3D Programming, 460 Pages	Rideout	2010	700.00
9789350230329	iPhone App Development: The Missing Manual, 360 Pgs	Hockenberry	2010	550.00
9788184048728	iPhone Game Development, 276 Pages	Zirkle	2009	425.00
9788184046922	iPhone SDK Application Development, 408 Pages	Zdziarski	2009	550.00
9789350239643	**iPhone: The Missing Manual, 6/ed, 560 Pages**	**Pogue**	**2013**	**825.00**
9789350233818	iPhoto '11: The Missing Manual, 408 Pages	Pogue	2011	600.00
9789350236055	**iPod: The Missing Manual, 10/ed, 348 Pages**	**Biersdorfer**	**2012**	**500.00**
9789350239919	**iPod: The Missing Manual, 11th Edition, 360 Pages**	**Biersdorfer**	**2013**	**550.00**
9788184042818	IPv6 Essentials, 2/ed, 450 Pages	Hagen	2006	600.00
9788173663024	IPv6 Network Administration, 316 Pages	Murphy	2005	325.00
9788173667374	J2EE Design Patterns, 390 Pages	Crawford	2003	550.00
9788173663437	J2ME in a Nutshell, 474 Pages	Topley	2002	450.00
9788173669293	Jakarta Commons Cookbook, 412 Pages	O'Brien	2004	375.00
9788173669484	Jakarta Struts Cookbook, 536 Pages	Siggelkow	2005	400.00
9788173667145	Jakarta Struts Pocket Reference, 142 Pages	Cavaness	2003	125.00
9788184043068	Java & XML, 3/ed, 496 Pages	McLaughlin	2006	450.00
9788173663796	Java & XSLT, 534 Pages	Burke	2001	350.00
9788173669361	Java Cookbook (Coverage of 1.5), 2/ed, 872 Pages	Darwin	2004	1,200.00
9789350232903	Java Cryptography, 388 Pages	Knudsen	2011	575.00
9788173666667	Java Database Best Practices, 304 Pages	Eckstein	2003	275.00
9789350233610	Java Distributed Computing, 408 Pages	Farley	2011	600.00
9789350238820	**Java EE 6 Pocket Guide, 224 Pages**	**Gupta**	**2012**	**225.00**
9788173665776	Java Enterprise Best Practices, 296 Pages	Eckstein	2002	275.00
9788184042870	Java Enterprise in a Nutshell, 3/ed, 906 Pages	Farley	2005	600.00
9788173668630	Java Examples in a Nutshell: A Tutorial Companion to Java in a Nutshell, 3/ed, 728 Pages	Flanagan	2004	400.00
9788173666681	Java Extreme Programming Cookbook, 296 Pages	Burke	2003	425.00
9788184042160	Java Generics and Collections, 308 Pages	Naftalin	2006	450.00
9788184041187	Java I/O, 2/ed, 740 Pages	Harold	2006	650.00
9788184042665	Java in a Nutshell, 5/ed, 1,266 Pages	Flanagan	2005	750.00
9788173662713	Java Internationalization, 456 Pages	Czarnecki	1998	675.00
9788184047349	Java Message Service, 2/ed, 348 Pages	Richards	2009	350.00
9788173663536	Java Network Programming, 3/ed, 770 Pages	Harold	2004	575.00
9788173665110	Java NIO, 308 Pages	Hitchens	2002	275.00
9788173665783	Java Performance Tuning, 2/ed, 600 Pages	Shirazi	2003	800.00
9788184044881	Java Pocket Guide, 208 Pages	Liguori	2008	200.00
9788184045031	Java Power Tools, 926 Pages	Smart	2008	950.00
9788173663819	Java RMI, 578 Pages	Grosso	2001	450.00
9788173664120	Java Security, 2/ed, 624 Pages	Oaks	2001	750.00
9788173668227	Java Servlet & JSP Cookbook, 756 Pages	Perry	2004	600.00
9788173662850	Java Servlet Programming 2/ed, 786 Pages	Hunter	2001	675.00
9788184047011	Java SOA Cookbook, 756 Pages	Hewitt	2009	600.00
9788173665684	Java Swing, 2/ed, 1,288 Pages	Loy	2002	850.00
9788173665929	Java Threads (Covers J2SE 5.0), 3/ed, 368 Pages	Oaks	2004	525.00
9788173663444	Java Web Services, 286 Pages	Chappell	2002	425.00
9788184047196	Java Web Services: Up and Running, 332 Pages	Kalin	2009	375.00
9789350230138	Java: The Good Parts, 212 Pages	Waldo	2010	325.00
9789350235621	JavaScript & jQuery: The Missing Manual, 2nd Edition, 560 Pages	McFarland	2011	550.00

ISBN	Title	Author	Year	Price
9788184045451	JavaScript and DHTML Cookbook, 2/ed, 620 Pages	Goodman	2008	475.00
9789350230688	JavaScript Cookbook, 574 Pages	Powers	2010	725.00
9789351100263	**JavaScript Enlightenment, 184 Pages**	**Lindley**	**2013**	**325.00**
9789351101291	**JavaScript for PHP Developers, 178 Pages**	**Stefanov**	**2013**	**300.00**
9789350231159	JavaScript Patterns, 260 Pages	Stefanov	2010	400.00
9789350237311	**JavaScript Pocket Reference, 3rd Edition, 296 Pages**	**Flanagan**	**2012**	**175.00**
9789351101253	**JavaScript Testing with Jasmine, 70 Pages**	**Hahn**	**2013**	**125.00**
9789350235065	JavaScript Web Applications, 304 Pages	MacCaw	2011	400.00
9789350233948	JavaScript: The Definitive Guide, 6/ed, 1,120 Pages	Flanagan	2011	825.00
9788184045222	JavaScript: The Good Parts, 186 Pages	Crockford	2008	275.00
9788184045659	JavaScript: The Missing Manual, 560 Pages	McFarland	2008	675.00
9788173669033	JavaServer Faces, 614 Pages	Bergsten	2004	750.00
9788173665301	JavaServer Pages (Covers JSP 2.0 & JSTL 1.1), 3/ed, 762 Pgs	Bergsten	2003	550.00
9788173663833	JavaServer Pages Pocket Reference, 96 Pages	Bergsten	2001	65.00
9788184040173	JBoss at Work: A Practical Guide, 318 Pages	Marrs	2005	475.00
9788173669460	JBoss: A Developer's Notebook, 182 Pages	Richards	2005	225.00
9788173666711	JDBC Pocket Reference, 160 Pages	Bales	2003	100.00
9789350234563	Jenkins: The Definitive Guide, 448 Pages	Smart	2011	650.00
9788173662508	Jini in a Nutshell, 340 Pages	Oaks	2000	425.00
9788184048759	jQuery Cookbook, 594 Pages	Experts	2009	725.00
9789350234570	jQuery Mobile, 152 Pages	Reid	2011	250.00
9789350236727	**jQuery Mobile: Up and Running, 288 Pages**	**Firtman**	**2012**	**375.00**
9789350232385	jQuery Pocket Reference, 176 Pages	Flanagan	2011	175.00
9789350237182	**jQuery UI, 260 Pages**	**Sarrion**	**2012**	**400.00**
9788184046427	JRuby Cookbook, 238 Pages	Edelson	2008	300.00
9789350239896	**Juniper Networks Warrior, 452 Pages**	**Southwick**	**2013**	**750.00**
9788173668609	JUnit Pocket Guide, 100 Pages	Beck	2004	100.00
9788184041163	JUNOS Cookbook, 682 Pages	Garrett	2006	450.00
9788184044997	JUNOS Enterprise Routing, 828 Pages	Marschke	2008	1,000.00
9788184047974	JUNOS Enterprise Switching, 772 Pages	Marschke	2009	1,150.00
9788184048193	JUNOS High Availability, 704 Pages	Sonderegger	2009	1,050.00
9789350231104	Junos Security, 872 Pages	Cameron	2010	1,300.00
9789350237656	**Just Spring Data, 88 Pages**	**Konda**	**2012**	**125.00**
9789350237090	**Just Spring Integration, 118 Pages**	**Konda**	**2012**	**200.00**
9789350234716	Just Spring, 84 Pages	Konda	2011	125.00
9788173665158	JXTA in a Nutshell: A Desktop Quick Reference, 422 Pages	Oaks	2002	225.00
9788173665608	Kerberos: The Definitive Guide, 280 Pages	Garman	2003	275.00
9788173669729	Killer Game Programming in Java, 986 Pages	Davison	2005	675.00
9789350236758	**Kindle Fire: The Missing Manual, 296 Pages**	**Meyers**	**2012**	**450.00**
9789350239483	**Kinect Hacks, 300 Pages**	**Jean**	**2012**	**450.00**
9788184040265	Knoppix Pocket Reference, 104 Pages	Rankin	2005	100.00
9788173666728	LDAP System Administration, 318 Pages	Carter	2003	400.00
9789351100867	**Lean Analytics, 456 Pages**	**Croll**	**2013**	**775.00**
9789350231364	Learning ActionScript 3.0: A Beginner's Guide, 2/ed, 480 Pages	Shupe	2010	1,075.00
9789350233788	Learning Android, 292 Pages	Gargenta	2011	450.00
9788184040456	Learning ASP.NET 2.0 with AJAX, 536 Pgs	Liberty	2007	400.00
9788184045666	Learning ASP.NET 3.5, 2/ed, 624 Pages	Liberty	2008	400.00
9788184046465	Learning C# 3.0, 708 Pages	Liberty	2008	450.00
9789350238059	**Learning CFEngine 3, 204 Pages**	**Zamboni**	**2012**	**325.00**
9789350239773	**Learning Cocoa with Objective-C, 3rd Edition, 380 Pages**	**Addison**	**2013**	**650.00**

ISBN	Title	Author	Year	Price
9789350231890	Learning Flex 4: Getting Up to Speed with Rich Internet Application Design and Development, 500 Pages	Cole	2010	1,125.00
9789351100614	**Learning from jQuery, 200 Pages**	**Macrae**	**2013**	**200.00**
9788173669637	Learning GNU Emacs, 3/ed, 544 Pages	Cameron	2004	450.00
9789350237083	**Learning iOS Programming, 2nd Edition, 448 Pages**	**Allan**	**2012**	**700.00**
9789351100737	**Learning iOS Programming, 3rd Edition, 472 Pages**	**Allan**	**2013**	**800.00**
9788184049718	Learning iPhone Programming, 396 Pages	Allan	2010	600.00
9788184047202	Learning JavaScript 2/ed, 412 Pages	Powers	2009	575.00
9789350238707	**Learning JavaScript Design Patterns, 268 Pages**	**Osmani**	**2012**	**400.00**
9788184042672	Learning MySQL, 632 Pages	Tahaghoghi	2006	750.00
9789350238714	**Learning Node, 412 Pages**	**Powers**	**2012**	**475.00**
9788184045970	Learning OpenCV: Computer Vision with the OpenCV Library, 592 Pages	Dr. Bradski	2008	725.00
9788173663918	Learning Oracle PL/SQL (Covers Oracle9i), 452 Pages	Pribyl	2001	325.00
9789350234341	Learning Perl, 6/ed, 412 Pages	Schwartz	2011	375.00
9788184043716	Learning PHP & MySQL, 2/ed: Step-by-Step Guide to Creating Database-Driven Web Sites, 444 Pages	Davis	2007	550.00
9789351100607	**Learning PHP Design Patterns, 384 Pages**	**Sanders**	**2013**	**550.00**
9788173667329	Learning PHP 5, 378 Pages	Sklar	2004	475.00
9789350239988	**Learning PHP, MySQL, JavaScript, and CSS, 2nd Edition, 600 Pages**	**Nixon**	**2013**	**650.00**
9788184048261	Learning Python, 4/ed, 1,230 Pages	Lutz	2009	775.00
9789350238493	**Learning Rails 3, 432 Pages**	**St. Laurent**	**2012**	**675.00**
9788184046458	Learning Rails, 458 Pages	St. Laurent	2008	450.00
9788184043341	Learning Ruby, 272 Pages	Fitzgerald	2007	300.00
9789350234594	Learning SPARQL, 280 Pages	DuCharme	2011	400.00
9788184047219	Learning SQL 2/ed, 352 Pages	Beaulieu	2009	325.00
9788184043044	Learning SQL on SQL Server 2005, 342 Pages	Bagui	2006	350.00
9788173668050	Learning the Bash Shell, 3/ed, 362 Pages	Newham	2005	375.00
9788173664236	Learning the UNIX Operating System, 5/ed, 174 Pages	Peek	2001	225.00
9788184045840	Learning the vi and Vim Editors, 7th Edition, 508 Pages	Robbins	2008	400.00
9788173660610	Learning the vi Editor 6/ed, 352 Pages	Lamb	1998	250.00
9788184042689	Learning UML 2.0, 300 Pages	Miles	2006	325.00
9789350239216	**Learning Unix for OS X Mountain Lion, 254 Pages**	**Taylor**	**2012**	**400.00**
9788184048292	Learning VBScript, 636 Pages	Lomax	2009	600.00
9788184043495	Learning WCF, 624 Pages	Bustamante	2007	650.00
9789350238912	**Learning Web Design, 4th Edition, 640 Pages**	**Robbins**	**2012**	**600.00**
9788184048964	Learning XML, 2nd Edition, 436 Pages	Ray	2009	650.00
9788184046472	Learning XNA 3.0: XNA 3.0 Game Development for the PC, Xbox 360, and Zune, 506 Pages	Reed	2008	500.00
9789350232415	Learning XNA 4.0: Game Development for the PC, Xbox 360, and Windows Phone 7, 558 Pages	Reed	2011	850.00
9789350238509	**LED Lighting, 88 Pages**	**Cangeloso**	**2012**	**125.00**
9788173660627	lex & yacc 2/ed, 392 Pages	Levine	1992	300.00
9788184044904	LINQ Pocket Reference, 188 Pages	Albahari	2008	150.00
9788173668449	Linux Cookbook, 590 Pages	Schroder	2004	825.00
9788184040166	Linux Desktop Pocket Guide, 202 Pages	Brickner	2005	150.00
9788173668494	Linux Device Drivers, 3/ed, 646 Pgs	Rubini	2005	525.00
9788184048278	Linux in a Nutshell 6/ed, 960 Pages	Siever	2009	600.00
9788184043525	Linux Kernel In A Nutshell, 216 Pages	Kroah	2006	300.00
9788173664540	Linux Network Administrator's Guide, 3/ed, 372 Pages	Kirch	2005	550.00
9788184044218	Linux Networking Cookbook, 654 Pages	Schroder	2007	575.00

ISBN	Title	Author	Year	Price
9789350237144	**Linux Pocket Guide, 2nd Edition 248 Pages**	**Barrett**	**2012**	**175.00**
9788173667183	Linux Security Cookbook, 340 Pages	Barrett	2003	325.00
9788184042887	Linux Server Security, 2/ed, 556 Pages	Bauer	2005	450.00
9788184043105	Linux System Administration, 310 Pages	Adelstein	2007	300.00
9788184043815	Linux System Programming: Talking Directly to the Kernel and C Library, 404 Pages	Love	2007	400.00
9788173668432	Linux Unwired, 322 Pages	Weeks	2004	300.00
9789350236604	**Little Book on CoffeeScript, The, 86 Pages**	**MacCaw**	**2012**	**125.00**
9788184048216	Living Green: The Missing Manual, 332 Pages	Conner	2009	475.00
9789350230558	LPI Linux Certification in a Nutshell, 3/ed, 540 Pages	Haeder	2010	750.00
9789351100751	**Mac Hacks, 348 Pages**	**Seibold**	**2013**	**575.00**
9789350235072	Mac OS X Lion Pocket Guide, 252 Pages	Seibold	2011	250.00
9789350235638	Mac OS X Lion: The Missing Manual, 952 Pages	Pogue	2011	1475.00
9788184048483	Mac OS X Snow Leopard, 924 Pages	Pogue	2009	1,375.00
9788184048704	Mac OS X Snow Leopard: Pocket Guide, 252 Pages	Seibold	2009	250.00
9789350236741	**Machine Learning for Hackers, 340 Pages**	**Conway**	**2012**	**525.00**
9789350235652	MacRuby: The Definitive Guide, 268 Pages	Aimonetti	2011	425.00
9789350237953	**Maintainable JavaScript, 260 Pages**	**Zakas**	**2012**	**400.00**
9789350236130	**Make a Mind-Controlled Arduino Robot, 114 Pages**	**Karvinen**	**2012**	**150.00**
9789351100324	**Make an Arduino-Controlled Robot, 274 Pages**	**Margolis**	**2013**	**450.00**
9789350233740	Make: Arduino Bots and Gadgets, 320 Pages	Karvinen	2011	650.00
9789350233207	Make: Electronics, 376 Pages	Platt	2011	450.00
9789350239926	**Make: Lego and Arduino Projects, 348 Pages**	**Beckler**	**2012**	**600.00**
9789350236789	**Making Android Accessories with IOIO, 88 Pages**	**Monk**	**2012**	**125.00**
9789350235706	Making Embedded Systems, 852 Pages	White	2011	425.00
9789350235058	Making Isometric Social Real-Time Games with HTML5, CSS3, and JavaScript, 176 Pages	Pagella	2011	275.00
9789350236734	**Making Musical Apps, 140 Pages**	**Brinkmann**	**2012**	**225.00**
9789350231401	Making Software: What Really Works, and Why We Believe It, 644 Pages	Oram	2010	750.00
9789350236284	**Making Things See, 464 Pages**	**Borenstein**	**2012**	**725.00**
9788173664656	Managing & Using MySQL, 2/ed, 448 Pages	Reese	2002	325.00
9789350234365	Managing Infrastructure with Puppet, 68 Pages	Loope	2011	100.00
9788173669583	Managing Projects with GNU Make, 3/ed, 310 Pages	Mecklenburg	2004	325.00
9789350236253	**Mapping with Drupal, 176 Pages**	**Palazzolo**	**2012**	**275.00**
9789350239810	**MapReduce Design Patterns, 272 Pages**	**Miner**	**2012**	**475.00**
9788173661167	Mastering Algorithms with C (B/CD), 572 Pages	Loudon	1999	500.00
9788173664618	Mastering Oracle SQL, 2/ed, 504 Pages	Mishra	2004	725.00
9788173666766	Mastering Perl for Bioinformatics, 406 Pages	Tisdall	2003	300.00
9788184043648	Mastering Perl, 458 Pages	Foy	2007	575.00
9788184043013	Mastering Regular Expressions, 3/ed, 556 Pages	Friedl	2006	625.00
9789350235614	Mastering Search Analytics, 428 Pages	Chaters	2011	650.00
9788184047028	Masterminds of Programming, 510 Pages	Biancuzzi	2009	450.00
9789350230305	Mathematica Cookbook, 848 Pages	Mangano	2010	1,275.00
9788173667916	Maven: A Developer's Notebook, 232 Pages	Massol	2005	325.00
9788184045987	Maven: The Definitive Guide, 484 Pages	Sonatype	2008	600.00
9788184042184	MCSE Core Elective Exams in a Nutshell, 604 Pages	Bhardwaj	2006	500.00
9788184041552	MCSE Core Required Exams in a Nutshell, 3/ed, 750 Pages	Stanek	2006	450.00
9789350235591	Meaningful Use and Beyond, 272 Pages	Uhlman	2011	425.00
9788184047479	Mercurial: The Definitive Guide, 300 Pages	O'Sullivan	2009	550.00
9789350230565	Microsoft Project 2010: The Missing Manual, 788 Pages	Biafore	2010	825.00

ISBN	Title	Author	Year	Price
9789350234372	Migrating Applications to IPv6, 72 Pages	York	2011	100.00
9789350232941	Mining the Social Web, 378 Pages	Russell	2011	575.00
9789350235201	MintDuino, 66 Pages	Kelly	2011	100.00
9788184048179	Mobile Design and Development, 352 Pages	Fling	2009	525.00
9789350236970	**Mobile Design Pattern Gallery, 296 Pages**	**Neil**	**2012**	**450.00**
9789350237595	**Mobile Development with C#, 192 Pages**	**Shackles**	**2012**	**300.00**
9789350237960	**Mobile JavaScript Application Development, 184 Pages**	**Kosmaczewski**	**2012**	**300.00**
9789350236413	**MongoDB and PHP, 104 Pages**	**Francia**	**2012**	**175.00**
9789351100744	**MongoDB Applied Design Patterns, 196 Pages**	**Copeland**	**2013**	**325.00**
9789350231128	MongoDB: The Definitive Guide, 240 Pages	Chodorow	2010	350.00
9789350234143	Motorola Xoom: The Missing Manual, 444 Pages	Gralla	2011	625.00
9788184042801	MySQL Cookbook, 2/ed, 990 Pages	DuBois	2006	1,200.00
9789350230695	MySQL High Availability, 644 Pages	Bell	2010	800.00
9788173668067	MySQL in a Nutshell, 358 Pages	Dyer	2005	325.00
9788184045444	MySQL Pocket Reference, 2/ed 148 Pages	Reese	2008	125.00
9788184041408	MySQL Stored Procedure Programming, 650 Pages	Harrison	2006	450.00
9789350236666	**MySQL Troubleshooting, 284 Pages**	**Smirnova**	**2012**	**300.00**
9788184047486	Natural Language Processing with Python, 522 Pages	Bird	2009	850.00
9788173665240	NetBeans: The Definitive Guide, 662 Pages	Boudreau	2002	825.00
9788184044256	Network Security Assessment: Know Your Network, 2/ed, 520 Pgs	McNab	2007	450.00
9788184042740	Network Security Hacks, 2/ed, 492 Pages	Lockhart	2006	425.00
9788173668395	Network Security Tools: Writing, Hacking, and Modifying Security Tools , 350 Pages	Dhanjani	2005	350.00
9788173663680	Network Troubleshooting Tools, 370 Pages	Sloan	2005	250.00
9789350234150	Network Warrior, 2nd Edition, 808 Pages	Donahue	2011	975.00
9789350238011	**Node for Front-End Developers, 76 Pages**	**Means**	**2012**	**125.00**
9789350237335	**Node: Up and Running, 220 Pages**	**Wilson**	**2012**	**350.00**
9788173667923	Nokia Smartphone Hacks: Tips & Tools for Your Smallest Computer, 418 Pages	Yuan	2005	400.00
9788173667848	NUnit Pocket Reference, 100 Pages	Hamilton	2004	100.00
9788173668265	Office 2003 XML, 596 Pages	Lenz	2004	450.00
9789350230701	Office 2010: The Missing Manual, 976 Pages	Conner	2010	800.00
9789350232880	Office 2011 for Macintosh: The Missing Manual, 840 Pages	Grover	2011	1,250.00
9789351100508	**Opa: Up and Running, 184 Pages**	**Binsztok**	**2013**	**325.00**
9788184049534	Open Government, 452 Pages	Lathrop	2010	675.00
9788173667725	Open Source for the Enterprise, 246 Pages	Woods	2005	250.00
9788184040296	Open Sources 2.0, 488 Pages	DiBona	2005	425.00
9788173667404	Optimizing Oracle Performance, 426 Pages	Milsap	2003	375.00
9788173669286	Oracle Applications Server 10g Essentials, 292 Pages	Greenwald	2004	275.00
9789350237892	**Oracle BAM 11gR1 Handbook, 260 Pages**	**Wang**	**2012**	**400.00**
9788173667077	Oracle Data Dictionary Pocket Reference, 150 Pages	Kreines	2003	125.00
9788173664175	Oracle DBA Checklist Pocket Reference, 88 Pages	RevealNet	2001	65.00
9788184040005	Oracle DBA Pocket Guide, 164 Pages	Kreines	2005	125.00
9788184044201	Oracle Essentials: Oracle Database 11g, 4/ed,422 Pages	Greenwald	2007	400.00
9788173664564	Oracle Initialization Parameters Pocket Reference (Oracle Database 10g), 128 Pgs	Kreines	2004	125.00
9788184045413	Oracle PL/SQL Best Practices, 2/ed, 308 Pages	Feuerstein	2008	375.00
9788173661181	Oracle PL/SQL Built-ins Pocket Reference, 78 Pages	Feuerstein	1998	60.00
9788184040357	Oracle PL/SQL for DBAs: Security, Scheduling, Performance & More Includes Oracle Database 10g, 466 Pages	Feuerstein	2005	625.00
9788184045420	Oracle PL/SQL Language Pocket Reference, 4/ed, 194 Pages	Feuerstein	2008	125.00
9788184049497	Oracle PL/SQL Programming, 5/ed, 1,246 Pages	Feuerstein	2010	700.00

ISBN	Title	Author	Year	Price
9788173662409	Oracle PL/SQL Programming: A Developer's Workbook, 576 Pages	Feuerstein	2000	575.00
9788173668111	Oracle Regular Expression Pocket Reference, 74 Pages	Burcham	2003	75.00
9788173661204	Oracle SAP Administration, 208 Pages	Burleson	1999	175.00
9788173666063	Oracle SQL*Plus: The Definitive Guide, 2/ed, 592 Pages	Gennick	2004	400.00
9788173661846	Oracle Utilities Pocket Reference, 136 Pages	Mishra	2003	100.00
9789350237748	**Orchard CMS: Up and Running, 148 Pages**	**Zablocki**	**2012**	**250.00**
9789350238516	**OS X Mountain Lion Pocket Guide, 284 Pages**	**Seibold**	**2012**	**275.00**
9789350238653	**OS X Mountain Lion: The Missing Manual, 908 Pages**	**Pogue**	**2012**	**1,400.00**
9789350234358	Packet Guide to Core Network Protocols, 180 Pages	Hartpence	2011	275.00
9789350235096	Packet Guide to Routing and Switching, 204 Pages	Hartpence	2011	300.00
9789351100713	**Packet Guide to Voice over IP, 260 Pages**	**Hartpence**	**2013**	**425.00**
9789350236802	**Parallel R, 140 Pages**	**Weston**	**2012**	**225.00**
9789350233771	PayPal APIs: Up and Running, 148 Pages	Balderas	2011	250.00
9788184042528	PC Annoyances, 2/ed: How To Fix The Most Annoying Things About Your Personal Computer, Wind & More, 268 Pages	Bass	2005	300.00
9788173667152	PC Hacks: 100 Industrial-Strength Tips & Tools, 316 Pages	Aspinwall	2004	300.00
9788173669736	PC Hardware Annoyances: How to Fix the Most ANNOYING Things About Your Computer Hardware, 276 Pages	Bigelow	2004	275.00
9788173665325	PC Hardware in a Nutshell: A Desktop Quick Reference, 3/ed, 848 Pgs	Thompson	2003	325.00
9788173667121	PDF Hacks: 100 Industrial-Strength Tips & Tools, 308 Pages	Steward	2004	300.00
9789350230169	Perl & LWP, 280 Pages	Burke	2010	350.00
9788173664465	Perl & XML, 224 Pages	Ray	2002	175.00
9788173661075	Perl 5 Pocket Reference, 3/ed, 96 Pages	Vromans	2001	70.00
9788184042764	Perl 6 and Parrot Essentials, 2/ed, 304 Pages	Randal	2004	325.00
9788173667336	Perl Cookbook, 2/ed, 976 Pages	Christiansen	2003	800.00
9789350230183	Perl Graphics Programming, 498 Pages	Wallace	2010	750.00
9788184041385	Perl Hacks, 310 Pages	Chromatic	2006	325.00
9789350234587	Perl Pocket Reference, 5/ed 120 Pages	Vromans	2011	125.00
9788173668364	Perl Testing: A Developer's Notebook, 212 Pages	Langworth	2005	300.00
9789350230411	Personal Investing: The Missing Manual, 268 Pages	Biafore	2010	400.00
9789350230343	Photoshop CS5: The Missing Manual, 836 Pages	Snider	2010	1,250.00
9789350235300	Photoshop Elements 10: The Missing Manual, 680 Pages	Brundage	2011	875.00
9789350235478	PHP & MySQL: The Missing Manual, 520 Pages	McLaughlin	2011	525.00
9788184043006	PHP Cookbook, 2/ed, 842 Pages	Sklar	2006	1,025.00
9788184040814	PHP Hacks: Tips & Tools for Creating Dynamic Web Sites, 468 Pages	Herrington	2005	400.00
9788184040234	PHP in a Nutshell, 370 Pages	Hudson	2005	450.00
9789350230176	PHP: The Good Parts, 194 Pages	MacIntyre	2010	300.00
9788184040258	PHPUnit Pocket Guide, 88 Pages	Bergmann	2005	100.00
9789350235218	Planning and Managing Drupal Projects, 120 Pages	Nordin	2011	175.00
9789350235089	Planning for IPv6, 104 Pages	Hagen	2011	175.00
9788173668715	Postfix: The Definitive Guide, 288 Pages	Dent	2003	275.00
9789350238523	**PostgreSQL: Up and Running, 184 Pages**	**Obe**	**2012**	**300.00**
9788184042948	PowerPoint 2007 For Starters: The Missing Manual, 325 Pages	Vander	2007	325.00
9788184042566	Powerpoint 2007: The Missing Manual, 502 Pages	Veer	2006	450.00
9788173660306	Practical C Programming 3/ed, 456 Pages	Oualline	1997	325.00
9788173666827	Practical C++ Programming, 2/ed, 582 Pages	Oualline	2002	225.00
9789350238424	**Practical Computer Vision with SimpleCV, 272 Pages**	**Demaagd**	**2012**	**425.00**
9788184040050	Practical Development Environments, 340 Pages	Doar	2005	325.00
9789350234211	Practical JIRA Administration, 116 Pages	Doar	2011	175.00
9789350234693	Practical JIRA Plugins, 136 Pages	Doar	2011	200.00

ISBN	Title	Author	Year	Price
9788173664397	Practical VoIP Using VOCAL, 532 Pages	Dang	2002	450.00
9789351100317	**Practical Zendesk Administration, 208 Pages**	**Vaughan**	**2013**	**350.00**
9789351100089	**Privacy and Big Data, 124 Pages**	**Craig**	**2013**	**200.00**
9788184042108	Process Improvement Essentials, 364 Pages	Persse, PhD	2006	400.00
9788184040227	Producing Open Sources Software, 302 Pages	Fogel	2005	325.00
9789350239780	**Programmer's Guide to Drupal, 180 Pages**	**Hodgdon**	**2013**	**225.00**
9788184045673	Programming .NET 3.5, 492 Pgs	Liberty	2008	400.00
9788184040340	Programming .NET Components, 2/ed (Covers .NET 2.0 & Visual Studio 2005), 656 Pages	Lowy	2005	425.00
9788173667206	Programming .NET Security, 704 Pages	Freeman	2003	550.00
9788173664380	Programming .NET Web Services, 500 Pages	Ferrara	2002	375.00
9789350233757	Programming Amazon EC2, 208 Pages	Vliet	2011	325.00
9788184045055	Programming Amazon Web Services: S3, EC2, SQS, FPS, and SimpleDB, 624 Pages	Murty	2008	600.00
9789350239193	**Programming Android, 2/ed, 584 Pages**	**Meike**	**2012**	**600.00**
9788184046113	Programming ASP.NET 3.5, 4/ed, 1,178 Pages	Liberty	2008	750.00
9788184043839	Programming ASP.NET AJAX: Build rich, Web 2.0-style UI with ASP.NET AJAX, 490 Pages	Wenz	2007	400.00
9789350239254	**Programming ASP.NET MVC 4, 508 Pages**	**Chadwick**	**2012**	**650.00**
9788184042085	Programming Atlas, 418 Pages	Wenz	2006	375.00
9789350230855	Programming C# 4.0, 6/ed, 880 Pages	Griffiths	2010	575.00
9788184043709	Programming Collective Intelligence: Building Smart Web 2.0 Applications, 376 Pages	Segaran	2007	475.00
9789350237663	**Programming Computer Vision with Python, 272 Pages**	**Solem**	**2012**	**425.00**
9788173660764	Programming Embedded Systems in C & C++, 198 Pages	Barr	1999	250.00
9788184042627	Programming Embedded Systems with C and GNU Development Tools, 2/ed, 340 Pages	Barr	2006	250.00
9789350230862	Programming Entity Framework, 2/ed, 936 Pages	Lerman	2010	1,075.00
9789350235935	Programming Entity Framework: Code First, 216 Pages	Miller	2011	350.00
9789350236673	**Programming Entity Framework: DbContext, 276 Pages**	**Miller**	**2012**	**425.00**
9788184048490	Programming F#, 424 Pages	Smith	2009	625.00
9788173669699	Programming Flash Communication Server, 842 Pages	Lesser	2005	600.00
9788184047233	Programming Flex 3, 674 Pages	Kazoun	2009	650.00
9789350233214	Programming Google App Engine, 416 Pages	Sanderson	2011	625.00
9789350239148	**Programming Hive, 368 Pages**	**Capriolo**	**2012**	**450.00**
9789350235904	Programming HTML5 Applications, 164 Pages	Kessin	2011	250.00
9789350236420	**Programming Interactivity, 2nd Edition, 752 Pages**	**Noble**	**2012**	**700.00**
9788184047981	Programming Interactivity, 756 Pages	Noble	2009	1,125.00
9789350234198	Programming iOS 4, 856 Pages	Neuburg	2011	1,000.00
9789350237137	**Programming iOS 5, 2nd Edition, 1,032 Pages**	**Neuburg**	**2012**	**1,500.00**
9789350230572	Programming Jabber, 500 Pages	Adams	2010	750.00
9788173668180	Programming Jakarta Struts 2/ed, 470 Pages	Cavaness	2004	575.00
9789350236505	**Programming Perl, 4th Edition, 1,204 Pages**	**Wall**	**2012**	**850.00**
9788184042719	Programming PHP, 2/ed, 425 Pages	Lerdorf	2006	500.00
9789350235317	Programming Pig, 242 Pages	Gates	2011	375.00
9789350232873	Programming Python, 4/ed, 1,652 Pages	Lutz	2011	1,100.00
9789350235171	Programming Razor, 140 Pages	Chadwick	2011	225.00
9788184048247	Programming Scala, 464 Pages	Qampler	2009	700.00
9789350235102	Programming Social Applications, 568 Pages	LeBlanc	2011	625.00
9788173667862	Programming SQL Server 2005, 600 Pages	Wildermuth	2006	400.00

9788184048186	Programming the iPhone User Experience, 208 Pages	Boudreaux	2009	300.00
9789350230718	Programming the Mobile Web, 532 Pages	Firtman	2010	675.00
9788173662379	Programming the Perl DBI, 372 Pages	Descartes	2000	350.00
9788184047950	Programming the Semantic Web, 320 Pages	Segaran	2009	475.00
9788184045253	Programming Visual Basic 2008, 798 Pages	Patrick	2008	550.00
9789350230947	Programming WCF Services, 3/ed, 936 Pages	Löwy	2010	725.00
9788173665738	Programming Web Services with Perl, 492 Pages	Ray	2002	400.00
9788173662041	Programming Web Services with SOAP, 268 Pages	Snell	2001	450.00
9789350230367	Programming Windows Azure, 388 Pages	Krishnan	2010	575.00
9788184043723	Programming WPF, 2/ed, 880 Pages	Sells	2007	725.00
9789351100904	**Pthreads Programming, 308 Pages**	**Nichols**	**2013**	**700.00**
9789350239902	**Puppet Types and Providers, 112 Pages**	**Liu**	**2013**	**200.00**
9788173664793	Python Cookbook (Covers Python 2.3 & 2.4), 2/ed, 852 Pages	Martelli	2005	600.00
9789351100065	**Python for Data Analysis, 488 Pages**	**McKinney**	**2013**	**500.00**
9788184045833	Python for Unix and Linux System Administration, 472 Pages	Gift	2008	450.00
9788184045406	Python in a Nutshell, 2/ed, 726 Pages	Martelli	2008	725.00
9788184048506	Python Pocket Reference, 4/ed, 226 Pages	Lutz	2009	275.00
9788173668487	qmail, 268 Pages	Levine	2004	275.00
9789350234952	Quick Guide to Flash Catalyst, 96 Pages	Elmansy	2011	150.00
9789350233795	R Cookbook, 460 Pages	Teetor	2011	700.00
9789350239827	**R Graphics Cookbook, 432 Pages**	**Chang**	**2012**	**725.00**
9789350239209	**R in a Nutshell, 2nd Edition, 744 Pages**	**Adler**	**2012**	**900.00**
9788184049435	RADIUS, 224 Pages	Hassell	2010	325.00
9788184042962	Rail Cookbook, 600 Pages	Orsini	2007	500.00
9788184045956	Rails Pocket Reference, 212 Pages	Berry	2008	150.00
9788184046090	Rails: Up and Running, 2/ed, 232 Pages	Tate	2008	300.00
9788184046489	Real World Haskell: Code You Can Believe In, 710 Pages	O'Sullivan	2008	850.00
9789350231913	Real World Instrumentation with Python: Automated Data Acquisition and Control Systems, 644 Pages	Hughes	2010	975.00
9788173666896	Real World Web Services, 230 Pages	Iverson	2004	325.00
9789350235119	Redis Cookbook, 96 Pages	Macedo	2011	150.00
9788184045857	Refactoring SQL Applications, 372 Pages	Faroult	2008	350.00
9788184043761	Regular Expression Pocket Reference, 2/ed, 126 Pages	Stubblebine	2007	150.00
9789350238691	**Regular Expressions Cookbook, 2nd Edition, 632**	**Goyvaerts**	**2012**	**675.00**
9788184047172	Regular Expressions Cookbook, 530 Pages	Goyvaerts	2009	800.00
9788184041378	Repairing and Upgrading Your PC, 462 Pages	Thompson	2006	350.00
9789351100010	**Resilience and Reliability on AWS, 180 Pages**	**Vliet**	**2013**	**300.00**
9789350237601	**Resource-Oriented Computing with NetKernel, 256 Pages**	**Geudens**	**2012**	**425.00**
9789350235645	REST API Design Rulebook, 136 Pages	Masse	2011	225.00
9789350231166	REST in Practice, 472 Pages	Webber	2010	700.00
9788184046410	RESTful .NET: Build and Consume RESTful Web Services with .NET 3.5, 324 Pages	Flanders	2008	500.00
9788184048698	RESTful Java with JAX-RS, 328 Pages	Burke	2009	500.00
9788184049558	RESTful Web Services Cookbook, 332 Pages	Allamaraju	2010	500.00
9788184043327	RESTful Web Services, 462 Pages	Richardson	2007	675.00
9788184040869	RFID Essentials, 276 Pages	Glover	2006	275.00
9788184047509	Ruby Best Practices, 347 Pages	Brown	2009	550.00
9788184041804	Ruby Cookbook, 920 Pages	Carlson	2006	650.00
9788184041996	Ruby on Rails: Up and Running, 196 Pages	Tate	2006	225.00
9788184043624	Ruby Pocket Reference, 182 Pages	Fitzgerald	2007	150.00

ISBN	Title	Author	Year	Price
9789350238042	**Running Lean, 2nd Edition, 256 Pages**	**Maurya**	**2012**	**400.00**
9788184042726	Running Linux, 5/ed, 986 Pages	Welsh	2005	875.00
9789350237670	**Safe C++, 160 Pages**	**Kushnir**	**2012**	**250.00**
9789350238004	**Sakai OAE Deployment and Management, 156 Pages**	**Whitney**	**2012**	**250.00**
9788173667053	Samba Pocket Reference, 2/ed, 146 Pages	Eckstein	2003	125.00
9789350234600	Scaling CouchDB, 92 Pages	Holt	2011	150.00
9789350239636	**SciPy and NumPy, 86 Pages**	**Bressert**	**2013**	**150.00**
9788184044935	ScreenOS Cookbook, 854 Pages	Brunner	2008	600.00
9788184047240	Search Engine Optimization for Flash, 294 Pages	Perkins	2009	350.00
9789350238776	**Search Patterns, 192 Pages**	**Callender**	**2012**	**400.00**
9788173667213	Secure Coding: Principles & Practices, 200 Pages	Graff	2003	225.00
9788184043600	Securing Ajax Applications, 266 Pages	Wells	2007	275.00
9788184040081	Security and Usability, 748 Pages	Cranor	2005	550.00
9788184047257	Security Monitoring, 262 Pages	Fry	2009	300.00
9788184043754	Security Power Tools, 872 Pages	Burns	2007	650.00
9788173668401	Security Warrior, 562 Pages	Peikari	2004	500.00
9788184049572	sed and awk Pocket Reference, 2/ed, 64 Pages	Robbins	2010	100.00
9788173660788	sed and awk, 2/ed, 440 Pages	Dougherty	1997	400.00
9789350239230	**Selectors, Specificity, and the Cascade, 104 Pages**	**Meyer**	**2012**	**175.00**
9788173669187	SELINUX NSA's Open Source Security Enhanced Linux, 264 Pgs	McCarty	2004	275.00
9788173668234	sendmail Cookbook, 418 Pages	Hunt	2003	400.00
9788184044225	sendmail, 4/ed, 1,324 Pages	Costales	2007	850.00
9788184048674	SEO Warrior, 512 Pages	Jerkovic	2009	775.00
9788173666865	Sequence Analysis in a Nutshell: A Guide to Common Tools & Databases (Covers EMBOSS 2.5.0), 310 Pages	Markel	2003	275.00
9789350236680	**SharePoint 2010 at Work, 284 Pages**	**Miller**	**2012**	**450.00**
9789350236451	**SharePoint 2010 for Project Management, 2nd Edition, 256 Pages**	**Raymond**	**2012**	**400.00**
9789350237175	**SharePoint Apps with LightSwitch, 96 Pages**	**Ferrill**	**2012**	**150.00**
9788184046144	SharePoint for Project Management, 266 Pages	Raymond	2008	300.00
9788173669835	SharePoint Office Pocket Guide, 94 Pages	Webb	2005	100.00
9788173667398	SharePoint User's Guide, 158 Pages	IDC	2005	150.00
9789350238646	**Shipping Greatness, 244 Pages**	**Mey**	**2012**	**350.00**
9789350236048	**Sinatra: Up and Running, 144 Pages**	**Harris**	**2012**	**225.00**
9788173669507	Snort Cookbook, 296 Pages	Orebaugh	2005	300.00
9788184043693	SOA in Practice: The Art of Distributed System Design, 358 Pgs	Josuttis	2007	525.00
9788173668197	Spidering Hacks: 100 Industrial - Strength Tips & Tools, 436 Pages	Hemenway	2003	350.00
9789351100294	**Spring Data, 332 Pages**	**Pollack**	**2013**	**575.00**
9788173668371	Spring: A Developer's Notebook, 202 Pages	Tate	2005	300.00
9789350236086	**SQL and Relational Theory: How to Write Accurate SQL Code, 2/ed, 472 Pgs**	**Date**	**2012**	**750.00**
9788184042207	SQL Hacks, 424 Pages	Cumming	2006	400.00
9788184047264	SQL IN A NUTSHELL 3/ed, 606 Pages	Kline	2009	500.00
9789350231920	SQL Pocket Guide, 3/ed, 224 Pages	Gennick	2010	225.00
9788173668241	SQL Tunning (Covers Oracle, DB2 & SQL Server), 356 Pages	Tow	2003	375.00
9788184040685	SQL Cookbook, 640 Pages	Molinaro	2005	475.00
9788184042795	SSH The Secure Shell: The Definitive Guide, 2/ed, 680 Pages	Barrett	2005	525.00
9788184045680	Statistics in a Nutshell: A Desktop Quick Reference, 492 Pages	Boslaugh	2008	250.00
9788173668579	STL Pocket Reference, 136 Pages	Lischner	2003	100.00
9788184045048	Subject To Change: Creating Great Products & Services for an Uncertain World: Adaptive Path on Design, 226 Pages	Merholz	2008	300.00
9789350234617	Supercharged JavaScript Graphics, 304 Pages	Cecco	2011	400.00

ISBN	Title	Author	Year	Price
9789350238769	**Surviving Orbit the DIY Way, 108 Pages**	**Antunes**	**2012**	**175.00**
9788184048520	Sustainable Network, The: The Accidental Answer for a Troubled Planet, 364 Pages	Sorensen	2009	575.00
9788184048315	SVG Essentials, 376 Pages	Eisenberg	2009	525.00
9788173664816	Swing Hacks, 554 Pages	Marinacci	2005	425.00
9788173665318	Switching to VoIP, 514 Pages	Wallingford	2005	450.00
9789350236031	**Tap, Move, Shake , 296 Pages**	**Moore**	**2012**	**475.00**
9789350239568	**Tapworthy: Designing Great iPhone Apps, 340 Pages**	**Clark**	**2012**	**600.00**
9788173660931	Tcl/Tk in a Nutshell: A Desktop Quick Reference, 480 Pages	Raines	1999	240.00
9788173664670	TCP/IP Network Administration 3/ed, 756 Pages	Hunt	2002	725.00
9789350238257	**Team Geek, 212 Pages**	**Fitzpatrick**	**2012**	**350.00**
9788173666513	Test Driving Linux: From Windows to Linux in 60 Seconds (B/CD), 372 Pages	Brickner	2005	350.00
9789351100881	**Testable JavaScript, 292 Pages**	**Trostler**	**2013**	**425.00**
9789350234389	Test-Driven Infrastructure with Chef, 111 Pages	Nelson-Smith	2011	175.00
9788184044232	The Art of Agile Development, 446 Pages	Shore	2007	600.00
9788184046946	The Art of Application Performance Testing, 174 Pages	Molyneaux	2009	300.00
9788184045963	The Art of Capacity Planning, 168 Pages	Allspaw	2008	200.00
9788184048209	The Art of Community, 412, Page	Bacon	2009	625.00
9788184047370	The Art of Concurrency, 321 Pages	Breshears	2009	575.00
9788184046953	The Art of Lean Software Development, 158 Pages	Hibbs	2009	200.00
9788173667831	The Art of Project Management, 512 Pages	Berkun	2005	575.00
9789350238677	The Art of SEO, 2/ed, 734 Pages	Enge	2009	700.00
9788184041415	The Art of SQL, 382 Pages	Faroult	2006	400.00
9789350238622	**The Connected Company, 324 Pages**	**Gray**	**2012**	**475.00**
9788184041811	The Internet: The Missing Manual, 466 Pages	Biersdorfer	2006	350.00
9789350232057	The Myths of Innovation, 268 Pages	Berkun	2011	400.00
9788184047516	The Myths of Security, 280 Pages	Viega	2009	475.00
9788184048711	The New Community Rules, 384 Pages	Weinberg	2009	575.00
9788184049053	The New How: Creating Business Solutions Through Collaborative Strategy	Nilofer	2010	450.00
9788184045581	The Productive Programmer, 238 Pages	Ford	2008	275.00
9788184041989	The Relational Database Dictionary, 126 Pages	Date	2006	150.00
9788184044928	The Ruby Programming Language, 460 Pages	Flanagan	2008	625.00
9788173661303	The Whole Internet: The Next Generation, 576 Pages	Conner/Krol	1999	425.00
9789350238035	**Think Complexity, 176 Pages**	**Downey**	**2012**	**275.00**
9789350238639	**Think Python, 316 Pages**	**Downey**	**2012**	**475.00**
9789350234457	Think Stats, 160 Pages	Downey	2011	250.00
9788184040302	Time Management for System Administrators, 238 Pages	Limoncelli	2005	250.00
9788173666032	TOAD Pocket Reference for Oracle, 2/ed, 136 Pages	McGrath	2005	125.00
9788184044041	Tomcat: The Definitive Guide, 2/ed (Cover TOMCAT 6.0), 358 Pgs	Brittain	2007	400.00
9789350234167	Transact-SQL Cookbook, 328 Pages	Gennick	2011	500.00
9788184047271	Twitter API: Up and Running, 429 Pages	Makice	2009	700.00
9789350235973	Twitter Book, The: 2nd Edition, 292 Pages	Milstein	2011	400.00
9788184041590	Ubuntu Hacks, 462 Pages	Oxer	2006	350.00
9788184040029	UML 2.0 in a Nutshell, 246 Pages	Pilone	2005	250.00
9788184042993	UML 2.0 Pocket Reference, 150 Pages	Pilone	2006	175.00
9788184040760	Understanding Linux Network Internals, 1,074 Pages	Benvenuti	2005	900.00
9788184043198	Understanding MySQL Internals, 208 Pages	Pachey	2007	300.00
9789350236383	**Understanding PaaS, 76 Pages**	**McGrath**	**2012**	**125.00**
9788184040838	Understanding the Linux Kernel (Cover Version 2.6), 3/ed, 954 Pgs	Bovet	2005	675.00
9788184041606	Unicode Explained, 692 Pages	Korpela	2006	525.00

ISBN	Title	Author	Year	Price
9788173666278	Unit Test Frameworks (B/CD), 222 Pages	Hamill	2004	225.00
9788184046434	Universal Design for Web Applications: Web Applications That Reach Everyone, 214 Pages	Chisholm	2008	300.00
9788184040609	Unix in a Nutshell, 4/ed, 992 Pages	Robbins	2005	500.00
9788173665653	Unix Power Tools, 3/ed, 1,162 Pages	Powers	2002	800.00
9788173666209	Upgrading to PHP 5 (Covers MySQL 4.1), 358 Pages	Trachtenberg	2004	350.00
9789350237281	**Using Drupal, 2nd Edition, 512 Pages**	**Byron**	**2012**	**625.00**
9788184047363	Using Google App Engine, 282 Pages	Severance	2009	350.00
9788184049008	Using Joomla, 428 Pages	Severdia	2010	650.00
9789350237168	**Using Mac OS X Lion Server, 240 Pages**	**Edge**	**2012**	**375.00**
9788184043037	Using Samba, 3/ed, 464 Pages	Carter	2007	450.00
9789350233191	Using SANs and NAS, 248 Pages	Preston	2011	375.00
9789350234709	Using the HTML5 Filesystem API, 96 Pages	Bidelman	2011	125.00
9789350238684	**Version Control with Git, 2/ed, 472 Pages**	**Loeliger**	**2012**	**600.00**
9788184047288	Version Control with Subversion 2/ed, 446 Pages	Pilato	2009	475.00
9788173662621	vi Editor Pocket Reference, 76 Pages	Robbins	1999	60.00
9789351100454	**View Updating and Relational Theory, 280 Pages**	**Date**	**2013**	**475.00**
9789350234396	Virtualization: A Manager's Guide, 96 Pages	Kusnetzky	2011	150.00
9788173660962	Visual Basic Controls in a Nutshell, 512 Pages	Dictor	1999	310.00
9789350237687	**VMware Cookbook, 2nd Edition, 292 Pages**	**Troy**	**2012**	**600.00**
9788184048681	VMware Cookbook, 316 Pages	Troy	2009	475.00
9788184040692	VOIP Hacks: Tips & Tools for Internet Telephony, 326 Pages	Wallingford	2006	325.00
9788184047356	Web 2.0 Architectures: What entrepreneurs and information architects need to know, 292 Pages	Nickull	2009	550.00
9788184045062	Web 2.0: A Strategy Guide: Business thinking and strategies behind successful Web 2.0 implementations, 302 Pages	Shuen	2008	350.00
9789351100799	**Web Audio API, 94 Pages**	**Smus**	**2013**	**150.00**
9788173669057	Web Database Application with PHP & MySQL (Covers PEAR, PHP 5 & MySQL 4.1), 2/ed, 828 Pages	Williams	2004	600.00
9788184040982	Web Design in a Nutshell: A Desktop Quick Reference, 3/ed, 826 Pages	Niederst	2006	450.00
9788184049046	Web Mapping Illustrated, 388 Pages	Mitchell	2005	575.00
9789350230589	Web Operations, 360 Pages	Allspaw	2010	550.00
9789350237977	**Web Performance Daybook Volume 2, 244 Pages**	**Stefanov**	**2012**	**400.00**
9788173663949	Web Security, Privacy & Commerce, 2/ed, 768 Pages	Garfinkel	2001	500.00
9788173663390	Web Services Essentials, 320 Pages	Cerami	2002	275.00
9788173667626	Web Site Cookbook, 262 Pages	Addison	2006	300.00
9789350237717	**Web Workers, 78 Pages**	**Green**	**2012**	**125.00**
9789350238738	**WebGL: Up and Running, 248 Pages**	**Parisi**	**2012**	**400.00**
9788184045628	Website Optimization, 408 Pages	King	2008	450.00
9788173661365	Win32 API Programming with Visual Basic (B/CD), 534 Pages	Roman	1999	700.00
9789350230299	Windows 7 Annoyances, 740 Pages	Karp	2010	900.00
9788184048537	Windows 7: The Definitive Guide, 1008 Pages	Stanek	2009	925.00
9788184049916	Windows 7: The Missing Manual, 924 Pages	Pogue	2010	450.00
9788184048339	Windows 7: Up and Running, 220 Pages	Wei-Meng Lee	2009	450.00
9789350239841	**Windows 8 Hacks, 440 Pages**	**Gralla**	**2013**	**750.00**
9789350239223	**Windows 8: Out of the Box, 160 Pages**	**Halsey**	**2012**	**250.00**
9789351100690	**Windows 8: The Missing Manual, 948 Pages**	**Pogue**	**2013**	**1,200.00**
9789350230930	Windows PowerShell Cookbook, 2/ed, 904 Pages	Holmes	2010	800.00
9789350238417	**Windows PowerShell for Developers, 344 Pages**	**Finke**	**2012**	**525.00**
9788184045239	Windows PowerShell Pocket Reference, 182 Pages	Holmes	2008	150.00

ISBN	Title	Author	Year	Price
9789350239797	**Windows PowerShell Pocket Reference, 2nd Edition, 196 Pages**	**Holmes**	**2013**	**225.00**
9788184045000	Windows Server 2008: The Definitive Guide, 508 Pages	Hassell	2008	675.00
9789350239834	Windows Server 2012: Up and Running, 276 Pages	Lynn	2013	475.00
9788173668838	Windows Server Hacks: 100 Industrial-Strength Tips & Tools , 328 Pages	Tulloch	2004	325.00
9788184042979	Windows Vista For Starters: The Missing Manual, 493 Pages	Pogue	2007	325.00
9788173669668	Windows XP Cookbook, 690 Pages	Allen	2005	500.00
9788184042931	Word 2007 For Starters: The Missing Manual, 372 Pages	Grover	2007	350.00
9788173666926	Word Pocket Guide, 160 Pages	Glenn	2003	125.00
9789350234068	Writing and Querying MapReduce Views in CouchDB, 100 Pages	Holt	2011	150.00
9788173665356	Writing Excel Macros with VBA, 2/ed, 580 Pages	Roman	2002	500.00
9789350234044	Writing Game Center Apps in iOS, 100 Pages	Nahavandipoor	2011	150.00
9788184044430	X Power Tools, 286 Pages	Tyler	2008	325.00
9788184042641	XML Pocket Reference, 3/ed, 198 Pages	Laurent	2005	175.00
9788173666155	XML Hacks: 100 Industrial-Strength Tips & Tools, 490 Pages	Fitzgerald	2004	425.00
9788173668456	XML in a Nutshell (Covers XML 1.1 & XInclude), 3/ed, 724 Pgs	Harold	2005	675.00
9788184047295	XMPP: The Definitive Guide, 324 Pages	Saint	2009	375.00
9788184043181	XQuery, 528 Pages	Walmsley	2007	500.00
9788173664908	XSLT 1.0 Pocket Reference, 188 Pages	Lenz	2005	150.00
9788184040784	XSLT Cookbook (Cover XSLT 1.0 & 2.0, 2/ed, 786 Pages	Mangano	2005	500.00
9789350237731	**YUI 3 Cookbook, 448 Pages**	**Goer**	**2012**	**700.00**
9789351100874	**ZeroMQ, 536 Pages**	**Hintjens**	**2013**	**900.00**

US EDITION AVAILABLE AT SPECIAL PRICE:

ISBN	Title	Author	Year	Price
9780596102364	Adobe Creative Suite 2 Workflow, 634 Pages	Alspach	2005	1,625.00
9780596006006	Adobe Encore DVD: In the Studio, 336 Pages	Dixon	2004	1,225.00
9780596529765	Adobe InDesign CS3 One-On-One (Book / DVD), 560 Pages	McClelland	2007	$44.00
9780596529758	Adobe Photoshop CS3 One-On-One (Book / DVD), 544 Pages	McClelland	2007	$40.00
9780596807979	**Adobe Photoshop CS5 One-on-One, 544 Pages**	**McClelland**	**2010**	**$49.99**
9781449382551	**Best Android Apps: The Guide for Discriminating Downloaders, 240 Pages**	**Hendrickson**	**2010**	**$19.99**
9780596101367	Building Extreme PCs, 192 Pages	Hardwidge	2006	1,200.00
9780596520748	Coding4Fun: 10 .NET Programming Projects for Wiimote, YouTube, World of Warcraft, and More, 512 Pages	Fernandez	2008	$39.00
9780596008499	Commercial Photoshop Retouching: In The Studio, 410 Pages	Honiball	2005	1,425.00
9780596008581	Creating Photomontages with Photoshop: A Designer's Notebook, 96 Pages	Collandre	2005	800.00
9780596008031	Designing Interfaces, 352 Pages	Tidwell	2005	$49.95
9780596528102	Designing Web Navigation: Optimizing the User Experience, 456 Pgs	Kalbach	2007	$40.00
9780596526801	Devices of the Soul Batting for Our Selves in an Age of Machines, 302 Pages	Talbott	2007	$18.00
9780596006662	Digital Photography Hacks: 100 Industrial - Strength Tips & Tools, 336 Pages	Story	2004	800.00
9780596100155	Digital Photography Pocket Guide, 3/ed, 160 Pages	Story	2005	450.00
9780596005474	Digital Photography: Expert Techniques, 496 Pages	Milburn	2003	1,375.00
9780596008413	Digital Photography: The Missing Manual, 432 Pages	Grover	2006	1,200.00
9780596009465	Digital Video Hacks: Tips & Tools for Shooting, Editing & Sharing, 426 Pages	Paul	2005	800.00
9780596005238	Digital Video Pocket Guide, 474 Pages	Story	2003	500.00
9780596510572	Dynamic Learning Dreamweaver CS3 (Book / DVD), 416 Pgs	Gerantabee	2007	$36.00
9780596510589	Dynamic Learning Flash CS3 (Book / DVD), 456 Pages	Gerantabee	2007	$36.00
9780596510619	Dynamic Learning: Photoshop CS3 (Book / DVD), 360 Pages	Smith	2007	$36.00
9780596102425	Fonts & Encodings, 1,037 Pages	Haralambous	2007	$48.00
9780596002879	Free As In Freedom: Richard Stallman's Crusade for Free Software, 243 Pages	Williams	2002	750.00

ISBN	Title	Author	Year	Price
9780596006624	Hackers & Painters: Big Ideas From the Computer Age, 276 Pgs	Graham	2004	700.00
9780596526856	Illustrated Guide to Astronomical Wonders: From Novice to Master Observer (DIY Science), 519 Pages	Thompson	2007	$24.00
9780596008598	Illustrations with Photoshop: A Designer's Notebook, 96 Pages	Rodarmor	2004	775.00
9780596100483	InDesign Production Cookbook, 224 Pages	Dabbs	2005	1,200.00
9780596007683	Just A Geek, 296 Pages	Wheaton	2004	700.00
9780596527877	Learning ActionScript 3.0: A Beginner's Guide, 382 Pages	Shupe	2008	$32.00
9780596517328	Learning Flex 3: Getting up to Speed with Rich Internet Applications (Adobe Developer Library), 304 Pages	Cole	2008	$32.00
9780596527525	Learning Web Design: A Beginner's Guide to (X)HTML, StyleSheets, and Web Graphics, 3/ed, 479 Pages	Robbins	2007	$36.00
9780596517717	Making Things Happen: Mastering Project Management (Theory in Practice), 408 Pages	Berkun	2008	$32.00
9780596007034	Mapping Hacks: Tips & Tools for Electronic Cartography, 574 Pgs	Erle	2005	900.00
9780596527051	Myths of Innovation, 196 Pages	Berkun	2007	$20.00
9780596002688	Oracle SQL Tuning Pocket Reference, 112 Pages	Gurry	2002	$9.95
9780596008604	Photo Retouching with Photoshop: A Designer's Notebook, 96 Pgs	CLEC'H	2004	775.00
9780596100209	Photoshop Blending Modes Cookbook for Digital Photographers, 176 Pages	Beardsworth	2005	1,025.00
9780596008512	Photoshop CS2 Raw: Using Adobe Camera Raw, Bridge, and Photoshop to Get the Most Out of Your Digital Camera, 206 Pgs	Aaland	2006	1,075.00
9780596515041	Photoshop CS3 Photo Effects Cookbook: 53 Easy-to-Follow Recipes for Digital Photographers, Designers, & Artists, 176 Pgs	Shelbourne	2007	$24.00
9780596510527	Photoshop CS3 Raw: Get the Most Out of the Raw Format with Adobe Photoshop, Camera Raw, and Bridge, 272 Pages	Aaland	2008	$28.00
9780596100216	Photoshop Filter Effects Encyclopedia, 176 Pages	Pring	2005	1,050.00
9780596100629	Photoshop Fine Art Effects Cookbook, 176 Pages	Beardsworth	2006	1,050.00
9780596100995	Photoshop Lightroom Adventure: Mastering Adobe's next-generation tool for digital photographers, 350 Pages	Aaland	2007	$32.00
9780596100223	Photoshop Photo Effects Cookbook, 176 Pages	Shelbourne	2005	1,025.00
9780596100308	Photoshop Retouching Cookbook for Digital Photographers, 176 Pages	Huggins	2005	1,025.00
9780596101138	Programming Windows Presentation Foundation, 430 Pages	Sells	2005	1,100.00
9780596007195	Revolution in the Valley, 324 Pages	Hertzfeld	2004	775.00
9780596523701	Stephen Johnson on Digital Photography, 320 Pages	Johnson	2006	1,500.00
9780596001087	The Cathedral & The Bazaar, 256 Pages	Raymond	2001	525.00
9780596100476	The Creative Digital Darkroom, 429 Pages	Eismann	2008	$40.00
9780596007331	We the Media: Grassroots Journalism by the People, for the People, 320 Pages	Gillmor	2004	775.00
9780596100834	Windows Seat, 152 Pages	Kost	2006	1,600.00

- Prices are subject to change without notice.
- All Prices are in Indian Rupees except where indicated in € (Euro Dollar) $ (US Dollar) and £ (Pound)€
- **Titles Released after January 2012 are marked in Bold.**